RACE, CLASS, GENDER, AND SEXUALITY:

The Big Questions

EDITED BY NAOMI ZACK, LAURIE SHRAGE, CRISPIN SARTWELL

D1572702

BLACKWELL
Publishers

Copyright © Blackwell Publishers Ltd, 1998

First published 1998

Reprinted 1999

2 4 6 8 10 9 7 5 3 1

Blackwell Publishers Inc.
350 Main Street
Malden, Massachusetts 02148
USA

Blackwell Publishers Ltd
108 Cowley Road
Oxford OX4 1JF
UK

Library of Congress Cataloging-in-Publication Data

Race, class, gender, and sexuality : the big questions / edited by
   Naomi Zack, Laurie Shrage, Crispin Sartwell
       p.   cm. — (Philosophy, the big questions : 7)
   Includes bibliographical references and index.
   ISBN 0-631-20874-7 (hdbk.) — ISBN 0-631-20875-5 (pbk.)
   1. Social problems.   2. Social classes.   3. Race relations.
   4. Sex role.   I. Zack, Naomi, 1944– . II. Shrage, Laurie, 1953– .
   III. Sartwell, Crispin, 1958– . IV. Series.
   HN18.R325   1998
   361.1—dc21   97-50241
                                               CIP

British Library Cataloguing in Publication Data

A CIP catalogue record for this book is available from the British Library.

Typeset in 10½ on 12½ pt Galliard
by Ace Filmsetting Ltd, Frome, Somerset
Printed in Great Britain by T. J. International, Padstow, Cornwall

This book is printed on acid-free paper.

Race, Class, Gender, and Sexuality: the Big Questions

Philosophy: The Big Questions

Series Editor: James P. Sterba, University of Notre Dame, Indiana

Designed to elicit a philosophical response in the mind of the student, this distinctive series of anthologies provides essential classical and contemporary readings that serve to make the central questions of philosophy come alive for today's students. It presents complete coverage of the Anglo-American tradition of philosophy, as well as the kinds of questions and challenges that it confronts today, both from other cultural traditions and from theoretical movements such as feminism and postmodernism.

Crispin Sartwell: For my daughter Emma

Laurie Shrage: To Hannah and Nathan

Naomi Zack: To my sons, Alex and Bradford

CONTENTS

CONTENTS

ABOUT THE EDITORS

Crispin Sartwell is Associate Professor of Humanities at Penn State, Capital College. He is the author of *The Art of Living: Aesthetics of the Ordinary in World Spiritual Traditions* (State University of New York Press, 1995); *Obscenity, Anarchy, Reality* (State University of New York Press, 1996); and *Act Like You Know: African-American Autobiography and White Identity* (forthcoming, University of Chicago Press).

Laurie Shrage is Professor and Chair in the Philosophy Department and teaches philosophy and women's studies at California State Polytechnic University, Pomona. She is the author of *Moral Dilemmas of Feminism: Prostitution, Adultery, and Abortion* (Routledge, 1994). She has published articles on ethnic and gender identity, equal opportunity and pay equality, feminist film aesthetics, and sex work. She has written *Brad, Who Used to be Barbara*, a children's book about trans-sexualism.

Naomi Zack is Associate Professor of Philosophy at the University at Albany, State University of New York. She is the author of *Race and Mixed Race* (Temple University Press, 1993), *Bachelors of Science: Seventeenth Century Identity, Then and Now* (Temple University Press, 1996), *Thinking About Race* (Wadsworth Publishing Co., 1998); and the editor of *American Mixed Race: The Culture of Microdiversity* (Rowman and Littlefield, 1995) and *RACE/SEX: Their Sameness, Difference and Interplay* (Routledge, 1997).

ACKNOWLEDGMENTS

Our thanks to James Sterba, series editor of *Philosophy: The Big Questions*, for first proposing this project. We are also grateful to Steve Smith at Blackwell Publishers for informed and responsive assistance in the execution of the guiding ideas. Thanks also to Mary Dortch for skilled trans-Atlantic desk-editing. Crispin Sartwell thanks Richard Abell and Judith Bradford. We all thank our co-editors.

For permission to publish copyright material in this book grateful acknowledgment is made to the following:

Kwame Anthony Appiah: for "The Uncompleted Argument: Du Bois and the Illusion of Race" in *Critical Inquiry* (Autumn 1985), to the author and The University of Chicago Press.

Christine Battersby: for "Stages on Kant's Way: Aesthetics, Morality, and the gendered Sublime" in *Feminism and Tradition in Aesthetics*, edited by Z. Brand and Carolyn Korsmeyer (1995), to The Pennsylvania State University Press.

Derrick Bell: for "The Real Status of Blacks Today" in *And We Are Not Saved* by Derrick Bell, copyright © 1987 by Basic Books, Inc., to Basic Books, a subsidiary of Perseus Books Group, LLC.

Allan Bérubé, with Florence Bérubé: for "Sunset Trailer Park" (November 1995) in *White Trash: Race and Class in America*, edited by Matt Wray and Annalee Newitz (Routledge, 1997), copyright © 1995 Allan Bérubé, to Allan Bérube.

Bernard Boxill: for "The Morality of Reparation" in *Social Theory and Practice*, volume 2, no. 1 (1972), pp. 113–22, to the author and publisher.

Frantz Fanon: for "The Fact of Blackness" in *Black Skin, White Masks*, translated by Charles Lam Markmann (Grove Weidenfeld, 1967), copyright © 1967 by Grove Press, Inc., to Grove/Atlantic, Inc.

Elizabeth Grosz: for "Refiguring Lesbian Desire" in *The Lesbian Postmodern*, edited by Laura Doan, copyright © 1994 by Columbia University Press, to the publisher.

David M. Halperin: for excerpts from *Saint Foucault: Towards a Gay Hagiography*, copyright © 1997 by David M. Halperin, to Oxford University Press, Inc.

Leonard Harris: for "The Status of Blacks in Academic Philosophy" in *The Journal of Blacks in Higher Education* (Winter 1994/5), to the author.

Virginia R. Harris: for "Prison of Color" in *Racism in the Lives of Women* edited by Jeanne Adleman and Gloria Enguídanos (1995), to The Howarth Press.

Renée Heberle: for "Deconstructive Strategies and the Movement Against Sexual Violence" in *Hypatia: A Journal of Feminist Philosophy*, volume 11, no. 4 (Fall 1996), to the author.

bell hooks: for "Talking Sex" in *Outlaw Culture: Resisting Representations* by bell hooks, copyright © 1994 by Gloria Watkins, to Routledge, Inc.

Patrick D. Hopkins: for "Gender Treachery: Homophobia, Masculinity, and Threatened Identities" in *Rethinking Masculinity: Philosophical Explorations in Light of Feminism*, edited by Larry May and Robert Strikwerda (Littlefield Adams Quality Paperbacks), copyright © 1996 by Rowan & Littlefield, to the publisher.

Joanna Kadi: for "Working-Class Culture" in *Thinking Class* by Joanna Kadi (1996), to South End Press, 116 Saint Botolph Street, Boston, Mass. 02115.

Robin D. G. Kelley: for "Confessions of a Nice Negro, or Why I Shaved My Head" in *Speak My Name: Black Men on Masculinity and the American Dream*, edited by Don Belton (Boston: Beacon Books, 1995) to the author.

John (Fire) Lame Deer and Richard Erdoes: for "The Green Frog Skin" in *Lame Deer Seeker of Visions*, copyright © 1994 by Pocket Books, copyright © 1972 by John (Fire) Lame Deer and Richard Erdoes, to Washington Square Press, a Publication of Pocket, a Division of Simon & Schuster.

Judith Lichtenberg: for "Racism in the Head, Racism in the World" in *Report from the Institute for Philosophy and Public Policy*, 12/1 (Spring/Summer 1992), to the publisher.

María Lugones and Elizabeth V. Spelman: for "Have We Got a Theory for You!" in *Hypatia Reborn: Essays in Feminist Philosophy*, edited by A. Y. al-Hibri and M. A. Simons (1990), to Indiana University Press.

Cherríe Moraga: for "Lo Que Nunca Paso Por Sus Labios" in *Loving in the War Years* by Cherríe Moraga (1983), to the author and South End Press, 116 Saint Botolph Street, Boston, Mass. 02115.

Lisa H. Newton: for "Reverse Discrimination as Unjustified" in *Ethics*, 83/4 (July 1973), to the author and The University of Chicago Press.

Linda Nicholson: for "Interpreting Gender" in *Signs*, 20/1 (Autumn 1994), to The University of Chicago Press.

Debra Satz: for "Markets in Women's Sexual Labor," in *Ethics*, 106/1 (October 1995), to the author and The University of Chicago Press.

Amy Tan: for "Mother Tongue" in *Under Western Eyes*, edited by Garrett Hongo (Anchor Doubleday, 1995). Originally published in *The Threepenny Review* (1989), copyright © 1989 by Amy Tan, to the author and the Sandra Dijkstra Literary Agency.

Max Weber: for selections from "Economy and Society" in *From Max Weber: Essays in Sociology* edited by H. H. Gerth and C. Wright Mills, translated by H. H. Gerth and C. Wright Mills, translation copyright 1946, 1958 by H. H.

Gerth and C. Wright Mills, to Oxford University Press, Inc.

Patricia J. Williams: for "Gilded Lilies and Liberal Guilt" in *Alchemy of Race and Rights* by Patricia J. Williams (Cambridge, Mass.: Harvard University Press), copyright © 1991 by the President and Fellows of Harvard College, to the publisher.

William Wimsatt: for "Aren't You in the Wrong Neighborhood?" in *Bomb the Suburbs* (2nd edition) (Subway and Elevated Press, 1994), to the author.

Naomi Zack: for "Mixed Black and White Race and Public Policy" in *Hypatia*, 10/1 (Winter 1995), to the author.

Every effort has been made to obtain permission from all copyright holders, but in some cases this has not proved possible at the time of going to press. The publishers therefore wish to thank those authors whose work is included without acknowledgment, and would be pleased to rectify any omissions brought to their attention at the earliest opportunity.

INTRODUCTION

Naomi Zack

Social Identities

This book is about the social identities of race, class, gender, and sexuality. Identity is the broadest subject in studies of human nature because it combines questions of how we seem to be to ourselves with how we operate as persons in society. Philosophers have found identity interesting in terms of several abstract amd general questions: What kind of thing in the world is a human being? What defines or distinguishes a person so that if every other aspect changes, that defining quality will guarantee that the same person is still present? Is the core of human identity something that we can experience only directly, in the "first-person" from the "inside," or is it something that others can observe about us from "outside" perspectives? Are we most truly our minds, our bodies, our behavior or some combination of these three things? Such abstract and general questions about human identity can be posed regardless of the time or place in which the subject lives. They are assumed to be universal questions about identity, about what we are.

In considering human identity as an aspect of human life in society, especially late twentieth-century American society, social categories and roles may be of more immediate everyday relevance than the universal or metaphysical categories addressed in the classic philosophical questions. In everyday life, most Americans are unconcerned about what it is that makes a person the same person or whether they are minds as opposed to bodies, or both, or something else. They are instead concerned with how the ways in which people are different affect their status and functioning in society. More specifically, most people accept what they take to be the facts of human difference and relate to others largely as members of the types and categories to which they seem to belong. This focus on the ways in which people differ in society, instead of on the ways in which they are the same, regardless of time and place, does not mean that sociology is more relevant than philosophy for understanding contemporary human identity. What it does mean, however, is that it may be useful to apply, or redirect, some of the philosophical questions about what endures through change and what it is that people most importantly are, to the categories of difference that are in wide use in society.

Redirection of philosophy from human sameness in a universal sense, to human difference in a social sense, raises a new set of philosophical questions about identity: Do the categories of human difference have natural or cultural origins? What are the defining characteristics of broad social categories, such as race, class, gender, and sexuality, to which people belong? Does membership in these categories completely define the person who belongs to them? Can the categories to which a person belongs change and is there room for overlap and interaction among categories?

So far, I have been using the term "category" to mean both race, class, gender, and sexuality, in their general senses, and specific types of race, class, gender, and sexuality, such as black, white, working class, female, or heterosexual. The universal questions about identity can be redirected again into questions of definition, sameness and change that apply to the specific types within the general categories.

However, there are limits to any system of human typing. All of us have ideas of ourselves and ways of interacting with others that seem to be typical of our race, class, gender, and sexuality. But we also vary as individuals and expect others to respect our uniqueness as members of a race or social class, as men or women, as heterosexuals or homosexuals. If strangers apply the categories to us and sort us into (what they think are) the appropriate types, we may feel diminished as human beings if our difference as individuals, as unique persons, is ignored.

Our identities of race, class, gender, and sexuality are partly made up by our own individual choices, partly influenced by the identities of others of the same group to which we belong, and partly influenced by members of groups different from our own. For example, if you are a man, you have your own ideas of what that means and much of your personal and social behavior, even your career and recreation choices, may express and define your masculinity. But your male peers, relatives and role models also influence what kind of a man you are, and so do your female peers, relatives and those who you accept as role models for women. Overall, if you are female, homosexual, white, Asian American, working class, upper class, disabled or whatever else may apply, your identity in the category that applies to you is made up in ways that combine self-image, same-group expectation and other-group image and expectation.

However, the range of personal choice may vary according to the types to which one belongs in the categories of race, class, gender, and sexuality. If one is a member of a type with a higher status – for example, male instead of female, white instead of black, heterosexual instead of homosexual, or middle class instead of working class, the range of personal choice will seem to be greater than if one belongs to the lower-status type. Also, where one lives, and when, and what subculture one belongs to, further affects social identity. Imagine, for example, the difference between being a black homosexual middle-class man in a southern city in 1940 and in 1998, or between belonging to the same types at the same times in New York City and San Francisco.

Of course, there are many other categories of difference to which people belong that make up their identities. Consider the categories of age (young, middle-aged or old), physical ability (able or disabled), health (mentally and physically well or ill). Thus in addition to race, class, gender, and sexuality, age, ability, and health are general components of identity that influence the formation of social roles in work and personal interactions. For example, your race and social class may influence the career you prepare for, and your age and physical ability may determine whether or not you can be a parent, while your race, class, and sexuality will partly determine whom you choose and are chosen by as a co-parent.

This Book

There are immediate reasons why the subject of this book is race, class, gender, and sexuality. In recent decades, partly owing to widespread social changes, there has been a new or revised interest in these categories and their specific types by scholars in the arts and sciences. Since the 1960s in the United States, there has been greater social *liberation* through increased economic and civic participation for disadvantaged types in the categories. More women have joined the work force and demanded full consideration as participating citizens in all aspects of American life. Nonwhites have been able to demand greater social justice and equality as the result of the civil rights legislation. Higher proportions of both women and nonwhites have attended college and entered the professions. Many members of the white working class have moved into the middle class through educational and economic advancement. During the same time, members of all category types have acquired more freedom to privately explore and express, and publicly identify, their sexuality.

At this point, it might help to define race, gender, class, and sexuality. Although there are no definitions that everyone would accept without qualification, the following will be useful for the sake of discussion, here.

Race: a physical and cultural typing that most Americans believe can be used to sort people into the four main groups of white, black, Asian, and Indian (Native American).

Class: a group that is distinctive from other groups owing to its members' wealth, occupations, incomes, level of formal education and lifestyle choices. The class and race a person belongs to is a rough but accurate predictor of his or her social status. Some scholars think race is a more important predictor of status or power, some think class. In the United States, most people think that social class identity is determined by money but they also acknowledge the importance of the educational level and occupation, not just of individuals but of their parents and grandparents, too.

Gender: masculine or feminine characteristics that include styles of appearance and habits, as well as social roles in romantic relationships, families, and other contexts of private and public life. Many feminist scholars believe that gender is the most important predictor of the degree of power and well-being that individuals enjoy in society; other scholars of liberation think that race and class are more determining. In contrast to gender, the term "sex" refers to the biological traits that result in an individual being male or female. An individual's sex is related to reproductive function as evidenced by the presence of ovaries or testicles or having XX (female) or XY (male) chromosomal markers. However, some feminist scholars believe that biological sex is a scientific idea that has resulted from cultural ideas about male and female gender.

Sexuality: orientation in sexual behavior, including the preferred sex of sexual partners, practices of monagamy or polygamy and styles of sexual behavior.

At this time, most people view race and sex as biologically determined. This is another way of saying that most people think that racial and sexual differences are "natural." By contrast, gender, especially the social roles assigned to human males and females, and class, are viewed as the products of culture; ethnicity is also viewed as a cultural product, in contrast to race. However, some contemporary scholars insist that sexual differences are culturally defined or "constructed" and others argue that racial differences are not biologically real.

There is a problem with the definitions offered above which is addressed in different ways by the writers in this collection. This is the problem of *essentialism*. Before modern science, it was believed that if something existed, especially if it was a natural object as opposed to a man-made object, it had an essence. The term "essence" was first used by the Greek philosopher, Aristotle (384–322 BC) to refer to a quality in a type of thing, shared by each member of that type that made it a member of the type. Thus every member of the groups of cats, dogs, trees, and bodies of water each had the essence of its group or kind. The British philosopher John Locke (1632–1794) is famous for arguing that essences do not exist in natural things themselves but are invented by the human mind, somewhat arbitrarily. Scientists in many fields, especially biology, define words for natural objects such as plants and animals, with words that refer to characteristics that objects must have in order to belong to the kinds that they do. But no one has ever discovered an essence as distinct from the specific traits shared by all members of a kind. For example, there are no cat essences although there are traits that all animals we call cats have in common.

The first scientists who studied human behavior attempted to follow the methodology of the physical sciences, because they began their studies after the physical sciences were generally accepted as successful inquiries. But some of the nineteenth-century scientists of human behavior and biology carried scientifically unconfirmed Aristotelian notions of essences into their work. Such essentialist thinking is evident to us now in early studies of sexual and racial difference, and of differences in social class. (This is putting the case neutrally because many scholars today argue that the nineteenth-century scientists of race, sex, and class were simply racist and misogynistic, as well as elitist.) To some extent, in ordinary life, many people still think of their own and others' racial, class, gender, and sexual identities in essentialist terms. They think that there is a white essence shared by all whites, a black essence shared by all blacks, masculine and feminine essences, essences of heterosexuality and homosexuality and essences of different social classes. In all of these cases, except perhaps for a chromosomally defined difference between males and females, not only are there no essences but there are not even collections of traits that all members of a group in question share.

To the extent that defining race, class, gender, and sexuality evokes ideas that there are essences of these things, all such definitions need to be accepted provisionally. Once the absence of essence is realized, it becomes necessary to account for how people have acquired such solid and seemingly deep identities of race, class, gender, and sexuality. Contemporary accounts of these identities sometimes refer to the ways in which dominant types in the categories benefit from assigning essential natures to subordinate types, for example, how men benefit by assigning essential natures to women that are of lesser social worth than their own, or how whites benefit by assigning essential natures to non-whites that are socially devalued. This kind of account in terms of self-serving motive leaves out the ways in which members of subordinate types comply with essentialist definitions of their types, revise them and invent new essences.

Another way of explaining ongoing beliefs in essentialism is by reference to ignorance and intellectual inertia: "common sense" always lags at least a century behind contemporary scientific views of the world. Finally, there are accounts of essentialist beliefs relying on the actual social rules and behaviors of ordinary life, which recreate and reinforce the essentialist beliefs.

A difficulty related to the unfounded beliefs in human essentialism in race, class, gender and sexuality is that in real life, the categories always *intersect*. In real life, no one is just – in the sense of only – black, white, middle class, male, female, heterosexual, homosexual or just anything else. Rather, people are black and male and working class, or black and female and middle class and lesbian, or white and male and working class and heterosexual, and so on. These real-life intersections make it misleading to talk about types of race, class, gender, and sexuality as *general abstractions* that could completely define whole persons.

Once intersection is taken into account, the complexity of social identity increases. Some writers claim that it is misleading to talk about any one category in isolation from the others, because individual identities are the results of combinations of categories in specific historical contexts. On this view, gender is determined by the effects of race and class on sex so that people of the same sex but different races and social classes may have different genders. For example, historically, there have been different feminine identities for black women who have worked outside of the home to support their families and white women who worked within their homes while their husbands supported them.

Another approach to category intersection emphasizes the ways in which a person's race, class, gender, and sexuality vary in importance over the course of a lifetime. For example, young children are more influenced by their gender than their race because their lives center on their families within which race is not an issue. But adolescents are more aware of their racial identities because they interact in a wider community. Young adults with new financial responsibilities may begin to develop identities of social class. Among the elderly, age may eclipse other types of identity. Obviously, this temporal view of intersection does not posit the mere passage of time as the determining factor on what categories are important but rather focuses on the events and contexts that change over time as a person grows up, matures, and ages.

Some feminists scholars and critical race theorists have argued that the intersection of oppressed types of categories, such as poverty (in class) and nonwhiteness (in race), do not merely add disadvantages but multiply them. The result of the multiplication of types oppression is the emergence of new types or categories of identity. For example, being both black and female would constitute a distinct category of race-gender. The only limit on the number of entities that this approach posits would be social recognition. However, social recognition of even new types within existing categories, such as bisexuals or people of mixed race, is often very difficult for those with the relevant experience to attain. Therefore, many new identities that result from intersection are not fully social but merely subjective and theoretical.

Some writers have argued that without the requirement of social recognition, individual or minority group identities would proliferate in ways that would undermine a socially intelligible system of identity based on race, class, gender, and sexuality, with a few clearly recognizable types within each category. Since it is social identity that is at issue here, the tension between individuals who do not fit into existing types or categories, and the majority of individuals who do fit in, can be a serious problem. Those who do not fit in require social recognition in order to function in society as what they believe themselves to be, but such recognition threatens to undermine the social order in which recognition takes place.

Finally, since there are no essences, the intersection of types cannot be used to account for real-life identities. This is because, even if, for example, one considers an Asian, female, working-class lesbian as an intersection of types within different categories (of race, gender, class, and sexuality), the category types themselves do not exist in pure, uniform forms before they are combined. We are not dealing with anything like primary colors or the table of the elements in talking about these social components of human identity. There is no reason to believe that any degree of observation, quantification, or verbal analysis will ever yield the kind of precision modeled on the subject matter and methods of the physical sciences.

One way of dealing with the problems caused by false essentialism, intersection, and "impurity" is not to expect too much from theories of human difference. Indeed, some writers, especially in the social sciences and literature, prefer not to deal with concepts of separate categories. Instead, they study existing communities or groups of people on a more direct empirical basis and describe how different aspects of their demographics influence their lives.

Perhaps these social scientists and writers have chosen the right paths of inquiry. The abstractions of types of race, class, gender, and sexuality do not take individual difference into account. Also, there are the other categories of age, ableness and wellness, not to mention types of religion and ethnicity, that this neat group of four categories excludes. So why bother with this project, why assemble this collection of readings about these four and expect students to learn from them? The answer is that race, class, gender, and sexuality do not represent mere variety but differences that influence how human beings treat one another in the most serious aspects of social life. That is, these categories have *moral* importance.

Many undergraduates in American colleges start out as moral relativists: they believe that what's right or wrong for me need not be right or wrong for you and that there is no way to decide an issue if you and I disagree on what is right or wrong. Most philosophy professors think that this is an overly simplified statement of differences in human values and choices because it leaves out the reasons why you or I think that something is right or wrong. According to philosophers, the truth about moral positions lies in these reasons; and to make moral disagreement into a mere matter of taste is just intellectual laziness. Some students get hooked on the philosophical processes of developing reasons for their moral opinions and constructing arguments around those reasons; others think that the request for reasons is just a word game that at best keeps disagreement cordial. Fortunately, this dispute between students and professors does not have to be settled here. The fact remains that moral matters involve benefit and harm to people. Many people are still benefited or harmed because of their types of race, class, gender, and sexuality.

These categories of social identity are therefore important. It is extremely difficult to build final encompassing theories about what they are, how they work, and how people should behave in regard to them. But nonetheless it is worth the effort to understand as much about them as we can. Even if the dimension of moral disagreement cannot be smoothed out to everyone's satisfaction, the issues of harm and benefit as they relate to the categories can be analyzed. Such analysis makes it possible to criticize present social reality. This criticism can empower people who are harmed by their categorizations, as well as increase awareness and strengthen pangs of conscience in those who do the harm. In this way, criticism may contribute to liberatory social change. As well, many find it interesting in its own right.

The book is divided into five parts: race, class, gender, sexuality, and intersections. Each part begins with an introduction that outlines the main contemporary topics of discussion among scholars in the field, and in some cases, the historical problems generated by the category in question. The themes of the readings are then connected to these scholarly and historical frameworks. Most of the readings date from the 1970s on but where contemporary discussions have roots in earlier sources, excerpts from those sources are included. There are "focus" questions before each reading and discussion questions at the end of all the readings in each part of book. A bibliography at the end of each part of the book suggests further readings in addition to the references listed in chapters.

The whole book has three editors and we have each been responsible for the parts that bear our names. This is a kind of division of labor that reflects our previous scholarly interests and publications, though we have also commented on and influenced the contributions of our colleagues in the process of putting the anthology together.

Note

My thanks to Laurie Shrage for editing help in clarifying the topics covered in this introduction.

PART ONE

RACE

edited by Naomi Zack

Race: Introduction to the Readings

The division of human beings into biological groups known as races is an idea in history dating from the late seventeenth century European colonial expansion into Africa and the Americas. Of course, differences based on religion, family ancestry, and geographical origins divided people in many ways for hundreds and even thousands of years before then. But the kinds of differences associated with race in a combined biological and cultural sense are unique to the modern period in the West.

In the European and American traditions, these ideas of race have had four main components: biological differences among groups, cultural differences among groups, unequal distributions of political and economic power whenever different groups have come together, and believed differences in the value or fundamental human worth of members of different groups.

The biological differences associated with race are commonly held to be the factual foundation of racial difference. Until the early twentieth century the cultural differences associated with race were believed to be inherited along with the biological differences. Since the 1920s the consensus among biological and social scientists has been that such cultural differences are not inherited but are the result of different historical circumstances. Where these differences amount to disadvantages among nonwhites, liberal thinkers today believe that they are the effects of white dominance over nonwhites; although conservative thinkers think that such differences in advantages are the result of choices made by individuals and values held, within nonwhite groups.

The differences in economic and political power that are associated with racial differences, as well as differences in social status, are the most serious part of the cultural differences associated with race. These inequalities in power between white and nonwhite racial groups motivate ongoing public debate about race and social justice.

The association of racial difference with that in fundamental human worth is a remnant of nineteenth-century hierarchical racial theories that were based on white supremacy. Today, all human ranking based on racial difference is believed to be racist by educated people of all races. However, there is considerable disagreement about exactly what racism is and what the best remedies for it are; some thinkers believe that racism is a kind of intentional ill-will while others believe that it is a kind of social structure.

Who are the principle characters in current problems involving race? If you asked most Americans this question, the answer would be, blacks and whites. But there are other races besides blacks and whites: Indians, Asians, and people of mixed race. Also, in reality, differences in racial types of identity are also constituted by ethnicity or the cultural traditions that are distinctive to varied groups and families. Hispanics, for example, are an American ethnic group with great racial variety among members. However, black–white racial problems seem to be the most severe, given a history of slavery, segregation, and poverty among African Americans, as well as strong feelings of distance between blacks and whites. A justification for focusing on black–white racial problems is a belief that if those problems could be solved, the solutions could be applied to racial problems between whites and Indians, and whites and Asians. The readings, here, reflect this kind of "optimism" although the student is encouraged to explore the problems unique to Asian Americans, Native American and Hispanic Americans, through the recommendations for further reading at the end of Part I. Despite common concerns, the authors of chapters in this part are not in agreement about how to address the different components of black and white racial difference; they have opposing ideas about what consitutes racial identity, racism, and social justice.

Derrick Bell's "The real status of blacks today" is an excerpt from his book, *And We Are Not Saved*. In this chapter, Bell's time-traveling heroine, Geneva Crenshaw, visits the delegates of the 1787 Constitutional Convention. The ensuing dialogues reveal how the early American idea of race was closely tied to beliefs in the sanctity of private property in ways that conflicted with other Enlightenment ideals of human equality and freedom. Slaves were a form of property, part of the capital of agricultural business in the South. The allowance for slavery in the US Constitution meant that the property interests of slave owners were considered more important than the fundamental rights of those enslaved.

The theories of black inferiority that were subsequently constructed, both during and after slavery, have been viewed by some writers as attempts to resolve this contradiction between doctrines of universal human rights and the institution of slavery: if blacks could be presented as less human than whites, then slavery and other forms of racist oppression could be presented as less evil than they were. However, there is an ironic, or what Kwame Anthony Appiah calls a "dialectical" aspect to identities based on racial difference. African American philosophers and activists, such as W. E. B. Du Bois (1868–1963), have attempted to create black racial identities, by making use of the identities imposed on blacks by whites who have oppressed them. In "The uncompleted argument: Du Bois and the illusion of race," Appiah explains how Du Bois tried to construct a liberatory concept of the black race, even though he knew that there was no foundation in science for a biological concept of race.

Appiah's explanation of why race is an illusion in scientific terms is woven into his interpretation of Du Bois. Appiah points out that the physical differences in human appearance that are ascribed to race in common sense are relatively unimportant biologically. Biologically, there is greater inherited variability within any of the socially recognized races than between any two of them. There is also no evidence that human differences in aptitude or ability are correlated with racial difference. Du Bois was aware of the failure of the concept of race to hold up under intellectual and scientific scrutiny. But he was reluctant to give it up because he believed that Negroes had a special destiny that could only be fulfilled through racial identity. A positive black racial identity would enable a level of achievement that would prove how white racists were wrong in their evaluation and treatment of blacks.

The African American destiny envisioned by Du Bois was made more attainable by the civil rights legislation of the mid-1960s, which outlawed discrimination on the basis of race in all public, civic, educational, and employment contexts. However, black and white racial groups do not yet enjoy social equality in the United States. There is also considerable disagreement about the degree of anti-black racism that remains and about appropriate remedies for it.

In her 1992 article, "Racism in the head, racism in the world," Judith Lichtenberg distinguishes between racism as deliberate ill will toward people of different races, and racism as a system of public and private practices that result in unequal treatment of people on the basis of race. Lichtenberg examines five kinds of "practices short of out-and-out racism" that are nonetheless discriminatory: different standards for people of different races; aversion to people of different races; stereotyping; accommodating racism in others; discrimination based on traits that are not in themselves racial but which correlate highly with racial difference (for example, discrimination against the hard-core poor who are disproportionately nonwhite).

In "The status of blacks in academic philosophy," Leonard Harris presents the stark statistics about the absence of blacks in philosophy departments in the most prestigious American universities. He suggests that part of the reason for this absence is that professional philosophers have not traditionally been interested in issues involving race.

Affirmative action is a public policy meant to remedy the fact that nonwhites and women have fewer opportunities than white males for higher education and professional employment. This is done by requiring the admission of members of minority racial groups (and also women) in educational and employment situations where they were previously absent or not present in proportion to their numbers in the wider population. The most contested form of affirmative action is preset "quotas" of nonwhites or women, but the policy has also been implemented through several other strategies: the creation of extra places for nonwhites and women; recruitment efforts to include minorities among qualified candidates for admission or hire; extra weight given to nonwhite race or female gender in assessing candidates of equal merit.

In "Reverse discrimination as unjustified" Lisa Newton argues that affirmative action practices are unjust because they do not treat all citizens equally, regardless of racial difference. Such equal treatment of citizens is a broad requirement for a lawful and orderly society. According to Newton, preferential treatment of nonwhite and female applicants is as unjust as discrimination against them, for two reasons: it is arbitrary in favoring those disadvantaged groups rather than others; there are no clear standards for the success of affirmative action policies.

Bernard Boxill presents arguments in favor of affirmative action in which the subjects of justice or injustice are groups with interlocking histories, rather than individuals who exist at the same time. In "The morality of reparation," Boxill claims that all members of a community are entitled to compensation for misfortunes that impair their opportunities to compete and participate fully in the community. For instance, victims of natural disasters, or people who suffer other misfortunes that are not their own fault are entitled to compensation. According to Boxill, those who have been wronged because of widescale social injustice deserve *reparation*, as well as compensation. Reparation consists of formal recognition of harm done by members of the oppressive group, and benefits confered on that basis.

The social categories of race, combined with racism, have had strong psychological effects on individuals. Although this subjective aspect of racial identity is shared by many people, it is a dimension of race and racism that is not always officially recognized. Frantz Fanon (1925–61) was a liberatory theorist who addressed the situations of non-whites in Africa, during and after European colonization. In an excerpt from "The fact of blackness," a chapter in *Black Skin, White Masks*, Fanon discusses the painful experience of being a black man in a white supremacist society. Fanon was dissatisfied with the identities imposed on blacks by colonizers but he was optimistic that protest and, if necessary, violent revolution, could lead to new identities that would allow for full development of human potential among the colonized.

Whites are not the only ones who practice psychologically harmful racism against blacks, because some aspects of racism become internalized by blacks themselves. In "Prison of color," Virgina Harris describes the damage to self-esteem that results from the color prejudice against dark skin which some blacks direct toward others. While the remarks and behavior of other blacks are the immediate cause of her pain and anger, the racism she experiences is an indirect result of white devaluations of blacks.

Problems with the scientific emptiness of race, with racism, and with nonwhite personal identity come together in the experience of mixed-race Americans. In "Mixed black and white race and public policy," I discuss the historical reasons for the American policy of not recognizing mixed black and white race. Belief in fundamental individual rights of freedom of expression and freedom of association would justify the recognition of mixed race identities. Mixed-race identities would be just as scientifically flimsy as the racial identities that are currently accepted socially, but they would also have the same liberatory jusfication: symbolization of lived experience; honoring of family history; resistance to racism.

Derrick Bell shows how the American founding fathers might have justified slavery. The title of the chapter suggests that there are analogous ways in which the present disadvantaged position of blacks could be rationalized by those in positions to end it.

Focus questions:
1 What did the delegates think that the main purpose of government was?
2 How did those who knew slavery was morally wrong continue to justify it?
3 Why does Bell think that aristocrats favored liberty and equality?

1   The Real Status of Blacks Today

Derrick Bell

The Chronicle of the Constitutional Contradiction

At the end of a journey back millions of light-years, I found myself standing quietly at the podium at the Constitutional Convention of 1787. It was late afternoon, and hot in that late summer way that makes it pleasant to stroll down a shaded country lane, but mighty oppressive in a large, crowded meeting room, particularly one where the doors are closed and locked to ensure secrecy.

The three dozen or so convention delegates looked tired. They had doubtless been meeting all day and now, clustered in small groups, were caucusing with their state delegations. So intense were their discussions that the few men who looked my way did not seem to see me. They knew this was a closed meeting, and thus could not readily take in the appearance, on what had just been an empty platform, of a tall stranger – a stranger who was not only a woman but also, all too clearly, black.

Though I knew I was protected by extraordinary forces, my hands were wet with nervous perspiration. Then I remembered why I was there. Taking a deep breath, I picked up the gavel and quickly struck the desktop twice, hard.

"Gentlemen," I said, "my name is Geneva Crenshaw, and I appear here to you as a representative of the late twentieth century to test whether the decisions you are making today might be altered if you were to know their future disastrous effect on the nation's people, both white and black."

For perhaps ten seconds, there was a shocked silence. Then the chamber exploded with shouts, exclamations, oaths. I fear the delegates' expressions of stunned surprise did no honor to their distinguished images. A warm welcome would have been too much to expect, but their shock at my sudden presence fumed into an angry commotion unrelieved by even a modicum of curiosity.

The delegates to the Constitutional Convention were, in the main, young and vigorous.[1] When I remained standing, unmoved by their strong language and dire threats, several particularly robust delegates charged toward the platform, determined to carry out the shouted orders: "Eject the Negro woman at once!"

Suddenly the hall was filled with the sound of martial music, blasting trumpets, and a deafening roll of snare drums. At the same time – as the delegates were almost upon me – a cylinder composed of thin vertical bars of red, white, and blue light descended swiftly and silently from the high ceiling, nicely encapsulating the podium and me.

The self-appointed ejection party neither slowed nor swerved, a courageous act they soon regretted. As each man reached and tried to pass through the transparent light shield, there was a loud hiss, quite like the sound that electrified bug zappers make on a warm summer evening. While not lethal, the shock each attacker received was sufficiently strong to knock him to the floor, stunned and shaking.

The injured delegates all seemed to recover quickly, except one who had tried to pierce the light shield with his sword. The weapon instantly glowed red hot and burned his hand. At that point, several delegates tried to rush out of the room either to escape or to seek help – but neither doors nor windows would open.

"Gentlemen," I repeated, but no one heard me in the turmoil of shouted orders, cries of outrage, and efforts to sound the alarm to those outside. Scanning the room, I saw a swarthy delegate cock his long pistol, aim carefully, and fire directly at me. But the ball hit the shield, ricocheted back into the room, and shattered an inkwell, splattering my intended assassin with red ink.

At that, one of the delegates, raising his hand, roared, "Silence!" and then turned to me. "Woman! Who are you and by what authority do you interrupt this gathering?"

"Gentlemen," I began, "delegates" – then paused and, with a slight smile, added, "fellow citizens, I – like some of you – am a Virginian, my forefathers having labored on the land holdings of your fellow patriot, the Honorable Thomas Jefferson. I have come to urge that, in your great work here, you not restrict the sweep of Mr Jefferson's self-evident truths that all men are equal and endowed by the Creator with inalienable rights, including 'Life, Liberty and the pursuit of Happiness.'" It was, I thought, a clever touch to invoke the name of Thomas Jefferson who, then serving as American minister to France, was not a member of the Virginia delegation.[2] But my remark could not overcome the offense of my presence.

"How dare you insert yourself in these deliberations?" a delegate demanded.

"I dare," I said, "because slavery is an evil that Jefferson, himself a slave owner and unconvinced that Africans are equal to whites, nevertheless found involved 'a perpetual exercise of the most boisterous passions, the most unremitting despotism on the one part, and degrading submissions on the other.' Slavery, Jefferson has written, brutalizes slave owner as well as slave and, worst of all, tends to undermine the 'only firm basis' of liberty, the conviction in the minds of the people that liberty is 'the gift of God.'[3]

"Gentlemen, it was also Thomas Jefferson who, considering the evil of slavery, wrote: 'I tremble for my country when I reflect that God is just; that his justice cannot sleep forever.'"[4]

There was a hush in the group. No one wanted to admit it, but the ambivalence on the slavery issue expressed by Jefferson obviously had meaning for at least some of those in the hall. It seemed the right moment to prove both that I was a visitor from the future and that Jefferson's troubled concern for his country had not been misplaced. In quick, broad strokes, I told them of the country's rapid growth, of how slavery had expanded rather than withered of its own accord, and finally of how its continued presence bred first suspicion and then enmity between those in the South who continued to rely on a plantation economy and those Northerners committed to industrial development using white wage workers. The entry into the Union of each new state, I explained, further dramatized the disparity between North and South. Inevitably, the differences led to armed conflict – a civil war that, for all its bloody costs, did not settle those differences, and they remain divisive even as we celebrate our two-hundredth anniversary as one nation.

"The stark truth is that the racial grief that persists today," I ended, "originated in the slavery institutionalized in the document you are drafting. Is this, gentlemen, an achievement for which you wish to be remembered?"

Oblivious to my plea, a delegate tried what he likely considered a sympathetic approach. "Geneva, be reasonable. Go and leave us to our work. We have heard the petitions of Africans and of abolitionists speaking in their behalf. Some here are sympathetic to these pleas for freedom. Others are not. But we have debated this issue at length, and after three months of difficult negotiations, compromises have been reached, decisions made, language drafted and approved. The matter is settled. Neither you nor whatever powers have sent you here can undo what is done."

I was not to be put off so easily. "Sirs," I said, "I have come to tell you that the matter of slavery will not be settled by your compromises. And even when it is ended by armed conflict and domestic turmoil far more devastating than that you hope to avoid here, the potential evil of giving priority to property over human rights will remain. Can you not address the contradiction in your words and deeds?"

"There is no contradiction," replied another delegate. "Gouverneur Morris of Pennsylvania, the Convention's most outspoken opponent of slavery, has admitted that 'life and liberty were generally said to be of more value, than property, . . . [but] an accurate view of the matter would nevertheless prove that property was the main object of Society.'"[5]

"A contradiction," another delegate added, "would occur were we to follow the course you urge. We are not unaware of the moral issues raised by slavery, but we have no response to the delegate from South Carolina, General Charles Cotesworth Pinckney, who has admonished us that 'property in slaves should not be exposed to danger under a government instituted for the protection of property.'"[6]

"Of what value is a government that does not secure its citizens in their persons and their property?" inquired another delegate. "Government, as Mr Pierce Butler from South Carolina has maintained here, 'was instituted principally for the protection of property and was itself . . . supported by property.'

Property, he reminded us, was 'the great object of government; the great cause of war; the great means of carrying it on.[7] And the whole South Carolina delegation joined him in making clear that 'the security the Southern states want is that their negroes may not be taken from them.'"[8]

"Your deliberations here have been secret," I replied. "And yet history has revealed what you here would hide. The Southern delegates have demanded the slavery compromises as their absolute precondition to forming a new government."

"And why should it not be so?" a delegate in the rear called out. "I do not represent the Southern point of view, and yet their rigidity on the slavery issue is wholly natural, stemming as it does from the commitment of their economy to labor-intensive agriculture. We are not surprised by the determined bargaining of the Georgia and South Carolina delegations, nor distressed that our Southern colleagues, in seeking the protection they have gained, seem untroubled by doubts about the policy and morality of slavery and the slave trade."

"Then," I countered, "you are not troubled by the knowledge that this document will be defended by your Southern colleagues in the South Carolina ratification debates, by admissions that 'Negroes were our wealth, our only resource'?"[9]

"Why, in God's name," the delegate responded, "should we be troubled by the truth, candidly stated? They have said no less in these chambers. General Charles Cotesworth Pinckney has flatly stated that 'South Carolina and Georgia cannot do without slaves.' And his cousin and fellow planter, Charles Pinckney, has added, 'The blacks are the laborers, the peasants of the Southern states.'"[10]

At this, an elderly delegate arose and rapped his cane on his chair for attention. "Woman, we would have you gone from this place. But if a record be made, that record should show that the economic benefits of slavery do not accrue only to the South. Plantation states provide a market for Northern factories, and the New England shipping industry and merchants participate in the slave trade. Northern states, moreover, utilize slaves in the fields, as domestics, and even as soldiers to defend against Indian raids."[11]

I shook my head. "Here you are then! Representatives from large and small states, slave states and those that have abolished slavery, all of you are protecting your property interests at the cost of your principles."

There was no response. The transparent shield protected my person, served as a language translator smoothing the differences in English usage, and provided a tranquilizing effect as it shimmered softly in the hot and humid room. Evidently, even this powerful mechanism could not bring the delegates to reassess their views on the slavery issue.

I asked, "Are you not concerned with the basic contradiction in your position: that you, who have gathered here in Philadelphia from each state in the confederacy, in fact represent and constitute major property holders? Do you not mind that your slogans of liberty and individual rights are basically guarantees that neither a strong government nor the masses will be able to interfere with your property rights and those of your class? This contradiction between what you espouse and what you here protect will be held against you by future citizens of this nation."[12]

"Unless we continue on our present course," a delegate called out, "there will be no nation whose origins can be criticized. These sessions were called because the country is teetering between anarchy and bankruptcy. The nation cannot meet its debts. And only a year ago, thousands of poor farmers in Massachusetts and elsewhere took up arms against the government."

"Indeed," I said, "I am aware of Shay's Rebellion, led by Daniel Shay, a former officer who served with distinction in the war against England. According to historians of my time, the inability of Congress to respond to Massachusetts's appeal for help provided 'the final argument to sway many Americans in favor of a stronger federal government.'[13] I understand the nature of the crisis that brings you here, but the compromises you make on the slavery issue are – "

"Young woman!" interrupted one of the older delegates. "Young woman, you say you understand. But I tell you that it is 'nearly impossible for anybody who has not been on the spot to conceive (from any description) what the delicacy and danger of our situation . . . [has] been. I am President of this Convention, drafted to the task against my wishes. I am here and I am ready to embrace any tolerable compromise that . . . [is] competent to save us from impending ruin.'"[14]

While so far I had recognized none of the delegates, the identity of this man – seated off by himself, and one of the few who had remained quiet through the bedlam that broke out after my arrival – was unmistakable.

"Thank you, General Washington," I responded. "I know that you, though a slave owner, are opposed to slavery. And yet you have said little during these meetings – to prevent, one may assume, your great prestige from unduly influencing debate. Future historians will say of your silence that you recognize that for you to throw the weight of your opinion against slavery might so hearten the opponents of the system, while discouraging its proponents, as to destroy all hope of compromise. This, would prevent the formation of the Union, and the Union, for you, is essential."[15]

"I will not respond to these presumptions," said General Washington, "but I will tell you now what I will say to others at a later time. There are in the new form some things, I will readily acknowledge, that never did, and I am persuaded never will, obtain my cordial approbation; but I did then conceive, and do now most firmly believe, that in the aggregate it is the best constitution, that can be obtained at this epoch, and that this, or a dissolution, awaits our choice, and is the only alternative."[16]

"Do you recognize," I asked, "that in order to gain unity among yourselves, your slavery compromises sacrifice freedom for the Africans who live amongst you and work for you? Such sacrifices of the rights of one group of human beings will, unless arrested here, become a difficult to-break pattern in the nation's politics."[17]

"Did you not listen to the general?" This man, I decided, must be James Madison. As the delegates calmed down, he had returned to a prominent seat in the front of the room directly in front of the podium. It was from this vantage point that he took notes of the proceedings which, when finally released in 1840, became the best record of the Convention.[18]

"I expect," Madison went on, "that many will question why I have agreed to the Constitution. And, like General Washington, I will answer: 'because I thought it safe to the liberties of the people, and the best that could be obtained from the jarring interests of States, and the miscellaneous opinions of Politicians; and because experience has proved that the real danger to America & to liberty lies in the defect of *energy and stability* in the present establishments of the United States.'"[19]

"Do not think," added a delegate from Massachusetts, "that this Convention has come easily to its conclusions on the matter that concerns you. Gouverneur Morris from Pennsylvania has said to us in the strongest terms: 'Domestic slavery is the most prominent feature in the aristocratic countenance of the proposed Constitution.[20] He warned again and again that 'the people of Pennsylvania will never agree to a representation of Negroes.'[21]

"Many of us shared Mr Morris's concern about basing apportionment on slaves as insisted by the Southern delegates. I recall with great sympathy his questions:

"Upon what principle is it that the slaves shall be computed in the representation? Are they men? Then make them citizens and let them vote? Are they property? Why then is no other property included? . . .

The admission of slaves into the Representation when fairly explained comes to this: that the inhabitant of Georgia and S.C. who goes to the Coast of Africa, and in defiance of the most sacred laws of humanity tears away his fellow creatures from their dearest connections & damns them to the most cruel bondages, shall have more votes in a Govt. instituted for protection of the rights of mankind, then the Citizen of Pa or N. Jersey who views with a laudable horror, so nefarious a practice.[22]

"I tell you, woman, this Convention was not unmoved at these words of Mr Morris's only a few weeks ago."

"Even so," I said, "the Convention has acquiesced when representatives of the Southern states adamantly insisted that the proposed new government not interfere with their property in slaves. And is it not so that, beyond a few speeches, the representatives of the Northern states have been, at best, ambivalent on the issue?"

"And why not?" interjected another delegate. "Slavery has provided the wealth that made independence possible. The profits from slavery funded the Revolution. It cannot be denied. At the time of the Revolution, the goods for which the United States demanded freedom were produced in very large measure by slave labor. Desperately needing assistance from other countries, we purchased this land from France with tobacco produced mainly by slave labor.[23] The nation's economic well-being depended on the institution, and its preservation is essential if the Constitution we are drafting is to be more than a useless document. At least, that is how we view the crisis we face."

To pierce the delegates' adamant front, I called on the oratorical talents that have, in the twentieth century, won me both praise and courtroom battles: "The real crisis you face should not be resolved by your recognition of slavery, an evil whose immorality will pollute the nation as it now stains your document. Despite your resort to euphemisms like persons to keep out of the Constitution such words as slave and slavery, you cannot evade the consequences of the ten different provisions you have placed in the Constitution for the purpose of protecting property in slaves.*

"Woman!" a delegate shouted from the rear of the room. "Explain to us how you, a black, have gotten free of your chains and gained the audacity to come here and teach white men anything."

I smiled, recognizing the eternal question. "Audacity," I replied, "is an antidote to your arrogance. Be assured: my knowledge, despite my race, is far greater than yours."

"But if my race and audacity offend you, then listen to your contemporaries who have opposed slavery in most moving terms. With all due respect, there are few in this company whose insight exceeds that of Abigail Adams who wrote her husband, John, during the Revolutionary War: 'I wish most sincerely there was not a slave in the province; it always appeared a most iniquitous scheme to me to fight ourselves for what we are daily robbing and plundering from those who have as good a right to freedom as we have.'[25] Mrs Adams's wish is, as you know, shared by many influential Americans who denounce slavery as a corrupting and morally unjustifiable practice.[26]

"Gentlemen," I continued, "how can you disagree with the view of the Maryland delegate Luther Martin that the slave trade and 'three-fifths' compromises

---

* The historian William Wiecek has listed the following direct and indirect accommodations to slavery contained in the Constitution:

1 Article I, Section 2: representatives in the House were apportioned among the states on the basis of population, computed by counting all free persons and three-fifths of the slaves (the "federal number," or "three-fifths," clause);

2 Article I, Section 2, and Article I, Section 9: two clauses requiring, redundantly, that direct taxes (including capitations) be apportioned among the states on the foregoing basis, the purpose being to prevent Congress from laying a head tax on slaves to encourage their emancipation;

3 Article I, Section 9: Congress was prohibited from abolishing the international slave trade to the United States before 1808;

4 Article IV, Section 2: the states were prohibited from emancipating fugitive slaves, who were to be returned on demand of the master;

5 Article I, Section 8: Congress empowered to provide for calling up the states' militias to suppress insurrections including slave uprisings;

6 Article IV, Section 4: the federal government was obliged to protect the states against domestic violence, including slave insurrections;

7 Article V: the provisions of Article I, Section 9, clauses 1 and 4 (pertaining to the slave trade and direct taxes) were made unamendable;

8 Article I, Section 9, and Article I, Section 10: these two clauses prohibited the federal government and the states from taxing exports, one purpose being to prevent them from taxing slavery indirectly by taxing the exported product of slave labor.[24]

'ought to be considered as a solemn mockery of, and insult to that God whose protection we had then implored, and . . . who views with equal eye the poor African slave and his American master'? I can tell you that Mr Martin will not only abandon these deliberations and refuse to sign the Constitution but also oppose its ratification in Maryland. And further, he will, in his opposition, expose the deal of the committee on which he served, under which New England states agrees to give the slave trade a twenty-year immunity from federal restrictions in exchange for Southern votes to eliminate restrictions on navigation acts. What is more, he will write that, to the rest of the world, it must appear 'absurd and disgraceful to the last degree, that we should *except* from the exercise of that power [to regulate commerce], the *only branch of commerce* which is *unjustifiable in its nature*, and *contrary* to the rights of *mankind.*'"[27]

"Again, woman," a Northern delegate assured me, "we have heard and considered all those who oppose slavery. Despite the remonstrations of the abolitionists – of whom few, I must add, believe Negroes to be the equal of white men, and even fewer would want the blacks to remain in this land were slavery abandoned – we have acted as we believe the situation demands."

"I cannot believe," I said, "that even a sincere belief in the superiority of the white race should suffice to condone so blatant a contradiction of your hallowed ideals."

"It should be apparent by now," said the delegate who had shot at me, but had now recovered his composure and shed his inkstained coat, "that we do not care what you think. Furthermore, if your people actually had the sensitivities of real human beings, you would realize that you are not wanted here and would have the decency to leave."

"I will not leave!" I said steadily, and waited while the delegates conferred.

Finally, a delegate responded to my challenge. "You have, by now, heard enough to realize that we have not lightly reached the compromises on slavery you so deplore. Perhaps we, with the responsibility of forming a radically new government in perilous times, see more clearly than is possible for you in hindsight that the unavoidable cost of our labors will be the need to accept and live with what you call a contradiction."

The delegate had gotten to his feet, and was walking slowly toward me as he spoke. "This contradiction is not lost on us. Surely we know, even though we are at pains not to mention it, that we have sacrificed the rights of some in the belief that this involuntary forfeiture is necessary to secure the rights for others in a society espousing, as its basic principle, the liberty of all."

He was standing directly in front of the shield now, ignoring its gentle hum, disregarding its known danger. "It grieves me," he continued, "that your presence here confirms my worst fears about the harm done to your people because the Constitution, while claiming to speak in an unequivocal voice, in fact promises freedom to whites and condemns blacks to slavery. But what alternative do we have? Unless we here frame a constitution that can first gain our signatures and then win ratification by the states, we shall soon have no nation. For better or worse, slavery has been the backbone of our economy, the source of much of our wealth. It was condoned in the colonies and recognized in the Articles of

Confederation. The majority of the delegates to this convention own slaves and must have that right protected if they and their states are to be included in the new government."

He paused and then asked, more out of frustration than defiance, "What better compromise on this issue can you offer than that which has been fashioned over so many hours of heated debate?"

The room was silent. The delegate, his statement made, his question presented, turned and walked slowly back to his seat. A few from his state touched his hand as he passed. Then all eyes turned to me.

I thanked the delegate for his question and then said, "The processes by which Northern states are even now abolishing slavery are known to you all.[28] What is lacking here is not legislative skill but the courage to recognize the evil of holding blacks in slavery – an evil that would be quickly and universally condemned were the subjects of bondage members of the Caucasian race. You fear that unless the slavery of blacks is recognized and given protection, the nation will not survive. And my message is that the compromises you are making here mean that the nation's survival will always be in doubt. For now in my own day, after two hundred years and despite bloody wars and the earnest efforts of committed people, the racial contradiction you sanction in this document remains and threatens to tear this country apart."

"Mr Chairman," said a delegate near the podium whose accent indicated that he was from the deep South, "this discussion grows tiresome and I resent to my very soul the presence in our midst of this offspring of slaves. If she accurately predicts the future fate of her race in this country, then our protection of slave property, which we deem essential for our survival, is easier to justify than in some later time when, as she implies, negroes remain subjugated even without the threats we face."

"Hear! Hear!" shouted a few delegates. "Bravo, Colonel!"

"It's all hypocrisy!" the Colonel shouted, his arms flailing the air, "sheer hypocrisy! Our Northern colleagues bemoan slavery while profiting from it as much as we in the South, meanwhile avoiding its costs and dangers. And our friends from Virginia, where slavery began, urge the end of importation – not out of humanitarian motivations, as their speeches suggest, but because they have sufficient slaves, and expect the value of their property will increase if further imports are barred.

"Mr George Mason, of the Virginia delegation, in his speech opposing the continued importation of slaves expressed fear that, if not barred, the people of Western lands, already crying for slaves, could get them through South Carolina and Georgia. He moans that: 'Slavery discourages arts & manufactures. The poor despise labor when performed by slaves. They prevent the immigration of Whites, who really enrich & strengthen a Country. They produce the most pernicious effect on manners.' Furthermore, according to Mr Mason, 'every master of slaves is born a petty tyrant. They bring the judgment of heaven on a Country . . . [and] by an inevitable chain of causes & effects providence punishes national sins, by national calamities.'[29]

"This, Mr Chairman, is nothing but hypocrisy or, worse, ignorance of history. We speak easily today of liberty, but the rise of liberty and equality in this country has been accompanied by the rise of slavery.[30] The negress who has seized our podium by diabolical force charges that we hold blacks slaves because we view them as inferior. Inferior in every way they surely are, but they were not slaves when Virginia was a new colony 150 years ago. Or, at least, their status was hardly worse than the luckless white indentured servants brought here from debtors' prisons and the poverty-ridden streets of England. Neither slave nor servant lived very long in that harsh, fever-ridden clime."

The Colonel, so close to the podium, steadfastly refused to speak to me or even to acknowledge my presence.

"In the beginning," he went on, "life was harsh, but the coming of tobacco to Virginia in 1617 turned a struggling colony into a place where great wealth could be made relatively quickly. To cultivate the labor-intense crop, large numbers of mainly white, male servants, indentured to their masters for a period of years, were imported. Blacks, too, were brought to the colony, both as slaves and as servants. They generally worked, ate, and slept with the white servants.

"As the years passed, more and more servants lived to gain their freedom, despite the practice of extending terms for any offence, large or small. They soon became a growing, poverty-stricken class, some of whom resigned themselves to working for wages; others preferred a meager living on dangerous frontier land or a hand-to-mouth existence, roaming from one county to another, renting a bit of land here, squatting on some there, dodging the tax collector, drinking, quarreling, stealing hogs, and enticing servants to run away with them."

"It is not extraordinary to suggest that the planters and those who governed Virginia were caught in a dilemma – a dilemma more like the contradiction we are accused of building into the Constitution than may at first meet the eye. They needed workers to maintain production in their fields, but young men were soon rebellious, without either land of their own or women, who were not seen as fit to work the fields. Moreover, the young workers were armed and had to be armed to repel attacks from Indians by land and from privateers and petty-thieving pirates by sea.

"The worst fears of Virginia's leaders were realized when, in 1676, a group of these former servants returned from a fruitless expedition against the Indians to attack their rulers in what was called Bacon's Rebellion. Governor William Berkeley bemoaned his lot in terms that defined the problem: 'How miserable that man is that Governes a People wher six parts of seaven at least are Poore Endebted Discontented and Armed.'[31]

"The solution came naturally and without decision. The planters purchased more slaves and imported fewer English servants. Slaves were more expensive initially, but their terms did not end, and their owners gained the benefits of the slaves' offspring. Africans, easily identified by color, could not hope to run away without being caught. The fear of pain and death could be and was substituted for the extension of terms as an incentive to force the slaves to work. They were not armed and could be held in chains.

"The fear of slave revolts increased as reliance on slavery grew and racial antipathy became more apparent. But this danger, while real, was less than that from restive and armed freedmen. Slaves did not have rising expectations, and no one told them they had rights. They had lost their freedom. Moreover, a woman could be made to work and have children every two years, thereby adding to the income of her master. Thus, many more women than indentured servants were imported.

"A free society divided between large landholders and small was much less riven by antagonisms than one divided between landholders and landless, masterless men. With the freedmen's expectations, sobriety, and status restored, he was no longer a man to be feared. That fact, together with the presence of a growing mass of alien slaves, tended to draw the white settlers closer together and to reduce the importance of the class difference between yeoman farmer and large plantation owner.

"Racial fears tended to lessen the economic and political differences between rich and poor whites. And as royal officials and tax collectors became more oppressive, both groups joined forces in protesting the import taxes on tobacco which provided income for the high and the low. The rich began to look to their less wealthy neighbors for political support against the English government and in local elections.

"Wealthy whites, of course, retained all their former prerogatives, but the creation of a black subclass enabled poor whites to identify with and support the policies of the upper class. With the, safe economic advantage provided by their slaves, large landowners were willing to grant poor whites a larger role in the political process."

"So, Colonel," I interrupted, "you are saying that slavery for blacks not only provided wealth for rich whites but, paradoxically, led also to greater freedom for poor whites. One of our twentieth-century historians, Edmund Morgan, has explained this paradox of slave owners espousing freedom and liberty:

> Aristocrats could more safely preach equality in a slave society than in a free one. Slaves did not become levering mobs, because their owners would see to it that they had no chance to. The apostrophes to equality were not addressed to them. And because Virginia's labor force was composed mainly of slaves, who had been isolated by race and removed from the political equation, the remaining free laborers and tenant farmers were too few in number to constitute a serious threat to the superiority of the men who assured them of their equality.

"In effect," I concluded, "what I call a contradiction here was deemed a solution then. Slavery enabled the rich to keep their lands, arrested discontent and repression of other Englishmen, strengthened their rights and nourished their attachment to liberty. But the solution, as Professor Morgan said, 'put an end to the process of turning Africans into Englishmen. The rights of Englishmen were preserved by destroying the rights of Africans.'"[33]

"Do you charge that our belief in individual liberty is feigned?" demanded a Virginian, outraged.

"It was Professor Morgan's point," I replied, "not that 'a belief in republican equality had to rest on slavery, but only that in Virginia (and probably in other southern colonies) it did. The most ardent American republicans were Virginians, and their ardor was not unrelated to their power over the men and women they held in bondage.' "[34]

And now, for the first time, the Colonel looked at me, amazed. "My thoughts on this slavery matter have confounded my mind for many years, and yet you summarize them in a few paragraphs. I must, after all, thank you." He walked back to his seat in a daze, neither commended nor condemned by his colleagues. Most, indeed, were deep in thought – but for a few delegates I noticed trying desperately to signal to passers by in the street. But I could not attend to them: my time, I knew, must be growing short.

"The Colonel," I began again, "has performed a valuable service. He has delineated the advantages of slavery as an institution in this country. And your lengthy debates here are but prelude to the struggles that will follow your incorporation of this moral evil into the nation's basic law."

"Woman! We implore you to allow us to continue our work. While we may be inconsistent about the Negro problem, we are convinced that this is the only way open to us. You asked that we let your people go. We cannot do that and still preserve the potential of this nation for good – a potential that requires us to recognize here and now what later generations may condemn as evil. And as we talk I wonder – are the problems of race in your time equally paradoxical?"

I longed to continue the debate, but never got the chance. Apparently someone outside had finally understood the delegates' signals for help, and had summoned the local militia. Hearing some commotion beyond the window, I turned to see a small cannon being rolled up, pointing straight at me. Then, in quick succession, the cannoneer lighted the fuse; the delegates dived under their desks; the cannon fired; and, with an ear-splitting roar, the cannonball broke against the light shield and splintered, leaving me and the shield intact.

I knew then my mission was over, and I returned to the twentieth century.

Notes

1 Samuel Eliot Morison, *The Oxford History of the American People* (New York: New American Library, 1965), p. 305.
2 See J. Miller, The Wolf By the Ears (New York: Free Press, 1977), p. 31.
3 Donald Robinson, *Slavery in the Structure of American Politics: 1756–1820* (New York: Harcourt Brace Jovanovich, 1971), p. 92, quoting from Thomas Jefferson, *Notes on the State of Virginia*, ed. T. Abernethy (1964) [or *Notes on the State of Virginia*, ed. William Harwood Peden (Chapel Hill, NC: University of North Carolina Press, 1954)].
4 Ibid.
5 Staughton Lynd, *Class Conflict, Slavery, and the United States Constitution* (Indianapolis, Ind.: Bobbs-Merrill, 1967), pp. 181–2 (quoting Max Farrand (ed.) *The Records of the Federal Convention of 1787* [1911] (New Haven, Conn.: Yale University Press, 1966), vol. I, p. 533).

6   See, for example, Lynd, *Class Conflict*, p. 182.
7   Robinson, *Slavery in the Structure of American Politics*, p. 185.
8   Farrand, *Records*, vol. I, p. xvi.
9   William Wiecek, *The Sources of Antislavery Constitutionalism in America: 1760–1848* (Ithaca, NY: Cornell University Press, 1977), pp. 63–4.
10   Robinson, *Slavery in the Structure of American Politics*, p. 210.
11   Ibid., pp. 55–7.
12   Charles Beard, *An Economic Interpetation of the Constitution of the United States* (New York: Macmillan, 1913), pp. 64–151. See also Pope McCorkle, "The historian as intellectual: Charles Beard and the Constitution reconsidered," *American Journal of Legal History* 38 (1984), p. 314, reviewing the criticism of Beard's work and finding validity in his thesis that the Framers primarily sought to advance the property interests of the wealthy.
13   Morison, *Oxford History*, p. 304.
14   Dumas Malone, *Jefferson and the Rights of Man* (Boston, Mass.: Little, Brown, 1951), p. 172 (letter from Washington to Thomas Jefferson, 31 August 1788).
15   W. Mazyck, *George Washington and the Negro* (Washington, DC: Associated Publishers 1932), p. 112.
16   Ibid.
17   Derrick Bell, *Race, Racism and American Law* (2d edn, Boston, Mass.: Little, Brown, 1980), pp. 29–30.
18   James Madison, quoted in Farrand, *Records*, vol. I, p. xvi.
19   Malone, *Jefferson*, p. 167 (letter written in 1788 from James Madison to Philip Mazzei).
20   *The Records of the Federal Convention of 1787* (rev. edn, New Haven, Conn: Yale University Press, 1937), vol. II, p. 222.
21   Gouverneur Morris, quoted in Robinson, *Slavery in the Structure of American Politics*, p. 200.
22   *The Records of the Federal Convention of 1787*, p. 222.
23   See Edmund Morgan, "Slavery and feedom: the American paradox," *Journal of American History* 59 (1972), pp. 1, 6.
24   See Wiecek, *Sources of Antislavery Constitutionalism*, pp. 62–3.
25   A. Leon Higginbotham, *In the Matter of Color: Race and the American Legal Process: The Colonial Period* (New York: Oxford University Press, 1978), p. 380.
26   Wiecek, *Sources of Antislavery Constitutionalism*, p. 42.
27   Luther Martin, quoted in David Brion Davis, *The Problem of Slavery in the Age of Revolution, 1770–1823* (Ithaca, NY: Cornell University Press, 1975), p. 323.
28   In the Northern states, slavery was abolished by constitutional provision in Vermont (1777), Ohio (1802), Illinois (1818), and Indiana (1816); by a judicial decision in Massachusetts (1783); by constitutional interpretation in New Hampshire (1857); and by gradual abolition acts in Pennsylvania (1780), Rhode Island (1784), Connecticut (1784 and 1797). New York (1799 and 1817), and New Jersey (1804). See L. Litwack, North of Slavery (Chicago: University of Chicago Press, 1961), pp. 3–20.
29   Broadus Mitchell and Louise Mitchell, *A Biography of the Constitution of the United States* (New York: Oxford University Press, 1964), pp. 100–1.
30   Morgan, "Slavery and freedom." The position taken by the Colonel is based on the motivation for American slavery set out in Professor Morgan's paper; he developed the thesis at greater length in his *Amerian Slavery, American Freedom* (New York: Norton, 1975).

31 Morgan, "Slavery and freedom," p. 22.
32 Morgan, *American Slavery, American Freedom*, pp. 380–1.
33 Morgan, "Slavery and freedom," p. 24.
34 Morgan, *American Slavery, American Freedom*, p. 381.

Kwame Anthony Appiah accomplishes two complex tasks in the progression of this article. He traces W. E. B. Du Bois's thoughts about the concept of race from 1897 to 1940; he clarifies the ways in which there is no such thing as race, according to scientists.

Focus questions:
1 What were Du Bois's different concepts of race throughout his career?
2 What problems are there with each of these concepts?
3 What are the scientific reasons for not believing in the existence of race?

2   The Uncompleted Argument: Du Bois and the Illusion of Race

Kwame Anthony Appiah

Contemporary biologists are not agreed on the question of whether there are any human races, despite the widespread scientific consensus on the underlying genetics. For most purposes, however, we can reasonably treat this issue as terminological. What most people in most cultures ordinarily believe about the significance of "racial" difference is quite remote, I think, from what the biologists *are* agreed on. Every reputable biologist will agree that human genetic variability between the populations of Africa and Europe and Asia is not much greater than that within those populations, though *how much* greater depends, in part, on the measure of genetic variability the biologist chooses. If biologists want to make interracial difference seem relatively large, they can say that "the population of genic variation attributable to racial differences is . . . 9–11%."[1] If they want to make it seem small, they can say that for two people who are both Caucasoid, the chances of difference in genetic constitution at one site on a given chromosome are currently estimated at about 14.3 percent, while for any two people taken at random from the human population, they are estimated at about 14.8 percent. (I discuss why this is considered a measure of genetic difference in the next section.) The statistical facts about the distribution of variant characteristics in human populations and subpopulations are the same, however the matter is expressed. Apart from the visible morphological characteristics of skin, hair, and bone, by which we are inclined to assign people to the broadest racial categories – black, white, yellow – there are few genetic characteristics to be found in the population of

England that are not found in similar proportions in Zaire or in China; and few (though more) that are found in Zaire but not in similar proportions in China or in England. All this, I repeat, is part of the consensus.[2] A more familiar part of the consensus is that the differences between peoples in language, moral affections, aesthetic attitudes, or political ideology – those differences which most deeply affect us in our dealing with each other – are not biologically determined to any significant degree.

These claims will, no doubt, seem outrageous to those who confuse the question of whether biological difference accounts for our differences with the question of whether biological similarity accounts for our similarities. Some of our similarities as human beings in these broadly cultural respects – the capacity to acquire human languages, for example, or, more specifically, the ability to smile – are to a significant degree biologically determined. We can study the biological basis for these cultural capacities and give biological explanations of our exercise of them. But if biological difference between human beings is unimportant in these explanations – and it is – then racial difference, as a species of biological difference, will not matter either.

In this essay I discuss the way in which W. E. B. Du Bois, who called his life story the "autobiography of a race concept" – came gradually, though never completely, to assimilate the unbiological nature of races. I have made these prefatory remarks partly because it is my experience that the biological evidence about race is not sufficiently known and appreciated but also because the foregoing statements are important in discussing Du Bois. Throughout his life, Du Bois was concerned not just with the meaning of race but with the truth about it. We are more inclined at present, however, not to express our understanding of the intellectual development of people and cultures as a movement toward the truth; I sketch some of the reasons for this at the end of the essay. I begin, therefore, by saying what I think the rough truth is about race, because, against the stream, I am disposed to argue that this struggle toward the truth is exactly what we find in the life of Du Bois. He can claim, in my view, to have thought longer, more engagedly, and more publicly about race than did any other social theorist of our century.

The Conservation of Races

Du Bois's first extended discussion of the concept of race is in "The Conservation of Races" (1897), a paper he delivered to the American Negro Academy in the year it was founded. The "American Negro," he declares, has "been led to . . . minimize race distinctions" because "back of most of the discussions of race with which he is familiar, have lurked certain assumptions as to his natural abilities, as to his political, intellectual and moral status, which he felt were wrong." He continues: "Nevertheless, in our calmer moments we must acknowledge that human beings are divided into races," even if when we "come to inquire into the essential difference of races we find it hard to come at once to any definite conclusion." For what it is worth, however, the "final word of science, so far, is that we have at least two, perhaps three, great families of human beings – the whites and Negroes, possibly the yellow race."[3]

Du Bois is not, however, satisfied with the final word of nineteenth-century science. For, as he thinks, what matter are not the "grosser physical differences of color, hair and bone" but the "differences – subtle, delicate and elusive, though they may be – which have silently but definitely separated men into groups."[4]

> While these subtle forces have generally followed the natural cleavage of common blood, descent and physical peculiarities, they have at other times swept across and ignored these. At all times, however, they have divided human beings into races, which, while they perhaps transcend scientific definition, nevertheless, are clearly defined to the eye of the historian and sociologist,
>
> If this be true, then the history of the world is the history, not of individuals, but of groups, not of nations, but of races. . . . What, then, is a race? It is a vast family of human beings, generally of common blood and language, always of common history, traditions and impulse, who are both voluntarily and in-voluntarily striving together for the accomplishment of certain more or less vividly conceived ideals of life.[5]

We have moved, then, away from the "scientific" – that is, biological and anthropological – conception of race to a sociohistorical notion. Using this socio-historical criterion – the sweep of which certainly encourages the thought that no biological or anthropological definition is possible – Du Bois considers that there are not three but eight "distinctly differentiated races, in the sense in which history tells us the word must be used."[6] The list is an odd one: Slavs, Teutons, English (both in Great Britain and America), Negroes (of Africa and, likewise, America), the Romance race, Semites, Hindus, and Mongolians.

> The question now is: What is the real distinction between these nations? Is it the physical differences of blood, color and cranial measurements? Certainly we must all acknowledge that physical differences play a great part. . . . But while race differences have followed mainly physical race lines, yet no mere physical distinc-tions would really define or explain the deeper differences – the cohesiveness and continuity of these groups. The deeper differences are spiritual, psychical, differ-ences – undoubtedly based on the physical, but infinitely transcending them.[7]

Each of the various races is "striving, . . . in its own way, to develop for civiliza-tion its particular message, its particular ideal, which shall help to guide the world nearer and nearer that perfection of human life for which we all long, that 'one far off Divine event.'"[8] For Du Bois, then, the problem for the Negro is the discovery and expression of the message of his or her race.

> The full, complete Negro message of the whole Negro race has not as yet been given to the world.
>
> The question is, then: how shall this message be delivered; how shall these various ideals be realized? The answer is plain: by the development of these race groups, not as individuals, but as races. . . . For the development of Negro genius,

of Negro literature and art, of Negro spirit, only Negroes bound and welded together, Negroes inspired by one vast ideal, can work out in its fullness the great message we have for humanity.

For this reason, the advance guard of the Negro people – the eight million people of Negro blood in the United States of America – must soon come to realize that if they are to take their just place in the van of Pan-Negroism, then their destiny is *not* absorption by the white Americans.[9]

Du Bois ends by proposing his Academy Creed, which begins with words that echo down almost a century of American race relations:

1   We believe that the Negro people, as a race, have a contribution to make to civilization and humanity, which no other race can make.
2   We believe it the duty of the Americans of Negro descent, as a body, to maintain their race identity until this mission of the Negro people is accomplished, and the ideal of human brotherhood has become a practical possibility.[10]

What can we make of this analysis and prescription? On the face of it, Du Bois's argument in "The Conservation of Races" is that "race" is not a scientific – that is, biological – concept. It is a sociohistorical concept. Sociohistorical races each have a "message" for humanity – a message which derives, in some way, from God's purpose in creating races. The Negro race has still to deliver its full message, and so it is the duty of Negroes to work together – through race organizations – so that this message can be delivered.

We do not need the theological underpinnings of this argument. What is essential is the thought that through common action Negroes can achieve, by virtue of their sociohistorical community, worthwhile ends which will not otherwise be achieved. On the face of it, then, Du Bois's strategy here is the antithesis in the classic dialectic of reaction to prejudice. The thesis in this dialectic – which Du Bois reports as the American Negro's attempt to "minimize race distinctions" – is the denial of difference. Du Bois's antithesis is the acceptance of difference, along with the claims that each group has its part to play; that the white race and its racial Other are related not as superior to inferior but as complementaries; and that the Negro message is, with the white one, part of the message of humankind.

I call this pattern the classic dialectic for a simple reason: we find it in feminism also – on the one hand, a simple claim to equality, a denial of substantial difference; on the other, a claim to a special message, revaluing the feminine Other not as the helpmeet of sexism, but as the New Woman. Because this is a classic dialectic, my reading of Du Bois's argument is a natural one. I believe that it is substantially correct. But to see that it is correct, we need to make clear that what Du Bois attempts, despite his own claims to the contrary, is not the transcendence of the nineteenth-century scientific conception of race – as we shall see, he relies on it – but rather, as the dialectic requires, a revaluation of the Negro race in the face of the sciences of racial inferiority. We can begin by analyzing the sources of tension in Du Bois's allegedly sociohistorical conception of race, which he explicitly sets over against the scientific conception. The tension is plain enough in his reference to "common blood"; for this, dressed up with fancy craniometry, a dose of melanin, and some measure for hair-curl, is what the scientific notion amounts to. If he has fully transcended the scientific notion, what is the role of this talk about "blood"?

We may leave aside for the moment the common "impulses" and the voluntary and involuntary "strivings." These must be due either to a shared biological inheritance, "based on the physical, but infinitely transcending" it; to a shared history; or, of course, to some combination of these. If Du Bois's notion is purely sociohistorical, then the issue is common history and traditions; otherwise, the issue is, at least in part, a common biology. We shall know which only when we understand the core of Du Bois's conception of race.

The claim that a race generally shares a common language is also plainly inessential: the "Romance" race is not of common language nor, more obviously, is the Negro. And "common blood" can mean little more than "of shared ancestry," which is already implied by talk of a "vast family." At the center of Du Bois's conception, then, is the claim that a race is "a vast family of human beings, . . . always of common history [and] traditions." So, if we want to understand Du Bois, our question must be: What is a family of common history?

We already see that the scientific notion, which presupposes common features in virtue of a common biology derived from a common descent, is not fully transcended. A family can, it is true, have adopted children, kin by social rather than biological law. By analogy, therefore, a vast human family might contain people joined not by biology but by an act of choice. But it is plain that Du Bois cannot have been contemplating this possibility: like all of his contemporaries, he would have taken for granted that race is a matter of birth. Indeed, to understand the talk of "family," we must distance ourselves from its sociological meaning. A family is almost always culturally defined only through either patrilineal or matrilineal descent. But if an individual drew a "conceptual" family tree back over five hundred years and assumed that he or she was descended from each ancestor in only one way, it would have more than a million branches at the top. Although in such a case many individuals would be represented by more than one branch – that far back we are all going to be descended from many people by more than one route – it is plain that either a matrilineal or patrilineal conception of our family histories drastically underrepresents the biological range of our ancestry. Biology and social convention go startlingly different ways. Let's pretend, secure in our republicanism, that the claim of the queen of England to the throne depends partly on a single line from one of her ancestors nine hundred years ago. If there were no overlaps in her family tree, there would be more than fifty thousand billion such lines, though there have never been that many people on the earth; even with reasonable assumptions about overlaps, there are millions of such lines. We chose one line, even though most of the population of England is probably descended from William the Conqueror by some uncharted route. Biology is democratic: all parents are equal. Thus, to speak of two people as being of common ancestry requires that before some historical point in the past, a large proportion of the branches in their respective family trees coincided.[11]

Already, then, Du Bois requires, as the scientific conception does, a common ancestry (in the sense just defined) with whatever – if anything – that ancestry biologically entails. But apparently this does not commit him to the scientific conception, for there are many groups of common ancestry – ranging from humanity in general to narrower groups such as the Slavs, Teutons, and Romance people taken together – which do not, for Du Bois, constitute races. Thus, Du Bois's "common history," which must be what is supposed to distinguish Slav from Teuton, is an essential part of his conception. The problem is whether a common history can be a criterion that distinguishes one group of human beings – extended in time – from another. Does adding a notion of common history allow us to make the distinctions between Slav and Teuton or between English and Negro? The answer is no.

Consider, for example, Du Bois himself. As the descendant of Dutch ancestors, why doesn't his relationship to the history of Holland in the fourteenth century (which he shares with all people of Dutch descent) make him a member of the Teutonic race? The answer is straightforward: the Dutch were not Negroes; Du Bois is. But it follows from this that the history of Africa is part of the common history of African Americans not simply because African Americans descended from various peoples who played a part in African history but rather because African history is the history of people of the same race.

My general point is this: in order to recognize two events at different times as part of the history of a single individual, we have to have a criterion for identity of the individual at each of those times, independent of his or her participation in the two events. In the same way, when we recognize two events as belonging to the history of one race, we have to have a criterion for membership in the race at those times, independent of the participation of the members in the two events. To put it more simply: sharing a common group history cannot be a criterion for being members of the same group, for we would have to be able to identify the group in order to identify its history. Someone in the fourteenth century could share a common history with me through our membership in a historically extended race only if something accounts both for his or her membership in the race in the fourteenth century and for mine in the twentieth. That something cannot, on pain of circularity, be the history of the race. Whatever holds Du Bois's races together conceptually cannot be a common history; it is only because they are bound together that members of a race at different times can share a history at all. If this is true, Du Bois's reference to a common history cannot be doing any work in his individuation of races. And once we have stripped away the sociohistorical elements from Du Bois's definition of race, we are left with the true criterion.

Consequently, not only the talk of language, which Du Bois admits is neither necessary (the Romance race speaks many languages) nor sufficient (African Americans and Americans generally speak the same language) for racial identity, must be expunged from the definition; now we have seen that talk of common history and traditions must go too. We are left with common descent and the common impulses and strivings that I put aside earlier. Since common descent and the characteristics that flow from it are part of the scientific conception of race, these impulses are all that remain to do the job that Du Bois had claimed for a sociohistorical conception: namely, to distinguish his conception from the biological one. Du Bois claims that the existence of races is "clearly defined to the eye of the historian and sociologist."[12] Since biology acknowledges common ancestry as a criterion, whatever extra insight is provided by sociohistorical understanding can be gained only by observing the common impulses and strivings. Reflection suggests, however, that this cannot be true. For what common impulses – whether voluntary or involuntary – do the Romance people share that the Teutons and the English do not?

Du Bois had read the historiography of the Anglo-Saxon school, which accounted for the democratic impulse in America by the racial tradition of the Anglo-Saxon moot. He had read American and British historians in earnest discussion of the "Latin" spirit of Romance peoples; and perhaps he had believed some of it. Here perhaps may be the source of the notion that history and sociology can observe the differing impulses of races.

In all these writings, however, such impulses are allegedly discovered to be the a posteriori of racial and national groups, not criteria of membership in them. It is, indeed, because the claim is a posteriori that historical evidence is relevant to it. And if we ask what common impulses history had detected that allow us to recognize the Negro, we will see that Du Bois's claim to have found a criterion of identity in these impulses is mere bravado. If, without evidence about his or her impulses, we can say who is a Negro, then it cannot be part of what it is to be a Negro that he or she has them; rather, it must be an a posteriori claim that people of a common race, defined by descent and biology, have impulses, for whatever reason, in common. Of course, the common impulses of a biologically defined group may be historically caused by common experiences – common history. But Du Bois's claim can only be that biologically defined races happen to share, for whatever reason, common impulses. The common impulses cannot be a criterion of group membership. And if that is so, we are left with the scientific conception.

How, then, is it possible for Du Bois's criteria to issue in eight groups, while the scientific conception issues in three? The reason is clear from the list. Slavs, Teutons, English, Hindus, and Romance peoples each live in a characteristic geographical region. (American English – and, for that matter, American Teutons, American Slavs, and American Romance people – share recent ancestry with their European "cousins" and thus share a relation to a place and certain languages and traditions.) Semites and Mongolians each inhabit a rather large geographical region also. Du Bois's talk of common history conceals his superaddition of a geographical criterion: group history is, in part, the history of people who have lived in the same place.[13]

The criterion Du Bois actually uses amounts to this: people are members of the same race if they share features in virtue of being descended largely from people of the same region. Those features may be physical – hence African

Americans are Negroes – or cultural – hence Anglo-Americans are English. Focusing on one sort of feature – "grosser . . . differences of color, hair and bone" – defines "whites and Negroes, possibly the yellow race" as the "final word of science, so far." Focusing on a different feature – language and shared customs – defines instead Teutons, Slavs, and Romance peoples. The tension in Du Bois's definition of race reflects the fact that, for the purposes of European historiography (of which his Harvard and University of Berlin training had made him aware), it was the latter that mattered; but for the purposes of American social and political life, it was the former.

The real difference in Du Bois's conception, therefore, is not that his definition of race is at odds with the scientific one. It is, rather, as the classic dialectic requires, that he assigns to race a moral and metaphysical significance different from that of his contemporaries. The distinctive claim is that the Negro race has a positive message, a message not only of difference but of value. And that, it seems to me, is the significance of the sociohistorical dimension: the strivings of a race are, as Du Bois viewed the matter, the stuff of history. "The history of the world is the history, not of individuals, but of groups, not of nations, but of races, and he who ignores or seeks to override the race idea in human history ignores and overrides the central thought of all history."[14] By studying history, we can discern the outlines of the message of each race.

Crisis: August 1911

We have seen that, for the purpose that concerned him most – understanding the status of the Negro – Du Bois was thrown back on the scientific definition of race, which he officially rejected. But the scientific definition (Du Bois's uneasiness with which is reflected in his remark that races "perhaps transcend scientific definition") was itself threatened as he spoke at the first meeting of the Negro Academy. In the later nineteenth century most thinking people (like too many even today) believed that what Du Bois called the "grosser differences" were a sign of an inherited racial essence which accounted for the intellectual and moral deficiency of the "lower" races. In "The Conservation of Races" Du Bois elected, in effect, to admit that color was a sign of a racial essence but to deny that the cultural capacities of the black-skinned, curly-haired members of humankind were inferior to those of the white-skinned, straighter-haired ones. But the collapse of the sciences of racial inferiority led Du Bois to deny the connection between cultural capacity and gross morphology – the familiar impulses and strivings of his earlier definition.

We can find evidence of his change of mind in an article in the August 1911 issue of the *Crisis*.

> The leading scientists of the world have come forward[15] . . . and laid down in categorical terms a series of propositions which may be summarized as follows:
> 1(a) It is not legitimate to argue from differences in physical characteristics to differences in mental characteristics. . . .

2(b) The civilization of a . . . race at any particular moment of time offers no index to its innate or inherited capacities.[16]

These results have been amply confirmed since then. And we do well, I think, to remind ourselves of the current picture.

Human characteristics are genetically determined, to the extent that they are determined, by sequences of DNA in the chromosomes – in other words, by genes.[17] The region of a chromosome occupied by a gene is called a locus. Some loci are occupied in different members of a population by different genes, each of which is called an allele; and a locus is said to be polymorphic in a population if there is at least one pair of alleles for it. Perhaps as many as half the loci in the human population are polymorphic; the rest, naturally enough, are monomorphic.

Many loci have not just two alleles but several, and each has a frequency in the population. Suppose a particular locus has n alleles, which we can call 1, 2, and so on up to n; then we can call their frequencies x_1, x_2, . . ., to x_n. If we consider two randomly chosen members of a population and look at the same locus on one chromosome of each of them, the probability that they will have the same allele at that locus is just the probability that they will both have the first allele (x_1^2) plus the probability that they will both have the second (x_2^2) plus the probability that they will both have the nth (x_n^2). We can call this number the expected homozygosity at that locus: it is just the proportion of people in the population who would be homozygous at that locus – having identical alleles at that locus on each of the relevant chromosomes – provided the population is mating at random.[18]

Now if we take the average value of the expected homozygosity for all loci, polymorphic and monomorphic (which, for some reason, tends to get labeled J), we have a measure of the chance that two people, taken at random from the population, will share the same allele at a locus on a chromosome taken at random. This is a good measure of how similar in biology a randomly chosen pair of individuals should be expected to be *and* a good (though rough) guide to how closely the populations are genetically related.

I can now express simply one measure of the extent to which members of the human populations we call races differ more from each other than they do from members of the same race. For example, the value of J for Caucasoids – based largely on samples from the English population – is estimated to be about 0.857, while that for the whole human population is estimated at 0.852.[19] The chances, in other words, that two people taken at random from the human population will have the same characteristic at a locus are about 85.2 percent, while the chances for two (white) people taken from the population of England are about 85.7 percent. And since 85.2 is 100 minus 14.8 and 85.7 is 100 minus 14.3, this is equivalent to what I said earlier: the chances of two people who are both Caucasoid differing in genetic constitution at one site on a given chromosome are about 14.3 percent, while for any two people taken at random from the human population they are about 14.8 percent. The conclusion is obvious: given only a person's race, it is hard to say what his or her biological characteristics will be, except in respect of the "grosser" features of color, hair, and bone (the genetics of which are, in any case, rather poorly understood) – features of "morphological differentiation," as the evolutionary biologist would say. As Nei and Roychoudhury express it, somewhat coyly, "The extent of genic differentiation between human races is not always correlated with the degree of morphological differentiation."[20]

To have established that race is relatively unimportant in explaining biological differences between people, where biological difference is measured in the proportion of differences in loci on the chromosome, is not yet to show that race is unimportant in explaining cultural difference. It could be that large differences in intellectual or moral capacity are caused by differences at very few loci and that at these loci all (or most) black-skinned people differ from all (or most) white-skinned or yellow-skinned ones. As it happens, there is little evidence for any such proposition and much against it. But suppose we had reason to believe it. In the biological conception of the human organism, in which characteristics are determined by the pattern of genes in interaction with environments, it is the presence of the alleles (which give rise to these moral and intellectual capacities) that accounts for the observed differences in those capacities in people in similar environments. So the characteristic racial morphology – skin and hair and bone – could only be a sign of those differences if it were (highly) correlated with those alleles. Furthermore, even if it were so correlated, the causal explanation of the differences would be that they differed in those alleles, not that they differed in race. Since there are no such strong correlations, even those who think that intellectual and moral character are strongly genetically determined must accept that race is at best a poor indicator of capacity.

But it was earlier evidence, pointing similarly to the conclusion that "the genic variation within and between the three major races of man . . . is small compared with the intraracial variation"[21] – and that differences in morphology were not correlated strongly with intellectual and moral capacity, that led Du Bois in the *Crisis* to an explicit rejection of the claim that biological race mattered for understanding the status of the Negro:

> So far at least as intellectual and moral aptitudes are concerned, we ought to speak of civilizations where we now speak of races. . . . Indeed, even the physical characteristics, excluding the skin color of a people, are to no small extent the direct result of the physical and social environment under which it is living. . . . These physical characteristics are furthermore too indefinite and elusive to serve as a basis for any rigid classification or division of human groups.[22]

This is straightforward enough. Yet it would be too swift a conclusion to suppose that Du Bois here expresses his deepest convictions. After 1911, he went on to advocate Pan-Africanism, as he had advocated Pan-Negroism in 1897, and whatever African Americans and Africans, from Ashanti to Zulu, share, it is not a single civilization.

Du Bois managed to maintain Pan-Africanism while officially rejecting talk of race as anything other than a synonym for color. We can see how he did this by turning to his second autobiography, Dusk of Dawn, published in 1940.

Dusk of Dawn

In *Dusk of Dawn* – the "essay toward an autobiography of a race concept" – Du Bois explicitly allies himself with the claim that race is not a scientific concept.

> It is easy to see that scientific definition of race is impossible; it is easy to prove that physical characteristics are not so inherited as to make it possible to divide the world into races; that ability is the monopoly of no known aristocracy; that the possibilities of human development cannot be circumscribed by color, nationality, or any conceivable definition of race.[23]

But we need no scientific definition, for

> all this has nothing to do with the plain fact that throughout the world today organized groups of men by monopoly of economic and physical power, legal enactment and intellectual training are limiting with determination and unflagging zeal the development of other groups; and that the concentration particularly of economic power today puts the majority of mankind into a slavery to the rest.[24]

Or, as he puts it pithily a little later, "the black man is a person who must ride 'Jim Crow' in Georgia."[25]

Yet, just a few pages earlier, he has explained why he remains a Pan-Africanist, committed to a political program which binds all this indefinable black race together. The passage is worth citing extensively. Du Bois begins with Countée Cullen's question, "What is Africa to me?" and answers,

> Once I should have answered the question simply: I should have said "fatherland" or perhaps better "motherland" because I was born in the century when the walls of race were clear and straight; when the world consisted of mut[u]ally exclusive races; and even though the edges might be blurred, there was no question of exact definition and understanding of the meaning of the word. . . .
>
> Since then [the writing of "The Conservation of Races"] the concept of race has so changed and presented so much of contradiction that as I face Africa I ask myself: what is it between us that constitutes a tie which I can feel better than I can explain? Africa is, of course, my fatherland. Yet neither my father nor my father's father ever saw Africa or knew its meaning or cared overmuch for it. My mother's folk were closer and yet their direct connection, in culture and race, became tenuous; still, my tie to Africa is strong. On this vast continent were born and lived a large portion of my direct ancestors going back a thousand years or more. The mark of their heritage is upon me in color and hair. These are obvious things, but of little meaning in themselves; only important as they stand for real and more subtle differences from other men. Whether they do or not, I do not know nor does science know today.
>
> But one thing is sure and that is the fact that since the fifteenth century these ancestors of mine and their other descendants have had a common history; have suffered a common disaster and have one long memory. The actual ties of heritage between the individuals of this group, varying with the ancestors that they have in common [with] many others: Europeans and Semites, perhaps Mongolians,

certainly American Indians. But the physical bond is least and the badge of color relatively unimportant save as a badge; the real essence of this kinship is its social heritage of slavery; the discrimination and insult; and this heritage binds together not simply the children of Africa, but extends through yellow Asia and into the South Seas. It is this unity that draws me to Africa.[26]

This passage is affecting, powerfully expressed. We might like to be able to follow it in its conclusions. But we should not; since the passage seduces us into error, we should begin distancing ourselves from the appeal of its argument by noticing how it echoes an earlier text. Color and hair are unimportant save "as they stand for real and more subtle differences," Du Bois says here, and we recall the "subtle forces" that "generally followed the natural cleavage of common blood, descent and physical peculiarities" of "The Conservation of Races." There it was an essential part of the argument that these subtle forces – "impulses" and "strivings" – were the common property of those who shared a "common blood"; here, Du Bois does "not know nor does science" whether this is so. But if it is not so, then, on Du Bois's own admission, these "obvious things" are "of little meaning." If they are of little meaning, then his mention of them marks, on the surface of his argument, the extent to which he cannot quite escape the appeal of the earlier conception of race.

Du Bois's yearning for the earlier conception which he prohibited himself from using accounts for the pathos of the gap between the unconfident certainty that Africa is "of course" his fatherland and the concession that it is not the land of his father or his father's father. What use is such a fatherland? What use is a motherland with which your own mother's connection is "tenuous"? What does it matter that a large portion of his ancestors have lived on that vast continent, if there is no subtler bond with them than brute – that is, culturally unmediated – biological descent and its entailed "badge" of hair and color?

Even in the passage that follows Du Bois's explicit disavowal of the scientific conception of race, the references to "common history" – the "one long memory," the "social heritage of slavery" – only leads us back into the now familiar move of substituting a sociohistorical conception of race for the biological one; but that is simply to bury the biological conception below the surface, not to transcend it. Because he never truly "speaks of civilization," Du Bois cannot ask if there is not in American culture – which undoubtedly *is* his culture – an African residue to take hold of and rejoice in, a subtle connection mediated not by genetics but by intentions, by meaning. Du Bois has no more conceptual resources here for explicating the unity of the Negro race – the Pan-African identity – than he had in "The Conservation of Races" half a century earlier. A glorious non sequitur must be submerged in the depths of the argument. It is easily brought to the surface.

If what Du Bois has in common with Africa is a history of "discrimination and insult," then this binds him, by his own account, to "yellow Asia and . . . the South Seas" also. How can something he shares with the whole nonwhite world bind him to only a part of it? Once we interrogate the argument here, a further suspicion arises that the claim to this bond may be based on a hyperbolic reading of the facts. Du Bois's experience of "discrimination and insult" in his American childhood and as an adult citizen of the industrialized world was different in character from that experienced by, say, Kwame Nkrumah in colonized West Africa; it is absent altogether in large parts of "yellow Asia." What Du Bois shares with the nonwhite world is not insult but the *badge* of insult; and the badge, without the insult, is the very skin and hair and bone which it is impossible to connect with a scientific definition of race.

Concluding Unscientific Postscript

Du Bois died in Nkrumah's Ghana, led there by the dream of Pan-Africanism and the reality of American racism. If he escaped that racism, he never completed the escape from race. The logic of his argument leads naturally to the final repudiation of race as a term of difference and to speaking instead "of civilizations where we now speak of races." The logic is the same logic that has brought us to speak of genders where we spoke of sexes, and a rational assessment of the evidence requires that we should endorse not only the logic but the premises of each argument. I have only sketched the evidence for these premises in the case of race, but it is all there in the scientific journals. Discussing Du Bois has been largely a pretext for adumbrating the argument he never quite managed to complete.

I think the argument is worth making because I believe that we – scholars in the academy – have not done enough to share it with our fellow citizens. One barrier facing those of us in the humanities has been methodological. Under Saussurian hegemony, we have too easily become accustomed to thinking of meaning as constituted by systems of differences purely internal to our endlessly structured *langues*.[27] Race, we all assume, is, like all other concepts, constructed by metaphor and metonymy; it stands in, metonymically, for the Other; it bears the weight, metaphorically, of other kinds of difference.

Yet, in our social lives away from the text-world of the academy, we too easily take reference for granted. Even if the concept of race *is* a structure of oppositions – white opposed to black (but also to yellow), Jew opposed to Gentile (but also to Arab) – it is a structure whose realization is, at best, problematic and, at worst, impossible. If we can now hope to understand the concept embodied in this system of oppositions, we are nowhere near finding referents for it. The truth is that there are no races: there is nothing in the world that can do all we ask "race" to do for us. The evil that is done is done by the concept and by easy – yet impossible – assumptions as to its application. What we miss through our obsession with the structure of relations of concepts is, simply, reality.

Talk of "race" is particularly distressing for those of us who take culture seriously. For, where race works – in places where "gross differences" of morphology are correlated with "subtle differences" of temperament, belief, and intention – it works as an attempt at a metonym for culture; and it does so only at the price of biologizing what is culture, or ideology. To call it "biologizing" is not to consign our concept of race to biology. What is present there is not our concept but our word only. Even the biologists who believe in human races use the term "race," as they say, "without any social implication."[28] What exists "out there" in the world – communities of meaning, shading variously into each other in the rich structure of the social world – is the province not of biology but of hermeneutic understanding.

I have examined these issues through the writings of Du Bois, with the burden of his scholarly inheritance, and have tried to transcend the system of oppositions that, had Du Bois accepted it, would have left him opposed to the (white) norm of form and value. In his early work, Du Bois took race for granted and sought to revalue one pole of the opposition of white to black. The received concept is a hierarchy, a vertical structure, and Du Bois wished to rotate the axis, to give race a "horizontal" reading. Challenge the assumption that there can be an axis, however oriented in the space of values, and the project fails for loss of presuppositions. In his later work, Du Bois – whose life's work was, in a sense, an attempt at just this impossible project – was unable to escape the notion of race he had explicitly rejected. We may borrow his own metaphor: though he saw the dawn coming, he never faced the sun. And we must surely admit that he is followed in this by many in our culture today; we too live in the dusk of that dawn.

Notes

1 Masatoshi Nei and Arun K. Roychoudhury, "Genetic relationship and evolution of human races," *Evolutionary Biology* 14 (1983), p. 11.
2 Ibid., pp. 1–59.
3 W. E. B. Du Bois, "The conservation of races," in Philip S. Foner (ed.) *W. E. B. Du Bois Speaks: Speeches and Addresses, 1890–1919* [1897] (New York: Pathfinder Press, 1970), pp. 73, 74, 75.
4 Ibid., p. 75.
5 Ibid., pp. 75–6.
6 Ibid., p. 76.
7 Ibid., p. 78.
8 Ibid.
9 Ibid., pp. 78, 79. This talk of racial absorption (and similar talk of racial extinction) reflects the idea that African Americans might disappear because their genetic heritage would be diluted by the white one. This idea might be considered absurd in any view propounding the notion of a racial essence: either a person has it or he/she doesn't. But this way of thinking conceives of racial essences as being like genes, though Mendelian genetics was not yet "rediscovered" when Du Bois wrote this piece. Du Bois is probably thinking of "passing for white"; in views of inheritance as the blending of parental "blood," the more that black "blood" is diluted, the more it is likely that *every* person of African descent in America *could* pass for white. That, of course, would be a kind of extinction of the Negro. It is interesting that those who discuss this issue assume that it would not cause the extinction of the white race also and the creation of a "hybridized" human race. But, as I say, such speculation is ruled out by the rise of Mendelian genetics.
10 Du Bois, "The conservation of races," p. 84.
11 I owe this way of thinking about the distance between social and biological ances-

try to chapter 6 of R. B. Le Page and A. Tabouret-Keller's forthcoming book, *Acts of Identity*. I am very grateful to R. B. Le Page for allowing me to see a typescript. [The book was published in 1985 in Cambridge and New York by Cambridge University Press: editor]

12 Du Bois, "The conservation of races," p. 75.

13 This seems to me the very notion that the biologists have ended up with: a population is a group of people (or, more generally, organisms) occupying a common region (or, more generally, an environmental niche), along with people largely descended from that original group who now live in other regions. See Nei and Roychoudbury, "Genetic differences between Caucasian, Negro, and Japanese populations," *Science* 177 (August 1972), pp. 434–5, and their "Genetic relationship," p. 4.

14 Du Bois, "The conservation of races," p. 75.

15 This claim was prompted by G. Spiller; see G. Spiller (ed.) *Papers in Inter-Racial Problems Communicated to the First Universal Races Congress Held at the University of London, July 26–29, 1911* [1911] (New York: Arno Press, 1969).

16 W. E. B. Du Bois, "Races," *Crisis* 2 4 (August 1911), pp. 157–9.

17 Strictly we should say that the character of an organism is fixed by genes, along with sequences of nucleic acid in the cytoplasm and some other features of the cytoplasm of the ovum. But these latter sources of human characteristics are largely swamped by the nucleic DNA and are, in any case, substantially similar in almost all people. It is the latter fact that accounts, I think, for their not being generally mentioned.

18 It follows from these definitions that where a locus is monomorphic, the expected homozygosity is going to be one.

19 These figures come from Nei and Roychoudhury, "Genetic relationship," and I have used the figures derived from looking at proteins, not blood-groups, since they claim these are likely to be more reliable. I have chosen a measure of "racial" biological difference that makes it look spectacularly small, but I would not wish to imply that it is not the case, as these authors say, that "genetic differentiation is real and generally statistically highly significant" (pp. 8, 11, and 41). I would dispute their claim that their work shows the existence of a biological basis for the classification of human races; what it shows is that human populations differ in their distributions of genes. That is a biological fact. The objection to using this fact as a basis of a system of classification is that far too many people don't fit into just one category that can be so defined.

20 Nei and Roychoudhury, "Genetic relationship," p. 44.

21 Ibid., p. 40.

22 Du Bois, "Races," p. 158.

23 W. E. B. Du Bois, *Dusk of Dawn: an Essay toward an Autobiography of a Race Concept* [1940] (New York: Schocken, 1968), p. 137.

24 Ibid., pp. 137–8.

25 Ibid., p. 153.

26 Ibid., pp. 116–17.

27 Post-structuralism is not a step forward here, as Terry Eagleton has observed (see *Literary Theory: an Introduction* (Oxford: Blackwell, 1983), pp. 143–4.

28 Nei and Roychoudhury, "Genetic relationship," p. 4.

Judith Lichtenberg suggests that what counts as racism depends on what race someone is. She then offers five categories of racist behavior that some whites would not recognize as racist.

Focus questions:
1 What is the difference between racism in the head and racism in the world?
2 For each of Lichtenberg's five types of "short of out-and-out" racism, explain why those who are affected by it and those who practice it might differ in calling it racism.

3   Racism in the Head, Racism in the World

Judith Lichtenberg

We're inclined to think that disputes about words are unimportant. We give up arguing with people when we see that our disagreements turn ("merely," we say) on terminology. It's hard to maintain this view, though, when the word in question is "racism."

Different perceptions among blacks and whites in our society about what racism is, and where it is, constitute an important source of racial tension. For many white Americans today, the word "racism" is a red flag. They don't see themselves as harboring animosity toward black people as such; they believe they hold to an ideal of equality, and of equal opportunity. So they feel insulted to be called racists, baffled by charges that we live in a racist society. A white supremacist would not be so wounded.

On the other hand, those who say our society is racist are not speaking rhetorically or hyperbolically. The claim that racism is dead or insignificant, in the face of overwhelming asymmetries between blacks and whites, in the face of the crisis of our inner cities and of the young black male, must produce anger or humiliation or incomprehension.

In general, white people today use the word "racism" to refer to the explicit conscious belief in racial superiority (typically white over black, but also sometimes black over white). For the most part, black people mean something different by racism: they mean a set of practices and institutions that result in the oppression of black people. Racism, on this view, is not a matter of what's in people's heads but of what happens in the world.

The white picture of the racist is the old-time Southern white supremacist, who proclaimed his beliefs proudly. Your typical late twentieth-century American is, at some important level, an egalitarian who rejects the supremacist creed. In her mind, then, she is not a racist.

That a person is not a racist in this sense makes a difference. Contrary to the pronouncements of some, things are worse when people explicitly believe and proclaim supremacist doctrines, and a special moral culpability attaches to holding such beliefs. But not to be a racist "in the head" is insufficient to prevent injustice and suffering that divides along racial lines.

The alternative view is that the evil we call racism is not fundamentally a matter of what's in people's heads, not a matter of their private, individual intentions, but rather a function of *public* institutions and practices that create or perpetuate social division and inequality. Who cares if your intentions are good if they reinforce or permit social discrimination and deprivation?

Racism as overt or out-and-out racism reflects a powerful strain in our attitudes toward moral responsibility. On this view, you are responsible only for what you intend; thus, if consciously you harbor no ill-will toward people of another race or background you are in that respect innocent. For those who would be deemed the oppressors, such a view is abetted by what psychologists call "cognitive dissonance" – essentially, the desire to reduce psychological discomfort. It is comfortable for white people to believe racism is dead just as long as they harbor no conscious feelings of antipathy or superiority to blacks. And, conversely, it is less painful for blacks, seeing what they see, to think otherwise.

In what follows I sketch five kinds of attitudes and practices short of out-and-out racism to which critics are calling attention when they use the word "racism" in the broad way that so irritates many white Americans.

Less-than-conscious Racism

Over the last thirty or forty years it has become publicly unacceptable, in most circles, to express racist views openly. (Even this assertion requires careful qualification. In a recent pair of focus groups conducted for People for the American Way, young whites talked openly about their negative views of blacks. The explicit avowal of racist views is more common than one might suppose, and may be on the rise.) When a view becomes publicly unexpressible, it often becomes privately unexpressible as well: what we won't say to others we may cease to think to ourselves. It doesn't follow, however, that such beliefs vanish altogether.

How do they manifest themselves? It's common for people to find – even without any awareness on their part – the behavior of a person of another race more threatening or obnoxious or stupid (or whatever) than they would the behavior of a member of their own group. And just as their threshold of intolerance may be lower for negative behavior, they may have higher standards for members of other groups than for their own when it comes to positive traits: thus the claim that women and minorities have to be "twice as good" as white males to get the same credit. A related phenomenon is what psychologists call "aversive racism." In an experiment by Samuel Gaertner, subjects received a phone call, seemingly a wrong number, from a person who said that his car had broken down, that he had just used his last dime and that he needed someone to call a tow truck for him. Young white liberals who presumably saw themselves as racially well-intentioned, were almost six times more likely to hang up on callers when the voice on the phone sounded black than when the person sounded white.

There's considerable evidence that murderers who kill white people are more likely to get the death penalty than those who kill black people, a disparity that implies the belief on the part of juries that white life is more valuable than black life. In general, you don't have to listen very carefully to hear the prejudices to which people give expression, often quite unawares, in talking about people who belong to other ethnic, racial, and religious groups.

Stereotyping

One way such views spill out is in ethnic or racial stereotypes. The stereotyper doesn't believe (or wouldn't say, anyway) that all blacks are less intelligent . . . more violent . . . lazier (choose one or more), or that all Jews are pushy or greedy, only that some, or most of those with whom she comes in contact, are. Or perhaps, to use an example of Adrian Piper's, she believes not that most black teenagers in running shoes are muggers but that most muggers are black teenagers in running shoes. In either case, she makes an inference about the person coming down the street toward her from a generalization she accepts about members of the group to which the person belongs. And that involves picking out some feature or features of the individual (in this case his blackness and youth) as most significant or noteworthy.

Two things can be said in defense of the white woman who crosses the street when she sees a group of black teenagers coming toward her. First, she might well do the same if the teenagers were white. In that case, her behavior does not constitute racial discrimination (though it might still be objectionable "ageism" or some other bias). Second, we need to analyze her thinking and her actions more carefully. She need not be thinking "These guys are black teenagers, therefore they are probably muggers." More likely she reasons "These guys are black teenagers, therefore the probability that they are muggers is greater than if they were ___ (fill in the blank: men in three-piece suits; gray-haired ladies; schoolchildren)" – and great enough to warrant taking the small and relatively inoffensive precaution of crossing the street.

Now the probability of black teenagers being muggers surely *is* greater than the probability of gray-haired ladies being muggers. The crucial question is: how much more probable does it have to be to justify the evasive behavior?

Obviously, questions of this kind have no simple answers. To evaluate behavior based on a racial or other group generalization, several matters are relevant. Among them are: (1) The particular behavior in question, and its costs to those stereotyped. Crossing the street is a minimal slight – if it's even noticed – and may be mitigated by a display of ulterior motivation, like inspecting the rosebushes on the other side. (2) This point is connected with another: is the behavior in question a merely private action, like the individual crossing the street, or is it the activity of a public official or institution? In that case, the threshold will be much higher, if indeed the behavior is permitted at all. A very damaging action done in an official capacity, like preventive detention, will be hardest of all to justify. (3) The costs or risks of not acting in the manner in question. Although the probability that the teenagers are muggers may be low, the risk if they are is great. (4) The available alternatives to the action or policy in question.

Stereotyping is morally problematic because in some forms it seems inevitable, yet at the same time faulty. We can't make our way in the world without relying on rules of thumb, generalizations that enable us to size up people and situations by correlating their characteristics with predictions about what we can expect to happen. But such generalizations are always flawed, because they attribute particular qualities to some people who don't possess them. To generalize is to overgeneralize.

Yet whatever its complexities, it is clear that the most common forms of racial and ethnic stereotyping are indefensible. It's not, after all, that most Jews are greedy or most blacks are violent, so that stereotyping merely goes a little too far by failing to recognize exceptions. Such broad, vulgar stereotyping offends by its "reckless willingness to believe" – the willingness to believe, for example, that (as a white college student in the People for the American Way study put it) *THEY* "have a chip on their shoulders," are "rowdy," "bring it [discrimination] on themselves."

Accommodating Other People's Racism

People sometimes justify discrimination not in terms of their own beliefs but in terms of other people's. A shopkeeper refuses to hire a black sales clerk not because he himself is prejudiced, but because his customers are, and he fears a decline in sales. A corporation refuses to sponsor a program featuring an interracial love affair, not, its representatives say, because they disapprove, but because their viewers do. Suppose for the sake of argument that the shopkeeper and the corporate executives speak the truth: they are not prejudiced, but their clients are. Whether or not we call the shopkeeper himself a racist there can be no doubt that he is perpetuating racism in the most direct way by reinforcing the harmful beliefs of his customers, and by discriminating against black people in his hiring practices. And were he to refuse to accommodate these beliefs, he might help to change other people's attitudes, and so the world.

"Secondary" Racism

Borrowing a term from Mary Anne Warren, we can define "secondary racism" as discrimination based not on race itself but according to race-correlated factors that unfairly affect racial minorities. (The term is misleading if it suggests that such practices are of secondary importance.) Accommodating other people's racism is one kind of secondary racism, but there are many other subtler and apparently more innocent forms as well. So, for example, the practices of hiring through personal connections, or of "last hired, first fired," need not be based on racist beliefs, but they nevertheless affect women and minorities disproportionately and irrespective of merit. The quite natural tendency to favor "one's own kind," which need not involve hostility toward "other kinds," is a form of secondary discrimination.

Similarly, entrance examinations and other tests may contain biases against some groups that are unintended by and opaque to their creators. Tests purporting to measure native intelligence may presume familiarity with objects known only by those coming from more privileged backgrounds. Crucial to this form of discrimination, which is at least part of what is meant by "institutional racism," is that the requirements are on their face race- (or gender-) neutral; that they nevertheless have a "disparate impact" on members of certain groups; and that the elements in question are by hypothesis irrelevent to the performance of the task at hand.

The Disadvantages of Being Disadvantaged

This last category has no common name, although it is perhaps the broadest and most intractable form by which racial inequalities are perpetuated. Whereas secondary racism involves discriminating (however inadvertently) on the basis of factors irrelevant to merit, this form employs criteria that are appropriate and relevant.

Most people would agree that we ought to admit people to jobs or schools on the basis of ability and talent, past or potential performance. Yet even if we could purge our screening devices of irrelevant biases, fewer blacks would gain entry than their numbers in the general population would suggest. They will on the whole be less competitive, given past deprivation, than their more privileged white counterparts. Our metaphors here are the vicious cycle, the downward spiral, the chicken and the egg.

Even if "racism-in-the-head" disappeared then, "racism-in-the-world" would not. One reason is the continued existence of facially race-neutral practices, like seniority systems and the old-boy network, that discriminate unfairly against minorities and women. The other reason is that people who as a historical consequence of overt racism have had substandard prenatal care, nutrition, housing, health services, and education, people who live in drug- and crime-infested neighborhoods, will on the whole fare less well than those more privileged.

Conclusion

"Racism" is inescapably a morally loaded term. To call a *person* a racist is to impugn his character by suggesting deliberate, malign discrimination, and it is therefore natural that those who think their hearts (or perhaps, in keeping with the foregoing metaphor, we should say their heads) are pure should take offense at the accusation.

Even if we were to agree that all racism is "in the head," however, overtly racist attitudes and beliefs do not exhaust its contents. Less-than-conscious attitudes and beliefs still play an important part in our mindsets. And even if individually such attitudes seem insignificant, collectively they add up to pervasive habits of behavior that can wreak injustice on whole groups of people.

At the same time, an individual whose attitudes and beliefs are not overly racist, are not even covertly racist, can inhabit a racist *society* or participate in racist *institutions*. A society or an institution is racist if it discriminates on grounds of race, either "primarily" or "secondarily," or if it perpetuates inequalities produced by primary or secondary racism. Sometimes, the society or the institution is so corrupt that a morally decent person arguably ought not have anything to do with it. More often, however, we hold individuals to less stringent standards. We want to know whether they simply go along with the objectionable practices, or if in the course of their involvement they do something to make the system less discriminatory. What can they do? How much ought they to do? That's another story.

Leonard Harris presents grim statistics concerning the presence of African Americans in philosophy departments in American universities.

Focus questions:
1 What are Harris's factual claims?
2 How does Harris think that these statistics are related to the traditional interests of philosophers?

---

4   The Status of Blacks in Academic Philosophy

Leonard Harris

The discipline of philosophy, particularly political philosophy, has always been an academic field that was particularly concerned with examining issues of ethics and justice. Yet, strangely, over a period of 400 years the morality of the slave trade never evoked much interest among Western civilization's great philosophers. The antislavery movement in this country, as well as in England, was essentially a religious movement. There was no sustained ethical or philosophical critique of slavery from the great seventeenth-century philosophers such as Descartes, Spinoza, and Pascal. Later, too, there were no treatises on the evils of racial subordination or white supremacy from nineteenth- or early twentieth-century philosophers such as Ralph Waldo Emerson, Jonathan Edwards, William James, and George Santayana.

The fact that philosophy has not addressed many of the issues of profound concern to blacks may be one main reason why so few African Americans have chosen to pursue philosophy in an academic setting. One notable exception was Alain Leroy Locke. Locke, whose father was a lawyer, was born in Philadelphia in 1885. He attended private elementary and high schools and went on to graduate *magna cum laude* from Harvard University in 1907. Locke then became the first African American Rhodes Scholar – an accomplishment that was not to be repeated by another black for half a century. After receiving a doctorate from Harvard in 1918, Locke became a major figure of the Harlem Renaissance. The publication of *The New Negro* in 1925 established Locke as the leading black philosopher of the day. As a professor at Howard University, Locke was a driving force behind Howard President Modercai Johnson's effort to convert the institution into a mecca for black intellectuals.

Over the centuries white academics never countenanced the possibility that blacks might have the intellectual skills to master abstract reasoning or have anything to offer on the profoundly difficult questions posed by metaphysics and philosophy. On this account, any black person seeking to pursue a Ph.D. in philosophy at a mainstream American institution was naive indeed. For whatever reason, very few blacks studied philosophy and this trend continues to this day. In 1990, there were 8,792 members of the American Philosophical Association (APA). A 1988 survey of the membership by its then executive director revealed that only 1.1 percent of the respondents were black.

Today there are no black philosophers on the faculties of any Ivy League university. The thirteen universities producing the majority of doctorates in philosophy between 1986 and 1991 did not have a single black faculty member above the level of assistant professor. These universities were Boston College, Brown University, Columbia University, Georgetown University, Guelph/McMaster University combined program, University of Massachusetts, University of Minnesota, SUNY Stony Brook, University of Notre Dame, University of Pittsburgh, University of Texas, Vanderbilt University, and the University of Wisconsin. The "Big Five" Catholic universities – Boston College, Catholic University, Fordham University, Georgetown University, and the University of Notre Dame – had only one nonwhite philosophy faculty member among them.

Most black philosophers today who do hold positions on university faculty

No black philosophers at the Ivy League schools (1994)

	Total philosophy faculty	*Black philosophy faculty*
Brown	14	0
Columbia	16	0
Cornell	14	0
Dartmouth	15	0
Harvard	21	0
Princeton	20	0
Univ. of Pennsylvania	12	0
Yale	12	0
Total	124	0

are employed in junior-level positions or at universities that do not award a doctorate in philosophy. Very few black philosophers sit on doctoral committees empowered to credential others in philosophy. Currently, there are ten African Americans authorized – not as a matter of courtesy but as a matter of their faculty rank – to sit on or chair a doctoral committee. They are Laurence Mordekhai Thomas and Georgette Sinkler at Syracuse University; Howard McGary, Kenneth Taylor, and Jorge Garcia at Rutgers University; Joseph Tolliver at the University of Arizona; Harvey Cormier at the University of Texas; Bernard Boxhill at the University of North Carolina; and Lewis Gordon and this article's author both at Purdue University. Seven of the ten are tenured. Only two of the ten have been tenured and empowered to sit on the doctoral committees for more than a decade.

The near total absence of blacks on the faculty of American universities will undoubtedly continue for the foreseeable future. Of the 274 doctorates in philosophy awarded in 1993 in the United States, only six went to blacks. Black colleges cannot be expected to pick up the slack. There are no graduate programs in philosophy at any black college or university in the United States.

Lisa Newton discusses both theoretical and practical problems with preferential treatment for women and minorities.

Focus questions:
1 What is the distinction between justice and equality?
2 What are the practical problems that preferential treatment might cause?

---

5   Reverse Discrimination as Unjustified

Lisa H. Newton

I have heard it argued that "simple justice" requires that we favor women and blacks in employment and educational opportunities, since women and blacks were "unjustly" excluded from such opportunities for so many years in the not so distant past. It is a strange argument, an example of a possible implication of a true proposition advanced to dispute the proposition itself, like an octopus absent-mindedly slicing off his head with a stray tentacle. A fatal confusion underlies this argument, a confusion fundamentally relevant to our understanding of the notion of the rule of law.

Two senses of justice and equality are involved in this confusion. The root notion of justice, progenitor of the other, is the one that Aristotle (*Nicomachean Ethics* 5.6; *Politics* 1.2; 3.1) assumes to be the foundation and proper virtue of the political association. It is the condition which free men establish among themselves when they "share a common life in order that their association bring them self-sufficiency" – the regulation of their relationship by law, and the establishment, by law, of equality before the law. Rule of law is the name and pattern of this justice; its equality stands against the inequalities – of wealth, talent, etc. – otherwise obtaining among its participants, who by virtue of that equality are called "citizens." It is an achievement – complete, or, more frequently, partial – of certain people in certain concrete situations. It is fragile and easily disrupted by powerful individuals who discover that the blind equality of rule of law is inconvenient for their interests. Despite its obvious instability, Aristotle assumed that the establishment of justice in this sense, the creation of citizenship, was a permanent possibility for men and that the resultant association of citizens was the natural home of the species. At levels below the political association, this rule-governed equality is easily found; it is exemplified by any group of children agreeing together to play a game. At the level of the political association, the attainment of this justice is more difficult, simply because the stakes are so much higher for each participant. The equality of citizenship is not something that happens of its own accord, and without the expenditure of a fair amount of effort it will collapse into the rule of a powerful few over an apathetic many. But at least it has been achieved, at some times in some places; it is always worth trying to achieve, and eminently worth trying to maintain, wherever and to whatever degree it has been brought into being,

Aristotle's parochialism is notorious; he really did not imagine that persons other than Greeks could associate freely in justice, and the only form of association he had in mind was the Greek *polis*. With the decline of the *polis* and the shift in the center of political thought, his notion of justice underwent a sea change. To be exact, it ceased to represent a political type and became a moral ideal: the ideal of equality as we know it. This ideal demands that all men be included in citizenship – that one Law govern all equally, that all men regard all other men as fellow citizens, with the same guarantees, rights, and protections. Briefly, it demands that the circle of citizenship achieved by any group be extended to include the entire human race. Properly understood, its effect on our associations can be excellent: it congratulates us on our achievement of rule of law as a process of government but refuses to let us remain complacent until we have expanded the associations to include others within the ambit of the rules, as often and as far as possible. While one man is a slave, none of us may feel truly free. We are constantly prodded by this ideal to look for possible unjustifiable discrimination, for inequalities not absolutely required for the functioning of the society and advantageous to all. And after twenty centuries of pressure, not at all constant, from this ideal, it might be said that some progress has been made. To take the cases in point for this problem, we are now prepared to assert, as Aristotle would never have been, the equality of sexes and of persons of different colors. The ambit of American citizenship, once restricted to white males of property, has been extended to include all adult free men, then all adult males including ex-slaves, then all women. The process of acquisition of full citizenship was for these groups a sporadic trail of half-measures, even now not complete; the steps on the road to full equality are marked by legislation and judicial decisions which are only recently concluded and still often not enforced. But the fact that we can now discuss the possibility of favoring such groups in hiring shows that over the area that concerns us, at least, full equality is presupposed as a basis for discussion. To that extent, they are full citizens, fully protected by the law of the land.

It is important for my argument that the moral ideal of equality be recognized as logically distinct from the condition (or virtue) of justice in the political sense. Justice in this sense exists *among* a citizenry, irrespective of the number of the populace included in that citizenry. Further, the moral ideal is parasitic upon the political virtue, for "equality" is unspecified – it means nothing until we are told in what respect that equality is to be realized. In a political context, "equality" is specified as "equal rights" – equal access to the public realm, public goods and offices, equal treatment under the law – in brief, the equality of citizenship. If citizenship is not a possibility, political equality is unintelligible. The ideal emerges as a generalization of the real condition and refers back to that condition for its content.

Now, if justice (Aristotle's justice in the political sense) is equal treatment under law for all citizens, what is injustice? Clearly, injustice is the violation of that equality, discriminating for or against a group of citizens, favoring them with special immunities and privileges or depriving them of those guaranteed to the others. When the southern employer refuses to hire blacks in white-collar jobs, when Wall Street will only hire women as secretaries with new titles, when Mississippi high schools routinely flunk all black boys above ninth grade, we have examples of injustice, and we work to restore the equality of the public realm by ensuring that equal opportunity will be provided in such cases in the future. But of course, when the employers and the schools *favor* women and blacks, the same injustice is done. Just as the previous discrimination did, this reverse discrimination violates the public equality which defines citizenship and destroys the rule of law for the areas in which these favors are granted. To the extent that we adopt a program of discrimination, reverse or otherwise, justice in the political sense is destroyed, and none of us, specifically affected or not, is a citizen, a bearer of rights – we are all petitioners for favors. And to the same extent, the ideal of equality is undermined, for it has content only where justice obtains, and by destroying justice we render the ideal meaningless. It is, then, an ironic paradox, if not a contradiction in terms, to assert that the ideal of equality justifies the violation of justice; it is as if one should argue, with William Buckley, that an ideal of humanity can justify the destruction of the human race.

Logically, the conclusion is simple enough: all discrimination is wrong prima facie because it violates justice, and that goes for reverse discrimination too. No violation of justice among the citizens may be justified (may overcome the prima facie objection) by appeal to the ideal of equality, for that ideal is logically dependent upon the notion of justice. Reverse discrimination, then, which attempts no other justification than an appeal to equality, is wrong. But let us try to make the conclusion more plausible by suggesting some of the implications of the suggested practice of reverse discrimination in employment and education. My argument will be that the problems raised there are insoluble, not only in practice but in principle.

We may argue, if we like, about what "discrimination" consists of. Do I discriminate against blacks if I admit none to my school when none of the black applicants are qualified by the tests I always give? How far must I go to root out cultural bias from my application forms and tests before I can say that I have not discriminated against those of different cultures? Can I assume that women are not strong enough to be roughnecks on my oil rigs, or must I test them individually? But this controversy, the most popular and well-argued aspect of the issue, is not as fatal as two others which cannot be avoided: if we are regarding the blacks as a "minority" victimized by discrimination, what is a "minority"? And for any group – blacks, women, whatever – that has been discriminated against, what amount of reverse discrimination wipes out the initial discrimination? Let us grant as true that women and blacks were discriminated against, even where laws forbade such discrimination, and grant for the sake of argument that a history of discrimination must be wiped out by reverse discrimination. What follows?

First, are there other groups which have been discriminated against? For they should have the same right of restitution. What about American Indians, Chicanos, Appalachian Mountain whites, Puerto Ricans, Jews, Cajuns, and Orientals? And if these are to be included, the principle according to which we specify a "minority" is simply the criterion of "ethnic (sub) group," and we're stuck with every hyphenated American in the lower-middle class clamoring for special privileges for *his* group – and with equal justification. For be it noted, when we run down the Harvard roster, we find not only a scarcity of blacks (in comparison with the proportion in the population) but an even more striking scarcity of those second-, third-, and fourth-generation ethnics who make up the loudest voice of Middle America. Shouldn't they demand *their* share? And eventually, the WASPs will have to form their own lobby, for they too are a minority. The point is simply this: there is no "majority" in America who will not mind giving up just a bit of their rights to make room for a favored minority. There are only other minorities, each of which is discriminated against by the favoring. The initial injustice is then repeated dozens of times, and if each minority is granted the same right of restitution as the others, an entire area of rule governance is dissolved into a pushing and shoving match between self-interested groups. Each works to catch the public eye and political popularity by whatever means of advertising and power politics lend themselves to the effort, to capitalize as much as possible on temporary popularity until the restless mob picks another group to feel sorry for. Hardly an edifying spectacle, and in the long run no one can benefit: the pie is no larger – it's just that instead of setting up and enforcing rules for getting a piece, we've turned the contest into a free-for-all, requiring much more effort for no larger a reward. It would be in the interests of all the participants to re-establish an objective rule to govern the process, carefully enforced and the same for all.

Second, supposing that we do manage to agree in general that women and blacks (and all the others) have some right of restitution, some right to a privileged place in the structure of opportunities for a while, how will we know when that while is up? How much privilege is enough? When will the guilt be gone, the price paid, the balance restored? What recompense is right for centuries of exclusion? What criterion tells us when we are done? Our experience with the Civil Rights movement shows us that agreement on these terms cannot be presupposed: a process that appears to some to be going at a mad gallop into a black takeover appears to the rest of us to be at a standstill. Should a practice of reverse discrimination be adopted, we may safely predict that just as some of us begin to see "a satisfactory start toward righting the balance," others of us will see that we "have already gone too far in the other direction" and will suggest that the discrimination ought to be reversed again. And such disagreement is inevitable, for the point is that we could not possibly have any criteria for evaluating the kind of recompense we have in mind. The context presumed by any discussion of restitution is the context of rule of law: law sets the rights of men and simultaneously sets the method for remedying the violation of those rights. You may exact suffering from others and/or damage payments for yourself if and only if the others have violated your rights; the suffering you have endured is not sufficient reason for them to suffer. And remedial rights exist only where there is law: primary human rights are useful guides to legislation but cannot stand as reasons for awarding remedies for injuries sustained. But then, the context presupposed by any discussion of restitution is the context of preexistent full citizenship. No remedial rights could exist for the excluded; neither in law nor in logic does there exist a right to *sue* for a standing to sue.

From these two considerations, then, the difficulties with reverse discrimination become evident. Restitution for a disadvantaged group whose rights under the law have been violated is possible by legal means, but restitution for a disadvantaged group whose grievance is that there was no law to protect them simply is not. First, outside of the area of justice defined by the law, no sense can be made of "the group's rights," for no law recognizes that group or the individuals in it, qua members, as bearers of rights (hence *any* group can constitute itself as a disadvantaged minority in some sense and demand similar restitution). Second, outside of the area of protection of law, no sense can be made of the violation of rights (hence the amount of the recompense cannot be decided by any objective criterion). For both reasons, the practice of reverse discrimination undermines the foundation of the very ideal in whose name it is advocated; it destroys justice, law, equality, and citizenship itself, and replaces them with power struggles and popularity contests.

Note

A version of this paper was read at a meeting of the Society for Women in Philosophy in Amherst, Massachusetts, November 5, 1972.

Bernard Boxill presents a moral argument about the collective responsibility of white Americans for harms suffered in the past by black Americans.

Focus questions:
1 What is the distinction between compensation and reparation?
2 What is the argument in favor of reparation to African Americans?

6 The Morality of Reparation

Bernard R. Boxill

In "Black Reparations – Two Views,"[1] Michael Harrington rejected and Arnold Kaufman endorsed James Forman's demand for $500 million in reparation from Christian churches and Jewish synagogues for their part in the exploitation of black people. Harrington's position involves two different points; he argues that reparation is irrelevant and unwarranted because even if it were made, it would do little to "even up incomes"; and he maintains that the *demand* for reparation will be counterproductive, since it will "divert precious political energies from the actual struggle" to even up incomes. Now, though Kaufman seemed to show good reason that, contra Harrington, the demand for reparation could be productive, I shall in the ensuing, completely disregard that issue. Whether the demand for reparation is counterproductive or not is a question the answer to which depends on the assessment of a large number of consequences which cannot be answered by philosophy alone.

In this paper I shall take issue with what I have distinguished as the first of Harrington's points, viz. that reparation is unwarranted and irrelevant because it would do little to even up incomes. I assume that, by implication, Harrington is not averse to special compensatory programs which will effectively raise the incomes of the poor; what he specifically opposes is reparation. By a discussion of the justification and aims of reparation and compensation, I shall now try to show that, though both are parts of justice, they have different aims, and hence compensation cannot replace reparation.

Let me begin with a discussion of how compensation may be justified. Because of the scarcity of positions and resources relative to aspiring individuals, every society that refuses to resort to paternalism or a strict regimentation of aspirations must incorporate competition among its members for scarce positions and resources. Given that freedom of choice necessitates at least the possibility of competition, I believe that justice requires that appropriate compensatory programs be instituted both to ensure that the competition is fair, and that the losers be protected.

If the minimum formal requirement of justice is that persons be given equal consideration, then it is clear that justice requires that compensatory programs be implemented in order to ensure that none of the participants suffers from a removable handicap. The same reasoning supports the contention that the losers in the competition be given, if necessary, sufficient compensation to enable them to re-enter the competition on equal terms with the others. In other words, the losers can demand equal opportunity as well as can the beginners.

In addition to providing compensation in the above cases, the community has the duty to provide compensation to the victims of accident where no one was in the wrong, and to the victims of "acts of God" such as floods, hurricanes, and earthquakes. Here again, the justification is that such compensation is required if it is necessary to ensure equality of opportunity.

Now, it should be noted that, in all the cases I have stated as requiring compensation, no prior injustice need have occurred. This is clear, of course, in the case of accidents and "acts of God"; but it is also the case that in a competition, even if everyone abides by the rules and acts fairly and justly, some will necessarily be losers. In such a case, I maintain, if the losers are rendered so destitute as to be unable to compete equally, they can demand compensation from the community. Such a right to compensation does not render the competition nugatory; the losers cannot demand success – they can demand only the minimum necessary to re-enter the competition. Neither is it the case that every failure has rights to compensation against the community. As we shall see, the right to compensation depends partly on the conviction that every individual has an equal right to pursue what he considers valuable; the wastrel or indolent man has signified what he values by what he has freely chosen to be. Thus, even if he seems a failure and considers himself a failure, he does not need or have a right of compensation. Finally, the case for compensation sketched is not necessarily paternalistic. It is not argued that society or government can decide what valuable things individuals should have and implement programs to see to it that they have them. Society must see to it that its members can pursue those things they consider valuable.

The justification of compensation rests on two premises: first, each individual is equal in dignity and worth to every other individual, and hence has a right, equal to that of any other, to arrange his life as he sees fit, and to pursue and acquire what he considers valuable; and second, the individuals involved must be members of a community. Both premises are necessary in order to show that compensation is both good and, in addition, mandatory or required by justice. One may, for example, concede that a man who is handicapped by some infirmity should receive compensation; but if the man is a member of no community, and if his infirmity is due to no injustice, then one would be hard put to find the party who could be legitimately forced to bear the cost of such compensation. Since persons can be legitimately compelled to do what justice dictates, then it would seem that in the absence of a community, and if the individual has suffered his handicap because of no injustice, that compensation cannot be part of justice. But given that the individual is a member of a community, then I maintain that he can legitimately demand compensation from that community. The members of a community are, in essential respects, members of a joint undertaking; the activities of the members of a community are interdependent and the community benefits from the efforts of its members even when such efforts do not bring the members what they individually aim at. It is legitimate to expect persons to follow the spirit and letter of rules and regulations, to work hard and honestly, to take calculated risks with their lives and fortunes, all of which helps society generally, only if such persons can demand compensation from society as a whole when necessary.

The case for rights of compensation depends, as I have argued above, on the fact that the individuals involved are members of a single community the very existence of which should imply a tacit agreement on the part of the whole to bear the costs of compensation. The case for reparation I shall try to show is more primitive in the sense that it depends only on the premise that every person has an equal right to pursue and acquire what he values. Recall that the crucial difference between compensation and reparation is that whereas the latter is due only after injustice, the former may be due when no one has acted unjustly to anyone else. It is this relative innocence of all the parties concerned which made it illegitimate, in the absence of prior commitments, to compel anyone to bear the cost of compensation.

In the case of reparation, however, this difficulty does not exist. When reparation is due, it is not the case that one is at fault, or that everyone is innocent; in such a case, necessarily, someone has infringed unjustly on another's right to pursue what he values. This could happen in several different ways, dispossession being perhaps the most obvious. When someone possesses something, he has signified by his choice that he values it. By taking it away from him one infringes on his equal right to pursue and possess what he values. On the other hand, if I thwart, unfairly, another's legitimate attempt to do or possess something, I have also acted unjustly; finally, an injustice has occurred when someone makes it impossible for others to pursue a legitimate goal, even if these others never actually attempt to achieve that goal. These examples of injustice differ in detail, but what they all have in common is that no supposition of prior commitment is necessary in order to be able to identify the parties who must bear the cost of reparation; it is simply and clearly the party who has acted unjustly.

The argument may, perhaps, be clarified by the ideas of a state of nature and a social contract. In the state of nature, as John Locke remarks, every man has the right to claim reparation from his injurer because of his right of self-preservation; if each man has a duty not to interfere in the rights of others, he has a duty to repair the results of his interference.[2] No social contract is required to legitimize compelling him to do so. But when compensation is due, i.e. when everyone has acted justly, and has done his duty, then a social contract or a prior agreement to help must be appealed to in order to legitimately compel an individual to help another.

The case for reparation thus requires for its justification less in the way of assumptions than the case for compensation. Examination of the justifications of reparation and compensation also reveals the difference in their aims.

The characteristic of compensatory programs is that they are essentially "forward looking"; by that I mean that such programs are intended to alleviate disabilities which stand in the way of some *future* good, *however* these disabilities may have come about. Thus, the history of injustices suffered by black and colonial people is quite irrelevant to their right to compensatory treatment. What is strictly relevant to this is that such compensatory treatment is necessary if some future goods such as increased happiness, equality of incomes, and so on, are to be secured. To put it another way, given the contingency of causal connections, the present condition of black and colonial people could have been produced in any one of a very large set of different causal sequences. Compensation is concerned with the remedying of the present situation however it may have been produced; and to know the present situation, and how to remedy it, it is not, strictly speaking, necessary to know just how it was brought about, or whether it was brought about by injustice.

On the other hand, the justification of reparation is essentially "backward looking"; reparation is due only when a breach of justice *has* occurred. Thus, as opposed to the case of compensation, the case for reparation to black and colonial people depends precisely on the fact that such people have been reduced to their present condition by a history of injustice. In sum, while the aim of compensation is to procure some future good, that of reparation is to rectify past injustices; and rectifying past injustices may not insure equality of opportunity.

The fact that reparation aims precisely at correcting a prior injustice suggests one further important difference between reparation and compensation. Part of what is involved in rectifying an injustice is an acknowledgement on the part of the transgressor that what he is doing is required of him because of his prior error. This concession of error seems required by the premise that every person is equal in worth and dignity. Without the acknowledgement of error, the injurer implies that the injured has been treated in a manner that befits him; hence, he cannot feel that the injured party is his equal. In such a case, even if the unjust party repairs the damage he has caused, justice does not yet obtain between himself and his victim. For, if it is true that when someone has done his duty nothing can be demanded of him, it follows that if, in my estimation, I have acted dutifully even when someone is injured as a result, then I must feel that nothing can be demanded of me and that any repairs I may make are gratuitous. If justice can be demanded, it follows that I cannot think that what I am doing is part of justice.

It will be objected, of course, that I have not shown in this situation that justice cannot obtain between injurer and victim, but only that the injurer does not *feel* that justice can hold between himself and the one he injures. The objection depends on the distinction between the objective transactions between the individuals and their subjective attitudes, and assumes that justice requires only the objective transactions. The model of justice presupposed by this objection is, no doubt, that justice requires equal treatment of equals, whereas the view I take is that justice requires equal consideration between equals; that is to say, justice requires not only that we *treat* people in a certain way, for whatever reason we please, but that we treat them as equals precisely because we believe they are our equals. In particular, justice requires that we acknowledge that our treatment of others can be required of us; thus, where an unjust injury has occurred, the injurer reaffirms his belief in the other's equality by conceding that repair can be demanded of him, and the injured rejects the allegation of his inferiority contained in the other's behavior by demanding reparation.

Consequently, when injustice has reduced a people of indigency, compensatory programs alone cannot be all that justice requires. Since the avowed aim of compensatory programs is forward looking, such programs *necessarily* cannot affirm that the help they give is required because of a prior injustice. This must be the case even if it is the unjustly injuring party who makes compensation. Thus, since the acknowledgment of error is required by justice as part of what it means to give equal consideration, compensatory programs cannot take the place of reparation.

In sum, *compensation* cannot be substituted for *reparation* where reparation is due, because they satisfy two differing requirements of justice. In addition, practically speaking, since it is by demanding and giving justice where it is due that the members of a community continually reaffirm their belief in each other's equality, a stable and equitable society is not possible without reparation being given and demanded when it is due.

Consider now the assertion that the present generation of white Americans owe the present generation of black Americans reparation for the injustices of slavery inflicted on the ancestors of the black population by the ancestors of the white population. To begin, consider the very simplest instance of a case where reparation may be said to be due: Tom has an indisputable moral right to possession of a certain item, say a bicycle, and Dick steals the bicycle from Tom. Here, clearly, Dick owes Tom, at least the bicycle and a concession of error, in reparation. Now complicate the case slightly; Dick steals the bicycle from Tom and "gives" it to Harry. Here again, even if he is innocent of complicity in the theft, and does not know that his "gift" was stolen, Harry must return the bicycle to Tom with the acknowledgment that, though innocent or blameless, he did not rightfully possess the bicycle. Consider a final complication; Dick steals the bicycle from Tom and gives it to Harry; in the meantime Tom dies, but leaves a will clearly conferring his right to ownership of the bicycle to his son, Jim. Here again we should have little hesitation in saying that Harry must return the bicycle to Jim.

Now, though it involves complications, the case for reparation under consideration is essentially the same as the one last mentioned: the slaves had an indisputable moral right to the products of their labour; these products were stolen from them by the slave masters who ultimately passed them on to their descendants; the slaves presumably have conferred their rights of ownership to the products of their labour to their descendants; thus, the descendants of slave masters are in possession of wealth to which the descendants of slaves have rights; hence, the descendants of slave masters must return this wealth to the descendants of slaves with a concession that they were not rightfully in possession of it.

It is not being claimed that the descendants of slaves must seek reparation from those among the white population who happen to be descendants of slave owners. This perhaps would be the case if slavery had produced for the slave owners merely specific hoards of gold, silver, or diamonds, which could be passed on in a very concrete way from father to son. As a matter of fact, slavery produced not merely specific hoards, but wealth which has been passed down mainly to descendants of the white community to the relative exclusion of the descendants of slaves. Thus, it is the white community as a whole that prevents the descendants of slaves from exercising their rights of ownership, and the white community as a whole that must bear the cost of reparation.

The above statement contains two distinguishable arguments. In the first argument the assertion is that each white person, individually, owes reparation to the black community because membership in the white community serves to identify an individual as a recipient of benefits to which the black community has a rightful claim. In the second argument, the conclusion is that the white community as a whole, considered as a kind of corporation or company, owes reparation to the black community.

In the first of the arguments sketched above, individuals are held liable to make reparation even if they have been merely passive recipients of benefits; that is, even if they have not deliberately chosen to accept the benefits in question. This argument invites the objection that, for the most part, white people are simply not in a position to choose to receive or refuse benefits belonging to the descendants of slaves and are, therefore, not culpable or blameable and hence not liable to make reparation. But this objection misses the point. The argument under consideration simply does not depend on or imply the claim that white people are culpable or blameable; the argument is that merely by being white, an individual receives benefits to which others have at least partial rights. In such cases, whatever one's choice or moral culpability, reparation must be made. Consider an extreme case: Harry has an unexpected heart attack and is taken unconscious to the hospital. In the same hospital Dick has recently died. A heart surgeon transplants the heart from Dick's dead body to Harry without permission from Dick's family. If Harry recovers, he must make suitable reparation to Dick's family, conceding that he is not in rightful possession of Dick's heart even if he had no part in choosing to receive it.

The second of the arguments distinguished above concluded that for the purpose in question, the white community can be regarded as a corporation or company which, as a whole, owes reparation to the sons of slaves. Certainly the white community resembles a corporation or company in some striking ways; like such companies, the white community has interests distinct from, and opposed to, other groups in the same society, and joint action is often taken by the members of the white community to protect and enhance their interests. Of course, there are differences; people are generally born into the white community and do not deliberately choose their membership in it; on the other hand, deliberate choice is often the standard procedure for gaining membership in a company. But this difference is unimportant; European immigrants often deliberately choose to become part of the white community in the United States for the obvious benefits this brings, and people often inherit shares and so, without deliberate choice, become members of a company. What is important here is not how deliberately one chooses to become part of a community or a company; what is relevant is that one chooses to continue to accept the benefits which circulate exclusively within the community, sees such benefits as belonging exclusively to the members of the community, identifies one's interests with those of the community, viewing them as opposed to those of others outside the community, and finally, takes joint action with other members of the community to protect such interests. In such a case, it seems not unfair to consider the present white population as members of a company that incurred debts before they were members of the company, and thus to ask them justly to bear the cost of such debts.

It may be objected that the case for reparation depends on the validity of inheritance; for, only if the sons of slaves inherit the rights of their ancestors can it be asserted that they have rights against the present white community. If the validity of inheritance is rejected, a somewhat different, but perhaps even stronger, argument for reparation can still be formulated. For if inheritance is rejected with the stipulation that the wealth of individuals be returned to the whole society at their deaths, then it is even clearer that the white community owes reparation to the black community. For the white community has appropriated, almost exclusively, the wealth from slavery in addition to the wealth from other sources; but such wealth belongs jointly to all members of the society, white as well as black; hence, it owes them reparation. The above formulation of the argument is entirely independent of the fact of slavery and extends the rights of the black community to its just portion of the total wealth of the society.

Notes

I am deeply indebted to Professor Thomas Hill, Jr., for helpful criticisms of earlier drafts of this paper.

1   Michael Harrington and Arnold Kaufman, "Black Reparations – Two Views," *Dissent* 16 (July–Aug. 1969), pp. 317–20.
2   John Locke, *Treatise of Civil Government and A Letter Concerning Toleration*, ed. Charles L. Sherman (New York: Appleton-Century Company, 1937), p. 9.

Frantz Fanon here discusses some of the personal pain and alienation that accompanies a black identity in a social system in which blacks are subordinate to whites.

Focus questions:
1 How does racism affect his bodily schema?
2 How does racism affect his status in society?

---

7   The Fact of Blackness

Frantz Fanon

"Dirty nigger!" Or simply, "Look, a Negro!"
    I came into the world imbued with the will to find a meaning in things, my

spirit filled with the desire to attain to the source of the world, and then I found that I was an object in the midst of other objects.

Sealed into that crushing objecthood, I turned beseechingly to others. Their attention was a liberation, running over my body suddenly abraded into nonbeing, endowing me once more with an agility that I had thought lost, and by taking me out of the world, restoring me to it. But just as I reached the other side, I stumbled, and the movements, the attitudes, the glances of the other fixed me there, in the sense in which a chemical solution is fixed by a dye. I was indignant; I demanded an explanation. Nothing happened. I burst apart. Now the fragments have been put together again by another self.

As long as the black man is among his own, he will have no occasion, except in minor internal conflicts, to experience his being through others. There is of course the moment of "being for others," of which Hegel speaks, but every ontology is made unattainable in a colonized and civilized society. It would seem that this fact has not been given sufficient attention by those who have discussed the question. In the *Weltanschauang* of a colonized people there is an impurity, a flaw that outlaws any ontological explanation. Someone may object that this is the case with every individual, but such an objection merely conceals a basic problem. Ontology – since it is finally admitted as leaving existence by the wayside – does not permit us to understand the being of the black man. For not only must the black man be black; he must be black in relation to the white man. Some critics will take it on themselves to remind us that this proposition has a converse. I say that this is false. The black man has no ontological resistance in the eyes of the white man. Overnight the Negro has been given two frames of reference within which he has had to place himself. His metaphysics, or, less pretentiously, his customs and the sources on which they were based, were wiped out because they were in conflict with a civilization that he did not know and that imposed itself on him.

The black man among his own in the twentieth century does not know at what moment his inferiority comes into being through the other. Of course I have talked about the black problem with friends, or, more rarely, with American Negroes. Together we protested, we asserted the equality of all men in the world. In the Antilles there was also that little gulf that exists among the almost-white, the mulatto, and the nigger. But I was satisfied with an intellectual understanding of these differences. It was not really dramatic. And then . . .

And then the occasion arose when I had to meet the white man's eyes. An unfamiliar weight burdened me. The real world challenged my claims. In the white world the man of color encounters difficulties in the development of his bodily schema. Consciousness of the body is solely a negating activity. It is a third-person consciousness. The body is surrounded by an atmosphere of certain uncertainty. I know that if I want to smoke, I shall have to reach out my right arm and take the pack of cigarettes lying at the other end of the table. The matches, however, are in the drawer on the left, and I shall have to lean back slightly. And all these movements are made not out of habit but out of implicit knowledge. A slow composition of my *self* as a body in the middle of a spatial and temporal world – such seems to be the schema. It does not impose itself on me; it is, rather, a definitive structuring of the self and of the world – definitive because it creates a real dialectic between my body and the world.

For several years certain laboratories have been trying to produce a serum for "denegrification"; with all the earnestness in the world, laboratories have sterilized their test tubes, checked their scales, and embarked on researches that might make it possible for the miserable Negro to whiten himself and thus to throw off the burden of that corporeal malediction. Below the corporeal schema I had sketched a historico-racial schema. The elements that I used had been provided for me not by "residual sensations and perceptions primarily of a tactile, vestibular, kinesthetic, and visual character,"[1] but by the other, the white man, who had woven me out of a thousand details, anecdotes, stories. I thought that what I had in hand was to construct a physiological self, to balance space, to localize sensations, and here I was called on for more.

"Look, a Negro!" It was an external stimulus that flicked over me as I passed by. I made a tight smile.

"Look, a Negro!" It was true. It amused me.

"Look, a Negro!" The circle was drawing a bit tighter. I made no secret of my amusement.

"Mama, see the Negro! I'm frightened!" Frightened! Frightened! Now they were beginning to be afraid of me. I made up my mind to laugh myself to tears, but laughter had become impossible.

I could no longer laugh, because I already knew that there were legends, stories, history, and above all *historicity*, which I had learned about from Jaspers. Then, assailed at various points, the corporeal schema crumbled, its place taken by a racial epidermal schema. In the train it was no longer a question of being aware of my body in the third person but in a triple person. In the train I was given not one but two, three places. I had already stopped being amused. It was not that I was finding febrile coordinates in the world. I existed triply: I occupied space. I moved toward the other . . . and the evanescent other, hostile but not opaque, transparent, not there, disappeared. Nausea . . .

I was responsible at the same time for my body, for my race, for my ancestors. I subjected myself to an objective examination, I discovered my blackness, my ethnic characteristics; and I was battered down by tom-toms, cannibalism, intellectual deficiency, fetishism, racial defects, slave-ships, and above all else, above all: "Sho' good eatin'."

On that day, completely dislocated, unable to be abroad with the other, the white man, who unmercifully imprisoned me, I took myself far off from my own presence, far indeed, and made myself an object. What else could it be for me but an amputation, an excision, a hemorrhage that spattered my whole body with black blood? But I did not want this revision, this thematization. All I wanted was to be a man among other men. I wanted to come lithe and young into a world that was ours and to help to build it together.

But I rejected all immunization of the emotions. I wanted to be a man, nothing but a man. Some identified me with ancestors of mine who had been enslaved or lynched: I decided to accept this. It was on the universal level of the intellect that I understood this inner kinship – was the grandson of slaves in exactly the same way in which President Lebrun was the grandson of tax-paying, hard-working peasants. In the main, the panic soon vanished.

In America, Negroes are segregated. In South America, Negroes are whipped in the streets, and Negro strikers are cut down by machine-guns. In West Africa, the Negro is an animal. And there beside me, my neighbor in the university, who was born in Algeria, told me: "As long as the Arab is treated like a man, no solution is possible."

"Understand, my dear boy, color prejudice is something I find utterly foreign . . . But of course, come in, sir, there is no color prejudice among us. . . . Quite, the Negro is a man like ourselves . . . It is not because he is black that he is less intelligent than we are. . . . I had a Senegalese buddy in the army who was really clever . . ."

Where am I to be classified? Or, if you prefer, tucked away?

"A Martinican, a native of 'our' old colonies."

Where shall I hide?

"Look at the nigger! . . . Mama, a Negro! . . . Hell, he's getting mad . . . Take no notice, sir, he does not know that you are as civilized as we . . ."

My body was given back to me sprawled out, distorted, recolored, clad in mourning in that white winter day. The Negro is an animal, the Negro is bad, the Negro is mean, the Negro is ugly; look, a nigger, it's cold, the nigger is shivering, the nigger is shivering because he is cold, the little boy is trembling because he is afraid of the nigger, the nigger is shivering with cold, that cold that goes through your bones, the handsome little boy is trembling because he thinks that the nigger is quivering with rage, the little white boy throws himself into his mother's arms: Mama, the nigger's going to eat me up.

All round me the white man, above the sky tears at its navel, the earth rasps under my feet, and there is a white song, a white song. All this whiteness that burns me . . .

I sit down at the fire and I become aware of my uniform. I had not seen it. It is indeed ugly. I stop there, for who can tell me what beauty is?

Where shall I find shelter from now on? I felt an easily identifiable flood mounting out of the countless facets of my being. I was about to be angry. The fire was long since out, and once more the nigger was trembling.

"Look how handsome that Negro is! . . ."

"Kiss the handsome Negro's ass, madame!"

Shame flooded her face. At last I was set free from my rumination. At the same time I accomplished two things: I identified my enemies and I made a scene. A grand slam. Now one would be able to laugh.

The field of battle having been marked out, I entered the lists.

What? While I was forgetting, forgiving, and wanting only to love, my message was flung back in my face like a slap. The white world, the only honorable one, barred me from all participation. A man was expected to behave like a man. I was expected to behave like a black man – or at least like a nigger. I shouted a greeting to the world and the world slashed away my joy. I was told to stay within bounds, to go back where I belonged.

They would see, then! I had warned them, anyway. Slavery? It was no longer even mentioned, that unpleasant memory. My supposed inferiority? A hoax that it was better to laugh at. I forgot it all, but only on condition that the world not protect itself against me any longer. I had incisors to test. I was sure they were strong. And besides . . .

What! When it was I who had every reason to hate, to despise, I was rejected? When I should have been begged, implored, I was denied the slightest recognition? I resolved, since it was impossible for me to get away from an *inborn complex*, to assert myself as a BLACK MAN. Since the other hesitated to recognize me, there remained only one solution: to make myself known.

In *Anti-Semite and Jew* (p. 95), Sartre says: "They [the Jews] have allowed themselves to be poisoned by the stereotype that others have of them, and they live in fear that their acts will correspond to this stereotype. . . . We may say that their conduct is perpetually overdetermined from the inside."

All the same, the Jew can be unknown in his Jewishness. He is not wholly what he is. One hopes, one waits. His actions, his behavior are the final determinant. He is a white man, and, apart from some rather debatable characteristics, he can sometimes go unnoticed. He belongs to the race of those who since the beginning of time have never known cannibalism. What an idea, to eat one's father! Simple enough, one has only not to be a nigger. Granted, the Jews are harassed – what am I thinking of? They are hunted down, exterminated, cremated. But these are little family quarrels. The Jew is disliked from the moment he is tracked down. But in my case everything takes on a *new* guise. I am given no chance. I am overdetermined from without. I am the slave not of the "idea" that others have of me but of my own appearance.

I move slowly in the world, accustomed now to seek no longer for upheaval. I progress by crawling. And already I am being dissected under white eyes, the only real eyes. I am *fixed*. Having adjusted their microtomes, they objectively cut away slices of my reality. I am laid bare. I feel, I see in those white faces that it is not a new man who has come in, but a new kind of man, a new genus. Why, it's a Negro!

I slip into corners, and my long antennae pick up the catch-phrases strewn over the surface of things – nigger underwear smells of nigger – nigger teeth are white – nigger feet are big – the nigger's barrel chest – I slip into corners, I remain silent, I strive for anonymity, for invisibility. Look, I will accept the lot, as long as no one notices me!

"Oh, I want you to meet my black friend . . . Aimé Césaire, a black man and a university graduate . . . Marian Anderson, the finest of Negro singers . . . Dr. Cobb, who invented white blood, is a Negro . . . Here, say hello to my friend from Martinique (be careful, he's extremely sensitive) . . ."

Shame. Shame and self-contempt. Nausea. When people like me, they tell me it is in spite of my color. When they dislike me, they point out that it is not because of my color. Either way, I am locked into the infernal circle.

I turn away from these inspectors of the Ark before the Flood and I attach myself to my brothers, Negroes like myself. To my horror, they too reject me. They are almost white. And besides they are about to marry white women. They will have children faintly tinged with brown. Who knows, perhaps little by little . . .

I had been dreaming.

"I want you to understand, sir, I am one of the best friends the Negro has in Lyon."

The evidence was there, unalterable. My blackness was there, dark and unarguable. And it tormented me, pursued me, disturbed me, angered me.

Negroes are savages, brutes, illiterates. But in my own case I knew that these statements were false. There was a myth of the Negro that had to be destroyed at all costs. The time had long since passed when a Negro priest was an occasion for wonder. We had physicians, professors, statesmen. Yes, but something out of the ordinary still clung to such cases. "We have, a Senegalese history teacher. He is quite bright . . . Our doctor is colored. He is very gentle."

It was always the Negro teacher, the Negro doctor; brittle as I was becoming, I shivered at the slightest pretext I knew, for instance, that if the physician made a mistake it would be the end of him and of all those who came after him. What could one expect, after all, from a Negro physician? As long as everything went well, he was praised to the skies, but look out, no nonsense, under any conditions! The black physician can never be sure how close he is to disgrace. I tell you, I was walled in: No exception was made for my refined manners, or my knowledge of literature, or my understanding of the quantum theory.

Note

1   Jean Lhermitte, *L'Image de notre corps* (Paris: Nouvelle Revue critique, 1939), p. 17.

Virginia Harris offers a first-person account of the color prejudice she has experienced from other black people as a result of her skin hue.

Focus questions:
1 What does Harris find upsetting about "colorism"?
2 What are her remedies for it?

---

8   Prison of Color

Virginia R. Harris

Colorism is the prejudicial or preferential treatment of same-race people based solely on their color.[1] I would add: colorism is to ascribe value and privilege to a same-race person based on lightness of color.

Clarence Thomas' stated preference for light-skinned women is colorism. A 1989 lawsuit brought against a dark-skinned supervisor because of alleged color discrimination by a light-skinned woman was colorism.[2] When my 80-year-old aunt, who dyes her hair, tells me I am too dark to wear my hair its natural gray, that is colorism (as well as ageism). Underdeveloping the pictures of dark-skinned people in my college year book so no one looked too dark was colorism.[3]

The phenomenon of ascribing worth based on color is generally attributed to African Americans, but colorism is active among all groups. In every group there are variations in color, with "value"[4] rated on the lightness of hue. Blonde and blue-eyed Aryan[5] is "preferable" to "swarthy" southern European. Traveling in China, I observed that the light Chinese were the Party members and functionaries, the dark Chinese were laborers and farmers. The Chinese assigned our group of eight American women rooms based on color. (Two dark-skinned African American women in one room, one light-skinned African American woman and a Chinese American in another, two blonde white women in a room, two brown-haired white women together, and two white women with almost black hair in the last room.) In New Mexico, the Hispanics[6] I met were adamant about not being Mexican and touted their Spanish (read white) heritage. A Filipino American friend, whose parents are Filipino, who was born in the Philippines, was told by darker Filipinos that she was "too light to be Filipino."[7] Light skin is prized. The belief that dark is evil, inherently less intelligent, and immoral is internalized.[8] People of color don't seem to recognize this as another racist divide-and-conquer tactic. By engaging in colorist behavior we collude in keeping white supremacy in place.

I have done considerable work to be aware of and rid myself of internalized racism. I am conscious of the many overt/covert/subtle ways internalized racism determined how I navigated a world bent on my destruction. I was therefore surprised at the extent and depth of the pain and hurt triggered by writing this paper. As much as racism from whites or cross-racial hostility[9] from other people of color hurts, my deepest hurt came at the hands of those who are like me – colored – Negro – Black – African American.

One night during the summer of 1991, watching television, I heard the following: "black is the glue that holds this country together."[10] My immediate reaction was, yes! A further thought: hatred of blackness will tear this country (the world?) apart. We live in and by a racial hierarchy with black at the bottom. No matter how bad things get, all non-blacks can unify around that fact, can hold still another truth to be self-evident – they ain't black. Richard Pryor, in the 1970s, did a monologue on how the Vietnamese immigrants were taught English. The first word learned? Nigger. The audience howled. I laughed, too. The truth of his statement still stares us all in the face.

My father used to say, "You can't throw mud on someone without getting your hands dirty." So, if I am glue, you are either glue or stuck to me. The best glue is invisible, flexible, does not deteriorate, has no odor, is non-toxic, and dries clear and fast. That definition aptly describes the image I tried to portray for many years, while at the same time fighting with every ounce of strength not to be held in my "place" – invisible, cohesive, and unshaken by racism (or any other form of oppression, for that matter). Racism and its legacy, colorism, made me struggle to be something I am not – white and male. I straightened my hair and tried to lighten my skin, while denying it: "I use Nadinola[11] because it's the only thing that controls these blackheads." No pun intended. It didn't work. I was still female. I was still dark.

When I was growing up, calling someone black was worse than calling them nigger. We sat on the porch steps and compared our colors. Who was the darkest? Who was "it" in a terrible game of degradation? I was "it" more times than not. I fought my sister and brother because they called me black. I generally got beaten up in those fights and then beaten again by my light-skinned mother for my loud, violent, attention-getting behavior. No matter the provocation, I had acted BLACK. The insidious irony is I am not darker than my brother and sister, I was made to THINK I was. Not only was racism outside waiting to rip me apart, the legacy of racism was active in our house. How did this come about? Why was it so important to make distinctions that don't exist?

My eyes itch from unshed tears. My parents' venom, born in their issues with color, spewed out – hidden, unspoken, violent – inside our house. I learned not to cry when I was hurt or in pain. My mother was the beat-you-until-you-cry type. I "showed" her. I could take the worst she could dish out – without crying. A victory, I thought.

A little history: My mother's father, one son of a slave and her master, blamed his mother for the circumstance of his birth. (None of his children could tell me her name.) He hated white people and dark-skinned people. He could have "passed," but never did – to my knowledge. Even though he married a dark-skinned woman, he told his children not to marry dark because black was evil and no good. All his sons complied. One daughter complied; another daughter married a dark-skinned man, divorced him, and was mistress to a white-skinned black man for over forty years. My mother didn't comply, but when angry with my dark-skinned father, said, "I should've listened to my father."

From the time I can remember everyone was described by color, down to a half or quarter shade darker than someone else.[12] If the person was dark, the description was negative, especially if the person was female. If for some reason the woman deserved a compliment, it was followed by ". . . but, she's so dark." "Marry light and improve the race," was the unequivocal message. All the men, on both sides of the family, in my parent's generation married light-skinned women. My father's "other women" were even lighter than my mother. All my male first cousins married white women. What a difference a generation made! To this day all my mother's sisters say color was not an issue in their family!

I got the message: no good, dark, ugly, not worth black men's attention, unattractive, and not wife material. I believed it. "I'll show them" became my watch phrase. I might be dark . . . but, just you wait and see. I excelled in school. The man I married, to whom I was "superior" by virtue of class and more education, was lighter than me, had all the necessary credentials (degreed professional), and paid me minimal attention. When my sister met him she asked, "How did you ever get a man like that?" She, on the other hand, married two very dark-skinned men. "The blacker the berry . . . ," she used to say. But was she trying to be the lighter one and therefore "superior" to those men based on her color? I wonder.

Black has been the glue that kept me stuck in a prison and in being victim. I am a dark-skinned woman who internalized the negativity society teaches about darkness. My internalized racism, colorism, and sexism have shaped an existence which I can only call a prison of color I wanted to be impenetrable, not feel the pain. So, I built walls to protect myself. They have gotten thick over the years and I am tightly bound inside a hated cell, my skin color. A posture created to "protect" myself from the excruciating pain of being black in a world where "biases . . . subscribe . . . Blackness as non-good 'Otherness.' "[13] The walls were my armor against the world where I did battle against everything, with everybody. The walls held me in place, restricted me like a girdle. Self-hatred is the tightest girdle anyone wears. I've been walled off, boxed in by my color, restricted in ways that are becoming clearer.

My prison – both protector and enslaver. Each wall familiar, like a face I remember, but can't recall the name. I pace this enclosure until I recall the names. ANGER. That's easy – smooth as glass, cold to the touch. I turn a corner. INVISIBILITY. A contradiction learned early – a wall of distorted mirrors. Another corner. INADEQUACY. A well-paved, smooth wall requiring constant maintenance to keep the image of inadequacy at bay. Another corner, another contradiction. OVER/UNDER ACHIEVING. A wall of different sizes and kinds of broken rocks set in the cement of control. The plight of a smart little black girl simultaneously applauded and slapped. ANGER and INADEQUACY confront each other as do INVISIBILITY and OVER/UNDER ACHIEVING.

I search for solace in this place that "protected" me in the past. But it feels so different! I thought the jagged edges, the hot acid rage were covered, hidden forever by the layers of control plastered over them. The internalized value system that states I am less than human because I am a descendant of Africa oozes out like pus from an infected cut. I've lived with the pain of being a woman, being black, being a victim, being hated, being angry, being invisible. I have survived in a world bent on my destruction. But, if I am to be free, I must know these walls and for what they stand.

ANGER – a friend – the only emotion allowed in my family. Righteous anger covering a pool of helpless, hopeless rage so close to the surface but rarely expressed. All the hurt and pain I've suppressed about how I was/am perceived and treated because of my color came screaming to the surface as I engaged with another dark-skinned woman to write this paper about colorism. I felt such rage (at her) I was unable to breathe. Rage burst to the surface because a dark-skinned woman had had a different experience with colorism than I had. I was catapulted back to my childhood where fist fights and worse were common fare.

My reaction in the present recalled an incident. Seven African American women talked about how color had affected our lives. We varied from beige to black-brown (the color we used to call "African" when we were ignorant of Africans' color variety). All seven of us had experienced the pain of being the "darkest" at one time or another. Two had experienced being the lightest, also. The black-brown woman was enraged. None of us could know and understand the kind of pain she had experienced. It was clear to me, at the time, that she needed to be the victim. I thought her rigid and closed-minded. All of us had painful experiences with colorism but she was unable to allow any of us our pain because her pain was so intense.

Six years later, I found myself acting out the same rigidity and closed-mindedness. My friend's different experience with being dark-skinned did not "validate" my pain. My pain felt even more intense in the comparison. The more we talked about our very different experiences with being dark-skinned black women, the more enraged I became. I held on to my old and new pain tenaciously, placed blame for all that pain on my friend. Not only was my hurt very deep, my need to hold on to that hurt was as deep. I needed to be the victim and I needed my friend to be responsible for my victimization. My parents and the community that hurt me when I was a child were gone, the system was too big and unyielding. If I allowed a different experience with colorism, somehow I would be erased. Not just my experience invalidated, but an erasure of SELF. Erasure slams me into the wall INVISIBILITY.

We African Americans are all colors. While racism distinguishes between us from dark to light, we still somehow become all the same. We are interchangeable in some instances, and in others not. It depends on the use the dominant culture has for us in the particular moment. Hollywood cast Sidney Poitier as Thurgood Marshall in a made-for-TV movie, erasing the white-skin privilege Marshall had traveling throughout the South in the 1940s and 1950s. "60 Minutes" did an expose about a New York employment agency's discrimination against blacks. The two African Americans who brought the suit were dark. The agency, to prove the charges false, gave a light-skinned black woman the "privilege" of recanting the charge. The abject pain on her face as she tried to rationalize a corporate memo that clearly implied, "discriminate, just don't get caught" was heartbreaking. How did she deal with that pain? Did she beat herself up, search for all the ways she failed? Did she make other black people responsible and render them invisible in order to feel she had some power? Was she able to hold it together so her bosses wouldn't know what she felt?

It is devastating when your illusionary world comes crashing down. The worst images reflected in those distorted mirrors haunt you. Feelings of INADEQUACY jump up like ghoulish Jacks-in-the-box, unexpected and terrifying. This wall's smooth surface is an illusion. INADEQUACY is wet tar that gets all over your best dress and you weren't even conscious of being near the wall. As I struggled to erase the belief that I was inadequate, I simultaneously erased pieces of mySELF. If I couldn't be a white male – the only thing that would make me adequate – I would best them at their own game – be more efficient, faster, take on more projects. I stood up to the power structure at work (all white men) – ignored my pain and hurt. I felt most adequate (powerful) when I proved white men (and later white women) wrong, using their own data and the statistical methods I'd learned in their universities, only to get stuck once again in the tar of INADEQUACY when the racism and sexism were dismissed and I was ignored. What had I done wrong? How could I make them see? Civil rights bills and Executive Orders provided some recourse for unfair treatment in the workplace. But what was the recourse in my life? I stood, feet sealed in cement, dodging feelings of inadequacy, but getting pummeled over and over again.

I built an elaborate system of musts and shoulds, none of which left me room to breathe, to BE. I stood rigidly on the "American" principles I had been taught even if white people didn't. I became the champion for causes of race and gender while denying how I was used by those in power to keep people of color and women under control. My option? Prove that the together, competent, get-things-done image was the real me.

The jagged rocks in the wall of OVER/UNDER ACHIEVING are splattered with the tar of INADEQUACY. We were taught in childhood that we had to prove we were twice as good to get ahead. Education was the key, so the more education one had . . . By the time I left graduate school unable to find a job, I said "twice as good to get half as much." It was clear to me that getting a Ph.D. had more to do with endurance than with ability. When I finally got a job in my field, my abilities were measured by the kind of research I did. But the kind of research I was assigned came through a white man's race/gender filter. If I completed a project quickly it was – scrutinized for mistakes, accuracy double-checked. After twelve years of "research" it dawned: Just because I majored in chemistry, I didn't have to work in it for the rest of my life. "How can you give up the prestige of chemistry for personnel?" I was asked. Easy. I never felt the "prestige" chemistry was supposed to afford me. All I felt was rage at being a glorified dishwasher. They told me I couldn't switch from science to administration, so I showed them. In personnel I saw the records documenting a history of extensive racism and heard my boss argue to pay a person of color (or woman) less money. My boss asked me, "Who do you think you are? What makes you think you have the credibility to make these kinds of charges?"

Twenty years later racism is alive and well. "This is a country where racism has been the longest standing national neurosis."[14] Without racism, colorism would not exist. I obscured my pain about colorism by fighting hard against racism. I thought if I fought hard enough, the pain would go away. It didn't. Writing this paper brought all the feelings to the surface with an intensity I never experienced in the past. The armor I'd worn against the pain no longer worked. I had no scapegoat or no object for the feelings. They were real. They were intense. They were mine.

I maintained two stances in the world. The outward one conquered obstacles, projected an "in charge" IMAGE. The inward one, a battered, dark-skinned child who believed she could do nothing to be acceptable, whose identity was her victimization. I wanted to be warm, protected, loved, and nurtured. I wanted a womb. I built a prison. I can continue to internalize the hatred I've learned from my family and the society. I can continue to turn it on myself and those like me. I can continue to envy those lighter than me, feel superior to those darker than me. I can continue to be an instrument of my destruction.

Yes, I could. But I choose to live a conscious life, making conscious choices to BE a whole person. Rejecting the value system where self-esteem and self-worth are based on being "better than," and where as an African American woman I am defined as "less than," would seem easy. But the power of the glue of hatred is greater than I ever imagined. It is a full-time, lifetime job undoing my socialization. I am learning to embrace all facets of who I am, to embrace a SELF rooted in BEing equitable in my soul, learning to nourish wellbeing and differentness in SELF and others.[15]

Notes

1   Alice Walker (1983). If the present looks like the past, what does the future look like? In *Search of Our Mother's Gardens* (New York: Harcourt Brace Jovanovich), p. 209.
2   *New York Times*, May 23, 1989, p. 1.
3   This reality hit home 33 years after the fact when showing a friend how much color determined women's popularity and recognition in the 1950s when I was in college. All (women's and men's) our colors were washed out to a medium gray. If light-skinned, the contrast in the photograph is sharper than if dark, where there is almost no contrast.
4   I use quotations marks here and throughout the manuscript to show irony, sometimes sarcastically and, finally, to show how language has been misused to further racism and other oppression.
5   Aryan has no validity as a racial term, it designates a family of languages. Hitler and the Nazis used the word to designate the "super race." Even though Hitler and many of the leading Nazis didn't fit the model superman, it was the standard to be achieved as evidenced by the breeding experiments conducted to produce as many blond blue-eyed members of the "master race" as possible. Through my eyes, this is still the standard to be met. I use Aryan here in its Nazi context.
6   The progressive Latino community in San Francisco no longer uses Hispanic, but uses Latino instead. The State continues to use Hispanic.
7   Conversation with Noemi Sohn, 1992.
8   Merlin Stone, *3000 Years of Racism* (New Sibylline Books, 1981), describes racism as a process that takes place in distinct and definable stages.
9   I use the term cross-racial hostility to differentiate the behavior of people of color toward each other from the racist behavior of whites toward people of color. See, Virginia R. Harris and Trinity A. Ordona, "Developing unity among women of color: crossing the barriers of internalized racism and cross-racial hostility," in Gloria Anzaldúa (ed.) *Making Face, Making Soul Haciendo Caras* (San Francisco: Aunt Lute Foundation Books, 1990), p. 304.
10   I spent weeks trying to track down the exact quote. I got the transcript and a video tape of the program; neither one has the statement on it. Since I am one of five people I know who watched the program and afterwards with whom I had discussions about the statement, I am sure it was not my imagination. What happened to the statement? One more in the series of distortions, misrepresentations, and censorship.
11   A bleaching cream, popular in the 1950s and still advertised in *Ebony* magazine.
12   Often, even now, when another African American woman, who is the same color as I am, describes another African American woman to me she generally says "darker than you," or "lighter than me," never the other way around.
13   Joyce Elaine King and Thomasyne Lightfoote Wilson, "Being the soul-freeing sub-

stance: a legacy of hope in Afro humanity," *Journal of Education* 172/2 (1990), p. 11.

14 Eleanor Holmes Norton, ". . . And the language is race," *Ms.* 2/4 (January–February 1992), p. 43.

15 King and Wilson, "Being the soul-freeing substance," p. 9.

I describe the American reality of mixed black and white race and present arguments for officially recognizing this identity.

Focus questions:
1 How is the non-recognition of mixed race identity connected to racist ideas of racial difference?
2 What are human rights arguments in favor of mixed race identity recognition?

---

9   Mixed Black and White Race and Public Policy

Naomi Zack

The American folk concept of race assumes the factual existence of races. However, biological science does not furnish empirical support for this assumption. Public policy derived from nineteenth century slave-owning patriarchy is the only foundation of the "one-drop rule" for black and white racial inheritance. In principle, Americans who are both black and white have a right to identify themselves racially. In fact, recent demographic changes and multiracial academic scholarship support this right.

There is so much myth involved in the classification of Americans into black and white racial categories that the facts about race are part of the subject of Racial Theory. Racial Theory is the intellectual structure within which it is possible to develop an understanding of how *race* is socially constructed. In that theoretical context, the ordinary concept of race in the United States, which purports to be about something hereditary and physical, has no scientific foundation; neither does this concept have an ethical rationale that ensures just treatment for individuals or a maximization of benefits for all concerned groups. In this essay, I mean to sketch the historical, empirical, and emancipatory context for permitting American individuals of mixed black and white race to identify themselves racially. Such permission would be a matter of future public policy in many different political, intellectual, scientific, and educational contexts – it would reflect a massive paradigm shift in emancipatory black and white racial thought and action, just as the historical denial of permission has reflected white racism and racial oppression. Because the case of black and white racial mixture has always been the site of the most stringent impositions of racial purity in

American culture, argument for self-identification in that case is an important beginning for unraveling racial mythology in general.

The One-drop Rule

The racial categories of black and white race form a rigid, asymmetrical classification system in the United States. On a folk level, it is assumed that an individual is either black or white, but not both.[1] However, there have been individuals acknowledged as having both black and white ancestors since seventeenth-century colonial days, so something besides the facts of heredity as they are understood in other cases of ancestral diversity must be at work here.[2] At work is the one-drop rule, which has been reflected in the United States census since 1920. According to the one-drop rule, an individual is racially black if he or she has one black ancestor anywhere in her genealogical line of descent, and this holds regardless of whether, or how many, white, Asian, or Native American ancestors were also present. By contrast, a person is white only if she has no nonwhite ancestors. That is the logic behind American racial designations, and its only basis is the public policy that was associated with black chattel slavery. Nevertheless, Americans assume that there are biological foundations for racial classifications. That there are no such foundations is worth a few minutes to review.

The Biology of Race

First of all, the "drop" in the one-drop rule refers to a drop of blood. It used to be believed that ancestors literally passed their blood on to their descendants and that this blood mixed with the blood of other ancestors whenever a child was conceived. We now know that this is nonsense: maternal and fetal blood circulate separately; blood is not passed on, but its type is copied genetically; there are no general racial blood types – human blood types are distinguished for transfusion purposes, and full siblings may have incompatible blood types.[3]

According to biological anthropologists, the racial unit is not an individual but a population that has more of some physical traits than other populations. There probably never have been pure races because racial populations have rarely been isolated from members of other racial populations. Social taboos may substitute for geographical isolation in breeding populations, but no such taboo has ever been completely effective; and even if such a taboo were effective, the physical traits that would be designated as racial traits would be a matter of cultural choice and not biology.[4] Biologically, there is no general genetic marker for race. There are genes associated with particular physical traits that have been socially designated as racial traits, but no gene for white race, black race, Asian race, or any other race has been scientifically identified during the centuries in which the modern idea of race has been in circulation.[5] It is important, in this regard, to note the contrast with sex. Although all individuals do not neatly divide into XX or XY on a chromosomal level because of borderline and more complex combinations of X and Y, nevertheless, X and Y are identifiable as general sexual markers that determine more specific sexual characteristics.[6] Even after all social constructions of sex and gender are filtered out, the overwhelming majority of individuals are XX or XY. This general XX-ness or XY-ness causes or explains less general physical character-istics, which themselves have underlying genes. For example, the presence of XX predicts the presence of the gene for ovaries. If it were the case that all of the specific physical sexual characteristics varied along continua and that XX and XY did not exist, then there would be no general genetic basis for sex. That is the situation with race. The specific physical characteristics that differ-ent cultures have designated as racial in different ways, vary, without any un-derlying general genetic marker that causes them or that can be used to explain their presence. Once one realizes this, it becomes clear that race is what cul-tures take it to be. As a general biological characteristic, which is how racist cultures construct race, race does not exist. But given racist constructions, race has a powerful social reality, and it is therefore an extraordinarily complex subject to both refer to and dissolve at the same time.

Due to the one-drop rule, an American classified as black may have more genes that cause physical characteristics considered to be white than an Ameri-can classified as white. The presence of a black ancestor does not ensure the presence of any of the genes of that ancestor beyond the second generation. This is because individuals get one-half of their genes from each parent, and there is no guarantee that they have genes from all four grandparents – the "racial" genes, that is, the genes underlying perceptible traits that the culture has designated as "racial" traits, might be just as likely to drop out as the non-racial ones. Lest it seem contradictory to speak – even in quotes – of racial genes in the same breath as a claim that there are no genes for race, it should be remembered that a racial gene is a gene for a trait that has been culturally deter-mined to be a racial trait. There is nothing specifically racial in a biological sense about a "racial" gene. "Racial" genes are genes that underlie skin color, hair texture, and other physical characteristics of human beings. They otherwise have nothing extra, physically or genetically, to distinguish them from other "nonracial" genetic differences, except that these "racial" genes have been des-ignated, picked out, identified, as "racial." Finally, it should also be noted that so-called racial genes do not get inherited in clumps. Most genes are subject to dispersal and recombination at conception, and the genes behind the physical traits that society has picked out as racial are no more likely to get passed on together than are genes for traits to which society attaches no racial signifi-cance.[7] This is why individuals who are otherwise presumed to be of the same race do not all have the same racial traits.

Groups of individuals from the same geographical area, such as a part of precolonial Africa, may share some biological traits among their members, such as dark brown skin and curly hair. But the designation of these traits as racial is a purely cultural construction. Ever since the colonial period racial designation has accompanied the oppression and exploitation, or domination, of the groups so designated. During the seventeenth, eighteenth, and nineteenth centuries, the domination of what are now called third world populations was practiced by Europeans on a global scale. The physical differences from Europeans of these third world peoples and the assumed difference in geographical origins of their ancestors became the basis of modern European concepts of race. Until the 1920s, social scientists also assumed the cultural difference among racially designated groups were physically inherited.[8]

The American History of the One-drop Rule

In colonial America, prisoners from Africa were worked as slaves, along with Europeans and Native Americans. By the end of the eighteenth century, these African slaves were known as "n"egroes – the 'n' was always lowercase until the Harlem Renaissance – and only "n"egroes could be enslaved in the United States.[9] By that time, those individuals who were then called "negroes" and who historians after the 1930s refer to as "Negroes," but who should probably be referred to as American slaves, had been conceptualised as a distinct race from whites, lower in biological hierarchy and intellectually and morally inferior to whites (Zack 1993: 116–22). So, first African prisoners were made slaves and then they were defined as a "race" of "negroes." Every member of this "race" of "negroes" was posited as having the characteristics of a population that was essentially different from the "white" population. (Unfortunately, the limitations of this essay preclude investigation of the development of cultural constructions of racial whiteness, not to mention the racialization of the indigenous American population.) Why was it necessary to posit that difference as a matter of public policy? Because the white population, as a matter of public policy, based on Enlightenment political theory, was constructed as having a human birthright of freedom (Immerwahr and Burke 1993: 26–7). The next conceptual step in the American racializing program, insofar as it was connected with the institution of slavery, entailed an identification of enslavement itself as a determinant of race.

The common assumption among contemporary historians is that in English North America, "Negroes" were enslaved because they were "n"egroes.[10] In fact, the situation was worse than that: African prisoners and their descendants were enslaved and kept in slavery for the simple reason that they or their ancestors were first enslaved. This was accomplished through the mediating concept of race, specifically the concept of "negro race."

The final North American public policy regarding the children of female slaves was beneficial to the economic interests of the owners of female slaves. As owners of living things, these owners wanted to have secure ownership of the offspring of what they already owned. Since only "n"egroes could be owned as slaves, the only way that they could own the children of their slaves were if those children were "n"egroes. As everyone has always known, the fathers of many children of women slaves were not slaves or "n"egroes. Therefore, to protect the economic interests of slave owners in English North America, the institution of slavery gave birth to the one-drop rule, as a matter of public policy. By contrast, in Louisiana under French rule and throughout Latin America, manumission of children with slave mothers and free white fathers was common all through the period of slavery. Those children were recognised as mixed black and white race.[11]

It became illegal to import slaves into the United Stares, in the 1830s. Then the cotton gin increased the speed with which cotton could be processed, and the need for slave labor to grow cotton increased. The large-scale miscegenation of the slave population due to generations of sexual exploitation of female slaves by free whites, as well as intraracial miscegenation within the "n"egro population, resulted in an otherwise embarrassing number of "whiter" slave offspring, who, if they were not automatically designated "n"egroes, because only "n"egroes could be enslaved, would have presented a disastrous loss of capital for the slave economy. After Louisiana came under the rule of Anglo Americans, and throughout slavery in the United States after the 1850s, all the children of slave mothers, regardless of their paternity, were assumed to have the racial status of their mothers. This was of course contrary to English custom and law, which supported patriarchal descent in all other matters of lineage and property (Zack 1993: 57–61).

Even though, originally, the economics of slavery determined the public policy of the one-drop rule, the abolition of slavery did not mitigate the application of this rule. Between the Civil War and 1915 the one-drop rule became the law in most states, where it was expressed in so-called anti-miscegenation laws that proscribed interracial marriage (Zack 1993: 79–82).[12] Ironically, this policy was locked in place among African Americans during the Harlem Renaissance, when many prominent mixed race black spokespersons explicitly took up Negro identities to the conceptual obliteration of their white ancestors. At the time, there was no choice in the matter because the United States census no longer recognised a category of mixed race; so anyone who was "black" according to the one-drop rule was not accepted as white in American society (Zack 1993: 95–112). Even though the antimiscegenation laws were struck down by the United States Supreme Court in 1967, the one-drop rule has never been successfully challenged as a basis for racial classification. Officially, and according to custom, an American is black given one black ancestor, no matter how many white ancestors she has and regardless of her social experiences.

Mixed Black and White Race and Present Public Policy: in Principle

The American history of racial categorization was unjust. Against the widespread understanding that the United States has a long history of racial injustice, this might occasion a yawn. However, we are still trapped in the rigidity of notions of biological racial difference that presuppose pseudoscientific ideas of race. And the one-drop rule is still public policy. Whites assume that this is how blacks want it, and blacks continue to reproduce it socially for a variety of reasons, including the preservation of hard-won affirmative action benefits that reinforce "pure" racial identities, family and community loyalty, and the continuing devaluation and oppression of individuals with African ancestry by individuals without African ancestry.

Nonetheless, many individuals of mixed black and white race, especially of first generation "mixture," experience the one-drop rule not only as racist in itself, against them, but as fundamentally supportive of the false categories of race. The whole idea of race requires an assumption of a population stable in certain physical characteristics, which will "breed true." That is, the idea of race rests on fantasies of racial purity.

The question is not whether it is better for an individual with black and white ancestors to be designated white, or partly black and partly white, than all black, because addressing the question in those terms accepts a foundation of the unjust treatment of blacks by whites. Rather, these are the pertinent questions: Since there is no such thing as race and our present legacy of racial categories is shot through with pseudoscience and racist habits and beliefs, how should "race" be determined? Who should decide what race I am to myself? How should anyone determine the "race" of another person? Notice that there are two levels to these questions. If race is a fiction, then the person of pure race is in the same position regarding these questions as the person of mixed race. But, if race is accepted or recognised as a social reality, then, in the context of the nonsense of the one-drop rule, the person of mixed black and white race presents a special problem to herself and others.

I would like to stay on the level that all notions of race are fictions, but I don't think that is yet feasible at this time in American culture. Therefore, I am provisionally going to go along with the fiction that there are such things as black and white race, as a basis on which to consider the ongoing one-drop rule from the standpoint of an individual of mixed black and white race. How should mixed black and white individuals identify themselves and be racially identified by others at this time?

I think that the only emancipatory answer to that question has to be provided by the individuals themselves. It has been estimated that between 75 percent and 90 percent of all African Americans have some white ancestry. Within this group, the group likely to self-identify as mixed race is probably no more than 10 percent or 15 percent (Williamson 1980: 9–16, 125). If, however, there is no scientific foundation to the concept of race, that is, if races do not exist, then neither do mixed races exist. The facts of racial mixture, namely the existence of individuals of mixed race, undermine the very notion of race, which presupposes racial "purity." Since there never have been pure races, it is impossible to calculate degrees of racial mixture. Still, despite these puzzles, on a folk level, Americans take race very seriously, and it is only fair that those individuals who do not fit into any one of the recognized racial categories have an opportunity to identify themselves, that is, to choose their own racial identities.

As it stands now, most people "choose" a racial identity after they have learned how others identity them. This is a passive process of choice, closer to socially approved assent than free choice. Children with a black parent and a white parent, and even greater degrees of racial diversity, are now obligated to "choose" which box to check as they move through the various institutional processes of racial identification in the culture. They choose the box that "best" applies to them, but nothing in official or social reality permits them a choice of *everything* that applies to them in racial terms.

Broadly speaking, even given the racial fictions in place, every person defines for herself what it means to be what she is racially by learning about her family history. Using present energy and making commitments for the future, she invents her racial identity at the same time that she tells herself she is discovering it. This is an existential point. The person of mixed race is as entitled to this existential process, with its self-defining illusion of invention masquerading as discovery, as is the person of presumptively pure race. In the present case, she has a right to be mixed race rather than black race or white race. At present, she can be white only if she lies about the presence of a black ancestor. And she can only eschew all racial identity, should she choose to invent herself on the ground of her discovery that race is a fiction, if she refuses to participate in many cultural contexts that might otherwise benefit her. This right for a mixed race person to be mixed race seems to be a fundamental requirement for psychological and social health, but it is as difficult to create a general justification for it as it is to justify the right of human beings to selfhood. In fact, the generality of the justification can only be anchored by something beyond American law and culture, as I will try to do in a moment. United States federal racial classification systems presently allow for only four racial categories – black, white, Asian and Native American, with an added ethnic rider of Hispanic or non-Hispanic. Where categories of "other" have been added to state forms, according to "Directive 15," the components of "other" in individual cases are reassessed, and if an individual has a black ancestor, the individual is reclassified as black (see Fernández 1995; Graham 1995).

In June 1993 the United States House of Representatives Subcommittee on Census, Statistics, and Postal Personnel heard public testimony concerning the inclusion of a multiracial category in the US census. As of this writing, the outcome of those hearings is inconclusive. It is not merely that even liberal public record keeping is constrained by outmoded concepts of race in the population at large. The inconclusiveness is further diffused by the expressed concern of African American interest groups that if part of their presently designated constituency of African Americans redesignates itself as multiracial, the remaining constituency will lose affirmative action gains (see Wright 1994). Nonetheless, many black and white mixed-race Americans continue to wonder whether one-drop black racial identification, based on biological fiction, should be supported at the expense of more accurate description and record keeping. It is difficult to see how anyone except the mixed-race individuals themselves would have a right to decide that matter.

According to international moral political rights theories, as stated in the United Nations Charter, the right of Americans of mixed race to identify themselves and be identified, that is, recognized, as a distinct racial category would seem to be related to other social and political rights of self-determination. The analogue to national self-determination in this political sense, for mixed black and white Americans, is racial self-identification. As with emerging nations, united within themselves by geography, self-identification precedes identification and recognition by others.

Mixed-race people do not constitute geographically continuous, potentially sovereign entitles as groups, so there is no issue of political independence at stake. But, neither do racially pure groups present a basis for national sovereignty – except within separatist movements; which in the United States, at least, have been motivated by extremist and supremacist ideologies. There has been, of course, some geographically based political districting of black racial interests in the United States in recent years for the presumed benefit of blacks. If some of the people in those districts revise their identification as racially mixed and not black, there is concern that the remaining blacks would not benefit as much as when the group was larger (Wright 1994). But the resulting groups could form coalitions. And the racism against blacks that presupposes nonexistent general differences among all members of racially designated populations will have been undermined to the extent that everyone publicly acknowledges that some American blacks have white ancestors and are therefore not, strictly speaking, "black." If all blacks are not black because some of them are also white, then the rigid differences that people mistakenly assume have a biological foundation would begin to soften in American folk thought. This would in turn undermine racism as a psychological attitude based on an assumption of strong physical difference.

Furthermore, the United Nations Charter expresses an international moral-political consensus that all individuals are entitled to the same rights, regardless of race and color (Article 2). If blacks and whites have a right to identify themselves as such, then so do mixed black and white individuals. The United Nations Charter also stipulates that no one may be compelled to belong to an association (Article 20, 2). If the one-drop rule does not have the biological foundation it has been assumed to have in American history, then no one should be compelled to be black. And, if race itself is a fiction, then no one should be compelled to identify herself or be identified by others in any way at all racially, if she so chooses. Failure to identify in some specific way racially, or in any way racially, ought not to put anyone at a disadvantage compared to those who do so identify.

In the context of freedom of association as stipulated by the United Nations Charter, racial identification has not yet been addressed because it has been assumed up to now that racial identification has a neutral, factual foundation. Indeed, the international theoretical work on race has primarily focused on the promulgation of the findings of the social and biological sciences of the first half of the twentieth century, which concluded that cultural differences among racial groups are matters of historical contingency rather than physical heredity.[13] But, since there is no empirical, factual foundation for the American one-drop rule of black racial classification, in many cases of mixed race, there are no neutral, factual determinants for racial identification. Given this absence of an assumed biological foundation for racial identification, if it is, for whatever reason, necessary that mixed-race individuals be identified by race, those individuals have a right to choose their racial identifications, based on the United Nations Charter right to freedom of association.

In situations where an individual's chosen racial designation is at odds with how others classify her, care should be taken by those others to refine the empirical basis on which they make their identifications. And in many cases, the reliance on socially coerced self-identification, that is, the one-drop rule, is so strong that experts will have to dispense with racial categories altogether. An interesting example of this is found in recent American Medical Association policy recommendations for the detection of sickle-cell anemia in infants. It was formerly believed that infants of nonwhite racial groups were at higher risk for this disease; however, medical practitioners have come to realise that they have no reliable criteria for identifying all infants racially, so the recommended procedure for detection is to test all infants for sickle-cell anemia, regardless of the racial group to which they seem to belong or are said to belong (Clinton 1991: 2158).

Mixed-race individuals would also have a right to reject all racial identification, just as a full right to freedom in religious affiliation would include the choice of no religious affiliation, or the choice of atheism. I have so far been suggesting that black and white mixed-race Americans would choose to identify as mixed race or nonracial. But even that is too stringent a projection once the false categories begin to crumble. Some people who are mixed black and white race will choose to be black. Others will choose to be white. And still others will choose to identify based on Asian or Native American ancestry.

Mixed Black and White Race and Present Public Policy: in Fact

Parallel to the foregoing theoretical justification for self-identification for individuals of mixed race, there is a demographic and grassroots basis for such self-identification that public policy theorists and planners need to allow into their awareness as specific contexts make relevant. Statistically, mixed-race births in the United States have increased 26 times as much as pure-race births over recent decades.[14] And now, for the first time in American history: due to the success of the Civil Rights movement, albeit incomplete and begrudged, there is a generation of mixed black and white individuals who are not ashamed of their racial origins, and whose parents do not experience a need to apologize for having brought them into the world.

Project RACE (Reclassify All Children Equally), an organisation originating from efforts to change racial designations of school children in Georgia, has been lobbying legislatures in recent years to include multiracial categories on the US census and in local record keeping. The membership of the Association of MultiEthnic Americans consists of mixed-race families and their children; they actively support one another through social and cultural events and newsletters in which they share their experiences in the larger society that does not recognize their existence as mixed race.[15]

When people from different racial categories have children, as they always have done despite the existence of social or legal strictures, and whether they do so as a result of exploitation, accident, ignorance, or love, fairness in a racial society require that those children receive the same degree of racial respect as presumptively racially pure children, especially since it is widely assumed that racial identities are constructed in childhood in ways closely connected with self esteem on deep motivational levels. It is not known to what extent the importance of a child's positive feelings about race is a result of racism in the culture. Neither is it known whether it would be consistent with other aspects of mental health and social adjustment for individuals to eschew all racial identity – even in a racist society. Before the studies can be conducted that will provide empirical answers to these questions, however, the conceptual framework or theoretical assumptions that would otherwise underlie such studies must be re-examined. There is no reason to believe that social scientists are not as burdened by racial mythology as other people.

At this time, for the first time in American academic letters, a small, rapidly increasing number of scholars from varied disciplines are beginning to discuss these issues of microdiversity, and the subject of mixed race is becoming a recognised addition to curricula that address diversity and multiculturalism: Paul Spickard (l989), F. James Davis (1991), Maria P. P. Root (1992), and I (1993, 1995) have recently published book-length works on the topic of mixed race in the United States; and further work is in press as of this writing. (The popular print media and commercial publishing houses are not far behind, or ahead, as the case may be.) The general scholarly topic is *Racial Theory*, the specialization at issue is *Mixed Race* (or *Multirace*), but in practical policy-making contexts, the facts that need to be addressed are the facts of *microdiversity*. The term "microdiversity" points to the reality that many individuals are racially diverse within themselves and not merely diverse as members of groups that are believed, in often erroneous ways, to be racially different from other groups.

The map of the emancipatory scholarship of microdiversity is now on the drawing board: it may be filled in by tracing out the complex varieties of microdiversity which exist in reality; or it may blaze a route to a neo-universalist rejection of the concept of race in both scholarly and popular culture. In historical analyses, microdiversity intersects with critique of patriarchy because the one-drop rule is a legacy of white male slave owners; and in feminist analyses of contemporary culture, microdiversity intersects with gender because mixed-race women are still stereotyped as exotic, erotic, and morally defective.

In terms of present practice and policy, microdiversity has indeterminate connections with affirmative action. Since the aim of both affirmative action and the scholarship of microdiversity is to improve the institutional situations of individuals who would otherwise be overlooked or abused, both become redundant if they succeed. In the meantime, if affirmative action is just and effective, the facts of microdiversity strengthen its mandate because people of mixed race have never before been positively acknowledged to exist. So long as Americans believe in races, they will believe in racial whiteness, and whites will probably continue to be generally better off than nonwhites. And if affirmative action programs continue to be the chosen strategy for achieving equality, then mixed race individuals, insofar as they do not belong to the white, privileged, dominant group, would continue to qualify as affirmative action clients (or "patients").

I want to close with a word of caution. Tigers have to be dismounted with great care. It's one thing to understand within a safe forum that race is a biological fiction. In American culture at large, the fiction of race continues to operate as fact, and in situations of backlash against emancipatory progress, the victims of racial oppression, nonwhites, are insulted and injured further for their progress against oppression. If those who practice such second-order oppression begin to employ the truth that race is a fiction, gains already secured against first-order oppression (or in redress of it) could be jeopardized. This is a risk many will find daunting, but the answer is not to back off from the truth but to realize that it will take a while to replace the fictitious cultural realities. If the truth about mixed black and white race and race in general were to be (affirmatively) taught throughout the American educational system, it would take about two generations to have a real effect on the culture – the first generation would learn it in school and teach it to their children.

Notes

1   For more comprehensive discussions of the inadequacy of the American folk concepts of black and white race, see Zack 1993, 1994.
2   For a book-length treatment of the history of mixed black and white race in the United States, conducted within the traditional racial paradigm, see Williamson 1980.
3   For the facts on blood and race, see Zack 1993, ch. 2 and references.
4   For a discussion of race and breeding, see Zack 1993, ch. 4.
5   For an argument about the *modernity* of contemporary concepts of race, see Bernal 1987, pp. 439–45, 454–5. See also Zack 1996, ch. 12.
6   For a discussion of the development of X and Y as chromosomal markers of sex, see Kelves 1985, pp. 238–50.
7   For discussions of variations in racial genes, see Dubinin 1965, pp. 68–83 and Dunn 1965, pp. 61–7.
8   For accounts and discussions of the history of the concept of race in the social sciences see Leiris 1965 and Wacker 1983.
9   For descriptions of nineteenth-century racial hierarchies and source references, see Zack 1993, pp. 58–61, 78–9.
10 For example, Immerwahr and Burke write, "Only blacks were slaves and slaves were slaves *because* they were black" (1993, 27).
11 The classic comparison of North and South America on this issue is Degler 1971.
12 For further details on the history of antimiscegenation laws, see Sickels (1972).
13 For the United Nations positions on race, culture, and heredity, sew "Four Statements on the race question" (drafted at Unesco House, Paris) in Kuper 1965, pp. 344–64.

14 For the statistics on the increase of mixed-race marriages and births, see Special Reports 1993, pp. 20–1.
15 See Project Race Newsletter, April 1993 (Roswell, Georgia).

References

Bernal, Martin (1987) *Black Athena*, New Brunswick, NJ: Rutgers University Press.

Clinton, Jarrett J. (1991) "From the agency for health care policy and research," *Journal of the American Medical Association* 70/18, p. 2158.

Davis, F. James (1991) *Who is Black?* University Park, Pa.: Pennsylvania State University Press.

Degler, Carl N. (1971) *Neither Black nor White: Slavery and Race Relations in Brazil and the United States*, New York: Macmillan.

Dubinin, N. P. (1965) "Race and contemporary genetics," in Kuper (ed.) *Race, Science and Society.*

Dunn, L. C. (1965) "Race and biology," in Kuper (ed.) *Race, Science and Society.*

Fernández, Carlos A. (1995) "Testimony of the Association of MultiEthnic Americans," in Zack, *American Mixed Race.*

Graham, Susan (1995) "The grass roots advocacy," in Zack, *American Mixed Race.*

Immerwahr, John and Michael Burke (1993) "Race and the modern philosophy course," *Teaching Philosophy* 16/1, pp. 26–7.

Kevles, Daniel J. (1985) *In the Name of Eugenics*, Berkeley, Calif.: University of California Press.

Kuper, Leo (ed.) (1965) *Race, Science, and Society*, New York: Columbia University Press.

Leiris, Michael (1965) "Race and culture," in Kuper (ed.) *Race, Science, and Society.*

Root, Maria P. P. (1992) *Racially Mixed People in America*, Newbury Park, Calif.: Sage.

Sickels, Robert J. (1972) *Race, Marriage and the Law*, Albuquerque, N. Mex.: University of New Mexico Press.

Special Reports (1993) *I-Pride Newsletter* 15 (January).

Spickard, Paul (1989) *Mixed Blood: Inter-marriage and Ethnic Identity in Twentieth-century America*, Madison, Wis.: University of Wisconsin Press.

Wacker, R. Fred (1983) *Ethnicity, Pluralism and Race*, Westport, Conn.: Greenwood.

Williamson, Joel (1980) *New People*, New York: Free Press.

Wright, Lawrence (1994) "One drop of blood," *New Yorker*, July 25, pp. 46–55.

Zack, Naomi (1993) *Race and Mixed Race*, Philadelphia, Pa.: Temple University Press.

—— (1994) "Race and philosophic meaning," *APA Newsletter on Philosophy and the Black Experience* 93, p. 2.

—— (ed.) (1995) *American Mixed Race: The Culture of Microdiversity*, Lanham, Md.: Roman and Littlefield.

—— (1996) *Bachelors of Science: Seventeenth-century Identity Then and Now*, Philadelphia, Pa.: Temple University Press.

Questions about Race

1. How is the history of black and white race relations still relevant to the position of blacks in American society today? If you don't think it is relevant, explain why.
2. What is the concept of race? In what ways is race an illusion? In what ways is it real?
3. Can you imagine a society without ideas of race? What would its advantages be? What would its disadvantages be? Could such a society come about or is it impossible?
4. How do you define racism? What are the advantages of your definition over other definitions?
5. Does the way in which one defines racism depend on what race one is? Explain how this works.
6. What ideas of justice are presupposed in the different positions on affirmative action?
7. What kinds of harm do you think deserve reparation? (Give examples and reasons.)
8. Describe several different forms of alienation between human beings that accompany racism.
9. Should mixed black and white Americans have a distinct racial identity?
10. What are some positive and empowering aspects of traditional racial identities (i.e. black, white, Asian, and Native American) that you think need to be preserved or strengthened?

Recommended Reading for Part One

Appiah, Anthony (1992) *In My Father's House*, Oxford: Oxford University Press (African identities based on race).

Bell, Linda and Blumenfeld, David (eds) (1994) *Overcoming Sexism and Racism*, Lanham, Md.: Rowman and Littlefield (includes diverse perspectives).

Butler, Robert Olen (1992) *A Good Scent from a Strange Mountain: Stories*, New York: H. Holt (Vietnamese experience in the US).

Churchill, Ward (1992) *Struggle for the Land*, Monroe, Me.: Common Courage Press (presents problems of dispossession among Native Americans).

Cross, W. E. (1991) *Shades of Black: Diversity in African-American Identity*, Philadelphia, Pa.: Temple University Press (about different black identities and effects of racism on blacks).

Davis, F. James (1991) *Who is Black?*, University Park, Pa.: Pennsylvania State University Press (explains mixed-race heritage of black Americans).

Du Bois, W. E. B. (1989) *The Souls of Black Folk*, New York: Penguin Books [1903] (classic source of black liberatory identity writing).

D'Souza, Dinesh (1995) *The End of Racism*, New York: Free Press (conservative perspective on racial issues).

Ezorsky, Gertrude (1991) *Racism and Justice*, Ithaca, NY: Cornell University Press (detailed arguments about affirmative action).

Funderburg, L. (1994) *Black, White, Other: Biracial Americans Talk About Race and*

Identity, New York: William Morrow (case studies).

Goldberg, David Theo (ed.) (1990) *Anatomy of Racism*, Minneapolis, Minn.: University of Minnesota Press (multidisciplinary writings on racism(s)).

Gordon, Lewis R. (1995) *Fanon and the Crisis of European Man: An Essay on Philosophy and the Human Sciences*, New York and London: Routledge (contemporary interpretation of Fanon as philosopher and social scientist).

Gould, Stephen Jay (1981) *The Mismeasure of Man*, New York: Norton (explains biased and fraudulent methods of nineteenth-century scientists of race).

Gwaltney, John Langston (1980) *Drylongso: A Self-Portrait of Black America*, New York: Vintage Books (interviews with traditional black Americans).

Harris, Leonard (ed.) (1989) *The Philosophy of Alain Locke*, Philadelphia, Pa.: Temple University Press (readings in pragmatism and liberatory race theory).

Ignatiev, Noel (1995) *How the Irish Became White: Irish-Americans and African-Americans in 19th Century Philadelphia*, New York: Verso (history of social construction of racial whiteness for Irish Americans).

Jaimes, M. A. (ed.) (1992) *The State of Native America*, Boston, Mass.: South End Press (readings in American Indian history and politics).

Lawson, Bill E. (1992) *The Underclass Question*, Philadelphia, Pa.: Temple University Press (about social problems of African American urban poor and moral and political problems raised by their plight).

Lewontin, Richard C. Rose, Steven and Kamin, Leon J. (1984) *Not in Our Genes*, New York: Pantheon Books (about the lack of a biological foundation for racial difference).

McBride, James (1996) *The Color of Water: A Black Man's Tribute to his White Mother*, New York: Riverhead Books (autobiographical account of discovered Jewish ancestry).

Pittman, John P. (ed.) (1996) *African-American Perspectives and Philosophical Traditions*, New York: Routledge (philosophical writings about African American identity and experience).

Root, M. P. P. (ed.) (1996) *The Multiracial Experience: Racial Borders as the New Frontier*, Thousand Oaks, Calif.: Sage (social science perspectives on mixed race).

___ (ed.) (1993) *Racially Mixed People in America*, Newbury Park, Calif.: Sage (social science perspectives on mixed race).

Russell, Kathy, Wilson, Midge and Hall, Ronald (1992) *The Color Complex The Politics of Skin Color Among African Americans*, New York: Harcourt Brace Jovanovich (racism about blackness, among blacks).

Thornton, Russell (1987) *American Indian Holocaust Survival: A Population History Since 1492*, Norman, Okla.: University of Oklahoma Press (American Indian identity from perspective of genocidal experiences).

Twain, Mark (1980) *The Tragedy of Pudd'nhead Wilson*, New York: Norton (classic American fictional account of nature versus nurture aspects of racial identity and difference).

Vaz, Kim Marie (ed.) (1995) *Black Women in America*, Thousand Oaks, Sage (social science and experiential perspectives).

West, Cornel (1993) *Race Matters*, Boston, Mass.: Beacon Press (on the importance of race in American society and its spiritual challenges).

Zack, Naomi (1993) *Race and Mixed Race*, Philadelphia, Pa.: Temple University Press (criticism of American racial categories).

—— (ed.) (1995) *American Mixed Race: The Culture of Microdiversity*, Roman and Littlefield: Lanham, Md. (multidisciplinary readings about mixed-race identities).

—— (ed.) (1997) *RACE/SEX: Their Sameness, Difference and Interplay*, New York: Routledge (original theoretical essays on racial identity and racism).

Zinn, Maxine Baca and Dill, Bonnie Thornton (eds) (1994) *Women of Color in U.S. Society*, Philadelphia, Pa.: Temple University Press (problems and experience of Hispanic, Asian, black and Native American women).

PART TWO

CLASS
edited by Crispin Sartwell

Class: Introduction to the Readings

Max Weber, in one of the readings collected here, defines "class" as a group of people who have a common interest or stake economically, whose life-chances are similarly affected by their position in the consumer or labor market. Since members of the same class have similar positions and hence similar interests in the economic world, they may form a community to push those interests forward: for example, labor unions, craft guilds, industrial associations. Another, much simpler, way to think about class, would be to distinguish classes by income levels: we could define "the poor" for example, as those with family incomes under $20,000 per year or "the rich" as those with family incomes over $200,000. That simple way to think about class is in fact very useful but perhaps somewhat misleading. For classical theorists such as Weber, class depends not only on income but on one's relation to the means of production: if you are a factory owner on the verge of bankruptcy you are still (for now!) a member of the ownership class. It is likely that you would support legislation that reduces the taxes on factory owners rather than legislation that reduces taxes for the poor, though you might join the ranks of the poor soon; for now, your interest, your stake, is with the class of owners.

For over a century – from the time the writings of Karl Marx became famous in the middle of the nineteenth century through the 1960s – class was the most important category of social analysis, particularly for the political left. For classical leftism – a political orientation that in general favored state ownership of at least some industries, aggressive social welfare programs, and redistribution of wealth through progressive taxation – class differences were the most significant source of social injustice. In the Marxist tradition and in work that builds on that tradition, the fundamental social relations were conceived to be economic relations and the fundamental mode of oppression was economic oppression. In fact, in classical Marxism, racism and sexism were held to be analyzable in economic terms: if white folks oppress black folks or men oppress women, it is fundamentally because it is in white men's economic interest to do so.

But for many leftists and other social critics, class is now out of fashion. One recent book is titled "The Death of Class," and many thinkers have remarked that social class is no longer conceived to be the only or even the fundamental unit of social analysis. There are at least two reasons for this decline. First, the rise of feminist theory, "queer" theory, race studies, and ethnic studies has tended to show that such modes of oppression and discrimination as sexism, heterosexism, and racism cannot very plausibly be reduced to economics. This is not to deny that there are economic factors at work in all these cases: the history of the slave, for example, and the history of the "housewife" or unpaid domestic laborer are certainly economic histories. But the best accounts of the supposed natural differences between the races or the genders, it is widely agreed, go beyond what is readily explicable through economic relations. In large measure, then, the focus of social analysts has shifted from class to these other categories.

Second, historical economic and political shifts have made it much more difficult to hold a Marxist-style view of class as the fundamental unit of social analysis. Marx, as we will see in the reading in this section, predicted that, as industrial capitalism developed, the owners of capital (the bourgeoisie) would become richer and richer while the laborers who worked in their factories (the proletariat) would become poorer and poorer. Eventually the conflict of the interests of these two classes would become obvious: the bourgeoisie's interest is to pay laborers as little as possible above subsistence, while the laborers' interest is to increase their own wages. This, Marx held, would bring on an inevitable class war that would end capitalism and lead eventually to a Communist paradise. His view was not entirely inaccurate. As factories became ever larger and more pervasive in the late nineteenth and early twentieth centuries, and as the personal fortunes of "robber barons" became ever more immense, labor organized into unions to fight for its share of the pie. Communist revolution swept much of Europe, Asia, Africa, and Latin America.

However, Marx's predictions turned out to be wrong for several reasons. First, the class situation itself has become ever more complicated. As the twentieth century progressed in the "developed" world, more and more people came to occupy what has been termed "the new class": a class of managers, consultants, and technical experts. This class makes more money than the proletariat or industrial laborer, and though the new class does not own the means of production and hence is not bourgeois on Marx's definition, it does not identify its interests with the proletariat. Partly, this class becomes dominant in the late-industrial or "postindustrial" economy of "first world" nations because industrial manufacturing and exploitation of labor has been shifted overseas to the "third world" while management structures remain in place and people require various services in the "first world." In contemporary capitalism one sees a complex class structure that Marx did not anticipate: there is still a massive gap between rich and poor, but in this gap there is a curve of incomes, and many people whose source of income is a wage rather than ownership (though there is likely to be investment as well) are very well off indeed. In addition, Communism itself has gone out of fashion historically in a very big way. The Berlin wall has fallen, the Soviet Union no longer exists, and even revolutionary groups in developing nations have backed away from Communist rhetoric. This in itself is no refutation of Marx, because the relation of these various regimes to Marxist theory was often tenuous and always problematic. But these historic events have contributed to Marxism's decline and hence also to the decline of class as a fundamental unit of social analysis.

Nevertheless, it is obvious that class remains an extremely important category for any survey of the social situation, particularly because the difficulties of what is now known as "the underclass" have been very hard to ameliorate. Violent crime, homelessness, drug addiction, and illiteracy are some of the problems faced by many of the members of this class even in the midst of a very productive economy, and these problems can be traced fundamentally to economic realities. We should not believe that class can be detached from such categories as ethnicity, gender, race, or sexual orientation, nor that all of these categories could somehow be reduced to class, as many Marxists once believed. But it is obvious that economic relations are deeply formative of all sorts of social relations and that "class consciousness" is alive and well. When a manual laborer says to a professor (and believe me this happens), "it must be nice not to work," he is crystallizing class attitudes and a class conflict: here between the "proletariat" and the "new class" of intellectual laborers. When well-paid executives express themselves baffled at how people can stand to be on welfare, or why poor folks "don't value education" or "family" or why they won't "work hard enough" to pull themselves up, they are expressing their own class values as well as class resentment against the poor or fear of the poor. When the Republicans push for a cut in capital gains tax and the Democrats push for tax cuts for higher education, they are representing the classes that fund them: the Republicans are representing the interests of the bourgeoisie or owners of capital while the Democrats are representing the "new class" of elite, extremely well-educated experts. So whether it is explicitly made a theme in our political and social lives, class continues to be a deeply important reality.

The first three extracts that follow are basic, extremely influential sources on class without which it is very hard to understand thinking about class today. The last four extracts move us toward and then into the contemporary class situation and the issues that surround it.

The first extract is from that hero of conservatives, Adam Smith. Smith set the tone for two hundred years of free market capitalist theory, and his views were formative for every economist who came after, including Marx. Smith argues that where there are not great inequalities of wealth there is little need for government authority, and hence that the fundamental reason for such authority is to protect the rich. In addition, Smith directly relates wealth to poverty, and argues that "for one very rich man there must be at least five hundred poor." That is, the wealth of a few is built out of the poverty of many. (Notice that by themselves these assertions might support very conservative or very radical conclusions: Smith's claim that political authority protects the rich might be used in a critique of that authority; the claim that wealth creates poverty is an observation made by Marx among many other leftists.) Smith then traces the reasons for inequality to "natural" differences: superiority of personal qualifications, superiority of age, superiority of fortune, and superiority of birth.

The Communist Manifesto of Marx and Engels, published in 1848, is one of the most influential documents in history, and provides a very clear summary of Marx and Engels' analysis of social life based on class relations. It traces the rise of industrial capitalism out of feudal economies, which involves the replacement of the feudal lords with the bourgeoisie as the ruling class and the replacement of the peasant or serf with the proletariat as the subordinate class. Hence, in germ, it sketches out Marx's "dialectical materialism," according to which history is driven inevitably in a certain direction by shifts in the forces of production and their accompanying class structures. *The Communist Manifesto* concludes by prescribing a solution to class struggle in capitalism, or rather by asserting what the necessary next stage will be: Communism. The greed of the capitalist class eventually becomes a barrier to efficient production, and a class struggle of the proletariat against the bourgeoisie leads to an era of extreme state power and "nonalienated" or satisfying labor.

Max Weber, in a difficult but important extract, gives a definition of class (summarized above) and discusses class in relation to the notion of community. The basic characterization of class given here has been massively influential, particularly within sociology. Weber argues (and Marx would agree) that classes are not "natural," as Smith held, but result from a given distribution of property and the structure of the economic order. This distribution and order can be changed by the rational association of members of the same class to transform the economic order. Classes are not the same as communities, and indeed members of the same class can be divided against one another as a strategy for domination. Weber argues implicitly that Marxist economic analysis of history in terms of class struggle was far too simplistic, and that other groups – status groups and political parties, for example – often cut across class but have often affected history profoundly. Such an analysis has been extended by admirers of Weber who hold that gender, race, sexual orientation, and ethnicity also create interest groups which join people of different classes and divide people of the same class.

At this point the readings leave the classical literature of class behind and begin to be more directly relevant to the current situation. In a passage from his important book *Tally's Corner*, Elliot Liebow describes the lives of poor black men living in the District of Columbia in the 1960s. Though such men were then, and are often now, condemned for not wanting to work and for failing to reside with or support their children, Liebow shows in detail why their decisions are rational given their options. In fact, given their labor situation, there is almost no prospect for such men to support a family, and the work available is often backbreaking and completely unrewarding. This piece remains a useful reply to certain stereotypes of the poor in general and the black poor in particular.

Dasiea Cavers-Huff and Janice Kollitz describe an interesting friendship between a black woman who was once on welfare and a white woman whose background is solidly middle class. They show how political positions often flow from social and economic positions, a point first made systematically by Marx. And though Cavers-Huff traces much of their difference to race, Kollitz traces much of it to class. Still, their friendship is a hopeful example of how such differences can be overcome on a personal level.

The extract from Patricia J. Williams explores some of these same attitudes, as well as the interaction between race and class. Williams, who is a professor of law, explores the concepts of ownership, visibility, privacy, contract, choice, and homelessness. Along the way, she describes her own experience of trying to discuss such issues in a personal way with law students who are themselves for the most part children of privilege. In her rapturous prose, Williams gets at these issues from several points of view simultaneously: legally, sociologically, and perhaps most importantly, personally.

The last excerpt is by Joanna Kadi. She explores the notion of "working-class culture," and in particular the fact that there is much working-class art, but that this art gets devalued by the upper and middle classes. She has in mind, first, crafts, such as sewing and cookery, and second, popular arts such as country music. Kadi's point is that some things gain a cultural value or cachet – and become "fine arts" – in large part because they are appreciated by the upper classes. Through the example of her own Arab-American aunt, who was a musician, dancer, and a mistress of flamboyant personal adornment, Kadi tries to contribute to a revaluation of working-class art. If we were to take Kadi's treatment seriously, we would have to throw into doubt the deepest assumptions that underpin the contemporary art world, such as the distinction between fine (or "great") art and popular art, and what it means to be an "expert" or even an artist.

Adam Smith (1723–90) was one of the most important political economists in history. Known for developing the basic economic laws of capitalism, including, for example, the relation of supply and demand, Smith, in this selection from his classic book *The Wealth of Nations*, argues that the origin of political authority is the defense of private wealth.

Focus questions:
1 In what ways does Smith relate the poverty of many to the wealth of a few?
2 What are the four "natural" sources of the subordination of some people to others, according to Smith?
3 What, for Smith, is the origin and purpose of civil government?

---

10   Civil Government is for Defence of Rich against Poor

Adam Smith

Among nations of hunters, as there is scarce any property, or at least none that exceeds the value of two or three days' labour, so there is seldom any established magistrate or any regular administration of justice. Men who have no property can injure one another only in their persons or reputations. But when one man kills, wounds, beats, or defames another, though he to whom the injury is done suffers, he who does it receives no benefit. It is otherwise with the injuries to property. The benefit of the person who does the injury is often equal to the loss of him who suffers it. Envy, malice, or resentment, are the only passions which can prompt one man to injure another in his person or reputation. But the greater part of men are not very frequently under the influence of those passions, and the very worst men are so only occasionally. As their gratification, too, how agreeable soever it may be to certain characters, is not attended with any real or permanent advantage, it is in greater part of men commonly restrained by prudential considerations. Men may live together in society with some tolerable degree of security, though there is no civil magistrate to protect them from the injustice of those passions. But avarice and ambition in the rich, in the poor the hatred of labour and the love of present ease and enjoyment, are the passions which prompt to invade property; passions much more steady in their operation, and much more universal in their influence. Wherever there is great property, there is great inequality. For one very rich man, there must be at least five hundred poor, and the affluence of the rich excites the indignation of the poor, who are often both driven by want and prompted by envy to invade his possessions. It is only under the shelter of the civil magistrate that the owner of that valuable property, which is acquired by the labour of many years, or perhaps of many successive generations, can sleep a single night in security. He is at all times surrounded by unknown enemies, whom, though he never provoked, he can never appease, and from whose injustice he can be protected only by the powerful arm of the civil magistrate continually held up to chastise it. The acquisition of valuable and extensive property, therefore, necessarily requires the establishment of civil government. Where there is no property, or at least none that exceeds the value of two or three days' labour, civil government is not so necessary.

Civil government supposes a certain subordination. But as the necessity of civil government gradually grows up with the acquisition of valuable property, so the principal causes which naturally introduce subordination gradually grow up with the growth of that valuable property. The cause of circumstances which naturally introduce subordination or which naturally, and antecedent to any civil institution, give some men some superiority over the greater part of their brethren, seem to be four in number.

The first of those causes or circumstances is the superiority of personal qualifications – of strength, beauty, and agility of body; of wisdom and virtue, of prudence, justice, fortitude, and moderation of mind. The qualifications of the body, unless supported by those of the mind, can give little authority in any period of society. He is a very strong man who, by mere strength of body, can force two weak ones to obey him. The qualifications of the mind can alone give very great authority. They are, however, invisible qualities; always disputable, and generally disputed. No society, whether barbarous or civilized, has ever found it convenient to settle the rules of precedency of rank and subordination according to those invisible qualities, but according to something that is more plain and palpable.

The second of those causes or circumstances is the superiority of age. An old man, provided his age is not so far advanced as to give suspicion of dotage, is everywhere more respected than a young man of equal rank, fortune, and abilities. Among nations of hunters, such as the native tribes of North America, age is the sole foundation of rank and precedency. Among them, father is the appellation of a superior; brother, of an equal; and son, of an inferior. In the most opulent and civilized nations, age regulates rank among those who are in every other respect equal, and among whom, therefore, there is nothing else to regulate it. Among brothers and among sisters the eldest always takes place; and in the succession of the paternal estate, everything which cannot be divided, but must go entire to one person, such as a title of honour, is in most cases given to the eldest. Age is a plain and palpable quality which admits of no dispute.

The third of those causes or circumstances is the superiority of fortune. The authority of riches, however, though great in every age of society, is perhaps greatest in the rudest age of society which admits of any considerable inequality of fortune. A Tartar chief, the increase of whose herds and flocks is sufficient to maintain a thousand men, cannot well employ that increase in any other way than in maintaining a thousand men. The rude state of his society does not afford him any manufactured produce, any trinkets or baubles of any kind, for which he can exchange that part of his rude produce which is over and above his own consumption. The 1,000 men whom he thus maintains, depending entirely upon him for their subsistence, must both obey his orders in war and submit to his jurisdiction in peace. He is necessarily both their general and their judge, and his chieftainship is the necessary effect of the superiority of his fortune. In an opulent and civilized society, a man may possess a much greater fortune, and yet not be able to command a dozen of people. Though the produce of his estate may be sufficient to maintain, and may perhaps actually maintain, more than 1,000 people, yet as those people pay for everything which they get from him, as he gives scarce anything to anybody but in exchange for an equivalent, there is scarce anybody who considers himself as entirely dependent upon him, and his authority extends only over a few menial servants. The authority of fortune, however, is very great even in an opulent and civilized society. That it is much greater than that, either of age, or of personal qualities, has been the constant complaint of every period of society which admitted of any considerable inequality of fortune. The first period of society, that of hunters, admits of no such inequality. Universal poverty establishes their universal equality, and the superiority either of age or of personal qualities, are the feeble, but the sole foundations of authority and subordination. There is therefore little or no authority or subordination in this period of society. The second period of society, that of shepherds, admits of very great inequalities of fortune, and there is no period in which the superiority of fortune gives so great authority to those who possess it. There is no period accordingly in which authority and subordination are more perfectly established. The authority of an Arabian scherif is very great; that of a Tartar khan altogether despotical.

The fourth of those causes or circumstances is the superiority of birth. Superiority of birth supposes an ancient superiority of fortune in the family of the person who claims it. All families are equally ancient; and the ancestors of the prince, though they may be better known, cannot well be more numerous than those of the beggar. Antiquity of family means everywhere the antiquity either founded upon wealth or accompanied with it. Upstart greatness is everywhere less respected than ancient greatness. The hatred of usurpers, the love of the family of an ancient monarch, are, in a great measure, founded upon the contempt which men naturally have for the former, and upon their veneration for the latter. As a military officer submits without reluctance to the authority of a superior by whom he has always been commanded, but cannot bear that his inferior should be set over his head, so men easily submit to a family to whom they and their ancestors have always submitted; but are fired with indignation when another family, in whom they had never acknowledged any such superiority, assumes a dominion over them.

The distinction of birth, being subsequent to the inequality of fortune, can have no place in nations of hunters, among whom all men, being equal in fortune, must likewise be very nearly equal in birth. The son of a wise and brave man may, indeed, even among them, be somewhat more respected than a man of equal merit who has the misfortune to be the son of a fool or a coward. The difference, however, will not be very great; and there never was, I believe, a great family in the world whose illustration was entirely derived from the inheritance of wisdom and virtue.

The distinction of birth not only may, but always does, take place among nations of shepherds. Such nations are always strangers to every sort of luxury, and great wealth can scarce ever be dissipated among them by improvident profusion. There are no nations accordingly who abound more in families revered and honoured on account of their descent from a long race of great and illustrious ancestors; because there are no nations among whom wealth is likely to continue longer in the same families.

Birth and fortune are evidently the two circumstances which principally set one man above another. They are the two great sources of personal distinction, and are therefore the principal causes which naturally establish authority and subordination among men. Among nations of shepherds both these causes operate with their full force. The great shepherd or herdsman, respected on account of his great wealth, and of the great number of those who depend upon him for subsistence, and revered on account of the nobleness of his birth and of the immemorial antiquity of his illustrious family, has a natural authority over all the inferior shepherds or herdsmen of his horde or clan. He can command the united force of a greater number of people than any of them. His military power is greater than that of any of them. In time of war they are all of them naturally disposed to muster themselves under his banner, rather than under that of any other person, and his birth and fortune thus naturally procure to him some sort of executive power. By commanding, too, the united force of a greater number of people than any of them, he is best able to compel any one of them who may have injured another to compensate the wrong. He is the person, therefore, to whom all those who are too weak to defend themselves naturally look up for protection. It is to him that they naturally complain of the injuries which they imagine have been done to them, and his interposition in such cases is more easily submitted to, even by the persons complained of, than that of any other person would be. His birth and fortune thus naturally procure him some sort of judicial authority.

It is in the age of shepherds, in the second period of society, that the inequality of fortune first begins to take place, and introduces among men a degree of authority and subordination which could not possibly exist before. It thereby introduces some degree of that civil government which is indispensably necessary for its own preservation: and it seems to do this naturally, and ever dependent of the consideration of that necessity. The consideration of that necessity comes, no doubt, afterwards to contribute very much to maintain and secure that authority and subordination. The rich, in particular, are necessarily interested to support that order of things, which can alone secure them in the possession of their own advantages. Men of inferior wealth combine to defend those of superior wealth in the possession of their property, in order that men of superior wealth may combine to defend them in the possession of theirs. All the inferior shepherds and herdsmen feel that the security of their own herds and flocks depends upon the security of those of the great shepherd or herdsman; and the maintenance of their lesser authority depends upon that of his greater authority, and that upon their subordination depends upon his power of keeping their inferiors in subordination to them. They constitute a sort of little nobility, who feel themselves interested to defend the property and to support the authority of their own little sovereign, in order that he may be able to defend their property and to support their authority. Civil government, so far as it is instituted for the security of property, is in reality instituted for the defence of the rich against the poor, or of those who have some property against those who have none at all.

Note

The title of the article is Smith's own.

Karl Marx (1818–83) and Friedrich Engels (1820–95) were economists and political thinkers of pervasive influence: their ideas affected the course of revolutions throughout the world. They were the inventors of modern Communism and a mode of historical analysis known as "dialectical materialism," according to which human beings are considered above all as economic producers and history is held to be determined by the conditions of production. Here, they trace the origins of capitalism and describe what they believe to be its inevitable decline. They then go on to describe the character of the Communist society they think will inevitably follow the end of capitalism.

Focus questions:

1 According to Marx and Engels, what is the basic class structure in capitalism?
2 What are the stages of capitalist development, and what point did Marx and Engels believe capitalism had reached when they wrote?
3 What will bring about the downfall of the capitalist mode of production, according to Marx and Engels?
4 What are the most important features of Communism?

---

11 Manifesto of the Communist Party

Karl Marx and Friedrich Engels

A spectre is haunting Europe – the spectre of Communism. All the Powers of old Europe have entered into a holy alliance to exorcise this spectre: Pope and

Czar, Metternich and Guizot, French Radicals and German police-spies.

Where is the party in opposition that has not been decried as Communistic by its opponents in power? Where the Opposition that has not hurled back the branding reproach of Communism, against the more advanced opposition parties, as well as against its reactionary adversaries?

Two things result from this fact.

I. Communism is already acknowledged by all European Powers to be itself a Power.

II. It is high time that Communists should openly, in the face of the whole world, publish their views, their aims, their tendencies, and meet this nursery tale of the Spectre of Communism with a Manifesto of the party itself.

To this end, Communists of various nationalities have assembled in London, and sketched the following Manifesto, to be published in the English, French, German, Italian, Flemish and Danish languages.

I. Bourgeois and Proletarians[1]

The history of all hitherto existing society[2] is the history of class struggles.

Freeman and slave, patrician and plebeian, lord and serf, guild-master[3] and journeyman, in a word, oppressor and oppressed, stood in constant opposition to one another, carried on an uninterrupted, now hidden, now open fight, a fight that each time ended, either in a revolutionary re-constitution of society at large, or in the common ruin of the contending classes.

In the earlier epochs of history, we find almost everywhere a complicated arrangement of society into various orders, a manifold gradation of social rank. In ancient Rome we have patricians, knights, plebeians, slaves; in the Middle Ages, feudal lords, vassals, guildmasters, journeymen, apprentices, serfs; in almost all of these classes, again, subordinate gradations.

The modern bourgeois society that has sprouted from the ruins of feudal society has not done away with class antagonisms. It has but established new classes, new conditions of oppression, new forms of struggle in place of the old ones.

Our epoch, the epoch of the bourgeoisie, possesses, however, this distinctive feature: it has simplified the class antagonisms: Society as a whole is more and more splitting up into two great hostile camps, into two great classes directly facing each other: Bourgeoisie and Proletariat.

From the serfs of the Middle Ages sprang the chartered burghers of the earliest towns. From these burgesses the first elements of the bourgeoisie were developed.

The discovery of America, the rounding of the Cape, opened up fresh ground for the rising bourgeoisie. The East-Indian and Chinese markets, the colonisation of America, trade with the colonies, the increase in the means of exchange and in commodities generally, gave to commerce, to navigation, to industry, an impulse never before known, and thereby, to the revolutionary element in the tottering feudal society, a rapid development.

The feudal system of industry, under which industrial production was monopolised by closed guilds, now no longer sufficed for the growing wants of the new markets. The manufacturing system took its place. The guild-masters were pushed on one side by the manufacturing middle class; division of labour between the different corporate guilds vanished in the face of division of labour in each single workshop.

Meantime the markets kept ever growing, the demand ever rising. Even manufacture no longer sufficed. Thereupon, steam and machinery revolutionised industrial production. The place of manufacture was taken by the giant, Modern Industry, the place of the industrial middle class, by industrial millionaires, the leaders of whole industrial armies, the modern bourgeois.

Modern industry has established the world-market, for which the discovery of America paved the way. This market has given an immense development to commerce, to navigation, to communication by land. This development has, in its turn, reacted on the extension of industry; and in proportion as industry, commerce, navigation, railways extended, in the same proportion the bourgeoisie developed, increased its capital, and pushed into the background every class handed down from the Middle Ages.

We see, therefore, how the modern bourgeoisie is itself the product of a long course of development, of a series of revolutions in the modes of production and of exchange.

Each step in the development of the bourgeoisie was accompanied by a corresponding political advance of that class. An oppressed class under the sway of the feudal nobility, an armed and self-governing association in the mediaeval commune;[4] here independent urban republic (as in Italy and Germany), there taxable "third estate" of the monarchy (as in France), afterwards, in the period of manufacture proper, serving either the semi-feudal or the absolute monarchy as a counterpoise against the nobility, and, in fact, cornerstone of the great monarchies in general, the bourgeoisie has at last, since the establishment of Modern Industry and of the world-market, conquered for itself, in the modern representative State, exclusive political sway. The executive of the modern State is but a committee for managing the common affairs of the whole bourgeoisie.

The bourgeoisie, historically, has played a most revolutionary part.

The bourgeoisie, wherever it has got the upper hand, has put an end to all feudal, patriarchal, idyllic relations. It has pitilessly torn asunder the motley feudal ties that bound man to his "natural superiors," and has left remaining no other nexus between man and man than naked self-interest, than callous "cash payment." It has drowned the most heavenly ecstasies of religious fervour, of chivalrous enthusiasm, of philistine sentimentalism, in the icy water of egotistical calculation. It has resolved personal worth into exchange value, and in place of the numberless indefeasible chartered freedoms, has set up that single, unconscionable freedom – Free Trade. In one word, for exploitation, veiled by religious and political illusions, it has substituted naked, shameless, direct, brutal exploitation.

The bourgeoisie has stripped of its halo every occupation hitherto honoured and looked up to with reverent awe. It has converted the physician, the lawyer, the priest, the poet, the man of science, into its paid wage-labourers.

The bourgeoisie has torn away from the family its sentimental veil, and has reduced the family relation to a mere money relation.

The bourgeoisie has disclosed how it came to pass that the brutal display of vigour in the Middle Ages, which Reactionists so much admire, found its fitting complement in the most slothful indolence. It has been the first to show what man's activity can bring about. It has accomplished wonders far surpassing Egyptian pyramids, Roman aqueducts, and Gothic cathedrals; it has conducted expeditions that put in the shade all former Exoduses of nations and crusades.

The bourgeoisie cannot exist without constantly revolutionising the instruments of production, and thereby the relations of production, and with them the whole relations of society. Conservation of the old modes of production in unaltered form, was, on the contrary, the first condition of existence for all earlier industrial classes. Constant revolutionising of production, uninterrupted disturbance of all social conditions, everlasting uncertainty, and agitation distinguish the bourgeois epoch from all earlier ones. All fixed, fast-frozen relations, with their train of ancient and venerable prejudices and opinions, are swept away, all new-formed ones become antiquated before they can ossify. All that is solid melts into air, all that is holy is profaned, and man is at last compelled to face with sober senses, his real conditions of life, and his relations with his kind.

The need of a constantly expanding market for its products chases the bourgeoisie over the whole surface of the globe. It must nestle everywhere, settle everywhere, establish connexions everywhere.

The bourgeoisie has through its exploitation of the world-market given a cosmopolitan character to production and consumption in every country. To the great chagrin of Reactionists, it has drawn from under the feet of industry the national ground on which it stood. All old-established national industries have been destroyed or are daily being destroyed. They are dislodged by new industries, whose introduction becomes a life and death question for all civilised nations, by industries that no longer work up indigenous raw material, but raw material drawn from the remotest zones; industries whose products are consumed, not only at home, but in every quarter of the globe. In place of the old wants, satisfied by the productions of the country, we find new wants, requiring for their satisfaction the products of distant lands and climes. In place of the old local and national seclusion and self-sufficiency, we have intercourse in every direction, universal interdependence of nations. And as in material, so also in intellectual production. The intellectual creations of individual nations become common property. National one-sidedness and narrow-mindedness become more and more impossible, and from the numerous national and local literatures, there arises a world literature.

The bourgeoisie, by the rapid improvement of all instruments of production, by the immensely facilitated means of communication, draws all, even the most barbarian, nations into civilisation. The cheap prices of its commodities are the heavy artillery with which it batters down all Chinese walls, with which it forces the barbarians' intensely obstinate hatred of foreigners to capitulate. It compels all nations, on pain of extinction, to adopt the bourgeois mode of production; it compels them to introduce what it calls civilisation into their midst, *i.e.*, to become bourgeois themselves. In one word, it creates a world after its own image.

The bourgeoisie has subjected the country to the rule of the towns. It has created enormous cities, has greatly increased the urban population as compared with the rural, and has thus rescued a considerable part of the population from the idiocy of rural life. Just as it has made the country dependent on the towns, so it has made barbarian and semi-barbarian countries dependent on the civilised ones, nations of peasants on nations of bourgeois, the East on the West.

The bourgeoisie keeps more and more doing away with the scattered state of the population, of the means of production, and of property. It has agglomerated population, centralised means of production, and has concentrated property in a few hands. The necessary consequence of this was political centralisation. Independent, or but loosely connected provinces, with separate interests, laws, governments and systems of taxation, became lumped together into one nation, with one government, one code of laws, one national class-interest, one frontier and one customs-tariff.

The bourgeoisie, during its rule of scarce one hundred years, has created more massive and more colossal productive forces than have all preceding generations together. Subjection of Nature's forces to man, machinery, application of chemistry to industry and agriculture, steam-navigation, railways, electric telegraphs, clearing of whole continents for cultivation, canalisation of rivers, whole populations conjured out of the ground – what earlier century had even a presentiment that such productive forces slumbered in the lap of social labour?

We see then: the means of production and of exchange, on whose foundation the bourgeoisie built itself up, were generated in feudal society. At a certain stage in the development of these means of production and of exchange, the conditions under which feudal society produced and exchanged, the feudal organisation of agriculture and manufacturing industry, in one word, the feudal relations of property became no longer compatible with the already developed productive forces; they became so many fetters. They had to be burst asunder; they were burst asunder.

Into their place stepped free competition, accompanied by a social and political constitution adapted to it, and by the economical and political sway of the bourgeois class.

A similar movement is going on before our own eyes. Modern bourgeois society with its relations of production, of exchange and of property, a society that has conjured up such gigantic means of production and of exchange, is like the sorcerer, who is no longer able to control the powers of the nether world whom he has called up by his spells. For many a decade past the history of industry and commerce is but the history of the revolt of modern productive forces against modern conditions of production, against the property relations that are the conditions for the existence of the bourgeoisie and of its rule. It is enough to mention the commercial crises that by their periodical return put on its trial, each time more threateningly, the existence of the entire bourgeois society. In these crises a great part not only of the existing products, but also of the previously created productive forces, are periodically destroyed. In these crises there breaks out an epidemic that, in all earlier epochs, would have seemed an absurdity – the epidemic of overproduction. Society suddenly finds itself put back into a state of momentary barbarism; it appears as if a famine, a universal war of devastation had cut off the supply of every means of subsistence; industry and commerce seem to be destroyed; and why? Because there is too much civilisation, too much means of subsistence, too much industry, too much commerce. The productive forces at the disposal of society no longer tend to further the development of the conditions of bourgeois property; on the contrary, they have become too powerful for these conditions, by which they are fettered, and so soon as they overcome these fetters they bring disorder into the whole of bourgeois society, endanger the existence of bourgeois property. The conditions of bourgeois society are too narrow to comprise the wealth created by them. And how does the bourgeoisie get over these crises? On the one hand by enforced destruction of a mass of productive forces; on the other, by the conquest of new markets, and by the more thorough exploitation of the old ones. That is to say, by paving the way for more extensive and more destructive crises, and by diminishing the means whereby crises are prevented.

The weapons with which the bourgeoisie felled feudalism to the ground are now turned against the bourgeoisie itself.

But not only has the bourgeoisie forged the weapons that bring death to itself; it has also called into existence the men who are to wield those weapons – the modern working class – the proletarians.

In proportion as the bourgeoisie, *i.e.*, capital, is developed, in the same proportion is the proletariat, the modern working class, developed – a class of labourers, who live only so long as they find work, and who find work only so long as their labour increases capital. These labourers, who must sell themselves piecemeal, are a commodity, like every other article of commerce, and are consequently exposed to all the vicissitudes of competition, to all the fluctuations of the market.

Owing to the extensive use of machinery and to division of labour, the work of the proletarians has lost all individual character, and consequently, all charm for the workman. He becomes an appendage of the machine, and it is only the most simple, most monotonous, and most easily acquired knack, that is required of him. Hence, the cost of production of a workman is restricted, almost entirely, to the means of subsistence that he requires for his maintenance, and for the propagation of his race. But the price of a commodity, and therefore also of labour,[5] is equal to its cost of production. In proportion, therefore, as the repulsiveness of the work increases, the wage decreases. Nay more, in proportion as the use of machinery and division of labour increases, in the same proportion the burden of toil also increases, whether by prolongation of the working hours, by increase of the work exacted in a given time or by increased speed of the machinery, etc.

Modern industry has converted the little workshop of the patriarchal master into the great factory of the industrial capitalist. Masses of labourers, crowded into the factory, are organised like soldiers. As privates of the industrial army they are placed under the command of a perfect hierarchy of officers and sergeants. Not only are they slaves of the bourgeois class, and of the bourgeois State; they are daily and hourly enslaved by the machine, by the over-looker, and, above all, by the individual bourgeois manufacturer himself. The more openly this despotism proclaims gain to be its end and aim, the more petty, the more hateful and the more embittering it is.

The less the skill and exertion of strength implied in manual labour, in other words, the more modern industry becomes developed, the more is the labour of men superseded by that of women. Differences of age and sex have no longer any distinctive social validity for the working class. All are instruments of labour, more or less expensive to use, according to their age and sex.

No sooner is the exploitation of the labourer by the manufacturer, so far, at an end, that he receives his wages in cash, than he is set upon by the other portions of the bourgeoisie, the landlord, the shopkeeper, the pawnbroker, etc.

The lower strata of the middle class – the small tradespeople, shopkeepers, and retired tradesmen generally, the handicraftsmen and peasants – all these sink gradually into the proletariat, partly because their diminutive capital does not suffice for the scale on which Modern Industry is carried on, and is swamped in the competition with the large capitalists, partly because their specialised skill is rendered worthless by new methods of production. Thus the proletariat is recruited from all classes of the population.

The proletariat goes through various stages of development. With its birth begins its struggle with the bourgeoisie. At first the contest is carried on by individual labourers, then by the workpeople of a factory, then by the operatives of one trade, in one locality, against the individual bourgeois who directly exploits them. They direct their attacks not against the bourgeois conditions of production, but against the instruments of production themselves; they destroy imported wares that compete with their labour, they smash to pieces machinery, they set factories ablaze, they seek to restore by force the vanished status of the workman of the Middle Ages.

At this stage the labourers still form an incoherent mass scattered over the whole country, and broken up by their mutual competition. If anywhere they unite to form more compact bodies, this is not yet the consequence of their own active union, but of the union of the bourgeoisie, which class, in order to attain its own political ends, is compelled to set the whole proletariat in motion, and is moreover yet, for a time, able to do so. At this stage, therefore, the proletarians do not fight their enemies, but the enemies of their enemies, the remnants of absolute monarchy, the landowners, the non-industrial bourgeois, the petty bourgeoisie. Thus the whole historical movement is concentrated in the hands of the bourgeoisie; every victory so obtained is a victory for the bourgeoisie.

But with the development of industry the proletariat not only increases in number; it becomes concentrated in greater masses, its strength grows, and it feels that strength more. The various interests and conditions of life within the ranks of the proletariat are more and more equalised, in proportion as machinery obliterates all distinctions of labour, and nearly everywhere reduces wages to the same low level. The growing competition among the bourgeois, and the resulting commercial crises, make the wages of the workers ever more fluctuating. The unceasing improvement of machinery, ever more rapidly developing, makes their livelihood more and more precarious; the collisions between individual workmen and individual bourgeois take more and more the character of collisions between two classes. Thereupon the workers begin to form combinations (Trades Unions) against the bourgeois; they club together in order to keep up the rate of wages; they found permanent associations in order to make provision beforehand for these occasional revolts. Here and there the contest breaks out into riots.

Now and then the workers are victorious, but only for a time. The real fruit of their battles lies, not in the immediate result, but in the ever-expanding union of the workers. This union is helped on by the improved means of communication that are created by modem industry and that place the workers of different localities in contact with one another. It was just this contact that was needed to centralise the numerous local struggles, all of the same character, into one national struggle between classes. But every class struggle is a political struggle. And that union, to attain which the burghers of the Middle Ages, with their miserable highways, required centuries, the modern proletarians, thanks to railways, achieve in a few years.

This organisation of the proletarians into a class, and consequently into a political party, is continually being upset again by the competition between the workers themselves. But it ever rises up again stronger, firmer, mightier. It compels legislative recognition of particular interests of the workers, by taking advantage of the divisions among the bourgeoisie itself. Thus the ten-hours' bill in England was carried.

Altogether collisions between the classes of the old society further, in many ways, the course of development of the proletariat. The bourgeoisie finds itself involved in a constant battle. At first with the aristocracy; later on, with those portions of the bourgeoisie itself, whose interests have become antagonistic to the progress of industry; at all times, with the bourgeoisie of foreign countries. In all these battles it sees itself compelled to appeal to the proletariat, to ask for its help, and thus, to drag it into the political arena. The bourgeoisie itself, therefore, supplies the proletariat with its own elements of political and general education, in other words, it furnishes the proletariat with weapons for fighting the bourgeoisie.

Further, as we have already seen, entire sections of the ruling classes are, by the advance of industry, precipitated into the proletariat, or are at least threatened in their conditions of existence. These also supply the proletariat with fresh elements of enlightenment and progress.

Finally, in times when the class struggle nears the decisive hour, the process of dissolution going on within the ruling class, in fact within the whole range of society, assumes such a violent, glaring character, that a small section of the ruling class cuts itself adrift, and joins the revolutionary class, the class that holds the future in its hands. Just as, therefore, at an earlier period, a section of the nobility went over to the bourgeoisie, so now a portion of the bourgeoisie goes over to the proletariat, and in particular, a portion of the bourgeois ideologists, who have raised themselves to the level of comprehending theoretically the historical movement as a whole.

Of all the classes that stand face to face with the bourgeoisie today, the proletariat alone is a really revolutionary class. The other classes decay and finally disappear in the face of Modern Industry; the proletariat is its special and essential product.

The lower middle class, the small manufacturer, the shopkeeper, the artisan, the peasant, all these fight against the bourgeoisie, to save from extinction their existence as fractions of the middle class. They are therefore not revolutionary, but conservative. Nay more, they are reactionary, for they try to roll back the wheel of history. If by chance they are revolutionary, they are so only in view of their impending transfer into the proletariat, they thus defend not their present, but their future interests, they desert their own standpoint to place themselves at that of the proletariat.

The "dangerous class," the social scum, that passively rotting mass thrown off by the lowest layers of old society, may, here and there, be swept into the movement by a proletarian revolution: its conditions of life, however, prepare it far more for the part of a bribed tool of reactionary intrigue.

In the conditions of the proletariat, those of old society at large are already virtually swamped. The proletarian is without property; his relation to his wife and children has no longer anything in common with the bourgeois family-relations: modern industrial labour, modern subjection to capital, the same in England as in France, in America as in Germany, has stripped him of every trace of national character. Law, morality, religion, are to him so many bourgeois prejudices, behind which lurk in ambush just as many bourgeois interests.

All the preceding classes that got the upper hand, sought to fortify their already acquired status by subjecting society at large to their conditions of appropriation. The proletarians cannot become masters of the productive forces of society, except by abolishing their own previous mode of appropriation, and thereby also every other previous mode of appropriation. They have nothing of their own to secure and to fortify; their mission is to destroy all previous securities for, and insurances of, individual property.

All previous historical movements were movements of minorities, or in the interests of minorities. The proletarian movement is the self-conscious, independent movement of the immense majority, in the interests of the immense majority. The proletariat, the lowest stratum of our present society, cannot stir, cannot raise itself up, without the whole superincumbent strata of official society being sprung into the air.

Though not in substance, yet in form, the struggle of the proletariat with the bourgeoisie is at first a national struggle. The proletariat of each country must, of course, first of all settle matters with its own bourgeoisie.

In depicting the most general phases of the development of the proletariat, we traced the more or less veiled civil war, raging within existing society, up to the point where that war breaks out into open revolution, and where the violent overthrow of the bourgeoisie lays the foundation for the sway of the proletariat.

Hitherto, every form of society has been based, as we have already seen, on the antagonism of oppressing and oppressed classes. But in order to oppress a class, certain conditions must be assured to it under which it can, at least, continue its slavish existence. The serf in the period of serfdom, raised himself to membership in the commune, just as the petty bourgeois, under the yoke of feudal absolutism, managed to develop into a bourgeois. The modern labourer, on the contrary, instead of rising with the progress of industry, sinks deeper and deeper below the conditions of existence of his own class. He becomes a pauper, and pauperism develops more rapidly than population and wealth. And here it becomes evident, that the bourgeoisie is unfit any longer to be the ruling class in society, and to impose its conditions of existence upon society as an overriding law. It is unfit to rule because it is incompetent to assure an existence to its slave within his slavery, because it cannot help letting him sink into such a state, that it has to feed him, instead of being fed by him. Society can no longer live under this bourgeoisie, in other words, its existence is no longer compatible with society.

The essential condition for the existence, and for the sway of the bourgeois class, is the formation and augmentation of capital; the condition for capital is wage-labour. Wage-labour rests exclusively on competition between the labourers. The advance of industry, whose involuntary promoter is the bourgeoisie, replaces the isolation of the labourers due to competition, by their revolutionary combination, due to association. The development of Modern Industry, therefore, cuts from under its feet the very foundation on which the bourgeoisie produces and appropriates products. What the bourgeoisie, therefore, produces, above all, is its own gravediggers. Its fall and the victory of the proletariat are equally inevitable.

II. Proletarians and Communists

In what relation do the Communists stand to the proletarians as a whole?

The Communists do not form a separate party opposed to other working-class parties.

They have no interests separate and apart from those of the proletariat as a whole.

They do not set up any sectarian principles of their own, by which to shape and mould the proletarian movement.

The Communists are distinguished from the other working-class parties by this only: (1) In the national struggles of the proletarians of the different countries, they point out and bring to the front the common interests of the entire proletariat, independently of all nationality. (2) In the various stages of development which the struggle of the working class against the bourgeoisie has to pass through, they always and everywhere represent the interests of the movement as a whole.

The Communists, therefore, are on the one hand, practically, the most advanced and resolute section of the working-class parties of every country, that section which pushes forward all others; on the other hand, theoretically, they have over the great mass of the proletariat the advantage of clearly understanding the line of march, the conditions, and the ultimate general results of the proletarian movement.

The immediate aim of the Communists is the same as that of all the other proletarian parties: formation of the proletariat into a class, overthrow of the bourgeois supremacy, conquest of political power by the proletariat.

The theoretical conclusions of the Communists are in no way based on ideas or principles that have been invented, or discovered, by this or that would-be universal reformer.

They merely express, in general terms, actual relations springing from an existing class struggle, from a historical movement going on under our very eyes. The abolition of existing property relations is not at all a distinctive feature of Communism.

All property relations in the past have continually been subject to historical change consequent upon the change in historical conditions.

The French Revolution, for example, abolished feudal property in favour of bourgeois property.

The distinguishing feature of Communism is not the abolition of property generally, but the abolition of bourgeois property. But modern bourgeois private property is the final and most complete expression of the system of producing and appropriating products, that is based on class antagonisms, on the exploitation of the many by the few.

In this sense, the theory of the Communists may be summed up in the single sentence: Abolition of private property.

We Communists have been reproached with the desire of abolishing the right of personally acquiring property as the fruit of a man's own labour, which property is alleged to be the groundwork of all personal freedom, activity and independence.

Hard-won, self-acquired, self-earned property! Do you mean the property of the petty artisan and of the small peasant, a form of property that preceded the bourgeois form? There is no need to abolish that; the development of industry has to a great extent already destroyed it, and is still destroying it daily.

Or do you mean modern bourgeois private property?

But does wage-labour create any property for the labourer? Not a bit. It creates capital, *i.e.*, that kind of property which exploits wage-labour, and which cannot increase except upon condition of begetting a new supply of wage-labour for fresh exploitation. Property, in its present form, is based on the antagonism of capital and wage-labour. Let us examine both sides of this antagonism.

To be a capitalist, is to have not only a purely personal, but a social *status* in production. Capital is a collective product, and only by the united action of many members, nay, in the last resort, only by the united action of all members of society, can it be set in motion.

Capital is, therefore, not a personal, it is a social power.

When, therefore, capital is converted into common property, into the property of all members of society, personal property is not thereby transformed into social property. It is only the social character of the property that is changed. It loses its class-character.

Let us now take wage-labour.

The average price of wage-labour is the minimum wage, *i.e.*, that quantum of the means of subsistence, which is absolutely requisite to keep the labourer in bare existence as a labourer. What, therefore, the wage-labourer appropriates by means of his labour, merely suffices to prolong and reproduce a bare existence. We by no means intend to abolish this personal appropriation of the products of labour, an appropriation that is made for the maintenance and reproduction of human life, and that leaves no surplus wherewith to command the labour of others. All that we want to do away with, is the miserable character of this appropriation, under which the labourer lives merely to increase capital, and is allowed to live only in so far as the interest of the ruling class requires it.

In bourgeois society, living labour is but a means to increase accumulated labour. In Communist society, accumulated labour is but a means to widen, to enrich, to promote the existence of the labourer.

In bourgeois society, therefore, the past dominates the present; in Communist society, the present dominates the past. In bourgeois society capital is independent and has individuality, while the living person is dependent and has no individuality.

And the abolition of this state of things is called by the bourgeois, abolition of individuality and freedom! And rightly so. The abolition of bourgeois individuality, bourgeois independence, and bourgeois freedom is undoubtedly aimed at.

By freedom is meant, under the present bourgeois conditions of production, free trade, free selling and buying.

But if selling and buying disappears, free selling and buying disappears also. This talk about free selling and buying, and all the other "brave words" or our bourgeoisie about freedom in general, have a meaning, if any, only in contrast with restricted selling and buying, with the fettered traders of the Middle Ages, but have no meaning when opposed to the Communistic abolition of buying and selling, of the bourgeois conditions of production, and of the bourgeoisie itself.

You are horrified at our intending to do away with private property. But in your existing society, private property is already done away with for nine-tenths of the population; its existence for the few is solely due to its non-existence in the hands of those nine tenths. You reproach us, therefore, with intending to do away with a form of property, the necessary condition for whose existence is the non-existence of any property for the immense majority of society.

In one word, you reproach us with intending to do away with your property. Precisely so; that is just what we intend.

From the moment when labour can no longer be converted into capital, money, or rent, into a social power capable of being monopolised, *i.e.*, from the moment when individual property can no longer be transformed into bourgeois property, into capital, from that moment, you say, individuality vanishes.

You must, therefore, confess that by "individual" you mean no other person than the bourgeois, than the middle-class owner of property. This person must, indeed, be swept out of the way, and made impossible.

Communism deprives no man of the power to appropriate the products of society; all that it does is to deprive him of the power to subjugate the labour of others by means of such appropriation.

It has been objected that upon the abolition of private property all work will cease, and universal laziness will overtake us.

According to this, bourgeois society ought long ago to have gone to the dogs through sheer idleness; for those of its members who work, acquire nothing, and those who acquire anything, do not work. The whole of this objection is but another expression of the tautology: that there can no longer be any wage-labour when there is no longer any capital.

All objections urged against the Communistic mode of producing and appropriating material products, have, in the same way, been urged against the Communistic modes of producing and appropriating intellectual products. Just as, to the bourgeois, the disappearance of class property is the disappearance of production itself, so the disappearance of class culture is to him identical with the disappearance of all culture.

That culture, the loss of which he laments, is, for the enormous majority, a mere training to act as a machine.

But don't wrangle with us so long as you apply, to our intended abolition of bourgeois property, the standard of your bourgeois notions of freedom, culture, law, &c. Your very ideas are but the outgrowth of the conditions of your bourgeois production and bourgeois property, just as your jurisprudence is but the will of your class made into a law for all, a will, whose essential character and direction are determined by the economical conditions of existence of your class.

The selfish misconception that induces you to transform into eternal laws of nature and of reason, the social forms springing from your present mode of production and form of property – historical relations that rise and disappear in the progress of production – this misconception you share with every ruling class that has preceded you. What you see clearly in the case of ancient property, what you admit in the case of feudal property, you are of course forbidden to admit in the case of your own bourgeois form of property.

Abolition of the family! Even the most radical flare up at this infamous proposal of the Communists.

On what foundation is the present family, the bourgeois family, based? On capital, on private gain. In its completely developed form this family exists only among the bourgeoisie. But this state of things finds its complement in the practical absence of the family among the proletarians, and in public prostitution.

The bourgeois family will vanish as a matter of course when its complement vanishes, and both will vanish with the vanishing of capital.

Do you charge us with wanting to stop the exploitation of children by their parents? To this crime we plead guilty.

But, you will say, we destroy the most hallowed of relations, when we replace home education by social.

And your education! Is not that also social, and determined by the social conditions under which you educate, by the intervention, direct or indirect, of society, by means of schools, &c.? The Communists have not invented the intervention of society in education; they do but seek to alter the character of that intervention, and to rescue education from the influence of the ruling class.

The bourgeois clap-trap about the family and education, about the hallowed co-relation of parent and child, becomes all the more disgusting, the more, by the action of Modern Industry, all family ties among the proletarians are torn asunder, and their children transformed into simple articles of commerce and instruments of labour.

But you Communists would introduce community of women, screams the whole bourgeoisie in chorus.

The bourgeois sees in his wife a mere instrument of production. He hears that the instruments of production are to be exploited in common, and, naturally, can come to no other conclusion than that the lot of being common to all will likewise fall to the women.

He has not even a suspicion that the real point aimed at is to do away with the status of women as mere instruments of production.

For the rest, nothing is more ridiculous than the virtuous indignation of our bourgeois at the community of women which, they pretend, is to be openly and officially established by the Communists. The Communists have no need to introduce community of women; it has existed almost from time immemorial.

Our bourgeois, not content with having the wives and daughters of their proletarians at their disposal, not to speak of common prostitutes, take the greatest pleasure in seducing each other's wives.

Bourgeois marriage is in reality a system of wives in common and thus, at the most, what the Communists might possibly be reproached with, is that they desire to introduce, in substitution for a hypocritically concealed, an openly legalised community of women. For the rest, it is self-evident that the abolition of the present system of production must bring with it the abolition of the community of women springing from that system, *i.e.*, of prostitution both public and private.

The Communists are further reproached with desiring to abolish countries and nationality.

The working men have no country. We cannot take from them what they have not got. Since the proletariat must first of all acquire political supremacy, must rise to be the leading class of the nation, must constitute itself *the* nation, it is, so far, itself national, though not in the bourgeois sense of the word.

National differences and antagonisms between peoples are daily more and more vanishing, owing to the development of the bourgeoisie, to freedom of commerce, to the world-market, to uniformity in the mode of production and in the conditions of life corresponding thereto.

The supremacy of the proletariat will cause them to vanish still faster. United action, of the leading civilised countries at least, is one of the first conditions for the emancipation of the proletariat.

In proportion as the exploitation of one individual by another is put an end to, the exploitation of one nation by another will also be put an end to. In proportion as the antagonism between classes within the nation vanishes, the hostility of one nation to another will come to an end.

The charges against Communism made from a religious, a philosophical, and, generally, from an ideological standpoint, are not deserving of serious examination.

Does it require deep intuition to comprehend that man's ideas, views and conceptions, in one word, man's consciousness, changes with every change in the conditions of his material existence, in his social relations and in his social life?

What else does the history of ideas prove, than that intellectual production changes its character in proportion as material production is changed? The ruling ideas of each age have ever been the ideas of its ruling class.

When people speak of ideas that revolutionise society, they do but express the fact, that within the old society, the elements of a new one have been created, and that the dissolution of the old ideas keeps even pace with the dissolution of the old conditions of existence.

When the ancient world was in its last throes, the ancient religions were overcome by Christianity. When Christian ideas succumbed in the 18th century to rationalist ideas, feudal society fought its death battle with the then revolutionary bourgeoisie. The ideas of religious liberty and freedom of conscience merely gave expression to the sway of free competition within the domain of knowledge.

"Undoubtedly," it will be said, "religious, moral, philosophical and juridical ideas have been modified in the course of historical development. But religion, morality, philosophy, political science, and law, constantly survived this change."

"There are, besides, eternal truths, such as Freedom, Justice, etc., that are common to all states of society. But Communism abolishes eternal truths, it abolishes all religion; and all morality, instead of constituting them on a new basis; it therefore acts in contradiction to all past historical experience."

What does this accusation reduce itself to? The history of all past society has consisted in the development of class antagonisms, antagonisms that assumed different forms at different epochs.

But whatever form they may have taken, one fact is common to all past ages, *viz.*, the exploitation of one part of society by the other. No wonder, then, that the social consciousness of past ages, despite all the multiplicity and variety it displays, moves within certain common forms, or general ideas, which cannot completely vanish except with the total disappearance of class antagonisms.

The Communist revolution is the most radical rupture with traditional property relations; no wonder that its development involves the most radical rupture with traditional ideas.

But let us have done with the bourgeois objections to Communism.

We have seen above, that the first step in the revolution by the working class, is to raise the proletariat to the position of ruling class, to win the battle of democracy.

The proletariat will use its political supremacy to wrest, by degrees, all capital from the bourgeoisie, to centralise all instruments of production in the hands of the State, *i.e.*, of the proletariat organised as the ruling class; and to increase the total of productive forces as rapidly as possible.

Of course, in the beginning, this cannot be effected except by means of despotic inroads on the rights of property, and on the conditions of bourgeois production; by means of measures, therefore, which appear economically insufficient and untenable, but which, in the course of the movement, outstrip themselves, necessitate further inroads upon the old social order, and are unavoidable as a means of entirely revolutionising the mode of production.

These measures will of course be different in different countries.

Nevertheless in the most advanced countries, the following will be pretty generally applicable.

1   Abolition of property in land and application of all rents of land to public purposes.
2   A heavy progressive or graduated income tax.
3   Abolition of all right of inheritance.
4   Confiscation of the property of all emigrants and rebels.
5   Centralisation of credit in the hands of the State, by means of a national bank with State capital and an exclusive monopoly.
6   Centralisation of the means of communication and transport in the hands of the State.
7   Extension of factories and instruments of production owned by the State; the bringing into cultivation of wastelands, and the improvement of the soil generally in accordance with a common plan.
8   Equal liability of all to labour. Establishment of industrial armies, especially for agriculture.
9   Combination of agriculture with manufacturing industries; gradual abolition of the distinction between town and country, by a more equable distribution of the population over the country.
10 Free education for all children in public schools. Abolition of children's factory labour in its present form. Combination of education with industrial production, &c., &c.

When, in the course of development, class distinctions have disappeared, and all production has been concentrated in the hands of a vast association of the whole nation, the public power will lose its political character. Political power, properly so called, is merely the organised power of one class for oppressing another. If the proletariat during its contest with the bourgeoisie is compelled, by the force of circumstances, to organise itself as a class, if, by means of a revolution, it makes itself the ruling class, and, as such, sweeps away by force the old conditions of production, then it will, along with these conditions, have swept away the conditions for the existence of class antagonisms and of classes generally, and will thereby have abolished its own supremacy as a class.

In place of the old bourgeois society, with its classes and class antagonisms, we shall have an association, in which the free development of each is the condition for the free development of all.

Notes

1 By bourgeoisie is meant the class of modern Capitalists, owners of the means of social production and employers of wage-labour. By proletariat, the class of modern wage-labourers who, having no means of production of their own, are reduced to selling their labour-power in order to live (Engels, English edition of 1888).

2 That is, all *written* history. In 1847, the pre-history of society, the social organisation existing previous to recorded history, was all but unknown. Since then, Haxthausen discovered common ownership of land in Russia, Maurer proved it to be the social foundation from which all Teutonic races started in history, and by and by village communities were found to be, or to have been the primitive form of society everywhere from India to Ireland. The inner organisation of this primitive Communistic society was laid bare, in its typical form, by Morgan's crowning discovery of the true nature of the *gens* and its relation to the *tribe*. With the dissolution of these primaeval communities society begins to be differentiated into separate and finally antagonistic classes. I have attempted to retrace this process of dissolution in: "Der Ursprung der Familie, des Privateigenthums und des Staats" (*The Origin of the Family, Private Property and the State*, 2nd edition, Stuttgart 1886. Engels, English edition of 1888).

3 Guild-master, that is, a full member of a guild, a master within, not a head of a guild (Engels, English edition of 1888).

4 "Commune" was the name taken, in France, by the nascent towns even before they had conquered from their feudal lords and masters local self government and political rights as the "Third Estate." Generally speaking, for the economical development of the bourgeoisie, England is here taken as the typical country; for its political development, France (Engels English edition of 1888).

This was the name given their urban communities by the townsmen of Italy and France, after they had purchased or wrested their initial rights of self-government from their feudal lords (Engels, German edition of 1890).

5 Subsequently Marx pointed out that the worker sells not his labour but his labour power.

Max Weber (1864–1920) is a key figure in the history of sociology. He strongly rejected Marxist-style economic determinism, arguing that other factors were just as important historically. Here he provides a general characterization of social class and sketches some of the limits of that notion for historical analysis.

Focus questions:
1 What is Weber's definition of "class"?
2 How does Weber distinguish class from community?
3 How, according to Weber, do status groups affect the "pure" operation of markets or class structures?

12   Economy and Society

Max Weber

1 Economically Determined Power and the Social Order

Law exists when there is a probability that an order will be upheld by a specific staff of men who will use physical or psychical compulsion with the intention of obtaining conformity with the order, or of inflicting sanctions for infringement of it.[1] The structure of every legal order directly influences the distribution of power, economic or otherwise, within its respective community. This is true of all legal orders and not only that of the state. In general, we understand by "power" the chance of a man or of a number of men to realize their own will in a communal action even against the resistance of others who are participating in the action.

"Economically conditioned" power is not, of course, identical with "power" as such. On the contrary, the emergence of economic power may be the consequence of power existing on other grounds. Man does not strive for power only in order to enrich himself economically. Power, including economic power, may be valued "for its own sake." Very frequently the striving for power is also conditioned by the social "honor" it entails. Not all power, however, entails social honor: The typical American Boss, as well as the typical big speculator, deliberately relinquishes social honor. Quite generally, "mere economic" power, and especially "naked" money power, is by no means a recognized basis of social honor. Nor is power the only basis of social honor. Indeed, social honor, or prestige, may even be the basis of political or economic power, and very frequently has been. Power, as well as honor, may be guaranteed by the legal order, but, at least normally, it is not their primary source. The legal order is rather an additional factor that enhances the chance to hold power or honor; but it cannot always secure them.

The way in which social honor is distributed in a community between typical groups participating in this distribution we may call the "social order." The social order and the economic order are, of course, similarly related to the "legal order." However, the social and the economic order are not identical. The economic order is for us merely the way in which economic goods and services are distributed and used. The social order is of course conditioned by the economic order to a high degree, and in its turn reacts upon it.

Now: "classes," "status groups," and "parties" are phenomena of the distribution of power within a community.

2 Determination of Class-situation by Market-situation

In our terminology, "classes" are not communities; they merely represent possible, and frequent, bases for communal action. We may speak of a "class" when (1) a number of people have in common a specific causal component of their life chances, in so far as (2) this component is represented exclusively by economic interests in the possession of goods and opportunities for income, and (3) is represented under the conditions of the commodity or labor markets. (These points refer to "class situation," which we may express more briefly as the typical chance for a supply of goods, external living conditions, and personal life experiences, in so far as this chance is determined by the amount and kind of power, or lack of such, to dispose of goods or skills for the sake of income in a given economic order. The term "class" refers to any group of people that is found in the same class situation.)

It is the most elemental economic fact that the way in which the disposition over material property is distributed among a plurality of people, meeting competitively in the market for the purpose of exchange, in itself creates specific life chances. According to the law of marginal utility this mode of distribution excludes the non-owners from competing for highly valued goods; it favors the owners and, in fact, gives to them a monopoly to acquire such goods. Other things being equal, this mode of distribution monopolizes the opportunities for profitable deals for all those who, provided with goods, do not necessarily have to exchange them. It increases, at least generally, their power in price wars with those who, being propertyless, have nothing to offer but their services in native form or goods in a form constituted through their own labor, and who above all are compelled to get rid of these products in order barely to subsist. This mode of distribution gives to the propertied a monopoly on the possibility of transferring property from the sphere of use as a "fortune," to the sphere of "capital goods"; that is, it gives them the entrepreneurial function and all chances to share directly or indirectly in returns on capital. All this holds true within the area in which pure market conditions prevail. "Property" and "lack of property" are, therefore, the basic categories of all class situations. It does not matter whether these two categories become effective in price wars or in competitive struggles.

Within these categories, however, class situations are further differentiated: on the one hand, according to the kind of property that is usable for returns; and, on the other hand, according to the kind of services that can be offered in the market. Ownership of domestic buildings; productive establishments; warehouses; stores; agriculturally usable land, large and small holdings – quantitative differences with possibly qualitative consequence –; ownership of mines; cattle; men (slaves), disposition over mobile instruments of production, or capital goods of all sorts, especially money or objects that can be exchanged for money easily and at any time; disposition over products of one's own labor or of others' labor differing according to their various distances from consumability; disposition over transferable monopolies of any kind – all these distinctions differentiate the class situations of the propertied just as does the "meaning" which they can and do give to the utilization of property, especially to property which has money equivalence. Accordingly, the propertied, for instance, may belong to the class of rentiers or to the class of entrepreneurs.

Those who have no property but who offer services are differentiated just as much according to their kinds of services as according to the way in which they make use of these services, in a continuous or discontinuous relation to a recipient. But always this is the generic connotation of the concept of class: that the kind of chance in the *market* is the decisive moment which presents a common condition for the individual's fate. "Class situation" is, in this sense, ultimately "market situation." The effect of naked possession *per se*, which among cattle breeders gives the nonowning slave or serf into the power of the cattle owner, is only a forerunner of real "class" formation. However, in the cattle loan and in the naked severity of the law of debts in such communities, for the first time mere "possession" as such emerges as decisive for the fate of the individual. This is very much in contrast to the agricultural communities based on labor. The creditor–debtor relation becomes the basis of "class situations" only in those cities where a "credit market," however primitive, with rates of interest increasing according to the extent of dearth and a factual monopolization of credits, is developed by a plutocracy. Therewith "class struggles" begin.

Those men whose fate is not determined by the chance of using goods or services for themselves on the market, e.g. slaves, are not, however, a "class" in the technical sense of the term. They are, rather, a "status group."

3 Communal Action Flowing from Class Interest

According to our terminology, the factor that creates "class" is unambiguously economic interest, and indeed, only those interests involved in the existence of the "market." Nevertheless, the concept of "class-interest" is an ambiguous one: even as an empirical concept it is ambiguous as soon as one understands by it something other than the factual direction of interests following with a certain probability from the class situation for a certain "average" of those people subjected to the class situation. The class situation and other circumstances remaining the same, the direction in which the individual worker, for instance, is likely to pursue his interests may vary widely, according to whether he is constitutionally qualified for the task at hand to a high, to an average, or to a low degree. In the same way, the direction of interests may vary according to whether or not a *communal* action of a larger or smaller portion of those commonly affected by the "class situation," or even an association among them, e.g. a "trade union," has grown out of the class situation from which the individual may or may not expect promising results. (Communal action refers to that action which is oriented to the feeling of the actors that they belong together. Societal action, on the other hand, is oriented to a rationally motivated adjustment of interests.) The rise of societal or even of communal action from a common class-situation is by no means a universal phenomenon.

The class situation may be restricted in its effects to the generation of essentially *similar* reactions, that is to say, within our terminology, of "mass actions." However, it may not have even this result. Furthermore, often merely an amorphous communal action emerges. For example, the "murmuring" of the workers known in ancient oriental ethics: the moral disapproval of the work-master's conduct, which in its practical significance was probably equivalent to an increasingly typical phenomenon of precisely the latest industrial development, namely, the "slow down" (the deliberate limiting of work effort) of laborers by virtue of tacit agreement. The degree in which "communal action" and possibly, "societal action," emerges from the "mass actions" of the members of a class is linked to general cultural conditions, especially to those of an intellectual sort. It is also linked to the extent of the contrasts that have already evolved, and is especially linked to the *transparency* of the connections between the causes and the consequences of the "class situation." For however different life chances may be, this fact in itself, according to all experience, by no means gives birth to "class action" (communal action by the members of a class). The fact of being conditioned and the results of the class situation must be distinctly recognizable. For only then the contrast of life chances can be felt not as an absolutely given fact to be accepted, but as a resultant from either (1) the given distribution of property, or (2) the structure of the concrete economic order. It is only then that people may react against the class structure not only through acts of an intermittent and irrational protest, but in the form of rational association. There have been "class situations" of the first category (1), of a specifically naked and transparent sort, in the urban centers of Antiquity and during the Middle Ages; especially then, when great fortunes were accumulated by factually monopolized trading in industrial products of these localities or in foodstuffs. Furthermore, under certain circumstances, in the rural economy of the most diverse periods, when agriculture was increasingly exploited in a profit-making manner. The most important historical example of the second category (2) is the class situation of the modern "proletariat."

4 Types of "Class Struggle"

Thus every class may be the carrier of any one of the possibly innumerable forms of "class action," but this is not necessarily so. In any case, a class does not in itself constitute a community. To treat "class" conceptually as having the same value as "community" leads to distortion. That men in the same class situation regularly react in mass actions to such tangible situations as economic ones in the direction of those interests that are most adequate to their average number is an important and after all simple fact for the understanding of historical events. Above all, this fact must not lead to that kind of pseudo-scientific operation with the concepts of "class" and "class interests" so frequently found these days, and which has found its most classic expression in the statement of a talented author, that the individual may be in error concerning his interests but that the "class" is "infallible" about its interests. Yet, if classes as such are not communities, nevertheless class situations emerge only on the basis of communalization. The communal action that brings forth class situations, however, is not basically action between members of the identical class; it is an action between members of different classes. Communal actions that directly determine the class situation of the worker and the entrepreneur are: the labor market, the commodities market, and the capitalistic enterprise. But, in its turn, the existence of a capitalistic enterprise presupposes that a very specific communal action exists and that it is specifically structured to protect the possession of goods *per se*, and especially the power of individuals to dispose, in principle freely, over the means of production. The existence of a capitalistic enterprise is preconditioned by a specific kind of "legal order." Each kind of class situation, and above all when it rests upon the power of property *per se*, will become most clearly efficacious when all other determinants of reciprocal relations are, as far as possible, eliminated in their significance. It is in this way that the utilization of the power of property in the market obtains its most sovereign importance.

Now "status groups" hinder the strict carrying through of the sheer market principle. In the present context they are of interest to us only from this one point of view. Before we briefly consider them, note that not much of a general nature can be said about the more specific kinds of antagonism between "classes" (in our meaning of the term). The great shift, which has been going on continuously in the past, and up to our times, may be summarized, although at the cost of some precision: the struggle in which class situations are effective has progressively shifted from consumption credit toward, first, competitive struggles in the commodity market and, then toward price wars on the labor market. The "class struggles" of antiquity – to the extent that they were genuine class struggles and not struggles between status groups – were initially carried on by indebted peasants, and perhaps also by artisans threatened by debt bondage and struggling against urban creditors. For debt bondage is the normal result of the differentiation of wealth in commercial cities, especially in sea-port cities. A similar situation has existed among cattle breeders. Debt relationships as such produced class action up to the time of Cataline. Along with this, and with an increase in provision of grain for the city by transporting it from the outside, the struggle over the means of sustenance emerged. It centered in the first place around the provision of bread and the determination of the price of bread. It lasted throughout antiquity and the entire Middle Ages. The propertyless as such flocked together against those who actually and supposedly were interested in the dearth of bread. This fight spread until it involved all those commodities essential to the way of life and to handicraft production. There were only incipient discussions of wage disputes in antiquity and in the Middle Ages. But they have been slowly increasing up into modern times. In the earlier periods they were completely secondary to slave rebellions as well as to fights in the commodity market.

The propertyless of antiquity and of the Middle Ages protested against monopolies, preemption, forestalling, and the withholding of goods from the market in order to raise prices. Today the central issue is the determination of the price of labor.

This transition is represented by the fight for access to the market and for the determination of the price of products. Such fights went on between merchants and workers in the putting-out system of domestic handicraft during the transition to modern times. Since it is quite a general phenomenon we must mention here that the class antagonisms that are conditioned through the market situation are usually most bitter between those who actually and directly participate as opponents in price wars. It is not the rentier, the share-holder, and the banker who suffer the ill will of the worker, but almost exclusively the manufacturer and the business executives who are the direct opponents of workers in price wars. This is so in spite of the fact that it is precisely the cash boxes of the rentier, the share-holder, and the banker into which the more or less "unearned" gains flow, rather than into the pockets of the manufacturers or of the business executives. This simple state of affairs has very frequently been decisive for the role the class situation has played in the formation of political parties. For example, it has made possible the varieties of patriarchal socialism and the frequent attempts – formerly, at least – of threatened status groups to form alliances with the proletariat against the "bourgeoisie."

Notes

1   *Wirtschaft und Gesellschaft*, part III, ch. 4, pp. 631–40. The first sentence in paragraph one and the several definitions in this chapter which are in brackets do not appear in the original text. They have been taken from other contexts of *Wirtschaft und Gesellschaft*.

The anthropologist Elliot Liebow, in this excerpt from his groundbreaking work *Tally's Corner,* published in 1967, describes the life of poor urban black men in intimate detail. In sketching their family and work lives, and the relations between the two, Liebow shows that such men are not lazy or irresponsible, but rather that their options are extremely limited.

Focus questions:
1 What sort of jobs can the men described by Liebow get?
2 What does Liebow mean by "the wage-theft" system?
3 How does Liebow describe the effect of these men's work and family lives on their self-image?

13   Men and Jobs

Elliot Liebow

A truck drives slowly down the street. The truck stops as it comes abreast of a man sitting on a cast-iron porch and the white driver calls out, asking if the man wants a day's work. The man shakes his head and the truck moves on up the block, stopping again whenever idling men come within calling distance of the driver. At the Carry-out corner, five men debate the question briefly and shake their heads no to the truck. The truck turns the corner and repeats the same performance up the next street. In the distance, one can see one man, then another, climb into the back of the truck and sit down. In starts and stops, the truck finally disappears.

What is it we have witnessed here? A labor scavenger rebuffed by his would-be prey? Lazy, irresponsible men turning down an honest day's pay for an honest day's work? Or a more complex phenomenon marking the intersection of economic forces, social values and individual states of mind and body?

Let us look again at the driver of the truck. He has been able to recruit only two or three men from each twenty or fifty he contacts. To him, it is clear that the others simply do not choose to work. Singly or in groups, belly-empty or belly-full, sullen or gregarious, drunk or sober, they confirm what he has read, heard and knows from his own experience: these men wouldn't take a job if it were handed to them on a platter.[1]

Quite apart from the question of whether or not this is true of some of the men he sees on the street, it is clearly not true of all of them. If it were, he would not have come here in the first place; or having come, he would have left with an empty truck. It is not even true of most of them, for most of the men he sees on the street this weekday morning do, in fact, have jobs. But since, at the moment, they are neither working nor sleeping, and since they hate the depressing room or apartment they live in, or because there is nothing to do there,[2] or because they want to get away from their wives or anyone else living there, they are out on the street, indistinguishable from those who do not have jobs or do not want them. Some, like Boley, a member of a trash-collection crew in a suburban housing development, work Saturdays and are off on this weekday. Some, like Sweets, work nights cleaning up middle-class trash, dirt, dishes and garbage, and mopping the floors of the office buildings, hotels, restaurants, toilets and other public places dirtied during the day. Some men work for retail businesses such as liquor stores which do not begin the day until ten o'clock. Some laborers, like Tally, have already come back from the job because the ground was too wet for pick and shovel or because the weather was too cold for pouring concrete. Other employed men stayed off the job today for personal reasons: Clarence to go to a funeral at eleven this morning and Sea Cat to answer a subpoena as a witness in a criminal proceeding.

Also on the street, unwitting contributors to the impression taken away by the truck driver, are the halt and the lame. The man on the cast-iron steps strokes one gnarled arthritic hand with the other and says he doesn't know whether or not he'll live long enough to be eligible for Social Security. He pauses, then adds matter-of-factly, "Most times, I don't care whether I do or don't." Stoopy's left leg was polio-withered in childhood. Raymond, who looks as if he could tear out a fire hydrant, coughs up blood if he bends or moves suddenly. The quiet man who hangs out in front of the Saratoga apartments has a steel hook strapped onto his left elbow. And had the man in the truck been able to look into the wine-clouded eyes of the man in the green cap, he would have realized that the man did not even understand he was being offered a day's work.

Others, having had jobs and been laid off, are drawing unemployment compensation (up to $44 per week) and have nothing to gain by accepting work which pays little more than this and frequently less.

Still others, like Bumdoodle the numbers man, are working hard at illegal ways of making money, hustlers who are on the street to turn a dollar any way they can: buying and selling sex, liquor, narcotics, stolen goods, or anything else that turns up.

Only a handful remains unaccounted for. There is Tonk, who cannot bring himself to take a job away from the corner, because, according to the other men, he suspects his wife will be unfaithful if given the opportunity. There is Stanton, who has not reported to work for four days now, not since Bernice disappeared. He bought a brand new knife against her return. She had done this twice before, he said, but not for so long and not without warning, and he had forgiven her. But this time, "I ain't got it in me to forgive her again." His rage and shame are there for all to see as he paces the Carry-out and the corner, day and night, hoping to catch a glimpse of her.

And finally, there are those like Arthur, able-bodied men who have no visible means of support, legal or illegal, who neither have jobs nor want them. The truck driver, among others, believes the Arthurs to be representative of all the men he sees idling on the street during his own working hours. They are not, but they cannot be dismissed simply because they are a small minority. It is not enough to explain them away as being lazy or irresponsible or both because an able-bodied man with responsibilities who refuses work is, by the truck driver's definition, lazy and irresponsible. Such an answer begs the question. It is descriptive of the facts; it does not explain them.

Moreover, despite their small numbers, the don't-work-and-don't-want-to-work minority is especially significant because they represent the strongest and clearest expression of those values and attitudes associated with making a living which, to varying degrees, are found throughout the streetcorner world. These men differ from the others in degree rather than in kind, the principal difference being that they are carrying out the implications of their values and experiences to their logical, inevitable conclusions. In this sense, the others have yet to come to terms with themselves and the world they live in.

Putting aside, for the moment, what the men say and feel, and looking at what they actually do and the choices they make, getting a job, keeping a job, and doing well at it is clearly of low priority. Arthur will not take a job at all. Leroy is supposed to be on his job at 4:00 p.m. but it is already 4:10 and he still cannot bring himself to leave the free games he has accumulated on the pinball machine in the Carry-out. Tonk started a construction job on Wednesday, worked Thursday and Friday, then didn't go back again. On the same kind of job, Sea Cat quit in the second week. Sweets had been working three months as a busboy in a restaurant, then quit without notice, not sure himself why he did so. A real estate agent, saying he was more interested in getting the job done than in the cost, asked Richard to give him an estimate on repairing and painting the inside of a house, but Richard, after looking over the job, somehow never got around to submitting an estimate. During one period, Tonk would not leave the corner to take a job because his wife might prove unfaithful; Stanton would not take a job because his woman had been unfaithful.

Thus, the man–job relationship is a tenuous one. At any given moment, a job may occupy a relatively low position on the streetcorner scale of real values. Getting a job may be subordinated to relations with women or to other non-job considerations; the commitment to a job one already has is frequently shallow and tentative.

The reasons are many. Some are objective and reside principally in the job; some are subjective and reside principally in the man. The line between them, however, is not a clear one. Behind the man's refusal to take a job or his decision to quit one is not a simple impulse or value choice but a complex combination of assessments of objective reality on the one hand, and values, attitudes and beliefs drawn from different levels of his experience on the other.

Objective economic considerations are frequently a controlling factor in a man's refusal to take a job. How much the job pays is a crucial question but seldom asked. He knows how much it pays. Working as a stock clerk, a delivery boy, or even behind the counter of liquor stores, drug stores and other retail businesses pays one dollar an hour. So, too, do most busboy, car-wash, janitorial and other jobs available to him. Some jobs, such as dishwasher, may dip as low as eighty cents an hour and others, such as elevator operator or work in a junk yard, may offer $1.15 or $1.25. Take-home pay for jobs such as these ranges from $35 to $50 a week, but a take-home pay of over $45 for a five-day week is the exception rather than the rule.

One of the principal advantages of these kinds of jobs is that they offer fairly regular work. Most of them involve essential services and are therefore some-what less responsive to business conditions than are some higher paying, less menial jobs. Most of them are also inside jobs not dependent on the weather, as are construction jobs and other higher-paying outside work.

Another seemingly important advantage of working in hotels, restaurants, office and apartment buildings and retail establishments is that they frequently offer an opportunity for stealing on the job. But stealing can be a two-edged sword. Apart from increasing the cost of the goods or services to the general public, a less obvious result is that the practice usually acts as a depressant on the employee's own wage level. Owners of small retail establishments and other employers frequently anticipate employee stealing and adjust the wage rate ac-cordingly. Tonk's employer explained why he was paying Tonk $35 for a 55–60 hour workweek. These men will all steal, he said. Although he keeps close watch on Tonk, he estimates that Tonk steals from $35 to $40 a week.[3] What he steals, when added to his regular earnings, brings his take-home pay to $70 or $75 per week. The employer said he did not mind this because Tonk is worth that much to the business. But if he were to pay Tonk outright the full value of his labor, Tonk would still be stealing $35–$40 per week and this, he said, the business simply would not support.

This wage arrangement, with stealing built-in, was satisfactory to both par-ties, with each one independently expressing his satisfaction. Such a wage-theft system, however, is not as balanced and equitable as it appears. Since the wage level rests on the premise that the employee will steal the unpaid value of his labor, the man who does not steal on the job is penalized. And furthermore, even if he does not steal, no one would believe him; the employer and others believe he steals because the system presumes it.

Nor is the man who steals, as he is expected to, as well off as he believes himself to be. The employer may occasionally close his eyes to the worker's stealing but not often and not for long. He is, after all, a businessman and cannot always find it within himself to let a man steal from him, even if the man is stealing his own wages. Moreover, it is only by keeping close watch on the worker that the employer can control how much is stolen and thereby protect himself against the employee's stealing more than he is worth. From this view-point, then, the employer is not in wage-theft collusion with the employee. In the case of Tonk, for instance, the employer was not actively abetting the theft. His estimate of how much Tonk was stealing was based on what he thought Tonk was able to steal despite his own best efforts to prevent him from stealing anything at all. Were he to have caught Tonk in the act of stealing, he would, of course, have fired him from the job and perhaps called the police as well. Thus, in an actual if not in a legal sense, all the elements of entrapment are present. The employer knowingly provides the conditions which entice (force) the em-ployee to steal the unpaid value of his labor, but at the same time he punishes him for theft if he catches him doing so.

Other consequences of the wage-theft system are even more damaging to the employee. Let us, for argument's sake, say that Tonk is in no danger of entrapment; that his employer is willing to wink at the stealing and that Tonk, for his part, is perfectly willing to earn a little, steal a little. Let us say, too, that he is paid $35 a week and allowed to steal $35. His money income – as measured by the goods and services he can purchase with it – is, of course, $70. But not all of his income is available to him for all purposes. He cannot draw on what he steals to build his self-respect or to measure his self-worth. For this, he can draw only on his earnings – the amount given him publicly and voluntarily in exchange for his labor. His "respect" and "self-worth" income remains at $35 – only half that of the man who also receives $70 but all of it in the form of wages. His earnings publicly measure the worth of his labor to his employer, and they are important to others and to himself in taking the measure of his worth as a man.[4]

With or without stealing, and quite apart from any interior processes going on in the man who refuses such a job or quits it casually and without apparent reason, the objective fact is that menial jobs in retailing or in the service trades simply do not pay enough to support a man and his family. This is not to say that the worker is underpaid; this may or may not be true. Whether he is or not, the plain fact is that, in such a job, he cannot make a living. Nor can he take much comfort in the fact that these jobs tend to offer more regular, steadier work. If he cannot live on the $45 or $50 he makes in one week, the longer he works, the longer he cannot live on what he makes.[5]

Construction work, even for unskilled laborers, usually pays better, with the hourly rate ranging from $1.50 to $2.60 an hour.[6] Importantly, too, good references, a good driving record, a tenth grade (or any high school) education, previous experience, the ability to "bring police clearance with you" are not normally required of laborers as they frequently are for some of the jobs in retailing or in the service trades.

Construction work, however, has its own objective disadvantages. It is, first of all, seasonal work for the great bulk of the laborers, beginning early in the spring and tapering off as winter weather sets in.[7] And even during the season the work is frequently irregular. Early or late in the season, snow or temperatures too low for concrete frequently sends the laborers back home, and during late spring or summer, a heavy rain on Tuesday or Wednesday, leaving a lot of water and mud behind it, can mean a two or three day workweek for the pick-and-shovel men and other unskilled laborers.[8]

The elements are not the only hazard. As the project moves from one construction stage to another, laborers – usually without warning – are laid off, sometimes permanently or sometimes for weeks at a time. The more fortunate or the better workers are told periodically to "take a walk for two, three days."

Both getting the construction job and getting to it are also relatively more difficult than is the case for the menial jobs in retailing and the service trades. Job competition is always fierce. In the city, the large construction projects are unionized. One has to have ready cash to get into the union to become eligible to work on these projects and, being eligible, one has to find an opening. Unless one "knows somebody," say a foreman or a laborer who knows the day before that they are going to take on new men in the morning, this can be a difficult and disheartening search.

Many of the nonunion jobs are in suburban Maryland or Virginia. The newspaper ads say, "Report ready to work to the trailer at the intersection of Rte. 11 and Old Bridge Rd., Bunston, Virginia (or Maryland)," but this location may be ten, fifteen, or even twenty-five miles from the Carry-out. Public transportation would require two or more hours to get there, if it services the area at all. Without access to a car or to a car-pool arrangement, it is not worthwhile reading the ad. So the men do not. Jobs such as these are usually filled by word of mouth information, beginning with someone who knows someone or who is himself working there and looking for a paying rider. Furthermore, nonunion jobs in outlying areas tend to be smaller projects of relatively short duration and to pay somewhat less than scale.

Still another objective factor is the work itself. For some men, whether the job be digging, mixing mortar, pushing a wheelbarrow, unloading materials, carrying and placing steel rods for reinforcing concrete, or building or laying concrete forms, the work is simply too hard. Men such as Tally and Wee Tom can make such work look like child's play; some of the older work-hardened men, such as Budder and Stanton, can do it too, although not without showing unmistakable signs of strain and weariness at the end of the workday. But those who lack the robustness of a Tally or the time-inured immunity of a Budder must either forego jobs such as these or pay a heavy toll to keep them. For Leroy, in his early twenties, almost six feet tall but weighing under 140 pounds, it would be as difficult to push a loaded wheelbarrow, or to unload and stack 96-pound bags of cement all day long, as it would be for Stoopy with his withered leg.

Heavy, backbreaking labor of the kind that used to be regularly associated with bull gangs or concrete gangs is no longer characteristic of laboring jobs, especially those with the larger, well-equipped construction companies. Brute strength is still required from time to time, as on smaller jobs where it is not economical to bring in heavy equipment or where the small, undercapitalized contractor has none to bring in. In many cases, however, the conveyor belt has replaced the wheelbarrow or the Georgia buggy, mechanized forklifts have eliminated heavy, manual lifting, and a variety of digging machines have replaced the pick and shovel. The result is fewer jobs for unskilled laborers and, in many cases, a work speed-up for those who do have jobs. Machines now set the pace formerly set by men. Formerly, a laborer pushed a wheelbarrow of wet cement to a particular spot, dumped it, and returned for another load. Another laborer, in hip boots, pushed the wet concrete around with a shovel or a hoe, getting it roughly level in preparation for the skilled finishers. He had relatively small loads to contend with and had only to keep up with the men pushing the wheelbarrows. Now, the job for the man pushing the wheelbarrow is gone and the wet concrete comes rushing down a chute at the man in the hip boots who must "spread it quick or drown."

Men who have been running an elevator, washing dishes, or "pulling trash" cannot easily move into laboring jobs. They lack the basic skills for "unskilled" construction labor, familiarity with tools and materials, and tricks of the trade without which hard jobs are made harder. Previously unused or untrained muscles rebel in pain against the new and insistent demands made upon them, seriously compromising the man's performance and testing his willingness to see the job through. A healthy, sturdy, active man of good intelligence requires from two to four weeks to break in on a construction job.[9] Even if he is willing somehow to bull his way through the first few weeks, it frequently happens that his foreman or the craftsman he services with materials and general assistance is not willing to wait that long for him to get into condition or to learn at a glance the difference in size between a rough $2 \leq \yen$ $8 \leq$ and a finished $2 \leq \yen$ $10 \leq$. The foreman and the craftsman are themselves "under the gun" and cannot "carry" the man when other men, who are already used to the work and who know the tools and materials, are lined up to take the job.

Sea Cat was "healthy, sturdy, active and of good intelligence." When a judge gave him six weeks in which to pay his wife $200 in back child-support payments, he left his grocery-store job in order to take a higher-paying job as a laborer, arranged for him by a foreman friend. During the first week the weather was bad and he worked only Wednesday and Friday, cursing the elements all the while for cheating him out of the money he could have made. The second week, the weather was fair but he quit at the end of the fourth day, saying frankly that the work was too hard for him. He went back to his job at the grocery store and took a second job working nights as a dishwasher in a restaurant,[10] earning little if any more at the two jobs than he would have earned as a laborer, and keeping at both of them until he had paid off his debts.

Tonk did not last as long as Sea Cat. No one made any predictions when he got a job in a parking lot, but when the men on the corner learned he was to start on a road construction job, estimates of how long he would last ranged from one to three weeks. Wednesday was his first day. He spent that evening and night at home. He did the same on Thursday. He worked Friday and spent Friday evening and part of Saturday draped over the mailbox on the corner. Sunday afternoon, Tonk decided he was not going to report on the job the next morning. He explained that after working three days, he knew enough about the job to know that it was too hard for him. He knew he wouldn't be able to keep up and he'd just as soon quit now as get fired later.

Logan was a tall, two-hundred-pound man in his late twenties. His back used to hurt him only on the job, he said, but now he can't straighten up for increasingly longer periods of time. He said he had traced this to the awkward walk he was forced to adopt by the loaded wheelbarrows which pull him down into a half-stoop. He's going to quit, he said, as soon as he can find another job. If he can't find one real soon, he guesses he'll quit anyway. It's not worth it, having to walk bent over and leaning to one side.

Sometimes, the strain and effort is greater than the man is willing to admit, even to himself. In the early summer of 1963, Richard was rooming at Nancy's place. His wife and children were "in the country" (his grandmother's home in Carolina), waiting for him to save up enough money so that he could bring them back to Washington and start over again after a disastrous attempt to "make it" in Philadelphia. Richard had gotten a job with a fence company in Virginia. It paid $1.60 an hour. The first few evenings, when he came home from work, he looked ill from exhaustion and the heat. Stanton said Richard would have to quit, "he's too small [thin] for that kind of work." Richard said he was doing OK and would stick with the job.

At Nancy's one night, when Richard had been working about two weeks, Nancy and three or four others were sitting around talking, drinking, and listening to music. Someone asked Nancy when was Richard going to bring his wife and children up from the country. Nancy said she didn't know, but it probably depended on how long it would take him to save up enough money. She said she didn't think he could stay with the fence job much longer. This morning, she said, the man Richard rode to work with knocked on the door and Richard didn't answer. She looked in his room. Richard was still asleep. Nancy tried to shake him awake. "No more digging!" Richard cried out. "No more digging! I can't do no more Goddamn digging!" When Nancy finally managed to wake him, he dressed quickly and went to work.

Richard stayed on the job two more weeks, then suddenly quit, ostensibly because his pay check was three dollars less than what he thought it should have been.

In summary of objective job considerations, then, the most important fact is that a man who is able and willing to work cannot earn enough money to support himself, his wife, and one or more children. A man's chances for working regularly are good only if he is willing to work for less than he can live on, and sometimes not even then. On some jobs, the wage rate is deceptively higher than on others, but the higher the wage rate, the more difficult it is to get the job, and the less the job security. Higher-paying construction work tends to be seasonal and, during the season, the amount of work available is highly sensitive to business and weather conditions and to the changing requirements of individual projects.[11] Moreover, high-paying construction jobs are frequently beyond the physical capacity of some of the men, and some of the low-paying jobs are scaled down even lower in accordance with the self-fulfilling assumption that the man will steal part of his wages on the job.[12]

Bernard assesses the objective job situation dispassionately over a cup of coffee, sometimes poking at the coffee with his spoon, sometimes staring at it as if, like a crystal ball, it holds tomorrow's secrets. He is twenty-seven years old. He and the woman with whom he lives have a baby son, and she has another child by another man. Bernard does odd jobs – mostly painting – but here it is the end of January, and his last job was with the Post Office during the Christmas mail rush. He would like postal work as a steady job, he says. It pays well (about $2.00 an hour) but he has twice failed the Post Office examination (he graduated from a Washington high school) and has given up the idea as an impractical one. He is supposed to see a man tonight about a job as a parking attendant for a large apartment house. The man told him to bring his birth certificate and driver's license, but his license was suspended because of a backlog of unpaid traffic fines. A friend promised to lend him some money this evening. If he gets it, he will pay the fines tomorrow morning and have his license reinstated. He hopes the man with the job will wait till tomorrow night.

A "security job" is what he really wants, he said. He would like to save up money for a taxicab. (But having twice failed the postal examination and having a bad driving record as well, it is highly doubtful that he could meet the qualifications or pass the written test.) That would be "a good life." He can always get a job in a restaurant or as a clerk in a drugstore but they don't pay enough, he said. He needs to take home at least $50 to $55 a week. He thinks he can get that much driving a truck somewhere . . . Sometimes he wishes he had stayed in the army . . . A security job, that's what he wants most of all, a real security job . . .

When we look at what the men bring to the job rather than at what the job offers the men, it is essential to keep in mind that we are not looking at men who come to the job fresh, just out of school perhaps, and newly prepared to undertake the task of making a living, or from another job where they earned a living and are prepared to do the same on this job. Each man comes to the job with a long job history characterized by his not being able to support himself and his family. Each man carries this knowledge, born of his experience, with him. He comes to the job flat and stale, wearied by the sameness of it all, convinced of his own incompetence, terrified of responsibility – of being tested still again and found wanting. Possible exceptions are the younger men not yet, or just, married. They suspect all this but have yet to have it confirmed by repeated personal experience over time. But those who are or have been married know it well. It is the experience of the individual and the group; of their fathers and probably their sons. Convinced of their inadequacies, not only do they not seek out those few better-paying jobs which test their resources, but they actively avoid them, gravitating in a mass to the menial, routine jobs which offer no challenge – and therefore pose no threat – to the already diminished images they have of themselves.

Thus Richard does not follow through on the real estate agent's offer. He is afraid to do on his own – minor plastering, replacing broken windows, other minor repairs and painting – exactly what he had been doing for months on a piecework basis under someone else (and which provided him with a solid base from which to derive a cost estimate).

Richard once offered an important clue to what may have gone on in his mind when the job offer was made. We were in the Carry-out, at a time when he was looking for work. He was talking about the kind of jobs available to him.

> I graduated from high school [Baltimore] but I don't know anything. I'm dumb. Most of the time I don't even say I graduated, 'cause then somebody asks me a question and I can't answer it, and they think I was lying about graduating. . . . They graduated me but I didn't know anything. I had lousy grades but I guess they wanted to get rid of me.
>
> I was at Margaret's house the other night and her little sister asked me to help her with her homework. She showed me some fractions and I knew right away I couldn't do them. I was ashamed so I told her I had to go to the bathroom.

And so it must have been, surely, with the real estate agent's offer. Convinced that "I'm dumb. . . . I don't know anything," he "knew right away" he couldn't do it, despite the fact that he had been doing just this sort of work all along.

Notes

1   By different methods, perhaps, some social scientists have also located the problem in the men themselves, in their unwillingness or lack of desire to work: To improve the underprivileged worker's performance, one must help him to learn to *want* . . . higher social goals for himself and his children. . . . The problem of changing the work habits and motivation of [lower class] people . . . is a problem of changing the goals, the ambitions, and the level of cultural and occupational aspiration of the underprivileged worker (Emphasis in original) (Allison Davis, "The motivation of the underprivileged worker," in William F. Whyte (ed.) *Industry and Society* (New York: McGraw-Hill, 1946)).

2   The comparison of sitting at home alone with being in jail is commonplace.

3   Exactly the same estimate as the one made by Tonk himself. On the basis of personal knowledge of the stealing routine employed by Tonk, however, I suspect the actual amount is considerably smaller.

4   Some public credit may accrue to the clever thief but not respect.

5   It might be profitable to compare, as Howard S. Becker suggests, gross aspects of income and housing costs in this particular area with those reported by Herbert Gans for the low-income working class in Boston's West End. In 1958, Gans reports, median income for the West Enders was just under $70 a week, a level considerably higher than that enjoyed by the people in the Carry-out neighborhood five years later. Gans himself rented a six-room apartment in the West End for $46 a month, about $10 more than the going rate for long-time residents. In the Carry-out neighborhood, rooms that could accommodate more than a cot and a miniature dresser – that is, rooms that qualified for family living – rented for $12 to $22 a week. Ignoring differences that really can't be ignored – the privacy and self-contained efficiency of the multi-room apartment as against the fragmented, public living of the rooming-house "apartment," with a public toilet on a floor always different from the one your room is on (no matter, it probably doesn't work, anyway) – and assuming comparable states of disrepair, the West Enders were paying $6 or $7 a month for a room that cost the Carry-outers at least $50 a month, and frequently more. Looking at housing costs as a percentage of income – and again ignoring what cannot be ignored: that what goes by the name of "housing" in the two areas is not at all the same thing – the median income West Ender could get a six-room apartment for about 12 percent of his income, while his 1963 Carry-out counterpart, with a weekly income of $60 (to choose a figure from the upper end of the income range), often paid 20–33 percent of his income for one room. See Herbert J. Gans, *The Urban Villagers* (New York: Free Press, 1962), pp. 10–13.

6   The higher amount is 1962 union scale for building laborers. According to the Wage Agreement Contract for Heavy Construction Laborers (Washington, DC, and vicinity) covering the period from May 1, 1963 to April 30, 1966, minimum hourly wage for heavy construction laborers was to go from $2.75 (May 1963) by annual increments to $2.92, effective November 1, 1965.

7   "Open-sky" work, such as building overpasses, highways, etc., in which the workers

and materials are directly exposed to the elements, traditionally begins in March and ends around Thanksgiving. The same is true for much of the street repair work and the laying of sewer, electric, gas, and telephone lines by the city and public utilities, all important employers of laborers. Between Thanksgiving and March, they retain only skeleton crews selected from their best, most reliable men.

8 In a recent year, the crime rate in Washington for the month of August jumped 18 percent over the preceding month. A veteran police officer explained the increase to David L. Bazelon, Chief Judge, US Court of Appeals for the District of Columbia. "It's quite simple. . . . You see, August was a very wet month. . . . These people wait on the street corner each morning around 6:00 or 6:30 for a truck to pick them up and take them to a construction site. If it's raining, that truck doesn't come, and the men are going to be idle that day. If the bad weather keeps up for three days . . . we know we are going to have trouble on our hands – and sure enough, there invariably follows a rash of purse-snatchings, house-breakings and the like. . . . These people have to eat like the rest of us, you know" (David L. Bazelon, Address to the Federal Bar Association, National Press Club, Washington, DC, April 30, 1963, p. 3).

9 Estimate of Mr Francis Greenfield, President of the International Hod Carriers, Building and Common Laborers' District Council of Washington, DC, and Vicinity. I am indebted to Mr Greenfield for several points in these paragraphs dealing with construction laborers.

10 Not a sinecure, even by streetcorner standards.

11 The overall result is that, in the long run, a Negro laborer's earnings are not substantially greater – and may be less – than those of the busboy, janitor, or stock clerk. Herman P. Miller, for example, reports that in 1960, 40 percent of all jobs held by Negro men were as laborers or in the service trades. The average annual wage for nonwhite nonfarm laborers was $2,400. The average earning of nonwhite service workers was $2,500 (*Rich Man, Poor Man* (New York: Crowell, 1964), p. 90). Francis Greenfield estimates that in the Washington vicinity, the 1965 earnings of the union laborer who works whenever work is available will be about $3,200. Even this figure is high for the man on the streetcorner. Union men in heavy construction are the aristocrats of the laborers. Casual day labor and jobs with small firms in the building and construction trades, or with firms in other industries, pay considerably less.

12 For an excellent discussion of the self-fulfilling assumption (or prophecy) as a social force, see "The self-fulfilling prophecy," ch. XI, in Robert K. Merton's *Social Theory and Social Structure* (New York: Free Press, 1957).

[Taken from: Elliot Liebow, *Tally's Corner* (Boston, Mass.: Little, Brown, 1967).]

In this piece, written especially for this volume, Cavers-Huff and Kollitz explore their friendship across boundaries of age, race, and above all class. Both seek to acknowledge the source of their values in their social location and to throw some of those values into question through their friendship.

Focus questions:

1 What attitudes of Cavers-Huff about white, middle-class people and about racism or classism were thrown into question in her friendship with Kollitz?

2 What attitudes toward African Americans and the poor did Kollitz throw into question through her friendship with Cavers-Huff?

3 What can one conclude about race and class from their friendship?

14 Seeing Ourselves Through the Eyes of the "Other": an Intellectual and Spiritual Journey

Dasiea Cavers-Huff and Janice Kollitz

Introduction

We have been close friends for a period of seven years. In many respects, it is an odd pairing: a fifty-something white woman, who has lived all her life in an upper-middle-class environment and a thirty-something black woman who has lived all her life (with the exception of the past seven years) at the very lowest rung of the socioeconomic ladder.

In addition, the white, upper-middle-class half of this pairing has consistently been quite politically conservative – both socially and fiscally – while the black member of this pair has been radically left-wing. All of this does not seem to make the deep and intense bonds of friendship/kinship that we share seem very likely.

We were instantly and undeniably drawn to one another. We have shared our stories, our educational experiences, our families, and, the most intimate aspects of our lives. Over the past seven years, we have become mother and daughter in the truest sense. In this essay, we would like to explore how this social, cultural, and, spiritual journey that we have taken has influenced our thinking on issues of race, gender, class, and culture.

Dasiea

Starting this essay was somewhat difficult for me, because as a black woman from the welfare class, who had gone on ultimately to write a dissertation in cognitive science – a branch of theoretical artificial intelligence research – I thought that I knew all (and perhaps more than I had ever wanted to know) about white folks. I really could not see, initially, what, if anything, I had learned about issues of class and culture from my association with Jan. I felt that I had at least three additional Ph.Ds: one each in racism, classism, and sexism. Always being the only black person in my classes in philosophy departments, always being the only black person in philosophy graduate programs, being probably the only black female in the country (and perhaps the world) to write a dissertation from the philosophy end of cognitive science, being the only black tenured professor in the Division of Humanities and Social Sciences at my college, being the only black person at myriad colloquia, receptions, cocktail parties, etc., I didn't think that there was a thing in the world that I had to learn about being black in a white society, being poor in a culture that values affluence, and being a woman in a "man's world." I also knew a lot about the advantages that accrued to being white.

But, through my association with Jan, I must say that my understanding of these issues has deepened. I always felt that racism stemmed either from irrational malevolence, gross ignorance, or both. Jan and I would have conversations about affirmative action, the role of law in society, welfare, the O. J. trial, and, I would always go away perplexed. Here was a woman that I really cared for; she is generous with both her time and resources; she is nurturing; she welcomed my husband and me into her home with open arms. We share holiday dinners; there are always gifts for us under her Christmas tree; she has never made me feel different, or lesser, because I was black and had grown up poor. In addition, she is an extremely intelligent and rational person, both being characteristics that I admire.

I found myself perplexed – how could an intelligent person of good will espouse doctrines that I had long associated with malevolent idiocy? I was left with a dilemma: how could my dear friend espouse views that I thought were basically inhumane, and still at the same time be one of the kindest and most humane people I had ever met? We debated issues endlessly. I could not understand how she could not see the systematic disadvantage that people of color lived under in this society: differential treatment in the educational, legal, economic, and social domains. Did she believe that I was the only black person in my graduate program and the only black tenured faculty member in my division in our college because I was the only black intelligent enough to occupy these positions? Was I one of only a handful of blacks who valued the job and economic security that a graduate degree and tenured faculty position could bring?

I would query her endlessly about occupational positions and social functions in which she had participated in her white middle-class world. She must have picked up the endemic racism and classism inherent in decisions, discussions, policies, and personal interactions that she had been privy to. This happens to me all the time in the white middle- and upper-middle-class circles that I move in, in the frequent use of the phrase "those people," the numerous situations I encounter in which people forget (or fail to be conscious of the fact) that I am black.

Case in point: I was having a discussion with one of our secretaries. We were two upper-middle-class women (although she works as a secretary, her family financial situation is quite good) discussing the difficulty of finding adequate household help (a not uncommon topic of discussion between upper-middle-class ladies like ourselves!). The secretary then proceeded to tell me that she feared that, in southern California, she would not be able to find a person with adequate English skills to work in her home, since she wanted to pay only $5 per hour for this type of work. The secretary then told me that to her astonishment, the agency sent a woman to her house to interview for the job and she was white! She turned to me and said with wide-eyed amazement "Dasiea! can you believe it, she was white! A white woman willing to work for $5 an hour; I can't believe it! And she speaks English as well! An English-speaking white woman who is willing to work for $5 an hour! It's too good to be true!" I was speechless with astonishment, but for a very different reason. I could not believe that she was saying these things to me, a Spanish-speaking black woman who had been off welfare for less than a decade. How many "English only" Constitutional amendment conversations had I had to endure? Some of these conversations took place with assimilationist Spanish-speakers, some were with members of my own family. How much anti-affirmative action raving had I had to suffer through in the company of both colleagues and friends? I was, myself, an affirmative action hire at my college. I was the recipient of minority-targeted funding during graduate school, as well.

I could not believe that my great friend was utterly insensitive to the daily slights and belittlements that I and my husband (and countless other blacks) endure while we are doing the much admired bootstrap routine. Then it hit me. She was neither malevolent, ignorant, insensitive, or any other horrible thing. She just didn't get it. She didn't get it. As close as we had become, this was the first such relationship she'd had. I, on the other hand, unless I wanted to be entirely socially isolated, had no choice but to befriend, live with, and on occasion date whites. I roomed with them, spent weekends and holidays in their homes, and even fell in love with one once upon a time.

Jan, on the other hand, simply assumed that blacks were no different, lived no differently, were treated no differently than whites. She told me that she was once naive enough to think that Dr King was a crackpot, and that people were lying about blacks not being able to use the same public facilities and accommodations. I was mystified by how all these things could be happening before her very eyes, and she be not able to see it. She said that it was because she lived in the San Francisco Bay area, which was quite multicultural, very different from the culture of, say, the deep South. I told her that in my experience, California, both northern and southern, was as racist a place as I had ever been (witness the landmark passage of anti-immigration and anti-affirmative action legislation by the voters of the state of California in 1994 and 1996, respectively).

I felt as if I were running my head up against a brick wall. As a researcher who studied human cognition, Jan's case was fascinating to me: the compartmentalization of her knowledge and feeling, and the (seemingly) flimsy justifications that she put forth in order to support views that, in my opinion, were quite racist. Very recently, during a conversation about affirmative action, Jan asked, "Wouldn't you rather be considered on the basis of your own merits; you definitely are an extremely competent person." I said, "From your lips to God's ears – if for once I could be considered solely on the basis my merits, if anyone could look past my blackness, it would be an extremely happy day."

From the depths of my perplexity, a solution to my dilemma began to emerge – and from my own experience, no less. In addition to being a black woman, I am also considered quite overweight for my height. (How lucky I am! The lowest organism on the body-conscious southern California food-chain, must be the fat, black female!) I was not always overweight, though. I gained the excess weight through corticosteroid treatment for a medical condition. Before the treatment, I was an athletically built woman with the hourglass figure that many women pay tens of thousands of dollars in cosmetic surgery to achieve. I was an arrogant bitch as well. I thought that fat people were lazy and undisci-plined. I would treat overweight people with what I know now to be intolerable rudeness.

If an overweight friend and I were having fun at my home, and I did not want her to leave, but she protested that she must, because she had not packed an overnight bag, I would tell her not to worry, she could wear something of mine (size 8). During shopping trips with women friends who were overweight, I would impulsively select a dress from the rack – inevitably a size 10, or the exquisitely cruel "one size fits all," and suggest that it would be perfect, and that she should try it on. My friend would then look down at the floor and mumble something about not having any money, or that the dress was not right for the occasion. Sometimes I would persist in my request that she try it, and my friend would reluctantly tell me that it wouldn't fit, and that nothing in the store would fit.

I was engaging in a culturally sanctioned practice of depersonalization. Peo-ple who are somehow outside of the cultural norm – a norm that demands that people be white, thin, literate, English-speaking, with perfectly functioning arms and legs – are objectified. This objectification is apparent in the language that we use: "the blacks," "the Hispanics," "the disabled," "the overweight." There is a failure to identify with these people as fully human. This objectification is so deeply ingrained that we even tend objectify and depersonalize ourselves. I was recently in the large-size specialty store where I purchase my clothing, and I was talking to my young, beautiful salesperson who weighed about 300 pounds. She was beautifully attired, vivacious, and quite sexy. This salesperson proceeded to tell me how much she hated her body, would not wear short pants or sleeve-less tops. My eyes started to fill with tears. I hurt very badly for the societal conditioning that led her to think of herself in this way. I gathered from her conversation that this woman felt unworthy to love or be loved or to take her rightful place alongside the "beautiful people." She couldn't see that she *was* one of the "beautiful people."

Through considering my role in perpetuating the societal practices of deper-sonalization and objectification I came to understand my friend Jan's earlier attitudes regarding people of color and poor people. I also understand, now, that it is not necessarily ignorance or malevolence that leads people to be racist, classist, size-ist, homophobic, ageist, etc. It is a deep inability to identify with experiences, bodies, financial situation etc., that are different from their own. In fact, racism, etc. are not irrational strategies given the prevailing cultural arche-types endemic to our culture.

This is the real value of my relationship with Jan. I identified with her as a person, I did not see her merely as an "old white woman" (I met her in my twenties, when anyone over 35 was old!), but as my dear friend and as a family member. During the course of this identification with her, I was able to arrive at the point of view that racism etc. are not due to a lack of intelligence, sensitivity, or good intentions, but that for the most part, the experiences of blacks and whites, those of the fat and the thin, those of the English speaker and the Span-ish speaker, are as foreign to one another as Martian culture would be to Earth-lings. The real value of the type of friendship that Jan and I share is that it reduces the depersonalization and objectification that leads to racist attitudes. The other becomes in a very literal sense one's self.

Jan

Before Dasiea and I became part of each other's lives I had not considered what life would be like for me if I had black skin. I had not considered living in a ghetto or living on welfare. I vehemently denied that I would discriminate against any group for their class, race, or gender. But as our friendship grew and I started understanding her perspectives, I realized that I unconsciously catego-rized people by groups; therefore, I depersonalized their stories and I treated them as objects.

In January of 1985, after raising and supporting eight children (my own three children from my first marriage and five stepchildren from my second marriage), earning and losing several fortunes, and lacking a college education, at age 47 I found myself in a terrible predicament. My permanently disabled husband could no longer provide half of the family income. My monthly ex-penses were more than my monthly earnings. I enrolled at Riverside Commu-nity College (RCC) as a first-year student so that I could improve my job skills and my income. In 1986, I earned an Associate of Arts degree and then en-rolled at California State University San Bernardino (CSUSB). In 1987, on my fiftieth birthday, I earned my Bachelor of Arts in English. I wanted to teach high school English but felt underprepared so I enrolled in CSUSB's Master of Arts in English Composition program. I found a job as a substitute teacher during daytime hours and attended graduate school at night. After finishing my coursework and becoming a candidate for the MA degree in 1988, I accepted a part-time job teaching first-year composition at Riverside Community College. In 1989, after I had received the MA, RCC offered me a short-term contract to fill the full-time position of a professor who had died two weeks into the new semester. Fortunately, in 1990, RCC hired me for a tenure track position.

When the college assigned me a permanent office, I found another new faculty member moving into the office directly across the hall: Dasiea Cavers-Huff, a philosopher. I immediately liked her sparkling energetic persona, her quick incisive comments, and her wonderful sense of humor. She is a natural communicator. She reminded me of my children and stepchildren because she liked the same pop culture icons my children enjoyed. Dasiea had moved from the University of Maryland to take the job at RCC and hadn't yet found a circle of friends her age. My maternal instincts kicked in so I informally "adopted" her, I invited her to join my family for birthdays, Thanksgiving, and Christmas. She fitted into my family just like I thought she would; my husband, children, and grandchildren also liked her immediately. After a short time, I realized she was one of the smartest people I knew and her superior education enhanced this innate intelligence.

After Dasiea settled into a cramped apartment and established a circle of friends, our mother–daughter relationship grew. I started maternal nagging, encouraging her to buy a house so that she could avoid excess income tax and start building a nest egg. I wanted her to have the same kind of stability my children were starting to establish. Her husband, Brian, quit his job in the East and joined her some months after she arrived in Riverside. I felt satisfied when Dasiea and Brian finally bought a beautiful suburban home in a good neighborhood. To me this was a natural event for an up-and-coming young couple. What I hadn't expected were the difficulties these young people faced in trying to qualify for a loan because they had black skin. Discriminating against people because of skin color was illegal. This couldn't happen in my America. Or could it? I didn't even think about my own skin color.

As I interacted with Dasiea, spending hours discussing race, class, and gender issues, I discovered we held divergent views. As a "canon promoting," fiscally conservative, white Anglo-Saxon Protestant, I needed to question the roots of my value system. I wanted to understand why Dasiea saw rampant racism everywhere she looked, because I didn't see it. Was my value system racist? Was my value system skewed because I'd always lived in middle- and upper-middle-class, mostly white communities? During the past seven years, I've come to understand my "world" better. I've also come to understand how Dasiea's "world" is different from mine.

Brian lacked the same kind of superior education Dasiea acquired in her "mostly white" school settings. Though he lacked a high school diploma, Brian wanted a college education. He decided to return to school and become a registered nurse. Earning a Bachelor of Science in nursing meant that Brian would need to play "catch-up." Brian became one of my English composition students so I "adopted" him too. Through Brian's struggles in the college setting, I learned some important elements about racism in a very unpleasant way. Because I supported Brian in an unjust situation, certain faculty members accused me of being unethical for not supporting the racist faculty member who injured him. These faculty members brought ethics violation charges against me in the college's Academic Senate. These charges included: "walking across campus with the [black] student in support of his position" and "being seen speaking to members of the press" about the situation. I became extremely upset when one faculty member poked her finger in my chest and said, "Give up on this one Jan; it's only one student." Only one student? This student was my "adopted" son and I felt like a mother lion ready to defend her young. I wanted to tear this bigot to pieces with my claws. She didn't convince me to give up but she did convince me that institutional racism is alive and well on college campuses. None of my children should be discriminated against for their color of skin. I could now empathize with the experience of being a victim of racism because I felt its sting; my so-called "liberal" colleagues were racist to the core.

What are the roots of my value system?

My mother's attitude influenced my daily socialization as a child, making me aware of class and gender discrimination. My undereducated mother lived by Emily Post's rules of etiquette: everything and everyone should behave in a "proper" manner. My mother always wanted to be perceived as upper class, so she kept up appearances so that people outside our family would think well of us. My mother believed girls should learn to cook, bake, sew, clean, and manage a household frugally. My mother believed children should learn to work, not play.

My father didn't seem to place the same importance on class that my mother did. Since my college-educated father spent hours teaching me "boy's" academic subjects (algebra, geometry, physics) and "boy's" tasks (mowing the lawn, fixing stuff with tools), I rejected the gender stereotype my mother promoted but I easily accepted the class stereotype. Throughout my life, I've always lived in a "better than average" neighborhood. Naturally, that is why I wanted my "adopted" daughter, Daisea, to buy a house in the same kind of better than average neighborhood because this is the proper middle-class thing to do.

Before we started our dialogue about race, class, and gender, I never once thought of Dasiea as someone raised in a lower-class structure. Why would I? She has impeccable manners, impeccable taste, and impeccable grooming (my mother's passion). She has a superior education and superior intelligence (my father's passion). She likes to discuss ideas (my passion). As far as I could tell, despite living in mostly "white" neighborhoods my entire life, they have always been segregated by class, not by race. Minorities who lived where I lived came from the middle and upper-middle classes and seemed, to me, to be fully accepted members of the community. Therefore, I considered minority neighbors, classmates, and friends to be equal to me in every way. My minority neighbors, classmates, and friends were all like the members of my family: hard working, frugal, and well educated. Because I grew up in the cosmopolitan San Francisco area, I didn't perceive black people to be injured by discrimination in my daily life. Black people rode the same buses I rode, drank from the same drinking fountains, seemed to have the all same privileges. The black people I knew personally lived middle- or upper-middle-class lives.

How did I become a self-defined "canon promoting," fiscally conservative WASP? First, I need to define what this phrase means. My paternal ancestors came in waves from England and Ireland and Wales, starting with the Morris family in the early seventeenth century. My ancestors fought the British in the Revolutionary War and fought the Confederacy in the Civil War. My maternal grandfather came to America from Germany in the nineteenth century as an indentured servant. Both my paternal and maternal ancestors believed in religious and political freedom from oppression for all people. I became a conservative defender of first amendment rights because of my family's values. They promoted the American Dream and the Yankee work ethic. They believed anyone could overcome oppression with hard work, determination, and excellent performance. My parents taught me to depend on myself and not complain or blame others when things went wrong. This value system made me believe that "victim mentality" was a curse to avoid.

My fiscally conservative ideas developed because of my Yankee work ethic. Like Thoreau, I believe that a government that "governs least, governs best." My parents taught me to be frugal and acquire wealth. I believe in entrepreneurship to improve my standard of living. The person who works harder and longer deserves rewards for this labor. I don't think the government should be in the business of playing Robin Hood. As a child, I was taught the importance of tithing: people should give 10 per cent of their earnings to help those less fortunate. I am not hard-hearted or unsympathetic; I always help others when I can but I feel used and abused when the government punishes me for my hard work by overtaxing me and giving my earnings to someone who abuses the system. Therefore, I'm in favor of welfare reform. I don't see welfare reform as a race issue. I see it as an opportunity to give people in the lowest socioeconomic classes those skills that will make them function successfully. However, I find myself disturbed by the government's anti-welfare direction in reform. I believe these policies are causing more ruptures in society: more racism, more sexism, and a new super underclass. The new plans for reform are punitive and unworkable. Bureaucrats have forgotten we need to teach people to fish before we take away today's meal.

I see gender inequalities everywhere, starting with my mother's attitudes about the woman's place. Because my father didn't buy into the stereotype, I learned to reject ideas that would impede my ability to succeed at anything I wanted to do. I feel strongly that affirmative action programs that have promoted "quotas" and allowed unqualified persons to take a job or college slot away from more qualified persons are racist and sexist in nature. I believe affirmative action programs have some merit because we need a vehicle to give the underrepresented an opportunity. But the reality of the last twenty years is an escalation of racism and sexism due to the Robin Hood mentality of these programs. A poor white man who has never owned a slave doesn't understand why he can't find a job; he blames the individual woman or minority who gets the job instead of blaming the system.

Why didn't I see the same rampant racism everywhere that Dasiea perceived? I guess I understood everything through my own experiences within my "canon promoting," fiscally conservative WASP perspective. Dasiea sees racism differently than I do because her experience leads her to different conclusions about people's motives.

Was my value system racist before I met Dasiea? Is my value system racist today? No! But my value system is class elitist because I've depersonalized people from lower classes. Was my value system skewed because I'd always lived in middle- and upper-middle-class, mostly white, communities? Dasiea pointed out that all my "minority" friends and neighbors appeared to be from my socio-economic group and class. Though I have many minority friends, they tend to be high achievers who share my values. My minority friends have, for the most part, exactly the same qualities I value in my WASP friends. Dasiea convinced me that I must start to look beyond my own experience. During the past seven years, I've come to understand my "world" better. I've also come to understand how Dasiea's "world" is different from mine.

In the end, because of my friendship with Dasiea, I've come to understand that we frequently take opposite sides in race, class, and gender arguments. Though we disagree about who is to blame for breakdowns in society and how to deal with welfare and affirmative action programs, we usually agree about the need for reform. Though we propose different ways to correct the problems, we are both looking for equity in race, class, and gender without infringing on the rights of others.

Patricia J. Williams, in this extract from her wondrous book *The Alchemy of Race and Rights*, tries to shed light on the imaginary notions that underlie attitudes toward the poor and homeless. Through concrete cases (including her own teaching experiences) and flights of abstraction, she shows how a powerful set of assumptions and stereotypes reinforces or makes possible the status quo.

Focus questions:
1 What is Williams's basic point about the concept of choice, and how does she use the case of rapists "choosing" to be castrated as an illustration of that point?
2 Why does Williams think that current attitudes toward wealth are "a formula for class war"?
3 What is the relation of wealth to privacy on Williams's account?

15　Gilded Lilies and Liberal Guilt

Patricia J. Williams

I am sitting in the library preparing a class on homelessness and the law. A student of mine, B., interrupts my writing. She is angry at me because she says my class is "out of control." She has been made to feel guilty, by the readings and the discussion, that her uncle is, as she describes him, "a slumlord." She says that the rich can't help who they are. I resent this interruption and snap at her: "They can help who they are as much" – and here I give B. back her own words of only a day or so before – "as poor people who are supposed to 'help' themselves out of poverty (as distinguished, of course, from helping themselves to any of the 'unearned' goodies of the wealthy)." I am very angry and it shows. I can feel how unprofessorial I must seem; looking into her eyes, I know I'll have to pay.

A few days later I receive a memo from the associate dean, expressing his concern about the way in which certain inappropriate "trumping moves" are being employed to "silence the more moderate members of the student body."

After the Civil War, when slaves were unowned – I hesitate to use the word emancipated even yet – they were also disowned: they were thrust out of the market and into a nowhere land that was not quite the mainstream labor market, and very much outside the marketplace of rights. They were placed beyond the bounds of valuation, in much the same way that the homeless are or that nomads and gypsies are, or tribal people who refuse to ascribe to the notion of private space and who refuse or are refused traditional jobs or stationary employment; they became like all those who cannot express themselves in the language of power and assertion and staked claims – all those who are nevertheless deserving of the dignity of social valuation, yet those who are so often denied survival itself.

I have been thinking about the unowning of blacks and their consignment to some collective public state of mind, known alternatively as "menace" or "burden" – about the degree to which it might be that public and private are economic notions, i.e., that the right to privacy might be a function of wealth. I wonder, still smarting from my encounter with B., if the concept of intimacy (assuming privacy is related to the drive for intimacy) is premised on socioeconomic status. B. was upset, I think, not because I actually insulted an uncle whom she loved and of whose existence I had no knowledge, but because the class discussion had threatened the deeply vested ordering of her world. She was saying: haves are entitled to privacy, in guarded, moated castles; have-nots must be out in the open – scrutinized, seen with their hands open and empty to make sure they're not pilfering. The rationale went something like: the poor are envious of the rich; the rich worked hard to get where they are or have more valuable social characteristics and therefore deserve it; they have suffered. B. kept saying just that: "My family suffered for what they have."

Perhaps, I finally decided, the best way to overcome all these divisions is indeed to acknowledge the suffering of the middle and upper classes. I think, in an odd moment of connection, of my Great-Aunt Mary who, back in the 1920s, decided that her lot in life would be better if she pretended to be a white woman. She left home, moved to Cambridge, Massachusetts, and married into one of the state's wealthiest families. While the marriage lasted, she sent her decidedly black daughter by a previous marriage to live with her sister, my Great-Aunt Sophie. Thirty years later, I grew up under the rather schizophrenic tutelage of these two aunts, one of whom had been a charwoman at Harvard University even as the other lived in splendor with one of its largest contributors. The gulf and yet the connection between the sisters is almost indescribable. The explicit sacrifice of family for money by each; the bonds, the tendrils, the need seeping up in odd, non-familial and quasi-familial ("just like family" is how the aunt who was the maid was described by the rich young men whose rooms she cleaned) expectations that were denied, in guilt, in half-conscious deference to the corruption of real family bonds. Their only contact with love, attention, and intimacy was always at the expense of their own children or family – each was in peonage to the other. There was in this a real exchange of mutual suffering.

I think about B.'s uncle the slumlord and the tax I seem to have extorted in her life's bargain not to think about him with guilt. I wonder at the price her uncle must have charged to begin with, in the agreement not to think of him in unheroic terms. And if the consideration in such an exchange is more than just money and material gain – if the real transaction is not for "salary" but for survival itself, for love and family and connection, then this becomes a contract of primal dimensions.

If both rich and poor are giving up life itself and yet both are deeply dissatis-fied, even suffering, they will never feel paid enough for their lot in life: what has gone on is not a trade or exchange, but a sacrifice. They have been victim-ized by a social construction that locks money into an impossible equation with "pricelessness," uniqueness. They have been locked into a socially constructed life-disappointment by the carrot of hope that somewhere, just ahead, there is satisfaction or sufficiency of payment. In the insistence on equation, more money eventually comes to equal the right to more intimacy, to have family. Yet since there is never "enough" money, family becomes out of reach, increasingly sus-pect as undeserved. Family becomes not figurative wealth (as in "my children are my jewels"), but the sign of literal wealth – that is, those who have family have money, or they are suspect, their welfare seen as undeserved theft. Such a bargain is nothing more than a trade of self-esteem for money. Money buys self-esteem. If you're poor, you can't be happy because you're the object of revulsion and ridicule; if you're poor, you can't be satisfied because that's equated with laziness; if you're poor, you can't accept it as fate because poverty is your fault; and if you're poor, you have to resent the upper classes because competi-tion – or economic revenge – is the name of the game, the only way out.

This is not merely a description of a class system; it is a formula for class war. Ideology aside, it is a formula bought by hopes of a lifestyle that will release us all from serfdom, show us into the promised land, and open the secrets of wealth and belonging. It is a formula that sprang forth from a hypothetical world in which the streets were paved with gold and where there were infinite resources. It is not a formula for a real world in which the reality of proximity comes crashing in on the illusion of privacy; or in which the desperation of isolation explodes into the mindless pleasantry of suburban good times. It is not a for-mula that works in a finite world.

I continue to ponder the equation of privacy with intimacy and of publicity with dispossession. Is not homelessness a metaphor for, as well as the manifes-tation of, collective disownership? I take my wondering to class and place it before my students. There are, I tell them, by conservative estimates 70,000 homeless people in New York City alone.[1] Although a disproportionate number of the homeless are black, this is not essentially a racial problem. Still I do see it as interwoven with the legacy of slavery, in its psychology of denial, in the notions of worth and unworthiness that go into the laws dealing with the home-less, in the ranking of "legitimate" needy and "illegitimate" homeless – these are familiar, cruel, blind games that make bastards and beggars of those who are in fact our family.

There are many homeless people on my street in New York, I tell my class full of non-New Yorkers. From the window of my home, I watch the well-heeled walk by the homeless. Some give money, most do not. From time to time, something especially visible or controversial happens with reference to the homelessness issue, and then the well-heeled give more or less, depending upon which way the sentiments are twisted. Mayor Koch puts up signs in the subway telling travelers not to give to panhandlers, that it's bad for tourism. Someone writes an editorial to say that the streets belong to taxpayers and that the homeless should pay rent for their use. A homeless child dies in her mother's arms. Small disenfranchisements give birth to large disenfranchisements, sympathies come and go.

There was a particularly well-publicized story about a homeless woman who gave birth to her child in the subway.[2] The state intervened and took away the child, saying that the mother was unfit because of her economic circumstances. The American Civil Liberties Union represented the mother in her attempt to maintain custody of the child. Although there is some law in New York to protect a newborn child from a mother's destitute circumstances, there is no law in the United States to provide a mother with the housing or health care or economic rights by which to provide for her child:

> While many European constitutions and the European Convention on Human Rights guarantee everyone the right to an education, the right to health care and even the right to a job or welfare payments, our Constitution does not.
> Our Bill of Rights guarantees the individual's right to be free of Governmental intrusions, not the individual's entitlements to Governmental support. The Supreme Court has uniformly rejected all claims to constitutional entitlements.[3]

My students always fight with me on this point. They tell me that this is the land of opportunity and everyone who works hard can get anything they want. (My students are all very hard workers.) I am not arguing, I tell them, that there are not laws that provide her with the opportunity to seek out a job and be successful at it. But if she does not find a job or is not successful at it, then she will have very little recourse, since the government has no obligation to provide for her. Friends working in the Department of Social Welfare in New York have told me that food stamps, for those lucky enough to get them (and most frequently this does not include the homeless), provided as of 1988 only 48 cents a meal. And in the wake of the October 1989 San Francisco earthquake, the Federal Emergency Management Agency actually turned the pre-quake homeless away from shelters, arguing that they were not the "crisis" homeless – those with homes destroyed by the quake – which FEMA was designed to serve. "'They have to differentiate between the quake-victim homeless and the pre-quake homeless,' [Barry Del Buono, executive director of the southern bay area's Emergency Housing Consortium] said, an exercise that underlines in his mind the inadequacy of federal response to homelessness in general."[4] It was also a distinction, conspicuous in the wake of the Reagan administration's Housing and Urban Development Agency scandal, in which those privileged enough to have had comfortable property interests to begin with became the "truly needy" after all.

It is thus, I tell my angry students, that the homeless have no real right to conjugal benefits, to family of their own, to anything like happiness, or to the good health that is necessary in order to enjoy life, appreciate liberty, and pursue happiness. Furthermore, our national and collective failure to provide guaranteed rights to food, shelter and medical care has significant costs that they will have to deal with in their lifetimes: both as a constitutional or a public matter, and in the overwhelming power of specialized economic interests, the power of so-called private interests.

It is the last few minutes of class, and my students are hungry and edgy. They growl with the restless urge to go shopping. I, who also love to shop, nevertheless run on and on: I am concerned, I say, about the way in which hunger, lack of education, and homelessness are devastating our communities, and particularly women, children, and black communities. I am alarmed by the denial that the very right to survive is being withheld, through untextualized constitutionalisms, governmental restraint, states rights, to say nothing of indigency's being characterized as a matter of choice.

I tell stories of the deep-rooted commonplaceness of our economically rationalized notions of humanity. Once I took the F train to 14th Street, where I saw an old beggar woman huddled against a pillar. Behind me, a pretty little girl of about 6 exclaimed, "Oh, daddy, there's someone who needs our help." The child was then led off by the hand, by her three-piece-suited father who patiently explained that giving money to the woman directly was "not the way we do things." Then he launched into a lecture on the United Way as succor for the masses. It was a first lesson in distributive justice: conditioned passivity, indirection, distance – statistical need positioned against actual need. I walked behind them for a little way, listening to him teach: responsiveness to immediate need was being devalued as wrong.

A few moments later, I saw another homeless person lying on a bench in the subway. He lay extended along its length, one leg bent to the floor, the other stretched out on the bench; one arm flung across his chest, the other crooked under his head. He was dressed poorly, but not as badly as some street people. He had a little beard and a complacent face. His mouth hung open, and his eyes – his eyes were half closed, yet open. His eyes were a startlingly vacant blue, heavy-lidded yet staring at the subway station ceiling, intense yet with no particular focus. They were the eyes, I thought, of a dead man. Then, I rationalized, no, he couldn't be. He's just sleeping as my mother used to, with the whites of her eyes showing, when she was sitting in her chair and didn't really want to fall asleep.

Then I looked at the face of another man who had seen what I saw, both of us still walking, never stopping for a second. I tried to flash worry at him. But he was seeking reassurance, which he took from my face despite myself. I could see him rationalize his concern away, in the flicker of an eye. We walked behind each other upstairs and three blocks down Broadway before I lost him and the conspiracy of our solidarity. Thus the man on the subway bench died twice: in body and in the spirit I had murdered.

(Deep inside, I am made insecure by the wandering gazes of my students. I wonder, as they obviously do, if all this is really related to law.) I think all this is related, I say aloud, to our ability to interpret laws. What we had engaged in was not merely a rationalization but an imposition of order – the ironclad imposition of a world view requiring adherence to fictional visions cloaked in the comfort of familiar truth-denying truisms: "I know a black family and they're making it"; "My grandfather came to this country with nothing and . . ."; "He'll just use it for booze or drugs," even though "he" looks hungry and asks for money for food. We, the passersby of the dispossessed, formed a society of sorts. We made, by our actions, a comfortable social compact whose bounds we did not transgress. We also made a bargain of the man who lay dead. We looked at each other for confirmation that he was not dead; we, the grim living, determined to make profit of the dead. There is great power in being able to see the world as one will and then to have that vision enacted. But if being is seeing for the subject, then being seen is the precise measure of existence for the object.

After class, my students rush to the dean to complain. They are not learning real law, they say, and they want someone else to give them remedial classes. How will they ever pass the bar with subway stories? I am called to the dean's office. (Even in his distress, he does not forget to offer me sherry.) I explain: The discussion of economic rights and civil liberties usually assumes at least two things – that equal protection guarantees equality of opportunity "blindly" for the benefit of those market actors who have exercised rational choices in wealth-maximizing ways; and that those who make irrational non-profit-motivated choices have chosen, and therefore deserve, to be poor. But I take as given two counterfacts: that in the United States we subsidize the wealthy in all kinds of ways, and we do so in a way that directly injures the poor; and that neither the state of indigency nor the state of wealth is necessarily or even frequently the result of freely exercised choice. I think that this wide divergence of professed ideals and day-to-day reality creates in us some costly degree of social schizophrenia. Over time, our relation to both the marketplace and to a sense of liberty – our view of ourselves as both free and free agents – has become tremendously complicated.

The dean offers me biscuits and a soft white cheese. This past summer, I tell him, I drove across the country with a friend who had never visited the United States before. His conclusion was that "Free is a magic word in America." At that moment we were on the highway just outside Las Vegas. He pointed to a sign on a roadside diner: "Free! All you can eat, only $7.99."

The sign was more than a joke. It symbolized the degree to which much of what we call "freedom" is either contradictory or meaningless. For example, when the Supreme Court, in the case of *Buckley* v. *Valeo*, held not only that it is undesirable to constrain the expenditure of money in political elections, but that such expenditure *is speech*,[5] what did that mean? The *Buckley* court seems to have gone one step beyond holding that money is related to access to expensive media; it seems to imply that if one could speak freely (without pecuniary cost, that is) but could not spend money, then one would still be "censored." But if expression is commodified in this fashion, then can it not be bought and sold? Is money itself communicative and of what? Is the introduction of money as a concept of expression something like introducing usury into our love lives? Can speech be usurious? Is money a form of language, in the way we think of speech as language? What does this imply for oaths, rituals, the swearing of attachments? Can we now say "political money" and "artistic money" and mean the same as when we say "political speech" and "artistic expression"? What does free speech or freedom itself mean, if it really has a price?

Here's what troubles me: we use money to express our valuation of things. We express equivalencies through money, and in that process of laying claim we introduce a powerful leveling device. Through reducing to commodified equivalencies, we can bargain away what is undesirable; we can purchase and create a market for what is desirable. But given the way we use money, we also dispense with the necessity of valuing or considering (for this is, at heart, the definition of "consideration,"[6] our economically derived conception of contract) whatever is outside the market.

The sherry is beginning to go to my head. If, I demand somewhat sharply of the dean, political discourse is a market phenomenon, what happens to those members of the polls who are outside the market – who cannot or will not be bought and sold? And what indeed is the impact of buying and selling on the polis that is within the marketplace of ideas? I say, jabbing the air with my finger, that the answer to all of this is increasingly apparent in the construction of American political discourse, not just in things like political action committees lobbying for legislation but in the pernicious degree to which advertising agencies and wheel-of-fortune popularity polls determine the course of world events – elections, health care, invasions, and whole wars. The focus of politics is shifted, in other words, from concepts such as service and duty to purchasers and the buying public. It is wealth-representative politics, the equivalent of what Robert Ellickson so appallingly endorsed in his article "Cities and Homeowners' Associations."[7] The focus of politics is shifted from amassing the greatest amount of intellectual or social or erotic capital to the simple amassing of capital.

It enables the wealthiest presidential candidates to purchase the soft fuzzy image of "I am a real American" and to hoard it like commodity wealth. It allows us to spurn those who do not express themselves through expenditure as undeserving. It allows speechwriters to become the property of presidents, almost like wives. And the harm I see in all of this is that it puts reality up for sale and makes meaning fungible: dishonest, empty, irresponsible.

An image that comes to mind is that of movie star Jessica Lange, who testified to Congress about the condition of farms in the United States because she had played a farmer's wife.[8] What on earth does "testimony" mean in that context? Similarly, the movie *Mississippi Burning*, in making history subservient to sales, purchased wholesale a new rendering of reality, of history, of experience; it provided a profound illustration of this commodity quantification, as mercenarily motivated political representation. Public discourse becomes privatized, speech becomes moneyed, money becomes the measure of our lives.

I pause for breath. The dean says quietly, "But money is real," and refills my glass.

I fail to heed the warning in his voice and continue rashly: Jean Baudrillard has said that the "secret of gambling is that money does not exist as a value."[9] It seems to me that the secret of the Madison Avenue stakes for which our legal and political futures are played, is that words do not exist as a value in the constitution of political currency.

In our legal and political system, words like "freedom" and "choice" are forms of currency. They function as the mediators by which we make all things equal, interchangeable. It is, therefore, not just what "freedom" means, but the relation it signals between each individual and the world. It is a word that levels difference.

Similarly, money itself signals a certain type of relationship. So perhaps it is not just money that is the problem, but the relationship it signals. The Tit for Tat. The purchasing of our liberties; the peonage of our citizenship. As one analyst describes it,

> In bourgeois ideology, history is negated by the process of exchange; in the equalization brought about by the need to determine that one ware is worth another ware, and everything has its price, that this equals that, history is replaced by an eternal stasis where values remain constant in an ideological tit for tat where the equal sign ensures a never-ending binary equilibrium in which a change on one side of the equation is always balanced by the algebraically obligatory change on the other. Everything becomes a perfect metaphor for everything else, for in the end all equations say the same thing and all equations say nothing. The emptiness behind the binary opposition is the emptiness behind the equation $0 = 0$. One thing is opposed to another thing in a two-fold opposition incapable of accommodating marginalities, third forces, or syntheses.[10]

The next day I get a note from the dean: he has received a variety of complaints about the polemical nature of my teaching and feels that my style is inappropriate in "the" law-school classroom. That night I go home, pour my own sherry, and write up my lecture notes for the next day's class, which on the next day I give, out of neither defiance nor defeat but because I don't have anything else to say.

In Brazil, I start, women are being asked to provide proof of sterilization before they can be hired. This comes in the wake of new legislation granting pregnant women four months of maternity leave. The law mostly affects poor rather than middle-class women, who "are able to return to work almost as quickly as they want because they can draw on a vast pool of poorly paid domestic servants, few of whom have social benefits . . . Such servants . . . also earned the right to maternity leave under the new laws. The Association for Domestic Workers in Rio de Janeiro believes this city alone has at least 300,000 nannies and maids, and the group has said it will now watch out for these women's interests."[11] In the United States we disguise the brutal directness of such bargains. We have employers in the private sector who, using arguments of fetal rights and protection, refuse to hire any woman capable of bearing a child.[12]

More troubling still, in the public sector we have the increasing phenomenon of sentencing hearings in which defendants in such cases as child abuse or rape are offered a "choice" between time in jail and sterilization.[13] The defendant is positioned as a purchaser, as "buying" her freedom by paying the price of her womb. And because that womb is in the position of money in this equivalence, it seems to many to be a form of expression, a voluntary and willing expenditure in the commerce of free choice. One of the more peculiar examples of this last is the case of Roscoe Brown, a black South Carolinian convicted of rape.[14] In an arrangement styled to resemble contract, Brown was offered a commutation of his thirty-year prison sentence if he agreed to be castrated. (Castration is not merely male sterilization, as in a vasectomy; it is the actual removal of the testes and was outlawed in South Carolina, even for slaves, in 1789.[15]) After spending some time in prison, Brown asked to be castrated. Civil libertarians intervened, and the case was appealed to the Supreme Court of South Carolina. Fortunately, the court ruled that the castration "option" would amount to cruel and unusual punishment. But the issue is not settled in other states.[16]

The question this case raised for me was the interpretation of the words "contract," "freedom of choice," and "autonomy." "In 1985," wrote the New York Times, "three convicted rapists in South Carolina were resentenced after the state Supreme Court said a judge's decision to *let* them *choose* castration over prison violated their rights to be free from cruel and unusual punishment" (emphasis added).[17] The vocabulary of allowance and option seems meaningless in the context of an imprisoned defendant dealing with a judge whose power is absolute. Yet in January 1989, on the Oprah Winfrey show, I saw Roscoe Brown's white lawyer vehemently arguing that Brown should be *allowed* to be castrated, that the refusal to allow the arrangement to go forward was unwarranted state intrusion into his privacy.

I have some difficulty in getting my students to understand why this might not be good private contract. There is a siege of questions, from faces full of sincerity, mouths round with worried wonder. "Why do you want to rob the defendant of his last little bit of freedom," asks one. "But the defendant chose the castration," says another.

I continue: It is true that the transaction was structured as a contract. The power of that structure, however, transforms the discourse from one of public obligation and consensus into one of privatized economy. This positioning renders invisible the force of the state, and invisible the enormous judicial whimsy exercised in the selection of such a currency. It allows us to think that the state is not putting the cut on its citizenry; it allows us to sustain the fiction, the half truth, that the cut is coming from the defendant's own mouth. It is he who is begging to be castrated. It is, as Sacvan Bercovitch has observed, Ahab's notion of covenant: "I do not order ye: ye will it."[18]

"But what if the defendant really, really wanted it?" insists another student. I respond by asking: what does the defendant's "really, really" wanting mean in such a context? Is there room to distinguish desire as a matter of autonomy and free will from the desire to submit? After all, the scenario of someone's really, really imploring to be castrated is very close to what, in another realm of sexual affairs, is called "dominance and submission." But is what the defendant wants the issue anyway? What else is at stake in a case that bears the name *People* [*the public*] v. *Roscoe Brown*?

I don't think it serves any interest to window-dress the enormous power and dominance of the state in transforming the public interest in consistent and fair sentencing into one of private desire. The private desire that comes out of the defendant's mouth is in fact the private whimsy of the judge. The inversion of having the defendant beg to be dominated does not make the state any less dominating; nor does the inversion serve to make the state submissive. The force of the state remains: the backdrop of incarceration is generally understood as signifying something quite different from an invisible hand or an economic incentive. Yet what does seem to be obscured is the fact that the state is creating a situation where it determines who shall have children or not; and the fact that judges are exercising unprecedented latitude to impose sentences without statutory authority. The problem with this is not simply that it breaks the rules but that it substitutes for the public discourse and full airing of what sort of force the state should use. Yet it is all of us who are on trial in criminal sentencing proceedings: do we really, really want the state to require a ransom of body parts?

This notion of privately purchased public rights comes out at a more complicated level in the recent Supreme Court decision to permit a state to choose whether or not it will protect its children from abuse[19] – this from a court that does not hesitate to "protect" minors from information about birth control and abortion. Here governmental responsibility is less rooted in the jurisprudence of enduring social compact than in that of short-term private contract. This view would impose no duty at all unless the state, like some arm's-length private transactor, has undertaken the obligation, has assumed the debt. The logical corollary is that if the state has not been paid, if there has been no consideration to support the state's activity for its citizens, then there is no obligation.

What does the state have to be paid in order to intervene in protecting a citizen from abuse? It is not as simple as taxes. What would a child have to introduce as currency by which care of the state would be made a right? This begins to resemble the argument advanced by Carl Wellman in "The growth of children's rights," where he maintains that children have no rights until they are grown enough to make the claim themselves.[20] Doesn't this mean that children don't have the price? Children and the poor make no considered bargains, and therefore they don't exist until they can buy and sell property. Before their emergence as property manipulators, there is no inducement, no exchange. The child's interests and the indigent's welfare become an incidental commodity to be purchased or not, an obligation for the government only if the right price is paid and the right laissez-faire subcontractors can be found to produce the thing purchased.

It is as if we lived in some supermarket state, a rich array of opportunities lining the shelves, the choices contingent only on the size of our budget. By this analogy, governmental goods and services all become fungible, equivalent. If there is no independent duty to provide welfare for our citizens, or if there is no community inspiration to provide it as a right, as a gift as some have characterized it, then the legislature becomes not the servant of the long-term public interest, but a slave to the buying public. Governmental actions become guided not by necessity but by trend. A municipal golf course, by such momentary consumerist vision, is as good a choice as child welfare (and certainly easier).

These bargained freedoms are perhaps nowhere better exemplified than in the words of President Bush's failed nominee for secretary of defence, John Tower. He promised, if you recall, to give up drinking if he got the job.[21] Not that he would give up drinking, period, or that he would give up drinking because it wrecked his homelife or because of public pressure, but that he would give it up *if.* Tit for tat. His sobriety was positioned as a commodity that we the public, through Congress, could purchase for the low, low price of our national defense. Like a used-car-salesman who will throw in air conditioning if you write the check Now, he dangled his sobriety like a bribe. The overexpended mental state we call "privacy" is destructive, not just as a concern about constitutional protections or civil liberties but also in the marketplace. It shifts emphasis from commerce among people for real things and becomes instead a system that transforms, in Francis Bacon's imagery, the idol of the marketplace into the idol of the theater.

Notes

1   David Lurie and Krzysztof Wodiczko, "Homeless vehicle project," *October* 47 (Winter 1988), p. 54.
2   "A homeless woman gives birth in subway," *New York Times*, March 22, 1989, p. B6.
3   Lloyd Cutler, "Pro-life? Then pay up," *New York Times*, July 7, 1989, p. A29.
4   Jay Mathews, "Earthquake swells ranks of homeless," *Washington Post*, October 27, 1989, p. A14.
5   424 U.S. 1 (1976). The Supreme Court states:

> While the independent expenditure ceiling thus fails to serve any substantial governmental interest in stemming the reality or appearance of corruption in the electoral process, it heavily burdens core First Amendment expression . . . Advocacy of the election or defeat of candidates for federal office is no less enticed to protection under the First Amendment than the discussion of policy generally or advocacy of the passage or defeat of legislation. (p. 39)
>
> It is argued, however, that the ancillary governmental interest in equalizing the relative ability of individuals and groups to influence the outcome of elections serves to justify the limitations on express advocacy of the election or defeat of candidates imposed by §602(e)(1)'s expenditure ceiling. But the concept that government may restrict the speech of some elements of our society in order to enhance the relative voice of others is wholly foreign to the First Amendment. (Ibid., pp. 47–9)

6   §71(a), *Restatement of the Law, Contracts (2d)* (St Paul: American Law Institute, 1982) provides: "To constitute consideration a performance or a return promise

must be bargained for." §79 further provides: "If the requirement of consideration is met, there is no additional requirement of (a) a gain, advantage, or benefit to the promisor or a loss, disadvantage, or detriment to the promisee, or (b) equivalence in the values exchanged; or (c) 'mutuality of obligation.'"

7   Robert Ellickson, "Cities and Homeowners' Associations," *University of Pennsylvania Law Review* 130 (1982), p. 1562. In encouraging consideration of a system of local elections in which voting power would be based on the "economic stake" in a community, Ellickson writes:

> Suppose that voting power in a suburb were to be reallocated from one-vote-per-resident to one-vote-per-acre. That reallocation would strengthen prodevelopment forces relative to antidevelopment forces because owners of undeveloped land would gain in political power. Assume more housing would be built. If exclusionary practices had previously pushed housing prices above competitive levels, housing prices would fall. It is possible that the gains low-income families would obtain from the drop in housing prices would outweigh other losses they would sustain from residing in a suburb that conferred voting power according to a formula that was facially disadvantageous to them. In other words, an apparently regressive voting system may have progressive distributional consequences.

8   See 131 *Congressional Record* S5727 (daily ed. May 9, 1985), statement of Jessica Lange.

9   Jean Baudrillard and Sylvère Lotringer, "Forget Baudrillard," in *Forget Foucault* (New York: Semiotext(e), 1987), p. 86.

10 John M. Brockman, "Bitburg deconstruction," *Philosophical Forum* 7 (1986), p. 160.

11 Marlise Simons, "Women in Brazil are now finding out sterilization may save their jobs," *New York Times*, December 7, 1988, p. A11.

12 See *U.A.W.* v. *Johnson Controls, Inc.*, 886 F.2d 871, 898–9 (7th Cir. 1989).

13 See, e.g., *Smith* v. *Superior Court*, 151 Ariz. 67, 725 P.2d 1101 (1986).

14 *State* v. *Brown*, 284 S.C. 411, 326 S.E.2d 410(1985).

15 See generally Winthrop Jordan, *White over Black* (Chapel Hill, NC: University of North Carolina Press, 1968), pp. 136–78 ("castration [for blacks] was dignified by specific legislative sanction as a lawful punishment in Antigua, the Carolinas, Bermuda, Virginia, Pennsylvania, and New Jersey," p. 154); John Dollard, *Caste and Class in a Southern Town* (Garden City, NY: Doubleday, 1957), pp. 134–72 (published originally in 1937, the author ominously and ambiguously reports that the mythology of exaggerated black potency is "further suspect because the same point seems to be coming up with respect to the Jews in Germany," p. 161).

16 See, e.g., "Judge suggests castration for convicted sex offender," *Los Angeles Daily Journal*, January 24, 1990, p. 26.

17 "Plan to sterilize women is debated," *New York Times*, September 25, 1988, p.35.

18 Sacvan Bercovitch, "Hawthorne's amorality of compromise," *Representations* 24 (1988), p. 21.

19 See *De Shaney* v. *Winnebago County Department of Social Services*, 109 S. Ct. 998, 1007 (1989); also Comment, "*De Shaney* v. *Winnebago County*: The Narrowing Scope of Constitutional Torts," *Maryland Law Review* 49 (1990), p. 463.

20 Carl Wellman, "The growth of children's rights," *Archiv fur Rechts und Sozialphilosophie* 70 (1984), p. 441.

21 "Tower takes vow he will not drink if he is confirmed," *New York Times*, February 27, 1989, p. A1.

Joanna Kadi, in this extract from her book *Think-ing Class*, argues for an appreciation of the art of the lower classes through the example of her own flamboyant Aunt Rose. If we took Kadi's approach seriously, we would have to reconsider our whole approach toward the arts, where fine arts such as symphonies and avant-garde paint-ing are highly valued whereas popular arts are devalued. Kadi suggests that the basis of this distinction is class snobbery.

Focus questions:
1 What does Aunt Rose do that makes Kadi con-sider her an artist?
2 What, according to Kadi, is the relation of art and activism?
3 What is the role of humor in Kadi's account?

16   Working-class Culture
not an oxymoron

Joanna Kadi

Clicking on the Keys

My Aunt Rose always had a whiskey within reach, smoked copiously, caked on the makeup, and wore so many bracelets she sounded like a rhythm section when she walked or, rather, teetered in her high heels. Her laugh could be heard three houses away. She refused to take off her sunglasses inside church, and fell asleep the moment the sermon began. Aunt Rose cooked and con-sumed huge amounts of Lebanese food, and loved to dance the debke.[1] A tal-ented pianist, she taught neighborhood children, played the organ at church every Sunday, and led our extended-family sing-alongs. I can still hear and see her clearly – long, painted fingernails clicking on the piano keys, whiskey and water within reach, raspy voice singing whatever song we clamored to hear. "Secondhand Rose" was always a big hit:

> Secondhand Rose
> I'm wearing secondhand clothes
> on Second Avenue
> Even Jake the plumber
> he's the man I adore
> had the noive to tell me
> he'd been married before . . .

Back then I didn't connect these activities to art or culture because I'd been indoctrinated with classist beliefs. My working-class family had no culture, no artistic gifts. Our Arabness made us a tad more interesting than our white neighbors, but even this "exotic" element couldn't outweigh class limitations and constraints. Like every other kid on the block, I knew that the general motors executive, in suit and tie, escorting his wife to the concert hall for an

153

evening of classical music was participating in a cultural event. The common-law heterosexual couple packing their kids, and the neighbors' kids, into a beat-up pick-up truck to attend a local square dance got sneers for being "such hillbillies,"[2] even if they didn't live anywhere near the hills.

What I learned simply mirrored dominant beliefs: rich people have culture, poor people don't. This is expressed in various ways, sometimes by advancing the idea of a split between arts and crafts, between high art and low art. Functional and accessible "crafts," no matter how beautiful, just can't compare with the expensive stuff safely locked away in a museum with a $10 admission charge.

The Working-class Person as an Artist

Social-change activists from the 1950s through the 1980s affected what's seen in museums, what's played on airwaves, and who's on stage. Today we reap the benefits of incredibly hard work done by people of color and/or women and/or working-class/poor people and/or queers[3] who organized and fought to open up the narrow parameters of public cultural expression.

These activists/artists met with tremendous resistance. Cultural arbiters with institutional power had no interest in hanging black women's quilts in museums or hearing Arab music in community orchestra halls. They dug in their heels, were polite and rude in turn, but kept saying no. Some activists continued to push on that front, while others opened galleries, held concerts, and planned exhibitions. As we established more community spaces, we also gained access to some museum walls and some prestigious stages.

Forced to include some of our art, curators and art "experts" had to figure out what to call it. They hadn't been faced with this before, since rich white men's art is just art. They came up with two categories – "traditional" and "ethnic." There are a couple of interesting points here. First, they held on to the power of classifying art/culture – they maintained hegemony over the power of naming. Second, their choice of "traditional" and "ethnic" merits examination.

These terms aren't total misrepresentations or totally inappropriate. "Traditional" captures the notion of an ongoing cultural activity that carries a long history. "Ethnic" clearly refers to artwork done by people of color, whether African, Native, Latino, or Asian (including Arab). In this race-conscious society, the term has the potential to interrupt the common and problematic practice of making people of color and our cultures invisible. But when used as the two definitive categories, "traditional" and "ethnic" skew reality. These categories appear to be mutually exclusive; they are not. Further, they position class outside the discussion's boundaries, keeping working-class and working-poor identities of particular artists hidden.

These categories allow the social silence around working-class/working-poor culture to continue. Art by poor white people is called traditional, a term often used to define quilts, carpentry, country-western music, and doll-making. Art by poor people of color (recent or long-term immigrants or Native Americans)[4] is described as ethnic art, whether located in fine-arts museums or natural-history museums. Everything from Hmong embroidery to Arab tile-making, from Yoruba music to Indonesian dance, falls into this category.

But the idea that valid, life-enhancing cultural expressions come from working-class people, whether "ethnic" or "American," still falls outside most people's conceptual framework. That idea can't fit into the narrow categories set up by self-appointed definers of culture, nor can it exist within elitist belief systems that insist poor people have no culture. Consequently, there's been little public interest to date in Joe Schmoe factory worker who has spent twenty years using watercolor paintings to document work on the line; he's not creating traditional art and can't be relegated to an ethnic group because he's white.

Cultural arbiters have decided they'll use our quilts, our music, and our embroidery only when defined and packaged according to their specifications. This leaves out huge numbers of artists like my Aunt Rose, whose cultural work couldn't be packaged or defined appropriately. Everything she did was too clearly and visibly working-class. Suppose someone showed interest in her ability to teach and lead the debke. They'd soon realize their mistake. Horrid presentation! Instead of a suitably modest, traditional Arab dress with intricate embroidery, or a suitably sexy belly-dancing outfit with cleavage showing, Aunt Rose wore lavish makeup, high heels, and short skirts, and backcombed her dyed, jet-black hair very high. Let's try something else. Hmm. Nix on the traditional category; she didn't embody the characteristics of the quiet, modest, working-class woman smiling sweetly while giving piano lessons to lovely little children. Instead, she dragged on cigarette after cigarette while she taught, and her incredibly long, brightly-painted fingernails tapped cheerily on the keys. (I didn't learn until later that "serious" piano players find this completely unacceptable.) Well, what about her ability to play from memory all the popular songs from the 1940s and 1950s, and to lead sing-alongs? Another no-go. According to restrictive definitions for ethnic art, a Lebanese woman singing "Secondhand Rose" with a full glass of whiskey and water beside her wasn't doing anything Arab. Especially with snow outside.

I believe present-day artists/activists must push past the static, false categories of traditional and ethnic, and broaden our definitions of art/culture. Class must inform our political work around culture; we need to become aware of how class integrates itself into cultural expression. Let's focus on artists' class identity and include art by working-class/working-poor people, of color and white. Shaping our work with this awareness will profoundly affect our political organizing, and allow us to create and follow guiding principles that more accurately reflect our identities and communities.

Art that Turns my Stomach

Do I think all working-class art is great? No. A lot of it falls into the "awful" category, along with so much middle-/upper-class art. By awful, I don't mean "ugly" or "unattractive." Ugly art can be emotionally disturbing, carry strong meaning and speak clearly about particular people and issues. That's not a problem. For me, awful art exhibits a lack of personal connection to its creator or its creator's community, means nothing to the artist, and may have been thrown together solely for cash or prestige (and I'm not criticizing the few working-class people who manage to make a living producing something rich people want to buy).

Class membership doesn't ensure awful art or good art. Class membership does ensure whose art, whose cultural expression, is valued and appreciated. Any talk about class and art necessarily entails talk about critics and criticism. Not surprisingly, the white, upper-middle-class sensibilities that have traditionally dominated the critics' world are unimpressed by and even hostile to working-class art and artists. Thus, awful art by upper-middle-class artists receives praise and legitimacy, while impressive art clearly exhibiting working-class form and content is passed over without comment, or has its many "flaws" scrupulously documented.

This is one reason social-change activists must involve ourselves in criticism, must respond to cultural work from a place of understanding class. Because I know about working-class/working-poor beliefs, values, and sensibilities regarding art and culture, I perceive more in our art than an upper- or middle-class critic who has no interest in moving outside the boundaries set by her profession. For example, I understand the importance we place on accessible arts and culture. I also know this ethic is completely at odds with the standards evoked by western art critics, and that working-class/working-poor people don't have the social and political power to implement this ethic anywhere except our own communities.

Those in power in our society have always asserted that art available to everyone isn't much good. According to capitalist ideology, rare, hard-to-find art— which is in part rare and hard-to find because of the art industry's organizing principles – is more valuable than common, easy-to-find art. Thus prices can be raised and profit margins pushed over the top. The making of rare, limited-edition prints (excuse me, but does anyone else find the term "limited edition" a bit pretentious for "not making any more copies"?) pays off again and again.

This makes sense within a capitalist framework, where profit is the key motivating factor. A whole set of meanings around particular items must be established and enacted. An industry of art dealers, art investors, and art "experts" backs up these ideas and puts them into practice.

The social construction of rarity[5] of is one of the operating principles behind institutionalized art standards. While capitalism didn't invent the idea of coveting rare art, it has developed and strengthened the concept to the point where the scrawl of a well-known artist on a small scrap of paper can bring in hundreds of thousands of dollars. Industry support seems to be equally or more important than talent in determining price.

While one segment of the market focuses on rare editions, another runs rampant with mass productions. Limitless, as opposed to limited, editions of paintings of flowers and cute white children are churned out day after day. Ceramic objects, glitzy wall decorations, and colored photographs of mountains can be had cheaply; this art for the masses is as carefully marketed and just as removed from the creative impulse as "rare" editions.[6] While mass-produced items bring in less profits, the quantity sold helps even the scales. Both segments of the market focus on profit. Neither is interested in the liberatory potential of art created by the people for the people.

Joining in Even When You Don't Want To

As I was driving home late one night from the queer country-western bar my lover and I frequent, an image of a ballet dancer popped into my head and I started thinking about the differences between two-stepping and ballet. A partnered dance done to country-western music, two-stepping involves taking two slow steps in time to the beat, followed by two quick steps. It's easy to learn (if hard to do well), and most people grasp the basics in one night. A dancer of average talent can teach others. Lessons are usually free or inexpensive.

My mind jumped from here to one of the earliest dances I learned – the debke.[7] After getting lessons from Aunt Rose, I watched, over the years, as she taught debke steps to new people who joined our extended-family gatherings. She insisted everyone dance – young or old, on crutches, shaky limbs, or healthy legs, it didn't matter. Time and again, Aunt Rose simply ignored protests based on age, ill health, or two left feet, and pulled people into the circle. While it takes time, skill, and commitment to do the debke well, usually people only need one lesson to reach a generalized skill level. One lesson from Aunt Rose offered that.

My aunt wanted everyone to participate because the debke can't be done alone, the party goes better if everyone's having fun, and dancing's more enjoyable than sitting on the sidelines. No money or special equipment was required, nor extra space; a church hall, a living room, a backyard sufficed. Aunt Rose praised all dancers, advanced and beginning. Differing skill levels didn't cause problems, because the activity's parameters are wide enough to incorporate differences. The ratio of women to men didn't matter, since it's a group dance without sex/gender divisions or heterosexual coupling.

Contrast this dance form with ballet. Outrageous admission prices,[8] highly gendered movement sequences, and the average person's inability to participate mark ballet as a middle- and upper-class art form. I don't want to trash ballet dancers, most of whom work very hard for little money and are themselves commodified; I want to analyze dance forms from different classes. For ballet, lots of money is needed for shoes, rental space, teachers' fees, and outfits. Costs for lessons are prohibitive, in part because it takes so long to learn. Few potential ballet dancers have an Aunt Rose available to teach basic skills in the living room. Instead, a specialized teacher must be found, and the more advanced the student, the more difficult the search.

Most people don't continue with ballet lessons because of difficulty and expense. Only the most determined will press on and "make it" in the highly competitive and stressful world of the middle- and upper-class art scene. Once lessons or expert-monitored rehearsals stop, ballet stops, since it's not a dance you can partake in sporadically.

In a sense, differences between debke and ballet generally capture differences between art/culture created and engaged in by rich people and poor people. Poor people are looking for group participation; rich people often chase performance and star status. Ballet dancers train for years in hopes of performing in high-priced venues; debke dancers and two-steppers are usually happy dancing once a week with friends.

The Artist as a Working-class Person

Exciting cultural work is emerging from marginalized communities, as we identify ourselves and each other, celebrate our cultures, discover our histories, resist oppression, struggle for liberation. One important aspect of our work is encouraging artistic and cultural expressions among group members. But how do we talk about class? Class differences mark significant splits among, for example, racial/ethnic groups. In and of themselves, these differences don't need to weaken or divide us. Weakening and division come when differences aren't acknowledged and taken seriously, when our own thinking about art and culture doesn't consider class.

Activists/artists have worked for years to create openings for art from marginalized communities. I'm intent on continuing this work, adding class awareness to organizing efforts, and bringing artists like Aunt Rose into the foreground. It's up to us to ensure community members don't get left behind, scorned, and belittled. The task of asking critical questions about art and culture, and insisting the class location of the artist matters, remains with those of us who started these discussions – cultural workers marginalized on the basis of our race, gender, sexuality, immigrant status, class, language. To do this, we need a strong and critical understanding of all aspects of our identities.

For example, within Arab-American communities there are a variety of types of artistic expression. Some of us, usually recent immigrants, create art that strongly reflects the land we just left. Others, whose families immigrated several generations ago, usually create art that is some conglomeration of aesthetics from the country in which we live, our class location, and our family's country of origin. This doesn't mean the art of the second group is less Arab-American – unless we make the mistake of setting up rigid categories of what qualifies as Arab within our own communities. In that case, artists like my Aunt Rose, whose creative outlets wove together reflections of life in a new country, her class experiences, and Lebanon, would be left out.

Giving Aunt Rose the Last Laugh

My Aunt Rose had a great sense of humor, a trait she shared with almost every working-class person I know. Humor holds an honored place as a long-lived form of working-class cultural expression that helps us survive and stay sane. It's a polished art form in our communities, and comes through not only in jokes but in music and storytelling. Both a critique of capitalism and a mild sense of self-deprecation run through our humor.

Aunt Rose told funny stories, about inept bosses complaining about her finger-nails tapping on typewriter keys, about piano students who didn't know the difference between the treble clef and the bass clef, about messing up a batch of grape leaves, about winning at poker and losing at bridge. After sharing these stories, she'd throw back her head and let loose with a raucous series of shrieks, slapping her thigh at the same time. Through all the crap she took as an Arab, a woman, a working-class person who labored as a secretary from the age of 15, she held that sense of humor close. In light of what I now know about class oppression, I connect her jokes to her art and perceive Aunt Rose as a working-class artist who let humor permeate her work, who never took herself too seri-ously, who added laughter to every sing-along and every debke lesson.

Aunt Rose died too young, reduced to skin and bones in a cold hospital room. Cancer, which continues to ravage working-class people of color, cut her down in her sixties. The disease attacked so quickly that I, living in another city, had no chance to say a real good-bye. When I reached her bedside, her mind was gone, and the stocky body that reflected our peasant roots in the same way mine does had wasted away to nothing.

We'd had our last real conversation several months earlier, after I'd been arrested for committing civil disobedience at a plant manufacturing parts for the cruise missile. Aunt Rose and I munched pretzels while curled up on her bright green and yellow couch, TV playing low in the background. I told her the whole story, hoping for an encouraging response; Aunt Rose didn't let me down.

"*They* arrested *you*!" she squawked. She threw back her head with the dyed black hair and let loose with those raucous shrieks. "They arrested you!" she repeated in the familiar tone that managed to mlx disgust for them and ap-proval for me. "Now that's a good one."

Notes

1 Traditional Arab folk dance.
2 Hillbillies, a term simply referring to people living in a hilly or backwoods region, has taken on an excessively negative meaning because of anti-rural and anti-work-ing-class oppression.
3 I use "and/or" to make it clear that people belong to one or more of these groups. Some people belong to all of these groups.
4 Non-Anglo "white" people, such as Sephardic Jews, also get put in this category.
5 Jan Binder coined the phrase and explained the idea of the social construction of rarity. She gave me a great deal of help in figuring out how to frame this essay, and this particular section. Jeff Nygaard provided further important ideas for this sec-tion. Thanks to him and Marjorie Huebner for their editing help.
6 I don't believe *all* high-priced paintings are uninspired but am trying to make sense of how they fit into the capitalist framework.

7   Interestingly, the debke and two-stepping have many things in common.
8   There is something hilarious about rich people paying upwards of $40 to watch from the sidelines while gay men throw too-skinny women in the air.

Questions about Class

1   What is a social class? Is social class an important concept for you in your own experience? How?
2   How does class relate to political power? Can political power be reduced to economic relations?
3   What new classes were generated at the beginning of capitalism? How has the class structure shifted since then?
4   Do you think it would be possible or desirable to live in a world without social classes, a world that was much more economically equal? What are some of the things we would gain in such a world? What are some of the things we would lose?
5   How would you describe your own class position? Can you easily categorize yourself as poor, middle class, or upper class, for example? Is that one of the most important things about you or is it relatively insignificant?
6   Describe the general attitudes of the rich and the middle classes toward the poor. Do you think these attitudes are accurate or fair? Why or why not?
7   What do you think should be done about poverty, if anything? Are welfare programs effective? What are some possible alternatives?
8   Think about how classes are depicted in the media. Often, working-class and poor people are romanticized, while rich people are ridiculed. Why do you think this is the case?
9   Do you have friends of different social classes? What difficulties do you think differences in social classes create for personal relationships?
10 How are the artistic achievements of working-class people different from those of the middle and upper classes? What are some of these achievements and how do they function within the culture as a whole?

Recommended Reading for Part Two

Breen, Richard (1995) *Class Stratification*, New York: Harvester Wheatsheaf (a multicultural perspective on class).

Coles, Robert (1967) *Children of Crisis*, Boston, Mass.: Little, Brown (a psychological and sociological study of poverty in the South).

Cottrell, Allin (1994) *Social Classes in Marxist Theory*, London: Routledge (a solid introduction to its subject).

Esping-Anderson, Gosta (1993) *Changing Classes*, London: Sage (an account of shifting class structures in postindustrial societies).

Gouldner, Alvin (1974) *The Future of Intellectuals and the Rise of the New Class*, New York: Seabury (a brilliant elaboration of and attack on Marxist theory).

Hacker, Andrew (1997) *Money: Who Has How Much and Why*, New York: Scribner (excellent, detailed treatment of the current American class structure).

Howell, Joseph (1973) *Hard Living on Clay Street*, New York: Anchor (portraits of blue-collar families in Washington, DC).

Lenin, V. I. (1987) *The Essential Works of Lenin*, New York: Dover (a collection of basic writings by the leader of the Russian revolution).

Marx, Karl and Engels, Friedrich (1978) *The Marx–Engels Reader*, ed. Robert Tucker, New York: Norton (a collection of basic writings).

Nozick, Robert (1974) *Anarchy, State and Utopia*, New York: Basic Books (features an attack on Rawls and a political theory that countenances much more inequality than does Rawls's).

Pakulski, Jan (1996) *The Death of Class*, London: Sage (describes the reasons why class analysis has become unfashionable).

Rawls, John (1971) *A Theory of Justice*, Cambridge, Mass.: Harvard University Press (a classic of political theory that discusses the best possible arrangement of economic inequalities).

Roemer, John (1982) *A General Theory of Exploitation and Class*, Cambridge, Mass.: Harvard (interesting in relation to the classical Marxist account).

Scott, John (1996) *Stratification and Power*, Cambridge, Mass.: Blackwell Publishers (relates class to wider issues of status and power).

Sennett, Richard and Cobb, Jonathan (1972) *The Hidden Injuries of Class*, New York: Vintage (a study of the social and psychological aspects of working-class America).

Sterne, Douglas (1957) *Work and Contemplation*, New York: Harper and Brothers (a discussion, from a Quaker point of view, of the aesthetics and spirituality of labor).

Terkel, Studs (1975) *Working*, New York: Avon (interviews with people about their jobs).

Weber, Max (1930) *The Protestant Ethic and the Spirit of Capitalism*, trans. Talcott Parsons, New York: Scribner (notable for its rejection of economic determinism).

Westgaard, John H. (1995) *Who Gets What?*, Cambridge, Mass.: Blackwell Publishers (an analysis of the hardening of inequality in the late twentieth century).

Wright, Erik Olin (1972) *Class Counts*, New York: Cambridge University Press (a sharp Marxist analysis).

PART THREE

GENDER

edited by Laurie Shrage

Gender: Introduction to the Readings

Patricia Williams relates the following incident:

> When I was living in California I had a student, S., who was very unhappy being a man and informed me of his intention to become a woman . . .
>
> After the sex-change operation, S. began to use the ladies' room. There was an enormous outcry from women students of all political persuasions, who "felt raped," in addition to the more academic assertions of some who "feared rape." In a complicated storm of homophobia, the men of the student body let it be known that they too "feared rape" and vowed to chase her out of any and all men's rooms . . .
>
> At the vortex of this torment, S. as human being who needed to go to the bathroom was lost.[1]

Can people change their sex or gender, or can they only pretend to? Is a male-to-female transsexual a woman or a man, or neither? As Williams's story shows, these questions are not merely academic but practical: we need to decide in some cases what bathroom someone like S. should use.

In our society today, some women and men are not only dressing and acting alike, they are also becoming one another. Indeed, the alleged problem of telling the boys from the girls has become intractable because the criteria of sex and gender assignment are now up for grabs. Can a girl have a penis (like RuPaul, or Dil in the movie *The Crying Game*)? Can a boy have breasts and a vagina, as well as long hair and a beard?

The existence of feminine men and masculine women is not new, yet there is a growing movement to gain acceptance for gender benders which is somewhat new. Should societies strive to be tolerant of people who change their sex, or who radically challenge the gender and body norms for their sex? The articles in this section will not resolve this question, but they begin to tease out the issues that can prepare us to address it constructively (i.e. without the barely controlled hysteria that often accompanies mainstream media discussion of this topic).

Philosophers writing on gender have examined a number of topics: are men more rational or better thinkers than women? Do women reason differently than men? Is philosophy as a discipline imaged as male in relation to other kinds of inquiry, and if so why? Do many philosophical accounts of reality, knowledge, beauty, or morality reflect male biases? How do bodies become gendered? What forms of injustice do people face because of their gender? Is our system of gender distinctions responsible for some kinds of inequality and injustice? What is the relationship between sex and gender? Is androgyny preferable to having the character traits of only one gender? Do minds, or only bodies, have gender properties? Should our legal system pay attention to gender differences? How do race and class distinctions complicate theories about women and men? Are gender distinctions and traits produced by culture or nature? The articles in this section cover some of these topics, including the relationship between sex and gender, whether it would be desirable to abolish gender distinctions, and male biases in philosophical accounts of art, reality, and the nature of philosophy itself.

GENDER

Patrick Hopkins's essay looks at how establishing one's manhood in American culture involves disassociating oneself from and denigrating girls and girlness. He argues that individuals who do not conform to established gender norms such as these threaten the general system of awarding male status. Gays, lesbians, bisexuals, cross-dressers, and feminists each challenge hegemonic ideals of masculinity and femininity and count as "gender traitors," according to Hopkins. Gender traitors are feared and hated in American society not merely because of the repressed "aberrant" desires of gender conformists, or because of the ignorance or political motives of heterosexuals, but because gender traitors challenge the male/female dichotomy that our norms of personhood require. Thus in order to address the social intolerance of gays, lesbians, and others, we need to question our acceptance of male/female dualism: the quasi-metaphysical idea that human beings can be sorted into two fundamentally different and recognizable sex-kinds.

Linda Nicholson's essay further explores the concept of "gender," as it has been deployed in the service of women's political struggles. Gender was initially used by feminist theorists to encompass alleged sex differences that are socially and culturally produced. Nicholson points out that this use of gender does not go far enough in challenging views that regard sex differences as biologically based, for it ultimately accepts that the sex categories we have in our culture are universal and part of nature. Yet this assumption is challenged by recent historical and ethnographic research, such as the work of Thomas Laqueur who claims that, in the pre-modern world, people saw differences between men and women as differences of degree, not kind. Also, anthropological research on some African and Native American societies shows that male and female social roles are not rigidly assigned on the basis of one's biological reproductive role or sexual body parts (i.e. genitals). Some anthropologists argue that a better way to make sense of Native American "berdache" practices is to attribute to these cultures non-binary concepts of gender that can comfortably make room for more than two genders.[2]

Nicholson examines how the weaker form of biological determinism in regard to sex (which she calls "biological foundationalism") is employed in the writings of radical and "difference" feminists – feminists who accept that women are fundamentally different from men but who place positive value on female qualities and abilities. She argues that biological foundationalism leads to feminist theories that treat women *in terms of their experience as women* as all alike. Such theories cannot account for differences between women from different historical periods or cultural backgrounds that are due not merely to differences of race, class, and so on, but also to different ways gender is patterned in different social contexts. In other words, gender, as a variable of social analysis, is not as easily separable or abstracted from race, class, and other social markers as feminists had earlier assumed. Rather, women's experiences *as women* are shaped by other social forces. Even within a single society women experience female socialization differently depending on their social location in terms of class, ethnicity, religion, physical ability, sexuality, and family idiosyncrasies, such as parents who raise their daughters as sons.

What this means for feminist theorizing, according to Nicholson, is that feminists can no longer fashion theories about women's lives across large distances of culture or history without attending carefully to where their generalizations break down. Moreover, since the category "woman" is not stable across history and cultures, the subjects of feminist investigation will vary in different contexts. Should feminists include, for example, Zuni berdache or contemporary transsexuals among the victims of patriarchy? Nicholson points out that the choices feminist theorists make in this regard are political choices, they are not matters that can be arbitrated by some neutral act of description.

Nicholson challenges feminists to acknowledge the political character of controlling the borders of gender categories. To contribute to this new way of thinking about gender, she proposes that "woman" be analyzed not as a category with necessary and sufficient conditions for membership, but as an idea that must be cashed out in terms of Wittgenstein's family resemblance model. On this model, the criteria for membership can vary in different contexts, but the shifting criteria contain similarities that constitute a "family" of related criteria. By treating "woman" as a category without rigid boundaries, Nicholson's proposal supports a feminist politics that is both more inclusive and more attentive to differences between women.

The next two essays have a different focus than the first two. As members of a "post-feminist" generation, we tend to think of gender as a characteristic of human beings. But prior to feminist theorists' use of gender as a basic tool of social analysis, gender was primarily thought of as a linguistic category or as a property of words. Gender or sex descriptors are often applied metaphorically to other things, such as electrical connectors and computer cables, or nature as a whole. The third and fourth readings in this section consider how gender metaphors enter into philosophical arguments and conceptions of philosophy as an enterprise.

Susan Shapiro's essay examines the gender metaphors employed by the philosopher Maimonides and also by earlier Greek philosophers. In opposing philosophy to rhetoric and depicting rhetoric as a dissembling female, philosophy emerges as male truth in Plato's works. Maimonides uses gender images to analyze the relationship between the mind and body, form and matter, and god and humans. The second term in each of these relationships is figured as a promiscuous wife that requires a controlling, forceful, and sometimes violent, husband to achieve a more perfect union. Such metaphors, according to Shapiro, serve to naturalize actual social arrangements between husbands and wives in which husbands brutalize wives into submission. Also, these metaphors can be used to bolster arguments about how a land such as Israel should be governed by monotheistic laws. Shapiro shows that these metaphors are not merely accidental or incidental to the views they support but are integral to the constitution of philosophy as a distinct kind of activity and to particular metaphysical theories.

Christine Battersby contributes to the feminist project of unveiling the male perspectives and biases that underlie much respected philosophical work. Her essay shows not only that the writings of Immanuel Kant reflect the prejudices against women common in his time, but that Kant imaginatively used and reinvigorated these prejudices to develop his philosophical views. Focusing on Kant's writings on aesthetics and ethics, Battersby examines how Kant's category of the sublime involves appropriating for men the culturally valued traits and capacities of reason, autonomy, activity, courage, transcendence, and power, and then relegating to women the culturally devalued capacities of taste, emotion, passivity, and fragility. Since sound aesthetic and moral judgments require the male capacities, few women on Kant's view are capable of forming them. In short, Battersby shows how, on Kant's view, philosophy is not just metaphorically male but is an activity suitable only for males.

Battersby ends by considering parts of Kant's writings about the sublime in nature where nature is imaged as female, and considers the influence this may have had on later writers of the romantic period who held a more uplifting view of femininity. Battersby questions whether it is the primary job of feminist or women philosophers to expose misogyny at the root of philosophical theorizing or whether feminist philosophers can reinvent philosophy from the perspectives of women.

Notes

1   Patricia Williams, *The Alchemy of Race and Rights*, Cambridge, Mass.: Harvard University Press, 1991, pp. 122–3.
2   See Will Roscoe, "How to become a berdache: toward a unified analysis of gender diversity," in *Third Sex, Third Gender*, New York: Zone Books, 1996.

Patrick Hopkins considers how the norms of gender identity in contemporary American society produce an intolerance for same-sex eroticism. He suggests that reducing homophobia may require challenging the idea that bodies have a gender or sex.

Focus questions:
1 What is "gender treachery," according to Hopkins?
2 How does same-sex eroticism threaten our dominant cultural definitions of masculinity and ultimately our conceptions of personhood, according to Hopkins?
3 How would the elimination of gender distinctions transform our society's preference for heterosexuality?

---

17   Gender Treachery: Homophobia, Masculinity, and Threatened Identities

---

Patrick D. Hopkins

One of my first critical insights into the pervasive structure of sex and gender categories occurred to me during my senior year of high school. The seating arrangement in my American Government class was typical – the "brains" up front and at the edge, the "jocks" at the back and in the center. Every day before and after class, the male jocks bandied insults back and forth. Typically, this "good-natured" fun included name-calling. Name-calling, like most pop-cultural phenomena, circulates in fads, with various names waxing and waning in popularity. During the time I was taking this class, the most popular insult/name was used over and over again, *ad nauseam*. What was the insult?

It was simply, "girl."

Suggestively, "girl" was the insult of choice among the male jocks. If a male student was annoying, they called him "girl." If he made a mistake during some athletic event, he was called "girl." Sometimes "girl" was used to challenge boys to do their masculine best ("don't let us down, girl"). Eventually, after its explicitly derogatory use, "girl" came to be used among the male jocks as merely a term of greeting ("hey, girl").

But the blatantly sexist use of the word "girl" as an insult was not the only thing that struck me as interesting in this case. There was something different about this school, which in retrospect leads to my insight. My high school was a conservative Christian institution; no profanity (of a defined type) was allowed. Using "bad" words was considered sinful, was against the rules, and was formally punished. There was, therefore, a regulated lack of access to the more commonly used insults available in secular schools. "Faggot," "queer," "homo," or "cocksucker" were not available for use unless one was willing to risk being overheard by school staff, and thus risk being punished. However, it is important to note that, for the most part, these words were not restricted because of any sense of hurtfulness to a particular group or because they expressed prejudice. They were restricted merely because they were "dirty" words, "filthy" words, gutter-language words, like "shit" or "asshole." "Girl" was not a dirty word, and so presented no risk. It was used flagrantly in the presence of staff members, and even used by staff members themselves.[1]

In a curious twist, the very restriction of discursive access to these more common profanities (in the name of morality and decency) reveals a deeper structure of all these significations. "Girl," as an allowable, non-profane substitute for "faggot," "homo," and "cocksucker," mirrors and thus reveals a common essence of these insults. It signifies "not-male," and as related to the male speaker, "not-me."

"Girl," like these other terms, signifies a failure of masculinity, a failure of living up to a gendered standard of behavior, and a gendered standard of identity. Whether it was the case that a "failure of masculinity" actually occurred (as in fumbling the football) or whether it was only the "good-natured" intimation that it would occur (challenging future masculine functioning), the use of such terms demonstrates that to levy a successful insult, it was enough for these young men to claim that their target was insufficiently male; he was inadequately masculine, inadequately gendered.[2]

This story can, of course, be subjected to countless analyses, countless interpretations. For my purposes here, however, I want to present this story as an illustration of how important gender is to the concept of one's self. For these young males, being a man was not merely another contingent feature of their personhood. They did not conceive of themselves as people who were also male. They were, or wanted to be, *Men*. "Person" could only be a less descriptive, more generic way of talking about humans in the abstract. But there are no abstract humans; there are no "persons," rigorously speaking. There are only men and women. Or so we believe.

In what follows, I use this insight into gendered identity to make a preliminary exploration of the relationships between masculinity and homophobia. I find that one way to read homophobia and heterosexism in men is in terms of homosexuality's threat to masculinity, which in light of the connection between gender and personal identity translates into a threat to what constitutes a man's sense of self. A genuine challenge to homophobia, therefore, will not result from or result in merely increased social tolerance, but will be situated in a fundamental challenge to traditional concepts of masculinity itself.

What it Means to be (a) Gendered Me

Categories of gender, in different ways, produce a multiplicity of other categories in a society. They affect – if not determine – labor, reproduction-associated responsibilities, childrearing roles, distributions of political power, economic status, sexual practices, uses of language, application of certain cognitive skills, possession of personality traits, spirituality and religious beliefs, and more. In fact, all members of a given society have their material and psychological statuses heavily determined by their identification as a particular gender. However, not only individuals' physical, economic, and sexual situations are determined by gender categories, but also their own sense of personal identity – their personhood. I use "personhood" here as a metaphor for describing individuals' beliefs about how they fit into a society, how they fit into a world, who and what they think they *are*.[3] Personhood is critically linked (or perhaps worse, uncritically linked) to the influence of the gender categories under which an individual develops.

Individuals' sense of personhood, their sense-of-self, is largely a result of their construction as members of particular social groups within society-at-large: religions, ethnicities, regional affinities, cultural heritages, classes, races, political parties, family lineages, etc. Some of the most pervasive, powerful, and hidden of these identity-constructing "groups" are the genders; pervasive because no individual escapes being gendered, powerful because so much else depends on gender, and hidden because gender is uncritically presented as a natural, biological given, about which much can be discovered but little can (or should) be altered. In most cultures, though not all, sex/gender identity, and thus much of personal identity, is regulated by a binary system – man and woman.[4] The socially meaningful categories of "men" and "women" are immediately extrapolated and constructed from the material of newborn human bodies – a culturally varied process that legitimates itself as purely "natural", even in all its variation.[5] To a very large extent, what it means to be a member of society, and thus what it means to be a person, *is* what it means to be a girl or boy, a man or woman. There is no such thing as a sexually or gender undifferentiated person.[6]

Identity is fundamentally relational. What it means to have a particular identity depends on what it means not to have some other identity, and by the kinds of relationships one has to other possible and actual identities. To have personhood, sense-of-self, regulated by a binary sex/gender system means that the one identity must be different from the other identity; a situation requiring that there be identifiable, performative, behavioral, and psychological characteristics that allow for clear differentiation. Binary identities demand criteria for differentiation.

For a "man" to qualify as a man, he must possess a certain (or worse, uncertain) number of demonstrable characteristics that make it clear that he is not a woman, and a woman must possess characteristics demonstrating she is not a man. These characteristics are, of course, culturally relative, and even intraculturally dynamic, but in late twentieth-century US culture the cluster of behaviors and qualities that situate men in relation to women include the by now well-known litany: (hetero)sexual prowess, sexual conquest of women, heading a nuclear family, siring children, physical and material competition with other men, independence, behavioral autonomy, rationality, strict emotional control, aggressiveness, obsession with success and status, a certain way of walking, a certain way of talking, having buddies rather than intimate friends, etc.[7]

Because personal identity (and all its concomitant social, political, religious, psychological, biological, and economic relations) is so heavily gendered, any threat to sex/gender categories is derivatively (though primarily non-consciously) interpreted as a threat to personal identity – a threat to what it means to *be* and especially what it means to *be me*. A threat to manhood (masculinity) is a threat to personhood (personal identity). Not surprisingly then, a threat to established gender categories, like most other serious threats, is often met with grave resistance, for challenging the regulatory operations of a gender system means to destabilize fundamental social, political, and personal categories (a profoundly anxiety-producing state), and society is always prejudiced toward the protection of established categories. Inertia is a force in culture as well as in physics.

There are many different threats to gendered identity, but I think they can all be generally grouped together under the rubric of "gender treachery."[8] A gender traitor can be thought of as anyone who violates the "rules" of gender identity/gender performance, i.e. someone who rejects or appears to reject the criteria by which the genders are differentiated.[9] At its most obvious, gender treachery occurs as homosexuality, bisexuality, cross-dressing, and feminist activism. Any of these traitorous activities may result in a serious reaction from those individuals and groups whose concept of personal and political identity is most deeply and thoroughly sexed by traditional binary categories.[10] However, homosexuality is particularly effective in producing the extreme (though not uncommon) reaction of homophobia – a response that is often manifested in acts of physical, economic, and verbal assault against perceived gender traitors, queers.[11] Homosexuals, intentionally or not, directly challenge assumptions concerning the relational aspects of the binary categories of sex/gender, and as such threaten individual identities. Since the homophobic reaction can be lethal and so theoretically suggestive, it deserves serious attention.

Homophobia/Heterosexism

Theorists debate the value of using the term "homophobia." For some, the "phobia" suffix codes anti-gay and anti-lesbian activity as appertaining to psychiatric discourse – the realm of irrationality, uncontrollable fear, a realm where moral responsibility or political critique seems inapplicable due to the clinical nature of the phobia.[12] We do not punish people for being claustrophobic; we do not accuse agoraphobics of ignorance or intolerance; why should we treat homophobics any differently?

Other terms have been used to describe the aggregation of prejudices against gays and lesbians, including homoerotophobia, homosexism, homonegativism, anti-homosexualism, anti-homosexuality, and homohatred.[13] "Heterosexism" has become the terminology of choice for some theorists, emphasizing similarities to racism and sexism. "Heterosexism" characterizes a political situation in which heterosexuality is presented and perceived as natural, moral, practical, and superior to any non-heterosexual option. As such, heterosexuals are *justly* accorded the privileges granted them – political power, sexual freedom, religious sanction, moral status, cultural validation, psychiatric and juridical non-interference, occupational and tax privilege, freedom to have or adopt children and raise families, civil rights protection, recourse against unfair hiring practices, public representation in media and entertainment industries, etc.

For many of us, however, "heterosexism," though accurate and useful, does not possess the rhetorical and emotional impact that "homophobia" does. "Heterosexism" is appropriate for describing why all television couples are straight, why marriage and joint tax returns are reserved for heterosexuals, why openly lesbian or gay candidates face inordinate difficulty in being elected to office, or why only heterosexuals can adopt children or be foster parents. But "heterosexism," though perhaps still technically accurate, does not seem strong enough to describe the scene of ten Texas teenage boys beating a gay man with nail-studded boards and stabbing him to death.[14] The blood pooling up on the ground beneath that dying body is evidence for something more than the protection of heterosexual privilege. It is evidence for a radical kind of evil.

It is neither my goal nor my desire here to set out specific definitions of homophobia. Though I will use the term primarily with reference to physical violence and strong verbal, economic, and juridical abuse against gays, I do not claim to establish a clear boundary between homophobia and heterosexism. No stable boundary could be set, nor would it be particularly useful to try to do so – they are not discrete. "Homophobia" and "heterosexism" are political words, political tools; they are ours to use as specific situations present specific needs.

However, for my purposes here, heterosexism – loosely characterized as valorizing and privileging heterosexuality (morally, economically, religiously, politically) – can be seen as the necessary precursor to homophobia. Heterosexism is the backdrop of the binary division into heterosexual and homosexual (parasitic on the man/woman binary), with, as usual, the first term of the binary good and second term bad. Heterosexism constructs the field of concepts and behaviors so that some heterosexists' hierarchical view of this binary will be reactionary, for a variety of reasons, thus becoming homophobic (read: violent/abusive/coercive). In the same way that a person doesn't have to be a member of a white supremacist organization to be racist, a person doesn't have to be homophobic to be heterosexist. This is not to say that heterosexism is not as bad as homophobia, but rather that though heterosexism presents less of an obvious, direct, personal physical threat to gays, it nonetheless situates the political arena such that homophobia can and is bound to exist. Heterosexism is culpable for the production of homophobia. Heterosexists are politically culpable for the production of homophobics.

But even when we choose to use the term "homophobia" for cases of brutality, fanatic claims, petitions for fascistic laws, or arbitrarily firing gay employees, this does not mean that we must always characterize homophobia as an irrational, psychiatric/clinical response. Such a characterization would be grossly inadequate. "Homophobia" has evolved as primarily a political term, not as a psychiatric one, and does not parallel claustrophobia or agoraphobia, for the political field is not the same.

Religious and political rhetorics of moral turpitude and moral danger do not attach to closed-in spaces or wide-open spaces in the way they attach to same-sex eroticism. In other words, the fear and abhorrence of homosexuals is often taught as a moral and practical virtue and political oppression is massed against gays and lesbians. As a result, oppositional strategies to homophobia must be located in political discourse, not just psychiatric or pop-psychiatric discourse. Homophobia is supported and subsidized by cultural and governmental institutions in ways that demand the need for a variety of analyses. Though homophobia may often seem irrational or semi-psychotic in appearance, it must not be dismissed as simply an obsessive individual psychological aberration. Homophobia is a product of institutional heterosexism and gendered identity.

How do people explain homophobia? And especially, though not exclusively, how do people in queer communities explain homophobia? Being the victims of it, what do they see in it? Why is it that some men react so strongly and so virulently to the mere presence of gay men?

The repression hypothesis

One of the most common explanations of homophobia among gay men is that of repressed homosexuality. Men who constantly make anti-gay slurs, tell anti-gay jokes, use anti-gay language, obsess about the dire political and moral impact of homosexuality on the family and country, or even who are known to attack gays physically are often thought to be repressing their own sexual attraction toward men. As a result of their terror in coming to grips with their own sexuality, they overcompensate, metastasizing into toxic, hypermasculine, ul-

PATRICK D. HOPKINS

tra-butch homophobes who seem to spend far more time worrying about homosexuality than openly gay men do.

This kind of repressed-homosexual explanation was aptly demonstrated by one of my straight undergraduate ethics professors. While teaching a section on sexual ethics, my professor and the entire class read a series in the college newspaper by our Young Republican student editor about how "the homosexuals" were taking over the country and converting all the children. Finally, after yet another repetition of the "but they can't have babies and they're unnatural" columns, my exasperated professor wrote a response to the paper, and after a lengthy list of counterarguments, ended by saying simply, "Methinks thou doth protest too much."

His intimation was clear. He believed that the Young Republican's arguments were more for his benefit than for his readers'. As the typical response goes among gays who hear men constantly ranting about the perils of homosexuality and the virtues of heterosexuality – "He's not trying to convince us. He's trying to convince himself."

I think for many men this theory of repression is accurate. It is not unusual for openly gay men to talk about their days in the closet and report that they were assertively heterosexist/homophobic – and that yes, they were desperately trying to convince themselves that they were really heterosexual. Sadly enough, many of these repressed homosexuals manage to maintain their repression at great cost to themselves and often at great cost to others. Some marry and live a lie, unfulfilled emotionally and sexually, deceiving their wives and children, sometimes having furtive, sexual affairs with other men. They manage psychologically to compartmentalize their erotic orientation and same-sex sexual experiences so radically that they live two separate, torturous lives. Some repressives become anti-gay activists and spend their lives trying to force gays and lesbians back into the closet, working against gay civil rights and protections.[15] Horrifyingly, some others undergo an even worse schism in their personalities, resulting in a bizarre, malignant, and persistent internalized war between homophobia and homophilia. This war can culminate in what John Money calls the exorcist syndrome, in which the repressive picks up, seduces, or even rapes a gay man, and then beats him or kills him in order to exorcise the repressive's "homosexual guilt."[16]

But while the repressive hypothesis is certainly accurate for some men, it is not accurate for all. I have no doubt that there are indubitably heterosexual men who hate and assault gays. To some extent, the explanation of repressed homosexuality may be wish fulfillment on the part of some gays. Forced by necessity of survival to be secretive and cryptic themselves, many gay men find it eminently reasonable to suspect any man of potential homosexual desire, and in fact, want such to be the case. It is reasonable, if optimistic, to hope that there are really more of you than there seem to be. And in light of the fact that many openly gay men report that they used to be homophobic themselves, the repression theory seems to be both empirically sound as well as emotionally attractive. There is also a certain sense of self-empowerment resulting from the repression hypothesis – out gays may see themselves as morally, cognitively, and emotionally superior to the men who continue to repress their sexuality. But homophobia is not so simple. What about those homophobes who clearly are not repressing their own homosexuality? What explanation fits them?

The irrationality/ignorance hypothesis

Another explanation, one in perfect keeping with the roots of the word, is that homophobia is an irrational fear, based in ignorance and resulting from social training.[17] This explanation is also popular among liberal heterosexuals as well as liberal lesbians and gays. The stereotype of this kind of cultural/developmental homophobia is that of a little boy who grows up in a poorly educated, very conservative family, often in a rural area, who hears his parents and other relatives talk about the fags on TV or the homo child molester they caught in the next county and how he ought to be "strung up and shot." As the little boy grows, he models his parents' behavior, identifying with their emotions and desiring to emulate them. Although the boy has no idea of what a "fag" or "homo" is, he nevertheless learns the appropriate cues for application of those terms to situations and individuals, and the emotions associated with that application. He begins to use them himself, often as a general-use insult (like young children calling each other "nigger" even when they do not know what it means). He learns that certain kinds of behaviors elicit being called a fag and that he can achieve a degree of peer approval when he uses those terms. So he stands on the playground at recess and calls the boy who takes piano lessons a homo; his friends laugh. He asks the girls who are jumping rope with another boy why they are playing with a faggot; his friends laugh. Simultaneously, of course, the boy is learning all the other dictums of traditional hetero-masculinity – girls are weak, boys are strong, girls play stupid games, boys play real games, girls that want to play football are weird, boys that do not want to play football are faggots. Eventually the boy learns the more complete definition of "faggot," "homo," "queer." Homos aren't just sissies who act like girls; they aren't just weak. They like to "do things" with other boys. Sick things. Perverted things.

A little knowledge is a very dangerous thing and the boy becomes a full-fledged homophobe who thinks boys who play the piano and do not like football want to touch him "down there." He learns that grown-up homos like to grab young boys and "do bad things to them." He learns that just as one can become a tougher, stronger, more masculine man by killing deer and by "slaughtering" the guys on the opposing football team, one can become more masculine, or prove one's masculinity, by verbally abusing or beating up queers.

Though this scenario may seem hyperbolic, it certainly does occur. I have seen it happen myself. The lesson that gets learned is that of the recurring conflict of essence and performance.

Essence: You (the little boy) have a natural, core, normal, good, essential identity; you are a *boy*, a *young man*, male, not-a-girl. This is just what you are. You were born this way. Little girls will like you. You have buddies. You're lucky. You are our son. It's natural and obvious that you will grow up and get married and be a *daddy*.

Performance: But even though you just *are* a little *boy*, even though it's perfectly natural, you must make sure you do not act (how? why?) like a girl. You must always make sure that you exhibit the right behavior for a boy (but isn't it natural?). Don't ever act like not-a-boy! Don't betray that which you are naturally, comfortably, normally. Don't not-be what you are. Perform like a man.

The stage is set. The child knows that he is a he and that being a he is a good, normal, natural thing. Being a he requires no effort. You just are a boy. But at the same time, there is lingering on the horizon the possibility, amorphous and not always spoken, that you might do something which violates what you are. It might be quiet – "Now put those down, son. Boys don't play with dolls." It might be loud – "What the hell are you doing playing with dolls like some sissy??!!" The little boy internalizes the expectations of masculinity.

This kind of explanation of homophobia, though useful and accurate for many purposes, tends to characterize homophobia as learned but completely irrational, unfounded, arbitrary, ignorant, counter-productive, and dysfunctional. However, such a simple analysis excludes much of the experience of the homophobe. It is not actually the case that the poor mindless homophobe simply veers through life distorting reality and obsessing over nothing, frothing at the mouth and seeing faggots behind every corner and homosexual conspiracies in every liberal platform, ruining his own life as well as others, In fact, homophobia is not dysfunctional in the way that agoraphobia is. Homophobia has functional characteristics.[18]

For example, in the story given above, the boy does not simply "catch" the obsessive, dysfunctional view of the world that his parents have. He learns that certain kinds of behaviors elicit rewarding emotions not only from his parents directly, but also from within himself when away from his parents. When the little boy plays with toy soldiers and pretends to slaughter communists or Indians, his parents smile, encourage him, and even play with him sometimes. If he plays house with his little sister, he is always the daddy and she is always the mommy and he pretends to get home from work and she pretends to have supper fixed for him – a game in which roles are correctly modeled and are thus emotionally rewarding – "I'm just like my daddy."

However, the emotional (and sometimes corporal) punishments function the same way. If the boy is caught playing with dolls, or pretending to be the mommy, he may be told that he is doing something wrong, or be punished, or may simply detect a sense of worry, disapproval, or distaste from his parents. Homophobic tendencies will be carried along with all the other traits of conservative masculinity. He will be "just like his daddy" when he calls some effeminate boy a sissy – an emotionally rewarding experience. He will receive approval from his peers when he pushes the class homo around – he will be tough and formidable in their eyes. And perhaps most importantly, he will be clearly and unambiguously performing the masculine role he perceives (correctly in context) to be so valued – an advantage in power, safety, admiration, and self-esteem. It is also in no small sense that homophobia can be functional in keeping other heterosexuals in line. The potential to accuse another boy of being a faggot, to threaten ostracism or physical assault, is a significant power.[19]

Thus, it is not the case that homophobia is somehow obviously dysfunctional on an individual or group level.[20] Homophobic activity carries with it certain rewards and a certain power to influence. In the case of the repressed homosexual, it externalizes the intra-psychic conflict and reaffirms a man's appearance of heterosexuality and thus his sense of stability, safety, and self. In the case of childhood modeling, homophobic activity wins approval from peers and authority figures, protects one from becoming the target of other homophobes, and reaffirms one's place in a larger context of gender appropriate behavior – protecting one's personal identity.

The political response hypothesis

The recognition that there are rational, functional aspects of homophobia (in a heteropatriarchal context) leads to a third explanation of homophobia that reverses the second. This theory says that queers are a genuine political threat to heterosexuals and really do intend to eliminate heterosexual privilege. Homophobia, therefore, is a rational political response.[21] Radical feminist lesbians and certain radical gay men directly challenge the hetero-male-dominated structure of society, rejecting patriarchal rule, conventional morality, and patriarchal modes of power distribution. All of the primary institutional sites of power that have maintained patriarchal domination – the state, the church, the family, the medical profession, the corporation – are being challenged from without by queers who do not want merely to be accepted, or tolerated, or left alone, but who want to dismantle heteropatriarchal society and build something different in its place. In response to liberal heterosexuals who promote the irrationalist theory of homophobia, supporters of this theory might say that many of the so-called "ignorant" and "false" stereotypes of queers are in fact correct, but they are not bad stereotypes; they are good and should be praised, should be revered, should replace heterosexual values. Yes lesbians do hate men. Yes, fags do want to destroy the nuclear family. Yes, dykes do want to convert children. Yes, homos are promiscuous.

The impetus for this theory of homophobia comes from lesbians and gays who view their sexuality as primarily a political identity, having chosen to reject heterosexuality and become lesbian or gay as a political act of resistance. They have chosen this identification because they want to fight, destroy, or separate from hetero-male-dominated society. According to this theory, homophobia is a perfectly rational, reasonable reaction to the presence of queers, because queers pose a genuine threat to the status of heterosexual privilege. It is only logical that heterosexuals would fight back, because if they do not fight back, their privilege, their power, and their dominance will be stripped away all the sooner.

There are people who seem, at least partially, to confirm this theory. It has been interesting to see that over the past ten years or so, it has become common for neo-conservative activist organizations to use the word "family" in their names. Among many gay, lesbian, and feminists activists, any organization with "Family" as part of its name is automatically suspected to be anti-gay, anti-lesbian, anti-feminist.[22] The frequency of the word "family" as an identification tag is seen as signifying a belief in the moral superiority of the traditional, heterosexual, nuclear family. This suggests that some "pro-family" activists trace and justify their anti-homosexual activism to the belief that lesbians and gays are threatening to destroy The Family and thus to destroy heterosexual morality.

It is also true that over the past twenty years or so, lesbian and gay thought has become radicalized in a variety of ways. Lesbians and gays have moved away from merely the hope of demedicalization and decriminalization to the hope of building cultures, ethics, practices, and politics of their own, hopes that include the destruction of heterosexist, or even heterosexual, society. There are some radical, separatist lesbians and separatist gays who view most human behavior in terms of rational, political aims, and for them homophobia is a predictable political response to their own oppositional politics. Nineteen ninety-two Republican presidential candidate Pat Buchanan was not simply being hyperbolic when he gravely predicted that the 1990s would be the decade of the radical homosexual. One of his campaign ads, featuring a film clip of near-nude, dancing, gay leathermen, formed the background for an attack on the grant policies of the National Endowment for the Arts. Such ads demonstrate that his homophobia is partially directed against queer-specific political and sexual challenges to his conservative Christian morality.

However, the political response hypothesis, like the others, accounts only for some homophobes, and I think, relatively few. This hypothesis suffers from too great a dose of modernist political rationalism. Like many traditional models of political activity, it overrationalizes the subjects involved. It assumes that members of the oppressor class interpret the world in political terms similar to that of members of an oppositional movement. Thus, the characterization of a homophobe is that of a rational individual with immoral goals who recognizes that the particular oppositional group of gays and lesbians is a genuine political threat to his or her power and privilege, and as such must take an active stand against that insurgent group. One of the best tactics for resisting the insurgents is terror – on individual levels with violence on institutional levels with oppressive laws, and on sociocultural levels with boogeyfag propaganda.[23]

While this model has merit and may be partially accurate in accounting for some homophobia, it endows homophobes (and homosexuals) with a hyperrationality that does not seem to be in evidence. Most homophobes, even those who openly admit their involvement in physical and verbal attacks on gays and lesbians, do not consider their activity to be political. Most of them, in fact, do not perceive any obvious threat from the people they attack. Gary Comstock claims that perpetrators of anti-queer violence typically list the "recreational, adventuresome aspect of pursuing, preying upon, and scaring lesbians and gay men" as the first and foremost reason for their behavior. Only secondarily and less often do they list things like the "wrongness of homosexuality" as a reason for their activity. But even this "wrongness" is not listed as an explanation or political justification for their behavior as much as a background assumption that functions as cultural permission.[24]

A recent television news program interviewed a perpetrator of anti-gay violence and, like Comstock's interviewee, he had little or no explanation for why
he was doing what he was doing except that it was fun. When asked how he
could have fun hurting people, he said that he had never really thought of
queers as real people. I think this suggests that interpreting all, or even most,
homophobic violence as conscious political activity ignores that much of the
"reasoning" behind homophobia, when there is any active reasoning at all,
relies on a very abstract and loosely integrated background of heterosexist assumptions. Many homophobes view gays and lesbians as politically, morally,
and economically insignificant. For those who have never had any personal interaction (positive or negative) with openly gay or lesbian folk, lesbian/gay
people may be such an abstract other that they do not enter into one's political
and moral consideration any more than people who kick dogs for fun consider
the political and moral significance of dogs, except perhaps in terms of legal
consequences.

Performing Gender and Gender Treachery

All three explanations of homophobia have one thing in common. They reside
on a field of unequal, binary, sexual and gender differentiation. Behind all homophobia, regardless of its development, expression, or motivation, is the background of heterosexism. Behind all heterosexism is the background of gendered
identities.

The gender category of men constructs its members around at least two conflicting characterizations of the essence of manhood. First, your masculinity
(being-a-man) is natural and healthy and innate. But second, you must stay
masculine – do not ever let your masculinity falter. So, although being a man is
seen as a natural and automatic state of affairs for a certain anatomical makeup,
masculinity is so valued, so valorized, so prized, and its loss such a terrible
thing, that one must always guard against losing it. Paradoxically, then, the
"naturalness" of being a man, of being masculine, is constantly guarding against
the danger of losing itself. Unaware, the "naturalness," the "rightness," of masculinity exposes its own uncertainties in its incessant self-monitoring – a self-
monitoring often accomplished by monitoring others. In fact, although the
stable performance of masculinity is presented as an *outcome* of being a man,
what arises in looking at heterosexism/homophobia is that being a man, or
continuing to be a man, is the *outcome* of performing masculinity. But of course,
not just anybody can make the performance. Anatomy is seen as prior even as
the performance is required to validate the anatomy. Thus the performance
produces the man, but the performance is also limited to and compulsory for a
"man."[25]

The insults of the male high school jocks are telling. Even though one is
recognized as a man (or boy) prior to evidenced masculinity, evidence must
also be forthcoming in order to merit that continued "unproblematic" status.
Whether performative evidence is provided with ease or with difficulty, it is

nonetheless a compulsory performance, as compulsory as the initial anatomically based gender assignment. But because (proof of) masculinity has to be maintained not merely by anatomical differentiation but by performance, the possibility of failure in the performance is always there. It is enough to insult, to challenge, to question personal identity, by implying that one is not being masculine enough.

The logic of masculinity is demanding – protect and maintain what you are intrinsically, or you could lose it, mutate, become something else. The insults of my student peers suggest that the "something else" is being a girl – a serious enough demotion in a patriarchal culture. But of course, this is metaphor. One does not actually become a girl; the power of prior anatomy is too spellbinding, even when the performance fails. The "something else" is a male without masculinity, a monster, a body without its essential spirit, a mutation with no specifiable identity.[26]

So one mutation, which is so offensive it becomes the template of all mutations, occurs when a man finds that his erotic orientation is toward other men.[27] If he acts on that erotic orientation, he violates a tenet of masculinity, he fails at masculinity, and most importantly, appears to reject standards by which real men are defined as selves, as subjects. In a binary gender system, however, to be unmasculine means to be feminine; that is the only other possibility. But even as a cultural transformation into the feminine is attempted, it appears to be seriously problematic; it is not without resistance that the unmasculine male is shunted off to the realm of the feminine, for though femininity is devalued as the repository of the unmasculine, its presence as a adiscernible nonmasculine essence/performance is required to maintain the boundary of masculinity, and "feminine essences" do not easily coincide with "male" bodies.

The male body, which is supposed to house masculine essence from the first time it is identified as male, is out of place in the realm of unmasculine. That body is a manifestation of confusion, a reminder of rejection, an arrogant affront to all that is good and true about men, real men, normal men, natural men. How could this "man" give up his natural power, his natural strength, his real self? Why is he rejecting what he should be, what I am?

If the male is neither masculine, nor feminine enough, what is he? He becomes a homosexual, a member of that relatively new species of creature, originally delineated by psychiatry, which does not simply engage in unmasculine behavior, but which has an essential, unmasculine essence; no positive essence of his own, mind you, but rather a negative essence, an absence of legitimate essence, and thus the absence of legitimate personhood.[28] But what is the response to a creature with an illegitimate essence, to a creature with the husk of a man but with the extremely present absence of masculinity? That depends entirely on the situatedness of the responder in the distribution of gender identities and personal identities.

The repressive sees and fears becoming *that*, and must distance himself from *that* by any means necessary, often overcompensating, revealing his repression through his obsession, sometimes through active malignancy – assaulting or killing or merely registering disgust at that which he hates embodied in that which he desires.[29]

The ignorant will dismiss *those* as not really human, creatures so unidentified that they do not merit the response given to genuine identities (whether positive or negative – even enemies have genuine, if hated, identities). *It* can be killed, can be beaten, can be played with, can be dismissed.

The heterosupremacist reactionary will raise the warning – *They* are dangerous! *They* are getting out of hand! *They* are here! *They* are threatening your homes, your churches, your families, your children! And in some sense the threat may be real; *they* really do reject many of the beliefs upon which the heterosupremacists' political and personal identities are maintained.

Fortunately, the logic of masculinity, like any other logic, is neither universal nor irresistibly stable. Not every individual classified as a male in this culture will be adequately represented in my sketchy characterization of masculine personhood. My characterization is not to be interpreted so much as an empirically accurate description of all men in this society as it is a description of the mythology of masculinity that informs all constructions of men, the masculine, the "self" in Western culture, and that which could threaten them. I do not claim that all heterosexual males are homophobic (although I do think that the vast majority of heterosexual males are heterosexist). While I describe three homophobic reactions to the identity threat represented by gay men (repression, abusive ignorant bigotry, political reactionism), these in no way exhaust the variety of male reactions.

Some men, though they hate and are sickened by gays, lack the bravado to do anything more about their hate than make private slurs. Others, particularly liberals, are tolerantly heterosexist; they have no "real" problem with gays provided they are discreet and replicate the model of conventional heterosexual morality and family. And then there is the rare, genuinely subversive heterosexual man, a kind of gender traitor himself, whose identity is not coextensive with his assignment as a man. Although comfortable with himself, he wouldn't mind being gay, or mind being a woman – those are not the categories by which he defines, or wants to define, his personhood.

Do not, however, take this as a disclaimer to the effect that homophobia is the exception, the out-of-nowhere, the unusual case. Heterosexism may be the father of homophobia, modeling in public what is done more blatantly in hiding, but hidden does not mean rare. Do not think that homophobes, even violent ones, are few and far between – occasional atavistics "suffering" from paleolithic conceptions of sex roles. Even though many instances of anti-gay/anti-lesbian crime go unreported due to fear of outing, lack of proof, fear of retaliation, or police hostility, evidence is accumulating that such crime is widespread and that violent attack is higher among gays and lesbians than for the population at large. In a recent Philadelphia study, 24 percent of gay men and 10 percent of lesbians *responding* said that they had been physically attacked – a victimization rate twice as high for lesbians and four times as high for gay men as for women and men in the urban population at large.[30] Economic threat and verbal assault are, of course, even more common.

The gender demographics of physical homophobic attack suggest something about the correlation between masculinity and homophobia. Consider the findings in a recent study on violence against lesbians and gays by Gary Comstock: (1) 94 percent of all attackers were male; (2) 99 percent of perpetrators who attacked gay men were male, while 83 percent of those who attacked lesbians were male; (3) while 15 percent of attacks on lesbians were made by women, only 1 percent of attacks on gay men were made by women.[31]

Homophobic violence seems to be predominantly a male activity. What is the relationship between homophobia and masculinity? Is the man who attacks gay men affirming or reaffirming, consciously or subconsciously, his own masculinity/heterosexuality and thus his own sense of self? How is masculinity implicated in homophobia?

I have suggested in this essay that one reading of homophobia is that queers pose a threat to (compulsory) masculinity and as such, pose a threat to men whose personhood is coextensive with their identity as men. Certainly, homophobia could not exist without the background assumptions of (heterosexist) masculine identity. There could be no fear or hatred of gays and lesbians if there were no concept of a proper gender identity and a proper sexual orientation. Masculinity assumes, essentializes, naturalizes, and privileges heterosexuality. A violation of heterosexuality can be seen as treachery against masculinity, which can register as an affront or threat to a man's core sense of self, a threat to his (male) identity. In this sense, homophobia requires masculinity (and femininity); it is necessarily parasitic on traditional categories of sex/gender identity. Homophobia is the malignant "correction" to a destabilizing deviation. Without gendered standards of identity, there could be nothing from which to deviate, and thus nothing to "correct."

If this reading is accurate, homophobia is not just a social prejudice (on the xenophobic/minoritarian model) that can be eliminated by education or tolerance training.[32] It will not be eliminated just by persuading people to be "more accepting." While these approaches may be helpful, they do not get at the basis of homophobia – binary gender systems and heterosexism. The only way to ensure that heterosexism and its virulent manifestation homophobia are genuinely eliminated is to eliminate the binary itself – challenge the assumption that one must be sexed or gendered to be a person. Eliminate the binary and it would be impossible to have heterosexism or homophobia, because hetero and homo would have no meaning. This does not mean humans would have to be "fused" into some androgynous entity ("androgyny" has no meaning without the binary). It means simply that identities would no longer be distributed according to anatomically based "sexes."

While this hope may seem utopian and may have theoretical problems of its own, it nonetheless suggests an approach to studies of masculinity that may be incommensurable with other approaches. When using the model of masculinity (and femininity) as a social construct that has no intrinsic interpretation, there seems to be little use in trying to reconstruct masculinity into more "positive" forms, at least as long as masculinity is somehow viewed as an intrinsically appropriate feature of certain bodies. To make masculinity "positive" could easily devolve into retracing the boundaries of appropriate behavior without challenging the compulsory nature of that behavior. Delving into mythology and folklore (along the lines of some of the men's movement models) to "rediscover" some archetypal masculine image upon which to base new male identities is not so much wrong or sexist as it is arbitrary. Discovering what it means, or should mean, to be a "real man" is an exercise in uselessness. A "real man" is nothing. A "real man" could be anything. This is not to say that searching through mythohistory for useful metaphors for living today is not useful. I believe that it is.[33] But such a search will never get anyone closer to being a "real man" or even to being just a "man." There is no such thing. Nor should there be.

For some of us who have been embattled our entire lives because our desires/performances/identities were "immorally" or "illegally" or "illegitimately" cross-coded with our anatomies, we fear the flight into "rediscovering" masculinity will be a repetition of what has gone before. Gendered epistemologies will only reproduce gendered identities. I personally do not want to be a "real man," or even an "unreal man." I want to be unmanned altogether. I want to evaluate courses of behavior and desire open to me on their pragmatic consequences, not on their appropriateness to my "sex." I want to delve into the wisdom of mythology, but without the prior restrictions of anatomy.

I want to betray gender.

Notes

I want to thank Larry May for his encouragement and editing suggestions throughout the writing of this paper. I also want to make it clear that although I think some of this essay is applicable to hatred and violence directed against lesbians (sometimes called lesbophobia), for the purposes of a volume specifically on masculinity I have deliberately (though not exclusively) focused on males and hatred and violence directed against gay males. Even with this focus, however, I am indebted to work on homophobia by lesbian researchers and theorists. In a future, more comprehensive project I will explore the oppression and marginalization of a wider variety of gender traitors. [This note refers to the book in which this chapter was first published, *Rethinking Masculinity* (1992): editor.]

1   Although the scope of this essay prevents a lengthy discussion, it should be pointed out that many male teachers and coaches call their students and team members "girls": to be playful, to be insulting, or to shame them into playing more roughly.
2   It should also be pointed out that gay men often use the word "girl" to refer to each other. In these cases, however, signifying a lack of masculinity is not registering insult. Often, it is expressing a sentiment of community – a community formed by the shared rejection of compulsory heterosexuality and compulsory forms of masculinity.
3   I deliberately sidestep the philosophical debate over the existence of a "self" in this discussion. While I am quite skeptical of the existence of any stable, core self, I do not think the argument in this paper turns on the answer to that problem. "Self" could simply be interpreted as a metaphor for social situatedness. In any case, I do not mean to suggest that subverting gender is a way to purify an essential human "self."

4   For work on Native American societies that do not operate with a simple gender binary, see Walter L. Williams, *The Spirit and the Flesh: Sexual Diversity in American Indian Culture* (Boston: Beacon Press, 1986) and Will Roscoe (ed.) *Living the Spirit: A Gay American Indian Anthology* (New York: St Martin's Press, 1988).

5   For works on the social construction of gender and sexuality see: Judith Butler, *Gender Trouble: Feminism and the Subversion of Identity* (New York: Routledge, 1990); Michel Foucault, *Herculine Barbin: Being the Recently Discovered Memoirs of a Nineteenth Century French Hermaphrodite* (New York: Pantheon, 1980); Michel Foucault, *The History of Sexuality, Vol. 1, An Introduction* (New York: Vintage Books, 1980); Monique Wittig, *The Straight Mind and Other Essays* (Boston, Mass.: Beacon Press, 1992). I do wish to point out that the notion of being "socially constructed" is often simplistically treated – even by its proponents – as merely a radical form of socialization which denies any constitutive influence of biology. Social constructivism does not have to imply irrealism or metaphysical idealism, however. It is possible consistently to hold that characteristics of bodies, including behaviors and cognitive abilities, are biologically produced and constrained while still holding that the *meanings* of these biologically-based differences are socially interpreted. For example, while skin color and physiognomy are largely biologically generated features of bodies, *race* is a social interpretation of these biological variations. Similarly, to say that sex and gender are socially constructed is not to say that there are not biologically determined differences among bodies with regard to reproductive capacities, cognition, size, strength, and appearance. It is to say that these differences mean nothing in and of themselves, but only achieve meaning after being socially interpreted. I am currently working on a paper that navigates a have-it-all position between social constructivism and biological realism.

6   In the United States and many other countries, if a baby is born with anatomical genital features that do not easily lend themselves to a classification within the gender/sex system in place, they are surgically and hormonally altered to fit into the categories of male or female, girl or boy.

7   I am grateful to Bob Strikwerda for pointing out that none of these characteristics taken by itself is absolutely necessary to be perceived as masculine in contemporary US culture (except perhaps heterosexuality). In fact, a man who possessed every characteristic would be seen as a parody.

8   I borrow the insightful term "gender treachery" from Margaret Atwood. In her brilliant dystopian novel, *The Handmaid's Tale* (Boston, Mass.: Houghton Mifflin, 1986), set in a post-fundamentalist Christian takeover America, criminals are executed and hanged on a public wall with the name of their crime around their necks for citizens to see. Homosexuals bear the placard "gender traitor."

9   It doesn't matter if this rejection is "deliberate" or not in the sense of direct refusal. Any deviant behavior can be seen as treacherous unless perhaps the individual admits "guilt" and seeks a "cure" or "forgiveness."

10 Someone might ask: But why those people most *thoroughly* sexed rather than those most insecure in their sexuality? My point here is a broad one about the categories of gender. Even those people who are insecure in their sexuality will be laboring under the compulsory ideal of traditional binary gender identities.

11 "Queers" – the name itself bespeaks curiosity, treachery, radical unidentifiability, the uncategorized, perverse entities, infectious otherness.

12 See Gregory M. Herek, "On heterosexual masculinity: some psychical consequences

of the social construction of gender and sexuality." *American Behavioral Scientist* 29/5 (May/June 1986), pp. 563–77.

13 For all these terms except "homohatred," see Gregory M. Herek, "Stigma, prejudice, and violence against lesbians and gay men," in J. C. Gonsiorek and J. D. Weinrich (eds) *Homosexuality: Research Implications for Public Policy* (London: Sage, 1991), pp. 60–80. For "homohatred," see Marshall Kirk and Hunter Madsen, *After the Ball: How America Will Conquer its Fear & Hatred of Gays in the 90s* (New York: Penguin Books, 1989).

14 See Jacob Smith Yang's article in *Gay Community News* 19/6 (August 18–24, 1991) p. 1. The brutal July 4 murder of Paul Broussard sparked an uproar in Houston's queer community over anti-gay violence and police indifference. To "quell the recent uproar," Houston police undertook an undercover operation in which officers posed as gay men in a well-known gay district. Although police were skeptical of gays' claims of the frequency of violence, within one hour of posing as gay men, undercover officers were sprayed with mace and attacked by punks wielding baseball bats.

15 See Kirk and Madsen, *After the Ball*, p. 127. They mention the case of Rose Mary Denman, a United Methodist minister who was a vocal opponent of the ordinations of gays and lesbians until she eventually acknowledged her own lesbianism. Upon announcing this, however, she was defrocked. Kirk and Madsen quote a *New York Times* article that states: "In retrospect, she attributed her previous vehement stand against ordaining homosexuals to the effects of denying her unacknowledged lesbian feelings."

16 See John Money, *Gay, Straight and In-Between: The Sexology of Erotic Orientation* (Oxford: Oxford University Press, 1988), pp. 109–10.

17 See Suzanne Pharr, *Homophobia: a Weapon of Sexism* (Little Rock, Ark.: Chardon Press, 1988) and also Kirk and Madsen, *After the Ball*. The stereotypical story is one I have elaborated on from Kirk and Madsen's book, ch. 2.

18 See Herek, "On heterosexual masculinity," especially pp. 572–3.

19 One can think of the typical scene where one boy challenges another boy to do something dangerous or cruel by claiming that if he does not do so, he is afraid – a sissy. Similarly, boys who are friends/peers of homophobes may be expected to engage in cruel physical or verbal behavior in order to appear strong, reliable, and most importantly of all, not faggots themselves. They know what happens to faggots.

20 See Herek, "On heterosexual masculinity," p. 573.

21 See Celia Kitzinger, *The Social Construction of Lesbianism* (London: Sage, 1987).

22 For example, in my own area of the country we have Rev. Don Wildmon's American Family Association, headquartered in Tupelo, Mississippi – an ultraconservative media watchdog group dedicated to the elimination of any media image not in keeping with right-wing Christian morality. Also, in Memphis, Tennessee, there is FLARE (Family Life America for Responsible Education Under God, Inc.), a group lobbying for Christian prayer in public schools, the elimination of sex education programs, and the installation of a "Family Life Curriculum" in public schools that would stress sexual abstinence and teach that the only form of morally acceptable sexual activity is married, heterosexual sex.

23 I borrow the term "boogeyfag" from David G. Powell's excellent unpublished manuscript, "Deviations of a queen: episodic gay theory." Powell deconstructs California Congressman Robert Dornan's claim that "The biggest mass murderers in history are gay."

24 Gary David Comstock, *Violence against Lesbians and Gay Men* (New York: Columbia University Press, 1991), p. 172.

25 For this analysis of masculinity and performance, I owe much to insights garnered from Judith Butler's article "Imitation and gender insubordiation," in Diana Fuss, *Inside/Out: Lesbian Theories, Gay Theories* (New York: Routledge, 1991).

26 I use the term "monster" here in a way similar to that of Donna Haraway in her essay "A cyborg manifesto: science, technology, and socialist-feminism in the late twentieth century," reprinted in her book *Simians, Cyborgs, and Women: The Reinvention of Nature* (New York: Routledge, 1991). Haraway says: "Monsters have always defined the limits of community in Western imaginations. The Centaurs and Amazons of ancient Greece established the limits of the centred polis of the Greek male human by their disruption of marriage and boundary pollutions of the warrior with animality and woman" (p. 180). I loosely use "monster" in referring to homosexuality in the sense that the homosexual disrupts gender boundaries and must therefore be categorized into its own species so as to prevent destabilizing those boundaries.

27 Aquinas, for example, viewed the "vice of sodomy" as the second worst "unnatural vice," worse even than rape – a view echoed in contemporary legal decisions such as *Bowers* v. *Hardwick* (106 S. Ct. 2841, 1986), which upheld the criminal status of homosexuality. See Arthur N. Gilbert, "Conceptions of homosexuality and sodomy in western history," in Salvatore J. Licata and Robert P. Peterson (eds) *The Gay Past: a Collection of Historical Essays* (New York: Harrington Park Press, 1985), pp. 57–68.

28 On the creation of homosexuality as a category, see Foucault, *The History of Sexuality*.

29 In this sense: The repressive hates the species "homosexual," but nonetheless desires the body "man." It is only an historically contingent construction that desiring a certain kind of body "makes" you a certain kind of person, "makes" you have a certain kind of "lifestyle." Unfortunately, it is also true that being a certain "kind" of person can carry with it serious dangers, as is the case for homosexuals.

30 See Comstock, *Violence against Lesbians and Gay Men*, p. 55.

31 Ibid., p. 59.

32 This is not to say that gays and lesbians are not often treated as a minority; good arguments have been made that they are. See Richard D. Mohr, "Gay studies as moral vision," *Educational Theory* 39/2 (1989).

33 In fact, I very much enjoy studies in applied mythology, particularly the work of Joseph Campbell. However, I am extremely skeptical about any application of mythology that characterizes itself as returning us to some primal experience of masculinity that contemporary culture has somehow marred or diminished. There is always the specter of essentialism in such moves.

Linda Nicholson argues that not only do gender norms vary across cultures but that there are no universal biological criteria of sex that cultures recognize in constructing and imposing gender norms. Nicholson formulates a Wittgensteinian "family resemblance" account of gender in order to provide feminists with a better conceptual tool for analyzing the social oppression of "women" while simultaneously acknowledging cultural and historical differences in the construction of this category.

Focus questions:
1 What is "biological foundationalism" with respect to gender, according to Nicholson?
2 Explain Nicholson's assertion that, in eighteenth-century Europe, the male/female distinction was elaborated increasingly as a binary one.
3 How is "woman" defined on a Wittgensteinian "family relationship" model?

18 Interpreting "Gender"

Linda J. Nicholson

"Gender" is a strange word within feminism. While many of us assume it has a clear and commonly understood meaning, it is actually used in at least two very different and, indeed, somewhat contradictory ways. On the one hand, "gender" was developed and is still often used as a contrast term to "sex," to depict that which is socially constructed as opposed to that which is biologically given. On this usage, "gender" is typically thought to refer to personality and behavior in distinction from the body. Here, "gender" and "sex" are understood as distinct. On the other hand, "gender" has increasingly become used to refer to any social construction having to do with the male/female distinction, including those constructions that separate "female" bodies from "male" bodies. This latter usage emerged when many came to realize that society shapes not only personality and behavior; it also shapes the ways in which the body appears. But if the body is itself always seen through social interpretation, then "sex" is not something that is separate from "gender," but is, rather, that which is subsumable under it. Joan Scott provides an eloquent description of this second understanding of "gender" where the subsumption of "sex" under "gender" is made clear:

> It follows then that gender is the social organization of sexual difference. But this does not mean that gender reflects or implements fixed and natural physical differences between women and men; rather gender is the knowledge that establishes meanings for bodily differences . . . We cannot see sexual differences except as a function of our knowledge about the body and that knowledge is not "pure," cannot be isolated from its implication in a broad range of discursive contexts.[1]

I want to argue that while this second understanding of gender has become more dominant within feminist discourse, the legacy of the first survives. The result is that "sex" subtly lingers in feminist theory as that which stands outside culture and history in framing the male/female distinction. To see how, we need to more fully elaborate the origins of the term "gender" itself.

"Gender" has its roots in the coming together of two ideas important within modern western thought: that of the material basis of self-identity and that of the social constitution of human character. By the time of the emergence of the "second wave" of feminism in the late 1960s, one legacy of the first idea was the conception, dominant in most industrialized societies, that the male/female distinction was caused by and expressed, in most essential respects, "the facts of biology." This conception was reflected in the fact that the word most commonly used to depict this distinction, "sex," was a word with strong biological associations. Early second-wave feminists correctly saw this concept as conceptually underpinning "sexism" in general. Because of its implicit claim that differences between women and men are rooted in biology, the concept of "sex" lent itself to the idea of the immutability of such differences and of the hopelessness of attempts for change. Feminists of the late 1960s drew on the idea of the social constitution of human character to undermine the power of this concept. Within English speaking countries, this was done by extending the meaning of the term "gender." Prior to the late 1960s, this was a term which had been used primarily to refer to the difference between feminine and masculine forms within language. As such, it conveyed strong associations about the role of society in distinguishing that which is coded "male" from that which is coded "female." Second-wave feminists extended the meaning of the term to refer now also to many of the differences between women and men exhibited in personality and behavior.

But most interesting is that "gender," at that time, was, by and large, not seen as a replacement for "sex"; it was viewed, rather, as a means to undermine the encompassing pretensions of "sex." Most feminists during the late 1960s and early 1970s accepted the premise that there existed real biological phenomena differentiating women and men which in all societies are used in similar ways to generate a male/female distinction. The new idea was only that many of the differences associated with women and men were neither of this type nor the direct effects of such. Thus "gender" was introduced as a concept to supplement "sex," not to replace it. Moreover, "gender" was not only viewed as not replacing "sex" but "sex" seemed essential in elaborating the very meaning of "gender." An example can be found in one of the most influential discussions of "gender" in early second-wave literature. In her important article, "The traffic in women," Gayle Rubin introduced the phrase "the sex/gender system" and defined it as "the set of arrangements upon which a society transforms biological sexuality into products of human activity, and in which these transformed sexual needs are satisfied."[2] Here, the biological is being assumed as the basis upon which cultural meanings are constructed. Thus, at the very moment the influence of the biological is being undermined, it is also being invoked.

Rubin's position in this essay is not idiosyncratic. Rather, it reflects an important feature of much twentieth-century thinking about "socialization," including the feminist application of such thinking to the male/female distinction. Many of those who accept the idea that character is socially formed, and thus reject the idea that it emanates from biology, do not necessarily reject the idea that biology is the site of character formation. In other words, they still view the physiological self as the "given" upon which specific characteristics are "superimposed"; it provides the location for establishing where specific social influences are to go. The feminist acceptance of such views meant that "sex" still retained an important role: it provided the site upon which "gender" was thought to be constructed.

Such a conception of the relationship between biology and socialization makes possible what can be described as a type of "coat rack" view of self-identity. Here the body is viewed as a type of rack upon which differing cultural artifacts, specifically those of personality and behavior, are thrown. Such a model made it possible for feminists to theorize the relationship between biology and personality in a way that kept some of the advantages of biological determinism while avoiding some of its disadvantages. If one thinks of the body as a type of "rack" upon which certain features of personality and behavior are "thrown," then one can think of the relation between the givens of the "rack" itself and what gets thrown upon it as both weaker than determinative but stronger than accidental. One does not *have to* throw coats and scarves upon a coat rack, one can, for example, throw sweaters, or even very different kinds of objects if one changes the material nature of the rack sufficiently. On the other hand, if, wherever one finds coat racks, one also finds coats and scarves, this will not require much explanation; after all, they are coat racks.

I label this view of the relationship between the body and personality and behavior "biological foundationalism" to indicate its difference and similarity with biological determinism. In common with "biological determinism" it postulates a more than accidental relationship between certain aspects of personality and behavior with biology. But in distinction from biological determinism, it allows for the possibility that the givens of biology can coexist without such aspects. Such an understanding of the relationship between biology and behavior and personality thus enabled feminists to maintain a claim often associated with biological determinism, that the constancies of nature are responsible for certain social constancies, without having to accept one of the crucial disadvantages of such a position from a feminist perspective, that such social constancies cannot be transformed.

Another crucial advantage of this view of the relation between biology and personality and behavior is that it enabled feminists to assume both commonalities and differences among women. If one thinks of the body as the common rack upon which different societies impose different norms of personality and behavior, then one can both explain how some of those norms might be the same in different societies and also explain how some other of those norms might be different. Again, while it is not surprising that one tends to find coats and scarves upon a coat rack, such apparel might very well come in different sizes and shapes.

I have gone to some lengths to elaborate "biological foundationalism" because I see this position, and the "coat rack" view of identity in general, as standing in the way of our truly understanding differences among women, differences among men, and differences regarding who gets counted as either.

Through the belief that "sex identity" represents that which is common across cultures, we have frequently falsely generalized that which is specific to modern western culture, or to certain groups within it. Moreover, it has been difficult identifying such faulty generalization as such, because of the alliance of all forms of "biological foundationalism" with social constructionism. Feminists have long come to see how claims about the biological causes of personality and behavior falsely generalize socially specific features of human personality and behavior onto all human societies. But "biological foundationalism" is not equivalent to biological determinism, for unlike the latter, it includes some element of social constructionism. Even the earliest feminist position which construes "sex" as independent of "gender," in using the term "gender" at all, allows for some social input into the construction of character. And, any position which recognizes at least some of what is associated with the male/female distinction as a social response, tends to theorize a certain amount of differences among women. However, while a "biological foundationalist," unlike a "biological determininist," position does allow for the recognition of differences among women, it does so in limited and problematic ways.

Most basically, it leads us to think of differences between women as coexisting, rather than intersecting with, differences of race, class, etc. Because of the assumption that commonalities of sex lend themselves to commonalities in gender, there is the tendency to think of gender as representing what women have in common and features of race, or class representing how women differ. In other words we are left with thinking that all women "in patriarchal societies" will be end up acting like coats and scarves though we may differ somewhat in relation to size and shape. We are thus led to develop what Elizabeth Spelman describes as an additive, or "pop bead" analysis of identity where all women share the gender "bead" but differ in relation to what other type "beads" are added on. But as she notes, such analyses typically describe the gender bead in terms of its most privileged manifestations. They also tend to depict the differences marking non-privileged women only in negative terms. Spelman describes some of these problems in regard to analyses of the relation of sexism and racism:

> In sum, according to an additive analysis of sexism and racism, all women are oppressed by sexism; some women are further oppressed by racism. Such an analysis distorts Black women's experiences of oppression by failing to note important differences between the contexts in which Black women and white women experience sexism. The additive analysis also suggests that a woman's racial identity can be "subtracted" from her combined sexual and racial identity.[3]

In other words, a dualistic approach obscures the possibility that what we are describing as commonalities may themselves be interlaced with differences. Who we are *as women* does not just differ in relation to accidental qualities, but differs at a deeper level. There are no common features emanating from biology.

In short, feminism needs to abandon biological foundationalism along with biological determinism. As I will shortly argue, the human population differs within itself not only in terms of social expectations about how we think, feel and act. There are also differences in the ways in which we understand the body. Consequently, we need to understand social variations in the male/female distinction as related to differences which go "all the way down," that is, as not just tied to the limited phenomena many of us associate with "gender" (i.e. to cultural stereotypes of personality and behavior), but as also tied to culturally various understandings of the body. This does not mean that the body disappears from feminist theory. Rather, it becomes a variable, rather than a constant, no longer able to ground claims about the male/female distinction across large sweeps of human history but still there as always potentially an important element in how the male/female distinction gets played out in any specific society.

To make my own position clear: I am not disclaiming the idea that all societies possess some form of a male/female distinction. All available evidence seems to indicate that they do. Nor am I rejecting the possibility that all societies relate this distinction in some way or another to the body. It is rather that differences in the meaning and importance of the body exist. These kinds of differences in turn affect the meaning of the male/female distinction. The consequence is that there appears no one set of criteria constituting "sex identity" from which one can extrapolate anything about the joys and oppressions of "being a woman." To think that there are, leads us astray. This is the basic argument of this essay. I would like to elaborate it in the following.

Historical Context

The tendency to think of sex identity as given, basic and common cross-culturally is a very powerful one. To weaken its hold on us requires some sense of its historical context. To the extent we can see sex identity as historically rooted, as the product of a belief system specific to modern western societies, to that extent might we come to appreciate the deep diversity in the forms through which the male/female distinction has and can come to be understood.

Let me begin this task by going back in European history to the early modern period. It was in the period from the seventeenth through the nineteenth centuries that there developed, particularly among "men of science," the tendency to think about people as matter in motion – physical beings, who are ultimately distinguishable from others by reference to the spatial and temporal coordinates we occupy. This meant a tendency to think about human beings in increasingly "thing-like" terms, that is, as both similar to the objects around us – because composed of the same substance, "matter" – and as separate from such objects and from each other – because of the distinctive spatial and temporal coordinates which each self occupies.[4]

But it is not only that the language of space and time became increasingly central as a means for providing identity to the self. The growing dominance of a materialist metaphysics also meant an increasing tendency to understand the "nature" of specific phenomena in terms of the specific configurations of matter they embody. The import of this for emerging views of self-identity was a growing tendency to understand the "nature" of human selves in terms of the specific configurations of matter which they too embodied. Thus the material or physical features of the body increasingly took on the role of providing testimony to the "nature" of the self it housed.

A word of qualification needs to be made about how such a claim should be understood in the context of seventeenth- and eighteenth-century thinking. In the late twentieth century, to think about the body taking on an increasing role in providing testimony to the "nature" of the self it houses, is to assume an increasing belief in biological determinism. However, what needs to be emphasized is that during the seventeenth and eighteenth centuries a growing sense of the self as "natural" or "material" conjoins two emphases which only in later centuries will become viewed by many as antithetical: a heightened consciousness of the body as a source of knowledge about the self and a sense of the self as shaped by the influences the self receives from the external world. Both emphases are present in the writings of many seventeenth- and eighteenth-century writers, but they are not seen, as they will frequently become later, as necessarily antithetical. A heightened consciousness of the self as bodily can be illustrated by the kinds of issues seventeenth- and eighteenth-century theorists increasingly thought relevant to attend to. Thus, for example, while an early seventeenth-century patriarchalist such as Sir Robert Filmer might use the Bible to justify women's subordination to men, the later natural law theorist John Locke would cite differences in male and female bodies to accomplish a related goal.[5] But "nature" for natural law theorists such as Locke did not just mean the body in distinction from other kinds of phenomena. It could also refer to the external influences provided by vision or education. Thus, while Locke might point to differences in women's and men's bodies to make a point, he could also in his writings on education view the minds of girls and boys as malleable in relation to the specific external influences they were subject to. In short, "materialism" at this point in history combines the seeds of what were later to become two very different and opposing traditions. On the one hand, out of seventeenth- and eighteenth-century materialism emerges a tradition which looks to the physical characteristics of the individual as a source of knowledge about the individual. On the other hand, seventeenth- and eighteenth-century materialists talk about processes which later come to be described as "socialization," that is, as that which shapes identity in opposition to the body. However, during late seventeenth- and eighteenth-century discourses these ways of thinking about the self are often conjoined within an overall naturalistic perspective. Ludmilla Jordanova makes a related point:

It had become clear by the end of the eighteenth century that living things and their environment were continually interacting and changing each other in the process . . . The customs and habits of day-to-day life such as diet, exercise and occupation, as well as more general social forces such as mode of government, were taken to have profound effects on all aspects of people's lives . . . The foundation to this was a naturalistic conceptual framework for understanding the physiological, mental and social aspects of human beings in a coordinated way. This framework underlay the relationship between nature, culture and gender in the period.[6]

As Jordanova notes, this tendency to view the bodily and the cultural as interrelated is expressed in the use of such eighteenth-century "bridging" concepts as "temperament," "habit," "constitution," and "sensibility."[7]

However, that during the seventeenth and eighteenth centuries a growing focus on the materiality of the self does not translate simply into what many today understand as biological determinism, does not negate the point that the body was increasingly emerging as a source of knowledge about the self in contrast to older theological views. And one way in which this focus on the body began to shift understandings of self-identity is that, particularly during the eighteenth century, the body increasingly began to be employed as a resource for attesting to the differentiated nature of human beings. One context where this is striking is in the emergence of the idea of "race." As many commentators have pointed out, "race" was only first employed as a means of categorizing human bodies in the late seventeenth century, and it was only in the eighteenth century with such publications as the influential *Natural System* by Carolus Linnaeus (1735) and Friedrich Blumenbach's *Generis humani varietate native liber* (*On the Natural Variety of Mankind*, 1776), that there began to be made what were taken to be authoritative racial divisions of human beings.[8] This does not mean that physical differences between, for example, Africans and Europeans were not noted by Europeans prior to the eighteenth century. They certainly were noted and used to justify slavery. But, as Winthrop Jordan points out, physical differences were only one of the differences noted and used by Europeans to justify slavery.[9] That Africans, from a European perspective, engaged in strange social practices and were "heathens," i.e. were not Christians, also provided justification in the European mind for the practice of taking Africans as slaves. In short, to note a physical difference, or even to attribute moral and political significance to it, is not the same as using it to "explain" basic divisions among the human population as the concept of "race" increasingly did from the late eighteenth century on.

The Sexed Body

The above example of "race" illustrates how the growing dominance of a materialist metaphysics did not mean the construction of new social distinctions *ex nihilo*, as it meant the elaboration and "explanation" of previously existing distinctions in new ways. Thus, in the case of "sex," the growth of a materialistic metaphysics did not create a male/female distinction. Such a distinction obviously existed in western Europe before the emergence of such a metaphysics. Moreover, an attention to physical differences played a role in the meaning of this distinction. However, the growth of a materialistic metaphysics also entailed changes, changes in the importance of physical characteristics and changes in their role. Most basically, it transformed the meaning of physical characteris-

tics from being a sign or marker of this distinction to being that which generated or caused it. Moreover, at the time such a metaphysics was increasingly
taking hold, other social changes were also occurring – such as an intensified
separation of a domestic and public sphere. Such changes meant that physical
characteristics became seen not only as causing the male/female distinction,
but in causing it as a very binary distinction. Let me begin elaborating these
points by turning to some of the recent work of Thomas Laqueur.

Laqueur, in his study of medical literature on the body from the Greeks
through the eighteenth century, identifies a significant change in this literature
in the course of the eighteenth century. Specifically, he identifies a view present
from the Greeks up until the eighteenth century, which while clearly diverse in
many respects, is similar in one important respect: it operates with what he
describes as a "one sex" view of the body. This contrasts with the "two sex"
view which begins to emerge during the course of the eighteenth century.
Whereas in the earlier view, the female body was seen as a lesser version of the
male body "along a vertical axis of infinite gradations," in the later view, the
female body becomes "an altogether different creature along a horizontal axis
whose middle ground was largely empty."[10]

That in the earlier view physical differences between the sexes are viewed as
differences of degree rather than of kind manifests itself in a variety of ways.
Whereas we, for example, view female sexual organs as different organs from
those of men, in the earlier view, these organs were viewed as less developed
versions of male organs. Thus, on the old view, the female vagina and cervix did
not constitute something distinct from the male penis; rather, together, they
constituted a less developed version of it. Similarly, on the old view, the process
of menstruation did not describe a process distinctive to women's lives. Rather,
menstruation was seen as just one more instance of the tendency of human
bodies to bleed, the orifice from which the blood emerged being perceived as
not very significant. Thus, it was thought that if a woman started vomiting
blood, she would stop menstruating.[11] Bleeding itself was viewed as one way
bodies in general got rid of an excess of nutriments. Since men were thought to
be cooler beings than women, they were thought to be less likely to possess
such a surplus and hence less likely to possess a need to bleed.[12] Similarly, Laqueur
points to Galen's argument that women must produce semen, since otherwise
Galen asks, there would be no reason for them to possess testicles, which they
clearly do.[13] In short, the organs, processes and fluids we think of as distinctive
to male and female bodies were rather thought of as convertible within a "generic corporeal economy of fluids and organs."[14]

This "generic corporeal economy of fluids and organs" began to give way to
a new "two sex" view. Laqueur describes aspects of the process:

> Organs that had shared a name – ovaries and testicles – were now linguistically
> distinguished. Organs that had not been distinguished by a name of their own –
> the vagina, for example, – were given one. Structures that had been thought com-
> mon to man and woman – the skeleton and the nervous system – were differenti-
> ated so as to correspond to the cultural male and female.[15]

That even a structure such as the skeleton would now be seen as different in women and men is illustrated in the work done by Londa Schiebinger. As Schiebinger notes, it was in 1796 that the German anatomist Samuel Thomas von Soemmerring produced what was one of the first illustrations of a female skeleton. This, she notes, is quite remarkable since many anatomists had been drawing illustrations of the human anatomy since the sixteenth century.[16] This drawing, however, was representative of a larger movement of the late eighteenth century where "discovering, describing and defining sex differences in every bone, muscle, nerve, and vein of the human body became a research priority in anatomic science."[17]

Another manifestation of this new "two sex" view was the delegitimation of the concept of "hermaphroditism." As Michel Foucault points out, hermaphroditism, in the eighteenth century, became a shrinking concept. Foucault notes that during this century the hermaphrodite of previous centuries became the "pseudo-hermaphrodite" whose "true" sexual identity only required sufficiently expert diagnosis.

> Biological theories of sexuality, juridical conceptions of the individual, forms of administrative control in modern nations, led little by little to rejecting the idea of a mixture of the two sexes in a single body, and consequently to limiting the free choice of indeterminate individuals. Henceforth, everybody was to have one and only one sex. Everybody was to have his or her primary, profound, determined and determining sexual identity; as for the elements of the other sex that might appear, they could only be accidental, superficial, or even quite simply illusory. From the medical point of view, this meant that when confronted with a hermaphrodite, the doctor was no longer concerned with recognizing the presence of the two sexes, juxtaposed or intermingled, or with knowing which of the two prevailed over the other, but rather with deciphering the true sex that was hidden beneath ambiguous appearances.[18]

But beyond the tendency to view the physical differences separating women and men in increasingly binary terms, was also the new tendency to see such physical differences as the cause of the male/female distinction itself. As Laqueur points out, it is not as though, in the older view, there did not exist a distinction, or that biology played no role in it. However, the distinction was seen not so much as "caused" by biology as being the logical expression of a certain cosmological order governed by difference, hierarchy, interrelation. Within this worldview, biological differences between women and men were perceived more as "markers" of the male/female distinction rather than as its basis or "cause." Laqueur points to the Aristotelian position as illustrative of the older view:

> Aristotle did not need the facts of sexual difference to support the claim that woman was a lesser being than man; it followed from the *a priori* truth that the material cause is inferior to the efficient cause. Of course males and females were in daily life identified by their corporeal characteristics, but the assertion that in generation the male was the efficient and the female the material cause was, in principle, not physically demonstrable; it was itself a restatement of what it *meant*

to be male or female. The specific nature of the ovaries or the uterus was thus only incidental to defining sexual difference. By the eighteenth century, this was no longer the case. The womb, which had been a sort of negative phallus, became the uterus – an organ whose fibers, nerves, and vasculature provided a naturalistic explanation and justification for the social status of women.[19]

In other words, when the Bible or Aristotle is the source of authority about how the relationship between women and men is to be understood, any asserted differences between women and men are to be justified primarily through reference to these texts. The body is not very important as a source. When, however, the texts of Aristotle and the Bible lose their authority, nature becomes the means for grounding any perceived distinction between women and men. And, in so far as the body is perceived as the representative of nature, it takes on the role of nature's "voice." This means that to the extent there is perceived a need for the male/female distinction to be constituted as a strongly binary one, the body must "speak" this distinction as a binary one. The consequence is a two sex view of the body.

In sum, during the eighteenth century there occurred a replacement of an understanding of women as lesser versions of men along an axis of infinite gradations to one where the relationship between women and men is perceived in more binary terms and where the body is thought of as the source of such binarism. The consequence is our idea of "sex identity" – a sharply differentiated male and female self rooted in a deeply differentiated body.

"Sex" and "Gender"

This concept of "sex identity" was dominant in most industrialized countries at the time of the emergence of second wave feminism. But there were also ideas around at the time which feminists could draw upon to begin to challenge it. In early sections of this essay I talked about the growing importance of a materialistic metaphysics in early modern western societies. Not mentioned was that the growth of such a metaphysics was never uncontested; many cultural and intellectual movements throughout western modernity have striven to prove the distinctiveness of human existence in relation to the rest of the physical world.[20] Some of these movements, particularly those grounded in religion, have continued to stress a religious, rather than physiological, grounding of the male/female distinction. Moreover, even from within a materialist metaphysics there emerged, prior to the growth of second-wave feminism, perspectives which challenged completely physiological understandings of "sex identity." In an earlier part of this essay I noted how many seventeenth- and eighteenth-century materialists put together two ideas which later often came to be seen as antithetical: the idea of the physiological basis of human "nature" and of the social construction of human character. In the nineteenth century, one theorist who combined both, that is, who maintained a strong materialism while also elaborating with great theoretical sophistication the idea of the social constitution of human character, was Karl Marx. He, along with many other nineteenth- and twentieth-century thinkers, contributed to a way of thinking about human character which acknowledged the deep importance of society in constituting character. Second-wave feminists could draw on this way of thinking to begin to challenge a pure physiological understanding of "sex identity." But, as I earlier claimed, while the challenge to this latter understanding of "sex identity" has been extensive in second-wave writings, it has also been incomplete. Still maintained is the idea that there exists some physiological "givens" which in all cultures are similarly used to distinguish women and men and which at least partially account for certain commonalities in the norms of personality and behavior affecting women and men in many societies. This position, which I have labelled "biological foundationalism," has enabled many feminists explicitly to reject biological determinism while holding onto a feature of biological determinism: the presumption of commonalities across cultures.

But what I am calling "biological foundationalism," rather than being understood as a single position, is best understood as representing a range of positions bounded on the one side by a strict biological determinism and on the other side by a complete social constructionism. One advantage of viewing "biological foundationalism" as representing a range of positions is that it counters a common tendency to think of "social constructionist" positions as all alike in the role that biology plays within them. Second-wave feminists have frequently assumed that as long as one acknowledged any distance at all from biological determinism, one thereby avoided all of the problems associated with this position. But the issue is more relative: second-wave positions have exhibited more or less distance from biological determinism and have exhibited more or less of the problems associated with that position – specifically its tendency to generate faulty generalizations which represent projections from the theorist's own cultural context – in accord with the degree they have exhibited such distance.

That one might be "more or less" of a social constructionist, follows from the point that any phenomenon can be thought to contribute "more or less" to a given outcome. Normally, we speak of "biological determinism" when a particular phenomenon is thought to be completely the consequence of biological factors. Thus, to be a "social constructionist" is merely to argue that society has some input into a given outcome. However, it is easy to see that from within such a perspective there might exist a range of positions on how important such input is. In the work of many second-wave theorists, "social constructionism" exists as almost a token position. While it allows for the presumption of a certain amount of difference among women, its minimal role entails that such difference is either restricted to the margins of human history or to depicting "secondary" qualities of "womanhood" – i.e. those that do not affect the basic definition of what it means to be a woman. To show how social constructionism can function in such a token way, let me now turn to the writings of two thinkers who are explicitly social constructionist yet who both use the body to create generalizations about women in ways not significantly different from biological determinism.

The first writer I would like to turn to is Robin Morgan in her introduction to *Sisterhood is Global*, "Planetary feminism: the politics of the 21st century."[21] In this essay, Morgan is explicit about the many ways women's lives vary across culture, race, nationality, etc. However, she also believes that certain commonalities exist amongst women. As she makes clear, such commonalities are for her not *determined* by biology, but are rather "the result of a common condition which, despite variations in degree, is experienced by all human beings who are born female."[22] While she never explicitly defines this common condition, she comes closest to doing so in the following passages:

> To many feminist theorists, the patriarchal control of women's bodies as the means of reproduction is the crux of the dilemma . . . The tragedy within the tragedy is that because we are regarded primarily as reproductive beings rather than full human beings, we are viewed in a (male-defined) sexual context, with the consequent epidemic of rape, sexual harassment, forced prostitution, and sexual traffick in women, with transacted marriage, institutionalized family structures, and the denial of individual women's own sexual expression.[23]

Passages such as these suggest that there is something about women's bodies, specifically our reproductive capacities, which, while not necessarily resulting in or determining a particular social outcome, nevertheless, sets the stage for or makes possible a certain range of male reactions across cultures which are common enough to lead to a certain commonality in women's experience as victims of such reactions. Again, this commonality in female bodies does not *determine* this range of reactions, in the sense that in *all* cultural contexts such a commonality would generate a reaction which was of this type, but nevertheless, this commonality does lead to this kind of reaction across many contexts. The difference between this type of a position and biological determinism is very slight. As I noted, biological determinism is commonly thought to apply only to contexts where a phenomenon is not affected by *any* variations in cultural context. Since Morgan is allowing that *some* variations in cultural context could affect the reaction, she is not here being a strict "biological determinist." But, since she believes that this commonality in female bodies leads to a common reaction across a wide range of cultural contexts, there is, in reality, only a small space which separates her position from a strict biological determinism. When we see that, within a theory, biology can have "more or less" of a determining influence, so can we also see that one can be "more or less" of a "social constructionist."

Another writer who explicitly rejects biological determinism but whose position also ends up being functionally close to it is Janice Raymond. In her book, *A Passion for Friends*, Raymond explicitly rejects the view that biology is the cause of women's uniqueness.

> Women have no biological edge on the more humane qualities of human existence, nor does women's uniqueness proceed from any biological differences from men. Rather, just as any cultural context distinguishes one group from another, women's "otherness" proceeds from women's culture.[24]

This position is also present in Raymond's earlier book, *The Transsexual Empire*.[25] However, what is very interesting about *The Transsexual Empire* is that much of the argument here, as was the case with Morgan's argument, rests on the assumption of an extremely invariant relationship between biology and character, though again, an invariance which is not of the usual biological determinist kind. In this work, Raymond is extremely critical of transsexuality in general, what she labels "the male-to-constructed female" in particular, and most especially those "male-to-constructed females" who call themselves "lesbian feminists." While many of Raymond's criticisms stem from the convincing position that modern medicine provides a very problematic ground for transcending gender, other parts of her criticism emerge from certain assumptions about an invariant relationship between biology and character. Specifically, Raymond doubts the veracity of claims on the part of any biological male to have "a female within him."

> The androgynous man and the transsexually constructed lesbian-feminist deceive women in much the same way, for they lead women into believing that they are truly one of us – this time not only one in behavior but one in spirit and conviction.[26]

For Raymond *all* women differ in certain important respects from *all* men. This is not because the biologies of either directly determine a certain character. Rather she believes that the possession of a particular kind of genitals, i.e. those labelled "female," generates certain kinds of reactions from others which are different in kind from the reactions generated by the possession of "male" genitals. The commonality among these reactions and their differences from those generated by male genitals are sufficient to ensure that no one born with male genitals can claim enough in common with those born with female genitals to warrant the label "female." Thus she claims:

> We know that we are woman who are born with female chromosomes and anatomy, and that whether or not we were socialized to be so-called normal women, patriarchy has treated and will treat us like women. Transsexuals have not had this same history. No man can have the history of being born and located in this culture as a woman. He can have the history of *wishing* to be a woman and of *acting* like a woman, but this gender experience is that of a transsexual, not of a woman.[27]

Raymond qualifies her claims in this passage to those living within patriarchal societies. But Raymond is assuming enough of a homogeneity of reaction across such societies such that biology, for all intents and purposes, becomes a "determinant" of character within such societies. To be sure, biology does not here *directly* generate character. But, since it invariably leads to certain common reactions, which have a specific effect on character, it becomes *in effect* a cause of character. In common with Morgan, Raymond is not claiming that biology generates specific consequences independent of culture. However, for both, variability within and among a wide range of societies becomes so muted that culture becomes a vanishing variable. The invocation of culture does, of course, allow these theorists to postulate differences existing side-by-side with the commonalities and it also leaves open the possibility of a distant society where biology might not have such effects. But in neither case does it interfere with the power of biological givens to generate important commonalities among women across a wide span of human history.

In the above I have focused on the writings of Robin Morgan and Janice Raymond for the purpose of illustration. The type of "biological foundationalism" exemplified in their writings is not unique to these two writers but represents a major tendency within second-wave theory, particularly in that tendency known as radical feminism. This is not surprising. Since the early 1970s, radical feminists have been in the vanguard of those who have stressed the similarites among women and their differences from men. But it is difficult justifying such claims without invoking biology in some way or other. During the 1970s, many radical feminists explicitly endorsed biological determinism.[28] Biological determinism became, however, increasingly distasteful among feminists for a variety of reasons. Not only did it possess an unpleasant association with anti-feminism, but it also seemed to disallow differences among women and – in the absence of feminist biological warfare – seemed to negate any hopes for change. The task became that of creating theory which allowed for differences among women, made at least theoretically possible the idea of a future without sexism, and yet also justified cross-cultural claims about women. Some version of a strong form of biological foundationalism became the answer for many radical feminists.

Radical feminist writings are a rich source of strong forms of biological foundationalism. However, even theories which pay more attention to cultural history and diversity than do those of many radical feminists often rely on some use of biological foundationalism to make critical moves. I claimed in the above that since the early 1970s, radical feminists have been in the vanguard of those who have wished to stress the commonalities among women and their differences from men. But beginning in the 1970s, early 1980s, much second-wave feminism began to move in such a direction, changing from what Iris Young has called a "humanistic" stance to a more "gynocentric" one.[29] The enormous attention given at this time to books such as Carol Gilligan's *In a Different Voice* and Nancy Chodorow's *The Reproduction of Mothering* can be said to follow from the usefulness of the former in elaborating differences between women and men and of the latter in accounting for it.[30] While both of these works strikingly exemplify a "difference" perspective, neither fits easily into the category of "radical feminism." However, in both of these works, as well as in others of this period which also emphasize difference, such as in the writings of such French feminists as Luce Irigiray, there is an interesting overlap with perspectives embodied in much radical feminist analysis. Specifically, in such works, a strong correlation is claimed between people with certain biological characteristics and people with certain character traits. To be sure, in a work such as Chodorow's *The Reproduction of Mothering* such claims are built upon a rich and complex story about *culture*: about how the possession of certain kinds of genitals gets one placed in a particular psycho-social dynamic only in specific types of circumstances and only in so far as those genitals possess certain kinds of meanings. Nevertheless, I would still describe a work such as *The Reproduction of Mothering* as "biologically foundationalist." I do so because its complex and sophisticated story of child development, as a story supposedly applicable about a wide range of cultures, rests on the assumption that the possession of certain kinds of genitals does possess a common enough meaning across this range of cultures to make possible the postulation of such a fundamentally homogeneous set of stories about child development. To assume that the cultural construction of the body functions as an unchanging variable across sweeps of human history and combines with other relatively static aspects of culture to create certain commonalities in personality formation across such history, suffices, on my account, to indicate some fairly significant version of biological foundationalism.

A problem running throughout the above theories, a problem which many commentators have pointed out, is that "a feminism of difference" tends to be "a feminism of uniformity." To say that "women are different from men in such and such ways" is to say that women *are* "such and such." But, inevitably, characterizations of women's "nature" or "essence" – even if this is described as a socially constructed "nature" or "essence" – tend to reflect the perspective of those making the characterizations. And since those who have the power to make such characterizations in contemporary European-based societies are often white, heterosexual and from the professional class, such characterizations tend to reflect the biases of those from these groups. It was thus not surprising that the gynocentric move of the 1970s soon gave way to outcries from women of color, lesbians and those of working-class backgrounds that the stories being told did not reflect their experiences. Thus Chodorow was soon critiqued for elaborating a basically heterosexual story and she, Gilligan and radical feminists such as Mary Daly have been accused of speaking primarily from a white, western, middle-class perspective.[31]

My argument is that in all those cases where feminist theory makes generalizations across large sweeps of history, what is, and must be, being assumed are common perspectives throughout such history about the meaning and import of female and male bodies. Many writers have pointed out how, in these types of theories, the specific content of the claim tends to reflect the culture of the theorist making the generalization. But also being borrowed from the theorist's cultural context, and making the generalization possible, is a specific understanding of the meaning of bodies and of their relation to culture: that bodies are always construed in specific ways and, in consequence, as setting in motion a particular story of character development or societal reaction. The methodological move here is not different from that employed by biological determinists: the assumed "givenness" and commonality of nature across culture is being drawn on to give credibility to the generality of the specific claim. In short, it is not only that certain specific ideas about women and men – that women are relational, nurturing and caring while men are aggressive and combative – are being falsely generalized, but also being falsely generalized, and indeed making these further generalizations about character possible, are certain specific assumptions about the body and its relation to character – that there are commonalities in the distinctive givens of the body which generate commonalities in the classification of human beings across cultures and in the reactions by others to those so classified. The problems associated with "a feminism of difference" are both reflected in and made possible by "biological foundationalism."

But the rejoinder might be made: what my argument is failing to allow for is that in many, if not most, historical contexts people *have* interpreted the body in relatively similar ways and this common interpretation has led to certain cross-cultural commonalities in the treatment of or experiences of women. True, it might be the case that some feminist scholarship falsely assumed the generalizability of some *specific* character traits found in contemporary middle-class western life, i.e., that women are more nurturant than men. However, it has not generally been problematic to assume, for contemporary western societies as well as for most others, that the possession of one of two possible kinds of bodies does lead to the labelling of some people as women and others as men and this labelling bears *some* common characteristics with *some* common effects.

This is a powerful response, but, I would claim, derives its power from a subtle misreading about how gender operates cross-culturally. Most every society known to western scholarship does appear to have some kind of a male/female distinction. Moreover, most appear to relate this distinction to some kind of bodily distinction between women and men. From such observations it is very tempting to move to the above claims. However, I would argue that such a move is faulty. And the reason is that "some kind of male/female distinction" and "some kind of bodily distinction" includes a wide range of possible subtle differences in the meaning of the male/female distinction and of how the bodily distinction works in relationship to it. Because these differences may be subtle, they are not necessarily the kinds of things which contemporary, western feminists will first see when they look at pre-modern European cultures or cultures not dominated by the influence of modern Europe. But subtle differences around such issues may contain important consequences in the very deep sense of what it means to be a man or woman. For example, certain Native American societies which have understood identity more in relation to spiritual forces than has been true of modern western, European-based societies have also allowed for some of those with male genitals to understand themselves and be understood by others as half man/half woman in ways this has not been possible within modern western European-based societies. Within these latter societies, the body has been interpreted as such an important signifier of identity that someone with female genitals has also not been thought to ever legitimately occupy the role of "husband"; whereas in many African societies this is not the case. In short, while all of these societies certainly possess some kind of a male/female distinction and also relate this distinction in some important way or another to the body, subtle differences in how the body itself is viewed may contain some very basic implications about what it means to be male or female and, consequently, important differences in the degree and ways in which sexism operates. In short, such subtle differences in the ways in which the body is read may relate to differences in what it means to be a man or woman which "go all the way down."[32]

But this point may be established not only by looking at the relation between contemporary western European-based societies and certain "exotic" others. Even within contemporary western European-based societies we can detect important tensions and conflicts in the meaning of the body and of how the body relates to male and female identity. While certainly these are societies which, over the last several centuries, have operated with a strongly binary male/female distinction and have based this distinction on an attributed, binary biology, they have also been societies which, in varying degrees, have also articulated notions of the self which deny differences among women and men, and this not just as a consequence of 1960s feminism. In part, this is manifest in the degree to which the belief that "women and men are fundamentally the same" is also a part of the hegemonic belief system of the societies in which many of us operate and has been available for feminists to draw on as an attack upon differences. Indeed, it is at least partly as a consequence of a general cultural tendency in some European-based societies to somewhat disassociate biology and character that feminism itself was made possible. One of the weaknesses of a difference-based feminism is that it cannot account for the phenomenon of such societies having produced feminists, that is, beings whose genitals, by virtue of the account, should have made us completely feminine, but whose actual political skills and/or presence in such previously male-dominated institutions as the academy must indicate a certain dosage of masculine socialization. Moreover, it seems inadequate to conceptualize such a dosage as merely an "add on" to certain "basic" commonalities. In short, it is because of a certain prior disassociation of biology and socialization that, at a very basic level, many of us are who we are.

In short, a feminism of difference, and the biological foundationalism on which it rests, contain, in contemporary European-based societies, elements of both truth and falsity. Because these are societies which, to a significant degree, perceive female and male genitals as binary and also link character to such genitals, people born with "male" genitals are likely to be different in many important respects from people born with "female" genitals. A feminism of difference, and the biological foundationalism on which it rests, are, however, also false not only because of the failure of both positions to recognize the historicity of their own insights but also, and related, because neither allows for the ways in which even within contemporary European-based societies, the belief system their insights reflect possess a multitude of cracks and fissures. Thus, a feminism of difference can provide no insight into those of us whose psyches are the manifestation of such cracks. Take, for example, those who are born with "male" genitals yet think of themselves as female. Janice Raymond, in *The Transsexual Empire*, claims that "male-to-constructed females" are motivated by the desire to seize control, at least symbolically, of women's power to reproduce.[33] She also claims that "female-to-constructed-males" are motivated by the desire to seize the general power given to men, that is, are "male-identified" to the extreme.[34] Assuming for the sake of discussion that such accounts are valid, they still leave unanswered such questions as why *some* women are so male-identified, or why only some men and not others wish to seize symbolic control of women's power to reproduce or do it in *this* way. Any appeals to "false consciousness," like their earlier Marxist counterparts, merely place the lack of an answer at a deeper level, since again, no account is made why some and not others succumb to "false consciousness."[35] Thus, even to the extent that the culture itself links gender to biology, a feminist analysis which follows this approach is unable to account for those who deviate.

Because a feminism of difference is both true and false within the societies in which many of us operate, the process of endorsing or rejecting it has certain strange elements. It is similar to looking at those pictures in psychology textbooks where one moment the picture looks like the head of a rabbit and the next moment it looks like the head of a duck. Within each "view" features stand out which had previously been hidden, and the momentary interpretation feels like the only possible one. Much of the power of books such as Chodorow's *The Reproduction of Mothering* and Gilligan's *In a Different Voice* lay in the fact that they generated radically new ways of viewing social relations. The problem, however, is that these new ways of configuring reality, while truly powerful, also missed so much. Like a lens which only illuminates certain aspects of what we see by shadowing others, these visions kept from sight the many contexts where we as women and men deviate from the generalizations these analyses generated – either because the cultural contexts of our childhoods were not ones where these generalizations were encompassing or because the specific psychic dynamics of our individual childhoods undermined any simple internalization of these generalizations. Thus it became impossible for women to acknowledge both the ways in which the generalizations generated from the analyses poorly captured their/our own notions of masculinity and femininity and also, even when they did, how their/our own psyches might embody masculine traits. Any acknowledgement of this latter deviation seemed to make one's membership in the feminist community particularly suspect.

This last point illuminates what is often forgotten in debates about the truth of such generalizations: since evidence can be accumulated both for their truth and their falsity, their endorsement or rejection is not a consequence of a dispassionate weighing of the "evidence." Rather, it is our disparate needs, both individual and collective, which push those of us who are women to see ourselves more or less like other women and different from men. At a collective level, the need for some to see themselves as very much like each other and different from men made a lot of things possible at a certain moment in history. Most importantly, it made it possible to uncover sexism in its depth and pervasiveness and to build communities of women organized around its eradication. However, it also contained some major weaknesses, most notably its tendency to eradicate differences among women. The question facing feminism today is whether we can generate new visions of gender which retain what has been positive in "a feminism of difference" while eliminating what has been negative.

How Then Do We Interpret "Woman"?

Within contemporary European-based societies there is a strong tendency to think in either/or ways regarding generalities: either there are commonalities which tie us all together *or* we are all just individuals. A large part of the appeal of theories which supported "a feminism of difference" was that they generated strong ammunition against that common societal tendency to dismiss the import of gender, to claim that feminism is not necessary since "we are all just individuals." "A feminism of difference" uncovered many important social patterns of gender, patterns which enabled many women to understand their circumstances in social rather than idiosyncratic terms.

My argument against "a feminism of difference" does not mean that we should stop searching for such patterns. It is rather that we understand them in different and more complex terms than we have tended to do, particularly that we become more attentive to the historicity of the patterns we uncover. As we search for that which is socially shared, we need to be simultaneously searching for the places where such patterns break down. My argument thus points to the replacement of claims about women as such or even women "in patriarchal societies" with claims about women in particular contexts.[36]

The idea that we can make claims about women which span large historical stretches has been facilitated by the idea that there is something common to the category of "woman" across such historical stretches: that all share, at some basic level, certain features of biology. Thus what I have called "biological foundationalism" gives content to the claim that there exist some common criteria defining what it means to be a woman. For political purposes such criteria are thought to enable us to differentiate enemy from ally and to provide the basis for feminism's political program. Thus there will be many who view my attack on "biological foundationalism" as an attack on feminism itself: if we do not possess some common criteria providing meaning to the word "woman" how can we generate a politics around this word? Does not feminist politics require that the word "woman" have some determinate meaning?

To counter this idea that feminist politics requires that "woman" possess some determinate meaning, I would like to borrow some ideas about language from Ludwig Wittgenstein. In arguing against a philosophy of language which claimed that meaning in general entailed such determinacy, Wittgenstein pointed to the word "game." He argued that it is impossible to come up with any one feature which is common to everything which is called a "game."

> For if you look at them [the proceedings that we call "games"] you will not see something that is common to *all*, but similarities, relationships, and a whole series of them at that . . . Look for example at board-games, with their multifarious relationships. Now pass to card-games; here you find many correspondences with the first group but many common features drop out, and others appear. When we pass next to ball-games, much that is common is retained, but much is lost . . . And the result of this examination is: we see a complicated network of similarities overlapping and cross-crossing: sometimes overall similarities, sometimes similarities of detail.[37]

Thus, the meaning of "game" is revealed not through the determination of some specific characteristic, or set of such, but through the elaboration of a complex network of characteristics, with different elements of this network being present in different cases. Wittgenstein used the phrase "family relationships" to describe such a network, since members of a family may resemble one another without necessarily sharing any one specific feature in common. Another metaphor which suggests the same point is that of a tapestry unified by overlapping threads of color but where no one particular color is found throughout the whole.[38]

I want to suggest that we think of the meaning of "woman" in the same way that Wittgenstein suggested we think about the meaning of "game," as a word whose meaning is not found through the elucidation of some specific characteristic but is found through the elaboration of a complex network of characteristics. This suggestion certainly allows for the fact that there might be some characteristics – such as possessing a vagina and being over a certain age – which play a dominant role within such a network over long periods of time. However, it also allows for the fact that the word may be used in contexts where such characteristics are not present, for example, in English-speaking countries prior to the adoption of the concept of "vagina," or in contemporary English-speaking societies to refer to those who do not have vaginas but who still feel themselves to be women, i.e. to transsexuals before a medical operation. Moreover, if our frame of reference is not only the English term "woman" but also all those words into which "woman" is translatable, then such a mode of thinking about the meaning of "woman" becomes even more helpful.

It is helpful mostly because of its non-arrogant stance towards meaning. As I mentioned, such a way of thinking about the meaning of "woman" and of its non-English cognates does not reject the idea that over stretches of history there will be patterns. To give up on the idea that "woman" has one clearly specifiable meaning does not entail that it has no meaning. Rather, this way of thinking about meaning works upon the assumption that such patterns are *found* within history and must be documented as such. We cannot presuppose that that meaning which is dominant in contemporary, industrialized western societies must be true everywhere or across stretches with indeterminate boundaries. Thus such a stance does not reject the idea that "the two sex" body has played an important role in structuring the male/female distinction and thus the meaning of "woman" over a certain portion of human history. But it does demand that we be clear about what exact portion that is and even within it, what are the contexts in which it does not apply. Moreover, because such a stance recognizes that the meaning of "woman" has changed over time, it also recognizes that those presently advocating non-traditional understandings of it, such as transsexuals, cannot be dismissed merely on the grounds that their interpretations contradict standard patterns. Janice Raymond claims that no one born without a vagina can claim to have had comparable experiences to those born with one. My question is: how can she know this? How can she know, for example, that some people's parents were not operating with a greater slippage between biology and character than is true for many in contemporary industrialized societies and thus really did provide to their children with "male" genitals experiences comparable to those born with vaginas? History is made by some having experiences which really are different from those which have predominated in the past.

Thus I am advocating that we think about the meaning of "woman" as illustrating a map of intersecting similarities and differences. Within such a map, the body does not disappear but rather becomes an historically specific variable whose meaning and import is recognized as potentially different in different historical contexts. Such a suggestion, in assuming that meaning is found rather than presupposed, also assumes that the search itself is not a research/political project which an individual scholar will be able to accomplish alone in her study. Rather, it implies an understanding of such a project as necessarily a collective effort undertaken by many in dialogue.

Moreover, as both the above reference to transsexuals and my earlier discussion of commonality among women and differences with men should indicate, it is a mistake to think of such a search as an "objective" task undertaken by scholars motivated only by the disinterested pursuit of truth. What we see and feel as commonalities and differences will at least partially depend on our diverse psychic needs and political goals. To articulate the meaning of a word, where any ambiguity exists, and where diverse consequences follow from diverse articulations, is a political act. Thus the articulation of the meaning of many concepts in our language, such as "mother," "education, "science," "democracy," while often described as merely descriptive acts, are, in actuality, stipulative. With a word as emotionally charged as that of "woman," where so much hangs on how its meaning is articulated, any claim about its meaning must be viewed as a political intervention.

But if elaborating the meaning of "woman" represents an ongoing task and an ongoing political struggle, does this not undermine the project of feminist politics? If those who call themselves feminists cannot even decide upon who "women" are, how can political demands be enacted in the name of women? Does not feminism require the very presupposition of unity around meaning which I am saying we cannot possess?

To respond to these concerns, let me suggest a slightly different way of understanding feminist politics than has often been taken for granted. Normally when we think of "coalition politics" we think of groups with clearly defined interests coming together on a temporary basis for purposes of mutual enhancement. On such a view, coalition politics is something which feminists enter into with "others." But we could think about "coalition politics" as something not merely external to feminist politics but as also internal to it. This means that we think about feminist politics as the coming together of those who want to work around the needs of "women" where such a concept is not understood as necessarily singular in meaning or commonly agreed upon. The "coalition" politics of such a movement would be formulated in the same way as "coalition politics" in general are formulated, as either comprised of lists of demands which take care of the diverse needs of the groups constituting the coalition, as comprised of demands articulated at a certain abstract level to include diversity, or as comprised of specific demands which diverse groups temporarily unite around. Indeed, such strategies are those which feminists have increasingly adopted over the past twenty-five-year period. Thus white feminists started talking about reproductive rights instead of abortion on demand when it became clear that many women of color saw access to prenatal care or freedom from involuntary sterilization as at least as relevant to their lives, if not more so, than access to abortion. In other words, feminist politics of the past twenty-five years has already been exhibiting internal coalitional strategies. Why cannot our theorization of "woman" reflect such a politics?

This type of politics does not demand that "woman" possess a singular meaning. Moreover, even when feminist politics does claim to speak on behalf of some one understanding of "woman," can it not explicitly acknowledge such an understanding as political and thus provisional, as open to whatever challenges others might put forth? In other words, can we not be clear that any claims we make on behalf of "women" or "women's interests" are stipulative rather than descriptive, as much based on an understanding of what we want women to be as on any collective survey on how those who call themselves women perceive themselves? Acknowledging the political character of such claims means, of course, abandoning the hope that it is easy determining whose definition of "women" or "women's interests" one will want to adopt. But, that determination has never been easy. Feminists, speaking in the name of "women," have often ignored the claims of right-wing women as they have also taken on ideals about "women's interests" from the male left. That white feminists in the US have increasingly felt it necessary to take seriously the demands of women of color and not the demands of white, conservative women is not because the former possess vaginas that the latter do not, but because the ideals of many of the former more closely conform to many of their own ideals than do those of the conservative women. Maybe it is time that we explicitly acknowledge that our claims about "women" are not based on some "given reality" but emerge from our own places within history and culture; they are political acts which reflect the contexts we emerge out of and the futures we would like to see.

Notes

This essay has been in the making for several years; consequently, it has a long and complex genealogy. For this reason I cannot begin to thank all of the people who have read or heard some ancestor to the present essay and who contributed a little or a lot to the birth of the present version. Many, many people will find much of this familiar. A few special thanks are, however, necessary. I would like to thank the Duke-UNC Chapel Hill Center for Research on Women for providing me with a Rockefeller Foundation Humanist in Residence Fellowship for 1991–2. That fellowship, combined with a University at Albany, State University of New York sabbatical gave me a year to think about many of the ideas in this essay. I also want to thank Steve Seidman for reading every draft and for intervening in the development of this essay at several crucial points.

1   Joan Scott, *Gender and the Politics of History* (New York: Columbia University Press, 1988), p. 2.

2   Gayle Rubin, "The traffic in women," in Rayna Reiter (ed.) *Toward an Anthropology of Women* (New York: Monthly Review Press, 1975), p. 159.

3   Elizabeth Spelman, *Inessential Woman: Problems of Exclusion in Feminist Thought* (Boston, Mass.: Beacon Press, 1988), p. 128.

4   While the growth of a materialist metaphysics may have contributed to the growth of that strong sense of individualism which many writers have linked to modern, western conceptions of the self, it would be a mistake to see such individualism merely as a result of the growth of such a metaphysics. Some writers, such as Charles Taylor, have pointed to an emerging sense of "inwardness," one aspect of such an individualism, as early as in the writings of Augustine. See Charles Taylor, *Sources of the Self: the Making of the Modern Identity* (Cambridge, Mass.: Harvard University Press, 1989), pp. 127–42. And according to Colin Morris, such a turn to a language of inwardness represents a widespread twelfth-century phenomenon. He notes the decline of this tendency in the mid-twelfth century followed by a gradual resurfacing culminating in the late fifteenth-century Italian Renaissance. See Colin Morris, *The Discovery of the Individual* (London: SPCK, 1972). Moreover, even in the period after the emergence of a materialistic metaphysics, social transformations other than the growth of such a metaphysics have contributed to the development of such a sense of individualism differently among different social groups.

5   For the reference to Filmer, see Gordon Schochet, *Patriarchalism in Political Thought* (Oxford: Basil Blackwell, 1975), p. 151 and p. 137. For Locke, see John Locke, *Two Treatises of Government*, ed. and with an introduction by Peter Laslett (New York: New American Library, 1965), p. 364 (par. 82).

6   Ludmilla Jordanova, *Sexual Visions: Images of Gender in Science and Medicine Between the Eighteenth and Twentieth Centuries* (Madison, Wis.: University of Wisconsin Press, 1989), pp. 25–6.

7   Jordanova, *Sexual Visions*, p. 27.

8   For discussions of this point see: Winthrop Jordan, *White Over Black: American Attitudes Toward the Negro, 1550–1812* (Chapel Hill. NC: University of North Carolina Press, 1968), pp. 217–18; Cornell West, "Towards a socialist theory of racism," in Cornell West (ed.) *Prophetic Fragments*, (Grand Rapids, Mich.: William B. Erdmans and Trenton, NJ: Africa World Press, 1988), p. 100; Lucius Outlaw in "Towards a critical theory of race," in David Theo Goldberg (ed.) *The Anatomy of Racism*, (Minneapolis, Minn.: University of Minnesota Press, 1990), p. 63 and Michael Banton and Jonathan Harwood, *The Race Concept* (New York: Praeger, 1975), p. 13.

9   Jordan, *White Over Black*, pp. 3–98.

10 Thomas Laqueur, *Making Sex: Body and Gender from the Greeks to Freud* (Cambridge, Mass.: Harvard University Press, 1990), p. 148.

11 Ibid., pp. 36–7.

12 Ibid., pp. 35–6.

13 Ibid., p. 40. Laqueur's reference is to Galen, *Peri spermatos (On the Seed)*, ed. K. G. Kuhn, 4.2.4, p. 622.

14 Laqueur, *Making Sex*, p. 35.

15 Ibid., pp. 149–50.

16 Londa Schiebinger, "Skeletons in the closet: the first illustrations of the female skeleton in eighteenth century anatomy," in Catherine Gallagher and Thomas Laqueur (eds) *The Making of the Modern Body: Sexuality and Society in the Nine-*

LINDA J. NICHOLSON

teenth Century (Berkeley, Calif.: University of California Press, 1987), p. 42.

17   Scheibinger, "Skeletons in the closet," p. 42.

18   Michel Foucault, *Herculine Barbin*, trans. Richard McDougal (New York: Pantheon, 1980), p. vii.

19   Laqueur, *Making Sex*, pp. 151–2.

20   Any elaboration of this opposition requires a book-length discussion. That a full-scale materialism was not easily endorsed in the very early period is most obviously indicated in the dualism of one of the most outspoken advocates of such a materialism, René Descartes. But even Descartes's position was considered much too radical by the "Cambridge Platonists." In the minds of many of these figures, a complete materialism left no room for God. For an informative discussion of religious tensions around the adoption of materialism through the modern period, see John Hedley Brooke, *Science and Religion: Some Historical Perspectives* (Cambridge: Cambridge University Press, 1991). In the late nineteenth century, other, non-religious arguments emerged against the utility of scientific modes of explanation in accounting for human behavior and social laws. This movement was pronounced in Germany and is represented in the writings of Wilhelm Dilthey.

21   It was as a consequence of reading Chandra Talpade Mohanty's very insightful discussion of Robin Morgan's Introduction to *Sisterhood is Powerful* that I thought of looking to Morgan's essay as a useful exemplar of biological foundationalism. See Chandra Talpade Mohanty, "Feminist encounters: locating the politics of experience," in Michele Barret and Anne Phillips (eds) *Destabilizing Theory*, ed. Michele Barret and Anne Phillips (Cambridge: Polity, 1992), pp. 74–92. I see the intent of Mohanty's analysis as very much overlapping with mine.

22   Robin Morgan, "Introduction/planetary feminism: the politics of the 21st century," in Robin Morgan (ed.) *Sisterhood is Global: the International Women's Movement Anthology* (Garden City, NY: Doubleday, 1984), p. 4.

23   Morgan, *Sisterhood is Global*, pp. 6 and 8.

24   Janice Raymond, *A Passion for Friends: Towards a Philosophy of Female Affection* (Boston, Mass.: Beacon, 1986), p. 21.

25   Janice Raymond, *The Transsexual Empire: the Making of the She-Male* (Boston, Mass.: Beacon, 1979).

26   Ibid., p. 100.

27   Ibid., p. 114.

28   One radical feminist theorist who explicitly endorsed biological determinism in the late 1970s is Mary Daly. In a 1979 interview in the feminist journal *Off Our Backs*, Daly responded to the question whether men's problems are rooted in biology with the response that she was inclined to think they were. See *Off Our Backs* IX 5 (May 1979), p. 23. This interview was brought to my attention by Carol Anne Douglas in *Love and Politics: Radical Feminist and Lesbian Theories* (San Francisco: ism Press, 1990). For other instances of this tendency within radical feminist theory during the 1970s see Alison Jaggar's useful discussion of biology and radical feminism in *Feminist Politics and Human Nature*, pp. 93–8.

29   Iris Marion Young, "Humanism, gynocentrism and feminist politics," in *Hypatia: A Journal of Feminist Philosophy* 3, a special issue of *Women's Studies International Forum* 8/3 (1985), pp. 173–83.

30   Carol Gilligan, *In a Different Voice: Psychological Theory and Women's Development* (Cambridge, Mass.: Harvard University Press, 1983); Nancy Chodorow, *The Reproduction of Mothering: Psychoanalysis and the Sociology of Gender* (Berkeley, Calif.: University of California Press, 1978).

31 Judith Lorber, in faulting Chodorow's work for not paying enough attention to social structural issues, explicitly raised questions about the class biases of *The Reproduction of Mothering*. Her more general points, however, would also apply to race. See her contribution to the critical symposium on *The Reproduction of Mothering* in *Signs* 6/3 (1981), pp. 482–6. Elizabeth Spelman focuses on the ways in which Chodorow's account insufficiently addressed race and class in *Inessential Woman*, pp. 80–113; Adrienne Rich notes the lacuna in Chodorow's analysis regarding lesbianism in "Compulsory heterosexuality and lesbian existence," *Signs* 5/4 (1980), pp. 635–7. Audre Lorde has raised issues of racism in relation to Mary Daly's *Gyn/Ecology* in "An open letter to Mary Daly," in Cherríe Moraga and Gloria Anzaldua (eds) *This Bridge Called My Back: Writings by Radical Women of Color* (Watertown, Mass.: Persephone Press, 1981), pp. 94–7. Spelman also looks at the ways in which Mary Daly's analysis tends to separate sexism and racism and make the latter secondary to the former in *Inessential Woman*, pp. 123–5. The separatism of radical lesbian feminist separatism has been criticized as ignoring issues of race. See, for example, The Combahee River Collective's "Black feminist statement" in *This Bridge Called My Back*, pp. 210–18. The class and race biases of Gilligan's work have been pointed to by John Broughton in "Women's rationality and men's virtues," *Social Research* 50/3 (1983), p. 634. I also develop this issue in my article in that same volume, "Women, morality and history," pp. 514–36.

32 On the ways in which the Native American berdache undermine European notions of gender see Walter I. Williams, *The Spirit and the Flesh: Sexual Diversity in American Indian Culture* (Boston, Mass.: Beacon Press, 1986) and Harriet Whitehead, "The bow and the burden strap: a new look at institutionalized homosexuality in Native North America," in Sherry B. Ortner and Harriet Whitehead (eds) *Sexual Meanings: The Cultural Construction of Gender and Sexuality* (Cambridge: Cambridge University Press, 1981), pp. 8–115. For a useful discussion of the phenomenon of female husbands see, Ifi Amadiume, *Male Daughters, Female Husbands: Gender and Sex in an African Society* (Atlantic Highlands, NJ: Zed Books, 1987). Igor Kopytoff in "Women's roles and existential identities," in Peggy Reeves Sanday and Ruth Gallagher Goodenough (eds) *Beyond the Second Sex: New Directions in the Anthropology of Gender* (Philadelphia, Pa.: University of Pennsylvania, 1990), pp. 77–98 provides an extremely provocative discussion of the relation between the phenomena of female husbands and broader issues concerning the nature of self-identity.

33 Raymond, *The Transsexual Empire*, pp. 28–9.

34 Ibid., pp. xxiii–xxv.

35 This general weakness in arguments which employ the concept of "false consciousness" was suggested to me by Marcia Lind.

36 Of course, the demand for particularity is always relative. As such, any demand for particularity cannot be interpreted in absolutist terms but only as a recommendation for a greater move in such a direction.

37 Ludwig Wittgenstein, *Philosophical Investigations*, trans. G. E. M. Anscombe (New York: Macmillan, 1953), par. 66, pp. 31e–32e.

38 The "tapestry" metaphor was first used in an article I co-authored with Nancy Fraser. See Nancy Fraser and Linda Nicholson, "Social criticism without philosophy: an encounter between feminism and postmodernism," in L. Nicholson (ed.) *Feminism/Postmodernism* (New York: Routledge, 1990).

Susan Shapiro shows how philosophical texts contain gender metaphors that are integral both to how philosophy is conceived as a discipline and to particular philosophical arguments. Focusing on the writings of the Jewish medieval philosopher Maimonides, Shapiro suggests that the gendering and sexualizing of the matter/form distinction supported social practices that subordinated women and it enabled some argumentative moves in a particular religious and cultural debate.

Focus questions:
1 How is matter like a "married harlot" for Maimonides?
2 How does the metaphor of the "married harlot" serve to legitimize wife-beating, according to Shapiro?
3 How does Maimonides use the metaphor of the unfaithful wife to condemn idolatry?

19 A Matter of Discipline: Reading for Gender in Jewish Philosophy

Susan E. Shapiro

Methodological Prelude

Reading for gender in Jewish philosophical texts is an uncommon critical practice. Yet, for both philosophical and feminist reasons, such a hermeneutic is importantly engaged. In this essay, I will first clarify what I mean by "reading for gender" and why I think such a practice should be undertaken. I will then, given the constraints of space, demonstrate what I am talking about by gesturing toward a reading of Maimonides' *Guide of the Perplexed* in these terms.[1]

Reading for gender requires attending to the rhetoricity and textuality of a work, that is, to its patterning of metaphors and other figures and tropes, and not only to its logic. This already represents a shift in certain, but not all, traditional philosophical practices. Rhetoric and poetics may be marginalized in Anglo-American philosophical styles of analysis and argument, but Jewish philosophy has long paid close attention to the role of stories and metaphors in its texts. However, even those who have noticed these metaphors and stories as part of their critical practice have, ultimately, made these aspects of the texts serve merely pedagogical, secondary functions in their interpretations. By contrast, the reading for rhetorics and poetics of gender in Jewish philosophical texts that I propose treats the relation between rhetoric and logic in the reverse; the logical arguments of a text are understood to be prefigured and, thus, made possible by its central rhetorical tropes. These tropes are, thus, considered constitutive and not secondary formations of the logic of philosophical texts.

Reading for gender, however, does not mean reading either for women or as a woman. To read for metaphors of "woman," "body," "gender relations," or "sexuality" is not to read for some actual woman or women that the text, some-how, represents. Nor does reading for gender mean reading as an "essentialized" woman reader who, as a woman, can (supposedly) locate the "feminine" stra-tum of the text. Rather, to read for gender is to read for constructions and performances of gender in these texts with an interest in the intellectual and cultural labor these tropes enact. It is to read, as well, with an interest in their consequences, both within these texts and for readers today. That is, the work performed by these gendered tropes will be found to be philosophical, requir-ing a rethinking of what we understand philosophical texts to be and how they, therefore, may best be read.

A genealogy of key tropes for gender and gender relations in Greek, Jewish, and Arabic philosophy will provide a context for the reading of Maimonides' *Guide of the Perplexed* undertaken here. In this essay, I will be able to indicate only the outlines and basic shape of this interpretive context. This reading, part of a larger work-in-process, makes clear, however, how such a genealogical read-ing works and why it is important. Finally, let me note that in making this turn to rhetoric I am not seeking to reduce other forms of discourse, such as logic, to "mere rhetoric." Rather, I am attempting to demonstrate rhetoric's constitu-tive relation to logic without, thereby, collapsing logic into rhetoric. To do so would simply reverse the usual effacement of rhetoric by logic, a reversal that would betray the critical purposes and potential of the rhetorical turn I propose to undertake.

A Genealogical Introduction

Attaching the unruly aspects of textuality and interpretation to women and the feminine is an ancient topos and philosophical practice. Indeed – as I have ar-gued elsewhere – the very disciplinarity of philosophy is in many respects con-structed through a marginalization and governance of such putatively disruptive and unreliable functions as rhetoric and poetics.[2] Plato, for example, distin-guishes philosophy – rhetoric made just through dialectic – and its other, un-ethical rhetoric: the cosmetic knack of mere appearance and deception. This originary disciplinary moment, thus, required a splitting within rhetoric. Through a dialectic of identity and difference, philosophy was built in opposition to rhetoric as its primary other. Philosophy thereby effaced its own rhetorical origins and character even as it relied on rhetoric to construct its own identity in opposition to her. The *locus classicus* for the constituting of philosophy over against mere rhetoric is Plato's *Gorgias*.[3]

> Socrates: Well then Gorgias, the activity [rhetoric] as a whole, it seems to me, is not an art, but the occupation of a shrewd and enterprising spirit, and of one naturally skilled in its dealings with men, and in sum and substance I call it "flat-tery." . . . There are then these four arts which always minister to what is best, one pair for the body, the other for the soul. But flattery perceiving this – I do not say by knowledge but by conjecture – has divided herself also into four branches, and

insinuating herself into the guise of each of these parts, pretends to be that which she impersonates. And having no thought for what is best, she regularly uses pleasure as a bait to catch folly and deceives it into believing that she is of supreme worth. . . . [T]his then I call a form of flattery, and I claim that this kind of thing is bad . . . because it aims at what is pleasant, ignoring the good, and I insist that it is not an art but a routine, because it can produce no principle in virtue of which it offers what it does, nor explain the nature thereof, and consequently is unable to point to the cause of each thing it offers. And I refuse the name of art to anything irrational. (*Gorgias* 245–7)

This feminine figuration of rhetoric, and its required masculine governance by dialectic to be made just, is a gender division and hierarchy built into the very emergence of philosophy as a discipline. Indeed, philosophy as such is constituted through this splitting of rational and irrational, and constituted further by the gendered splits upon which it is based (soul and body, the good and pleasure, truth and illusion) in which the former term both characterizes and governs (that is, disciplines) the latter term. It is a disciplinary practice repeated throughout the history of both philosophy and the art of rhetoric. Yet, in this Greek context, the association of deception with the nature of the feminine may find its genealogy in the story of Zeus's creation of Pandora as a punishment to mankind. Hesiod wrote of Pandora's fabrication in two places, the *Theogony* and *Works and Days*. I will quote here from the briefer account, *Theogony*:

The famous Lame God plastered up some clay / To look like a shy virgin just like Zeus wanted, And Athena, the Owl-eyed Goddess, / Got her all dressed up in silvery clothes and with her hands draped a veil from her head, / An intricate thing, wonderful to look at. . . . He made this lovely evil to balance the good, / Then led her off to the other gods and men Gorgeous in the finery of the owl-eyed daughter / Sired in power. And they were stunned, Immortal gods and mortal men, when they saw / The sheer deception, irresistible to men. From her is the race of female women, / The deadly race and population of women, A great infestation among mortal men. . . . / That's just how Zeus, the high lord of thunder, Made women as a curse to mortal men, / Evil conspirators. And he added another evil To offset the good. Whoever escapes marriage / And women's harm, comes to deadly old age Without any son to support him. . . . / Then again, whoever marries. As fated, and gets a good wife, compatible, / Has a life that is balanced between evil and good, A constant struggle. But if he marries the abusive kind, / He lives with pain in his heart all down the line, / Pain in spirit and mind, incurable evil. / There's no way to get around the mind of Zeus.[4]

Pandora is a cosmetic creature, made to deceive and ensnare man through that which is pleasing, not good. Pandora is impersonation herself, a "shrewd and enterprising spirit, naturally skilled in dealing with men."[5] It is not at all difficult to hear and see this "female woman," Pandora, in Plato's characterization of rhetoric as a mere deceptive knack of appearing to be that which she is not. Plato's trope of deceptive femininity and its connection to lies and rhetoric, thus seems to find its root, its genealogy, in the figure of Pandora.[6] Mastering Pandora's deceptive and dangerous powers is part of the work of philosophy. It is no surprise, therefore, to find dialectic governing rhetoric in masculine terms, reasserting the power of men over Pandora.[7] The disciplining of rhetoric in Plato's – and, certainly not only Plato's – thought, thus, is accomplished by the mutual configuration of body and discourse through a gender system in which maleness is considered superior to, and more trustworthy than, femaleness and in which, as a rule, men should govern women.

Jewish Philosophy: Intersecting Genealogies

The practice of marginalizing the body and the feminine is evident in Jewish philosophy as well, with important consequences both for the gendering of the Jewish philosophical subject and for the lives of Jewish women and men. Through an examination of selected aspects of the writings of Moses Maimonides, I will demonstrate how this practice of engendering philosophy works in Jewish thought and with what cultural and social consequences. (I am not, however, thereby claiming to characterize all of Jewish philosophy. Rather, here, I separate out a genealogy of one of its most important strands.) I will pay close attention, especially, to how this practice of marginalizing the body and the feminine is instituted and naturalized through figures and tropes of gender difference and hierarchy. I will do this with an eye to the repetition of the earlier disciplining of rhetoric in these terms in Greek thought, now overlaid by the intersection of these tropes with the imagination of idolatry as the dangerous other.

In turning to the works of Maimonides, I will focus on his use of the "married harlot" as a metaphor for matter in the *Guide of the Perplexed*. In so doing, I am purposely selecting one metaphor – a gendered one – through which to represent the relation between body and soul. I am not interested here in the other ways in which Maimonides represents this relationship. Likewise, I am not asserting that this metaphor represents all that Maimonides has to say (even implicitly) about women and female sexuality.[8] I am interested, rather, in tracing the genealogy of a specific trope of female character and sexuality and its various disciplinary roles. Thus, the metaphor of the "married harlot," while of interest in itself, is important, I will argue, in ways that go beyond the literary scope of the *Guide of the Perplexed*. I am interested not only in how this metaphor resonates with Plato's figuration of rhetoric or with Aristotle's understandings of desire but in how it serves other functions within specifically Jewish thought.

For Maimonides, "matter" is considered the source of all corruption (at least, in the sublunar realm). "Form" is considered permanent and, in and of itself, free of all corruption. Because reason and soul must be embodied, form is necessarily tied to matter. Maimonides' asceticism does not go to the extreme of separating body and soul, matter and reason, in this world. The Jewish man must not be celibate but, rather, must marry and have children. The relation between body and reason, matter and form, is itself figured as a marriage, a marriage in which form rules matter, reason rules body, and "husband" rules "wife." Consider in this regard the following key text from the *Guide of the Perplexed*:

> How extraordinary is what Solomon said in his wisdom when likening matter to a married harlot [Prov. 6: 26], for matter is in no way found without form and is consequently always like a married woman who is never separated from a man and is never free. However, notwithstanding her being a married woman, she never ceases to seek another man to substitute for her husband, and she deceives and draws him on in every way until he obtains from her what her husband used to obtain. This is the state of matter. For whatever form is found in it, does but prepare it to receive another form. And it does not cease to move with a view to putting off that form that actually is in it and to obtaining another form; and the selfsame state obtains after that other form has been obtained in actu. It has then become clear that all passing-away and corruption or deficiency are due solely to matter. (*Guide* Bk III: 8)

This metaphor of matter as a married harlot is a bit distracting.[9] What are the implications and genealogy of Maimonides' development of the trope in this way? One strand of its genealogy may be located in a metaphoric development of Aristotle's distinguishing of the respective cosmological roles of matter and particularized privation, in which the latter is figured as a kind of "evil agent." Aristotle sets up an analogy between the relationship of form and matter to male and female as follows: "The truth is that what desires the form is matter, as the female desires the male and the ugly the beautiful – only the ugly or the female not per se but per accidens" (*Physics* Bk I, ch. 9, 192a22–3). Matter's desire for form is, according to Aristotle, for "something divine, good, desirable." The cosmological building blocks or elements are the same in Aristotle's and Maimonides' thought and both figure their relation through the desire of matter for form. But Aristotle's version is a milder analogy whereas Maimonides' metaphor of matter as a "married harlot" is both more specific and more extreme. Maimonides develops this trope of female matter desiring male form not only into a tropics of monogamous marriage but into an asymmetrical marriage between matter as the unfaithful, indeed, nymphomaniacal harlot wife and form as the faithful, always cuckolded husband. Thus, of the three existents subject to generation and corruption in the sublunar realm (matter, form, and particularized privation), it is matter that Maimonides figures most negatively. Matter is the sole cause of corruption (Maimonides follows Plato more than Aristotle in this regard), and its figuration as the harlot wife of form further feminizes and sexualizes this corruption.[10]

The problem, for Maimonides, is how to make matter as good (that is, as obedient to form or reason) as possible. In this way, form will be less corrupted in its relations with matter. It is here that we see the masculine governance of reason reappear, to discipline the married harlot, that is, the male philosopher's body. As Maimonides notes, "he [God] granted . . . the human form . . . power, dominion, rule, and control over matter, in order that it subjugate it, quell its impulses, and bring it back to the best and most harmonious state that is possible."[11]

That the subject of this disciplining is not literally a wife but, as it were, "only" a figurative one – the feminized body of the male philosopher subjugated in its "marriage" to his reason – does not mean that this marriage metaphor is either neutral or benign. In a brief glance at the genealogy of this trope, we find that the rule of the master's masculine reason over the defective or nonauthoritative reason of the females in his household is to be found first, of course, in Aristotle's *Politics* (1254b13–14, Jowett trans.: "Further the male is by nature superior and the female inferior; and the one rules and other is ruled"). This gender hierarchy resonates as well with Plato's mastering of rhetoric as dialectic's feminized other in the *Gorgias*. Should there be a question of what Maimonides' interpretation of woman's nonauthoritative deliberative or practical reason might be – as there is in Aristotle scholarship on this issue – the implications of the metaphor of the "married harlot" seems clear. It is not that woman does not have reason. Nor that it does not function. Rather, woman's reason is weak and fails to have authority over her more powerful, especially sexual, passions.[12] What this trope makes evident, in any case, is that matter's inconstancy and moral corruption is due to its, as it were, "female sexuality," here imagined as promiscuous to the point of nymphomania. Again, we must recall that in the context of the *Guide of the Perplexed*, the matter referred to is that of the male philosopher whose body is thus feminized and in need of masculine disciplining by reason and the commandments. Perhaps the most extreme example of this disciplining is to be found in the *Guide of the Perplexed* Part III: 49:

If a man becomes sexually excited without having intended it, he is obliged to direct his mind to some other thought and to reflect on something else until this sexual excitement passes away. The *Sages, may their memory be blessed*, say in their precepts, which perfect the virtuous: *My son, if this abominable one affects you, drag him to the house of study. If he is of iron, he will melt. If he is of stone, he will break into pieces. For it is said: Is not my word like as fire? saith the Lord; and like a hammer that breaketh the rock in pieces?* [The Sage] says to his son with a view to giving him a rule of conduct: If you feel sexual excitement and suffer because of it, *go to the house of study*, read, take part in discussions, put questions, and be asked in your turn, for then this suffering will indubitably pass away. Marvel at this expression, *this abominable one*, and what an *abomination* this is! . . . Similarly with regard to *circumcision*, one of the reasons for it is, in my opinion, the wish to bring about a decrease in sexual intercourse and a weakening of the organ in question, so that this activity be diminished and the organ be in as quiet a state as possible. . . . In fact this *commandment* has not been prescribed with a view to perfecting what is defective congenitally, but to perfecting what is defective morally. The bodily pain caused to that member is the real purpose of circumcision. . . . The fact that circumcision weakens the faculty of sexual excitement and sometimes perhaps diminishes the pleasure is indubitable. . . . The *Sages, may their memory be blessed*, have explicitly stated: *It is hard for a woman with whom an uncircumcised man has had sexual intercourse to separate from him.* In my opinion this is the strongest of the reasons for *circumcision*. Who first began to perform this act, if not *Abraham* who was celebrated for his chastity . . . , with reference to his dictum: *Behold now, I know that thou art a fair woman to look upon.*[13]

While Maimonides is clearly concerned in this passage with disciplining the male body, he accomplishes this through reference to two kinds of "women." Undisciplined male desire is exemplified by the uncircumcised man, but it is the difficulty of "a woman . . . to separate from him" that represents the very excess of this desire. In this way, the male body is feminized. Like an overly passionate woman, the male body requires disciplining. And Abraham's chastity, exemplified through his circumcision, his properly governed body, is portrayed as a "fair woman to look upon." The excessively passionate woman and the fair woman represent two opposed states of the male body: undisciplined passion versus properly governed passion. The passionate woman is the uncircumcised male and is like the "married harlot," whereas the "fair woman" is the circumcised male and is like the "woman of virtue." In the "marriage" of the male philosopher's reason and body, the commandments – especially circumcision – play an integral role.

Although the consequences of this "marriage" trope, thus, may not be benign for men, it is, as I have already suggested, not thereby without negative consequences for women. There are social and cultural consequences for the tropes philosophers – and others – use to prefigure and make possible their more "properly" logical arguments. As is evident in the text about circumcision (quoted directly above), the disciplining of the male body is itself feminized. As the text and argument continue, Maimonides further intensifies the related metaphor of the "husband's" rule over his "wife"

As for [Solomon's] dictum, "A woman of virtue who can find" [Prov. 31: 10], . . . if it so happens that the matter of a man is excellent, and suitable, neither dominating him nor corrupting his constitution, that matter is an excellent gift. To sum up: it is easy . . . to control suitable matter. If it is unsuitable, it is not impossible for someone trained to quell it. For this reason, Solomon . . . inculcated all these exhortations. Also the commandments and prohibitions of the Law are only intended to quell all the impulses of matter.

In Hesiod's view of marriage, the quality of life for the husband depends on the kind of wife to whom he is married. Hesiod speaks of the "good wife" and an "abusive kind" of wife. In Maimonides' marriage metaphor, matter is figured as a "woman of virtue" or as a "married harlot." While Maimonides portrays "marriage" to suitable matter as a gift, the "husband's" fate depends on more than just the kind and quality of his "wife." Maimonides' "husband" has at his disposal all the commandments and prohibitions of the Law, with which he may quell, discipline, and control unsuitable matter. Even a "woman of virtue" will also always already be a "married harlot" (except, perhaps, for the prophetic virtue finally achieved by Moses). Therefore, the "husband" is enabled to rule his "wife" one way or the other.

So, what difference does it make? One might suggest at this point that this is all much ado about metaphor – metaphors, furthermore, that apparently refer not to actual women but to the body of the male philosopher! And what do metaphors have to do with disciplined philosophical argument, anyway?

To address this question about the role of metaphor in philosophical argument, I will first shift the genre of discourse a bit and consider a text from Maimonides' legal writings. In Chapter 21 of his *Treatise on Marriage* from the *Mishneh Torah*,[14] Maimonides describes the various kinds of work that a wife, and only a wife, must perform for her husband. These include spinning wool; washing his face, hands, and feet; pouring his cup for him; spreading his couch; and waiting on him. If they are poor, she has additional obligations to bake bread, cook food, wash clothes, nurse her child, put fodder before her husband's mount, and attend to the grinding of corn. "A wife who refuses to perform any kind of work that she is obligated to do," Maimonides tells us, "may be compelled to perform it, even by scourging her with a rod." A husband may legally batter his wife with a rod to discipline her, to "quell" her unruliness. However, when a man is to be compelled by the rod, it can be administered only by the court and never, under any circumstances, at the behest of his wife or, indeed, by any woman.

The asymmetry of the marriage metaphor in which husband rules over wife in Maimonides' philosophical work, the *Guide of the Perplexed*, is shown to be no "mere metaphor." As his ruling in the *Mishneh Torah* demonstrates, this asymmetry is violent in its consequences for actual wives and women. I am not suggesting that Maimonides required the metaphor of the "married harlot" to hold this position on wife beating. Nor do I argue that he held this position on the permissibility, even desirability, of wife beating simply because of his metaphoric disciplining of matter as a "married harlot" in the *Guide of the Perplexed*. The metaphor didn't make him do it. Rather, I am suggesting that this trope of marriage in his philosophical work fails to offer corrective resistance to his understandings of marriage in the *Mishneh Torah* and that it further reinforces, rationalizes, and justifies such violence against wives and women. Metaphors matter. They have consequences.

How, then, are we to read the metaphors, figures, and tropes that prefigure and configure philosophical texts? Are we to read them as secondary ornamentation, as elaborations or affectations added to a logical ediface of an already built and freestanding argument? Certainly, that is how these philosophical texts, from Plato's on, would have us read – rather, not read – them. But we have already noted that philosophical discourse instituted a disciplinary opposition between rhetoric and philosophy that was accomplished through figures of gender hierarchy in which the masculine rules over and governs the feminine. Minimally, the very circularity of these claims should suggest the importance of adjudicating between these opposing positions – either that metaphors are marginal and secondary to logic or that metaphors prefigure, make possible, and are, thus, constitutive of philosophical argument. A choice between these two alternatives must be made through examining, among other matters, their respective social consequences and, at a minimum, by undertaking a hermeneutic of suspicion of what political, social, and cultural interests are being served through these discursive arrangements.

I have already indicated the negative consequences of these metaphors for women's lives. I will further suggest that the unarticulated values that undergird, make possible, and shore up philosophical argument are to be found precisely in the seemingly peripheral metaphors, figures, and tropes of philosophical texts. These figures and tropes perform intellectual and cultural labor that is necessary if the so-called properly philosophical work of these texts is to be done. It is labor, furthermore, that only these figures and tropes can perform. The labor of these tropes, however, must be effaced if philosophy is to fulfill its disciplinary telos or dream of self-sufficiency and mastery.[15] Reading for metaphors, for figures and tropes, and for the effaced intellectual and cultural labor they perform in philosophical texts is a way of reading these texts "otherwise," through a redemptive critique. It is to read them for the sake of a transformation of their very subject, their disciplinarity, and their effects.[16]

One of the ways of getting at these figures and tropes by reading otherwise is through their genealogy. That is, one may ask, as I have here: What economies of thought and practice are being established, institutionalized, and maintained through the workings of particular figures or tropes in a given text, say that of the metaphor in the *Guide of the Perplexed* of matter as a "married harlot" who must be disciplined to approximate the "woman of virtue"? I have already traced these tropes within both Greek and Jewish texts. To address this question more fully, it is necessary to turn now to a genealogy of the trope of the "married harlot" at the intersection of Greek and Jewish texts. While in this limited space I cannot adequately focus on the cultural location of this meeting, it is important to note that this intersection occurs in the context of Arabic philosophy.

Jews writing in Arabic or Judeo-Arabic were subjects in a dramatic cultural dynamic and exchange.[17] Admiring much in Arabic culture and thought, Jewish writers were both accommodating and appropriative. Yet, these adaptations were also driven by competition and the need for self-justification. This was, certainly, the case for a Jewish philosopher such as Maimonides. Idolatry was a central issue in Muslim thought; indeed, Judaism was seen as not sufficiently iconoclastic by comparison. It was in this cultural and religious context that Maimonides wrote the *Guide of the Perplexed*, a text whose project as a whole may fairly be described as a critique of idolatrous worship, interpretation, and belief.

In Part I of the *Guide of the Perplexed*, Maimonides systematically reinterprets scriptural references to God that are corporeal, either apparently or implicitly so. In this way, he forestalls possible idolatrous consequences; these bodily references could result in worshipping, as it were, the "wrong" God or wrongly conceiving of the "right" God. The critique of idolatry is the necessary precondition of true discourse about or addressed to God, inasmuch as this "true" discourse entails an iconoclastic understanding of the limits of discourse to represent – or to refer at all – to God. Maimonides' asceticism

READING FOR GENDER IN JEWISH PHILOSOPHY

about bodily terms in scripture that appear to refer or relate to God has, there-fore, to do (at least in part) with his concern that they not be misinterpreted through a literal reading, improperly to impute that God is corporeal. This linguistic asceticism is related to Maimonides' suspicions of the imaginative faculty (except in its productive and reliable use in prophecy). His critique of idolatry is further instituted by the insistence that these bodily terms be read figuratively and that these figures, in turn, be arranged and ruled by logic. This discursive hierarchy, certainly, is related to the general denegration of rhetoric in favor of logic by the Arabic philosophers of his milieu who medi-ated (and altogether made possible) Maimonides' knowledge of Greek philo-sophical texts and traditions.[18] Especially for the philosopher, a proper suspicion and reading of these bodily terms as figurative is emphasized in which, as I have already noted, logic rules over poetic and rhetorical forms of speech. Logic so disciplines in order to guard against idolatrous misinterpretations wherein God has a body (and thus, is not one but many). In Jewish philoso-phy, this is the theological scandal *par excellence*. It is a scandal, however, that is risked in the very contact of Jewish and Greek thought that the *Guide of the Perplexed* marks.

It is at this intersection that the genealogy of the metaphor of the "married harlot" becomes both evident and significant. For it is precisely idolatry that has been figured (in the biblical books of Ezekiel, Hosea, and Jeremiah) through the metaphor of Israel as the unfaithful wife of God, who goes a-whoring after other, foreign gods and thereby breaks the Covenant, with catastrophic conse-quences. Ezekiel 16: 15–26, 28–34 resonates with the *Guide of the Perplexed*'s characterization of matter as a nymphomaniacal, "married harlot" in Part III: 8:[19]

> But confident in your beauty and fame, you played the harlot: you lavished your favors, [Israel], on every passerby; they were his. . . . You played the whore with your neighbors, the lustful Egyptians – you multiplied your harlotries to anger Me. . . . In your insatiable lust you also played the whore with the Assyrians; you played the whore with them, but were still unsated. You multiplied your harlotries with Chaldea, that land of traders; yet even with this you were not satisfied. . . . [You were like] the adulterous wife who welcomes strangers instead of her hus-band.

Aristotle employed a more subtle and less specific metaphor of matter as a woman desiring a man (that is, form) in the *Physics*. This metaphoric usage, however, would not work in the *Guide of the Perplexed*, because if the problem-atic of idolatry is to be introduced into the constitution of matter and its rela-tion to form, matter must be married, even if unfaithfully. Without, as it were, the regulative ideal of Israel's monogamous marriage to God, all one would have is a radical, because unlimited, polytheism. And because God is incorpo-real, body and matter become associated with the other of God, with the idola-trous. The connection between idolatry and sexuality (especially, female sexuality) goes back to Exodus 34: 15–16: "You must not make a covenant with the inhabitants of the land, for they will lust after their gods and invite you, and you will eat of their sacrifices. And when you take wives from among their daughters for your sons, their daughters will lust after their gods and will cause your sons to lust after their gods." It is interesting to note that the problem of idolatry in Exodus is figured in terms of "foreign women" and their seductive importation of other gods. Even in the incident of the Golden Calf, the Midrash insists that the Hebrew women refused to yield their jewelry for the purposes of molding this idol. It is most striking, therefore, that by the time of the prophets, the problem of idolatry was figured in the endogamous terms of Hebrew women's disloyalty, faithlessness, and adultery.

If Aristotle's metaphor of desiring matter is to be made to work at all in the context of a Jewish argument against idolatry such as Maimonides', matter will have to be married to form the way Israel is married to God. The problem is that idolatry – as the desire for other gods or "husbands" – seems to be the state of matter (and of Israel?) as such. As matter (and as Israel), she is married, even if a harlot. And just as disciplining by her "husband" is required to keep or make matter obedient to form, so are God's commandments and laws necessary to keep Israel faithful, to make her a more virtuous "wife" of God. The metaphor of matter as a "married harlot" thereby unites Greek and Jewish thought, tying together in one figure the sins of Israel, the imagination, idolatry, and undisciplined, unethical mattter.[20] Like the disciplining of feminized rhetoric as the other of philosophy in Plato's *Gorgias*, and the rule of the male's reason over his wife (and her nonauthoritative reason) in the household of Aristotle's *Politics*, the disciplining of matter – the wayward wife of form – and of Israel – the unfaithful wife of God – through the commandments of the Law so as to make each one more a "woman of virtue" is performed in Maimonides' *Guide of the Perplexed* through a hierarchy of gender relations, in which male rules female and the masculine supplements and corrects the feminine.[21]

A significant part of the intellectual, indeed philosophical, labor that the trope of the "married harlot" performs in the *Guide of the Perplexed*, then, is to connect Greek and Jewish thinking about matter in an anti-idolatrous text. Different cosmological views, biblical and Greek, are thus made to inhabit the same text – however uncomfortably. The seams of their contradictions are, as it were, sewn together by metaphors (of the "married harlot" and the "woman of virtue"), giving the texture of the *Guide of the Perplexed*'s arguments a conservative and normative appearance. By reproducing a gender hierarchy in which men rule over women in Greek and Jewish, as well as Muslim, cultures, a sense of order and stability is given to an otherwise innovative and, possibly, disruptive philosophical enterprise. Further, in its attempts to appropriate as well as to surpass Muslim and Arabic culture, the *Guide of the Perplexed* trades on these gendered tropes in order to enact this double cultural exchange. The *Guide of the Perplexed*, apparently conserving both Jewish and Greek traditions and (cosmological) positions, radically transforms them through their juxtaposition in that hybrid genre written, in this case, in Judeo-Arabic: "Jewish philosophy."

Notes

I thank Laura Levitt and Miriam Peskowitz for providing this essay such a welcome home [originally in *Judaism Since Gender* (1997): editor]. I am fortunate in both their friendship and intellectual companionship, traces of which are, happily, to be found throughout this essay.

1 Moses Maimonides, *The Guide of the Perplexed*, trans. Shlomo Pines (Chicago: University of Chicago Press, 1963).

2 See my "Rhetoric as ideology critique: the Gadamer–Habermas debate reinvented," *Journal of the American Academy of Religion* 62/1, pp. 123–50.

3 Plato, *Gorgias* 463–6, trans. W. D. Woodhead, in *Plato: The Collected Dialogues*, ed. Edith Hamilton and Huntington Cairns (Princeton, NJ: Princeton University Press, 1961), pp. 245–8.

4 Hesiod, *The Theogony*, trans. Stanley Lombardo, in Contemporary Civilization Reader (New York: American Heritage, 1994), pp. 23–4.

5 As Nicole Loraux notes, "The shimmering veil that Athena uses to cover her protégée and the chiseled diadem that Hephaistos makes for her, add up to equivalents of woman herself. . . . Her veil does not conceal anything other than a woman: not a god, a demon, or a man. It hides nothing, because the woman has no interior to conceal. In short, in the *Theogony*, the first woman *is* her adornments – she has no body" (Nicole Loraux, T*he Children of Athena: Athenian Ideas about Citizenship and the Division between the Sexes* (Princeton, NJ: Princeton University Press, 1993), pp. 80–1). Froma Zeitlin puts the matter differently: "Bodiliness is what most defines her in the cultural system that associates her with the physical processes of birth and death and stresses the material dimensions of her experience, as exemplified, above all, in Hesiod's canonical myth of how the first woman, Pandora, was created. Men have bodies, to be sure, but in the gender system the role of representing the corporeal side of life in its helplessness and submission to constraints is primarily assigned to women" (Froma Zeitlin, "Playing the other: theatre, theatricality, and the feminine in Greek drama," in Froma Zeitlin (ed.) *Nothing to Do with Dionysos* (Princeton, NJ: Princeton University Press, 1990), p. 74).

6 As Froma Zeitlin notes, "Fashioned at the orders of Zeus as punishment for Prometheus's deceptive theft of celestial fire for men, the female is the first imitation and the living counterpart to that original deception. . . . Artifact and artifice herself, Pandora installs the woman as *eidolon* in the frame of human culture, equipped by her 'unnatural' nature to seduce and enchant, to delight and deceive." Zeitlin continues with a – for us – relevant quotation from Pietro Pucci: "Pandora emblematizes the beginning of rhetoric; but at the same time she also stands for the rhetoric of the beginning. . . . The text [Hesiod's *Theogony*] implies both the human dawn unmarked by imitation and rhetoric and a turning point that initiates the beautiful, imitative rhetorical process." Zeitlin properly reminds us, however, that in Hesiod's time (ca. 700 BCE), rhetoric had not yet been invented. "But his [Hesiod's] negative view of Pandora," she continues, ". . . can still serve as a preview of the later philosophical thought, which in testing the world of physical appearances, finds it deceptive precisely in the two spheres of carnal eros and artistic mimesis, specifically in the art of rhetoric itself" (Froma Zeitlin, "Travesties of gender and genre in Aristophanes' *Themorphoriazousae*," in Froma I. Zeitlin, *Playing the Other: Gender and Society in Classical Greek Literature* (Chicago: University of Chicago Press, 1996) pp. 412–13). See also her

"Signifying difference: the case of Hesiod's Pandora," in *Playing the Other*, pp. 53–86.

7   That such a reassertion of power is fated to fail is integral to Hesiod's account of Pandora's creation and nature.

8   For an informative discussion of some of these issues, see W. Zev Harvey, "Sex and health in Maimonides," in Fred Rosner and Samuel S. Kottek (eds) *Moses Maimonides: Physician, Scientist, and Philosopher* (Northvale, NJ: Jason Aronson, 1993), pp. 33–9.

9   I use the term "distracting" here to denote that the reader's attention is distracted by this metaphor away from certain philosophical problems implicit is this discussion, e.g. the question of whether the world is created or eternal in "both directions." Attention is redirected, instead, to matters of sexuality, gender, and marriage. Some readers of this metaphor may have found, as I will suggest below, its implications comforting, giving a sense of familiarity precisely where Jewish and Greek views would seem profoundly to conflict. (And, of course, the *Guide of the Perplexed* was written for various kinds and levels of readers. One might certainly argue – as has been suggested by those of a Straussian persuasion, as well as others – that these metaphors are directed to the many who can't understand the philosophical argument and claims of the *Guide of the Perplexed* and for whom such knowledge would have dangerous consequences. In this brief essay, I cannot address these issues of the varieties of audience response more fully, separating out between different kinds of reception of the metaphors of the *Guide of the Perplexed*.) However, for feminist readers, such metaphors are, certainly, not comforting. Rather, they raise questions for reading that precisely reveal the seams in the argument and the text that these metaphors were meant to conceal.

10   See Isaak Heinemann, "Scientific allegorization during the Jewish Middle Ages," in Alfred Jospe (ed.) *Studies in Jewish Thought: An Anthology of German Jewish Scholarship* (Detroit, Mich.: Wayne State University Press, 1981), esp. pp. 255–6: "The words of the prophets, even if taken literally, contain very useful things, but in their deeper meaning they contain the complete scientific truth. Thus 'the strange woman' in Prov. 7: 5 ff. designates matter (according to III, 8, bad, unreceptive matter in contrast to good matter, the symbol of which is the good woman in Prov. 31: 10ff.). The literal meaning is in no way meant to be disdainful. Indeed, Solomon wrote the book 'as a warning against unchastity and gluttony' (III, 8). But there is a good connection between this literal and the deeper significance, for it is matter which degrades the spirit. The interpretation is based on Plato's comparison of matter with a woman." But, as Shlomo Pines notes, "I 17 refers to Matter having been called a female by Plato and the philosophers who preceded him. With respect to Plato this is not quite accurate, as the Receptacle – a term that was sometimes interpreted as signifying Matter – is designated in the *Timaeus* (51A) as Mother. However, Maimonides may have followed some later Platonistic interpretation" (Shlomo Pines, "Translator's Introduction: the philosophic sources of *The Guide of the Perplexed*," in Moses Maimonides, *The Guide of the Perplexed* (Chicago: University of Chicago Press, 1963), p. lxxvi). Alfred Ivry follows up this insight further in his essay "Maimonides and Neoplatonism: challenge and response," in Lenn G. Goodman (ed.) *Neoplatonism and Jewish Thought* (Albany, NY: SUNY Press, 1992) pp. 137–56. As Ivry notes on pages 152–3, "The indeterminate, 'free' status of matter, then, is not a positive value in Avicenna's scheme, and it is not surprising that the evil in the world

is linked by him directly to matter: unlicensed, uncontrolled, unmodified (by form), matter is seen as a cause of evil in the world. Yet beyond this, the very presence of matter, as the symbol of potentiality and change, is antagonistic to all that God represents."

11 Maimonides, *Guide of the Perplexed*, Part III: 8, p. 432.

12 If this were, in fact, not already the more reasonable reading of Aristotle on this question of woman's nonauthoritative reason, I would hesitate more in reading this position into such a figurative treatment of matter as woman – specifically, as "married harlot" – in Maimonides' thought. See, e.g., Deborah K. W. Modrak, "Aristotle: women, deliberation, and naure," in Bat-Ami Bar On (ed.) *Engendering Origins: Critical Feminist Readings in Plato and Aristotle* (Albany, NY: SUNY Press, 1994), pp. 207–22; and Christine M. Senack, "Aristotle on the woman's soul, in ibid., pp. 223–36. See also Nancy Tuana, "Mutilated men: Aristotle," in her *Woman and the History of Philosophy* (New York: Paragon House, 1992), esp. pp. 28–9.

13 Maimonides, *Guide of the Perplexed*, p. 608 (italics in the Pines translation).

14 Moses Maimonides, ch. XXI of *Laws Concerning Marriage* Treatise I in *The Book of Women, Code of Maimonides (Mishneh Torah)*, Book IV, ed. Leon Nemoy and trans. Isaac Klein, Yale Judaica Series, vol. 19 (New Haven: Yale University Press, 1972), pp. 130–5, esp. Item 10 on pp. 131–3. I would like to thank Ruth Sandberg, Leonard and Ethel Assistant Professor of Rabbinics, Graetz College, for bringing this passage to my attention.

15 As Michele le Doeuff suggests, "Philosophical discourse is inscribed and declared its status as philosophy through a break with myth, fable, the poetic, the domain of the image. . . . Philosophy has always arrogated to itself the right or task of speaking about itself, of having a discourse about its own discourse and its (legitimate or other) modes, writing a commentary on its own texts. This metadiscourse regularly affirms the nonphilosophical character of thought in images. But this attempted exclusion always fails, for 'in fact, Socrates talks about laden asses, blacksmiths, cobblers, tanners'. Various strategies have been pursued to exorcize this inner scandal. One of them consists in projecting the shameful side of philosophy on to an Other. . . . [W]hether the image is seen as radically heterogeneous to, or completely isomorphous with, the corpus of concepts it translates into the Other's language, the status of an element within philosophical work is denied it. It is not part of the enterprise. In either case it falls within what Foucault calls the teratology of a knowledge – and the good reader, who has passed through the philosophical discipline, will know he should pass it by" (Michele le Doeuff, *The Philosophical Imaginary*, trans. Colin Gordon (Stanford: Stanford University Press, 1989), esp. pp. 1–6).

16 See my "Rhetoric as ideology critique" for a discussion of the role of rhetoric in redemptive critique.

17 Ross Brann, *The Compunctious Poet: Cultural Ambiguity and Hebrew Poetry in Muslim Spain* (Baltimore, Md.: Johns Hopkins University Press, 1991).

18 As Brann notes in The Compunctious Poet, pp. 72–3: "Attitudes toward poetry, such as we expressed in Judeo-Arabic poetic theory, were deeply influenced by the Arabic glosses on Aristotle's epistemology. The implications of the relationship between poetry and philosophy in literary theory were profound. Medieval speculative philosophers living in Islamic domains read Aristotle in such a way as to relegate the rhetorical arts, including poetry, to the bottom of the scale in the hierarchy of the intellect. According to the influential thinker al-Farabi (d. ca.

950), for example, the use of persuasion (rhetoric) and imaginative representation (poetry) in shaping the theological opinions of the masses (who are incapable of grasping dialectical proofs) is an indication of the inferior logic and lowly status of rhetoric. Furthermore, . . . al-Farabi defines a wholly false statement as poetic and imitative. Since poetry lacks logical rigor, deals only with imitations (mimesis), and does not contribute to cognitive knowledge, philosophy defined it as an artistic enterprise (*sina a*) that bordered on meaningless activity. Jewish thinkers followed al-Farabi in dismissing poetry to an intellectual exile remote from philosophical truth. Moses Maimonides (1135–204) . . . describes poetry in his treatise on logic as an art 'that praise[s] and blame[s] things in no ways other than by means of imitations." The fact that Maimonides' views of rhetoric and logic were derived from Arabic thought and that his knowledge of Greek philosophy was, of course, utterly dependent on its Arabic mediation, is a very important and, alas, in this brief essay, an underexplored site and link at the intersection of the two genealogies I am tracing here, that is, Greek philosophical and the Jewish scriptural texts and traditions. See also Arthur M. Lesley, "A survey of medieval Hebrew rhetoric" in David R. Blumenthal (ed.) *Approaches to Judaism in Medieval Times*, Brown Judaic Studies, no. 54 (Chico, Calif.: Scholars Press, 1984), pp. 107–33; and Deborah L. Black, *Logic and Aristotle's* Rhetoric *and* Poetics *in Medieval Arabic Philosophy* (Leiden: E. J. Brill, 1990), as well as Arthur Hyman (ed.) *Essays in Medieval Jewish and Islamic Philosophy* (New York: KTAV Publishing House, 1977).

19 The relevant text from Maimonides is "How extraordinary is what *Solomon* said in his wisdom when likening matter to *a married harlot*, for matter is in no way found without form and is consequently always like *a married woman* who is never separated from a man and is never *free*. However, notwithstanding her being *a married woman*, she never ceases to seek for another man to substitute for her husband, and she deceives and draws him on in every way until he obtains from her what her husband used to obtain. This is the state of matter. For whatever form is found in it, does but prepare it to receive another form. And it does not cease to move with a view to putting off that form that actually is in it and to obtaining another form; and the selfsame state obtains after that other form has been obtained in actu" (Maimonides, *Guide of the Perplexed*, p. 431 (italics in the Pines translation).

20 This disciplining of matter and of Israel does not finally resolve their inherent tendency to idolatry and promiscuity but, rather, merely holds it temporarily in check (except in the case of Moses). I thank Natalie Kampen for raising this question and for her most helpful close reading of this essay.

21 Again, as I have already noted, it is important to recognize the Arabic context for this intersection. I must, alas, defer treatment of this subject to another occasion.

While I don't enter here into the question of which texts of Greek philosophy Maimonides had access to and when, I will note that I am not suggesting that he had direct access to Aristotle's *Politics*, but that he probably had it in part through the mediation of Arabic philosophy. I have benefited from the comments and suggestions of Peter Awn and Elizabeth Castelli, for which I thank them both.

[Taken from: *Judaism Since Gender*, ed. Laura Levitt and Miriam Peskowitz (London: Routledge, 1997).]

Christine Battersby ·examines Immanuel Kant's notion of the sublime in order to demonstrate how human intellectual, moral, and creative capacities were assigned according to gender in the European Enlightenment period. Battersby shows how the development of particular moral and aesthetic concepts in philosophy is tied to viewing females as distinct but inferior creatures.

Focus questions:
1 How does Kant's notion of the sublime reflect both the devaluation of qualities considered feminine and the inferiority of human beings who are female?
2 How might a "woman-centered philosophy" valorize capacities and traits we associate with women? Must philosophy be either female-centered or male-centered?

20 Stages on Kant's Way: Aesthetics, Morality, and the Gendered Sublime

Christine Battersby

For the eighteenth-century Scots, "moral philosophy" encompassed both ethical and aesthetical enquiries, and the French *philosophes* also moved easily between the two realms. It was only really with Kant[1] that the distinction between ethical and aesthetic attitudes to the world was sharpened. But this division would work to the disadvantage of women who frequently found themselves entirely excluded from the ethical sphere, or granted a different – inferior – form of moral consciousness. Thus, Freud remarks: "I cannot evade the notion (though I hesitate to give it expression) that for women the level of what is ethically normal is different from what it is in men. Their super-ego is never so inexorable, so impersonal, so independent of its emotional origins as we require it to be in men."[2]

For Freud, female "character-traits" include showing "less sense of justice than men," being "less ready to submit to the great exigencies of life," and being "more often influenced in their judgements by feelings of affection or hostility." These prejudices of 1925 are prefigured in Kant's views, expressed most clearly in an early work of 1764. There we are told that women do not distinguish between good and bad actions on the basis of a moral sense, but by means of aesthetic taste:

> The virtue of a woman is a *beautiful virtue*. That of the male sex should be a *noble virtue*. Women will avoid the wicked not because it is unright, but because it is ugly; and virtuous actions mean to them such as are morally beautiful. Nothing of duty, nothing of compulsion, nothing of obligation! . . . I hardly believe that the fair sex is capable of principles, and I hope by that not to offend, for these are also extremely rare in the male. (*O*, p. 81 (2: 231–2))

Women have traditionally been confined to the stage of consciousness that post-Kantian philosophers termed the "aesthetic." As Judge William put it in

Kierkegaard's *Stages on Life's Way*, "A feminine soul does not have and should not have reflection the way a man does"; rather "in her immediacy, woman is essentially esthetic."[3] It is, therefore, ironic that although the present-day opponents of feminism have been able to grasp that there might be a place for feminist ethics or feminist political theory within the discipline of philosophy, there is much more hostility to the notion of feminist aesthetics. Nor is it only from outside feminism that such opposition has originated. One of the most important feminist art historians, Griselda Pollock, has argued that feminists should "stop merely juggling the aesthetic criteria for appreciating art" and "reject all of this evaluative criticism."[4] In literary criticism there has also been too quick a move to neutral ground "beyond" feminist aesthetics.[5] Whereas feminists emerging from the Marxist and socialist traditions have wanted to legitimize value judgments in ethics and politics, feminist aesthetics has been regarded as necessarily ahistorical and essentialist in approach, as conservative, or, at best, confused.[6]

This hostility to a feminist aesthetics is produced, at least in part, by the acceptance of an idea that Kant developed in his later work: the *Critique of Judgment* (1790). There Kant argued – in a way that he did not in the 1764 essay – that a truly aesthetic value judgement must be "disinterested"; it must abstract from all use value and material value, and concentrate solely on the object or artwork considered as form. I shall here address the question of whether or not feminist philosophers should accept Kantian markers for the boundary between the aesthetic and nonaesthetic realms. I shall look at the way gender operates at the point in Kant's philosophy at which the aesthetic and ethical attitudes intersect: in the experience of the sublime. As we shall see, the later developments within the Kantian system mean that women fit comfortably neither side of the aesthetic/ethical divide and, indeed, fall outside personhood altogether.

Those who have addressed the question of gender in Kant's philosophy have looked primarily at that other boundary: between the moral and the political. What has been explored is the tension that exists between Kant's moral notion of freedom (as a requirement to respect all rational beings), and his political conception of freedom, which would limit the rights of citizenship to those adult males who are their "own masters."[7] Susan Mendus has argued that the paradoxicality of Kant's position on women cannot simply be explained away by reference to more general fault lines that run across the Kantian system: described variously by Kant's commentators as being "between conservatism and radicalism; idealism and pragmatism, rationalism and empiricism." Instead, Kant's comments on female nature in *Anthropology* (1798) are read by Mendus as "merely ludicrous," a result of "prejudice" and "bigotry" that could come only from a lack of experience of women.[8]

It is, however, important to recognize that Kant's comments on women are in a sense a compromise between conservatism and radicalism. And we can understand this point most clearly by focusing on that other boundary: the sublime. Kant's aesthetic theories also both reflect and resist the revolutionary: registering the radical breakdowns in gender categories that occurred toward the end of the eighteenth century, but also providing new rationalizations for an ancient sexual conservatism.

In *Gender and Genius*, I showed how notions of sex difference were fundamentally revised during the so-called Enlightenment period, as both Christianity and Aristotelianism lost their authority. Emotion, strong imagination, wildness, and powerful sexual appetite – characteristics previously despised and associated with females – were revalued when located in the bodies of an elite of males.[9] Male geniuses were promoted as "sublime" and godlike creators, while women found themselves confined to the (distinctly inferior) category of the "beautiful" by the new aesthetic vocabularies and gender distinctions that came into play during this period. Instinct, madness, the primitive, and the capricious remained "feminine" characteristics and were admired (in psychically androgynous males); but they were no longer thought of as specifically *female* characteristics. During the Renaissance, it had been woman who was represented as the sexually greedy partner. But by the mid-nineteenth century, the ideal bourgeois woman was an "angel in the house," totally lacking in sexual appetite. During the transitional phase of the Enlightenment, woman was increasingly deprived of sisterhood with the wild and threatening aspects of nature. "Beauty" linked women with delicacy, gentleness, softness, tenderness, and charm.

During the late eighteenth century unimproved nature gained a male face as it became more admired. Mary Wollstonecraft – one of the writers most enthralled by the "sublime" – was not being simply eccentric when she referred to the "Father of nature."[10] The "sublime" was often explicitly, and nearly always implicitly, gendered as male. Thus, in his influential *A Philosophical Enquiry into the Origin of our Ideas of the Sublime and Beautiful* (1757), Edmund Burke seems to have deliberately adopted the language of sexual power to explain the psychological thrill that comes from the sublime. The latter is exemplified by kings and commanders discharging their terrible strength and destroying all obstacles in their paths, as well as by the grandeur of the Alps.[11] By contrast, the "beautiful" – small, smooth, delicate, and graceful – is claimed to be what men (= males) love in the opposite sex (*Enquiry*, pp. 42–3, 112ff.). In much of the aesthetic literature of the period, the sublime is described as a natural force that overpowers and overwhelms the spectator by a kind of mental rape.

The spectator was passive, but so was the genius himself. Since art (even poetry, music, and tragedy) was conceptualized as an essentially mimetic activity, the genius remained little more than a privileged spectator of the sublime. Shakespeare, for example, was presented as the archetypal "natural" genius who produced his works as painlessly, as effortlessly, and as automatically as a bird on a bough in a forest produces its song. He was sublime because his subject matter was sublime: blasted heaths, ghosts, storms, shipwrecks, and terrible passions. Shakespeare was a lawless, wild "child of nature" who broke all the rules of neoclassical drama, and who was nonetheless still (mysteriously) awe-inspiring. Shakespeare was a "primitive": untutored; artless; producing his works in a blank ecstasy of imaginative and passionate inspiration; merely imitating the strong emotions that nature induced in him.

The Romantics switched the emphasis away from the reactions of a passive spectator to the actions of the artistic producer. In particular, they abandoned the notion that a sublime artwork simply overwhelms the mind of the audience with the refracted thrills of nature. However, they continued to describe that producer in language that suggested the genius retained elements of the old passivity. In the passive/active state of "intellectual intuition," the Romantic genius was provided with privileged access to the sublime and to the infinite power of nature. Indeed, the Romantics inherited from the pre-Romantics a taste for "nature" in its most savage and unimproved mode: for primeval and desolate landscapes, untouched by agriculture and untamed by gardening. Gaunt mountains, thunder and lightning, the immensity of the ocean – all remained "sublime" and were contrasted with the delicacy and "beauty" of the tranquil and cultivated valleys.[12] None of the passivity – and "femininity" – of that contact with the sublime rendered the archetypal genius female, however. Though like a woman, he was not a woman.

Kant's pre-critical essay, *Observations on the Feeling of the Beautiful and the Sublime* (1764), and his *Critique of Judgment* (1790) are positioned at this pre-Romantic and Romantic divide. *Observations* is a straightforwardly pre-Romantic text; but the Third Critique builds on the epistemological groundwork of Kant's earlier *Critique of Pure Reason* (1781) and reverses previous ontological dependencies by making nature dependent on man. This is Kant's so-called Copernican revolution, which was so important for the German Romantics and for Coleridge. There are, however, constancies, as well as change, in Kant's position, and one of the constancies is the duty Kant imposes on women not to render themselves sublime.

The differentiation between the characteristics considered "beautiful" (and typical of ideal females) and characteristics designated "sublime" (and typical of a male cultural elite) became a dominant topic in eighteenth-century "moral" philosophy. Into this tradition of theorizing sex differences Kant's *Observations* neatly fits:

> The fair sex has just as much understanding as the male, but it is a *beautiful understanding*, whereas ours should be a *deep understanding*, an expression which signifies identity with the sublime.
>
> To the beauty of all actions belongs above all the mark that they display facility, and appear to be accomplished without painful toil. On the other hand, strivings and surmounted difficulties arouse admiration and belong to the sublime. Deep meditation and a long-sustained reflection are noble but difficult, and do not well befit a person in whom unconstrained charms should show nothing else than a beautiful nature. Laborious learning or a painful pondering, even if a woman should greatly succeed in it, destroy the merits that are proper to her sex. (*O*, p. 78 (2: 229)

It is the difficult, the challenging, and the overcoming of obstacles that Kant most values; these are characteristics identified with the "sublime," and restricted to male human beings. Although Kant goes on to indicate that some (few) women are capable of the sublime, he judges this to be unnatural and "disgusting" (*ekelhaft*) (*O*, p. 83 (2: 233)). "A woman who has a head full of Greek" or who indulges in arguments about mechanics "might as well even have a beard" (*O*, 78 (2: 229–30)). Her knowledge makes her ugly: makes her unable to carry out her aesthetic duties of being charming, being beautiful, and appealing to the sexual appetites of the males – thereby helping nature to propagate the race. There is thus a difference in this early work between Kant's claim about women's moral capacities – that women just do not happen to be able to follow moral principles – and his aesthetical claim that women should never attempt the sublime. In this early Kantian work we are already in a Kierkegaardian mode: facility, ease (and hence immediacy) are aesthetic duties for women. The question that raises itself for the aesthetic/ethical boundary is not, therefore, simply to do with Kant's "factual" errors about female nature, but about the duty that Kant imposes on women to remain in the immediate, and to leave their powers of reason undeveloped.

In Kant's later writings women continue to have a duty to remain outside the sublime, even though the gendering of human excellence disrupts and disturbs the whole of his critical system. Kant could not avoid these stresses, since he was revolutionary enough to accept the new anti-Aristotelian accounts of human excellence and also revolutionary enough to refuse the traditional Christian accounts that made goodness and beauty absolutes, dependent solely on God for their universal validity. But Kant was also conservative enough to have retained the older accounts of female nature: his women have a lust to dominate, have sexual appetites as strong as those of the men, and have strong emotions and instincts that must be governed and harnessed. Kant's woman is not in herself beautiful or in harmony with man's ends and purposes as a social creature. Woman – like Nature – has to be reconstructed in accordance with man's will and man's imagination. Thus in the *Anthropology* Kant would claim that in primitive societies woman is no more than a domestic animal, a *Hausthier* (*A*, p. 168 (7: 304)). It is only civilization that has rendered her a tender, delicate, domestic, nurturing – "beautiful" – companion for the male.

In *Religion within the Limits of Reason Alone* (1793) Kant divides the determining forces of human behavior into three main types: (1) animality/*Thierheit* (instinctual drives, passions etc.); (2) humanity/*Menschheit* (the ability to judge, reason, and posit ends for action based on a comparison between the self and others); and (3) personality/*Persönlichkeit* (the capacity to act in accordance with the dictates of reason and the will).[13] Reading Kant's remarks about women in the *Anthropology* and elsewhere in the light of this division it becomes clear that for Kant women are both fully animal and fully human, but he sees no need for them to develop the potential for personality. Thus, if we compare Kant's essay "An answer to the question: 'What is Enlightenment?'" with his approval of women (of whatever age) remaining in tutelage, we see that "Enlightenment" (defined as freedom from tutelage) is for Kant an inappropriate goal for women. Within the public sphere, husbands (or other males) are required to act as women's guardians.[14]

In a Kantian society it is the task of the males – particularly husbands – to discipline the anarchic forces implicit in female nature. Far from being bizarre and eccentric prejudices "almost wholly uncluttered by any actual experience," as Mendus supposes (1987: 35), Kant's views in the *Anthropology* show that he has interpreted his experience of women through the older stereotypes of female nature still in play during the eighteenth century. Rousseau is the most obvious influence; but the reader attuned to Enlightenment rhetoric can also find persistent echoes of Hume and the whole *Spectator* tradition of domesticating women into becoming suitable wives for male citizens who are their "own masters."[15]

In the Kantian universe it is the individual person who legislates moral and aesthetic values through his own will and through the play of his faculties. By the time he writes his critical philosophy, however, Kant is taking a stand against empiricism (with its emphasis on passivity, sensibility, and affectivity), as well as against the *Sturm und Drang* accounts that made the male subject as arbitrary, capricious, and irrational a creature as a Renaissance female. Thus Kant's later critical writings continued to have a strongly charged sexual subtext. Kant was attempting to return to the older notions of maleness that were uncontaminated by the newly revalued passions and irrationality. To this end, he adopted a kind of radical conservatism that was recognized as having revolutionary implications by his contemporaries. Thus Goethe praised Kant for his "immortal service" of having "brought us all back from that effeminacy in which we were wallowing."[16] To understand this "immortal service" more fully it will be necessary to summarize Kant's account of the differences between the beautiful and the sublime in the *Critique of Judgment*. This will help us understand how Kant's position had changed since *Observations*, and how he manipulated the transcendental ego – apparently gender-neutral, in that it is no more than a logical construct – to fit onto the body of a human male.

In the pre-critical *Observations* woman was among the paradigm examples of the "beautiful." In the Third Critique, by contrast, it is objects in nature that have become the paradigm, and a special analysis is required to explain how the term "beautiful" can be applied to human beings at all. Kant's examples of the sublime in the Third Critique have also changed so as to place less emphasis on (male, European) humans and more on natural objects. However, great military commanders and geniuses still count as sublime – along with bold, overhanging, and threatening rocks; clouds piled up in the sky; great waterfalls; storm-ridden seas; earthquakes and volcanoes (*CJ*, sect. 28, pp. 100–2 (5: 260–3)). All of these would also have qualified as "sublime" in *Observations*, but Kant no longer describes the sublime as a passive response to the overwhelming, the powerful, the massive, and the colossal.[17] In the *Critique* it is not objects in nature that are *in themselves* sublime or beautiful; rather, these are qualities read on to nature by human beings (*CJ*, sect. 1, p. 37; sect. 26, p. 95 (5: 203, 256)).

In *Observations* Kant could see no transcendent element in the human response to beauty. It was all just a matter of *Reiz* – normally translated as "charm" but better rendered as "attraction" – and Kant quite specifically made sexual attraction the underlying *Reiz* (*O*, pp. 86ff. (2: 235ff.)). In the *Critique of Judgment*, on the other hand, beauty has a transcendent element: it is consistent with attraction (including sexual attraction), but a response is aesthetic insofar as the experiencing subject abstracts from all *Reiz* – and hence from all use value and material value – and concentrates solely on the form of the object. The pure aesthetic reaction is "disinterested." And, since such a pure response will not generate the peculiar feeling of the sublime, the latter can never be as purely aesthetic as the appreciation of beauty (*CJ*, sect. 13, p. 59; sect. 14, p. 62 (5: 223, 226)).

The pleasure in the beautiful comes from the mind's creation of a (phenomenal) reality that seems purposively designed to accord with human capacities (*CJ*, sect. 10, pp. 54ff. (5: 219ff.)). Beauty – and this will include an appreciation of *Frauenzimmern* (a rather derogatory term for women that takes their shape or "frame" as their most salient characteristic – involves pleasure in constructing and forming nature in such a way that it seems non-threatening. The sublime, by contrast, involves registering nature as a noumenal, superhuman, nonconstructed infinity: it involves *Rührung* (usually translated as "emotion" but better rendered as "psychic disturbance" or "turbulence"). The sublime involves an enjoyment of the threatening: an awareness of danger, an attitude of respect (*Achtung*) for that which could overwhelm the ego (*CJ*, sect. 27, pp. 96ff. (5: 257ff.)).

The appreciation of the sublime is the negation of fear: it requires both an appreciation of the terribleness of the object surveyed and a (simultaneous) transcendence of terror (*CJ*, sect. 28, pp. 99–100 (5: 260–1)). For Kant such pleasures are closed off to all except the "moral man" who has been educated into confidence in the power of his own ego over nature (*CJ*, sect. 29, pp. 104ff. (5: 264ff.)). According to Kant, this will exclude those who have been taken over by the spirit of trade (*Handelsgeist*), by base self-interest (*Eigennutz*), softness (*Weichlichkeit*), and cowardice (*Feigheit*) (*CJ*, sect. 28, p. 102 (5: 263)). A "tender [*weich*] though weak [*schwach*] soul" (that is, an ideal woman) could never have the right attitude of mind; but the non-ideal woman would also be unlikely to qualify. Kant is scathing about all cringing, ingratiating, abject creatures who have no confidence in their own strengths, and about those who are only concerned with mental ease and pleasure. Such attitudes are not even compatible, Kant says, with the (still distinctly second-rate) category of the beautiful (*CJ*, sect. 29, pp. 113–14 (5: 273–4)).

Kant's analysis of the sublime is thus intimately connected with his (gendered) notion of personality. A man proves his superior moral excellence by his ability to experience the sublime. And it is significant to note in this context that *Achtung* – the attitude of respect that is an integral part of the experience of the sublime – is also a key term in Kant's moral philosophy. It is that feeling (which is not strictly a feeling) that accompanies the adoption of the universal law (and hence that is required in our dealings with other persons).[18] Through his analysis of the sublime Kant escapes from his previously deontological system of ethics into aretaics. He redraws the gender divide in the Third Critique by returning to Greek notions of warrior virtues. War, we are told, is both sublime and more likely than long periods of peace to produce men capable of experiencing the sublime (*CJ*, sect. 28, p. 102 (5: 262–3)).

As in the *Observations*, Kant does not make it a logical impossibility for a woman to thrill to the sublime; but there is no inference that women should be educated into the kinds of courage and self-confidence that would enable them to rise above fear. On the contrary, Kant claims in the *Anthropology* that it is important for women to be timorous in the face of physical danger. Since the future of the human race is in the hands – or, rather, the womb – of women, to ensure the continuance of the species women should be concerned with their own physical safety (*A*, 169 (7: 306)). But this is an important rider to the Kantian system, because such feelings will debar women from developing *Achtung*: that reverential attitude necessary for experiencing the sublime; for acting in accordance with universal duty; for imaginative access to the noumenal realm, and hence for visionary insights of a religious nature. Kant's women are thus not incapable of becoming "persons" in the full sense that Kant outlines in his *Religion*, but have no duty to do so. On the contrary, although Kant's women count as "humans," their duty is to remain also akin to his instinct-driven "animals."

Kant concludes this point in the *Anthropology* not by demanding that women's weakness should be corrected by women themselves, but instead by requiring males to act as the protectors of women. Since Kant then goes on immediately to make reference to a kind of "cultivated propriety" that masquerades as true (duty-based) virtue, we can be sure that Kant had recognized the implications of this gendering of human excellence. Here, in the context of thinking about women and children, Kant condones actions motivated by feeling as integral to human culture and refinement.

Kant's comments on gender show him registering the importance of emotion to bodily and species survival; but only to one-half of the human race. Since it is clearly unsatisfactory for him to have devised a "universal duty" that excludes women, Kant's system of morality requires major revision. In this context, however, it is worth noting that Kant makes some useful points about the different attitudes that are open to those educated into bodily transcendence and those encouraged to respect their bodily desires and emotions. We could allow that, in our society, models of virtue and personhood are indeed gendered – or that the experience of the "sublime" might indeed be different for women – without, in any way, endorsing Kant's conservative conclusions about female nature.

If, in our society, a typically "female" response to the infinite and overwhelming involves immanence, rather than transcendence, it would disappear from literary histories that use Kantian markers to demarcate the contours of that contact with the unrepresentable that constitutes the sublime. This seems to be what has gone wrong with Timothy Gould's attempt to develop "a feminist perspective on the Kantian sublime." He simply accepts that "the experience of the sublime was initially the province of male writers."[19] And the same is true of Patricia Yaeger's recent account of the "feminine" or "pre-Oedipal" sublime, since she supposes these genres limited to "recent decades."[20]

The poetry of Karoline von Günderode (1780–1806) and the prose of her friend, Bettina von Arnim (née Bettine Brentano, 1785–1859), effectively show that such critics are viewing history through eyes that take the male writer as both norm and ideal. Günderode was immersed in the philosophy of Kant, Schelling, and Novalis, and used her mystical poetry and dramas to appropriate the sublime for female writers – a point not lost on Bettina who tried in her novel *Die Günderode* (1840) to position Karoline in her life and tragic suicide as the epitome of the female sublime.[21] . . .

Kant has often been attacked for leaving no room at all for emotion and for sexuality in his moral and aesthetic theory. Günderode's ability to negotiate the Kantian sublime indicates that such blanket dismissals of Kant as rationalistic are too simplistic. She manipulates the Kantian sublime so as to counterpoise "male" positions of transcendence (up in the heavens) by an emotional inter-penetration with the earth (which she describes as a womb).[22] To understand how such reversals might be possible within a Kantian frame, it is necessary to refute a number of charges commonly leveled against Kant by recent feminist philosophers.

Robin May Schott, for example, has criticized Kant for portraying "the ideal man as a highly disciplined, apathetic creature who values pain above pleasure, whose greatest enjoyment consists in the relaxation following work, and who finds no place for love in his life."[23] But this criticism rests on a simple misun-derstanding of Kant's praise of "apathy": a state of mind that Kant is careful to explain did not for the Stoics involve indifference to emotion, but which in-stead involved the transcendence of emotion.[24] Similarly when Schott criticizes Kant for delineating emotion as "an intoxicant which one has to sleep off" and passion as putting the self "in chains," she registers Kant's distinction between an affect (*Affekt*) and a passion (*Leidenschaft*), but without apparently grasping that Kant graded emotions (such as anger) above passions (such as hatred). Emotions are affects, says Kant, that come before reflection and can therefore be transcended once reason comes into play. Much worse are passions – "*appe-tite* grown into permanent inclination" – which exist alongside reason and are indulged with a "calmness" that "leaves room for reflection." Passion is con-demned as a vice; emotion, by contrast, is "childish" and "weak" but, since it is natural, is not in itself morally evil.[25]

What is wrong with Kant's account of emotion and of sexuality from a femi-nist point of view is not simply that he downgrades so-called feminine charac-teristics of mind, as Schott's analysis would suggest; but rather, that he tries to re-establish the old (Aristotelian) sexual polarities that bind rationality, creativ-ity, and the highest moral duties to the bodies of an elite of males. Kant implic-itly lines up all women on the side of "weakness." Women either cannot – or should not – transcend fear. Males should ideally transcend fear, and only the (male) human being who has reached these lofty heights can be said to repre-sent the universal – and make valid judgments of taste – or to be fully moral.

Similar remarks apply to Kant's comments on sexual desire. Schott suggests that Kant has a hostility toward sex analogous to that of the Christian mystics. She claims that Kant is so reluctant to mention the sexual act that he uses nine-teen different Latin phrases on one page, rather than discuss it in his own tongue (*Cognition*, p. 113). But in the *Lectures on Ethics*, Kant's Latin phrases serve to make more explicit his detailed catalogue and grading – in German – of the variety of sexual perversions. Kant's text continues the German "natural law" tradition of finding justifications for social order that do not rest simply on divine law. Thus Kant's assertion that masturbation, male homosexuality, lesbianism, and intercourse with animals are vices more heinous than incest is established on the basis of an appeal to reason, not to God or simply to instinctive repulsion.[26]

In the same series of *Lectures* Kant argues against those who promote the "mortification of the flesh." Bodies require discipline; but "discipline can be of one of two kinds: we may have to strengthen the body, or we may have to weaken it." The "fanatical and monkish" virtues of starving and wasting the flesh are compared unfavourably with those of Diogenes. "We must harden our body as Diogenes did" (p. 158). It is probable that Kant did not know that Diogenes was famous for his acts of public masturbation (Kant's most terrible vice), as well as for living simply in his barrel. Nevertheless, Diogenes is a most interesting choice of hero. Kant suggests here – as he will also argue in his *Religion* – that it is not man's animal nature as such that is evil, but rather the failure of a man to harden himself (and it is surely a himself) into a person.[27]

Can male sexuality be controlled? And how about female sexuality? These are the questions that require urgent answers once the traditional Aristotelian and Christian answers have been rejected. Kant speculates that the origin of evil in society comes from the fact that males mature sexually in their mid-teens, but cannot (on average) afford to get married until their mid-twenties.[28] It is not that Kant's ideal male lacks desire, as Schott suggests, but that he transcends and controls desire. He also controls and governs female sexuality, even though charm (*Reiz*, and hence sexual attractiveness) is still registered in the *Anthropology* as integral to female nature (*A*, p. 169 (7: 305)).

Sarah Kofman has some interesting observations to make on Kant's attitude to male desire. Nonetheless, although her critique is a good deal more subtle than that of Schott, her psychoanalytical reading of Kant depoliticizes his attempts to re-establish the links between human excellence and maleness. Kofman analyzes a passage in the Third Critique where Kant claims: "Perhaps nothing more sublime was ever said and no sublimer thought ever expressed than the famous inscription on the Temple of Isis (Mother Nature): 'I am all that is and that was and that shall be, and no mortal hath lifted my veil' "(*CJ*, sect. 49, p. 160n. (5: 315n)). The veiling of Mother Nature in this passage is interpreted as a fear of castration: the veil concealing the lack of the penis.[29] And this fetishistic fear is read as both an aspect of Kant's warped sexuality and also as typical of the underlying misogyny of Enlightenment man's "respect" for women. But reading Kant's allusion in a more historically specific way, we see that it is one of the many places in his critical writings where Kant's apparently radical "Copernican revolution" is used to buttress traditional gender hierarchies.

As I have already indicated, for the pre-Romantics the sublime in nature has a distinctly masculine persona, and Kant himself seemed to endorse this position in his *Observations*. In the Third Critique, however, Kant keeps all the standard examples of the sublime in nature – referring to Burke with evident approval – but also deprives raw nature of the masculine face descried by Burke, and that Mary Wollstonecraft had gone so far as to personify as the "Father of nature." For Kant, by contrast, nature is a mother. She is the undisclosed (and forever undiscoverable) reality: the infinity of possibilities that entice and beckon the transcendental imagination that fashions Nature as an inexhaustible whole.

This regendering of the sublime in nature as feminine sparked a kind of dialogue between Kant and his contemporaries. The issue was the proper relation (or distance) between true maleness and nature, and what constitutes a passive relation to matter. In an essay that appeared one year after Kant's *Critique of Judgment*, Schiller reused the image of a veiled Isis, suggesting that the Egyptians once had direct access to "sublime" truths about "the unity of God and the refutation of paganism." Although we are told that the key to these mysteries is lost, Schiller also indicates that particular symbols and rituals were passed down to Moses by Egyptian priests who had access to the inner sanctum of the temples of Isis and Serapis.

> At the base of an old statue of Isis one read the words: "I am what there is." And on a pyramid at Sais the remarkable ancient inscription was found: "I am all, what is, what was, what shall be; no mortal has lifted my veil." No one was permitted to enter the temple of Serapis who did not bear on his chest or forehead the name Joa – or I-ha-ho – a name resembling in sound the Hebraic Jehova and probably also having the same meaning.[30]

Those who were initiated into these mysteries were called "beholders [*Anschauer*] or Epoptes" because the discovery of this hidden truth "can be compared to a passage from darkness to light, and perhaps also because they really and truly looked at the newly discovered truths in sensuous images." In Egypt "the first revelation" made to the young initiate into the mysteries of the temple was Joa's name: "He is alone and to himself and to him alone all things owe their existence" (in Pfefferkorn 1988: 120).

For Schiller, nature and its creator seem to collapse into each other, and are alternatively female (Isis) then male (Joa). But the beholders of the sublime – those who seek the truth and seek to follow Moses in linking the ancient mysteries of Eleusis and Samothrace with those of "the Brotherhood of Freemasons" – are male. Indeed, for Schiller it is no more than a contingent (historical) fact that no male now is sublime enough to negotiate the way out of the darkness of the cave of Platonic illusion, to see the truth in sensuous images – and remain sane. He thus, in principle, allows access to a noumenal realm that is not constructed by man's transcendental imagination, and (taking a cue from Plato's discussion of divine madness in *Phaedrus*) romanticizes the hierophant who had the audacity to uncover one of the mysteries and "was said to have suddenly gone mad" (Pfefferkorn 1988: 120–1).

This scenario reappears four years later in Schiller's poem "The veiled image at Sais." Behind the veil is "the truth"; but the "oracle" has decreed that truth has to reveal herself and cannot be gained by any mortal who actively wills that knowledge. Schiller's young, daring novice will not, however, respect Isis, and takes her by force:

"Let there be under it what may. I'll raise
This veil" – He shouts out loud – "and I shall see!"
Shall see!
Shouts back sarcastic'ly an echo.
He speaks it and then raises up the veil.
What, you may ask, saw he beneath it?
I do not know. The priests they found him there
By the next day, unconscious and so pale
He lay prone at the statue's pedestal.
What he had seen and what he learned
He never said. The gladness of his life
Had left his side for ever
And to an early grave took him despair.[31]

Resisting the temptation to read this poem psychoanalytically, I shall instead position it as a contribution to a philosophical debate about access to the noumenal, and hence about intellectual intuition and a kind of (male) passivity. In his critical writings, Kant had reserved the capacity of intellectual intuition for unknowable – but not unthinkable – superhuman beings (including God). Schiller, by contrast, does not deny man (males) the capacity to see what is hidden behind the veil of appearances; he only denies that there are now males strong enough – sublime enough – to actively seek the truth in the manner of Moses. Unless the male is passive, and is simply granted a vision of the truth behind the veil – by a kind of neo-Platonic inspiration – Nature will punish him.

For Schiller, access to the sublime involves passivity and activity, along with a *male* viewing position that is linked to the transcendental imagination. Indeed, the latter seems to be presupposed in all the permutations on this theme by male artists at this time. Thus, Mozart's *Magic Flute* (1791) involves ceremonies of initiation into the temple of Isis via a symbolization of the "brotherly" rites of Masonry. Female Masons existed in separate Lodges, but were assigned a position of inferior insight by both the libretto and score of Mozart's opera. As Renée Lorraine explains, masculine and feminine principles are yoked together in the opera, but in ways that privilege male adepts and patrilineal traditions and downgrade their female counterparts.[32]

Although less misogynistic, similar themes can be detected in "The novices at Sais," a story Novalis started in 1798. Via his hero Hyacinth, Novalis identifies with the feminine: lifting the veil of the goddess at Sais and finding truth in the form of Roseblossom, the girl he loves. Since the rose was the symbol of female initiation into the rites of Masonry, and was also an important symbol in the libretto of the *Magic Flute*, there are both Masonic and Mozartian echoes to the far-off music that accompanies the climax of initiation for Novalis's young male novice.[33] Novalis echoes Schiller, but reverses the implications, since his elite male novice is permitted to "raise the veil" without punishment or madness.

Novalis allies "truth" with "woman"; but we should not be misled into thinking that Novalis's celebration of the feminine involves a fundamental abandonment of the links between maleness and sublimity. A fragment not included in the story emphasizes this point: "One succeeded – he raised the veil of the goddess at Sais – But what did he see? he saw – miracle of miracle – himself."[34] Hyacinth's discovery of his own self and his union with his female counterpart, Roseblossom, can act as parallels in the different versions of the story, since Novalis's hero retains his identity as a male who simply appropriates the feminine as the object of his own (male) quest. Novalis might seek to transcend normal (masculine, reason-based) access to the truth that is hidden behind the veil of appearances, but femininity and passivity are not his starting-point. Rather, Novalis presents us with a hero, male enough (sublime enough) to take nature by force, to seek out the noumenal, and be rewarded with the double blessing of finding his true self and attaining a mystical union with his beloved. It is the supra-rational (but sane) male who achieves sublimity, not the female.

In *Gender and Genius* I explored the androgyny of the *male* Romantic genius, with a *male* body and a counteractive "feminine" side. This allowed a variety of male alliances with the sublime – all of which negotiated femininity, but erased (as no more than an echo) the female writers who were contemporaneously expressing their own experiences of the demonic and numinous. Karoline von Günderode's metaphoric imagery privileged the female who lifts the "holy veil" of Isis–Nature; but Karoline's voice was not heard – even though Bettina von Arnim attempted to amplify the sound by emphasizing the symbolic dimensions of Karoline's dagger through her heart. For both Karoline and Bettina a woman could be sublime; but only by embracing tragedy and renouncing her own identity within the sphere of the domestic and the "femininity" of the beautiful.[35] The female sublime was not silenced but was pushed behind a veil of logical impossibility through which no sound could penetrate. Thus, the question of whether a man was male enough/sublime enough/genius enough to lift Isis's veil became a trope of Romantic and post-Romantic writing. Even Hitler would claim in *Mein Kampf* to have "lifted a corner of nature's gigantic veil."[36]

Kant himself refused to feminize the male. Thus, when he returns to the figure of a veiled Isis in 1796 in "On a newly arisen superior tone in philosophy" – also discussed by Kofman – it is in the context of allying himself more nearly to Aristotle than to the neo-Platonists. The essay starts with a dig at Masonic tradition, and moves on to contrast Aristotelian "labor" (*Arbeit*) with the lazy mysticism of recent neo-Platonists whose philosophy prioritizes ease, passivity, inspiration, and intellectual intuition for a fanciful elite.[37] It is not a veiled Isis, nor "metaphysical sublimation" that "emasculates" reason, says Kant (with astonishing explicitness). Emasculation (*Entmannung*) comes from a false relation to the real: from claiming that the veil of Isis is thin enough for us to be able to sense what is beneath.[38] The veiled Isis must remain as inexhaustible labor (the sublime), and not be allied with that which is given as determinate (beauty). The sublime demands a reason that is male: unemasculated by an apparently penetrative act of intellectual intuition that merely signifies a passive and dependent relationship to matter.

Nature, and the moral law, with which Isis is here allied, are regulative ideas that cannot be exhausted by any particular experience – not even by the sum of experiences. Those "mighty men who claim to have seized the goddess by the train of her veils and overpowered her" are simply giving themselves airs.[39] The truly mighty men acknowledge and kneel before "the veiled goddess . . . that is the moral law in us in its invulnerable majesty." They "hear her voice" and "understand her commandments," but they recognize the impossibility of discovering "whether she comes from man and originates in the all-powerfulness of his own reason, or if she emanates from some other powerful being whose nature is unknown to him."[40] Nature must be constructed in such a way that is consistent with its invention by man, the lawgiver; but it is also consistent with the laws of a supersensible (and unknowable) God who brought it into existence.

Nature/matter/the law/*what* is created are personified as female. The divine – or semi-divine – formative force that creates Nature is not "emasculated" by this act of creation, but only by a failure to regulate distance between man and matter. Kant's claim that the purest moral and aesthetic judgments are concerned only with "form" (a priori, and a good thing) and not with "matter" (a potentially entrapping empirical thing) in effect re-established the ancient Greek links between "form" and "maleness" and "matter" and "femaleness." Feminists have every reason to be suspicious of such a linkage. Since Kant's delineation of the subject areas of ethics and aesthetics rests on this distinction, feminists will also need to ask a much more radical question: of whether we should accept, revise, or altogether reject this Kantian divide.

I hope this initial exploration of the "sublime" – the place at which Kantian borders seem to break down – will help feminists understand that it is a mistake to collapse into a monolithic model of "fetishistic fear," the variety of ways that the female has been downgraded in aesthetic, ethical, and metaphysical thought since the Enlightenment. Romanticism grew out of Kantianism, and I therefore find it easy to resist the reading of Kant as simple defender of reason (and hence as emotionally and imaginatively paralyzed) that is currently fashionable amongst those feminists and postmodernists who lump Kant with other "Enlightenment" thinkers. This is not the Kant that I have been influenced by – and whom I also oppose. There are gaps in the Kantian system, gaps occupied by the "unrepresentable": by emotion, sexual desire, and even by a powerful feminine "Isis" as the construct (and limits of) the imagination. It was in these gaps that Romanticism flowered and in which women Romantics drew breath.

But none of this makes the Kantian universe a space in which I, as a feminist philosopher, can move freely. The "feminine" principle idealized by the Romantics is not a feminist starting-point. And neither is Kant's refusal to rape Isis as the Mother of Nature. Much feminist philosophy has evolved along lines that Margolis has identified as a "psychoanalytically informed hermeneutics of suspicion"; but for me this is not enough.[41] Use of methods derived from any of Ricoeur's three "masters of suspicion" '(who include Marx and Nietzsche, as well as Freud) might bring a useful skepticism to philosophical texts, and expose *inter alia* the hidden gender-assumptions of both their truth claims and the rhetoric they employ.[42] But such techniques cannot solve the philosophical problems that remain once the finger of suspicion has been pointed – not least, because the thought of all three "masters" took male bodies, minds, and life experiences as both ideal and norm. And the same is true of those more recent "masters" of suspicion: Derrida, Foucault, Habermas, and Lyotard.

I do not see why I should assent to Margolis's dismissal: "Of course, feminism may invent new such strategies [for opposing ontological invariance or cognitive transparency], but those strategies could never remain feminist." Margolis is prepared to allow that feminist philosophy has now moved beyond "a first confused phase of an exploratory sort"; but he condemns me to a fate of negativity, of forever acting out of skepticism and suspicion. Is that all that feminist philosophy has to offer? I'm afraid my own suspicions are directed to the eagerness with which he elides a "post-post-structuralist aesthetics" with a "postfeminist aesthetics," and looks forward to the latter![43]

My own feminist philosophy asks, by contrast, what a woman-centered philosophy would be like. It asks, for example, how to think through the form/matter distinction, space, time, personhood – and the sublime – in ways that prioritize female life patterns, not the "feminine" Otherness mythologized and embraced by so many post-Kantian philosophers. It's not an easy task. And, since I would claim that there is no "outside" to language or to ideology (only competing languages and ideologies that together constitute a heteronomous whole), I would insist that one of the primary ways to transform the present lies in the possibility of a radical encounter with the past. Distinctively female traditions of argument and art have been written out of history, and continue to be erased by monolithic theories of "phallogocentric" discourse or of closed "periods" of time, such as "the Enlightenment" or "modernism." History has been defined using parameters taken from a few privileged (male) writers and artists. Some, at least, of the productions of these past generations of women remain, however. Opening ourselves up to this impossible past also transforms the way we perceive women speaking/writing/creating now.[44]

Notes

1 Relevant volume and page numbers in *Kants Gesammelte Schriften*, 29 vols (Berlin: Preussische Akademie der Wissenschaften, 1900–85) are recorded within brackets. In-text references to Immanuel Kant's works are abbreviated as follows: A = *Anthropology from a Pragmatic Point of View* [1798], trans. Mary J. Gregor (The Hague: Nijhoff, 1974); CJ = *Critique of Judgment* [1790], trans. J. H. Bernard (New York: Hafner, 1951); O = *Observations on the Feeling of the Beautiful and the Sublime* [1764], trans. John T. Goldthwait (Berkeley and Los Angeles. Calif.: University of California Press, 1960).

2 Sigmund Freud, "Some psychical consequences of the anatomical distinction between the sexes," in *Pelican Freud Library 7: On Sexuality* [1925], trans. James Strachey (Harmondsworth: Penguin Books, 1977), p. 342.

3 Søren Kierkegaard, "Some reflections on marriage, " in *Stages on Life's Way* [1845] ed. and trans. Howard V. Hong and E. H. Hong (Princeton, NJ: Princeton University Press, 1988), p. 166.

4 Griselda Pollock, *Vision and Difference* (London: Routledge, 1988), p. 26. For a more detailed critique of such positions, see C. Battersby, "Situating the aesthetic:

a feminist defence," in Andrew Benjamin and P. Osborne (eds) *Thinking Art* (London Institute of Contemporary Arts, ICA documents no. 10, 1991), pp. 31–43.

5   See, for example, Rita Felski, *Beyond Feminist Aesthetics* (London: Hutchinson Radius, 1989).

6   For signs of change see, however, additions to the 2nd edition of Janet Wolff, *Aesthetics and the Sociology of Art* (London: Macmillan, 1993).

7   Kant, *On the Old Saw: That May Be Right in Theory But It Won't Work in Practice* [1793], trans. E. B. Ashton (Philadelphia, Pa.: University of Pennsylvania Press, 1974), p. 59 (8: 291).

8   Susan Mendus, "Kant: 'an honest but narrow-minded bourgeois?'," in Ellen Kennedy and S. Mendus (eds) *Women in Western Political Philosophy* (Brighton: Harvester, 1987), pp. 22, 38–9, 35.

9   C. Battersby, *Gender and Genius: Towards a Feminist Aesthetics* (London: Women's Press, 1989; Indiana University Press, 1990).

10 Mary Wollstonecraft, "The cave of fancy," in *Posthumous Works* [1787] (Clifton, NJ: Augustus M. Kelley, 1972), 2: p. 107.

11 Edmund Burke, *A Philosophical Enquiry into the Origin of our Ideas of the Sublime and Beautiful* [1757], ed. James T. Boulton (Oxford: Basil Blackwell, 1987), pp. 164ff.

12 Later in the eighteenth century, the "picturesque" was developed as an intermediate category, designed to fit between the Burkean beautiful and the sublime. Its gender logic – and the problem it poses for feminists seeking to reclaim the sublime – is analyzed by C. Battersby, "Gender and the picturesque: recording ruins in the landscape of patriarchy," in Jane Brettle and S. Rice (eds) *Public Bodies/Private States* (Manchester: Manchester University Press, 1994).

13 I. Kant, *Religion within the Limits of Reason Alone* [1793], trans. Theodore M. Greene and H. H. Hudson (New York: Harper Torchbooks, 1960), pp. 21ff. (6: 26ff.).

14 Compare Kant's essay "An answer to the question 'What is Enlightenment?'" [1784] in Lewis White Beck (ed.) *Kant on History* (Indianapolis, Ind.: Bobbs-Merrill, 1963), pp. 3–10 (8: 35–42) with *Anthropology*, pp. 79–80 (7: 209).

15 For Hume on gender, see C. Battersby, "An enquiry concerning the Humean woman," *Philosophy* 56 (1981), pp. 79–80; also *Gender and Genius* for the *Spectator*, etc.

16 Goethe's letter to Chancellor von Müller (29 April 1818), quoted in Ernst Cassirer, *Kant's Life and Thought* [1918], trans. James Haden (New Haven, Conn.: Yale University Press, 1981), p. 270. Cassirer obviously agrees with Goethe's sentiments, since he praises effusively Kant's "completely virile way of thinking" and his opposition to "the effeminacy and over-softness that he saw in control all around him."

17 For a list of sublime objects in *Observations*, see pp. 47–50 (2: 208–10).

18 I. Kant, *Critique of Practical Reason* [1788], trans. T. K. Abbott (London: Longmans, 1909), pp. 167–70 (5: 75–8). Also *Foundations of the Metaphysics of Morals* [1785], trans. Lewis White Beck (Indianapolis, Ind.: Library of Liberal Arts, 1959), pp. 17n.–18n. (4: 401n.). Kant had clearly changed his mind to some extent about *Achtung* between the Second and Third Critiques, since in the cited passage from the Second Critique Kant also insists that respect is only accorded to persons, and not to objects.

19 Timothy Gould, "Intensity and its audiences," in P. Z. Brand and C. Korsmeyer (eds) *Feminism and Tradition in Aesthetics* (University Park, Pa.: Pennsylvania University Press, 1995).

20 See Patricia Yaeger, "Toward a female sublime," in Linda Kauffman (ed.) *Gender and Theory* (Oxford: Basil Blackwell, 1989), pp. 191ff. A more extended critique of Yaeger is included in C. Battersby, "Unblocking the Oedipal: Karoline von Günderode and the female sublime," in S. Ledger, Josephine McDonagh, and J. Spencer (eds) *Political Gender: Texts and Contexts* (Hemel Hempstead: Harvester Wheatsheaf, 1994).

21 Bettina von Arnim's *Die Günderode* was a work of fiction, but was based on actual letters between her and Karoline von Günderode (also spelled Günderrode). As such, it was an exact counterpart to the earlier Goethe's *Letters to a Child* (1835) in which Bettina situated Goethe as the paradigm (sublime) genius. Christa Wolf also semifictionalizes Günderode in her 1979 novel *Kein Ort, Nirgends* (*No Place on Earth*). Wolf has also edited and written on Günderode in *Der Schatten eines Traumes* (1979), and in her edition of Bettine von Arnim, *Die Günderode* (1983). [Christine Battersby's translation of Günderode's "Once I lived a sweet life" appears in Brand and Korsmeyer, *Feminism and Tradition*: ed.]

22 For a more detailed analysis of Günderode's sublime, see my "Unblocking the Oedipal."

23 Robin May Schott, *Cognition and Eros: A Critique of the Kantian Paradigm* (Boston, Mass.: Beacon, 1988), p. 109.

24 *Metaphysical Elements of Ethics*, printed with Abbott's trans. of *Critique of Practical Reason* (1797, op. cit.), sect. 17, pp. 319–20 (6: sect. 16, pp. 408–9). Abbott's translation is weak at this point, and perhaps contributes to leading Schott astray.

25 Schott, 105–6; Kant, *Metaphysical Elements*, sect. 16, p. 319 (6: sect. 15, pp. 407–8). As well as feminist critiques of Kant, there are feminist defences of his position that are also far too extreme. I certainly would not support Ursula Pia Jauch's reading of Kant as "a feminist 'avant la lettre'," in her *Immanuel Kant zur Geschlechterdifferenz* (Vienna: Passagen, 1988).

26 Kant, *Lectures on Ethics* [1775–81], trans. Louis Infield (collated 1930; New York: Harper and Row, 1963), pp. 69–71.

27 Kant, *Religion*, pp. 30–1 (6: 34–6).

28 "Conjectural beginning of human history," [1786] in Beck, *Kant on History*, p. 61 and n. 2 (8: 116 and n.).

29 Sarah Kofman, from *Le Respect des Femmes*, trans. as "The economy of respect: Kant and respect for women," in *Social Research* 49 (1982), pp. 383–404.

30 Friedrich von Schiller, "Die Sendung Moses," *Thalia* [1791] trans. in Kristin Pfefferkorn, *Novalis: a Romantic's Theory of Language and Poetry* (New Haven, Conn.: Yale University Press, 1988), p. 120.

31 Schiller, "Das verschleierte Bild zu Sais," *Die Horen* [1795], in Pfefferkorn, *Novalis*, pp. 125–6.

32 See Renée Lorraine, "A history of music," in Brand and Korsmeyer, *Feminism and Tradition*.

33 See plate 9 (a woman's Masonic apron, decorated with roses) and "Commentaries on the plates," in Jacques Chailley, *The Magic Flute, Masonic Opera*, trans. Herbert Weinstock (New York: Knopf, 1971; London: Gollancz, 1972).

34 Novalis (Georg Friedrich Philipp von Hardenberg), *Vermischte Fragmente* III, ii, 584, no. 250 in Pfefferkorn, 1988, pp. 126, 220; fragment relating to "Die Lehrlinge zu Sais." My discussion of Isis is greatly indebted to Pfefferkorn, although some of the gender and philosophical context given here complicates Pfefferkorn's thesis.

35 Margarete Lazarowicz has noted that the metaphor of Nature as a veiled Isis anchors Günderode's use of mythological imagery. See her *Karoline von Günderrode:*

Porträt einer Fremden (Frankfurt: Peter Lang, 1986), n. 108 and pp. 168ff. For Günderode, the veil of Nature is "thick" (as it is for Kant); but, unlike Kant, she indicates that it can be lifted by those few whose lives are "undivided" in their surrender to the power of the virgin Isis. The priestess of Apollo is made the paradigm example of one who has raised the "holy veil, " and who is taken over by the sublime, which uses her as its mouthpiece. Karoline thus goes beyond Novalis both in privileging the female initiate into the sublime and in suggesting – via her portrait of Cassandra in her drama *Magic and Destiny* (1805) – that such a surrender would produce tragedy in a woman's life by placing her outside the realm of the domestic.

36 Adolf Hitler, *Mein Kampf* (Boston, 1943), p. 287; quoted in Susan Griffin, *Pornography and Silence* (London: Women's Press, 1981), p. 168.
37 "On a newly arisen superior tone in philosophy," in *Raising the Tone of Philosophy* [1796], trans. and ed. Peter Fenves (Baltimore, Md.: Johns Hopkins University Press, 1993), pp. 51ff. (8: 389ff.). Fenves's translation has only recently appeared; I am therefore grateful to my colleague Tony Phelan for allowing me access to the first draft of his own translation of "Von einem neuerdings erhobenen vornehmen Ton in der Philosophie."
38 Ibid., pp. 64ff. (8: 399ff.).
39 Ibid., pp. 66n. (8: 401n.), amended translation.
40 Ibid., pp. 71 (8: 405), amended translation.
41 Joseph Margolis, "Reconciling analytic and feminist philosophy and aesthetics," in Brand and Korsmeyer, *Feminism and Tradition*.
42 Introduction to Paul Ricoeur, *Hermeneutics and the Human Sciences*, ed. and trans. John B. Thompson (Cambridge: Cambridge University Press, 1981), p. 6.
43 Margolis, "Reconciling analytic and feminist philosophy," in Brand and Korsmeyer, *Feminism and Tradition*, p. 428.
44 Preliminary versions of this paper have been presented at the Universities of Amsterdam, Southampton, and Warwick and the British Society for Eighteenth Century Studies in London. I am grateful to participants for comments that extended the range of my analysis.

Questions about Gender

1 What are some obvious ways that men and women are treated differently – within families, schools, religious and political institutions, and the work force?
2 Would you change your sex or gender if you could? Why or why not?
3 Is there a conflict in viewing masculinity both as a set of traits that develop naturally in male-bodied individuals and as something that continually needs to be proven and socially rewarded?
4 Do lesbians pose the same threat to male gender norms as gay men?
5 What is the difference between gender and biological sex?
6 Does Nicholson's account of gender recognize male-to-female transsexuals as women? Explain.
7 Explain how the Greeks configured philosophy as male, according to Shapiro.
8 Is the gender imagery invoked by philosophers such as Maimonides or Plato inci-

dental to or required for their articulations and justifications of claims about the relationship between the mind and body or humans and god?

9 Give your own examples of things that are "sublime" and things that are "beautiful," and then compare your two lists (e.g. music by the Rolling Stones? Princess Diana's gowns? drag racing? etc.)

10 How can one show that intellectual and physical prowess in a woman is not grotesque?

Recommended Reading for Part Three

Beauvoir, Simone de (1974) *The Second Sex*, trans. H. M. Parshley, New York: Vintage Books (classic feminist work providing historical and philosophical analysis of the position of woman in society).

Bordo, Susan (1988) "Feminist skepticism and the 'maleness' of philosophy," *Journal of Philosophy*, vol. 85, no. 5 (argues that concern for difference need not lead to the avoidance of generalizations about women).

Brod, Harry (ed.) (1987) *The Making of Masculinities: The New Men's Studies*, Boston, Mass.: Allen and Unwin (contributions from men's studies to theories of gender identity).

—— (ed.) (1988) *A Mensch Among Men: Explorations in Jewish Masculinity*, Freedom, Calif.: Crossing Press (explores constructions of masculinity in Jewish contexts).

Butler, Judith (1990) *Gender Trouble*, New York: Routledge (questions the naturalness of gender using postmodern philosophical, literary, and psychoanalytic theory).

Chodorow, Nancy (1995) "Gender as a personal and cultural construction," *Signs*, vol. 20, no. 3 (Spring) (a feminist psychological account of gender using psychoanalytic theory and clinical experience).

Clatterbaugh, Kenneth (ed.) (1990) *Contemporary Perspectives on Masculinity: Men, Women, and Politics in Modern Society*, Boulder, Colo.: Westview (explores conservative and progressive views of masculinity, and their critique by the contemporary men's movement).

Code, Lorraine (1991) *What Can She Know*, Ithaca, NY: Cornell University Press (examines the relationship between gender and intellectual capacities).

Collins, Patricia Hill (1991) *Black Feminist Thought*, New York: Routledge (feminist critique of culturally dominant images of black women).

Gilmore, David (ed.) (1990) *Manhood in the Making: Cultural Concepts of Masculinity*, New Haven, Conn.: Yale University Press (looks at how male identity and masculinity are understood in different societies).

Grimshaw, Jean (1986) *Philosophy and Feminist Thinking*, Minneapolis, Minn.: University of Minnesota Press (investigates the ways philosophy is regarded as male).

Hale, Jacob (1996) "Are lesbians women?," *Hypatia*, vol. 11, no. 2 (Spring) (critiques view that lesbians are not "women" in some importance sense).

Harding, Sandra (1986) *The Science Question in Feminism*, Ithaca, NY: Cornell University Press (the import of gender for scientific objectivity).

Hawkesworth, Mary (1997) "Confounding gender," *Signs*, vol. 22, no. 3 (Spring) (shows how recent theories about gender reproduce culturally entrenched assumptions about gender).

hooks, bell (1990) *Yearning: Race, Gender, and Cultural Politics*, Boston, Mass.: South End Press (essays on black masculinity, and cultural representations of gender and race).

Jaggar, Alison and Bordo, Susan (eds) (1989) *Gender/Body/Knowledge*, New Brunswick, NJ: Rutgers University Press (essays on gender and the body, and gender and knowledge).

James, Stanlie and Busia, Abena (eds) (1993) *Theorizing Black Feminisms*, London: Routledge (black feminist perspectives on gender and the possibilities for social change).

Keller, Evelyn Fox (1985) *Reflections on Gender and Science*, New Haven, Conn.: Yale University Press (the impact of gender on scientific inquiry and philosophical conceptions of knowledge).

Le Doeuff, Michèle (1991) *Hipparchia's Choice: an Essay Concerning Women, Philosophy, etc.*, Cambridge, Mass.: Blackwell Publishers (explores the challenges of being a woman and a philosopher).

Lloyd, Genevieve (1984) *The Man of Reason: "Male" and "Female" in Western Philosophy*, Minneapolis, Minn.: University of Minnesota Press (investigates the relationship between gender and rationality).

Mahowald, Mary (ed.) (1983) *Philosophy of Woman*, Indianapolis, Ind.: Hackett (classic philosophical texts on the nature of women).

May, Larry and Strikwerda, Robert (eds) (1992) *Rethinking Masculinity: Philosophical Explorations in Light of Feminism*, Lanham, Md.: Littlefield Adams (philosophical analysis of male gender roles and norms and their transformation).

Nicholson, Linda (1986) *Gender and History*, New York: Columbia University Press (shows how contemporary debates on gender issues emerged historically).

Okin, Susan Moller (1989) *Justice, Gender, and the Family*, New York: Basic Books (examines the injustices created by the way girls and boys, women and men are treated within families).

—— (1996) "Sexual orientation, gender, and families: dichotomizing differences," *Hypatia*, vol. 11, no. 1 (Winter) (argues that as the social importance of gender is diminished so will intolerance of same-sex sexual partners).

Rajan, Rajeswari Sunder (1993) *Real and Imagined Women: Gender, Culture, and Postcolonialism*, New York: Routledge (critiques common and sensationalized images of third-world women, focusing on women in colonial and postcolonial India).

Rhode, Deborah (1989) *Justice and Gender*, Cambridge, Mass.: Harvard University Press (analyzes how gender distinctions have been encoded in American law for the past century).

Rothblatt, Martine (1995) *The Apartheid of Sex: A Manifesto on the Freedom of Gender*, New York: Crown Publishers (argues for a continuum view of male/female difference and gender identity).

Scheman, Naomi (1993) *Engenderings*, New York: Routledge (essays on gender, knowledge, and emotions).

Spelman, Elizabeth (1988) *Inessential Woman*, Boston, Mass.: Beacon Press (analyzes problems in feminist accounts of the relationship between gender and race).

Tuana, Nancy (1992) *Woman and the History of Philosophy*, New York: Paragon House (considers how women and qualities associated with women are treated in the theories of major philosophers).

Vetterling-Braggin, Mary (ed.) (1982) *"Femininity," "Masculinity," and "Androgyny,"* Totowa, NJ: Littlefield, Adams, and Company (essays on the origins of gender traits and different models of gender diversity).

Warren, Mary Anne (1985) *Gendercide*, Totowa, NJ: Rowman and Allanheld (analysis of the moral implications of using abortion to increase the number of male children).

Young, Iris (1990) *Throwing Like a Girl and Other Essays in Feminist Philosophy and Social Theory*, Bloomington, Ind.: Indiana University Press (phenomenological account of gender identity).

Zack, Naomi (ed.) (1997) *Race/Sex: Their Sameness, Difference, and Interplay*, New York: Routledge (several essays exploring how gender is related to race, ethnicity, and biological sex).

PART FOUR

SEXUALITY

edited by Laurie Shrage

Sexuality: Introduction to the Readings

Philosophical discussions of sexuality fall mostly into two categories: debates about the morality of particular sexual practices and debates about the nature of sexual desire and experience. The first category includes discussions of the appropriate moral and social response to prostitution, pornography, same-sex eroticism, sado-masochism, sexual harassment, rape, adultery, and premarital sex. The second includes discussion of the meaning and purpose of sexual intimacy, the nature of sexual attraction and erotic experience, the consequences and dynamics of sexual objectification, the features of sexual perversion, the relationship between sex and love, and the role of the mind, body, culture, and nature in sexual behavior. Philosophical accounts of sexuality go back at least as far as Plato, who, in several works, considered higher and lower forms of sexual experience, the origin of different types of sexual desire, and the proper norms governing sexual relationships.

Many philosophical accounts of sexuality seem absurd today, such as Plato's notion that the highest forms of sexuality involved intellectual production and transcendence of the body – a theory in which philosophers are in essence the best lovers. Arthur Schopenhauer argued that sexual attraction represents a natural force that serves to insure that the bodily and mental characteristics of future generations will conform to some human ideal. His theory basically says that you're sexually attracted to those people with whom you could make beautiful babies, people whose traits ameliorate your imperfections. This theory takes the notion that opposites attract to its logical extreme (e.g. tall people are attracted to short people, shy to socially bold people, long nosed to short nosed people, masculine to feminine people, etc.). Immanuel Kant thought that sex involved treating another person as a mere means to one's own pleasure, but that the commitment of marriage could redeem sexual acts. This seems to be another version of the Catholic doctrine that it's better to commit a lesser sin (sex for pleasure in marriage) than a worse sin (sex for pleasure outside of marriage).

In the late twentieth century, sexuality is frequently taken to be an attribute that defines a person in a particular way. A person can be gay, lesbian, bisexual, heterosexual, a fetishist, or a pro (professional sex worker). As a category of identity, sexuality refers to sexual desires and behavior that distinguish people into different kinds. Many social scientific studies of sexuality tend to investigate sexuality in this sense, especially forms of sexuality regarded as socially deviant. In response, some philosophical studies of sexuality aim to critique psychological and sociological accounts that analyze culturally unacceptable sexual behaviors in terms of deviance, abnormality, and illness.

The selections in this section consider scientific accounts of sexuality, the nature of sexual desire, feminist critiques of patriarchal sexual norms, commerce in sex, and sexual assault. David Halperin's essay builds on Michel Foucault's notion that scientific accounts of sexuality invent or produce the very phenomena they claim to investigate. According to Halperin, there were no homosexuals until roughly a hundred years ago, when behavioral scientists introduced the concept. This is not to say that there were no homosexual behaviors prior to then, only that homosexuality and heterosexuality were not markers for different types of persons. Halperin shows how scientific and cultural debates about homosexuals are internally inconsistent and contradictory. Yet instead of entering into a point-by-point debate with social scientists about the nature of homosexuality, Halperin investigates, in a Foucauldian manner, the power relations that led to the stigmatization and social marginalization of people who have sexual partners of the same sex. According to Halperin, the invention of the homosexual made possible the invention of the heterosexual: a type of sexual being defined in opposition to the homosexual. In this conceptual economy, the heterosexual can claim to be everything that the homosexual is not: if the homosexual is abnormal, the heterosexual is normal; if the homosexual is sick, the heterosexual is healthy; if the homosexual is unnatural, the heterosexual is natural; if the male homosexual is feminine, the male heterosexual is masculine; and if the female homosexual is masculine, the female heterosexual is feminine. As an unnatural being, the homosexual becomes an object of interest that non-homosexuals authorize themselves to inquire about and understand (how are homosexuals brought into being, how do they have sex, how are their relationships like those of heterosexuals, etc.). Heterosexuality becomes the unquestioned true sexuality whose origins and dynamics stand in no need of investigation. Halperin's research suggests that to overcome homophobia, we need to interrogate the homosexual/heterosexual distinction.

Elizabeth Grosz's essay attempts to explore lesbian sexuality without getting bogged down in the usual debates about who is or isn't a lesbian and whether lesbians have good sex. Instead she focuses on models of sexual desire and asks if they can illuminate lesbian desire. One influential philosophical model of desire represents it as a relationship between a subject and an object where the subject perceives the object to possess something not present in the subject but whose possession would make the subject more perfect or complete. Grosz finds this model of desire inadequate for understanding lesbian desire because it suggests that people desire what is different from them, such as men desiring women, where women function as the Other. Also, on this model of desire, the natural subjects of desire are presumed male while the objects are coded female. If women actually desire sexually on this model they are masculinized or they merely possess the feminine desire to be the object of someone's desire. For women to desire women sexually, they must assume the male subject position, which implicitly heterosexualizes desire. In addition, by understanding desire as a relation between a subject and an object, this model represents one term of the relationship (the feminine term) as a place-holder for things that are substitutable and replaceable. On this model then, men desire women as objects whom they can replace when the women no longer satisfy or possess what the subject is missing.

Grosz attempts to rejuvenate a less influential model of desire where desire is conceived as a creative force that shapes reality, rather than as an internal striving that is obstructed by an external reality. Desire involves not the filling of some emptiness but the addition of new entities or the production of new relations between components or subjects. Desire does not come about from a sense of incompleteness but is a source of energy needed to generate and invent. On this model, sexuality involves not some dialectic between interior states of frustration and fulfillment but it involves an activity in which subjects relate to one another, and explore pleasuring themselves, through their bodies. Given that this model posits relations among subjects who are not inherently sexed or dichotomized, it makes better sense of women's desire for union with other women. The primary question for lesbians, according to Grosz, should be not who identifies as one, but what forms of intimacy and pleasure lesbian desire makes possible.

Debra Satz considers the morality of treating sex as a commodity that can be bought or sold on the open market. She asks whether marketing sexual labor or skills is different in a morally relevant way from marketing secretarial or nursing skills. Her essay examines two common arguments that aim to support the notion that marketing sex is different: (1) that the social costs of markets in sex outweigh their potential benefits, and (2) market exchanges of sex degrade the provider and dehumanize sexual intimacy. Satz rejects the first argument because it fails to capture what many people find morally objectionable about prostitution, and it fails to consider whether the social costs of prostitution stem from the background conditions in which it operates. Satz also rejects the second argument because it fails to acknowledge that market exchanges of sex are not always desperate or coerced exchanges, and that some prostitutes report enjoying and taking pride in their work. Also, while prostitution may promote inferior forms of human sexual intimacy, many kinds of work promote inferior human relationships and dull or damage human capacities. For instance, working in most unskilled, minimum-wage jobs in America today is likely to damage our capacities for creativity and collective governance.

According to Satz, there is nothing that distinguishes markets in sex from markets in other commodities except that markets in sex, in some social environments, can reproduce social inequalities between women and men. In a social context in which the primary buyers of sex are men and the primary providers are women, markets in sex reinforce the idea that women's sexuality exists to serve male sexual needs, an idea that renders women the social subordinates and sexual servants of men. Also, prostitutes and their work are stigmatized in our society, and few contemporary forms of prostitution challenge the social stigmas that workers in this industry must bear. Satz concludes by supporting the decriminalization of prostitution, since the punitive systems of control that are currently in force do not address the gender inequalities that both contribute to and are an effect of prostitution. Instead of criminalizing the sale of sex, Satz formulates guidelines for regulating markets in sex.

bell hooks considers how the plurality of feminist views about sex have been reduced by the media to two: old feminist man-hating sex prudes and new feminist men-loving sexually liberated playmates. According to hooks, most feminists are neither anti-sex man-haters or pro-sex men-lovers, rather feminists have developed views and practices that challenge men to change the way they interact sexually with women. hooks describes her experience with *Esquire* magazine to show how the media suppress more complex and challenging feminist views about male sexual behavior, and instead pander to public tastes for simplistic stereotypes and sexist, racist, and heterosexist cultural images.

hooks reflects on the difficulties feminists face when attempting to intervene in mass cultural dialogues about sex. Feminists who attempt to critique masculine sexual norms are viewed in terms of those very norms: either a woman can be a passive sexual object for a man or she can sexually objectify a man. Similarly, when black feminists speak openly about sex, they risk being subsumed under cultural stereotypes that portray women of color as sexually loose. These representational strategies, as well as the strategy of representing all women who oppose the sexual status quo as man haters, serve a conservative political agenda that opposes any feminist reform of our cultural institutions.

hooks suggests that in order to initiate a more nuanced public conversation about gender and sexuality, feminists must attempt to communicate with a larger audience through art, literature, and film. Their failure to do this allows the media to get away with their either/or distorted messages about feminists. Feminists should not recede from talking about sex publicly, though they need to find ways to subvert efforts to caricature them to fit patriarchal ideologies.

Renée Heberle's article also considers the difficulties faced in fostering constructive, broad public discussion about gender and sex. Heberle analyzes the "speaking out" strategies of the anti-rape movement and suggests that they may inadvertently reinforce the entrenched cultural belief that all women are rapable and all men are potential rapists. Speaking out about sexual violence aims to make the public aware of the extent of sexual abuse and assault, so that serious efforts will be made to reduce and eliminate sexual violence. The primary form of "speaking out" promoted by the anti-rape movement has involved individual women sharing personal stories about their own or another woman's victimization. Heberle suggests that the public telling of these stories does not always produce an empathetic, soul-searching response. Rather, these stories project an image of vulnerable women ravished by dangerous men that many accept as natural and inevitable. Indeed, emphasizing women's sexual victimization by men reinforces some of the basic assumptions of a rape culture mentality.

Heberle argues that anti-rape activists need to reconsider their strategies of speaking out about sexual violence. Perhaps stories need to be heard about women who resist sexual violence, women who are less vulnerable and more dangerous, to counter the image of woman as rapable. Telling such stories runs the risk that women who do not successfully resist sexual assault will be seen as blameworthy or less admirable. This risk can be minimized by simultaneously pointing out how absurd it is to hold women responsible for the sexual assaults committed against them, whether they fight back or not. By promoting images of women who are not easy targets for victimization, the anti-rape movement would challenge entrenched cultural beliefs about the extent of male power.

FourDavid Halperin discusses Michel Foucault's account of sexuality and its relation to queer theory, and gay and lesbian political resistance. Halperin shows how Foucault's ideas provide the basis for a powerful critique of culturally authoritative medical, moral, scientific, and legal conversations or practices regarding homosexuality.

Focus questions:
1 How does the dynamic of being in or out of the closet reflect the difficulties of managing information about one's stigmatized sexuality? Why does a person's heterosexuality not have to be hidden or revealed?
2 How is sexuality produced by particular knowledge practices?
3 How does the sorting of human beings into the mutually exclusive categories of homosexual and heterosexual create and maintain social hierarchy, according to Halperin?

21 Saint Foucault

David M. Halperin

Homphobic discourses contain no fixed propositional content. They are composed of a potentially infinite number of different but functionally interchangeable assertions, such that whenever any one assertion is falsified or disqualified another one – even one with a content exactly contrary to the original one – can be neatly and effectively substituted for it. A good example of the opportunistic and propositionally indeterminate nature of homophobic discourses is provided by the history of legal disputes over whether homosexuality constitutes an "immutable characteristic." The story begins in the nineteenth century, when German gay-rights advocates who were attempting to decriminalize sodomy decided it would be to their advantage to represent homosexuality to their contemporaries as a natural condition into which a minority of individuals are born rather than as a sin or moral failing or acquired perversity for which homosexuals themselves should be held criminally liable; these militants succeeded so well in convincing the early sexologists of their view that a number of influential, mid- and late-nineteenth-century accounts of "sexual inversion" relied for their data on the self-representations of gay polemicists. That victory did not bring about the reform of the Prussian penal code – despite some initial, and quite promising, results. It did diminish the practice of sending homosexuals to jail for fixed terms; from now on, instead, they would be incarcerated for life in insane asylums – and ultimately exterminated in concentration camps by the Nazis – as members of a degenerate *species*. Judicial history has recently been repeating itself in the United States. American courts have ruled repeatedly that homosexuals possess no rights, as a minority group, to equal protection under the law, in part because homosexuality – unlike race or gender, supposedly – is not an "immutable characteristic." At the same time, the courts have held that homosexuals as a group do share at least one immutable characteristic: by definition we all commit sodomy, apparently, which is a felony in half of the United States. As of April 15, 1991 (when my information runs out), four separate judicial decisions had, on the basis of such reasoning, legally defined homosexuals to be criminals *as a class*.[1] In short, if homosexuality *is* an immutable characteristic, we lose our civil rights, and if homosexuality is *not* an immutable characteristic, we lose our civil rights. Anyone for rational argument on these terms?

Homophobic discourses are incoherent, then, but their incoherence, far from incapacitating them, turns out to empower them. In fact, homophobic discourses operate strategically *by means of* logical contradictions. The logical contradictions internal to homophobic discourses give rise to a series of double binds which function – incoherently, to be sure, but nonetheless effectively and systematically – to impair the lives of lesbians and gay men.

The best illustration of this phenomenon is provided by what Eve Kosofsky Sedgwick has memorably called the "epistemology of the closet."[2] Sedgwick has shown that the closet is an impossibly contradictory place: you can't be in it, and you can't be out of it. You can't be in it because – so long as you *are* in the closet – you can never be certain of the extent to which you have actually succeeded in keeping your homosexuality secret; after all, one effect of being in the closet is that you are precluded from knowing whether people are treating you as straight because you have managed to fool them and they do not suspect you of being gay, or whether they are treating you as straight because they are playing along with you and enjoying the epistemological privilege that your ignorance of their knowledge affords them. But if you can never be in the closet, you can't ever be out of it either, because those who have once enjoyed the epistemological privilege constituted by their knowledge of your ignorance of their knowledge typically refuse to give up that privilege, and insist on constructing your sexuality as a secret to which they have special access, a secret which always gives itself away to their superior and knowing gaze.[3] By that means they contrive to consolidate their claim to a superior knowingness about sexual matters, a knowingness that is not only distinct from knowledge but is actually opposed to it, is actually a form of ignorance, insofar as it conceals from the knowing the political nature of their own considerable stakes in preserving the epistemology of the closet as well as in maintaining the corresponding and exactly opposite epistemological construction of heterosexuality as *both* an obvious fact that can be universally known without "flaunting itself" *and* a form of personal life that can remain protectively private without constituting a secret truth.

The closet is an impossibly contradictory place, moreover, because when you *do* come out, it's both too soon and too late. You can tell that it's too soon by the frequency with which the affirmation of your homosexuality is greeted with impatient dismissal, which may take either an abusive form – of the "Why do you have to shove it in our faces?" variety – or, in better circles, the supremely urbane form of feigned boredom and indifference: "Why did you imagine that we would be interested in knowing such an inconsequential and trivial fact about you?"[4] (Of course, you told them *not* because you thought they would be interested – although in fact they obviously *are* interested, intensely interested – but because you didn't want them to presume that you were straight.) Nonetheless, whenever you do come out of the closet, it's also already too late, because if you had been honest you would have come out earlier.

That double bind operates not only informally, in personal relations, but institutionally – for instance, in the courts. I quote Eve Kosofsky Sedgwick's powerful account of one particularly telling example.

> In Montgomery County, Maryland, in 1973, an eighth-grade earth science teacher named Acanfora was transferred to a nonteaching position by the Board of Education when they learned he was gay. When Acanfora spoke to the news media, such as "60 Minutes" and the Public Broadcasting System, about his situation, he was refused a new contract entirely. Acanfora sued. The federal district court that first heard his case supported the action and rationale of the Board of Education, holding that Acanfora's recourse to the media had brought undue attention to himself and his sexuality, to a degree that would be deleterious to the educational process. The Fourth Circuit Court of Appeals disagreed. They considered Acanfora's public disclosures to be protected speech under the First Amendment. Although they overruled the lower court's rationale, however, the appellate court affirmed its decision not to allow Acanfora to return to teaching. Indeed, they denied his standing to bring the suit in the first place, on the grounds that he had failed to note on his original employment application that he had been, in college, an officer of a student homophile organization – a notation that would, as school officials admitted in court, have prevented his ever being hired. The rationale for keeping Acanfora out of his classroom was thus no longer that he had disclosed too much about his homosexuality, but quite the opposite, that he had not disclosed enough. The Supreme Court declined to entertain an appeal.
>
> It is striking that each of the two rulings in *Acanfora* emphasized that the teacher's homosexuality "itself" would not have provided an acceptable ground for denying him employment. Each of the courts relied in its decision on an implicit distinction between the supposedly protected and bracketable fact of Acanfora's homosexuality proper, on the one hand, and on the other hand his highly vulnerable management of information about it. So very vulnerable does this latter exercise prove to be, however, and vulnerable to such a contradictory array of interdictions, that the space for simply existing as a gay person who is a teacher is in fact bayonetted through and through, from both sides, by the vectors of a disclosure at once compulsory and forbidden.[5]

Sedgwick's whole account of the epistemology of the closet owes a great deal, as she acknowledges, to Foucault. It is inspired, specifically, by a passage in *The History of Sexuality, Volume I*, which Sedgwick quotes at the outset of her study:

> Silence itself . . . is less the absolute limit of discourse . . . than an element that functions alongside the things said. . . . There is no binary division to be made between what one says and what one does not say; we must try to determine the different ways of not saying such things, how those who can and those who cannot speak of them are distributed, which type of discourse is authorized, or what form of discretion is required in either case.

But Sedgwick's entire project can perhaps be summed up more precisely by transposing Foucault's terms and suggesting instead that Sedgwick does for "knowledge" and "ignorance" what Foucault himself did for "speech" and "silence." One has only to substitute "ignorance" for "silence" and "epistemology" for "discourse" in the concluding sentence of the passage Sedgwick quotes in order to grasp this point: "There is not one but many silences," Foucault writes, "and they are an integral part of the strategies that underlie and permeate discourses."[6]

The great virtue of Sedgwick's analysis is that it delivers lesbians and gay men from the temptation to play what is ultimately a mug's game of refuting the routine slanders and fantasies produced by the discourses of homophobia. The reason it is pointless to refute the lies of homophobia is not that they are difficult or impossible to refute – on the contrary, taken one at a time they are easily falsifiable, as I've already suggested – but that refuting them does nothing to impair the strategic functioning of discourses that operate precisely by deploying a series of mutually contradictory premises in such a way that any one of them can be substituted for any other, as different circumstances may require, without changing the final outcome of the argument. Sedgwick's account recalls us, specifically, from our natural impulse to try and win, move by move, the game of homophobic truth being played against us and to respond to each fresh defeat in this losing game by determining to play it harder, better, more intelligently, more truthfully. Sedgwick encourages us, instead, to stop playing long enough to stand back from the game, to look at all its rules in their totality, and to examine our entire strategic situation: how the game has been set up, on what terms most favorable to whom, with what consequences for which of its players. In this she exemplifies the basic method of Foucauldian discourse analysis, which is to refuse to engage with the content of particular authoritative discourses – in this case, with the content of homophobic discourses – and to analyze discourses in terms of their overall strategies.

Foucault's tendency to analyze discourses not substantively but strategically dates back to his early work on "madness and unreason." In the original preface to *Madness and Civilization*, for example, Foucault describes his project, famously, as follows:

> In the serene world of mental illness, modern man no longer communicates with the madman. . . . As for a common language, there is no such thing; or rather, there is no such thing any longer; the constitution of madness as a mental illness, at the end of the eighteenth century, affords the evidence of a broken dialogue, posits the separation as already effected, and thrusts into oblivion all those stammered, imperfect words without fixed syntax in which the exchange between madness and reason was made. The language of psychiatry, which is a monologue of reason *about* madness, has been established only on the basis of such a silence.
>   I have not tried to write the history of that language, but rather the archaeology of that silence.[7]

Rather than examine and critique the representations or concepts of madness produced by psychiatric scientists, in other words, Foucault inquires into the process whereby madness came to occupy its present discursive position *vis-à-vis* reason and rationality – how it came to be de-authorized, silenced, relegated to the status of a voiceless object of scientific discourse, and positioned both institutionally and discursively in relation to evolving practices of reason. Madness, on Foucault's view, is not a thing but a relation. As Foucault explained in an interview in *Le Monde* on July 22, 1961, "Madness cannot be found in a wild state. Madness exists only within a society, it does not exist outside the forms of sensibility which isolate it and the forms of repulsion which exclude it or capture it."[8] Madness, in effect, is a by-product of the processes that constructed the modern form of reason itself: madness is constituted in such a way as to answer to the functional requirements of reason (which comes to define itself as the knowledge of the difference between reason and madness) and thereby furnishes an element indispensable to the discursive and institutional operation of reason.[9] Or, as Roland Barthes, reviewing Foucault's book, put it, "[M]adness is not an object of understanding, whose history must be rediscovered; it is nothing more, if you like, than this understanding itself."[10] And Michel Serres, in his own review, went further: "[T]he object of archaic psychiatric knowledge is not so much the madman . . . as a projection of the classical cultural universe on to the space of confinement."[11] Substitute "homosexuality" for "madness" and "heterosexuality" for "reason" in these formulations and you have (despite the obvious disanalogies between the two sets of terms) many of the grounding axioms of contemporary queer theory.

In *The History of Sexuality, Volume I*, Foucault took the same approach to "sexuality" as he had to "madness": he treats sexuality not as a thing, a natural reality, but as the necessary instrument and determinate effect of an entire series of discursive and political strategies. "Sexuality," he writes, "must not be thought of as a kind of natural given which power tries to hold in check, or as an obscure domain which knowledge tries gradually to uncover."[12] Sexuality, in the first instance at least, is nothing more than "the correlative of that slowly developed discursive practice which constitutes the *scientia sexualis*"; its essential features correspond "to the functional requirements of a discourse that must produce its truth."[13] If sexuality is located by that discourse in nature, in bodies – in what, in other words, are the most literal and objective of realities[14] that positivism can conceive – that is because sexuality is defined by its function, which is to ground the discourse of which it is the object. Without a stable object to study, there can be no positive science of sexuality. It is part of the function of sexuality, in its role as "a specific domain of truth,"[15] to provide an epistemological anchor for that science, a secure ground of knowledge on which the new science of sexuality can be built.

Foucault's shift of perspective, his insistence on writing the history of sexuality "from the viewpoint of a history of discourses"[16] rather than from the viewpoint of the history of science,[17] enables him both to denaturalize and to politicize sexuality. Conceived according to Foucault in discursive terms, sexuality can now be analyzed according to the strategies immanent in its discursive operation. When sexuality is viewed from that angle, it appears not as a natural drive but instead (as we have seen) as "an especially concentrated point of traversal for relations of power." Sexuality is in fact part of an "apparatus" or "device" (*dispositif*)[18] that serves to connect new forms of power and knowledge with new objects and new domains. It can therefore be described as "a great surface network in which the stimulation of bodies, the intensification of pleasures, the incitement to discourse, the formation of special knowledges, the strengthening of controls and resistances, are linked to one another, in accordance with a few major strategies of knowledge and power."[19] The political importance of sex consists in the way it supports the modern regime of "bio-power," which Foucault defines, contrasting it with the old regime of "power over life and death," as an "entire political technology of life." "Bio-power" refers to the modern political procedure of regulating human life by means of expert techniques (statistics, demographics, eugenics, sterilization, etc.) – techniques that make possible a strategic alliance between specialized knowledge and institutionalized power in the state's management of life. Sex contributes to this technology, specifically, by connecting the body and the nation, linking "the procedures of power that characterized the disciplines" of sexuality (the "anatomo-politics of the human body") with "an entire series of . . . regulatory controls: a bio-politics of the population."[20]

Foucault's conceptual reorientation of sexuality, his transformation of it from an object of knowledge into a cumulative effect of power – "the sum of effects produced in bodies, behaviors, and social relations by a certain apparatus that emerges from a complex political technology" – enables him effectively to displace conventional ontologies of the sexual and thereby to resist the pre-emptive claims of various modern expert knowledges, of positivist epistemologies that constitute sexuality as a (or as the) real thing, an objective natural phenomenon to be known by the mind. Foucault's own discursive counterpractice seeks to remove sexuality from among the objects of knowledge and thereby to de-authorize those branches of expertise grounded in a scientific or quasi-scientific understanding of it; it also seeks to delegitimate those regulatory disciplines whose power acquires the guise of legitimate authority by basing itself on a privileged access to the "truth" of sexuality. By analyzing modern knowledge practices in terms of the strategies of power immanent in them, and by treating "sexuality" accordingly not as a determinate thing in itself but as a *positivity* produced by those knowledge practices and situated by their epistemic operations in the place of the real, Foucault politicizes both truth and the body: he reconstitutes knowledge and sexuality as sites of contestation, thereby opening up new opportunities for both scholarly and political intervention.

The political implications of Foucault's discursive approach to sexuality have not been lost on lesbians and gay men,[22] who for too long have been the objects rather than the subjects of expert discourses of sexuality – who have been the objects, in particular, of murderously pathologizing, criminalizing, and moralizing discourses, one of whose comparatively minor effects has been to de-authorize our subjective experiences and to delegitimate our claims to be able to speak knowledgeably about our own lives. (To be sure, we no longer live in an era when reputable books can be published with such titles as *The Homosexuals: as Seen by Themselves and Thirty Authorities*,[23] but a glance at the recent scientific literature reveals a plethora of equally idiotic and authoritative publications: "Physical and biochemical characteristics of homosexual men," for example, demonstrates that "homosexuals" have "less subcutaneous fat and smaller muscle/bone development," narrower shoulders in relation to pelvic width, and lesser muscular strength, among many other things, than heterosexuals; "Female homosexuality and body build" establishes that "homosexual women have narrower hips, increased arm and leg girths, less subcutaneous fat, and more muscle than heterosexual women.")[24] It is not surprising, therefore, that a number of lesbian and gay critical and cultural theorists have tended to follow Foucault's example and to resist, being drawn in by what he called the *bavardage*, or "chatter,"[25] of psychiatry, sexology, criminology, and social science. Like Sedgwick, they have concerned themselves less with refuting homophobic discourses than with describing how those discourses have been constituted, how they function, how they have constructed their subjects and objects, how they participate in the legitimation of oppressive social practices and how they manage to make their own operations invisible.[26] In a sense, all gay-positive analysis of the discursive, epistemological, and institutional operations of homophobia begins where Foucault left off: its inaugural gesture, as I already suggested, is to do for the relation between "heterosexuality" and "homosexuality" what Foucault did for the relation between "reason" and "madness."

How can such a discursive or strategic analysis help to explain the puzzling features of homophobic discourse already noted – namely, its paradoxical combination of incoherence, propositional indeterminacy, and social efficacy? Lesbian and gay theorists, influenced by Foucault, have advanced two related explanations, the first in a deconstructive and the second in a psychoanalytic mode. The modes are distinguishable, but they are in fact often and easily combined.[27] According to the first, "the homosexual" is not a stable or autonomous term but a supplement to the definition of "the heterosexual" – a means of stabilizing heterosexual identity.[28] According to the second, "the homosexual" is an imaginary "Other," whose flamboyant "difference" deflects attention from the contradictions inherent in the construction of heterosexuality; heterosexuality thrives precisely by preserving and consolidating its internal contradictions at the same time as it preserves and consolidates its own ignorance of them, and it does that by constructing and deploying the figure of "the homosexual."[29] I'll expand on each of these two points in turn.

The heterosexual/homosexual binarism is itself a homophobic production, just as the man/woman binarism is a sexist production. Each consists of two terms, the first of which is unmarked and unproblematized – it designates "the category to which everyone is assumed to belong" (unless someone is specifically marked as different) – whereas the second term is marked and problematized: it designates a category of persons whom *something differenti-ates* from normal, unmarked people.[30] The marked (or queer) term ultimately functions not as a means of denominating a real or determinate class of persons but as a means of delimiting and defining – by negation and opposition – the unmarked term. If the term "homosexuality" turns out, as we have seen, not to describe a single, stable *thing* but to operate as a placeholder for a set of mutually incompatible, logically contradictory predicates, whose impossible conjunction does not refer to some paradoxical phenomenon in the world so much as it marks out the limits of the opposed term, "heterosexuality," that is because homosexuality and heterosexuality do not represent a true pair, two mutually referential contraries, but a hierarchical opposition in which heterosexuality defines itself implicitly by constituting itself as the negation of homosexuality.[31] Heterosexuality defines itself without problematizing itself, it elevates itself as a privileged and unmarked term, by abjecting and problematizing homosexuality. Heterosexuality, then, *depends* on homosexuality to lend it substance – and to enable it to acquire *by* default its status *as* a default, as a *lack of difference* or an *absence of abnormality*.[32] ("A source of heterosexual comfort," Paul Morrison suggests: " 'Whatever else you might say about [heterosexuality], at least it's not that.' " But also "a source of heterosexual anxiety: 'There is nothing else to say about it but that.' ")[33] Although the unmarked term claims a kind of precedence or priority over the marked term, the very logic of supplementarity entails the unmarked term's dependence on the marked term: the unmarked term needs the marked term in order to generate itself as unmarked. In that sense the marked term turns out to be structurally and logically prior to the unmarked one. (In the case of heterosexuality and homosexuality, the marked term's priority to the unmarked term is not only structural or logical but historical as well: the invention of the term and the concept of homosexuality preceded by some years the invention of the term and concept of heterosexuality – which was originally the name of a perversion (what we now call bisexuality) and only gradually came to occupy its familiar place as the polar opposite of homosexuality.)[34] "Homosexual," like "woman,"[35] is not a name that refers to a "natural kind" of thing; it's a discursive, and homophobic, construction that has come to be misrecognized as an object under the epistemological regime known as realism. Which is not, of course, to say that homosexuality is unreal. On the contrary, constructions are very real.[36] People live by them, after all – and nowadays, increasingly, they die from them. You can't get more real than that. But if homosexuality is a reality, it is a constructed reality, a social and not a natural reality. The social world contains many realities that do not exist by nature.

"The homosexual," then, is not the name of a natural kind but a projection, a conceptual and semiotic dumping ground for all sorts of mutually incompatible, logically contradictory notions. These contradictory notions not only serve to define the binary opposite of homosexuality by (and as a) default; they also put into play a series of double binds that are uniquely oppressive to those who fall under the description of "homosexual," double binds whose operation is underwritten and sustained by socially entrenched discursive and institutional practices. As constructed by homophobic discourse, "the homosexual" is indeed an impossibly – and, it now appears, fatally – contradictory creature. For "the homosexual" is simultaneously (1) a social misfit, (2) an unnatural monster or freak, (3) a moral failure, and (4) a sexual pervert. Now it is of course impossible, under a post-Kantian system of ethics at least, for anyone to be all of those things at the same time – to be, for example, both *sick* and *blameworthy* in respect of the same defect – but no matter: such attributes may be mutually incompatible in logical terms, but they turn out to be perfectly compatible in practical, that is to say political, terms. Not only do they not cancel out one another in practice, they actually reinforce one another and work together systematically to produce, over and over again, the same effect: namely, the abjection of "the homosexual."

But if the logical contradictions internal to "the homosexual," as the term and concept are deployed in the political economy of sexual discourse, are crippling to those unfortunates who fall under that designation, they also enable – correspondingly – a crucially *empowering* incoherence to attach to the unmarked term and concept of "the heterosexual." They serve to define heterosexuality, implicitly and therefore all the more efficaciously, as simultaneously (1) a social norm, (2) a perfectly natural condition into which everyone is born and into which everyone grows up if no catastrophic accident interferes with normal, healthy development, (3) a highly laudable accomplishment that one is entitled to take pride in and for which one deserves no small amount of personal and social credit, and (4) a frighteningly unstable and precarious state that can easily be overthrown – by such contingent events as coming into contact with a gay or lesbian role model, being seduced by a member of the same sex during adolescence, hearing homosexuality spoken of too often, or having a gay man as a primary school teacher (as if there is anyone who has ever had a *non-gay* man as a primary school teacher) – and that therefore needs to be militantly protected, defended, and safeguarded by a constant mobilization of social forces.

What allows those mutually incompatible and internally contradictory notions about heterosexuality not only to coexist but to thrive, to reinforce one another, and to be politically efficacious is their privileged invisibility and the ignorance that surrounds them. The crucial, empowering incoherence at the core of heterosexuality and its definition never becomes visible because heterosexuality itself is never an *object* of knowledge, a target of scrutiny in its own right, so much as it is a *condition* for the supposedly objective, disinterested knowledge of *other* objects, especially homosexuality, which it constantly produces as a manipulably and spectacularly contradictory figure of transgression so as to deflect attention – by means of accusation – from its own incoherence.[37] (If there are no academic Departments of Heterosexual Studies, even in our more liberal universities, that is not only because all branches of the human sciences are already, to a greater or lesser degree, departments of heterosexual studies but also because heterosexuality has thus far largely escaped becoming a *problem* that needs to be studied and understood.)[38] By constituting homosexuality as an object of knowledge, heterosexuality also constitutes itself as a privileged stance of subjectivity – as the very condition of knowing – and thereby avoids becoming an object of knowledge itself, the target of a possible critique.[39] In this, it is of course unlike homo-sexuality, which is a perennial object of inquiry but never a viable subjective stance, never a disinterested, nonpartisan, legitimate position from which to speak, and is therefore never authorized except as the occasional voice of an already discounted and devalued subcultural minority. Thus heterosexual-ity can be a repository for all sorts of contradictory notions without forfeiting its privileges. For the notions that go into heterosexuality, however contra-dictory they may be, turn out not to be collectively disabling because they operate not as a set of double binds but as a set of mutually authorizing credentials which, despite their patchwork quality, become all the more un-impeachable for *never having to be presented*. Indeed, if heterosexual creden-tials ever *do* have to be presented, they not only fail to work but tend to invalidate themselves in the process: as all the world knows, there's no quicker or surer way to compromise your own heterosexuality than by proclaiming it. After all, if you really were straight, why would you have to say so? (Hetero-sexuality, not homosexuality, then, is truly "the love that dare not speak its name.")[40]

Notes

1   See Janet E. Halley, "Misreading sodomy: a critique of the classification of 'homo-sexuals' in federal equal protection law," in Julia Epstein and Kristina Straub (eds) *Body Guards: The Cultural Politics of Gender Ambiguity*, pp. 351–77; see also Janet E. Halley, "The construction of heterosexuality," in Michael Warner (ed.) *Fear of a Queer Planet: Queer Politics and Social Theory* (Minneapolis, Minn.: University of Minnesota Press, 1993), pp. 82–102, esp. 93–4.

2   Eve Kosofsky Sedgwick, *Epistemology of the Closet* (Berkeley, Calif.: University of California Press, 1990).

3   The characterization of the sexuality of the nineteenth-century homosexual as "a secret that always gave itself away" is, of course, Foucault's: see *The History of Sexuality, Vol. I*, trans. Robert Hurley (New York: Pantheon, 1978), p. 43. For an example of the heterosexist tactic of imposing secrecy on a homosexual's sexuality, all the better to expose it, see George Steiner's comments on Foucault's death in *The New Yorker*, March 17, 1986, p. 105: "Certain enforced secrecies and evasions veiled his personal existence. This obsessive inquirer into disease and sexuality – into the mind's constructs of Eros and into the effects of such constructs on the body politic and on the individual flesh – was done to death by the most hideous and symbolically charged of current diseases [*sic*]." As Ed Cohen, who quotes this vengeful passage ("Foucauldian Necrologies: 'Gay' 'politics'? Politically gay?" *Textual Practice* 2/1 (Spring 1988), p. 99 n. 12), remarks, Steiner's own veiled allu-sions to the supposedly well-guarded but transparent secret of Foucault's homosexuality are particularly curious inasmuch as Steiner had published, only four years earlier, in a volume that Steiner himself had coedited, a lengthy interview with Foucault devoted to the topic of homosexuality, a topic which Foucault had addressed from the perspective of an openly gay man: "Sexual choice, sexual act: an

interview with Michel Foucault," in Robert Boyers and George Steiner (eds) *Homosexuality: Sacrilege, Vision, Politics,* special issue of *Salmagundi* 58–9 (1982–3), pp. 10–24; reprinted in Sylvère Lotringer (ed.) *Foucault Live (Interviews 1966–84),* (New York: Semiotext(e), 1989), pp. 211–32, and in Michel Foucault, *Politics, Philosophy, Culture: Interviews and Other Writings, 1977–1984,* trans. Alan Sheridan et al., ed. with introduction by Lawrence D. Kritzman (New York: Routledge, 1988), pp. 286–303.

4   On urbanity as a homophobic tactic, see the brilliant analysis by D. A. Miller, "Sontag's urbanity," *The Lesbian and Gay Studies Reader,* esp. p. 215.

5   Sedgwick, *Epistemology of the Closet,* pp. 69–70.

6   Foucault, *The History of Sexuality, Vol. I,* p. 27; Sedgwick, *Epistemology of the Closet,* p. 3.

7   Michel Foucault, *Madness and Civilization: a History of Insanity in the Age of Reason,* trans. Richard Howard (New York: Pantheon, 1965), pp. x–xi (emphasis in original).

8   Quoted in David Macey, *The Lives of Michel Foucault* (London: Hutchinson, 1993), pp. 114–15.

9   See Foucault, *Remarks on Marx: Conversations with Duccio Trombadori,* trans. R. James Goldstein and James Cascaito (New York: Semiotext(e), 1991), pp. 63–5, esp. p. 65.

>   To the construction of the object madness, there corresponded a rational subject who "knew" about madness and who understood it. In *The History of Madness* I tried to understand this kind of collective, plural experience which was defined between the sixteenth and nineteenth centuries and which was marked by the interaction between the birth of "rational" man who recognizes and "knows" madness, and madness itself as an object susceptible of being understood and determined.

10   Roland Barthes, "Savoir et folie," *Critique* 17 (1961), pp. 915–22; reprinted in Barthes, *Essais critiques* (Paris: Seuil, 1964), quoted in Didier Eribon, *Michel Foucault,* trans. Betsy Wing (Cambridge, Mass.: Harvard University Press, 1991) p. 117.

11   Michel Serres, "Géométrie de la folie," *Le Mercure de France* (August 1962), pp. 682–96; (September 1962), pp. 62–81; quoted in Macey, *Lives of Michel Foucault,* p. 117.

12   Foucault, *The History of Sexuality, Vol. I,* p. 105.

13   Ibid., p. 68.

14   See D. A. Miller, "The late Jane Austen," *Raritan* 10.1 (Summer 1990), pp. 55–79, esp. p. 57: "All the deployments of the 'bio-power' that characterizes our modernity depend on the supposition that the most effective take on the subject is rooted in its body, insinuated within this body's 'naturally given' imperatives. Metaphorizing the body begins and ends with literalizing the meanings the body is thus made to bear."

15   "comme domaine de vérité spécifique": *La Volonté de savoir,* p. 92; cf. *The History of Sexuality, Vol. I,* p. 69.

16   Foucault, *The History of Sexuality, Vol. I,* p. 69.

17   For a critical history of sexology as a science, see Janice M. Irvine, *Disorders of Desire: Sex and Gender in Modern American Sexology* (Philadelphia, Pa.: Temple University Press, 1990).

18   Foucault's emphasis is unfortunately lost on Anglophone readers, because his English translator Robert Hurley renders *dispositif* in the title of Part IV of *The History of Sexuality, Vol. I,* as "deployment" but elsewhere (including a much-quoted pas-

sage on p. 105), as "construct." See note 6 to "Saint Foucault," in David M. Halperin, *Saint Foucault: Towards a Gay Hagiography* (New York: Oxford University Press, 1995).

19   Foucault, *The History of Sexuality, Vol. I*, pp. 105–6.

20   Ibid., pp. 139–45.

21   Foucault, *La Volonté de savoir*, p. 168; cf. *The History of Sexuality, Vol. I*, p. 127.

22   For an early appreciation of the political usefulness of Foucault, see the characteristically prescient remarks by Gayle Rubin, "Thinking sex: notes for a radical theory of the politics of sexuality," in Carole S. Vance (ed.) *Pleasure and Danger: Exploring Female Sexuality* (Boston: Routledge and Kegan Paul, 1984), pp. 267–319, esp. pp. 276–8, 284–8; reprinted, with revisions, in Henry Abelove, Michèle Aina Barale, and David M. Halperin (eds) *The Lesbian and Gay Studies Reader* (New York: Routledge, 1993), pp. 3–44, esp. pp. 10–11, 16–19.

23   A. M. Krich (ed.) *The Homosexuals: as Seen by Themselves and Thirty Authorities* [1954], 6th paperback edn (New York: Citadel Press, 1968). The book's cover adds the following notation: "A comprehensive, revealing inquiry into the cause and cure of homoerotic manifestations in men and women with *case histories* and *autobiographical accounts.*"

24   Ray B. Evans, "Physical and biochemical characteristics of homosexual men," *Journal of Consulting and Clinical Psychology* 39/1 (1972), pp. 140–7; Muriel Wilson Perkins, "Female homosexuality and body build," *Archives of Sexual Behavior* 10/4 (1981), pp. 337–45 (I quote from the abstracts of the two articles).

25   E.g. Foucault, *Surveiller et punir*, p. 311 (*Discipline and Punish: The Birth of the Prison*, trans. Alan Sheridan (New York: Pantheon, 1978), p. 304): "the chatter of criminology."

26   "Maurice Florence" (namely Michel Foucault and François Ewald), "Foucault," in Denis Huisman (ed.) *Dictionnaire des philosophes*, (Paris: Presses Universitaires de France, 1984), 1: 942–4; trans. Catherine Porter in Gary Gutting (ed.) *The Cambridge Companion to Foucault* (Cambridge: Cambridge University Press, 1994) , pp. 314–19, esp. p. 3l7:

> [T]o refuse the universals of "madness," "delinquency," or "sexuality" does not mean that these notions refer to nothing at all, nor that they are only chimeras invented in the interest of a dubious cause. . . . [Rather, it] entails wondering about the conditions that make it possible, according to the rules of truth-telling, to recognize a subject as mentally ill or to cause subjects to recognize the most essential part of themselves in the modality of their sexual desire.

Cf. Judith Butler, "Critically queer," *GLQ* 1 (1993/4), pp. 17–32; reprinted in Judith Butler, *Bodies That Matter: On the Discursive Limits of "Sex"* (New York: Routledge, 1993), pp. 223–42: "My understanding of Foucault's notion of genealogy is that it is a specifically philosophical exercise in exposing and tracing the installation and operation of false universals" (p. 282 n. 8).

27   For distinguished recent examples of this synthesis, see Lee Edelman, *Homographesis: Essays in Gay Literary and Cultural Theory* (New York: Routledge, 1994), and Butler, *Bodies That Matter.*

28   Harold Beaver, "Homosexual signs (*In Memory of Roland Barthes*)," *Critical Inquiry* 8 (1981/2), pp. 99–119, esp. pp. 115–16; Sedgwick, *Epistemology of the Closet*, esp. pp. 9–11; Simon Watney, "Troubleshooters," *Artforum* 30/3 (November 1991), pp. 16–18, esp. p. 17: "Homosexual identity should thus be understood as a *strategic position that privileges heterosexuality*" (emphasis in original); Halley, "The construction of heterosexuality."

29   See, for example, Michael Warner, "Homo-narcissism; or, heterosexuality," in Joseph

A. Boone and Michael Cadden (eds) *Engendering Men: the Question of Male Feminist Criticism* (New York: Routledge, 1990), pp. 190–206, 313–15; D. A. Miller, "Anal *Rope*"; Lee Edelman, "Tearooms and sympathy, or, the epistemology of the water closet," in Andrew Parker, Mary Russo, Doris Sommer, and Patricia Yaeger (eds) *Nationalisms and Sexualities* (New York: Routledge, 1992), pp. 263–84; reprinted, with revisions, in Abelove et al., *The Lesbian and Gay Studies Reader*, pp. 553–74, and in Edelman, *Homographesis*, pp. 148–70.

30 Halley, "Misreading sodomy," p. 361.

31 Cf. Jacques Derrida, *The Truth in Painting*, trans. Geoff Bennington and Ian McLeod (Chicago: University of Chicago Press, 1987), esp. pp. 332–5, 373–9, on the strange relations or irrelations among and within the terms *two, the pair, parity, the couple, the double, fetishism, homosexuality, heterosexuality, and bisexuality.*

32 Halley, "The construction of heterosexuality."

33 Paul Morrison, "End pleasure," *GLQ* 1 (1993/4), pp. 53–78 (quotation on p. 57).

34 Jonathan Katz, *Gay/Lesbian Almanac: a New Documentary* (New York: Harper and Row, 1983) pp. 147–50; David M. Halperin, *One Hundred Years of Homosexuality* (New York: Routledge, 1990), p. 17, and p. 158 n. 17.

35 For an elaboration of this point, see Judith Butler, *Gender Trouble: Feminism and the Subversion of Identity* (New York: Routledge, 1990).

36 I owe this formulation to an unpublished paper by Robert Padgug.

37 On the practice concealing and exculpating oneself by accusing others, see Eve Kosofsky Sedgwick's remarks on Proust in *Epistemology of the Closet*, pp. 222–30.

38 The notable exceptions include Sigmund Freud, *Three Essays on the Theory of Sexuality*, especially the famous 1915 footnote to the paragraph on "The sexual aim of inverts" in Section 1a of the first essay: "Thus from the point of view of psychoanalysis the exclusive sexual interest felt by men for women is also a problem that needs elucidating and is not a self-evident fact." See Freud, *Three Essays on the Theory of Sexuality*, trans. and ed. James Strachey, intro. Steven Marcus (New York: Basic Books, 1975), p. 12. See also Alfred C. Kinsey, Wardell B. Pomeroy, and Clyde E. Martin, *Sexual Behavior in the Human Male* (Philadelphia, Pa.: B. Saunders, 1948); William H. Masters, *Heterosexuality* (New York: HarperCollins, 1994).

39 The history of the concept of sexual perversion abundantly illustrates this point: see Arnold I. Davidson, "Closing up the corpses: diseases of sexuality and the emergence of the psychiatric style of reasoning," in George Boolos (ed.) *Meaning and Method: Essays in Honor of Hilary Putnam* (Cambridge: Cambridge University Press, 1990), pp. 295–325, esp. pp. 308–9. See also Halley, "The construction of heterosexuality."

40 Paul Morrison, *Sexual Subjects* (New York: Oxford University Press, forthcoming).

Elizabeth Grosz examines traditional philosophical accounts of desire – as a longing for something one lacks – and rejects these accounts as inadequate for theorizing lesbian desire. She then explores a conception of desire as a kind of fuel that can create or unite things, and employs it to develop an account of lesbian sexuality and desire.

Focus questions:

1 What problems does Grosz find with accounts that construe sexual desire in terms of seeking to fill a lack?
2 How does an account of desire in the positive terms of energizing the creation and uniting of things, rather than the negative terms of filling an unfillable lack, change our picture of sexuality?
3 Many view lesbian sex as replicating heterosexual sex in that, in the former, a woman takes on a man's role. How would Grosz respond to those who see lesbian couples and sex in this way?

22   Refiguring Lesbian Desire

Elizabeth Grosz

> *I knew you'd be a good lover when I noticed you always smelt books before you read them – especially hardbacks . . . now make love to me.*
>
> (Mary Fallon, *Working Hot*)

Experimental Thought

A great deal of work has been published in the last decade in the area now known as lesbian and gay studies. Much of this work has been exceptionally powerful and worthwhile in both political and intellectual terms. A whole series of issues vital not just for lesbian and gay studies but also for understanding the structures of heterosexuality and, indeed, for understanding the notion of subjectivity or identity in broader terms have been engaged with, analyzed, and discussed. Many of these key issues center around questions of the structures of social power, of sexuality and the processes involved in the production of an identity: essentialism versus constructionism;[1] coalitionist politics versus separatism; the alignments of lesbians with feminists versus their alignments with gay male activists; the entwinement of "alternative" sexual and lifestyle practices with what it is they attempt to challenge and move beyond (for example, the current debates about the political status of lesbian s/m, of drag, and issues in what is now understood as lesbian or sexual ethics and whether these are transgressive or recuperative practices) have now been fairly thoroughly debated, if not entirely successfully resolved.[2] I do not plan to make any particular contribution to the richness and complexity of these debates. While I am impressed with the scholarship, knowledge, and political sense made by many working in this area, these issues will not be the ones that concern me here.

I have, for once, the luxury of being able to undertake a wildly speculative paper, one that is openly experimental (in concepts, if not in style) and in which I have no guarantee that my claims will make sense, that my arguments are cogent, or that my position is "politically correct." I figured that at least once in my professional life I could – indeed, I must – take the risk of being totally wrong, of committing some heinous theoretical blunder, of going way out on a limb, instead of being very careful, covering myself from rearguard criticism, knowing in advance that at least some of my claims have popular support or general credibility. Why now? Because it seems to me that in a topic as personally important to me as refiguring and rethinking lesbian desire I need to go beyond the more typical theoretical models and paradigms used to explain and assess the social, political, sexual, and economic positions of lesbians and gay men in order to see if something different, something new, another way of seeing things, might serve to characterize lesbian desire beyond its usual models of representation.

Thus I don't really want to talk about lesbian or gay "identities," whether these are considered as unified, a priori totalities (the essentialism position) or as "fractured or dislocated multiplicities" (the so-called postmodern and/or psychoanalytic positions). I don't want to talk about lesbian psychologies, about the psychical genesis of lesbian desires, or about the meaning, signification, or representation of these desires (this already differentiates my paper from the vast bulk of material now beginning to pour out of the lesbian and gay studies industry, including my own previous forays into the terrain).[3]

In short, I don't want to discuss lesbian identity or desire in terms of a psychical depth or interiority, or in terms of a genesis, development or processes of constitution, history or etiology. I am much less interested in where lesbian desire comes from, how it emerges, and the ways in which it develops than in where it is going to, its possibilities, its open-ended future. I am interested in how to embrace this openness, to welcome unknown readings, new claims, provocative analyses – to make things happen, to move fixed positions, to transform our everyday expectations and our habitual conceptual schemas.

Nor am I here interested in notions of sexual morality, in discovering a "true" sexuality or an "ideologically sound one." I am not interested in judging the sexual practices, fantasies, and desires of others – but I am interested in what kinds of terms may be appropriate for understanding my own. Thus I am not concerned with adjudicating what is transgressive or recuperative or to what extent drag, sexual role playing, butch-femme relations, etc., etc., participate in phallocentrism or heterosexism or serve to undermine them. *All* sexual practices, in any case, are made possible and function within the constraints of heterosexism and phallocentrism, but this indeed is the condition of any effective transgression of them: we must no longer understand them as megalithic systems that function in immutability and perfection. Rather, they are contradictory systems, fraught with complexities, ambiguities, and vulnerabilities that can and should be used to strategically discern significant sites of contestation. My project is thus not to analyze or explain lesbian desire but rather to experiment with an idea, or a series of them, to see how far they can go, what they enable us to rethink, to recontextualize, to see in a different way – a kind of excessive analysis, one that goes beyond a well-charted terrain with Nietzschean joy.

I want to explore here two issues that I believe are deeply interrelated: can feminist theory sustain its ability to think innovatively and experimentally, playing with views, positions, models, frameworks – even frameworks that may be treated with caution or suspicion – in order to see how far they take us in rethinking what has been taken for the truth or orthodoxy (even if it is now feminists who, at least in some cases, supply and validate these truths or orthodoxies), in redoing the social and cultural order? And can feminist theory find an adequate, i.e., an experimental or hitherto unworked-out, way of (re)thinking lesbianism and lesbian desire? In short, can feminist theory move beyond the constraints imposed by psychoanalysis, by theories of representation and signification, and by notions of the functioning of power relations – all of which implicitly presume the notion of a masculine or sexually neutral (which also means masculine) subject and the ontology of lack and depth? Can feminist theory eschew the notion of depth? Can we think desire beyond the logic of lack and acquisition, a logic that has rendered women the repositories, the passive receptacles of men's needs, anxieties, and desires? Can desire be refigured in terms of surfaces and surface effects?

The Ontology of Lack

My problem is how to conceive of desire, particularly, how to think desire as a "proper" province of women. The most acute way in which this question can be formulated is to ask the question: how to conceive lesbian desire given that lesbian desire is the pre-eminent and most unambiguous exemplar of *women's* desires, women's desire(s) for other women? In what terms is desire to be understood so that it can be attributed to and conceived of in terms of women? This is not really an idle or perverse question though it may seem so at first sight. I am asking how it is that a notion like desire, which has been almost exclusively understood in male (and commonly heterocentric) terms, can be transformed so that it is capable of accommodating the very category on whose exclusion it has previously been based. Desire has up to now functioned only through the surreptitious exclusion of women (and hence lesbians). How can this concept be dramatically stretched to include as subject what it has previously designated only by the position of object, to make what is considered passivity into an activity?

There are, in my understanding, three irresolvable problems associated with the notions of desire we have generally inherited in the West. These three problems signal that desire must be thoroughly overhauled if it is to be capable of accommodating women's desires and those desires – whatever they might be – that specify and distinguish lesbianism. These I can indicate only briefly although they clearly warrant a much more thorough investigation.

In the first place, the concept of desire has had an illustrious history beginning with the writings of Plato, especially in the *Symposium*, where Plato explains that desire is a lack in man's being, an imperfection or flaw in human existence. For him, desire is both a shortcoming and a vindication of human endeavor. Desire is considered a yearning for access to the good and the beautiful, which man lacks. It is thus simultaneously the emblem of atrophy and of progress toward the Idea. Born of *penia* (poverty) and *poros* (wealth), of inadequacy and excess together, this Platonic understanding of desire remains the dominant one within our received history of thought, even today. This trajectory for thinking desire reaches a major, modern turning point in Hegel's understanding of desire in *The Phenomenology of Spirit*, where Hegel conceives of desire as a unique lack that, unlike other lacks, can function only if it remains unfilled. It is therefore a lack with a peculiar object all its own – its object is always another desire. The only object desire can desire is an object that will not fill the lack or provide complete satisfaction. To provide desire with its object is to annihilate it. Desire desires to be desired. Thus, for Hegel, the only object that both satisfies desire yet perpetuates it is not an object but another desire. The desire of the other is thus the only appropriate object of desire.

Freud himself and the psychoanalytic theory following him are the heirs to this tradition of conceiving of desire in negative terms, in terms of an absence, and it is largely through psychoanalytic theory – in which, for example, Lacan reads Freud quite explicitly in terms of Hegel's understanding of desire – that this conception of desire continues to be the dominant one in feminist, lesbian, and gay studies. Freud modifies the Platonic understanding of desire while nonetheless remaining faithful to its terms: the lack constitutive of desire is not an inherent feature of the subject (as Hegel assumed) but is now a function of (social) reality. Desire is the movement of substitution that creates a series of equivalent objects to fill a primordial lack. In seeking to replace an (impossible) plenitude, a lost completion originating (at least in fantasy) in the early mother/ child dyad, desire will create a realm of objects that can be substituted for the primal (lost, forbidden) object. Desire's endless chain is an effect of an oedipalizing process that requires that the child relinquishes its incestual attachments through creating an endless network of replacements, substitutes, and representations of the perpetually absent object.

Now this notion of desire as an absence, lack, or hole, an abyss seeking to be engulfed, stuffed to satisfaction, is not only uniquely useful in capitalist models of acquisition, propriety, and ownership (seeing the object of desire on the model of the consumable commodity), but it also inherently sexualizes desire, coding it in terms of the prevailing characteristics attributed to the masculine/feminine opposition, presence and absence. Desire, like female sexuality itself, is insatiable, boundless, relentless, a gaping hole that cannot be filled or can only be temporarily filled; it suffers an inherent dependence on its object(s), a fundamental incompletion without them. I would suggest that the metaphorics of desire on such models[4] are in fact coded as a sexual polarization. Where desire is given a negative status, it is hardly surprising that it becomes or is coded in terms similar to the ones attributed to femininity. Moreover, it is precisely such a model, where desire lacks, yearns, seeks, without ever being capable of finding itself and its equilibrium, that enables the two sexes to be understood as (biological, sexual, social and psychical) complements of each other – each is presumed to complete, to fill up, the lack of the other. The model of completion provided here corresponds to or is congruent with the logic regulating the goal posited by Aristophanes' hermaphrodite. Such a model, in other words, performs an act of violence: for any consideration of the autonomy of the two sexes, particularly the autonomy of women is rendered impossible within a model of complementarity. It feminizes, heterosexualizes, and binarizes desire at an ontological and epistemological level. The activity of this model of complementarily is merely a reaction to its perceived shortcomings, its own failure to sustain itself.

If this is the primary model of desire we in the West have inherited over millennia, this problem seems to me to be complicit with a second problem, a problem that can, this time, be more narrowly circumscribed and represented by a single corpus of writing. This second problem I see with the notion of desire as it is commonly understood can be most readily articulated with reference to a psychoanalytic account of desire, which in this context can be used as a shorthand version for – indeed, as a symptom of – a broader cultural and intellectual tradition. In such models – the most notable certainly being Freud's – desire is, as he describes it, inherently masculine. There is only male or rather masculine libido; there is only desire as an activity (activity being, for Freud, correlated with masculinity); in this case, the notion of female desire is oxymoronic.

Freud does get around this complication in a variety of ingenious ways: for him the so-called normal or heterosexual response on the part of woman is to give up the (masculine, phallic, anaclitic) desire to love and to substitute for it the passive aim of being loved and desired. This constitutes women's adult, secondary version of their primary narcissism;[5] by contrast, the woman suffering from the "masculinity complex" retains an active relation to desire at the cost of abandoning any self-representation as feminine or castrated. In exchange for the activity and phallic status she refuses to renounce – and while retaining the structure of virile desire – she abandons femininity. When she loves and desires, she does so not as a woman but as a man.

This understanding of female "inversion" (both literally and metaphorically) permeates the two case studies of female homosexuality Freud undertook – his study of Dora (1905) (which he recognized too late as a study of *homosexual* desire, that is, well after Dora had left him) and the study of the young female homosexual (1920), in which he can only represent the young woman's love relations to "her lady" on the model of the chivalrous male lover. In short, insofar as the woman occupies the feminine position, she can only take the place of the object of desire and never that of the subject of desire; insofar as she takes the position of the subject of desire, the subject who desires, she must renounce any position as feminine.[6] The idea of feminine desire or even female desire is contradictory. It is thus rather surprising, given the inherent impossibility of psychoanalysis to adequately provide the terms by which an analysis of women and of female desire is possible, that it nevertheless provides the basis for a disproportionately large number of texts within the field of lesbian and gay studies.

The third problem with this dominant notion of desire is of course bound up with the other two. It could be described as the implicit "hommo-sexuality"[7] of desire. Here the claim is not, as I have just argued, that desire is inherently masculine insofar as it is defined as necessarily active; in addition to its phallo-centrism there is a claim about the circuits of exchange in which desire func-tions. Irigaray argues that what psychoanalysis articulates as the imposition of oedipalization is in fact the (re)production of a circuit of symbolic exchange in which women function only as objects, commodities, or goods. In this circuit women, as it were, serve as the excuse, the intermediary, the linkage point be-tween one man and another. As evidence, she cites the fascination of many men with prostitution, with the idea of sharing a woman that other men have "had."[8]

Moreover, gay male relations are partly persecuted in our culture, she claims, because they (or many of them) make explicit the fundamentally *hommo-sexual* nature of exchange itself – including the exchange constituted as desire – that is, they make clear that the stakes do not involve women themselves. If desire is a lack, and if it functions by way of the substitution of one impossible/unsatisfying object after another, then what is significant about desire is not the objects to which it attaches itself but rather the flows and dynamics of its circulation, the paths, detours, and returns its undergoes. If Irigaray is correct in her readings of psychoanalytic discourse as representative of Western philosophical thought, and more generally in terms of its underlying investments in phallocentrism, then it also follows that these circuits of exchange are, like desire and sexual difference itself in patriarchal cultures, governed and regulated with respect to the phallus. These circuits are hommo-sexual, for and between men.

It is now clear, I hope, why there may be a problem using theories like psychoa-nalysis – as many lesbian theorists have done[9] – to explain the psychic and sexual economies of lesbians even if psychoanalysis could provide an explanation/ac-count of male homosexuality (which seems dubious to me, given Freud's pre-sumption of the primitive, maternally oriented heterosexuality as the "origin" of male desire). In the terms we have most readily available, it seems impossible to think lesbian desire. To think desire is difficult enough: desire has never been thoroughly reconsidered as an intensity, innervation, positivity, or force. Wom-en's desire is inconceivable within models attributing to desire the status of an activity: women function (for men) as objects of desire. To think lesbian desire thus involves surmounting both of these obstacles; while it is possible to experi-ence it, to have/to be it, psychoanalysis, theories of interiority, and, indeed, socio-logical, literary, and representational accounts – accounts that attempt to explain or assess it – are all required to do so in the very terms and within the very frame-works making this unthinkable. For this reason I would propose a temporary aban-donment of the attempt to understand and explain lesbian desire and instead propose the development of very different models by which to experiment with it, that is, to understand desire not in terms of what is missing or absent, not in terms of a depth, latency, or interiority but in terms of surfaces and intensities.

Refiguring Desire

If the dominant or received notions of desire from Plato to Freud and Lacan have construed desire as a lack or negativity, there is a minor or subordinated tradition within Western thought that has seen desire in quite different terms. In contrast to the negative model that dooms desire to consumption, incorporation, dissatisfaction, destruction of the object, there is a tradition – we may for our purposes date it from Spinoza[10] – of seeing desire primarily as production rather than as lack. Here, desire cannot be identified with an object whose attainment provides satisfaction but with processes that produce. In contrast to Freud, for Spinoza reality does not prohibit desire but is produced by it.[11] Desire is the force of positive production, the energy that creates things, makes alliances, and forges interactions between things. Where Hegelian desire attempts to internalize and obliterate its objects, Spinozist desire assembles things, joins, or unjoins them. Thus, on the one hand, desire is a pure absence striving for an impossible completion, fated evermore to play out or repeat its primal or founding loss; on the other hand, we have a notion of desire as a pure positivity, as production, forging connections, making things, as non-fantasmatic, as real. If Freud and psychoanalytic theory can act as representatives of the first and dominant understanding of desire as a lack, then Deleuze and Guattari can be seen to represent the second broad trajectory. And it is to some of their work I now wish to turn, acknowledging that in the space that I have here, I am unable to do justice to the richness and complexity of their works. What follows must therefore be considered as notes pointing toward a further investigation.

At first sight it may appear that I am simply substituting one evil (Deleuze and Guattari's rhizomatics) for another (Freudian and Lacanian psychoanalysis), that I am throwing away what feminists, and many lesbian feminists, have found the most appealing of all theoretical models. I do not do so lightly, having myself invested a great deal of time in psychoanalytic theory. In spite of well-recognized problems – problems I have discussed elsewhere and that others have dealt with as well[12] – I believe that their work does not have to be followed faithfully to be of use in dealing with issues that they do not, or perhaps even cannot, deal with themselves, most specifically the question of lesbian desire. Nevertheless, because they refuse to understand desire in negative terms, because they refuse to structure it with reference to a singular signifier – i.e., the phallus – and because they allow desire to be understood not just as feeling or affect but also as doing and making, I believe that Deleuze and Guattari may have quite a lot to contribute to refiguring lesbian desire.

Following Nietzsche and Spinoza, Deleuze understands desire as immanent, positive, and productive, as inherently full. Instead of a yearning, desire is seen as an actualization, a series of practices, action, production, bringing together components, making machines, creating reality: "Desire is a relation of effectuation, not of satisfaction," as Colin Gordon put it (1981: 32). Desire is primary, not lack. It is not produced as an effect of frustration but is primitive and given; it is not opposed to and does not postdate reality, but it produces reality. It does not take a particular object for itself whose attainment provides it with satisfaction; rather, it aims at nothing in particular, above and beyond its own self-expansion, its own proliferation. It assembles things out of singularities and breaks down things, assemblages, into their singularities: "If desire produces, its product is real. If desire is productive, it can be so in reality, and of reality" (Deleuze and Guattari 1977: 26).

As production, desire does not provide blueprints, models, ideals, or goals. Rather, it experiments, it makes: it is fundamentally aleatory, inventive. Such a theory cannot but be of interest for feminist theory insofar as women are the traditional repositories of the lack constitutive of desire and insofar as the oppositions between presence and absence, between reality and fantasy, have conventionally constrained women to occupy the place of men's other. Lack only makes sense to the (male) subject insofar as some other (woman) personifies and embodies it for him. Such a model of desire, when explicitly sexualized, reveals the impossibility of understanding lesbian desire. Any model of desire that dispenses with a reliance on lack seems to be a positive step forward and for that reason alone worthy of further investigation.

Lesbian Bodies and Pleasure

The terms by which lesbianism and lesbian desire are commonly understood seem to me problematic: it is no longer adequate to think them in terms of psychology, especially given that the dominant psychological models – psychoanalytic ones – are so inadequate for thinking femininity. So, in attempting to go the other way, I want to be able to provide a reading of lesbianism, or at least of lesbian sexuality and desire, in terms of bodies, pleasures, surfaces, intensities, as suggested by Deleuze and Guattari, Lyotard, and others.

There are a number of features of lesbian theory and of characterizations of lesbian desire that I would consequently like to avoid. In the first place, I wish to avoid the sentimentality and romanticism so commonly involved in thinking lesbian relationships. While I can understand the political need to validate and valorize lesbian relations in a culture openly hostile to lesbianism, I think it is also politically important to remain open to self-criticism and thus to change and growth. Lesbian relationships are no better, nor any worse, than the complexities involved in all sociosexual interrelations. Nor are they in any sense a solution to patriarchal forms of sexuality, because lesbianism and gay male sexuality are, as much as heterosexuality, products of patriarchy. There is no pure sexuality, no inherently transgressive sexual practice, no sexuality beyond or outside the limits of patriarchal models. This is not, however, to say that all forms of human sexuality are equally invested in patriarchal values, for there are clearly many different kinds of subversion and transgression, many types of sexual aberration that cannot be assimilated into historically determinate norms and ideals. It is not only utopian but also naive to take the moral high ground in proclaiming for oneself the right to judge the transgressive or other status of desire and sexuality: the function of moral evaluations of the sexual terrain can only be one of policing and prohibition, which does not deal with and does not explain the very desire for and energy of transgression.

In the second place, I would like to avoid seeing lesbian relations in terms of a binary or polarized model: this means abandoning many of the dominant models of sexual relations between women. In short, I want to avoid seeing lesbian sexual partners either as imaginary, mirror-stage duplicates, narcissistic doubles, self-reflections, bound to each other through mutual identification and self-recognition or in terms of complementarity with the lovers complementing each other's sexual style and role – butch-femme and bottom-top couplings.

In the third place, I would also like to avoid models that privilege genitality over other forms of sexuality. While it is clear that genitality remains a major site of intensity, in a phallic model it is the only true sexuality. I would like to use a model or framework in which sexual relationships are contiguous with and a part of other relationships – those of the writer to pen and paper, of the body-builder to weights, of the bureaucrat to files. The bedroom is no more the privileged site of sexuality than any other space; sexuality and desire are part of the intensity and passion of life itself.

In the fourth place, I want to avoid the kinds of narrow judgmentalism that suggest that any kind of sexuality or desire is better, more political, more radical, more transgressive than another and the kinds of feminist analysis that seek to judge the morality and ethics of the sexual practices of others, adjudicating what is wrong if not what is right.

And fifth, I want to look at lesbian relations and, if possible, at all social relations in terms of bodies, energies, movements, and inscriptions rather than in terms of ideologies, the inculcation of ideas, the transmission of systems of belief or representations, modes of socialization, or social reproduction, flattening depth, reducing it to surface effects.

Sexuality and desire, then, are not fantasies, wishes, hopes, aspirations (although no doubt these are some of their components), but they are energies, excitations, impulses, actions, movements, practices, moments, pulses of feeling. The sites most intensely invested always occur at a conjunction, an interruption, a point of machinic connection; they are always surface effects between one thing and another – between a hand and a breast, a tongue and a cunt, a mouth and food, a nose and a rose. In order to understand this notion, we have to abandon our habitual understanding of entities as the integrated totality of parts, and instead we must focus on the elements, the parts, outside their integration or organization; we must look beyond the organism to the organs comprising it. In looking at the interlocking of two such parts – fingers and velvet, toes and sand – there is not, as psychoanalysis suggests, a predesignated erotogenic zone, a site always ready and able to function as erotic. Rather, the coming together of two surfaces produces a tracing that imbues both of them with eros or libido, making bits of bodies, its parts, or particular surfaces throb, intensify, for their own sake and not for the benefit of the entity or organism as a whole. In other words, they come to have a life of their own, functioning according to their own rhythms, intensities, pulsations, and movements. Their value is always provisional and temporary, ephemeral and fleeting; they may fire the organism, infiltrate other zones and surfaces with their intensity, but they are unsustainable – they have no memory. They are not a recorded or a recording activity.

These body relations are not (as much of gay male culture presumes) anonymous, quick encounters; rather, each is a relation to a singularity or particularity, always specific, never generalizable. Neither anonymous nor yet entirely personal, each is still an intimacy of encounter, a pleasure/unpleasure of and for itself. Encounters, interfaces between one part and another of bodies or bodies and things, produce the erotogenic surface, inscribe it as a surface, linger on and around it for their evanescent effects: like torture, diet, clothing, and exercise, sexual encounters mark or inscribe the body's surface, and in doing so they produce an intensity that is in no way innate or given. Probably one of the most interesting and undervalued theorists of the erotic and of desire is Alphonso Lingis, whose wonderful texts shimmer with the very intensity he describes:

> The libidinal excitations do not invest a pregiven surface; they extend a libidinal surface. This surface is not the surface of a depth, the contour enclosing an interior. The excitations do not function as signals, as sensations. Their free mobility is horizontal and continually annexes whatever is tangent to the libidinal body. On this surface exterior and interior are continuous; its spatiality that of a Moebius strip. The excitations extend a continuity of convexities and concavities, probing fingers, facial contours, and orifices, swelling thighs and mouths, everywhere glands surfacing, and what was protuberance and tumescence on the last contact can now be fold, cavity, squeezed breasts, soles of feet forming still another mouth. Feeling one's way across the outer face of this Moebius strip one finds oneself on the inner face – all surface still and not inwardness. (Lingis 1985: 76)

To relate through someone to something else, or to relate through something to someone: not to relate to some one and only one, without mediation. To use the machinic connections a body part forms with another, whether it be organic or inorganic, to form an intensity, an investment of libido, is to see desire and sexuality as productive. Productive, though in no way reproductive, for this pleasure can serve no other purpose, can have no other function than its own augmentation, its own proliferation: a production, then, that makes but reproduces nothing – a truly nomad desire unfettered by anything external, for anything can form part of its circuit and be absorbed into its operations.

If we are looking at intensities and surfaces rather than latencies and depths, then it is not the relation between an impulse and its absent other – its fantasies, wishes, hoped-for objects – that interests us; rather, it is the spread or distribution, the quantity and quality of intensities relative to each other, their patterns, their contiguities that are most significant. It is their effects rather than any intentions that occupy our focus, what they make and do rather than what they mean or represent. They transform themselves, undergo metamorphoses, become something else, never retain an identity or purpose. Others, human subjects, women, are not simply the privileged objects of desire: through women's bodies to relate to other things to make connections.

While I cannot give a "real life illustration," I can at least refer to one of Australia's few postmodern lesbian writers, Mary Fallon:

> Stroking my whole body all night long until your fingers became fine sprays of white flowers until they became fine silver wires electrifying my epidermis until they became delicate instruments of torture and the night wore on for

too many hours and I loved you irritably as dawn reprieved us we are two live-wire
women wound and sprung together we are neither of us afraid of the metamorphoses transmogrifications the meltings the juices squelching in the body out of
the body – a split fruit of a woman we are neither of us is afraid to sink our teeth
into the peach it's not love or sex it's just that we are collaborating every night on
a book called The Pleasures of the Flesh Made Simple. (Fallon 1989: 87)

One "thing" transmutes into another, becomes something else through its
connections with something or someone outside. Fingers becoming flowers,
becoming silver, becoming torture instruments. This is precisely what the
Deleuzian notion of "becoming" entails: entry into an arrangement, an as-
semblage of other fragments, other things, becoming bound up in some other
production, forming part of a machine, becoming a component in a series
of flows and breaks, of varying speeds and intensities. To "become animal"
(or, more contentiously, to "become woman") does not involve imitating,
reproducing, or tracing the animal (woman) and becoming like it. Rather,
it involves entering into relation with a third term and with it to form a
machine that enters into relations with a machine composed of "animal"
components.[13] Becomings then are not a broad general trajectory of development but always concrete and specific, becoming something, something
momentary, provisional, something inherently unstable and changing. It is
not a question of being (animal, woman, lesbian), of attaining a definite status
as a thing, a permanent fixture, nor of clinging to, having an identity, but of
moving, changing, being swept beyond one singular position into a multiplicity of flows or into what Deleuze and Guattari have described as "a thousand
tiny sexes": to liberate the myriad of flows, to proliferate connections, to intensify.

Becoming lesbian, if I can put it this way, is thus no longer or not simply
a question of being lesbian, of identifying with that being known as a lesbian,
of residing in a position or identity. The question is not am I – or are you –
a lesbian but, rather, what kinds of lesbian connections, what kinds of
lesbian-machine, we invest our time, energy, and bodies in, what kinds of
sexuality we invest ourselves in, with what other kinds of bodies, with what
bodies of our own, and with what effects? What it is that together, in parts
and bits and interconnections, we can make that is new, that is exploratory, that opens up further spaces, induces further intensities, speeds up, ener-
vates, and proliferates production (production of the body, production of the
world)?

While what I am putting forth here is a positive view, it is not, in my opinion,
a utopian one: it is not a prophecy of the future, a vision of things to come, an
ideal or goal to aspire to. It is a way of looking at things and doing things with
concepts and ideas in the same ways we do them with bodies and pleasures, a
way of leveling, of flattening the hierarchical relations between ideas and things,
qualities and entities, of eliminating the privilege of the human over the animal,
the organic over the inorganic, the male over the female, the straight over the
"bent" – of making them level and interactive, rendering them productive and

innovative, experimental and provocative. That is the most we can hope for from knowledge. Or desire.

Notes

1 In my understanding, a mistaken bifurcation or division is created between so-called essentialists and constructionists insofar as constructionism is inherently bound up with notions of essence. To be consistent, constructionism must explain what the "raw materials" of the construction consist in; these raw materials must, by definition, be essential insofar as they precondition and make possible the processes of social construction.

2 The work of a number of feminists in this area is clearly laudable and provides a model or ideal for politically engaged knowledges. In this context, see the work of Butler, de Lauretis, and Fuss.

3 See, for example, my paper "Lesbian fetishism?" (1991).

4 Such models are of course not the only ones spawned by Western thought; alternative models, which see desire as a positivity, a production or making, while considerably rarer in our received history, nonetheless still develop and have exerted their influence in the writings of, among others, Spinoza, Nietzsche, Deleuze, and Lyotard, as I will discuss in more detail below.

5 I have tried to elaborate in considerable detail the differences between masculine, anaclitic forms of love/desire and feminine/narcissistic forms in my *Jacques Lacan: a Feminist Introduction* (1990), ch. 5.

6 This idea has been effectively explored in Jacqueline Rose's penetrating analysis of Freud's treatment of Dora (1985).

7 See Irigaray, *This Sex Which Is Not One* (1985); Grosz, *Sexual Subversions* (1989), and Whitford, *Luce Irigaray* (1991).

8 See Irigaray, "Commodities among themselves" and "Women on the market" (in *This Sex Which Is Not One*).

> Implicitly condemned by the social order [the prostitute] is implicitly tolerated. . . . In her case, the qualities of woman's body are "useful." However, these qualities have "value" only because they serve as the locus of relations – hidden ones – between men. Prostitution amounts to the *usage that is exchanged*. Usage that is not merely potential: it has already been realized. The woman's body is valuable because it has already been used. In the extreme case, the more it has served, the more it is worth. . . . [It] has become once again no more than a vehicle for relations among men. (1985: 186)

9 See the works of Butler, De Lauretis, and Fuss.

10 I am grateful to Moira Gatens for her research on Spinoza, which has been invaluable to me in this paper and in reconceiving corporeality. See Gatens, *Feminism and Philosophy*.

> 11 The mind endeavours to persist in its being for an indefinite period. . . . This endeavour . . . when referred to the mind and the body in conjunction . . . is called *appetite*; it is, in fact, nothing else but man's essence, from the nature of which necessarily follow all those results which tend to its preservation. . . . Further, between appetite and desire, there is no difference . . . we deem a thing to be good, because we strive for it, wish for it, long for it or desire it. (Spinoza, *The Ethics*, 3: x)

12 Rosi Braidotti articulates with considerable subtlety and sophistication many common reservations regarding Deleuze and Guattari's work, most especially concern-

ing their appropriation of the metaphorics of femininity ("becoming-woman") as a kind of betrayal of feminist interests:

> Deleuze's desiring machines amalgamate men and women into a new supposedly gender-free sexuality; . . . this drive towards a post-gender subjectivity, this urge to transcend sexual difference to reach a stage of multiple differentiation is not fully convincing. . . . Is the bypassing of gender in favour of a dispersed polysexuality not a very masculine move? . . . When this "becoming-woman" is disembodied to the extent that it bears no connection to the struggles, the experiences, the discursivity of real-life women, what good is it for feminist practice? Deleuze's multiple sexuality assumes that women conform to a masculine model which claims to get rid of sexual difference. (1991: 120–1)

13   "The actor Robert De Niro walks 'like' a crab in a certain sequence: but, he says, it is not a question of his imitating a crab; it is a question of making something that has to do with the crab enter into composition with the image, with the speed of the image" (Deleuze and Guattari 1987: 274).

References

Braidotti, Rosi (1991) *Patterns of Dissonance: a Study of Women in Contemporary Philosophy*, trans. Elizabeth Guild, Cambridge: Polity Press.

Butler, Judith (1990) *Gender Trouble: Feminism and the Subversion of Identity*, New York and London: Routledge.

—— (1991) "Imitation and gender insubordination," in Diana Fuss (ed.) *Inside/Out: Lesbian Theories, Gay Theories*, New York and London: Routledge, pp. 13–31.

Creet, Julia (1991) "Daughter of the movement: the psychodynamics of lesbian s/m fantasy," *differences* 5/2, pp. 135–59.

de Lauretis, Teresa (1987) "The female body and heterosexual presumption," *Semiotica* 67/3–4.

—— (1988) "Sexual indifference and lesbian representation," *Theatre Journal* 40/2.

Deleuze, Gilles (1989) *Masochism: Coldness and Cruelty*, trans. Jean McNeil, New York: Zone Books.

Deleuze, Gilles and Guattari, Felix (1977) *Anti-Oedipus: Capitalism and Schizophrenia*, vol. 1, trans. Mark Seem, Minneapolis, Minn.: University of Minnesota Press.

—— and —— (1987) *A Thousand Plateaus: Capitalism and Schizophrenia*, vol. 2, trans. Brian Massumi, Minneapolis, Minn.: University of Minnesota Press.

Fallon, Mary (1989) *Working Hot*, Melbourne: Sybella Press.

Freud, Sigmund [1905] "Fragment of an analysis of a case of hysteria," in *The Standard Edition of the Complete Psychological Works of Sigmund Freud*, trans. and ed. James Strachey, vol. 7, London: Hogarth Press, 1953–74, pp. 1–122.

—— [1920] "The psychogenesis of a case of homosexuality in a woman," in *The Standard Edition of the Complete Psychological Works of Sigmund Freud*, trans. and ed. James Strachey, vol. 18, London: Hogarth Press, 1953–74, pp. 145–72.

Frye, Marilyn (1984) *The Politics of Reality: Essays in Feminist Theory*, Trumansburgh, NY: Crossings Press.

Fuss, Diana (1989) *Essentially Speaking: Feminism, Nature, and Difference*, New York and London: Routledge.

—— (1991) *Inside/Out: Lesbian Theories, Gay Theories*, New York and London: Routledge.

Gatens, Moira (1991) *Feminism and Philosophy: Perspectives in Equality and Difference*, Cambridge: Polity Press.

Gordon, Colin (1981) "The subtracting machine," *I & C 8*.

Grosz, Elizabeth (1989) *Sexual Subversions: Three French Feminists*, Sydney: Allen and Unwin.

—— (1990) *Jacques Lacan: a Feminist Introduction*, New York and London: Routledge.

—— (1991) "Lesbian fetishism?," *differences* 5/2, pp. 39–54.

—— (forthcoming) "A thousand tiny sexes: feminism and rhizomatics," in Constantin Boundas and Dorothea Olkowski (eds) *Gilles Deleuze: the Theater of Philosophy.*

Irigaray, Luce (1985) *This Sex Which Is Not One*, trans. Catherine Porter, Ithaca, NY: Cornell University Press.

King, Katie (1990) "Producing sex, theory, and culture: gay/straight remappings in contemporary feminism," in Marianne Hirsch and Evelyn Fox Keller (eds) *Conflicts in Feminism*, New York and London: Routledge, pp. 82–101.

Lingis, Alphonso (1985) *Libido: the French Existential Theories.* Bloomington, Ind.: Indiana University Press.

Rose, Jacqueline (1985) "Dora: fragment of an analysis," in Charles Bertheimer and Claire Kahane (eds) *Dora's Case: Freud–Hysteria–Feminism*, New York: Columbia University Press, pp. 128–47.

Whitford, Margaret (1991) *Luce Irigaray: Philosophy in the Feminine*, London and New York: Routledge.

Debra Satz considers the standard philosophical and feminist objections to prostitution and points out their weaknesses. She argues that, if prostitution is wrong, it is wrong because its practice in particular cultural contexts contributes to the social inequality of women.

Focus questions:

1 Does the work of a prostitute involve a greater loss of bodily sovereignty than the work of a dancer, secretary, assembly-line worker, or mother?

2 What are the social costs of prostitution? Do these costs indicate a need to prohibit prostitution or to regulate it?

3 How does Satz support the thesis that prostitution can affect the way all women are viewed in a society?

---

23   Markets in Women's Sexual Labor

Debra Satz

There is a widely shared intuition that markets are inappropriate for some kinds of human endeavor: that some things simply should not be bought and sold. For example, virtually everyone believes that love and friendship should have no price. The sale of other human capacities is disputed, but many people believe that there is something about sexual and reproductive activities that makes their sale inappropriate. I have called the thesis supported by this intuition the asymmetry thesis.[1] Those who hold the asymmetry thesis believe that markets in reproduction and sex are asymmetric to other labor markets. They think that treating sexual and reproductive capacities as commodities, as goods to be developed and exchanged for a price, is worse than treating our other capacities as commodities. They think that there is something wrong with commercial surrogacy and prostitution that is not wrong with teaching and professional sports.

The intuition that there is a distinction between markets in different human capacities is a deep one, even among people who ultimately think that the distinction does not justify legally forbidding sales of reproductive capacity and sex. I accept this intuition, which I continue to probe in this article. In particular, I ask: What justifies taking an asymmetric attitude toward markets in our sexual capacities? What, if anything, is problematic about a woman selling her sexual as opposed to her secretarial labor? And, if the apparent asymmetry can be explained and justified, what implications follow for public policy?

In this article, I sketch and criticize two popular approaches to these questions. The first, which I call the economic approach, attributes the wrongness of prostitution to its consequences for efficiency or welfare. The important feature of this approach is its treatment of sex as a morally indifferent matter: sexual labor is not to be treated as a commodity if and only if such treatment fails to be efficient or welfare maximizing. The second, the "essentialist" approach, by contrast, stresses that sales of sexual labor are wrong because they are inherently alienating or damaging to human happiness. In contrast to these two ways of thinking about the immorality of prostitution, I will argue that the most plausible support for the asymmetry thesis stems from the role of commercialized sex and reproduction in sustaining a social world in which women form a subordinated group. Prostitution is wrong insofar as the sale of women's sexual labor reinforces broad patterns of sex discrimination. My argument thus stresses neither efficiency nor sexuality's intrinsic value but, rather, equality. In particular, I argue that contemporary prostitution contributes to, and also instantiates, the perception of women as socially inferior to men.

On the basis of my analysis of prostitution's wrongness, there is no simple conclusion as to what its legal status ought to be. Both criminalization and decriminalization may have the effect of exacerbating the inequalities in virtue of which I claim that prostitution is wrong. Nonetheless, my argument does have implications for the form of prostitution's regulation, if legal, and its prohibition and penalties, if illegal. Overall, my argument tends to support decriminalization.

The argument I will put forward here is qualified and tentative in its practical conclusions, but its theoretical point is not. I will argue that the most plausible account of prostitution's wrongness turns on its relationship to the pervasive social inequality between men and women. If, in fact, no causal relationship obtains between prostitution and gender inequality, then I do not think that prostitution is morally troubling.[2] This is a controversial claim. In my evaluation of prostitution, consideration of the actual social conditions which many, if not most, women face plays a crucial role. It will follow from my analysis that male prostitution raises distinct issues and is not connected to injustice in the same way as female prostitution.

On my view, prostitution is not wrong irrespective of its cultural and economic context. Moreover, prostitution is a complex phenomenon. I begin, accordingly, with the question, Who is a prostitute?

Who is a Prostitute?

While much has been written on the history of prostitution, and some empirical studies of prostitutes themselves have been undertaken, the few philosophers writing on this subject have tended to treat prostitution as if the term referred to something as obvious as "table."[3] But it does not. Not only is it hard to draw a sharp line between prostitution and practices which look like prostitution, but as historians of the subject have emphasized, prostitution today is also a very different phenomenon from earlier forms of commercial sex.[4] In particular, the idea of prostitution as a specialized occupation of an outcast and stigmatized group is of relatively recent origin.[5]

While all contemporary prostitutes are stigmatized as outsiders, prostitution itself has an internal hierarchy based on class, race, and gender. The majority of prostitutes – and all those who walk the streets – are poor. The majority of streetwalkers in the United States are poor black women. These women are a world apart from prostitution's upper tier. Consider three cases: a streetwalker in Boston, a call girl on Park Avenue, and a male prostitute in San Francisco's tenderloin district. In what way do these three lives resemble one another? Consider the three cases:

1. A fourteen-year-old girl prostitutes herself to support her boyfriend's heroin addiction. Later, she works the streets to support her own habit. She begins, like most teenage streetwalkers, to rely on a pimp for protection. She is uneducated and is frequently subjected to violence in her relationships and with her customers. She also receives no social security, no sick leave or maternity leave, and – most important – no control as to whether or not she has sex with a man. The latter is decided by her pimp.

2. Now imagine the life of a Park Avenue call girl. Many call girls drift into prostitution after "run of the mill promiscuity," led neither by material want nor lack of alternatives.[6] Some are young college graduates, who upon graduation earn money by prostitution while searching for other jobs. Call girls can earn between $30,000 and $100,000 annually. These women have control over the entire amount they earn as well as an unusual degree of independence, far greater than in most other forms of work. They can also decide who they wish to have sex with and when they wish to do so.[7] There is little resemblance between their lives and that of the Boston streetwalker.

3. Finally, consider the increasing number of male prostitutes. Most male prostitutes (but not all) sell sex to other men.[8] Often the men who buy such sex are themselves married. Unfortunately, there is little information on male prostitutes; it has not been well studied as either a historical or a contemporary phenomenon.[9] What we do know suggests that like their female counterparts, male prostitutes cover the economic spectrum. Two important differences be-

tween male and female prostitutes are that men are more likely to work only part time and that they are not generally subject to the violence of male pimps; they tend to work on their own.

Are these three cases distinct? Many critics of prostitution have assumed that all prostitutes were women who entered the practice under circumstances which included abuse and economic desperation. But that is a false assumption: the critics have mistaken a part of the practice for the whole.[10] For example, although women who walk the streets are the most visible, they constitute only about 20 percent of the prostitute population in the United States.[11]

The varying circumstances of prostitution are important because they force us to consider carefully what we think may be wrong with prostitution. For example, in the first case, the factors which seem crucial to our response of condemnation are the miserable background conditions, the prostitute's vulnerability to violence at the hands of her pimp or client, her age, and her lack of control over whether she has sex with a client. These conditions could be redressed through regulation without forbidding commercial sexual exchanges between consenting adults.[12] The second class of prostitution stands in sharp contrast. These women engage in what seems to be a voluntary activity, chosen among a range of decent alternatives. Many of these women sell their sexual capacities without coercion or regret. The third case rebuts arguments that prostitution has no other purpose than to subordinate women.

In the next section, I explore three alternative explanations of prostitution's wrongness, which I refer to respectively as economic, essentialist, and egalitarian.

What is Wrong with Prostitution?

The economic approach

Economists generally frame their questions about the best way to distribute a good without reference to its intrinsic qualities. They tend to focus on the quantitative features of a good and not its qualities.[13] Economists tend to endorse interference with a market in some good only when the results of that market are inefficient or have adverse effects on welfare.

An economic approach to prostitution does not specify a priori that certain sales are wrong: no act of commodification is ruled out in advance.[14] Rather, this approach focuses on the costs and benefits that accompany such sales. An economic approach to contracts will justify inalienability rules – rules which forbid individuals from entering into certain transactions – in cases where there are costly externalities to those transactions and in general where such transactions are inefficient. The economic approach thus supports the asymmetry thesis when the net social costs of prostitution are greater than the net social costs incurred by the sale of other human capacities.

What are the costs of prostitution? In the first place, the parties to a commercial sex transaction share possible costs of disease and guilt.[15] Prostitution also has costs to third parties: a man who frequents a prostitute dissipates financial resources which might otherwise be directed to his family; in a society which values intimate marriage, infidelity costs a man's wife or companion in terms of mistrust and suffering (and therefore prostitution may sometimes lead to marital instability); and prostitutes often have diseases which can be spread to others. Perhaps the largest third-party costs to prostitution are "moralisms":[16] many people find the practice morally offensive and are pained by its existence. (Note that "moralisms" refers to people's preferences about moral issues and not to morality as such.)

The economic approach generates a contingent case for the asymmetry thesis, focusing on prostitution's "moral" costs in terms of public opinion or the welfare costs to prostitutes or the population as a whole (e.g. through the spread of diseases). Consideration of the limitations on sexual freedom which can be justified from a welfare standpoint can be illuminating and forces us to think about the actual effects of sexual regulations.[17] Nevertheless, I want to register three objections to this approach to justifying the asymmetry thesis.

First, and most obvious, both markets and contractual exchanges function within a regime of property rights and legal entitlements. The economic approach ignores the background system of distribution within which prostitution occurs. Some background systems, however, are unjust. How do we know whether prostitution itself is part of a morally acceptable system of property rights and entitlements?

Second, this type of approach seems disabled from making sense of distinctions between goods in cases where these distinctions do not seem to reflect mere differences in the net sum of costs and benefits. The sale of certain goods seems to many people simply unthinkable – human life, for example. While it may be possible to justify prohibitions on slavery by appeal to costs and benefits (and even count moralisms in the sum), the problem is that such justification makes contingent an outcome which reasonable people do not hold contingently. It also makes little sense, phenomenologically, to describe the moral repugnance people feel toward slavery as "just a cost."[18]

Let me elaborate this point. There seems to be a fundamental difference between the "goods" of my person and my external goods, a difference whose nature is not completely explained by appeal to information failures and externalities. "Human capital" is not just another form of capital. For example, my relationship with my body and my capacities is more intimate than my relationship with most external things. The economic approach fails to capture this distinction.

Richard Posner – one of the foremost practitioners of the economic approach to law – illustrates the limits of the economic approach when he views a rapist as a "sex thief."[19] He thus overlooks the fact that rape is a crime of violence and assault.[20] He also ignores the qualitative differences between my relationship with my body and my car. But that there are such differences is obvious. The circumstances in which I sell my capacities have a much more profound effect on who I am and who I become – through effects on my desires, capacities, and values – than the circumstances in which I sell my Honda Civic. Moreover, the idea of sovereignty over body and mind is closely related to the idea of personal integrity, which is a crucial element of any reasonable scheme of liberty. The liberty to exercise sovereignty over my car has a lesser place in any reasonable scheme of liberties than the liberty to be sovereign over my body and mind.[21]

Third, some goods seem to have a special status which requires that they be shielded from the market if their social meaning or role is to be preserved. The sale of citizenship rights or friendship does not simply produce costs and benefits: it transforms the nature of the goods sold. In this sense, the market is not a neutral mechanism of exchange: there are some goods whose sale transforms or destroys their initial meaning.

These objections resonate with objections to prostitution for which its wrongness is not adequately captured by summing up contingent welfare costs and benefits. These objections resonate with moralist and egalitarian concerns. Below I survey two other types of arguments which can be used to support the asymmetry thesis: (1) essentialist arguments that the sale of sexual labor is intrinsically wrong because it is alienating or contrary to human flourishing and happiness; and (2) my own egalitarian argument that the sale of sex is wrong because, given the background conditions within which it occurs, it tends to reinforce gender inequality. I thus claim that contemporary prostitution is wrong because it promotes injustice, and not because it makes people less happy.

The essentialist approach

Economists abstract from the qualities of the goods that they consider. By contrast essentialists hold that there is something intrinsic to the sphere of sex and intimacy that accounts for the distinction we mark between it and other types of labor. Prostitution is not wrong simply because it causes harm; prostitution constitutes a harm. Essentialists hold that there is some intrinsic property of sex which makes its commodification wrong. Specific arguments differ, however, in what they take this property to be. I will consider two popular versions of essentialism: the first stresses the close connection between sex and the self; the second stresses the close connection between sex and human flourishing.[22]

Some feminist critics of prostitution have argued that sexual and reproductive capacities are more crucially tied to the nature of our selves than our other capacities.[23] The sale of sex is taken to cut deeper into the self, to involve a more total alienation from the self. As Carole Pateman puts it, "When a prostitute contracts out use of her body she is thus selling *herself* in a very real sense. Women's selves are involved in prostitution in a different manner from the involvement of the self in other occupations."[24] The realization of women's selfhood requires, on this view, that some of the capacities embodied in their persons, including their sexuality, remain "market-inalienable."[25]

Consider an analogous strategy for accounting for the value of bodily integrity in terms of its relationship to our personhood. It seems right to say that a world in which the boundaries of our bodies were not (more or less) secure would be a world in which our sense of self would be fundamentally shaken.

Damage to, and violation of, our bodies affects us in a "deeper" way, a more significant way, than damage to our external property. Robbing my body of a kidney is a violation different in kind than robbing my house of a stereo, however expensive. Distributing kidneys from healthy people to sick people through a lottery is a far different act than using a lottery to distribute door prizes.[26]

But this analogy can only be the first step in an argument in favor of treating either our organs or sexual capacities as market-inalienable. Most liberals think that individual sovereignty over mind and body is crucial for the exercise of fundamental liberties. Thus, in the absence of clear harms, most liberals would reject legal bans on voluntary sales of body parts or sexual capacities. Indeed, the usual justification of such bans is harm to self: such sales are presumed to be "desperate exchanges" that the individual herself would reasonably want to foreclose. American law blocks voluntary sales of individual organs and body parts but not sales of blood on the assumption that only the former sales are likely to be so harmful to the individual that given any reasonable alternative, she herself would refrain from such sales.

Whatever the plausibility of such a claim with respect to body parts, it is considerably weaker when applied to sex (or blood). There is no strong evidence that prostitution is, at least in the United States, a desperate exchange. In part this reflects the fact that the relationship people have with their sexual capacities is far more diverse than the relationship they have with their body parts. For some people, sexuality is a realm of ecstatic communion with another, for others it is little more than a sport or distraction. Some people will find consenting to be sexually used by another person enjoyable or adequately compensated by a wage. Even for the same person, sex can be the source of a range of experiences.

Of course, the point cannot simply be that, as an empirical matter, people have differing conceptions of sexuality. The critics of prostitution grant that. The point is whether, and within what range, this diversity is desirable.[27]

Let us assume, then, in the absence of compelling counterargument, that an individual can exercise sovereignty through the sale of her sexual capacities. Margaret Radin raises a distinct worry about the effects of widespread prostitution on human flourishing. Radin's argument stresses that widespread sex markets would promote inferior forms of personhood. She says that we can see this is the case if we "reflect on what we know now about human life and choose the best from among the conceptions available to us."[28] If prostitution were to become common, Radin argues, it would have adverse effects on a form of personhood which itself is intrinsically valuable. For example, if the signs of affection and intimacy were frequently detached from their usual meaning, such signs might well become more ambiguous and easy to manipulate. The marks of an intimate relationship (physical intimacy, terms of endearment, etc.) would no longer signal the existence of intimacy. In that case, by obscuring the nature of sexual relationships, prostitution might undermine our ability to apply the criteria for coercion and informational failure.[29] Individuals might more easily enter into damaging relationships and lead less fulfilling lives as a result.

Radin is committed to a form of perfectionism which rules out the social

practice of prostitution as incompatible with the highest forms of human development and flourishing. But why should perfectionists condemn prostitution
while tolerating practices such as monotonous assembly line work where human beings are often mere appendages to machines? Monotonous wage labor,
moreover, is far more widespread than prostitution.[30] Can a consistent perfec-
tionist give reasons for differentiating sexual markets from other labor markets?

It is difficult to draw a line between our various capacities such that only
sexual and reproductive capacities are essential to the flourishing self. In a money
economy like our own, we each sell the use of many human capacities. Writers
sell the use of their ability to write, advertisers sell the use of their ability to write
jingles, and musicians sell the use of their ability to write and perform symphonies. Aren't these capacities also closely tied to our personhood and its higher
capacities?[31] Yet the mere alienation of the use of these capacities, even when
widespread, does not seem to threaten personal flourishing.

An alternative version of the essentialist thesis views the commodification of
sex as an assault on personal dignity.[32] Prostitution degrades the prostitute.
Elizabeth Anderson, for example, discusses the effect of commodification on
the nature of sex as a shared good, based on the recognition of mutual attraction. In commercial sex, each party now values the other only instrumentally,
not intrinsically. And, while both parties are thus prevented from enjoying a
shared good, it is worse for the prostitute. The customer merely surrenders a
certain amount of cash; the prostitute cedes her body: the prostitute is thus
degraded to the status of a thing. Call this the degradation objection.

I share the intuition that the failure to treat others as persons is morally significant; it is wrong to treat people as mere things. But I am skeptical as to
whether this intuition supports the conclusion that prostitution is wrong. Consider the contrast between slavery and prostitution. Slavery was, in Orlando
Patterson's memorable phrase, a form of "social death": it denied to enslaved
individuals the ability to press claims, to be – in their own right – sources of
value and interest. But the mere sale of the use of someone's capacities does not
necessarily involve a failure of this kind, on the part of either the buyer or the
seller.[33] Many forms of labor, perhaps most, cede some control of a person's
body to others. Such control can range from requirements to be in a certain
place at a certain time (e.g. reporting to the office), to requirements that a
person (e.g. a professional athlete) eat certain foods and get certain amounts of
sleep, or maintain good humor in the face of the offensive behavior of others
(e.g. airline stewardesses). Some control of our capacities by others does not
seem to be ipso facto destructive of our dignity.[34] Whether the purchase of a
form of human labor power will have this negative consequence will depend on
background social macrolevel and microlevel institutions. Minimum wages,
worker participation and control, health and safety regulations, maternity and
paternity leave, restrictions on specific performance, and the right to "exit"
one's job are all features which attenuate the objectionable aspects of treating
people's labor as a mere economic input. The advocates of prostitution's wrongness in virtue of its connection to self-hood, flourishing and degradation have
not shown that a system of regulated prostitution would be unable to respond

to their worries. In particular, they have not established that there is something wrong with prostitution irrespective of its cultural and historical context.

There is, however, another way of interpreting the degradation objection which draws a connection between the current practice of prostitution and the lesser social status of women.[35] This connection is not a matter of the logic of prostitution per se but of the fact that contemporary prostitution degrades women by treating them as the sexual servants of men. In current prostitution, prostitutes are overwhelmingly women and their clients are almost exclusively men. Prostitution, in conceiving of a class of women as needed to satisfy male sexual desire, represents women as sexual servants to men. The degradation objection, so understood, can be seen as a way of expressing an egalitarian concern since there is no reciprocal ideology which represents men as servicing women's sexual needs. It is to this egalitarian understanding of prostitution's wrongness that I turn in the next section.

The egalitarian approach

While the essentialists rightly call our attention to the different relation we have with our capacities and external things, they overstate the nature of the difference between our sexual capacities and our other capacities with respect to our personhood, flourishing, and dignity.[36] They are also insufficiently attentive to the background conditions in which commercial sex exchanges take place. A third account of prostitution's wrongness stresses its causal relationship to gender inequality. I have defended this line of argument with respect to markets in women's reproductive labor.[37] Can this argument be extended to cover prostitution as well?

The answer hinges in part on how we conceive of gender inequality. On my view, there are two important dimensions of gender inequality, often conflated. The first dimension concerns inequalities in the distribution of income, wealth, and opportunity. In most nations, including the United States, women form an economically and socially disadvantaged group. The statistics regarding these disadvantages, even in the United States, are grim.

1. *Income inequality.* In 1992, given equal hours of work, women in the United States earned on average 66 cents for every dollar earned by a man.[38] Seventy-five percent of full-time working women (as opposed to 37 percent of full-time working men) earn less than $20,000.

2. *Job segregation*: Women are less likely than men to fill socially rewarding, high-paying jobs. Despite the increasing entrance of women into previously gender-segregated occupations, 46 percent of all working women are employed in service and administrative support jobs such as secretaries, waitresses, and health aides. In the United States and Canada, the extent of job segregation in the lowest-paying occupations is increasing.[40]

3. *Poverty.* In 1989, one out of five families were headed by women. One-third of such women-headed families live below the poverty line, which was $13,359 for a family of four in 1990.[41] In the United States, fathers currently owe mothers $24 billion in unpaid child support.

4. *Unequal division of labor in the family.* Within the family, women spend disproportionate amounts of time on housework and rearing children. According to one recent study, wives employed full time outside the home do 70 percent of the housework; full-time housewives do 83 percent.[43] The unequal family division of labor is itself caused by and causes labor market inequality: given the lower wages of working women, it is more costly for men to participate in household labor.

Inequalities in income and opportunity form an important part of the backdrop against which prostitution must be viewed. While there are many possible routes into prostitution, the largest number of women who participate in it are poor, young, and uneducated. Labor market inequalities will be part of any plausible explanation of why many women "choose" to enter into prostitution.

The second dimension of gender inequality does not concern income and opportunity but status.[44] In many contemporary contexts, women are viewed and treated as inferior to men. This inferior treatment proceeds via several distinct mechanisms.

1. *Negative stereotyping.* Stereotypes persist as to the types of jobs and responsibilities a woman can assume. Extensive studies have shown that people typically believe that men are more dominant, assertive, and instrumentally rational than women. Gender shapes beliefs about a person's capacities: women are thought to be less intelligent than their male equals.[45]

2. *Unequal power.* Men are able to asymmetrically sanction women. The paradigm case of this is violence. Women are subjected to greater amounts of violence by men than is the reverse: every fifteen seconds a woman is battered in the United States. Battering causes more injury (excluding deaths) to women than car accidents, rape, and muggings combined.[46] Four million women a year are physically assaulted by their male partners.[47]

3. *Marginalization.* People who are marginalized are excluded from, or absent from, core productive social roles in society – roles which convey self-respect and meaningful contribution.[48] At the extremes, marginalized women lack the means for their basic survival: they are dependent on state welfare or male partners to secure the basic necessities of life. Less severely marginalized women lack access to central and important social roles. Their activities are confined to peripheral spheres of social organization. For example, the total number of women who have served in Congress since its inception through 1992 is 134. The total number of men is 11,096. In one-third of governments worldwide, there are no women in the decision-making bodies of the country.[49]

4. *Stigma.* A woman's gender is associated, in some contexts, with stigma, a badge of dishonor. Consider rape. In crimes of rape, the complainant's past behavior and character are central in determining whether a crime has actually occurred. This is not true of other crimes: "mail fraud" (pun intended) is not dismissed because of the bad judgment or naïveté of the victims. Society views rape differently, I suggest, because many people think that women really want to be forced into sex. Women's lower status thus influences the way that rape is seen.

Both forms of inequality – income inequality and status inequality – potentially bear on the question of prostitution's wrongness. Women's decisions to enter into prostitution must be viewed against the background of their unequal life chances and their unequal opportunities for income and rewarding work. The extent to which women face a highly constrained range of options will surely be relevant to whether, and to what degree, we view their choices as autonomous. Some women may actually loathe or judge as inferior the lives of prostitution they "choose." Economic inequality may thus shape prostitution.

We can also ask, Does prostitution itself shape employment inequalities between men and women? In general, whenever there are significant inequalities between groups, those on the disadvantageous side will be disproportionately allocated to subordinate positions. What they do, the positions they occupy, will serve to reinforce negative and disempowering images of themselves. In this sense, prostitution can have an effect on labor-market inequality, associating women with certain stereotypes. For example, images reinforced by prostitution may make it less likely for women to be hired in certain jobs. Admittedly the effect of prostitution on labor market inequality, if it exists at all, will be small. Other roles which women disproportionately occupy – secretaries, housecleaners, babysitters, waitresses, and saleswomen – will be far more significant in reinforcing (as well as constituting) a gender-segregated division of labor.

I do not think it is plausible to attribute to prostitution a direct causal role in income inequality between men and women. But I believe that it is plausible to maintain that prostitution makes an important and direct contribution to women's inferior social status. Prostitution shapes and is itself shaped by custom and culture, by cultural meanings about the importance of sex, about the nature of women's sexuality and male desire.[50]

If prostitution is wrong it is because of its effects on how men perceive women and on how women perceive themselves. In our society, prostitution represents women as the sexual servants of men. It supports and embodies the widely held belief that men have strong sex drives which must be satisfied – largely through gaining access to some woman's body. This belief underlies the mistaken idea that prostitution is the "oldest" profession, since it is seen as a necessary consequence of human (i.e. male) nature. It also underlies the traditional conception of marriage, in which a man owned not only his wife's property but her body as well. It should not fail to startle us that until recently, most states did not recognize the possibility of "real rape" in marriage.[51] (Marital rape remains legal in two states: North Carolina and Oklahoma.)

Why is the idea that women must service men's sexual needs an image of inequality and not mere difference? My argument suggests that there are two primary, contextual reasons:

First, in our culture, there is no reciprocal social practice which represents men as serving women's sexual needs. Men are gigolos and paid escorts – but their sexuality is not seen as an independent capacity whose use women can buy. It is not part of the identity of a class of men that they will service women's sexual desires. Indeed, male prostitutes overwhelmingly service other men and not women. Men are not depicted as fully capable of commercially alienating their sexuality to women; but prostitution depicts women as sexual servants of men.

Second, the idea that prostitution embodies an idea of women as inferior is strongly suggested by the high incidence of rape and violence against prostitutes, as well as the fact that few men seek out or even contemplate prostitutes as potential marriage partners. While all women in our society are potential targets of rape and violence, the mortality rates for women engaged in streetwalking prostitution are roughly forty times higher than that of nonprostitute women.[52]

My suggestion is that prostitution depicts an image of gender inequality, by constituting one class of women as inferior. Prostitution is a "theater" of inequality – it displays for us a practice in which women are subordinated to men. This is especially the case where women are forcibly controlled by their (male) pimps. It follows from my conception of prostitution that it need not have such a negative effect when the prostitute is male. More research needs to be done on popular images and conceptions of gay male prostitutes, as well as on the extremely small number of male prostitutes who have women clients.

The negative image of women who participate in prostitution, the image of their inferior status, is objectionable in itself. It constitutes an important form of inequality – unequal status – based on attitudes of superiority and disrespect. Unfortunately, this form of inequality has largely been ignored by political philosophers and economists who have focused instead on inequalities in income and opportunity. Moreover, this form of inequality is not confined to prostitutes. I believe that the negative image of women prostitutes has third party effects: it shapes and influences the way women as a whole are seen. This hypothesis is, of course, an empirical one. It has not been tested largely because of the lack of studies of men who go to prostitutes. Most extant studies of prostitution examine the behavior and motivations of the women who enter into the practice, a fact which itself raises the suspicion that prostitution is viewed as "a problem about the women who are prostitutes . . . [rather than] a problem about the men who demand to buy them."[53] In these studies, male gender identity is taken as a given.

To investigate prostitution's negative image effects on female prostitutes and on women generally we need research on the following questions: (1) What are the attitudes of men who visit women prostitutes toward prostitutes? How do their attitudes compare with the attitudes of men who do not visit prostitutes toward women prostitutes? (2) What are the attitudes of men who visit women prostitutes toward women generally? What are the attitudes of men who do not visit women prostitutes toward women generally? (3) What are the attitudes of women toward women prostitutes? (4) What are the attitudes of the men and women involved in prostitution toward themselves? (5) Given the large proportion of African-American women who participate in prostitution, in what ways does prostitution contribute to male attitudes toward these women? (6) Does prostitution contribute to or diminish the likelihood of crimes of sexual violence? (7) What can we learn about these questions through cross-national studies? How do attitudes in the United States about women prostitutes compare with those in countries with more egalitarian wage policies or less status inequality between men and women?

The answers to these questions will reflect social facts about our culture. Whatever plausibility there is to the hypothesis that prostitution causally contributes to gender status inequality, it gains this plausibility from its surrounding cultural context.

I can imagine hypothetical circumstances in which prostitution would not have a negative image effect, where it could mark a reclaiming of women's sexuality. Margo St James and other members of Call Off Your Old Tired Ethics (COYOTE) have argued that prostitutes can function as sex therapists, fulfilling a legitimate social need as well as providing a source of experiment and alternative conceptions of sexuality and gender.[54] I agree that in a different culture, with different assumptions about men's and women's gender identities, prostitution might not have unequalizing effects. But I think that St James and others have minimized the cultural stereotypes that surround contemporary prostitution and their power over the shape of the practice. Prostitution, as we know it, is not separable from the larger surrounding culture which marginalizes, stereotypes, and stigmatizes women. Rather than providing an alternative conception of sexuality, I think that we need to look carefully at what men and women actually learn in prostitution. I do not believe that ethnographic studies of prostitution would support COYOTE's claim that prostitution contributes to images of women's dignity and equal standing.

If, through its negative image of women as sexual servants of men, prostitution reinforces women's inferior status in society, then it is wrong. Even though men can be and are prostitutes, I think that it is unlikely that we will find such negative image effects on men as a group. Individual men may be degraded in individual acts of prostitution: men as a group are not.

Granting all of the above, one objection to the equality approach to prostitution's wrongness remains. Is prostitution's negative image effect greater than that produced by other professions in which women largely service men, for example, secretarial labor? What is special about prostitution?

The negative image effect undoubtedly operates outside the domain of prostitution. But there are two significant differences between prostitution and other gender-segregated professions.

First, most people believe that prostitution, unlike secretarial work, is especially objectionable. Holding such moral views of prostitution constant, if prostitution continues to be primarily a female occupation, then the existence of prostitution will disproportionately fuel negative images of women.[55] Second, and relatedly, the particular image of women in prostitution is more of an image of inferiority than that of a secretary. The image embodies a greater amount of objectification, of representing the prostitute as an object without a will of her own. Prostitutes are far more likely to be victims of violence than are secretaries: as I mentioned, the mortality rate of women in prostitution is forty times that of other women. Prostitutes are also far more likely to be raped: a prostitute's "no" does not, to the male she services, mean no.

My claim is that, unless such arguments about prostitution's causal role in sustaining a form of gender inequality can be supported, I am not persuaded that something is morally wrong with markets in sex. In particular, I do not find arguments about the necessary relationship between commercial sex and diminished flourishing and degradation convincing. If prostitution is wrong, it is not because of its effects on happiness or personhood (effects which are shared with other forms of wage-labor); rather, it is because the sale of women's sexual labor may have adverse consequences for achieving a significant form of equality between men and women. My argument for the asymmetry thesis, if correct, connects prostitution to injustice. I now turn to the question of whether, even if we assume that prostitution is wrong under current conditions, it should remain illegal.

Should Prostitution be Legalized?

It is important to distinguish between prostitution's wrongness and the legal response that we are entitled to make to that wrongness. Even if prostitution is wrong, we may not be justified in prohibiting it if that prohibition makes the facts in virtue of which it is wrong worse, or if its costs are too great for other important values, such as autonomy and privacy. For example, even if someone accepts that the contemporary division of labor in the family is wrong, they may still reasonably object to government surveillance of the family's division of household chores. To determine whether such surveillance is justified, we need know more about the fundamental interests at stake, the costs of surveillance and the availability of alternative mechanisms for promoting equality in families. While I think that there is no acceptable view which would advocate governmental surveillance of family chores, there remain a range of plausible views about the appropriate scope of state intervention and, indeed, the appropriate scope of equality considerations.[56]

It is also important to keep in mind that in the case of prostitution, as with pornography and hate speech, narrowing the discussion of solutions to the single question of whether to ban or not to ban shows a poverty of imagination. There are many ways of challenging existing cultural values about the appropriate division of labor in the family and the nature of women's sexual and reproductive capacities – for example, education, consciousness-raising groups, changes in employee leave policies, comparable worth programs, etc. The law is not the only way to provide women with incentives to refrain from participating in prostitution. Nonetheless, we do need to decide what the best legal policy toward prostitution should be.

I begin with an assessment of the policy which we now have. The United States is one of the few developed Western countries which criminalizes prostitution.[57] Denmark, the Netherlands, West Germany, Sweden, Switzerland, and Austria all have legalized prostitution, although in some of these countries it is restricted by local ordinances.[58] Where prostitution is permitted, it is closely regulated.

Suppose that we accept that gender equality is a legitimate goal of social policy. The question is whether the current legal prohibition on prostitution in the United States promotes gender equality. The answer I think is that it clearly does not. The current legal policies in the United States arguably exacerbate the factors in virtue of which prostitution is wrong.

The current prohibition on prostitution renders the women who engage in the practice vulnerable. First, the participants in the practice seek assistance from pimps in lieu of the contractual and legal remedies which are denied them. Male pimps may protect women prostitutes from their customers and from the police, but the system of pimp-run prostitution has enormous negative effects on the women at the lowest rungs of prostitution. Second, prohibition of prostitution raises the dilemma of the "double bind": if we prevent prostitution without greater redistribution of income, wealth, and opportunities, we deprive poor women of one way – in some circumstances the only way – of improving their condition.[59] Analogously, we do not solve the problem of homelessness by criminalizing it.

Furthermore, women are disproportionately punished for engaging in commercial sex acts. Many state laws make it a worse crime to sell sex than to buy it. Consequently, pimps and clients ("johns") are rarely prosecuted. In some jurisdictions, patronizing a prostitute is not illegal. The record of arrests and convictions is also highly asymmetric. Ninety percent of all convicted prostitutes are women. Studies have shown that male prostitutes are arrested with less frequency than female prostitutes and receive shorter sentences. One study of the judicial processing of 2,859 male and female prostitutes found that judges were more likely to find defendants guilty if they were female.[60]

Not does the current legal prohibition on prostitution unambiguously benefit women as a class because the cultural meaning of current governmental prohibition of prostitution is unclear. While an unrestricted regime of prostitution – a pricing system in women's sexual attributes – could have negative external consequences on women's self-perceptions and perceptions by men, state prohibition can also reflect a view of women which contributes to their inequality. For example, some people support state regulation because they believe that women's sexuality is for purposes of reproduction, a claim tied to traditional ideas about women's proper role.

There is an additional reason why banning prostitution seems an inadequate response to the problem of gender inequality and which suggests a lack of parallel with the case of commercial surrogacy. Banning prostitution would not by itself – does not – eliminate it. While there is reason to think that making commercial surrogacy arrangements illegal or unenforceable would diminish their occurrence, no such evidence exists about prostitution. No city has eliminated prostitution merely through criminalization. Instead, criminalized prostitution thrives as a black market activity in which pimps substitute for law as the mechanism for enforcing contracts. It thereby makes the lives of prostitutes worse than they might otherwise be and without clearly counteracting prostitution's largely negative image of women.

If we decide to ban prostitution, these problems must be addressed. If we decide not to ban prostitution (either by legalizing it or decriminalizing it), then we must be careful to regulate the practice to address its negative effects. Certain restrictions on advertising and recruitment will be needed in order to address the negative image effects that an unrestricted regime of prostitution would perpetuate. But the current regime of prostitution has negative effects on the prostitutes themselves. It places their sexual capacities largely under the control of men. In order to promote women's autonomy, the law needs to ensure that certain restrictions – in effect, a Bill of Rights for Women – are in place.

1 No woman should be forced, either by law or by private persons, to have sex against her will. (Recall that it is only quite recently that the courts have recognized the existence of marital rape.) A woman who sells sex must be able to refuse to give it; she must not be coerced by law or private persons to perform.
2 No woman should be denied access, either by law or by private persons, to contraception or to treatment for sexually transmitted diseases, particularly AIDS, or to abortion (at least in the first trimester).
3 The law should ensure that a woman has adequate information before she agrees to sexual intercourse. The risks of venereal and other sexually transmitted diseases, the risks of pregnancy, and the laws protecting a woman's right to refuse sex should all be generally available.
4 Minimum age of consent laws for sexual intercourse should be enforced. These laws should ensure that women (and men) are protected from coercion and do not enter into sexual relationships until they are in a position to understand what they are consenting to.
5 The law should promote women's control over their own sexuality by prohibiting brokerage. If what is wrong with prostitution is its relation to gender inequality, then it is crucial that the law be brought to bear primarily on the men who profit from the use of women's sexual capacities.

Each of these principles is meant to establish and protect a woman's right to control her sexual and reproductive capacities and not to give control of these capacities to others. Each of these principles is meant to protect the conditions for women's consent to sex, whether commercial or not. Each of these principles also seeks to counter the degradation of women in prostitution by mitigating its nature as a form of female servitude. In addition, given that a woman's choices are shaped both by the range of available opportunities and by the distribution of entitlements in society, it is crucial to attend to the economic position of women in American society and those social and economic factors which produce the unequal life chances of men and women.

Conclusion

If the arguments I have offered here are correct, then prostitution is wrong in virtue of its contributions to perpetuating a pervasive form of inequality. In different circumstances, with different assumptions about women and their role in society, I do not think that prostitution would be especially troubling – no more troubling than many other labor markets currently allowed. It follows, then, that in other circumstances, the asymmetry thesis would be denied or less strongly felt. While the idea that prostitution is intrinsically degrading is a powerful intuition (and like many such intuitions, it persists even after its proponents undergo what Richard Brandt has termed "cognitive therapy," in which errors of fact and inference are corrected), I believe that this intuition is itself bound up with well-entrenched views of male gender identity and women's sexual role in the context of that identity.[62] If we are troubled by prostitution, as I think we should be, then we should direct much of our energy to putting forward alternative models of egalitarian relations between men and women.

Notes

I am grateful to the support of a Rockefeller Fellowship at Princeton University's Center for Human Values. Earlier versions of this article were presented at Swarthmore College, Princeton University, and Oxford University. I am grateful to the audiences at these institutions and in particular to Elizabeth Anderson, Michael Blake, C. A. J. Coady, Amy Gutmann, George Kateb, Andrew Koppelman, Arthur Kuflik, Peter de Marneffe, Thomas Pogge, Adam Swift, Stuart White, and Elisabeth Wood. I also thank two anonymous reviewers at *Ethics* as well as the editors of the journal.

1   Debra Satz, "Markets in women's reproductive labor," *Philosophy and Public Affairs* 21 (1992), pp. 107–31.
2   What would remain troubling would be the miserable and unjust background circumstances in which much prostitution occurs. That is, if there were gender equality between the sexes but a substantial group of very poor men and women were selling sex, this would indeed be troubling. We should be suspicious of any labor contract entered into under circumstances of desperation.
3   Laurie Shrage, "Should feminists oppose prostitution?" *Ethics* 99 (1989), pp. 347–61, is an important exception. See also her new book, *Moral Dilemmas of Feminism: Prostitution, Adultery and Abortion* (New York: Routledge, 1994).
4   The fact that monetary exchange plays a role in maintaining many intimate relationships is a point underscored by George Bernard Shaw in *Mrs. Warren's Profession* (New York: Garland, 1981).
5   Compare Judith Walkowitz, *Prostitution and Victorian Society* (Cambridge: Cambridge University Press, 1980); Ruth Rosen, *Prostitution in America: 1900–1918* (Baltimore, Md.: Johns Hopkins University Press, 1982); B. Hobson, *Uneasy Virtue: the Politics of Prostitution and the American Reform Tradition* (Chicago: University of Chicago Press, 1990).
6   John Decker, *Prostitution: Regulation and Control* (Littleton, Colo.: Rothman, 1979), p. 191.
7   Compare Harold Greenwald, *The Elegant Prostitute: a Social and Psychoanalytic Study* (New York: Walker, 1970), p. 10.
8   For discussion of male prostitutes who sell sex to women, see H. Smith and B. Van der Horst, "For women only – how it feels to be a male hooker," *Village Voice* (March 7, 1977). Dictionary and common usage tends to identify prostitutes with women. Men who sell sex to women are generally referred to as "gigolos," not

"prostitutes." The former term encompasses the sale of companionship as well as sex.

9 Male prostitutes merit only a dozen pages in John Decker's monumental study of prostitution. See also D. Drew and J. Drake, *Boys for Sale: a Sociological Study of Boy Prostitution* (Deer Park, NY: Brown Book Co., 1969); D. Deisher, "Young male prostitutes," *Journal of American Medical Association* 212 (1970), pp. 1661–6; Gita Sereny, *The Invisible Children: Child Prostitution in America, West Germany and Great Britain* (London: Deutsch, 1984). I am grateful to Vincent DiGirolamo for bringing these works to my attention.

10 Compare Kathleen Barry, *Female Sexual Slavery* (New York: Avon, 1979). If we consider prostitution as an international phenomenon, then a majority of prostitutes are desperately poor and abused women. Nevertheless, there is a significant minority who are not. Furthermore, if prostitution were legalized, it is possible that the minimum condition of prostitutes in at least some countries would be raised.

11 Priscilla Alexander, "Prostitution: a difficult issue for feminists," in Alexander and F. Delacoste (eds) *Writings by Women in the Sex Industry* (Pittsburgh: Cleis, 1987).

12 Moreover, to the extent that the desperate background conditions are the problem it is not apparent that outlawing prostitution is the solution. Banning prostitution may only remove a poor woman's best option: it in no way eradicates the circumstances which led her to such a choice. See M. Radin, "Market-inalienability," *Harvard Law Review* 100 (1987), pp. 1849–937, on the problem of the "double bind."

13 Sometimes the qualitative aspects of a good have quantitative effects and so for that reason need to be taken into account. It is difficult, e.g., to establish a market in used cars given the uncertainties of ascertaining their qualitative condition. Compare George Akerlof, "The market for lemons: qualitative uncertainty and the market mechanism," *Quarterly Journal of Economics* 84 (1970), pp. 488–500.

14 For an attempt to understand human sexuality as a whole through the economic approach, see Richard Posner, *Sex and Reason* (Cambridge, Mass.: Harvard University Press, 1992).

15 Although two-thirds of prostitutes surveyed say that they have no regrets about choice of work. Compare Decker, pp. 165–6. This figure is hard to interpret, given the high costs of thinking that one has made a bad choice of occupation and the lack of decent employment alternatives for many prostitutes.

16 See Guido Calabresi and A. Douglas Melamed, "Property rules, liability rules and inalienability: one view of the cathedral," *Harvard Law Review* 85 (1972), pp. 1089–128.

17 Economic analysis fails to justify the laws we now have regarding prostitution. See below.

18 See Radin, "Market-inalienability," pp. 1884ff.

19 Posner, *Sex and Reason*, p. 182. See also R. Posner, "An eonomic theory of the criminal law," *Columbia Law Review* 85 (1985), pp. 1193–231. "The prohibition against rape is to the sex and marriage 'market' as the prohibition against theft is to explicit markets in goods and services" (p. 1199).

20 His approach in fact suggests that rape be seen as a "benefit" to the rapist, a suggestion that I think we should be loathe to follow.

21 I do not mean to claim however that such sovereignty over the body is absolute.

22 This section draws from and enlarges upon Satz, "Markets in women's reproductive labor."

23   Prostitution is, however, an issue which continues to divide feminists as well as prostitutes and former prostitutes. On the one side, some feminists see prostitution as dehumanizing and alienating and linked to male domination. This is the view taken by the prostitute organization Women Hurt in Systems of Prostitution Engaged in Revolt (WHISPER). On the other side, some feminists see sex markets as affirming a woman's right to autonomy, sexual pleasure, and economic welfare. This is the view taken by the prostitute organization COYOTE.

24   Carole Pateman, *The Sexual Contract* (Stanford, Calif.: Stanford University Press, 1988), p. 207; emphasis added.

25   The phrase is Radin's.

26   J. Harris, "The survival lottery," *Philosophy* 50 (1975), pp. 81–7.

27   As an example of the ways in which the diversity of sexual experience has been culturally productive, see Lynn Hunt (ed.) *The Invention of Pornography* (New York: Zone, 1993). Many of the essays in this volume illustrate the ways in which pornography has historically contributed to broader social criticism.

28   Radin, "Market-inalienability," p. 1884.

29   An objection along these lines is raised by Margaret Baldwin ("Split at the root: feminist discourses of law reform," *Yale Journal of Law and Feminism* 5 (1992), pp. 47–120). Baldwin worries that prostitution undermines our ability to understand a woman's capacity to consent to sex. Baldwin asks, Will a prostitute's consent to sex be seen as consent to a twenty dollar payment? Will courts determine sentences in rape trials involving prostitutes as the equivalent of parking fine violations (e.g. as another twenty dollar payment)? Aren't prostitutes liable to have their fundamental interests in bodily integrity discounted? I think Baldwin's worry is a real one, especially in the context of the current stigmatization of prostitutes. It could be resolved, in part, by withholding information about a woman's profession from rape trials.

30   Radin is herself fairly consistent in her hostility to many forms of wage labor. She has a complicated view about decommodification in nonideal circumstances which I cannot discuss here.

31   Also notice that many forms of labor we make inalienable – e.g., bans on mercenaries – cannot be justified by that labor's relationship to our personhood.

32   Elizabeth Anderson, *Value in Ethics and Economics* (Cambridge, Mass.: Harvard University Press, 1993), p. 45.

33   Actually, the prostitute's humanity is a part of the sex transaction itself. Whereas Posner's economic approach places sex with another person on the same scale as sex with a sheep, for many people the latter is not a form of sex at all (*Sex and Reason*). Moreover, in its worst forms, the prostitute's humanity (and gender) may be crucial to the john's experience of himself as superior to her. See Catherine MacKinnon, *Toward a Feminist Theory of the State* (Cambridge, Mass.: Harvard University Press, 1989).

34   Although this statement might have to be qualified in the light of empirical research. Arlie Hochschild, e.g., has found that the sale of "emotional labor" by airline stewardesses and insurance salesmen distorts their responses to pain and frustration (*The Managed Heart: the Commercialization of Human Feeling* (New York: Basic Books, 1983)).

35   I owe this point to Elizabeth Anderson, who stressed the need to distinguish between different versions of the degradation objection and suggested some lines of interpretation (conversation with author, Oxford University, July 1994).

36   More generally, they raise questions about the desirability of a world in which

people use and exploit each other as they use and exploit other natural objects, insofar as this is compatible with Pareto improvements.

37 See Satz, "Markets in women's reproduction labor."

38 US Department of Labor, Women's Bureau (Washington, DC: Government Printing Office, 1992).

39 D. Taylor, "Women: an analysis," in *Women: a World Report* (London: Methuen, 1985). Taylor reports that while on a world scale women "perform nearly two-thirds of all working hours [they] receive only one tenth of the world income and own less than one percent of world resources."

40 J. David-McNeil, "The changing economic status of the female labor force in Canada," in Economic Council of Canada (ed.) *Towards Equity: Proceedings of a Colloquium on the Economic Status of Women in the Labor Market,*" (Ottawa: Canadian Government Publication Centre, 1985).

41 S. Rix (ed.) *The American Woman, 1990–91* (New York: Norton, 1990), cited in Woman's Action Coalition (ed.) *WAC Stats: The Facts about Women* (New York: New Press, 1993), p. 41.

42 Report of the Federal Office of Child Support Enforcement, 1990.

43 Rix, *American Woman*. Note also that the time women spend doing housework has not declined since the 1920s despite the invention of labor saving technologies (e.g. laundry machines and dishwashers).

44 My views about this aspect of gender inequality have been greatly clarified in discussions and correspondence with Elizabeth Anderson and Elisabeth Wood during 1994.

45 See Paul Rosenkrantz, Susan Vogel, Helen Bees, Inge Broverman, and David Broverman, "Sex-role stereotypes and self-concepts in college students," *Journal of Consulting and Clinical Psychology* 32 (1968), pp. 286–95.

46 L. Heise, "Gender violence as a health issue" (Violence, Health and Development Project, Center for Women's Global Leadership, Rutgers University, New Brunswick, NJ, 1992).

47 L. Heise, "Violence against women: the missing agenda," in *Women's Health: A Global Perspective* (New York: Westview, 1992), cited in Woman's Action Coalition, *WAC Stats*, p. 55. More than one-third of female homicide victims are killed by their husbands or boyfriends.

48 I am indebted here to the discussion of Iris Young in *Justice and the Politics of Difference* (Princeton, NJ: Princeton University Press, 1990).

49 Ruth Leger Sivard, *Women . . . a World Survey* (Washington, DC: World Priorities, 1985).

50 Shrage ("Should feminists oppose prostitution?) argues that prostitution perpetuates the following beliefs which oppress women: (1) the universal possession of a potent sex drive; (2) the "natural" dominance of men; (3) the pollution of women by sexual contact; and (4) the reification of sexual practice.

51 Susan Estrich, *Real Rape* (Cambridge, Mass.: Harvard University Press, 1987).,

52 Baldwin, "Split at the root," p. 75. Compare the Canadian Report on Prostitution and Pornography; also M. Silbert, "Sexual assault on prostitutes," research report to the *National Center for the Prevention and Control of Rape*, November 1980, for a study of street prostitutes in which 70 percent of those surveyed reported that they had been raped while walking the streets.

53 Carole Pateman, "Defending prostitution: charges against Ericsson," *Ethics* 93 (1983) pp. 561–5, p. 563.

54 See also, S. Schwartzenbach, "Contractarians and feminists debate prostitution," *New York University Review of Law and Social Change* 18 (1990–1), pp. 103–30.

55 I owe this point to Arthur Kuflik.
56 For example, does the fact that racist joke-telling reinforces negative stereotypes
and perpetuates racial prejudice and inequality justify legal bans on such joke telling? What are the limits on what we can justifiably use the state to do in the name
of equality? This is a difficult question. I only note here that arguments which
justify state banning of prostitution can be consistent with the endorsement of
stringent protections for speech. This is because speech and expression are arguably connected with basic fundamental human interests – with forming and articulating conceptions of value, with gathering information, with testifying on matters
of conscience – in a way that prostitution (and some speech, e.g. commercial speech)
is not. Even if we assume, as I think we should, that people have fundamental
interests in having control over certain aspects of their bodies and lives, it does not
follow that they have a fundamental interest in being free to sell themselves, their
body parts, or any of their particular capacities.
57 Prostitution is legalized only in several jurisdictions in Nevada.
58 These countries have more pay equity between men and women than does the
United States. This might be taken to undermine an argument about prostitution's role in contributing to income inequality. Moreover, women's status is lower
in some societies which repress prostitution (such as those of the Islamic nations)
than in those which do not (such as those of the Scandinavian nations). But given
the variety of cultural, economic, and political factors and mechanisms which need
to be taken into account, we need to be very careful in drawing hasty conclusions.
Legalizing prostitution might have negative effects on gender equality in the United
States, even if legal prostitution does not correlate with gender inequality in other
countries. There are many differences between the United States and European
societies which make it implausible to think that one factor can alone be explana-
tory with respect to gender inequality.
59 Radin, "Market-inalienability," pp. 1915ff.
60 J. Lindquist et al., "Judicial processing of males and females charged with prostitution," *Journal of Criminal Justice* 17 (1989), pp. 277–91. Several state laws banning prostitution have been challenged on equal protection grounds. These statistics
support the idea that prostitution's negative image effect has disporportionate bearing on male and female prostitutes.
61 In this section, I have benefited from reading Cass Sunstein, "Gender difference,
reproduction and the law" (University of Chicago Law School, 1992, unpublished
manuscript). Sunstein believes that someone committed to gender equality will,
most likely, advocate a legal ban on prostitution.

bell hooks examines the way progressive feminist thinking about sex is represented in the mainstream media. She shows how a male-oriented magazine like *Esquire* distorts and appropriates progressive feminist voices on sexuality in order to counter their full impact and thus maintain the sexual status quo. She points to the need for a more nuanced public dialogue about gender and sexual liberation.

Focus questions:
1 How does the conventional sexual practice involving the aggressive seduction of women fail to acknowledge women as full sexual agents?
2 hooks suggests that feminists have not only criticized patriarchal sexual speech (pornography) but have developed a positive vision of liberatory sexual relations that is rarely glimpsed by the mainstream media. How does this vision differ from that of the "do me" feminists that *Esquire* promotes?
3 How did hooks's racial identity affect the *Esquire* reporter's interpretation or deliberate use of her comments about sex?

24 Talking Sex
Beyond the Patriarchal Phallic Imaginary

bell hooks

Women who grew to womanhood at the peak of contemporary feminist movement know that at that moment in time, sexual liberation was on the feminist agenda. The right to make decisions about our bodies was primary, as were reproductive rights, particularly the right to abort an unplanned for unwanted fetus, and yet it was also important to claim the body as a site of pleasure. The feminist movement I embraced as a young coed at Stanford University highlighted the body. Refusing to shave, we let hair grow on our legs and under our armpits. We chose whether or not to wear panties. We gave up bras, girdles, and slips. We had all-girl parties, grown-up sleepovers. We slept together. We had sex. We did it with girls and boys. We did it across race, class, nationality. We did it in groups. We watched each other doing it. We did it with the men in our lives differently. We let them celebrate with us the discovery of female sexual agency. We let them know the joys and ecstasy of mutual sexual choice. We embraced nakedness. We reclaimed the female body as a site of power and possibility.

We were the generation of the birth-control pill. We saw female freedom as intimately and always tied to the issue of body rights. We believed that women would never be free if we did not have the right to recover our bodies from sexual slavery, from the prison of patriarchy. We were not taking back the night; we were claiming it, claiming the dark in resistance to the bourgeois sexist world of repression, order, boredom, and fixed social roles. In the dark, we were finding new ways to see ourselves as women. We were charting a journey from slavery to freedom. We were making revolution. Our bodies were the occupied countries we liberated.

It was this vision of contemporary feminist movement I shared with *Esquire* magazine when interviewed by Tad Friend. Consistently, I shared with him the reality that many feminists have always been and are into sex. I emphatically stated that I repudiated the notion of a "new feminism" and saw it being created in the mass media mainly as a marketing ploy to advance the opportunistic concerns of individual women while simultaneously acting as an agent of antifeminist backlash by undermining feminism's radical/revolutionary gains. "New feminism" is being brought to us as a product that works effectively to set women against one another, to engage us in competition wars over which brand of feminism is more effective. Large numbers of feminist thinkers and activists oppose the exploitative, hedonistic consumerism that is repackaging feminism as a commodity and selling it to us full of toxic components (a little bit of poisonous, patriarchal thinking sprinkled here and there), but we feel powerless to change this trend. Many of us feel we have never had a voice in the mainstream media, and that our counterhegemonic standpoints rarely gain a wider public hearing. For years, I was among those feminist thinkers who felt reluctant to engage the mass media (by appearing on radio programs, television shows, or speaking with journalists) for fear of cooptation by editing processes which can be used to slant any message in the direction desired by the producers. That turning away from the mass media (to the degree that the mainstream media showed any interest in presenting our views) has been a gap that made it easier for reformists and liberal advocates for gender equality to assume the public spotlight and shape public opinion about feminist thinking.

The patriarchal-dominated mass media is far more interested in promoting the views of women who want both to claim feminism and repudiate it at the same time. Hence, the success of Camille Paglia, Katie Roiphe, and to some extent Naomi Wolf. Seen as the more liberal feminist voices countering those taken to embody strident, narrow anti-sex standpoints (e.g. Catharine MacKinnon, Andrea Dworkin), these women are offered up by the white male-dominated mass media as the hope of feminism. And they are the individuals that the mass media most often turns to when it desires to hear the feminist voice speak. These women are all white. For the most part, they come from privileged class backgrounds, were educated at elite institutions, and take conservative positions on most gender issues. They in no way represent radical or revolutionary feminist standpoints. And these standpoints are the ones the mass media rarely wants to call attention to. Feminist women of color must still struggle to break through the barriers of racism and white supremacy to make our voices heard. Some of us have been willing to engage the mass media, out of fear that this "new feminism" will erase our voices and our concerns by attempting to universalize the category "woman" while simultaneously deflecting attention away from the ways differences created by race and class hierarchies disrupt an unrealistic vision of commonality.

Strategic engagement with subversive politics of representation makes it necessary for us to intervene by actively participating in mainstream public dia-

logues about feminist movement. It was this standpoint that informed my decision to talk with *Esquire*. Even though the sexist perspectives commonly conveyed by articles in this magazine made me reluctant to speak with them, I had
been assured by a feminist comrade – a black female – that the white male
reporter could be trusted to represent our views fairly, that his intention was
not to distort, pervert or mock. When I spoke with Tad Friend, I was told that
he was doing a piece on different attitudes among feminists towards sexuality.
It was my understanding that this was the primary focus of his discussion. When
the article appeared in the February 1994 issue of *Esquire*, I found my comments had been distorted, perverted – that indeed the article intentionally mocks
those presumably "old feminists" who are not "down" with the pro-sex "new
feminists." Not having heard Friend use the phrase "do-me" (a bit of eating-
the-other white cultural appropriation of funky black R&B I would have "dissed,"
had it been shared by Tad when he spoke with me), I could not object to his use
of these phrases. During our phone interview he showed no knowledge of the
contributions black women had made to feminist theory, even though he positively presented himself as striving to be inclusive, a stance I welcomed. Not
being in any way a man-hater or a believer in racial separatism, I was pleased to
engage in a discussion about feminism and sexuality with a young white male
from a privileged class background who seemed genuinely interested in learning. These dialogues across difference are important for education for critical
consciousness. They are necessary if we are ever to change the structures of
racism, sexism, and class elitism which exclude and do not promote solidarity
across difference. With generosity and warmth, I engaged in a lively discussion
with Friend about feminism and sexuality.

Over and over again in our conversation, I passionately addressed the dangers of a conservative politics of representation that eagerly exploits the idea of
a "new feminism" that is more pro-sex and pro-male. My repudiation of the
idea of "new feminism," as well as most of the ideas I discussed with Friend,
were in no way conveyed in his article (which he never showed me before publishing). Reading the *Esquire* piece, I found myself and my ideas exploited in
the conventional ways white supremacist, capitalist patriarchy consistently de-
ploys to perpetuate the devaluation of feminism and black womanhood. Friend
violated my confidence by doing exactly what I requested he not do, which is
exploit my comments to reinforce the vision of "new feminism that is being
pushed by privileged white girls." Acting in a similar manner to that of racist
white women in feminist movement, he exploited my presence and my words
to appear more inclusive and therefore more politically correct even as he discounted the meaning and substance of both. Although all the white women
whose words and images are highlighted used sexually explicit street vernacular
in their quotes, only mine are extracted and used to "represent" my major
points – even though they were actually witty asides I made to explain a point
Friend claimed not to understand, to want "broken down" to a more basic
level.

By highlighting this quote, making the black female's voice and body exemplify rough, raw, vernacular speech, he continues the racist/sexist representa-

tion of black women as the oversexed "hot pussies" I critique in *Black Looks*, juxtaposing it, by way of contrast, with the racist/sexist image of white women as being less sexually raw, more repressed. Of course, all the white women quoted in the body of the article, speak in a graphic heterosexist vernacular. At this white male-dominated magazine, some individuals decided that it was acceptable to highlight a black female using sexually explicit speech while downplaying white women doing the same, a strategy that helps keep in place neat little racist/sexist stereotypes about the differences between white and black women. My point here is not to suggest that women should not use sexually explicit street vernacular (that was certainly one of the freedoms feminists fought for at the onset of the movement), but to interrogate the way my use of this language was distorted by a process of decontextualization.

Friend attributes to me a quote which reads: "If all we have to choose from is the limp dick or the super hard dick we're in trouble. We need a versatile dick who admits that intercourse isn't all there is to sexuality, who can negotiate rough sex on Monday, eating pussy on Tuesday, and cuddling on Wednesday." Rewritten by Friend, my use of black street vernacular is turned into white parody. Never having thought that I myself "need a versatile dick," I shared with Friend my sense that heterosexual women want a man who can be versatile. To use the phrase "a versatile man" is to evoke a vision of action and agency, of male willingness to change and alter behavior. The phrase a "versatile dick" dehumanizes. Friend changed my words to make it appear that I support female objectification of men, denying their full personhood and reducing them to their anatomy. I am hard-pressed to understand how "dicks" negotiate anything, since the very word "negotiate" emphasizes communication and consent. Friend distorts this statement so as to make my words affirm identification with a phallic mindset, thereby evoking tired racist/sexist stereotypes of emasculating and castrating pseudo-masculine and ultimately undesirable – hard, black females.

In like manner, I shared with him that "women can't just ask men to give up sexist objectification if we want a hard dick and a tight butt – and many of us do. We must change the way we desire. We must not objectify." Dropping the last two sentences without using punctuation to indicate that he has left something out, as well as changing my words and including his own, Friend toys with my ideas, reshaping them so that I am made to appear supportive of patriarchal notions of sexual pleasure and sexist/heterosexist thinking that I in no way condone. Yet, despite Friend's deliberate distortion of my highlighted quote, its radical intentionality remains intact. It makes clear that sexist men must undergo a process of feminist revolution if they want to be capable of satisfying the needs of feminist women who experience our most intense sexual pleasure in an oppositional space outside the patriarchal phallic imaginary. It is this feminist vision of liberatory heterosexuality that seems to terrify men.

No wonder, then, that women who want to be sexual with men are perversely reinventing feminism so that it will satisfy patriarchal desires, so that it can be incorporated into a sexist phallic imaginary in such a way that male sexual agency as we now know it will never need to change. Representing a larger structure of white male power, Tad Friend, in conjunction with those who edited and published this piece, show contempt for any radical or revolutionary feminist practice that upholds dialogue and engagement with men, that sees men as comrades in struggle. Contrary to what this magazine and the mass media in general project in complicity with opportunistic white female allies (e.g. Camille Paglia, Naomi Wolf), older feminists like myself were supporting the inclusion of men in feminist movement (actually writing and publishing articles to push this point) years ago. Contrary to *Esquire*'s suggestion that there is "a new generation of women, who are embracing sex (and men!)," we are witnessing a new generation of women who, like their sexist male counterparts, are aggressively ahistorical and unaware of the long tradition of radical/revolutionary feminist thought that celebrates inclusiveness and liberatory sexuality. Both these groups prefer to seek out the most conservative, narrow-minded feminist thought on sex and men, then arrogantly use these images to represent the movement.

Their refusal even to acknowledge the existence of progressive feminist thought about sex and sexuality allows them to sensationalize these issues even as they effectively use the image of the "do-me" feminists to assault the many women who stand against patriarchy and phallocentrism. *Esquire* magazine goes to great lengths to place me in the "do-me" category precisely because many sexist men remain unable to accept that women (and our male allies) who repudiate patriarchy assert sexual agency in new and exciting ways that are mutually humanizing and satistfying. It has always served the interest of the patriarchal status quo for men to represent the feminist woman as antisex and antimale. Even though the real lives of women active in feminist movement never conformed to this representation, it continues to prevail in the popular imagination because the subjugated knowledge that embracing feminism intensifies sexual pleasure for men and women in this society, no matter our sexual practice, is dangerous information. Too many folks might want to convert to feminist thought if they knew firsthand the powerful and passionate positive transformation it would create in every area of their sexual lives. It is better for patriarchy to try and make us believe that the only real sex available to feminist women who like men must be negotiated using the same old patriarchal modes of seduction that are perpetually unsatisfying to all women.

Patriarchal publications can successfully push this propagandistic message, as the *Esquire* issue does, precisely because powerful discussions of feminism and sexuality are not taking place continually, everywhere. Talking sex in meta-language and theoretical prose does not capture the imagination of masses of folks who are working daily to understand how their lives have been affected by shifting gender roles and expectations and how sexism fucks us all up, folks who just want to know what feminism is really all about and whether or not it can rescue us from the abyss of loneliness and sexual death. Living as we do in an antisex culture, with patriarchy as the most well organized and institutionalized attack on our sexual agency and imaginations, it is downright perverse and frightening that the mass media can convince anyone that feminism is the cause of women turning away from men or from heterosexual sex. Heterosexual women turned on by feminist movement learn how to move away from sexually dead encounters with patriarchal men who eroticize exploitative power and domination scenarios that in no way embrace female sexual agency, but these women do so not to give up sex but to make sex new, different, liberatory, and fun. Lack of critical vigilance within feminist movement made everyone unmindful of the ongoing need to document this shift positively. Were many more of us documenting our sex lives in art, literature, film and other media, there would be an abundance of counter-hegemonic evidence to disprove the popular sexist stereotype that women in feminist movement are antisex and antimen. By conceding the turf of sexuality to the phallocentric sexist media, feminists – whether liberal or radical – become complicit with conservative repression of public discourse of sexuality. If nothing else, articles such as the *Esquire* piece should serve as pointed reminders that radical/revolutionary feminists must always keep alive a dynamic public discussion of sexuality.

Collectively, many feminists stopped talking about sex publicly because such talk exposed not only our differences, our contradictions, it revealed that we had not yet produced visionary models of liberatory sexuality that fully reconciled issues of power and domination with our will to end systemic, sexist sexual exploitation and oppression. As the feminist pro-sex collective voice retreated into silence, sometimes pushed into the background by the puritanical violence of antisex conservative gender rights propaganda, the individual voices of narrowly focused thinkers like privileged white law professor Catharine MacKinnon, to give just one example, claimed to represent feminist perspectives on sexuality. Only folks outside feminist movement accept these voices as representative, yet these voices continue to speak the feminist speech that the mass media most wants to hear. It delights in the sound of these voices because they are easier to belittle, make fun of, and finally dismiss. Obviously one-dimensional and often ruthlessly dogmatic, these voices are usually antisex, antipleasure, utterly lacking in humor. They deny the reality of contradictions and insist on an unattainable perfectionism in human behavior. It is no wonder, then, that the public voices of puritanical, reformist feminism turn most folks off. However, we do not effectively counter the negative impact of this message by embracing outmoded sexist visions of female sexual agency and pleasure.

I hear nothing sexually open or radical in the statement attributed to Lisa Palac in *Esquire*, who declares "I say to men, 'Okay, pretend you're a burglar and you've broken in here and you throw me down on the bed and make me suck your cock!' They're horrified – it goes against all they've been taught: No, no, it would degrade you! Exactly. Degrade me when I ask you to." The eroticization of sex as degradation, especially dick-sucking, and the equation of that chosen "degradation" with pleasure is merely an unimaginative reworking of stale patriarchal, pornographic fantasies that do not become more exciting or liberatory if women are the agents of their projection and realization. Most of the women quoted in *Esquire* display a lack of sexual imagination, since they primarily conceive of sexual agency only by inverting the patriarchal standpoint and claiming it as their own. Their comments were so pathetically male-identified that it was scary to think that readers might actually be convinced they were an expression of feminist, female, sexual agency. However, they were intended to excite the male imagination, and no doubt many men get off fantasizing that the feminist sexual revolution would not really change anything, just make it easier for everybody to occupy the space of the patriarchal phallic imaginary.

No doubt it was just such a moment of ecstatic masturbatory reverie that led Tad Friend to declare: "The do-me feminists are choosing locker-room talk to shift discussion from the failures of men to the failures of feminism, from the paradigm of sexual abuse to the paradigm of sexual pleasure." This kind of either/or binary thinking mirrors the narrow-minded dogmatic thinking it claims to critique. Revolutionary feminism does not focus on the failures of men, but rather on the violence of patriarchy and the pain of sexist exploitation and oppression. It calls out sexual abuse to transform the space of the erotic so that sexual pleasure can be sustained and ongoing, so that female agency can exist as an inalienable right. Revolutionary feminism embraces men who are able to change, who are capable of responding mutually in a subject-to-subject encounter where desire and fulfillment are in no way linked to coercive subjugation. This feminist vision of the sexual imaginary is the space few men seem able to enter.

Renée Heberle considers whether the strategies employed by the movement to end sexual violence have been effective. She argues that the public sharing of stories that aim to prove the reality of sexual violence and the victim's suffering work to reinforce cultural beliefs in the sexual allure of women and the inevitability of male sexual aggression – beliefs which contribute to the problem of rape. She suggests that women who have resisted and neutralized sexual assault be encouraged to speak out in order to challenge myths about male power and female vulnerability.

Focus questions:
1 What do anti-rape activists hope to achieve by calling attention to the sexual victimization of women by men? What dangers are there in this strategy?
2 What defines a "rape culture" and what sorts of interventions are needed to transform it, according to Heberle?
3 Anthropologists report that there is at least one society in which men fear rape by gangs of women. How might knowledge of this society serve the purposes of the movement to end sexual violence against women?

---

25 Deconstructive Strategies and the Movement against Sexual Violence

---

Renée Heberle

This essay considers the social effects of the strategy of "speaking out" about sexual violence to transform rape culture. I articulate the paradox that women's identification as victims in the public sphere reinscribes the gendered norms that enable the

victimization of women. I suggest we create a more diversified public narrative of
sexual violence and sexuality within the context of the movement against sexual vio-
lence in order to deconstruct masculinist power in feminine victimization.

The movement against sexual violence works to expose the reality of rape culture[1] through the narration of women's experiences in the public sphere in
speakouts and through the media.[2] Women are encouraged by movement activists and theorists to tell of their experience, not only for purposes of inform-
ing the public, but to authorize social and legal interventions in what is argued
to be a culture saturated by images and practices of sexual violence against
women.[3] This project of exposure is not without risks, however. One of those
risks is that as the ever-enlarged map of women's sexual suffering is pieced
together, it becomes, in effect, the social insignia of male power.

   I draw upon Elaine Scarry's analysis (1985) of the relationship between pain
and modern forms of power as a resource to help understand this peculiar logic
and the effects of representing sexual violence. Her examination of the structure of modern forms of torture and the quality of pain resonates profoundly
with women's descriptions of being battered and sexually abused. Further, I
suggest that her thinking about the relationship between power and the representation of suffering, should caution us about the political effects of efforts to
express the reality of rape culture.[4] I ask whether the strategy of speaking out, of
telling stories of women's sexual suffering, will necessarily achieve the transformation advocates claim is immanent to its goal of persuading society of its reality as a rape culture.[5] Scarry's discussion of pain and power combined with
Sharon Marcus's recent critique of the concrete effects on movement strategy
of the insistence on the "reality" of sexual violence leads me to argue for a self-
consciously performative and deconstructive approach to the political project of
representing the experience of sexual violence.

I

In a recent collection of essays about the movement against sexual violence
titled *Transforming a Rape Culture*, women's stories are explicitly discussed as
critical to movement strategy: "A generation into the anti-rape movement, we
have a history born out of speakouts, rallies, consciousness-raising groups, and
volunteer hotlines in church basements . . . Some [states] have coalitions for
mass education, for support, and for maintaining the growth and focus of the
movement" (Buchwald et al. 1995: 51). We say that the issue of sexual violence
must be personalized. We put faces on the numbers and familiarize the public
with the everyday details of women's experience of living with sexual violence.
Women who have been raped or battered volunteer nationally and locally to tell
their stories on the street or in meeting halls over and over again. Details of
survival and the negotiation of horror are described. Speaking out about the
reality of sexual suffering is encouraged in the name of persuading society as to
its reality as a rape culture. The immediate call in response to increased levels of

violence is for more speech. If society has not yet been persuaded as to its reality as a rape culture, more stories must be told and retold and the reality continually pieced together like a strange puzzle that resists finishing. The stories provide testimony to the reality of rape culture. They will, it is thought, encourage the eradication of images and practices of sexual violence altogether. Women express their pain and victimization because of their outrage, and to move toward healing themselves through the catharsis of recognition. But they also express themselves out of the conviction that once society understands the truth about itself, it will transform its terms of existence.[6]

With the relatively widespread exposure, discussion, and moral condemnation of sexual violence, through speakouts but also through popular culture, the incidents have not decreased. In spite of increased punitive measures and an increased willingness to intervene in the "private" sphere[7] there has been a steady rise in reports of sexual violence over the last twenty years. Participants in the movement respond to this increase by pointing to incremental reforms in legal, social, and cultural life that improve the chances of women reporting, escaping, and receiving some form of limited justice. There may not be an actual increase, rather more women are identifying what happened to them as criminal violence and speaking out about it. We say the increase shows rape culture to be more embedded than we could have imagined twenty years ago when its terms were first described by feminist activists. The effort to persuade society of the truth and experiential reality of sexual violence and abuse through naming, describing, and speaking out is said to be more critical than ever to the success of strategies to stop sexual violence and abuse. Thus the emphasis on speaking out is not questioned in itself; instead it is said not to have worked *yet*.

But what if in emphasizing the strategy of piecing together our reality as a rape culture through speakouts and detailed descriptions of experience, we participate in setting up the event of sexual violence as a defining moment of women's possibilities for being in the world? What if, in our empathic responses to women's suffering and insistence that "it could happen to any of us" we participate in conferring a monolithic reality onto an otherwise phantasmatic, illegitimate, and therefore fragile edifice of masculinist dominance rent with contradiction and internal conflict? What if there is an immanent fragility to masculinist dominance that has been obscured by the construction of a *political* strategy grounded upon the exposure of women's suffering?[8] Simply put, what if this strategy furthers the reification of masculinist dominance?

II

Elaine Scarry's analysis of torture inspires my exploration of this counterintuitive claim.[9] Her work helps me think about sexual violence against women as a necessary tool deployed in the name of stabilizing the otherwise fragile edifice of masculinist power – creating its fictions but also enabling its material effects in the world. A number of feminist discussions of patriarchy describe its shifting terms of existence and indicate that patriarchy is never finally successful in its project of dominance.[10] It is constantly reinventing itself and reconstituting the terms of its legitimacy in the face of threats from actual historical women. Sexual violence is part of this process. How does the pain inflicted through sexual violence become reinvested in patriarchal dominance?

In *The Body in Pain: the Making and Unmaking of the World*, Scarry (1985) constructs a materialist world view. She builds a vision of a social world of discourse and mutual understanding as constituted through objects.[11] For Scarry, if a human feeling has no object external to itself, it will not be effectively or pleasurably projected into the world through language but will resist language. Scarry argues pain is such an experience. Unlike any other experience we associate with feeling, pain has no object to which it refers. Pain happens to us. It is not an achievement in relation to the object world. Desire, love, distaste, even orgasm is an achievement in relation to fantasy or an object (Scarry 1985: 5). Pain therefore resists objectification in description or in explanation more profoundly than other sensations. We cannot share it through the objective world by pointing to something associated with the experience. We find pain resists projection as a reality through the language of comparison, analogy, or other typical strategies of communication.

We attempt to express pain for many reasons, mostly because we want it to stop. Human rights advocates bear witness to others' pain and try to be a voice for otherwise voiceless victims of pain. Patients try to describe their pain to doctors as if it will help in an otherwise physiological diagnosis. We try to describe pain in courtrooms in personal injury cases and sometimes to achieve more severe sentences for defendants in criminal cases. But in spite of the constant efforts in history to represent pain to the world, Scarry argues that pain may be the one instance where one person, she who is in pain, experiences something like absolute certainty and another, she who listens and even tries to empathize, experiences something like absolute doubt (Scarry 1985: 4). Sentient beings may all experience pain, but it is not shared in discourse in the same ways other feelings are shared, even if not fully or adequately represented.

Scarry argues that pain not only resists representation but actively works to destroy language. It exists in a destructive tension with our ability to communicate and is thus all the more significant for politics. Scarry's immediate moral and political concern is how pain is ritually used to reinforce the reality of the otherwise phantasmatic power of illegitimate political regimes. She argues that they use ritualized practices of torture, which in destroying the world of the prisoner (the social being – potentially disruptive and challenging) create the world of the state. It is "the conversion of absolute pain into the fiction of absolute power" (Scarry 1985: 27). Scarry says:

> In the very processes it uses to produce pain within the body of the prisoner, it bestows visibility on the structure and enormity of what is usually private and incommunicable, contained within the boundaries of the sufferer's body. It then goes on to deny, to falsify, the reality of the very thing it has itself objectified by a perceptual shift which converts the visions of suffering into the wholly illusory but, to the torturers and the regime they represent, wholly convincing spectacle of power. The physical pain is so incontestably real that it seems to confer its

quality of "incontestable reality" on that power that has brought it into being. It is, of course, precisely because the reality of that power is so highly contestable, the regime so unstable, that torture is being used. (Scarry 1985: 27)

Across the set of inversions that occur between pain and power in the context of torture, pain becomes power. The prisoner's world is systematically and ritualistically destroyed; she is separated from the objects in the world, material and ideological, through the subversion of their uses as torture weapons. Her contact with objects and ideas is no longer sure or safe. She thus loses her sense of place and/or identity. If she speaks the words of the torturer in confession, the world sees her as further split off from what made her real outside the torture chamber. Those who confess are identified as betrayers, as weak. Even those with a strong sense of empathy may not avoid having a sense of disappointment in the prisoner for speaking. This participates in enlarging the world of the torturer and thus the power of the regime he represents. The outside world accepts the power of the torturer as "having succeeded in making the prisoner speak," thus further destroying the object world of the prisoner and enlarging the territory of the state. "Power is cautious. It covers itself. It bases itself in another's pain and prevents all recognition that there is 'another' by looped circles that ensure its own solipsism" (Scarry 1985: 59). Thus Scarry argues that the immanent and often inapparent instability of a regime goes hand in hand with the use of torture. Torture as a practice is simultaneously at the extreme edges of politics and central to state power in modernity.

Scarry makes the connection between the silence of pain and the needs of state power. She tries to capture the politics embedded in inflicting pain and the struggle over the representation of pain. While I am not making a literal comparison between the practice of torture and sexual violence, the struggle Scarry describes over the representation of the truth of pain resonates profoundly with women's efforts to describe the experience of sexual violence. The response to the exposure of sexual violence, the persistent interrogation of the veracity of women's claims, whether they "wanted it" and "why didn't they leave?" resonates, albeit on a more subtle level of cruelty and complicity, with the junta's declarations that the subversives provoke violence, that their torture and disappearance never occurred the way eyewitnesses claim it did, or that they were in the wrong place at the wrong time. The denial of the "truth" of women's stories of sexual violence has justifiably led feminism to take up the project of representing that truth to the world, to insisting on the reality of sexual violence.

However, in this struggle, the expectation that the experience of suffering inevitably *is* or *will be* transparent to representation and social understanding, and that there are only gains to be had in the articulation of that experience, has gone unchallenged. Scarry's description shows how torture is useful to the regime beyond being a punishment for resistance. The reality of the pain of torture is translated into the spectacle of the regime's power through the struggle over the terms of representation. This spectacle shores up an otherwise phantasmatic and illegitimate power of the state.

What if, following Scarry's arguments, sexual violence were shown to be the sign of the instability of masculinity rather than the sign of the totality of patriarchal power? What if sexual violence were argued to signify the limits of patriarchy, rather than to represent its totalizing authority or power over women as a system?[12] It would not make it any less severe. In fact, it would show just how much is invested by patriarchy in sustaining the "reality" of sexual violence and constituting its devastating effects on women's bodies as real and thus impenetrable. On the politicized terrain of gender relations the reality of women's pain may translate into the reality of male power. It has been argued by many that sexual violence is the means by which men can control the sexual "otherness" and potentially threatening powers of women, that men live in fear of the feminine principle as something that undermines their sense of place in the world and use sexual violence to undermine the power of the feminine. But I do not assume in advance the relative power of women as autonomous from men. My argument is limited to observing that continued insistence upon the reality or truth of women's pain as a political strategy to authorize further action may contribute to sustaining the reality of masculinist power – rather than doing what is intuitively and understandably expected, that is, making men stop raping and beating women.

If we consider Scarry's analysis of pain and power, we can say that sexual violence represents the limits of masculinist hegemony. It is in part due to the unrepresentability of the pain inflicted – the psychic and the sentient pain – that masculinity is able to render sexual violence as social and political power. Society, saturated as it is with masculinist power, always already understands the logic of sexual violence even if it cannot know the self-identical truth of women's experience of sexual violence.

We thus should be conscious of the performative and interventionist quality of our representations rather than assuming we are telling society something it did not already know. In the politicized context of the struggle against sexual violence, as we try to finish the puzzle that will represent the reality of masculinist sexual violence to the world, we risk participating in the construction of the spectacle of women's sexual suffering.

If it is in the reduction of a victim's world through the infliction of pain that the perpetrator enlarges his territorial space psychically and physically (Scarry 1985: 37), then in fighting sexual violence, women must recolonize the space taken from them. This does not mean we render women individually responsible for what happens to them. It means taking every initiative to expose sexual violence as the signifier of the impotence of masculinist social power rather than as the "reality" of masculinist social power.

The limits placed on women's agency through totalizing interpretations of the "reality" of sexual violence may encourage feminists to continue to turn to the very social and political institutions which continue to represent public patriarchy. Through the years, for what are clearly pragmatic reasons, women have with increasing frequency turned to the "legitimate" violence and paternalistic protection of the state. They turn to the courts for punitive justice against batterers and to the social service industry for physical and psychic sustenance.

Feminism knows that these institutions are the representative sites of patriarchal rule, but antiviolence advocates argue for the pragmatic necessity of turning to them in order to cope with the immediacy and "reality" of sexual violence.[13]

Turning to these institutions offers increased legitimacy to the violence of the state in general and to racist and patriarchal norms *vis-à-vis* justice and freedom of movement for women in particular. Advocating strong policing strategies as a means of protection places feminist critiques of the racist/patriarchal state in the background in light of the "reality" of sexual violence.[14] Further, going to the state can be extremely isolating and removes responsibility from society for combatting sexual violence. It literally individuates women as vulnerable objects of masculinist power (women have to argue their immanent vulnerability in order to prove they were raped and in need of services) and disallows public acknowledgement of the complex logic of sexual violence writ large.[15] At best it offers individual women a limited sense of safety and some (increasingly limited) resources. In the long run, however, state-centered, bureaucratic, and legalistic strategies may do more to normalize violence as a constitutive aspect of political life than to prevent sexual violence as a constitutive aspect of social life.

Scarry's theory of the inversions of pain and power which invest the reality of pain in the reality of power encourages us to take note of the fragility of the edifice of masculine power. It has been shown that sexual violence escalates to murderous proportions when batterers fear a woman's imminent withdrawal or separation. Women who are battered risk death when they become pregnant, attempt to leave, or file for divorce. In these situations, batterers experience a lack of control and try, through violence, to gain it back – to establish the certainty of "their woman's" commitment. Violence often manifests itself in blows to the woman's stomach to cause a miscarriage. Pregnancy appears as a form of separation and therefore a threat to male power (Jones 1994; Schneider 1992; Walker 1984, 1989). In response to this, the movement often advocates further protectionist strategies in alliance with a masculinist state. The question I raise is not whether those are necessary in the moment for individual women in danger, but whether the habit of continually pointing to the immediacy and "reality" of the problem as the grounds for creating global social and political policy further shores up masculinist forms of social power and its ability to define the limits of women's lives. Remembering the reasons for earlier feminist insistence upon autonomy from the state and inventing alternatives may point us in a direction of isolating sexual violence as a cultural phenomenon due to its inability to affect the terms on which women live their lives (Schechter 1982).

Further, self-consciously performative narratives that represent diverse experiences of sexual violence to the social world can emerge if we take seriously the significance of the multiple sites from which women experience sexual violence and include stories of resistance which subvert the images of women as vulnerable. The insistence on commonality and identity among women given their experiences of sexual violence precludes attention to what differences among women can tell us about the terms on which sexual violence is possible. The deconstructive narrative exposes the naturalized social truths about gender and victimization that are embedded in the events of sexual violence itself rather than seeing only the immutable and singular "reality" of sexual violence for all women in common.

III

Sharon Marcus is also concerned with the representation of sexual violence as the "reality" of women's lives. She argues that this as much as guarantees that the rape will always have already happened *before* the social world is held to account and leaves women in the situation of proving the violence of the event after the fact.

> To treat rape simply as one of [quoting Mary Hawkesworth, 1989] "the realities that circumscribe women's lives" can mean to consider rape as terrifyingly unnameable and unrepresentable, a reality that lies beyond our grasp and which we can only experience as grasping and encircling us. In its efforts to convey the horror and iniquity of rape, such a view often concurs with masculinist culture in its designation of rape as a fate worse than or tantamount to, death; the apocalyptic tone which it adopts implies that rape can only be feared or legally repaired, not fought. (Marcus 1992: 387)

To counter this tendency, Marcus relies on the postmodern contention that gender dominance is enacted through language and discursive strategies. Like Judith Butler (1990), Marcus argues that iterative linguistic and physical habits and practices engender us as masculine and feminine identities. We are always already creating the (necessarily unstable) terrain on which gender works. How might her approach contribute to the project of demobilizing masculinist social power that I suggest above?

Marcus's approach treats sexual violence as a variable practice of dominance rather than as an immutable reality of gendered identity. She argues that the movement focuses too much on the experience of a rape that has already happened at the expense of exposing and thus strategically demobilizing cultural scripts that constitute women as rapable.

I think the most useful insight in Marcus's discussion is how easily talk of the reality of rape slides into an assumption of the inevitability of rape. Insistence on the reality of rape as a foundation for political action serves to reify the inevitability of the physical act by eliding its socially constructed quality. Marcus argues that the "success" of rape is dependent upon a sequence of events that can be interrupted but that contemporary constructions of the event treat it as if the outcome were inevitable. She reiterates a point feminists have made before, that men's bodies *become* weapons and tools of violence and women's bodies *become* objects of violence; there is nothing intrinsic or ahistorical or natural about the differential in male/female recourse to or capacity for violence. But she expands the point in arguing the *linguistic* enactment of desire and sexuality that informs the scenario that becomes rape.

Marcus thus advises women to become subjects of violence, not only by practicing reactive self-defence techniques, but through the concrete practice of intervening in any cultural and linguistic inscription of their bodies as always already rapable (Marcus 1992: 389). She criticizes anti-rape literature that advises caution in avoiding sites where rape might happen and against resistance in the event that it does happen because it reinscribes women's bodies as essentially vulnerable.[16] If women took the advice of most rape-prevention manuals to heart, they would live lives of utter caution and defensiveness in the interest of protecting their bodies from violation.

Marcus argues for the denaturing of the sexual aspect of sexual violence so that it might be "read" as a script and thereby interrupted. She refers to the empirical research by Pauline Bart and Patricia O'Brien (1985) that shows how women who respond in aggressive ways not traditionally associated with feminine behavior are more likely to avoid rape. This implies rapists have particular expectations which can be interrupted as women successfully expose, through subverting, what Marcus calls "the gendered grammars of violence" (Marcus 1992: 393). Marcus argues if rape is conceived of as a script women will develop increasing numbers of strategies of often unexpected and therefore effective interventions. If rape is instead conceived of as an event with no immanent structure but only an inevitable outcome, intervention becomes next to impossible.

This is not only a semantic difference. Because it is sexual violence, rape has internal contradictions and gaps in its logic of progression as a performance that women can take advantage of. Feminists have persuasively argued that rape is different than other forms of violence because it functions to differentiate masculinity from the feminine. However, another reason to recognize the sexual difference in rape is that it renders it all the more fragile.[17] Sexuality has a complex and deeply embedded, albeit permeable, script which is quite different than the scripts of generalized violences people commit outside of the terms of gender and sex. Male sexuality is not monolithic or self-assured. The drive to rape ought to be shown to be a signifier of the contradictions immanent in masculinist conceptions of sexuality and not only significant in demonstrating the dangerous potential of their dominance over women as gendered beings. The permeability of the sexual in "sexual violence" should be emphasized as the movement discusses anti-rape strategies.

There are historically concrete reasons to take apart the assumed "reality" that is the event of sexual violence – to interrupt its apparently seamless effect on women's lives – to find where differences in the experiences of women even *vis-à vis* sexual violence disrupt totalizing patriarchal images of women as embodied and available sex. If sexual violence shores up patriarchy at its edges, its terms will shift as patriarchy is threatened within changing historical contexts. The movement against sexual violence therefore should not make the success of our project dependent upon finally piecing together the puzzle that is the reality of rape culture, but should view its shifts across time and historical context as opportunities to interrupt its effectivity in proscribing the terms on which women live their lives. One strategic shift the movement might make in light of this argument is to emphasize the diverse experiences women have of sexual violence, rather than thinking that we must conceptualize what we find in common as a grounds for legitimacy. Speakouts rarely if ever include stories from women who self-identify as having successfully resisted assault. Women practice self-defense and educate one another in other contexts about strategies of resistance, but stories from women who successfully practice self-defense are not yet heard publicly through the movement against sexual violence. The difficulty with this may be that survivors of "successful" or completed rapes may feel inadequate or second guess themselves if there are stories other than victimization and survival included. Further, society may take this as an opportunity to place greater onus on women to resist. But hearing the different stories women have to tell does not necessarily engage us in an exercise of comparison and contrast about which woman did the "right" thing or was the quickest thinker. What a woman does when she is under attack or in a battering relationship is *always* the right thing. The movement must continue to find ways to enforce that as an article of faith at the societal level. Then on the politicized terrain of speaking out about sexual violence we may be able to hear in different women's strategies, failures, and successes increased possibilities for prevention and resistance in the moment.

Further, when women who are battered act violently in self-defense it becomes news. It becomes a story about an innocent woman being victimized who, out of irrational desperation, strikes back and happens to kill her abuser. Encouraging stories of successful prevention and resistance as reasonable and necessary rather than as only desperate and irrational can lead to increased knowledge about the contradictions and fissures in the logic of the rape script and contribute to the general deconstruction of identifications of women with real sexual vulnerability and men with real sexual power.[18]

IV

Sharon Marcus says that the crime of sexual violence, and rape in particular, is not that it steals something away from us that was always already there (Marcus 1992: 399). If sexuality is essentially always already there, it becomes a static property of the self. This understanding limits the terrain laid out by the movement against sexual violence to defensive and protectionist strategies,[19] and the injustice of sexual violence will continue to depend upon normative assumptions about the purity of female sexuality. Instead, Marcus argues that the crime of sexual violence is that it makes us into things to be taken. Feminist struggles against sexual violence therefore must be inventive acts of political will, not conditioned upon the essential value of sexuality as a property found in common across time and differences. We will then be prepared for the continuing public contest over the terms of sexuality.

Through interpreting and interrupting the experience of sexual violence, feminism intervenes in distinct and critical ways with dominant discourses and assumptions about gender and sexuality that unjustly shore up male power; it does not only "discover" a previously hidden or underlying reality of women's lives within an undifferentiated patriarchy. Understood in this way, the struggle against sexual violence may become a terrain for renewed discussion in feminism about sexual possibilities rather than being limited to a defense of vulnerable bodies against sexual aggression. The movement against sexual violence may then move further toward redeeming and reinventing the terms of sexuality in modernity.

Notes

1 Susan Griffin (1977) coined the term "rape culture" to describe the general environment created by the threat and the experience of sexual violence whose terms women must internalize in order to live safely in the world.

2 This essay is part of a work in progress that studies the politics of bearing witness and offering historical meaning to sexual suffering in modernity. I thank William Rose for his substantive comments and editorial advice.

3 This has been identified with a specifically "feminist" way of doing the political work of consciousness-raising with the individual woman and with society as a whole. However, as these strategies have more recently been taken up by some I would hesitate to call "feminist" and others who should reject the description, I am going to refer to the "movement" as including anyone who commits themselves to intervening in rape culture, whether it be through legal strategies, shelters, grassroots organizing, church-supported activities, or making public policy. I will also use "we" when referring to the movement because I consider myself a part of it.

4 I cannot go into Scarry's extraordinary and eloquent descriptions of the impact of torture on the body and voice of the victim. I will only assert that the abuse of the body in order to destroy the autonomous use of the voice is one of the logics and effects of sexual violence and battering. Therefore, this essay should not be taken as an argument against giving voice to suffering or bearing witness to suffering, only a cautionary discussion about the use and abuse by power of representations of pain.

5 That transformation is often articulated as one that will result in a "safer" world, one in which mutual respect and mutual obligation govern sexuality rather than attitudes of taking or objectification of the other. The sex debates, arguments about violence in sex and arguments about pornography among feminists, articulate a number of different visions for how to create a sexually liberated future (Vance 1984). Thus the vision of "safety" is not common to all feminists concerned with questions of sexuality and sexual violence, but it does govern the discourse of what I am calling the movement.

6 There is in fact an awareness or self-consciousness within movement politics of the intrinsically political quality of narrative and speech, though activists hesitate to describe it as such. A discursive terrain has been more or less deliberately developed to allow for the representation of violations previously held in silence or obscured within the realm of private affairs. This discourse is understood as a means to make society take public or social responsibility for them and change the course of history. Further, the framing of an imperative to "believe the woman" in response to the time-honored and deeply embedded assumption that women lie about their desire for sex, indicates the movement in some way understands women's descriptions of their experience as acts of political will rather than as mere expressions or reflections of reality.

7 Social service and policing procedures have changed drastically over the years, indi-

cating a shift in society's willingness to pierce the veil of privacy that has masked private violence for so many years. See Fineman and Mykitiuk (1994) and Sherman et al. (1992) for discussions and descriptions of social policy and policing with particular attention to battering.

8 I emphasize the particularity of the political here because I am concerned with the investments of power in the phenomenon of sexual violence and whether oppositional strategies are taking into account the complex forms taken by those investments. I am considering the political effects of speaking out about sexual violence rather than denying its therapeutic and cathartic effects.

9 I do not equate sexual violence with torture, nor am I interested in comparing them as events. They are singularly different though sexual violence may be torturous and torturers make use of sexual violence, not only against women but against men as well.

10 Feminist critiques of theories that assume a social totality or universal condition argue for more specific and particular discussions of the terms on which masculinist dominance remains possible given specific historical and structural challenges. Feminists of color and postmodern feminists move us toward a less totalizing map of women's situatedness in the world.

11 Scarry's form of materialism is less progressivist than that found in Marxist theory, which presumes a creative or transformative relationship to the world as that which drives social change and development. Scarry constructs a materialism that is not progressivist but founds itself in the simpler humanist impulse to defeat suffering. Her materialism is founded in the sensuous relationship between bodies and the material world which results in social movement or creation as a means to alter conditions of lack, discomfort, or suffering. The "making of the world" is a project of creating conditions that improve our sensual relationship to the external world.

12 This is not to say individual men are impotent or weak in carrying out acts of sexual violence, any more than it is to say that individual torturers are not invested with extraordinary power in the context of the individualized violences carried out against their victims. Rather it is to say that the social power their practices invoke is phantasmatic and illegitimate.

13 If we accept the terms of crime and punishment set up by the liberal state, it makes a great deal of political sense. Heavier sentences are imposed for far less onerous crimes than sexual assault, which directly implicates the system of sentencing in the devaluation of women's lives. Thus some feminists may feel it logical to "compete" on these grounds. I do not accept those terms however, and argue we must find other means of struggle. See Robert Cover's classic article, "Violence and the Word" for a devastating critique of the "legitimate violence of the state as essentially destructive of lives and possibilities" (Cover 1986).

14 This has also limited opportunities for alliances to be made around race and gendered struggles for justice. The black community, including black women, have justifiable reasons for not turning to the state for justice when it is the state and the police who so often violate their rights in the name of justice. The heavy penalties against black men for the rape of white women and the relatively light penalties against white men for the rape of black women is a good example.

15 Kristin Bumiller (1990) reads the trial of the Big Dan gang rape case to show how the rape was constituted through the trial as an individualized tragedy rather than acknowledged as the result of complex social logics of class and gender relations.

16 See the appendix of Russell (1975) for a good example of rape-prevention literature published by a San Francisco area rape crisis center which advises perpetual

vigilance and cautious behavior in light of an all-consuming threat against women's bodies.

17   It has been empirically shown that men who rape think about it and experience it as a sexual act. Twenty years ago Diana Russell interviewed rape victims and rapists in order to show that, while from the victim's perspective rape is traumatic and stigmatizing, from the rapist's perspective it is a relatively predictable response to an "uncontrollable" desire for sex. Rapists often speak of themselves as loving women or merely wanting to show women "what they have" (Russell 1975; Scully 1990). However, men also use rape specifically as an act of violence against a particular woman, particularly in the context of intimate or "domestic" violence. In these testimonies of torture-like situations, men use sex as a weapon among others against women.

18   This is not a strategy that will help us in the legal context. The law demands that victims be victims through and through before rendering its limited forms of justice. Because the law needs victims in order to render justice it perpetuates the very gender arrangements that create the terms that make sexual violence possible in the first place. Therefore the legal system will never be instrumental in eradicating sexual violence, only in managing it. Rather than normalizing strategies of representation that fit the needs of the legal system, the movement against sexual violence should find new alternatives to its increasing dependence on the legal system.

19   Catharine MacKinnon's comparison of sexuality to work invokes the image of sexuality as a unified property of the self which can thus be taken from the self (MacKinnon 1987, 1989, 1990).

References

Bart, Pauline and O'Brien, Patricia (1985) *Stopping Rape: Successful Survival Strategies*, New York: Pergamon Press.

Buchwald, Emilie, Fletcher, Pamela and Roth, Martha (eds) (1995) *Transforming a Rape Culture*, Minneapolis, Minn.: Milkweed Editions.

Bumiller, Kristin (1990) "Fallen angels: the representation of violence against women in legal culture?" *International Journal of the Sociology of Law* 18, pp. 125–42.

Butler, Judith (1990) *Gender Trouble*, New York: Routledge.

Cover, Robert (1986) "Violence and the word," *Yale Law Journal* 95, pp. 1601–29.

Fineman, Martha Albertson and Mykitiuk, Roxanne (eds) *The Public Nature of Private Violence*, New York: Routledge.

Griffin, Susan (1977) "Rape: the all-American crime," in Duncan Chappell, Robley Geis, and Gilbert Geis (eds) *Forcible Rape: the Crime, the Victim, and the Offender*, New York: Columbia University Press.

Hawkesworth, Mary E. (1989) "Knower, knowing, known: feminist theory and claims of truth," *Signs* 14/3, pp. 533–57.

Jones, Ann (1994) *Next Time She'll be Dead: Battering and How to Stop it*, Boston, Mass.: Beacon Press.

MacKinnon, Catharine (1987) *Feminism Unomodified*, Cambridge, Mass.: Harvard University Press.

—— (1989) *Towards a Feminist Theory of the State*, Cambridge, Mass.: Harvard University Press.

—— (1990) "Does sexuality have a history?," *Michigan Quarterly Review* 30/1, pp. 1–11.

Mahoney, Martha R. (1991) "Legal images of battered women: redefining the issue of separation," *Michigan Law Review* 90/1, pp. 1–94.

Marcus, Sharon (1992) "Fighting bodies, fighting words: a theory and politics of rape prevention," in Judith Butler and Joan Scott (eds) *Feminists Theorize the Political*, New York: Routledge.

Russell, Diana E. H. (1975) *The Politics of Rape: the Victim's Perspective*, New York: Stein and Day.

Scarry, Elaine (1985) *The Body in Pain: the Making and Unmaking of the World*, London: Oxford University Press.

Schechter, Susan (1982) *Women and Male Violence: the Visions and Struggles of the Battered Women's Movement*, Boston, Mass.: South End Press.

Schneider, Elizabeth (1992) "Particularity and generality: challenges of feminist theory and practice in work on woman-abuse," *New York Univerwsity Law Review* 67/3, pp. 520–68.

Scott, Joan (1992) "Experience," in Judith Butler and Joan Scott (eds) *Feminists Theorize the Political*, New York: Routledge.

Scully, Diana (1990) *Understanding Sexual Violence: a Study of Convicted Rapists*, Cambridge: Unwin Hyman.

Sherman, Lawrence, Schmidt, Janet D., and Rogan, Dennis P. (1992) *Policing Domestic Violence: Experiments and Dilemmas*, New York: Free Press.

Vance, Carol (ed.) (1984) *Pleasure and Danger*, New York: Routledge and Kegan Paul.

Walker, Lenore (1984) *The Battered Woman Syndrome*, New York: Springer Publishing.

—— (1989) *Terrifying Love: Why Battered Women Kill and How Society Responds*, New York: Harper and Row.

Questions about Sexuality

1   Is sexuality a function of innate human drives that can be known and controlled by experts or are human sexual desires and needs shaped and imposed by culture?

2   Should the private bodily sensations and pleasures that we take to constitute non-reproductive sexual experience be regulated by the state?

3   Does sexual desire involve a longing for something one lacks? (For Aristophanes, sexual desire represents a longing for a person's other half that he or she originally possessed; for Freud, sexual desire involves a longing for a penis, if one is a woman, and (re-)union with one's mother if one is a man.)

4   In many films and other artistic productions, women are shown as the objects of someone's sexual desires and not as subjects with their own sexual desires. When women are represented as sexual subjects or agents, what do they generally desire?

5   Should a capitalist society prohibit some goods from being exchanged on the open market, such as sex, babies, bodily organs, or certain drugs? If so, why?

6   If prostitution were decriminalized, should certain forms of it remain illegal: e.g. prostitution that involves minors, prostitution that involves "unsafe sex," or prostitution that involves adultery?

7   Does political liberation require sexual liberation?

8   Is the practice of sexually objectifying men a good or useful feminist tool or should feminists avoid it? Explain.

9   Does the high frequency of male sexual assault against women in American society suggest that there is a political component to sexual assault? Is rape a way that men act individually and collectively to keep women in "their place"?

10 Anti-rape activists have pointed to the occurrence of male-on-male rape, and the sexual assault of babies, children, and the elderly to challenge the theory that rape is caused by the failure of men to control their desire for the sexuality that some women's bodies offer plus men's ability to take advantage of their superior strength to obtain it. What effect would telling the stories of these victims have on transforming our rape culture?

Recommended Reading for Part Four

Allen, Jeffner (ed.) (1990) *Lesbian Philosophies and Cultures*, Albany, NY: State University of New York Press (philosophical issues raised by lesbian experience).

Allen, Jeffner and Young, Iris (eds) (1989) *Thinking Muse: Feminism and Modern French Philosophy*, Bloomington, Ind.: Indiana University Press (feminist critiques of theories of sexuality by de Beauvoir, Merleau-Ponty, Sartre, and Foucault).

Baird, Robert and Rosenbaum, Stuart (eds) (1991) *Pornography: Private Right or Public Menace?*, Buffalo, NY: Prometheus Books (feminist, libertarian, and religious perspectives on pornography).

Brison, Susan (1993) "Surviving sexual assault," *Journal of Social Philosophy*, 24/1 (Spring) (philosophical assessment of the harm caused by rape).

Card, Claudia (ed.) (1992) *Hypatia: Special Issue on Lesbian Philosophy*, 7/4 (Fall) (analyses of lesbian identity and moral perspectives).

Copp, David and Wendell, Susan (eds) (1983) *Pornography and Censorship*, Buffalo, NY: Prometheus Books (essays about the morality, effects, and censorship of pornography).

Davis, Karen Elizabeth (1990) "I love myself when I am laughing: a new paradigm for sex," *Journal of Social Philosophy*, 21/2 and 3 (Fall/Winter) (argues against sexual desire as hunger account and analyses eroticism in terms of laughter).

Delacoste, Frédérique and Alexander, Priscilla (eds) (1987) *Sex Work: Writings By Women in the Sex Industry*, San Francisco, Calif.: Cleis Press (essays on prostitution by sex workers).

Estrich, Susan (1987) *Real Rape*, Cambridge, Mass.: Harvard University Press (analyzes the inadequacies of current laws on rape).

Foucault, Michel (1990) *The History of Sexuality, Vol. I: An Introduction*, trans. Robert Hurley, New York: Vintage Books (analyzes our obsession with sex as an effect of power).

Francis, Leslie (ed.) (1996) *Date Rape: Feminism, Philosophy, and the Law*, University Park, Pa.: Pennsylvania State University Press (philosophical analyses of acquaintance rape).

Gruen, Lori and Panichas, George (eds) (1997) *Sex, Morality, and the Law*, New York: Routledge (opposing perspectives on lesbian and gay sexuality, prostitution, pornography, sexual harassment, and rape).

Hopkins, Patrick (1994) "Rethinking sadomasochism: feminism, interpretation, and simulation," *Hypatia*, 9/1 (Winter) (critiques radical feminist opposition to s/m).

Kaplan, Morris (1997) *Sexual Justice: Democratic Citizenship and the Politics of Desire*, New York: Routledge (argues that democracy entails equality for gays and lesbians).

Koertge, Noretta (ed.) (1985) *Philosophy and Homosexuality*, New York: Harrington Park Press (definitions and origins of sexual orientation).

LeMoncheck, Linda (1985) *Dehumanizing Women: Treating Persons as Sex Objects*, Totowa, NJ: Roman and Allanheld (conceptual and moral analysis of sexual objectification).

MacKinnon, Catharine (1989) *Toward a Feminist Theory of the State*, Cambridge, Mass.: Harvard University Press (radical feminist account of pornography and rape).

May, Larry and Strikwerda, Robert (eds) (1994) "Men in groups: collective responsibility for rape," *Hypatia*, 9/2 (Spring) (investigates responsibility for rape).

Mohr, Richard (1988) *Gays/Justice: a Study of Ethics, Society, and Law*, New York: Columbia University Press (philosophical issues raised by the gay rights movement).

Nussbaum, Martha (1995) "Objectification," *Philosophy and Public Affairs*, 24/4 (Fall) (philosophical and literary analysis of sexual objectification).

Pateman, Carole (1988) *The Sexual Contract*, Stanford, Calif.: Stanford University Press (argument against prostitution).

Posner, Richard (1992) *Sex and Reason*, Cambridge, Mass.: Harvard University Press (free market legal analysis of different forms of sex).

Schott, Robin May (1993) *Cognition and Eros*, University Park, Pa.: Pennsylvania State University Press (feminist critique of traditional philosophical views on women and sexuality).

Shrage, Laurie (1994) *Moral Dilemmas of Feminism: Prostitution, Adultery, and Abortion*, New York Routledge (provides a feminist and culturally relativistic account of prostitution and adultery).

Soble, Alan (ed.) (1991) *The Philosophy of Sex*, Savage, Md.: Rowman and Littlefield (articles on sexual perversion, privacy, masturbation, adultery, rape, prostitution, and pornography).

Stein, Edward (ed.) (1992) *Forms of Desire: Sexual Orientation and the Social Constructionist Controversy*, New York: Routledge (debate about the causes of sexual identity).

Tong, Rosemarie (1984) *Women, Sex, and the Law*, Totowa, NJ: Rowman and Allanheld (feminist legal analyses of pornography, prostitution, sexual harassment, and rape).

Trevas, Robert, Zucker, Arthur, and Borchert, Donald (eds) *Philosophy of Sex and Love*, Upper Saddle River, NJ: Prentice Hall (articles on relationship between sex and love, adultery, sexual perversion, prostitution, pornography, sexual harassment, and rape).

Vance, Carole (ed) (1989) *Pleasure and Danger: Exploring Female Sexuality*, London: Pandora (topics range from voyeurism to sex and children).

Wall, Edmund (ed.) (1992) *Sexual Harassment*, Buffalo, NY: Prometheus Books (causal accounts and legal responses to sexual harassment in different settings).

West, Cornel (1993) *Race Matters*, Boston, Mass.: Beacon Press (chapter on black sexuality).

Zatz, Noah (1997) "Sex work/sex act: law, labor and desire in constructions of prostitution," *Signs* 22/2 (Winter) (argument for decriminalizing prostitution).

PART FIVE

INTERSECTIONS

edited by Crispin Sartwell

Intersections: Introduction to the Readings

The categories of race, gender, class, and sexual orientation are abstractions. No one is just a woman, for example, or just a rich person, or just a white person, or just a bisexual. Real people occupy many roles and identities simultaneously. That is what this section is about: the ways the identities discussed in the previous sections interact in particular human lives. Most of the selections in this part are personal narratives of social location that show how social identities intersect in complex ways in individuals.

There is no such thing as a "pure" social identity, and this is something we have seen in each of the previous sections. Many of the selections on class also raised issues about race and gender, and the selections on race and gender raised issues about class. Theorists refer to these identities as "interactive variables": in a given person, each factor in social identity affects all the others. The gender system in the African American community, for example, is not the same as the gender system in the white community, for a variety of historical reasons. So what it means to be a woman for a black woman is not necessarily the same as what it means to be a woman for a white woman, and what it means to be a man for a black man is not necessarily the same as what it means to be a man for a white man. To take another example: what it means to be a gay man is very different in wealthy communities than it is in poor communities. It may be much easier, for example, for a wealthy person to stay "in the closet"; wealth can be used to buy privacy or to clean up scandals. And the sorts of heterosexism faced by poor gay men is likely to be very different than that faced by wealthy ones: while a poor community may include explicit homophobes who are in your face (of course, it may also include various mechanisms of support), a wealthy community may be no less heterosexist but much less obvious about it. So the sorts of oppression that our two hypothetical gay men face are different, and their homosexuality is also different.

This makes the task of intellectual and consciousness-raising endeavors such as feminism and critical race studies very difficult indeed. A program that tries, for example, to put forward the interests of "all gay people" or "all women" or "all black people" is likely to find that it represents the interests, at best, of only one sort of gay person or woman or black person. So in trying to take into account the experiences and the interests of groups that are diverse, feminism, critical race theory, and gay studies have had to get more and more complicated; they have had to begin to listen to divergent voices, and they have had to give up some of their central tenets. The identities to which they appealed – "woman," "gay person," "poor person," "black person" – were too simple: so simple, in fact, that many or even most people those movements tried to represent did not find themselves represented.

Black feminists have pointed out that when white feminists raised "women's issues" they were often white women's issues rather than black women's issues. For example, the feminist movement of the 1960s and 1970s was concerned as much as anything with allowing women to enter the workforce on an equal basis with men. There was a critique of the role of the "housewife" as being a relic of patriarchal oppression; the work of a housewife was supposed to be unpaid and unrewarding, with little scope for personal development. What should have been clear to everyone from the start was that this was not an issue for all women; it was an issue almost exclusively for middle- and upper-class white heterosexual women. Black women had been working outside the home for generations – indeed since their arrival on this continent – and some black feminists, such as Patricia Hill Collins, pointed out that a goal of many black women was to perform domestic labor for their own families rather than for white middle- and upper-class families. In other words, some African American women who identified themselves as feminists thought that housewives had a pretty good life. The issues facing black women in virtue of their gender are very different than the issues facing white women.

There was and continues to be a backlash within the feminist movement against the criticisms of the movement by women of color and poor women; it is sometimes held that black feminists, for example, are not concerned with "women's" issues but with racial issues and that the feminist movement should return from "identity politics" (which in this case means politics based on the social identities of race, class, and sexual orientation) to issues such as daycare, abortion, equal pay with men, and the "glass ceiling" that stops women's careers at a certain level. These issues are important. But it must be kept in mind that they are of different significance in different communities and that to a woman who has worked all her life as a maid, the fact that someone can't make vice president does not look like a crisis. Furthermore, to identify the issues pertinent to white middle-class women as "women's issues" per se is to exclude whole groups of women not only from feminism but from womanhood. To which we might hear the African American antislavery activist Sojourner Truth respond: "Ain't I a woman?"

That is an example of a much larger concern: that the "normal" or "pure" examples of many categories are in fact not normal or pure at all but white and middle class. Some feminists identified the issues of white middle-class women as the women's issues. Likewise, some white male commentators dismiss the concerns of, say, Chicana lesbians as being parochial and concerned only with "identity politics," as though white heterosexual men had no particular racial or sexual identity. Indeed, the racial and sexual identity of a white heterosexual man is no less pronounced than that of a Chicana lesbian, and there is no reason beyond historical contingencies why it ought to be regarded as more normative. But it is normative, which is to say that it is invisible as an identity, that it tends to be conceived as the identity from which every other identity is a divergence or of which every other identity is a distortion. That has been obvious even in this book: while many of the writers we have included have tried to say what it means to be a woman, or an African American, or gay, very few have tried to say what it means to be a white heterosexual man. Indeed, the whole question has an almost absurd ring to it because a white heterosexual man is not conceived to have a particular identity at all, but is supposed to be a sort of universal human norm. Think, for example, of the norm, rarely called into question in political debates, of the nuclear family. "Family values" are supposed to be a neutral ground on which we can all agree. But the picture of the family is, at least often, freighted with various identities: it is middle-class, and in it two heterosexual parents raise their biological children. The fact that other cultures (for example, African cultures) have very different family structures of equal legitimacy is rarely pointed out.

Every person lives at various intesections in the sense used here. I am not only a man; I am a middle-class white man. But identities are also much more complicated than that: each person has her own, for one thing. Even if identities are socially constructed – that is, not found naturally in people but a result of their circumstances among and trainings by other people – no two people have exactly the same identity because no two people have exactly the same social relations to exactly the same people. Say two men are both lawyers doing similar work at major law firms in New York, making the same salary, both married with one child, both black, and so on. Nevertheless, they are connected in different ways to different people and they are not, interchangeable: if they switched lives, for example, their wives and children would notice the difference. So even if, again, identities are socially constructed, they are also individual. We have been using "social identity" to mean race, gender, class, and sexual orientation, but each person also occupies a *particular* social location that no one else occupies, and each person also has a personal identity, even if that is also socially constructed.

In addition, individual identities are mobile, often radically so. Persons who believe themselves to be heterosexual may find that they are gay. People can change classes, and with a little luck today's corporate raider is tomorrow's street person. People can marry outside of their class or race and enter into a different community, and perhaps produce children who are "interstitial," who do not fall clearly into either category or who have elements of both identities. People can get caught between communities, languages, identities: speak English on the job, say, and Chinese at home; act and in fact be middle-class at the job and act and in fact be working-class at home. People can have sex change operations, or undergo less radical transformations, as when a white kid romanticizes black culture and tries to act black and enter into black communities, or when a black man from the ghetto enters the boardroom and tries to act white. None of these things should be conceived to be failures or evidences of personal inauthenticity; potentially they are all opportunities for exploration as well as indications that rigid social identities cannot be maintained, that people cannot simply be consigned and confined to categories.

More widely, there are aspects of social identities that can be shared by many people which do not immediately fall into any of the categories discussed in this book so far. "Ethnicity," for example, is a concept that can be central to identity. It is not the same as race. Race is supposedly biological, but ethnicity is a matter of culture and background. For example, Hispanic persons are often held to share an ethnicity (this is in the US white community; it is fair to say that in their own communities they are held to display many ethnicities – Puerto Rican, Chicano, Spanish, and so on – another demonstration that such identities are socially constructed). On the other hand, Hispanic people are racially diverse: there are black, white, Native, and Asian Hispanics. There are also regional identities to contend with: the American south, for example, has its own distinctive linguistic practices, values, artistic expressions, and so forth. What it means to be a black person living in Meridian, Mississippi and what it means to be a black person living in Detroit are different but related things. For that matter, what it means to be a white person living in Meridian and what it means to be a white person living in Detroit are two different and related things, and the differences among white people in different regions is related to the differences among black people in different regions. What it means to be white in Meridian is different than what it means to be white in Detroit in part because what it means to be black is different in the two places, and vice versa. Perhaps, for example, black people in Meridian are more deferential to white people than they are in Detroit; perhaps black people in Detroit are more hostile. This makes a white person feel his or her whiteness in different ways.

Obviously, any selection of materials on these potentially limitless complications of identity can only scratch the surface. The readings here are an attempt to survey a range of intersectional identities and a range of ways of experiencing and expressing intersectional social locations. With one or two exceptions these readings are personal: they try to show what it is like to be the person who is writing; they emerge from deep reflection on the personal experience of social identity. But they are also theoretically rich; they bring personal experience to bear on an account or a sense of what identity is in general, how it is made, what it means, and perhaps how it can be compromised or ripped apart at need.

The first selection is by the novelist Amy Tan. In her finely-wrought prose she describes linguistic intersectionality. While her mother speaks a Chinese American vernacular, and Tan herself can slide into such a vernacular effortlessly, she has learned to use a more "mainstream" English outside the home. While many people would find Tan's mother's language stereotypical or symptomatic of a lack of intelligence, Tan celebrates it as an expressive vehicle of great richness. As you read this you might want to think also about the response of many white people to African American vernacular speech.

Robin D. G. Kelley, in a very funny piece called "Confessions of nice negro," describes the flavors of black masculinity, a particular intersection of race and gender. As mentioned above, what it means to be a man is different to some extent for black men than it is for white men, and black men are often stereotyped as being dangerous and violent. Kelley describes himself as anything but that; nevertheless, people react to him as if he were, especially after he shaves his head. He finds this amusing if also disturbing, and actually enjoys being a black man playing a black man.

The Lakota holy man Lame Deer discusses differences in the traditional attitudes of the members of his tribe and European Americans that bear on class. He describes European American culture as obsessed with money and says that this has led to various cultural and ecological disasters, both for his people and for the European Americans themselves. This reading is meant to illustrate the fact that different cultures have radically different class systems, or even that there are cultures that have no class system at all, at least in the classic sense put forward by such figures as Marx and Weber. Marx held that such systems were more or less a universal human condition, but that claim will not stand up in a multicultural perspective.

William Upski Wimsatt refers to himself as a "Wigger" or "white nigger." This selection from his book *Bomb the Suburbs* investigates the possibilities and the limits of race mobility as Wimsatt tries to enter the black community, especially through his appreciation of and participation in hip hop music and culture. In the process Wimsatt sheds light on the social construction of both white and black identities.

Allan Bérubé, in a piece written with his mother Florence, writes about growing up as "white trash" in a New Jersey trailer park. He describes the pleasures of this existence, its racial codings, the attitudes of other people toward the residents of the trailer park, and also the ambition of those residents to "better" themselves. In addition, Bérubé describes coming to a sense of his own gay identity within the race and class situation in which he found himself. Finally, he discusses how he came to view his own background as campy (so unhip as to be hip: think of polyester leisure suits) and as something to be celebrated aesthetically.

Robert Hughes expresses great reservations about the multiplying of identities in contemporary America and in particular about the "politically correct" language that emerges out of this multiplication. He attacks some of the ridiculous excesses of identity politics and the extreme sensitivity of some people to the mildest perceived slight. In addition, he decries the debasement of language to which this leads: a kind of mealy-mouthed string of euphemisms in which it is almost impossible to say anything interesting. Although in other parts of the book from which the extract is taken Hughes attacks the political right, his criticism here is aimed squarely at the left.

María Lugones and Elizabeth Spelman write from two different locations: Lugones describes her voice as "Hispana" and Spelman describes hers as "white Anglo". They write about the same thing, however: the omission of voices other than white, middle-class voices from feminist theory. They argue that there is no single "woman's voice" that should be constructed or presented in feminism, but that there are as many voices as there are social locations from which women can speak. Lugones in particular argues passionately that women such as herself often feel left out of feminist discourse because they have very different concerns than the white women who dominate the feminist movement. In the early days of feminism, when getting any woman's voice heard at all was a considerable achievement, holding that there was a single woman's voice or set of concerns was perhaps understandable though ultimately indefensible. But at this point any claim of anyone to speak for all women (and for that matter any claim of anyone to speak for all men, or all African Americans) ought to be regarded with great suspicion. The paper is an excellent illustration of its own argument, for the theoretical points emerge only in a dialogue between different voices. Ultimately a theory about someone (women, for example) is responsible to the people it is a theory about (women, for example, of different sorts).

Cherríe Moraga has a very complex identity indeed: she is half Chicana and half Anglo, and a lesbian. Here she discusses the various factors that go into making this identity: from the traditional sexism of some Chicano culture, to her economic situation, to her awakening to her homosexuality and other aspects of her sexual identity. This is a richly literary and wonderfully erotic piece, as well as an astute piece of political analysis. Finally, she connects sexuality and politics to spirituality, which she describes as "feeding people in all their hungers."

Amy Tan describes the experience of being caught between two language communities: the Chinese American vernacular of her mother and the "proper English" of her work as a writer. She celebrates both, and celebrates also her mobility between them.

Focus questions:
1 What are some of the problems or discomforts Tan identifies in her linguistic mobility?
2 Why does Tan think, finally, that being caught between two languages is a good thing, an opportunity?

26   Mother Tongue

Amy Tan

I am not a scholar of English or literature. I cannot give you much more than personal opinions on the English language and its variations in this country or others.

I am a writer. And by that definition, I am someone who has always loved language. I am fascinated by language in daily life. I spend a great deal of my time thinking about the power of language – the way it can evoke an emotion, a visual image, a complex idea, or a simple truth. Language is the tool of my trade. And I use them all – all the Englishes I grew up with.

Recently, I was made keenly aware of the different Englishes I do use. I was giving a talk to a large group of people, the same talk I had already given to half a dozen other groups. The nature of the talk was about my writing, my life, and my book *The Joy Luck Club*. The talk was going along well enough, until I remembered one major difference that made the whole talk sound wrong. My mother was in the room. And it was perhaps the first time she had heard me give a lengthy speech, using the kind of English I have never used with her. I was saying things like "The intersection of memory upon imagination" and "There is an aspect of my fiction that relates to thus-and-thus" – a speech filled with carefully wrought grammatical phrases, burdened, it suddenly seemed to me, with nominalized forms, past perfect tenses, conditional phrases, all the forms of standard English that I had learned in school and through books, the forms of English I did not use at home with my mother.

Just last week, I was walking down the street with my mother, and I again found myself conscious of the English I was using, the English I do use with her. We were talking about the price of new and used furniture and I heard myself saying this: "Not waste money that way." My husband was with us as well, and he didn't notice any switch in my English. And then I realized why. It's because over the twenty years we've been together I've often used that same kind of English with him, and sometimes he even uses it with me. It has become our language of intimacy, a different sort of English that relates to family talk, the language I grew up with.

So you'll have some idea of what this family talk I heard sounds like, I'll quote what my mother said during a recent conversation which I videotaped and then transcribed. During this conversation, my mother was talking about a political gangster in Shanghai who had the same last name as her family's, Du, and how the gangster in his early years wanted to be adopted by her family, which was rich by comparison. Later, the gangster became more powerful, far richer than my mother's family, and one day showed up at my mother's wedding to pay his respects. Here's what she said in part:

"Du Yusong having business like fruit stand. Like off the street kind. He is Du like Du Zong – but not Tsung-ming Island people. The local people call putong, the river east side, he belong to that side local people. That man want to ask Du Zong father take him in like become own family. Du Zong father wasn't look down on him, but didn't take seriously, until that man big like become a mafia. Now important person, very hard to inviting him. Chinese way, came only to show respect, don't stay for dinner. Respect for making big celebration, he shows up. Mean gives lots of respect. Chinese custom. Chinese social life that way. If too important won't have to stay too long. He come to my wedding. I didn't see, I heard it. I gone to boy's side, they have YMCA dinner. Chinese age I was nineteen."

You should know that my mother's expressive command of English belies how much she actually understands. She reads the *Forbes* report, listens to *Wall Street Week*, converses daily with her stockbroker, reads all of Shirley MacLaine's books with ease – all kinds of things I can't begin to understand. Yet some of my friends tell me they understand 50 percent of what my mother says. Some say they understand 80 to 90 percent. Some say they understand none of it, as if she were speaking pure Chinese. But to me, my mother's English is perfectly clear, perfectly natural. It's my mother tongue. Her language, as I hear it, is vivid, direct, full of observation and imagery. That was the language that helped shape the way I saw things, expressed things, made sense of the world.

Lately, I've been giving more thought to the kind of English my mother speaks. Like others, I have described it to people as "broken" or "fractured" English. But I wince when I say that. It has always bothered me that I can think of no way to describe it other than "broken," as if it were damaged and needed to be fixed, as if it lacked a certain wholeness and soundness. I've heard other terms used, "limited English," for example. But they seem just as bad, as if everything is limited, including people's perceptions of the limited English speaker.

I know this for a fact, because when I was growing up, my mother's "limited" English limited *my* perception of her. I was ashamed of her English. I believed that her English reflected the quality of what she had to say. That is, because she expressed them imperfectly her thoughts were imperfect. And I had plenty of empirical evidence to support me: the fact that people in department stores, at banks, and at restaurants did not take her seriously, did not give her good service, pretended not to understand her, or even acted as if they did not hear her.

My mother has long realized the limitations of her English as well. When I was fifteen, she used to have me call people on the phone to pretend I was she. In this guise, I was forced to ask for information or even to complain and yell at people who had been rude to her. One time it was a call to her stockbroker in New York. She had cashed out her small portfolio and it just so happened we were going to go to New York the next week, our very first trip outside California. I had to get on the phone and say in an adolescent voice that was not very convincing, "This is Mrs Tan."

And my mother was standing in the back whispering loudly, "Why he don't send me check, already two weeks late. So mad he lie to me losing me money."

And then I said in perfect English, "Yes, I'm getting rather concerned. You had agreed to send the check two weeks ago, but it hasn't arrived."

Then she began to talk more loudly. "What he want, I come to New York tell him front of his boss, you cheating me?" And I was trying to calm her down, make her be quiet, while telling the stockbroker, "I can't tolerate any more excuses. If I don't receive the check immediately, I am going to have to speak to your manager when I'm in New York next week." And sure enough, the following week there we were in front of this astonished stockbroker, and I was sitting there red-faced and quiet, and my mother, the real Mrs Tan, was shouting at his boss in her impeccable broken English.

We used a similar routine just five days ago, for a situation that was far less humorous. My mother had gone to the hospital for an appointment, to find out about a benign brain tumor a CAT scan had revealed a month ago. She said she had spoken very good English, her best English, no mistakes. Still, she said, the hospital did not apologize when they said they had lost the CAT scan and she had come for nothing. She said they did not seem to have any sympathy when she told them she was anxious to know the exact diagnosis, since her husband and son had both died of brain tumors. She said they would not give her any more information until the next time and she would have to make another appointment for that. So she said she would not leave until the doctor called her daughter. She wouldn't budge. And when the doctor finally called her daughter, me, who spoke in perfect English – lo and behold – we had assurances the CAT scan would be found, promises that a conference call on Monday would be held, and apologies for any suffering my mother had gone through for a most regrettable mistake.

I think my mother's English almost had an effect on limiting my possibilities in life as well. Sociologists and linguists probably will tell you that a person's developing language skills are more influenced by peers. But I do think that the language spoken in the family, especially in immigrant families which are more insular, plays a large role in shaping the language of the child. And I believe that it affected my results on achievement tests, IQ tests, and the SAT. While my English skills were never judged as poor, compared to math, English could not be considered my strong suit. In grade school I did moderately well, getting perhaps B's, sometimes B-pluses, in English and scoring perhaps in the sixtieth or seventieth percentile on achievement tests. But those scores were not good enough to override the opinion that my true abilities lay in math and science, because in those areas I achieved A's and scored in the ninetieth percentile or higher.

This was understandable. Math is precise; there is only one correct answer. Whereas, for me at least, the answers on English tests were always a judgment call, a matter of opinion and personal experience. Those tests were constructed around items like fill-in-the-blank sentence completion, such as "Even though Tom was ___, Mary thought he was ___." And the correct answer always seemed to be the most bland combinations of thoughts, for example, "Even though Tom was shy, Mary thought he was charming," with the grammatical structure "even though" limiting the correct answer to some sort of semantic opposites, so you wouldn't get answers like "Even though Tom was foolish, Mary thought he was ridiculous." Well, according to my mother, there were very few limitations as to what Tom could have been and what Mary might have thought of him. So I never did well on tests like that.

The same was true with word analogies, pairs of words in which you were supposed to find some sort of logical, semantic relationship – for example, "*Sunset* is to *nightfall* as ___ is to ___." And here you would be presented with a list of four possible pairs, one of which showed the same kind of relationship: *red* is to *stoplight, bus* is to *arrival, chills* is to *fever, yawn* is to *boring*. Well, I could never think that way. I knew what the tests were asking, but I could not block out of my mind the images already created by the first pair, "*sunset* is to *nightfall*" and I would see a burst of colors against a darkening sky, the moon rising, the lowering of a curtain of stars. And all the other pairs of words – *red, bus, stoplight, boring* – just threw up a mass of confusing images, making it impossible for me to sort out something as logical as saying: "A sunset precedes nightfall" is the same as "a chill precedes a fever." The only way I would have gotten that answer right would have been to imagine an associative situation, for example, my being disobedient and staying out past sunset, catching a chill at night, which turns into feverish pneumonia as punishment, which indeed did happen to me.

I have been thinking about all this lately, about my mother's English, about achievement tests. Because lately I've been asked, as a writer, why there are not more Asian Americans represented in American literature. Why are there few Asian Americans enrolled in creative writing programs? Why do so many Chinese students go into engineering? Well, these are broad sociological questions I can't begin to answer. But I have noticed in surveys – in fact, just last week –

that Asian students, as a whole, always do significantly better on math achievement tests than in English. And this makes me think that there are other Asian American students whose English spoken in the home might also be described as "broken" or "limited." And perhaps they also have teachers who are steering them away from writing and into math and science, which is what happened to me.

Fortunately, I happen to be rebellious in nature and enjoy the challenge of disproving assumptions made about me. I became an English major my first year in college, after being enrolled as premed. I started writing nonfiction as a freelancer the week after I was told by my former boss that writing was my worst skill and I should hone my talents toward account management.

But it wasn't until 1985 that I finally began to write fiction. And at first I wrote using what I thought to be wittily crafted sentences, sentences that would finally prove I had mastery over the English language. Here's an example from the first draft of a story that later made its way into *The Joy Luck Club*, but without this line: "That was my mental quandary in its nascent state." A terrible line, which I can barely pronounce.

Fortunately, for reasons I won't get into today, I later decided I should envision a reader for the stories I would write. And the reader I decided upon was my mother, because these were stories about mothers. So with this reader in mind – and in fact she did read my early drafts – I began to write stories using all the Englishes I grew up with: the English I spoke to my mother, which for lack of a better term might be described as "simple"; the English she used with me, which for lack of a better term might be described as "broken"; my translation of her Chinese, which could certainly be described as "watered down"; and what I imagined to be her translation of her Chinese if she could speak in perfect English, her internal language, and for that I sought to preserve the essence, but neither an English nor a Chinese structure. I wanted to capture what language ability tests can never reveal: her intent, her passion, her imagery, the rhythms of her speech and the nature of her thoughts.

Apart from what any critic had to say about my writing, I knew I had succeeded where it counted when my mother finished reading my book and gave me her verdict: "So easy to read."

Robin D. G. Kelley, in this delightful piece, describes some of the attitudes toward black masculinity. Even as he bemoans the stereotypes, he takes a certain delight in playing with them.

Focus questions:
1 Do you agree with Kelley that many people think that black men are hypermasculine and potentially violent? How have these attitudes affected your behavior?
2 A shaved head might be termed a "signifier," that is, a symbol of something. What does it symbolize? What are some other signifiers of race or gender having to do with grooming or adornment?

27 Confessions of a Nice Negro, or Why I Shaved My Head

Robin D. G. Kelley

It happened just the other day – two days into the new year, to be exact. I had dashed into the deserted lobby of an Ann Arbor movie theater, pulling the door behind me to escape the freezing winds Michigan residents have come to know so well. Behind the counter knelt a young white teenager filling the popcorn bin with bags of that awful pre-popped stuff. Hardly the enthusiastic employee; from a distance it looked like she was lost in deep thought. The generous display of body piercing suggested an X-generation flowerchild – perhaps an anthropology major into acid jazz and environmentalism, I thought. Sporting a black New York Yankees baseball cap and a black-and-beige scarf over my nose and mouth, I must have looked like I had stepped out of a John Singleton film. And because I was already late, I rushed madly toward the ticket counter.

The flower child was startled: "I don't have anything in the cash register," she blurted as she pulled the bag of popcorn in front of her for protection.

"Huh? I just want one ticket for *Little Women*, please – the two-fifteen show. My wife and daughter should already be in there." I slowly gestured to the theater door and gave her one of those innocent childlike glances I used to give my mom when I wanted to sit on her lap.

"Oh god . . . I'm so sorry. A reflex. Just one ticket? You only missed the first twenty minutes. Enjoy the show."

Enjoy the show? Barely 1995 and here we go again. Another bout with racism in a so-called liberal college town; another racial drama in which I play the prime suspect. And yet I have to confess the situation was pretty funny. Just two hours earlier I couldn't persuade Elleza, my four-year-old daughter, to put her toys away; time-out did nothing, yelling had no effect, and the evil stare made no impact whatsoever. Thoroughly frustrated, I had only one option left: "Okay, I'm gonna tell Mommy!" Of course it worked.

So those five seconds as a media-made black man felt kind of good. I know it's a product of racism. I know that the myth of black male violence has resulted in the deaths of many innocent boys and men of darker hue. I know that the power to scare is not real power. I know all that – after all, I study this stuff for a living! For the moment, though, it felt good. (Besides, the ability to scare with your body can come in handy, especially when you're trying to get a good seat in a theater or avoid long lines.)

I shouldn't admit this, but I take particular pleasure in putting fear into people on the lookout for black male criminality mainly because those moments are so rare for me. Indeed, my *inability* to employ black-maleness as a weapon is the story of my life. Why I don't possess it, or rather possess so little of it, escapes me. I grew up poor in Harlem and Afrodena (the Negro West Side of Pasadena/Altadena, California). My mom was single during my formative preadolescent years, and for a brief moment she even received a welfare check. A hard life makes a hard nigga, so I've been told.

Never an egghead or a dork, as a teenager I was pretty cool. I did the house-party circuit on Friday and Saturday nights and used to stroll down the block toting the serious Radio Raheem boombox. Why, I even invaded move theaters in the company of ten or fifteen hooded and high-topped black bodies, colonizing the balconies and occupying two seats per person. Armed with popcorn and Raisinettes as our missiles of choice, we dared any usher to ask us to leave. Those of us who had cars (we called them hoopties or rides back in the day) spent our lunch hours and precious class time hanging out in the school parking lot, running down our Die Hards to pump up Cameo, Funkadelic, Grandmaster Flash from our car stereos. I sported dickies and Levis, picked up that gangsta stroll, and when the shag came in style I was with it – always armed with a silk scarf to ensure that my hair was laid. Granted, I vomited after drinking malt liquor for the first time and my only hit of a joint ended abruptly in an asthma attack. But I was cool.

Sure, I was cool, but nobody feared me. That I'm relatively short with dimples and curly hair, speak softly in a rather medium to high-pitched voice, and have a "girl's name" doesn't help matters. And everyone knows that light skin is less threatening to white people than blue-black or midnight brown. Besides, growing up with a soft-spoken, uncharacteristically passive West Indian mother deep into East Indian religions, a mother who sometimes walked barefoot in the streets of Harlem, a mother who insisted on proper diction and never, ever, ever used a swear word, screwed me up royally. I could never curse right. My mouth had trouble forming the words – "fuck" always came out as "fock" and "goddamn" always sounded like it's spelled, not "gotdayum," the way my Pasadena homies pronounced it in their Calabama twang. I don't even recall saying the word "bitch" unless I was quoting somebody or some authorless vernacular rhyme. For some unknown reason, that word scared me.

Moms dressed me up in the coolest mod outfits – short pant suits with matching hats, Nehru jackets, those sixties British-looking turtlenecks. Sure, she got some of that stuff from John's Bargain Store or Goodwill, but I always looked "cute." More stylish than roguish. Kinda like W. E. B. Du Bois as a toddler, or those turn-of-the-century photos of middle-class West Indian boys who grow up to become prime ministers or poets. Ghetto ethnographers back in the late sixties and early seventies would not have found me or my family very "authentic," especially if they had discovered that one of my middle names is Gibran, after the Lebanese poet Kahlil Gibran.

Everybody seemed to like me. Teachers liked me, kids liked me; I even fell in with some notorious teenage criminals at Pasadena High School because *they* liked me. I remember one memorable night in the ninth grade when I went down to the Pasadena Boys' Club to take photos of some of my partners on the basketball team. On my way home some big kids, eleventh-graders to be exact, tried to take my camera. The ringleader pulled out a knife and gently poked it against my chest. I told them it was my stepfather's camera and if I came home without it he'd kick my ass for a week. Miraculously, this launched a whole conversation about stepfathers and how messed up they are, which must have made them feel sorry for me. Within minutes we were cool; they let me go unmolested and I had made another friend.

In affairs of the heart, however, "being liked" had the opposite effect. I can only recall having had four fights in my entire life, all of which were with girls who supposedly liked me but thoroughly beat my behind. Sadly, my record in the boxing ring of puppy love is still 0–4. By the time I graduated to serious dating, being a nice guy seemed like the root of all my romantic problems. I resisted jealousy, tried to be understanding, brought flowers and balloons, opened doors, wrote poems and songs, and seemed to always be on my knees for one reason or another. If you've ever watched "Love Connection" or read *Cosmopolitan*, you know the rest of the story: I practically never had sex and most of the women I dated left me in the cold for roughnecks. My last girlfriend in high school, the woman I took to my prom, the woman I once thought I'd die for, tried to show me the light: "Why do you always ask me what I want? Why don't you just *tell* me what you want me to do? Why don't you take charge and *be a man*? If you want to be a real man you can't be nice all the time!"

I always thought she was wrong; being nice has nothing to do with being a man. While I still think she's wrong, it's an established fact that our culture links manhood to terror and power, and that black men are frequently imaged as the ultimate in hypermasculinity. But the black man as the prototype of violent hypermasculinity is as much a fiction as the happy Sambo. No matter what critics and stand-up comics might say, I know from experience that not all black men – and here I'm only speaking of well-lighted or daytime situations – generate fear. Who scares and who doesn't has a lot to do with the body in question; it is dependent on factors such as age, skin color, size, clothes, hairstyle, and even the sound of one's voice. The cops who beat Rodney King and the jury who acquitted King's assailants openly admitted that the size, shape, and color of his body automatically made him a threat to the officers' safety.

On the other hand, the threatening black male body can take the most incongruous forms. Some of the hardest brothas on my block in West Pasadena kept their perms in pink rollers and hairnets. It was not unusual to see young black men in public with curlers, tank-top undershirts, sweatpants, black mid-calf dress socks, and Stacey Adams shoes, hanging out on the corner or on the basketball court. And we all knew that these brothas were not to be messed with. The rest of the world probably knows it by now, too, since black males in curlers are occasionally featured on "Cops" and "America's Most Wanted" as notorious drug dealers or heartless pimps.)

Whatever the source of this ineffable terror, my body simply lacked it. Indeed, the older I got and the more ensconced I became in the world of academia, the less threatening I seemed. Marrying and having a child also reduced the threat factor. By the time I hit my late twenties, my wife, Diedra, and I found ourselves in the awkward position of being everyone's favorite Negroes. I don't know how many times we've attended dinner parties where we were the only African Americans in the room. Occasionally there were others, but we seemed to have a monopoly on the dinner party invitations. This not only happened in Ann Arbor, where there is a small but substantial black population to choose from, but in the Negro mecca of Atlanta, Georgia. Our hosts always felt comfortable asking us "sensitive" questions about race that they would not dare ask other black colleagues and friends: What do African Americans think about Farrakahn? Ben Chavis? Nelson Mandela? Most of my black students are very conservative and career-oriented – why is that? How can we mend the relations between blacks and Jews? Do you celebrate Kwanzaa? Do you put anything in your hair to make it that way? What are the starting salaries for young black faculty nowadays?

Of course, these sorts of exchanges appear regularly in most black autobiographies. As soon as they're comfortable, it is not uncommon for white people to take the opportunity to find out everything they've always wanted to know about "us" (which also applies to other people of color, I'm sure) but were afraid to ask. That they feel perfectly at ease asking dumb or unanswerable questions is not simply a case of (mis)perceived racelessness. Being a "nice Negro" has a lot to do with gender, and my peculiar form of "left-feminist-funny-guy" masculinity – a little Kevin Hooks, some Bobby McFerrin, a dash of Woody Allen – is regarded as less threatening than that of most other black men.

Not that I mind the soft-sensitive masculine persona – after all, it is the genuine me, a product of my mother's heroic and revolutionary child-rearing style. But there are moments when I wish I could invoke the intimidation factor of blackmaleness on demand. If I only had that look – that Malcolm X/Mike Tyson/Ice Cube/Larry Fishburne/Bigger Thomas/Fruit of Islam look – I could keep the stupid questions at bay, make college administrators tremble, and scare editors into submission. Subconsciously, I decided that I had to do something about my image. Then, as if by magic, my wish was fulfilled.

Actually, it began as an accident involving a pair of electric clippers and sleep deprivation – a bad auto-cut gone awry. With my lowtop fade on the verge of a Sly Stone afro, I was in desperate need of a trim. Diedra didn't have the time to do it, and as it was February (Black History Month), I was on the chitlin' lecture circuit and couldn't spare forty-five minutes at a barber shop, so I elected to do it myself. Standing in a well-lighted bathroom, armed with two mirrors, I started trimming. Despite a steady hand and what I've always believed was a good eye, my hair turned out lopsided. I kept trimming and trimming to correct my error, but as my flattop sank lower, a yellow patch of scalp began to rise above the surrounding hair, like one of those big granite mounds dotting the grassy knolls of Central Park. A nice yarmulke could have covered it, but that would have been more difficult to explain than a bald spot. So, bearing in mind role models like Michael Jordan, Charles Barkley, Stanley Crouch, and Onyx (then the hip-hop group of the hour), I decided to take it all off.

I didn't think much of it at first, but the new style accomplished what years of evil stares and carefully crafted sartorial statements could not: I began to scare people. The effect was immediate and dramatic. Passing strangers avoided me and smiled less frequently. Those who did smile or make eye contact seemed to be deliberately trying to disarm me – a common strategy taught in campus rape-prevention centers. Scaring people was fun for a while, but I especially enjoyed standing in line at the supermarket with my bald head, baggy pants, high-top Reeboks, and long black hooded down coat, humming old standards like "Darn That Dream," "A Foggy Day," and "I Could Write a Book." Now *that* brought some stares. I must have been convincing, since I adore those songs and have been humming them ever since I can remember. No simple case of cultural hybridity here, just your average menace to society with a deep appreciation for Gershwin, Rodgers and Hart, Van Heusen, Cole Porter, and Jerome Kern.

Among my colleagues, my bald head became the lead subject of every conversation. "You look older, more mature." "With that new cut you come across as much more serious than usual." "You really look quite rugged and masculine with a bald head." My close friends dispensed with the euphemisms and went straight to the point: "Damn. You look scary!" The most painful comment was that I looked like a "B-Boy wannabe" and was "too old for that shit." I had to remind my friend that I'm an OBB (Original B-Boy), that I was in the eleventh grade in 1979 when the Sugar Hill Gang dropped "Rapper's Delight," and that *his* tired behind was in graduate school at the time. Besides, B-Boy was not the intent.

In the end, however, I got more questions than comments. Was I in crisis? Did I want to talk? What was I trying to say by shaving my head? What was the political point of my actions? Once the novelty passed, I began getting those "speak for the race" questions that irritated the hell out of me when I had hair. Why have *black men* begun to shave their heads in greater numbers? Why have so many black athletes decided to shave their heads? Does this new trend have some kind of phallic meaning? Against my better judgment, I found myself coming up with answers to these questions – call it an academician's reflex. I don't remember exactly what I said, but it usually began with black prizefighter Jack Johnson, America's real life "baaad nigger" of the early twentieth century, whose head was always shaved and greased, and ended with the hip-hop community's embrace of an outlaw status. Whatever it was, it made sense at the time.

The publicity photo for my recent book, *Race Rebels*, clearly generated the most controversy among my colleagues. It diverged dramatically from the photo on my first book, where I look particularly innocent, almost angelic. In that first photo I smiled just enough to make my dimples visible; my eyes gazed away from the camera in sort of a dreamy, contemplative pose; my haircut was nondescript and the natural sunlight had a kind of halo effect. The Izod shirt was the icing on the cake. By contrast, the photograph for *Race Rebels* (which Diedra set up and shot, by the way) has me looking directly into the camera, arms folded, bald head glistening from baby oil and rear window light, with a grimace that could give Snoop Doggy Dogg a run for his money. The lens made my arms appear much larger than they really are, creating a kind of Popeye effect. Soon after the book came out, I received several e-mail messages about the photo. A particularly memorable one came from a friend and fellow historian in Australia. In the course of explaining to me how he had corrected one of his students who had read an essay of mine and presumed I was a woman, he wrote: "Mind you, the photo in your book should make things clear – the angle and foreshortening of the arms, and the hairstyle make it one of the more masculine author photos I've seen recently????!!!!!!"

My publisher really milked this photo, which actually fit well with the book's title. For the American Studies Association meeting in Nashville, Tennessee, which took place the week the book came out, my publisher bought a full-page ad on the back cover of an ASA handout, with my mug staring dead at you. Everywhere I turned – in hotel elevators, hallways, lobbies, meeting rooms – I saw myself, and it was not exactly a pretty sight. The quality of the reproduction (essentially a high-contrast xerox) made me appear harder, meaner, and crazier than the original photograph.

The situation became even stranger since I had decided to abandon the skinhead look and grow my hair back. In fact, by the time of the ASA meeting I was on the road (since abandoned) toward a big Black Power Afro – a retro style that at the time seemed to be making a comeback. Worse still, I had come to participate in a round-table discussion on black hair! My paper, titled "Nap Time: Historicizing the Afro," explored the political implications of competing narratives of the Afro's origins and meaning. Overall, it was a terrific session; the room was packed and the discussion was stimulating. But inevitably the question came up: "Although this isn't directly related to his paper, I'd like to find out from Professor Kelley why he shaved his head. Professor Kelley, given the panel's topic and in light of the current ads floating about with your picture on them, can you shed some light on what is attractive to black men about baldness?" The question was posed by a very distinguished and widely read African American literary scholar. Hardly the naif, he knew the answers as well as I did, but wanted to generate a public discussion. And he succeeded. For ten minutes the audience ran the gamut of issues revolving around race, gender, sexuality, and the politics of style. Even the issue of bald heads as phallic symbols came up. "It's probably true," I said, "but when I was cutting my hair at three-o'clock in the morning I wasn't thinking 'penis.'" Eventually the discussion drifted from black masculinity to the tremendous workloads of minority scholars, which, in all honesty, was the source of my baldness in the first place. Unlike the golden old days, when doing hair was highly ritualized and completely integrated into daily life, we're so busy mentoring and publishing and speaking and fighting that we have very little time to attend to our heads.

Beyond the session itself, that ad continued to haunt me during the entire conference. Every ten minutes, or so it seemed, someone came up to me and offered unsolicited commentary on the photo. One person slyly suggested that in order to make the picture complete I should have posed with an Uzi. When I approached a very good friend of mine, a historian who is partly my Jewish mother and partly my confidante and *always* looking out for my best interests, the first words out of her mouth were, "Robin, I hate that picture! It's the worst picture of you I've ever seen. It doesn't do you justice. Why did you let them use it?"

"It's not that bad," I replied. "Diedra likes it – she took the picture. You just don't like my bald head."

"No, that's not it. I like the bald look on some men, and you have a very nice head. The problem is the photo and the fact that I know what kind of person you are. None of your gentleness and lovability comes out in that picture. Now, don't get a swelled head when I say this, but you have a delightful face and expression that makes people feel good, even when you're talking about serious stuff. The way you smile, there's something unbelievably safe about you."

It was a painful compliment. And yet I knew deep down that she was telling the truth. I've always been unbelievably safe, not just because of my look but because of my actions. Not that I consciously try to put people at ease, to erase conflict and difference, to remain silent on sensitive issues. I can't quite put my finger on it. Perhaps it's my mother's politeness drills? Perhaps it's a manifestation of my continuing bout with shyness? Maybe it has something to do with the sense of joy I get from stimulating conversations? Or maybe it's linked to the fact that my mom refused to raise me in a manner boys are accustomed to? Most likely it is a product of cultural capital – the fact that I *can* speak the language, (re)cite the texts, exhibit the manners and mannerisms that are inherent to bourgeois academic culture. My colleagues identify with me because I can talk intelligently about their scholarship on their terms, which invariably has the effect of creating an illusion of brilliance. As Frantz Fanon said in *Black Skin, White Masks*, the mere fact that he was an articulate *black* man who read a lot rendered him a stunning specimen of erudition in the eyes of his fellow intellectuals in Paris.

Whatever the source of my ineffable lovability, I've learned that it's not entirely a bad thing. In fact, the rest of the world could look a little deeper, beyond the hardcore exterior – the wide bodies, the carefully constructed grimaces, the performance of terror – they would find many, many brothas much nicer and smarter than myself. The problem lies in a racist culture, a highly gendered racist culture, that is so deeply enmeshed in the fabric of daily life that it's practically invisible. The very existence of the "nice Negro," like the model-minority myth pinned on Asian Americans, renders the war on those "other," hardcore niggas justifiable and even palatable. In a little-known essay on the public image of world champion boxer Joe Louis, the radical Trinidadian writer C. L. R. James put it best: "This attempt to hold up Louis as a model Negro has strong overtones of condescension and race prejudice. It implies: 'See! When a Negro knows how to conduct himself, he gets on very well and we all love him.' From there the next step is: 'If only all Negroes behaved like Joe, the race problem would be solved.'"[1]

Of course we all know this is a bunch of fiction. Behaving "like Joe" was merely a code for deference and patience, which is all the more remarkable given his vocation. Unlike his predecessor Jack Johnson – the bald-headed prize fighter who transgresed racial boundaries by sleeping with and even marrying white women, who refused to apologize for his "outrageous" behavior, who boasted of his prowess in every facet of life (he even wrapped gauze around his penis to make it appear bigger under his boxing shorts) – Joe Louis was America's hero. As James put it, he was a credit to his race, "I mean the human race."[2] (Re)presented as a humble Alabama boy, God-fearing and devoid of hatred, Louis was constructed in the press as a raceless man whose masculinity was put to good, patriotic use. To many of his white fans, he was a man in the ring and a boy – a good boy – outside of it. To many black folks, he was a hero because he had the license to kick white men's butts and yet maintain the admiration and respect of a nation. Thus, despite similarities in race, class, and vocation, and their common iconization, Louis and Johnson exhibited public behavior that reflected radically different masculinities.

Here, then, is a lesson we cannot ignore. There is some truth in the implication that race (or gender) conflict is partly linked to behavior and how certain behavior is perceived. If our society, for example, could dispense with rigid, archaic notions of appropriate masculine and feminine behavior, perhaps we might create a world that nurtures, encourages, and even rewards nice guys. If violence were not so central to American culture – to the way manhood is defined, to the way in which the state keeps African American men in check, to the way men interact with women, to the way oppressed peoples interact with one another – perhaps we might see the withering away of white fears of black men. Perhaps young black men wouldn't feel the need to adopt hardened, threatening postures merely to survive in a Doggy-Dogg world. Not that black men ought to become colored equivalents of Alan Alda. Rather, black men ought to be whomever or whatever they want to be, without unwarranted criticism or societal pressures to conform to a particular definition of manhood. They could finally dress down without suspicion, talk loudly without surveillance, and love each other without sanction. Fortunately, such a transformation would also mean the long-awaited death of the "nice Negro."

Not in my lifetime. Any fool can look around and see that the situation for race and gender relations in general, and for black males in particular, has taken a turn for the worse – and relief is nowhere in sight. In the meantime, I will make the most of my "nice Negro" status. When it's all said and done, there is nothing romantic or interesting about playing Bigger Thomas. Maybe I can't persuade a well-dressed white couple to give up their box seats, but at least they'll listen to me. For now. . . .

Notes

1   C. L. R. James, "Joe Louis and Jack Johnson," *Labor Action*, July 1, 1946.
2   Ibid.
[Taken from: *Speak My Name: Black Men on Masculinity and the American Dream*, ed.
    Don Belton (Boston, Mass.: Beacon Books, 1995).]

Lame Deer, a Lakota holy man and former rodeo clown, criminal, and activist among other things, condemns white America's obsession with "green frog skins": money. In the process he shows that the traditional class structure among the Lakota is very different than that of the white world, or even, perhaps, that there is no class structure at all in traditional Lakota culture.

Focus questions:
1 How does Lame Deer's attitude toward money differ from that of white culture? What does he think are the drawbacks of white attitudes?
2 What does Lame Deer believe about white practices of ownership and consumerism?

---

28   The Green Frog Skin

John (Fire) Lame Deer and Richard Erdoes

The green frog skin – that's what I call a dollar bill. In our attitude toward it lies the biggest difference between Indians and whites. My grandparents grew up in an Indian world without money. Just before the Custer battle the white soldiers had received their pay. Their pockets were full of green paper and they had no place to spend it. What were their last thoughts as an Indian bullet or arrow hit them? I guess they were thinking of all that money going to waste, of not having had a chance to enjoy it, of a bunch of dumb savages getting their paws on that hard-earned pay. That must have hurt them more than the arrow between their ribs.

The close hand-to-hand fighting, with a thousand horses gally-hooting all over the place, had covered the battlefield with an enormous cloud of dust, and in it the green frog skins of the soldiers were whirling around like snowflakes in a blizzard. Now, what did the Indians do with all that money? They gave it to their children to play with, to fold those strange bits of colored paper into all kinds of shapes, making them into toy buffalo and horses. Somebody was enjoying that money after all. The books tell of one soldier who survived. He got away, but he went crazy and some women watched him from a distance as he killed himself. The writers always say he must have been afraid of being captured and tortured, but that's all wrong.

Can't you see it? There he is, bellied down in a gully, watching what is going on. He sees the kids playing with the money, tearing it up, the women using it to fire up some dried buffalo chips to cook on, the men lighting their pipes with green frog skins, but mostly all those beautiful dollar bills floating away with the

dust and the wind. It's this sight that drove that poor soldier crazy. He's clutch-
ing his head, hollering, "Goddam, Jesus Christ Almighty, look at them dumb,
stupid, red sons of bitches wasting all that dough!" He watches till he can't stand
it any longer, and then he blows his brains out with a six-shooter. It would make
a great scene in a movie, but it would take an Indian mind to get the point.

The green frog skin – that was what the fight was all about. The gold of the
Black Hills, the gold in every clump of grass. Each day you can see ranch hands
riding over this land. They have a bagful of grain hanging from their saddle
horns, and whenever they see a prairie-dog hole they toss a handful of oats in it,
like a kind little old lady feeding the pigeons in one of your city parks. Only the
oats for the prairie dogs are poisoned with strychnine. What happens to the
prairie dog after he has eaten this grain is not a pleasant thing to watch. The
prairie dogs are poisoned, because they eat grass. A thousand of them eat up as
much grass in a year as a cow. So if the rancher can kill that many prairie dogs he
can run one more head of cattle, make a little more money. When he looks at a
prairie dog he sees only a green frog skin getting away from him.

For the white man each blade of grass or spring of water has a price tag on it.
And that is the trouble, because look at what happens. The bobcats and coyotes
which used to feed on prairie dogs now have to go after a stray lamb or a
crippled calf. The rancher calls the pest-control officer to kill these animals. This
man shoots some rabbits and puts them out as bait with a piece of wood stuck
in them. That stick has an explosive charge which shoots some cyanide into the
mouth of the coyote who tugs at it. The officer has been trained to be careful.
He puts a printed warning on each stick reading, "Danger, Explosive, Poison!"
The trouble is that our dogs can't read, and some of our children can't either.

And the prairie becomes a thing without life – no more prairie dogs, no more
badgers, foxes, coyotes. The big birds of prey used to feed on prairie dogs, too.
So you hardly see an eagle these days. The bald eagle is your symbol. You see
him on your money, but your money is killing him. When a people start killing
off their own symbols they are in a bad way.

The Sioux have a name for white men. They call them *wasicun* – fat-takers. It
is a good name, because you have taken the fat of the land. But it does not seem
to have agreed with you. Right now you don't look so healthy – overweight,
yes, but not healthy. Americans are bred like stuffed geese – to be consumers,
not human beings. The moment they stop consuming and buying, the frog-
skin world has no more use for them. They have become frogs themselves.
Some cruel child has stuffed a cigar into their mouths and they have to keep
puffing and puffing until they explode. Fat-taking is a bad thing, even for the
taker. It is especially bad for Indians who are forced to live in this frog-skin
world which they did not make and for which they have no use.

You, Richard, are an artist. That's one reason we get along well. Artists are the
Indians of the white world. They are called dreamers who live in the clouds, improvident people who can't hold onto their money, people who don't want to
face "reality." They say the same things about Indians. How the hell do these
frog-skin people know what reality is? The world in which you paint a picture in
your mind, a picture which shows things different from what your eyes see, that is

the world from which I get my visions. I tell you this is the real world, not the Green Frog Skin World. That's only a bad dream, a streamlined, smog-filled nightmare.

Because we refuse to step out of our reality into this frog-skin illusion, we are called dumb, lazy, improvident, immature, other-worldly. It makes me happy to be called "other-worldly," and it should make you so. It's a good thing our reality is different from theirs. I remember one white man looking at my grandfather's vest. It was made of black velvet and had ten-dollar gold coins for buttons. The white man had a fit, saying over and over again, "Only a crazy Indian would think of that, using good money for buttons, a man who hasn't got a pot to piss in!" But Grandpa wasn't a bit crazy and he had learned to know the value of money as well as anybody. But money exists to give a man pleasure. Well, it pleasured Grandpa to put a few golden Indian heads on his vest. That made sense.

I knew a well-educated Indian who had come back to his reservation after working for many years in a big city. With his life savings he opened a cafeteria and gas station. All day long the cars lined up. "Hey, Uncle, fill her up. I can't pay, but you are rich; you let me have it free." And the same thing over at the cafeteria: "Say, Uncle, let me have one of them barbecued-beef sandwiches. Don't bother to write up a bill for a relation of yours."

The owner had done very well living and working in the white man's way among white people. But now he was an Indian again, back among Indians. He couldn't say "no" to a poor relative, and the whole reservation was just one big mass of poor relatives, people who called him Uncle and Cousin regardless of the degree of their relationship. He couldn't refuse them and his education couldn't help him in this situation. We aren't divided up into separate, neat little families – Pa, Ma, kids, and to hell with everybody else. The whole damn tribe is one big family; that's our kind of reality.

It wasn't long before this Indian businessman was broke and in debt. But this man was smart, white-educated. So he found a way out. He hired a white waitress and a white gas-station attendant and spread the word that he had been forced to sell the business to white owners. From then on he did well. Everybody paid, because they knew white men don't give anything away for free.

I once heard of an Indian who lost a leg in an industrial accident. He got about fifteen thousand dollars in insurance money. In no time his place was overrun with more than a hundred hungry relatives. They came in old jalopies, in buckboards, on horseback or on foot. From morning to night a pick-up truck was making round trips between his place and the nearest store, hauling beef and bread and crates of beer to keep all of those lean bellies full. In the end they bought a few scrub steers and did their own butchering. The fun lasted a few weeks, then the money was gone. A day after that the relatives were gone, too. That man had no regrets. He said he wished he'd lose his other leg so that he could start all over again. This man had become quite a hero, even to other tribes, and he was welcome everywhere.

I made up a new proverb: "Indians chase the vision, white men chase the dollar." We are lousy raw material from which to form a capitalist. We could do it easily, but then we would stop being Indians. We would just be ordinary citizens with a slightly darker skin. That's a high price to pay, my friend, too high. We make lousy farmers, too, because deep down within us lingers a feeling that land, water, air, the earth and what lies beneath its surface cannot be owned as someone's private property. That belongs to everybody, and if man wants to survive, he had better come around to this Indian point of view, the sooner the better, because there isn't much time left to think it over.

I always remember listening to my first radio. That was in the little town of Interior, way back in the twenties. There was a sign over a door: "Listen to wireless music from Sioux Falls – 300 miles away! $1.50 per person." You had to plunk that much down to be allowed inside this café to give your ears a treat. We saw a guy fooling around with a needle on a crystal and heard a tinny, crackling voice saying something about winter feed, corn and the price of prime hogs. At that moment an old Indian spoke up. "They took the land and the water, now they own the air, too." So we have the green frog-skin world in which all things have a price tag.

Indians don't like to haggle. A long argument about money is painful. But we can drive a shrewd bargain. My uncle, Poor Thunder, bred a special brand of Appaloosas. At that time you could get a saddle-broken horse for twenty bucks, not one of Poor Thunder's Appaloosas. If a white man came and asked for a price my uncle would tell him it was seventy-five dollars per head. The buyer used to scratch his head and say the price was too high. They always came back in a day or two, because these horses were really something. But when they returned with cash in their hands my uncle would tell them, "That was yesterday's price. Now it will cost you a hundred dollars." If they were foolish enough to do some more head-scratching the price would go up to 125 dollars. But the cheerful buyer who didn't haggle, who made up his mind at once, got ten bucks off. Uncle loved his ponies. He once told me, "An Indian can love one horse so much, he'll die for it." He had a great head for business – he was one hell of a horse trader – but he gave most of what he got away to his poor relations. The trader in him couldn't get the better of the Indian.

Old Uncle would sometimes leave a heifer or steer in front of a poor cousin's house. He used to tell me, "There's more to food than just passing through your body. There are spirits in the food, watching over it. If you are stingy, that spirit will go away thinking 'that bastard is so tight, I'll leave.' But if you share your food with others, this good spirit will always stay around." I was brought up to regard food as something sacred. I can foresee a day when all you have to give us are capsules with some chemicals and vitamins instead of food, with the missionaries telling us to fold our hands over a few tablets on our plates, saying, "Heavenly Father, bless our daily pill." I'm glad I won't be around to see it.

I'd rather have a glass of *mini-sha*, red water, with one of my neighbors. He is an old wino but very generous. He'll share his last bottle with a friend. He told me, "The whisky can't get away from me. The more I give away, the more it comes. I've got to be careful, or I'll drown in it."

The anthropologists are always saying that there is still too much of the old buffalo hunter in us. Share your food, share your goods, or the tribe will perish. That was good for yesterday. Today it's saying "No, no, no" to a poor cousin.

That's the practical thing to do. Trying always to remake people in one's own image is a white man's disease. I can't cure that. I tell those anthros, "You have green frog skins on your brains. If we Indians were such filthy savages as you tell us, we should have eaten you up when you first came to this turtle continent. Then I could have some peace and quiet now." That shuts them up for a while.

They are also wagging their fingers at us when we have a give-away feast. What they are trying to tell us is that poor people can't afford to be generous. But we hold onto our *otuhan*, our give-aways, because they help us to remain Indians. All the big events in our lives – birth and death, joy and sadness – can be occasions for a give-away. We don't believe in a family getting wealthy through inheritance. Better give away a dead person's belongings. That way he, or she, will be remembered.

If a man loses his wife, his friends come and help him cry. He cries for four days, but no longer, because life must go on, and if he cries too much the spirits will give him something extra to cry about. Not so long ago I saw an old lady who still cut her hair short to mourn for a dead grandson. After four days she and her husband emptied the whole house. They gave away the grand piano, the TV, even their bed. They were sitting on the bare floor calling out to the people coming to pay their respects, "Say, brother, sister, do you need this thing? If it is useful to you, take it." Only the empty walls were left at the end of the day. Friends gave them a new bed. A *wopila* – a thanksgiving for something good that happened to a person – is also a time for giving away things. But your white man's day of thanksgiving – that's a day of mourning for the Indians, nothing to be thankful for.

You put "In God We Trust" on your money. I'm glad you left the Great Spirit out of it. What you want to use your God for is your own business. I tried to show you that the green frog skin is something that keeps whites and Indians apart. But even a medicine man like myself has to have some money, because you force me to live in your make-believe world where I can't get along without it. Which means that I have to be two persons living in two different worlds. I don't like it, but I can't help it. I will try to tell you how I managed this. Whether I have been successful at it you may judge for yourself.

As long as I still had some of the horses and cattle left which my father had given me, I had no thought about earning money. I roamed. I didn't let myself get swallowed up by the frog-skin world, but I was curious enough to explore it. I liked to go to town on horseback. I used to pick up my pals on the way, like Ben Rifle, who later became a congressman. We played around the little reservation towns called Wososo, or Upper Cut Meat. I was like an elk dreamer with a power to charm the girls. I had a good voice and liked to sing Indian. My grandparents had taught me all the old songs. I had no education, but always I was thinking, finding out, trying to fit what I saw and heard into my kind of reality.

Then the day came when I swapped or sold the last of my livestock. I was almost happy. Now I no longer had any property to take care of, to tie me down. Now I could be what I wanted – a real Sioux, an *ikce wicasa*, a common, wild, natural human being. How such a creature could survive in frog-skin land was something I would have to find out. I thought I'd do some hunting to keep meat on my table. I found out that I needed a hunting license if I wanted to go after deer or antelope. The idea of an Indian having to pay for a fancy piece of paper in order to be allowed to hunt on his own land to feed his own, genuine, red man's belly seemed like a bad joke to me. It made me laugh, but it also made me angry. The same people who had killed off the buffalo, who were chopping up the last wild horses into dog food, now were telling me that I was a danger to wildlife preservation if I wanted some red meat on my table, that I had to be regulated. Why couldn't I be satisfied with the starches they were handing out to us? They told me I should be flattered, that having to buy a license put me up there on the same level with the white gentleman hunter. I answered, through an interpreter, that I was no goddam sportsman, just a hungry, common, natural Indian who did not like fancy stamped papers and knew of only one way he could use them.

I was not the only one to feel this way. Most Indians would have been ashamed to hunt with a license. So we did without. The only catch was that there was really not much game left. A few hungry Indians, when they came across some white man's scrub steer, pretended that he had antlers and there was a little bit of "night-butchering" on the reservation, and some people were eating "slow elk." There was some satisfaction in this, like stealing horses from the Crow Indians in the good old days.

No matter how much I hated it I had to face up to the fact that I would have to earn some money. I was like many other fullbloods. I didn't want a steady job in an office or factory. I thought myself too good for that, not because I was stuck up but simply because any human being is too good for that kind of no-life, even white people. I trained myself to need and want as little as could be so that I wouldn't have to work except when I felt like it. That way I got along fine with plenty of spare time to think, to ask, to learn, to listen, to count coup on the girls.

Wimsatt describes the experience of being white and being a minority: he went to school and later hung around in neighborhoods that were mostly black. He romanticized black culture – and in particular black music – and here describes the possibilities and limits of race mobility: in some sense he tried to become black.

Focus questions:

1 What attracts Wimsatt to black culture?
2 What sorts of things does Wimsatt do to try to identify with black culture?
3 What does Wimsatt believe are the limits on race mobility?

---

29 Aren't You in the Wrong Neighborhood?

William Upski Wimsatt

The six-flat condo I grew up in was perfectly integrated: two white families, two black, and two mixed. The apartments across the street were home to many black youngsters. Yet even in these harmonious circumstances, whether by parental design, personal preference, or simple habit, my playmates of choice were almost always white. For all my fascination, I knew little of black people. Even in places like Hyde Park, most whites never do.

By age 11, curiosity got the better of me. I joined the neighborhood baseball league, and transferred to Kenwood Academy, a public magnet school. Like most of Hyde Park's public institutions, both were about nine-tenths black. One of my classmates at Kenwood, Mike Davis, went on to become the only white student at Morehouse College. Within a few years, the experiences I had would allow me to outgrow my first layer of naïveté, the one that most white Americans, including most of the whites at Kenwood, don't realize they are still wearing.

Midway through grammar school, I made a discovery. Michael Jackson, Prince, and most of the other rock stars I stood admiring one day in the record store display window, were black. From this massive insight followed others. Practically all of the wittiest, the coolest, the strongest, the most agile, and the most precocious kids I knew were black (in part this was because most of the whites I knew were unusually dull and spoiled). In the locker room, the black boys really did seem to have bigger dicks. Although it has been proven untrue scientifically, you couldn't have told me that at the time. Next to them, my voice was flat, my personality dull, my lifestyle bland, my complexion pallid. I didn't yet know race was the national obsession. I thought obsessing about blacks was, like masturbation, my dirty little secret.

As embarrassing as all of this was, its importance shouldn't be overlooked. The most promising thing about spilled milk is that it has ventured from its container. The most promising thing about the Cool White, the white b-boy, the wannabe (or to update Norman Mailer's term, the white nigga), is that he is defying in some way the circumstances of his birth. He harbors curiosity and admiration for a people his people have stepped on. He lives by his fascinations rather than his habits, his awkwardness rather than his cool. But it is the desire to be cool that drives him. And it is this desire – not only his guilt – that blacks must use to judo some of his power away from him.

My romanticization of blacks was also a way to elevate myself. If blacks were the superior race, then by association, I too was superior. This conceit, shared by all wiggers, is founded on (what seems to us our rare) ability to mingle with blacks who other whites find inaccessible. In fact, we flatter ourselves; fitting in requires no uncommon talent. The main reason more whites don't become wiggers – instead of just white rap fans – is that getting down with blacks, like any relationship, requires that precious, ego-endangering resource: effort.

Effort is why the White B-boy, the Wigger, rather than the white liberal is at the center of my attention. The white liberal is a worthless frustration to black efforts; he has never put any skin on the line and he never will. The white missionary has guts, but he also has his own agenda, whether religious or ideological. The white b-boy, at his best, avoids the drawbacks of both. He has the zeal of the missionary, but he lacks a firm agenda. And unlike both, he knows blacks first as people, not as issues.

How thrilling it was to be the only white kid who knew that " 11th and Hamilton" meant the juvenile court and detention center, and knew the calendar number, reputation, and drinking habits of the judges there. How critical it was to understand that "I'm going to kick your white ass" is not so much a threat as a test. How illuminating to eat dinner as a friend in the houses of kids who thought Hyde Park was a place to tease, taunt, and take bikes from white people (especially the ones who did their best to avoid black teenagers).

But I didn't infiltrate black teenage society instantly. Much of my initiation came from the loose-knit bunch of kids at my school who were into hip-hop. Partly popular, partly outcasts, our interracial band of troublemakers grew up on hip-hop together.

Unlike sports or music, the more conventional ports of entry into blackness, hip-hop was a total culture. It involved art, music, sport, risk, media, teenage foolishness, mischief, and an instant city-wide network of homeys. For the first year or so, most of my break-dancing and graffiti partners were white, Mexican, or Puerto Rican. By ninth grade, when breakdancing died and most of my white friends, after one or two arrests, had abandoned hip-hop and graffiti for drugs and skateboarding – activities I found dull in comparison – I immersed myself deeper into the city-wide family of graffiti writers, rappers, dancers, DJs, and delinquents.

Imagine what an adventure it must have been for a 13-year-old upper middle-class white kid with over-protective parents to steal and stash cases of spray paint, sneak out at night, travel all over the city (I wonder how white moms in passing cars explained me!), run from the cops, dodge trains in subway tunnels, walk alone through the projects, pick up girls at all-black dances, and commit other crimes for which the statute of limitations has not yet passed. And on top of that, to be accepted by all but the bitterest of the blacks. I was almost instantly and undeservingly made welcome, either directly in the form of: "Brother," "Cool white boy," "That white boy crazy," "You black," "You my nigga," or indirectly, as in "Aren't you in the wrong neighborhood?" or "What (gang) you ride?" etc. – and all the non-verbal comments which meant the same thing.

My favorite of these was told by a white police officer who was writing me up at the 21st district: "Shit. (scribble scribble) I marked down that you were black. You must be the first white kid I've arrested in . . . a long time. Stick with your own kind if you know what I mean." In reply to his mistake, I waited until he had left his office, then mistakenly tore down the anti-graffiti poster hanging on his wall, and shoved it down my pants.

One day my Little League coach arranged for our rag-tag baseball team to scrimmage against a well-trained white suburban team. Warming up, I remember feeling proud to be the only white boy on this black team, and felt certain that our raw city talent would prevail. Within a few innings, we lost by slaughter rule. It was then that I realized for the first time in no uncertain terms that black people did not rule the world.

Experiences like this fed the missionary in me. The small cruelties of elementary school cliques, if not our own families, teach all of us how it feels to be the outcast or the underdog. While some of us spend our lives escaping this feeling, and some inflict the feeling onto others à la Napoleon, others take to the Gandhi role.

What began as a social infatuation with blacks and hip-hop slowly evolved into a political agenda. Sent back to University of Chicago High School Sophomore year for bad grades and behavior, I found the social scene so boring, and myself so out of place that I turned to loner activities like reading and writing. Frustrated by the inequalities of my two worlds, I gravitated toward what are unappealingly called "political activism" and "community service."

My own need was to be accepted by both worlds, to change them, perhaps to integrate them; but as anyone who's tried it knows, challenging people mainly just alienates them. Whites were the hardest to talk to. For blacks at least, their goal was universally understood: they had to make it in the white world and uplift the race. This was a core value of American society, and one that needed no justification.

But why should whites want to change, to climb down the social ladder – to slay their fears? To brook adventure? To become more worldly? As much as we may admire romantic motives such as these in our heroes (Robinson Crusoe, Tom Sawyer) we look on them as abnormal and suspicious in real life. Most of us would rather play it safe. As my grandmother says: "That's crazy, running around in the gutter with the blacks all night. Why would you want to lower yourself running with the niggers?"

Besides, in heroes all qualities are believed to come effortlessly. The reluctant detective is dragged into the case, dragged into bed with the beautiful client. For most of us, unfortunately, adventure and discovery generally require not just risk, but effort.

Where black people tend to take constructive criticism constructively, and read candor as a sign of respect, whites tend to have the opposite response. Challenge is taken as unfriendly, a threat, something to be avoided. Defensiveness betrays their underlying shame. Even now, when non-hip-hop acquaintances ask me what my favorite kind of music is, I try to avoid the subject. "Everything," I lie.

On matters of race, I naturally found it easier to talk to blacks. As recently as two years ago, I was DJing radio shows and writing under pen-names as though I was black. In one article, I scripted myself as the ghost of Malcolm X who humbles an ego-trippin modern-day black kid for not studying history. Another article I wrote even prompted a white boy from Oxnard, California, to mail a whiny letter to the editor, complaining about my anti-white sentiment.

My extreme view had to be tempered with an opposite and extreme view: blacks are stupider than whites. I don't recall the first time I thought that, probably pretty early on, and often times I still imagine pseudo-scientifically that it is true. Usually it is based on an observed instance of black stupidity, but I could pretty much rationalize it out of thin air, or even contrary to the facts at hand. My mind wants to believe in hierarchy. I am unable to imagine equality, unable to love blacks without simultaneously hating them. The same mind that believes a dumb black dude has the potential of an Einstein has to restrain itself from shouting "nigger" when he goes to see a brilliant black scholar give a lecture.

All that shit those great racial healers talk about just doesn't click with me inside. It is with this schizophrenic mind that I, and to some degree all, Americans try to forge for ourselves a sensible opinion on race. Usually it doesn't work. One of my first racial causes – imagine this! – was to dismantle black people's stereotypes of *me*. The wind at my back, I actually believed that I was doing black people a favor by showing them I had rhythm. Why couldn't these blacks – the few who wouldn't accept me – wake up and realize that I was down with them?

The main way I expressed my downness, it turned out, was to dis anyone who wasn't as down as I was, especially anyone associated with house music, R&B, the Fresh Prince, anyone at all except for the hardest of hardcore b-boys. Hell, I even dissed them. At age 14, when, as Dres of Black Sheep says, "I dreamt I was *hard*," I initiated a battle with Orko, one of the kings of Chicago graffiti, a quick-witted Jheri-Kurl writer who was not much bigger than me physically, but four years my senior and straight out of jail. The battle turned nasty when I defaced a rooftop with a suggestive message about a certain female family member. "My mama just died!" he shouted when he finally caught up to me, catching me off guard long enough to apply a coat of spray paint to my face. The color he chose, "beige,' almost perfectly matched my skin – a sharp reminder that I was not just any graffiti writer, but a white graffiti writer, from a good home, and with a fraction of Orko's problems.

I learned this lesson slowly. It was during a phase when I was trying to analogize the black experience in my own experience. Around the time of the Orko incident, I had changed my graffiti name to Jew 2 and began wearing a Star-of-David medallion. Jews had been oppressed too, hadn't we? And wasn't Israel right next to Africa? My short experiment in contrived cultural chauvinism (being a Jew was not, after all, a big part of my daily life) ended one day after gym class in the Kenwood locker room. I was on friendly, if adversarial, terms with Abnar Farrakhan (son of Minister Louis Farrakhan), one of the coolest, toughest, and most intelligent kids at Kenwood. One day Abnar started talking shit about Jews, basically to get a rise out of me. I called him nigger, basically to get a rise out of his father that night at the dinner table. We got in each other's face and he body-slammed me.

The next summer, community service programs had channeled my aggression into a more enlightened scheme. Instead of battling against black kids, I would educate them – not on math or science, you understand, but on themselves. Their music, their history, their politics, their culture, and their problems, which always fell into three conveniently demonizable categories: racists, sell-outs, and suckers – none of which included me. Like the black who assimilates into the white world, my mission was to blend in and defy the stereotypes of my race. The only difference was, where white culture was built on black people's backs, black culture was built on white people's scraps. I was the president of General Electric mailing his $35 pledge to Greenpeace.

Hadn't I Just Been a Special White Boy?

All the while, I was so preoccupied, as all explorers are, with my own experiences, that it took a long time to notice some basic insights about how black people see the world. Not that they think as a group, but there are patterns.

I was going deeper into the ghetto, later at night, for longer periods of time, and more and more frequently, alone. How was I able to do this when in integrated Hyde Park, my own neighborhood, the blacks were already so hostile? Weren't the blacks in my neighborhood just the tip of the iceberg? Weren't blacks in the ghetto far more angry and violent toward whites, just as the whites who lived in all-white neighborhoods would terrorize any black family who tried to move in? Hadn't I just been lucky – a *special* white boy?

For the first few years I thought so. But after a couple of times getting into fights with black dudes in Hyde Park, and the lack of static I encountered in the ghetto, I began to wonder. The only time anyone had ever fucked with me in the ghetto I was waiting for a bus at the 55th/Garfield El station where a lot of whites catch the bus into Hyde Park. It took a long time to occur to me that these guys had fucked with me not because I was in the ghetto, but because it seemed to them that I, like all the other white people who wait at that bus stop, was trying to get away from the ghetto. The whites who do stick around are the poverty pimps – police, landlords, school teachers, and social workers – and only until they pick up their checks.

Where once I found black behavior offensive, I finally began to see that it was in fact *defensive*. This insight was corroborated from another angle when I went to hear Abnar's dad, Minister Louis Farrakhan, give a public speech at the Nation of Islam National Center on 73rd and Stony Island. From a crowd of maybe 20,000, not more than five to ten whites. While the people sitting next to me cheered furiously when Farrakhan spoke against the white man, more than one of them – the very same people – made it a point to be friendly to me, shake my hand, and call me "brother". And because I had to leave before the end, the FOI security guard who escorted me to the door put his arm around me and asked me how I liked the speech.

The reason for the apparent paradox was clear. Even the most militant blacks don't hate whites individually just because we're white. They have a double consciousness. They believe, as Farrakhan says, that white folks should be regarded with the same suspicion as snakes: not all of them are bad, but you don't want to go around picking up snakes to try to find a good one. So when someone makes anti-white generalizations, black people know to interpret it correctly as overstatement, the overstatement of someone who is tired of biking into the wind. White people, however, take the rhetoric literally. It becomes their excuse for not bothering to become one of the whites who militant blacks don't hate. For his part, Farrakhan is a moderating force in American race relations. A lot of people are ready to hear something far more extremist than what he's actually saying. He doesn't abuse the demagogue role. We ought to thank our lucky stars he isn't calling for an all-out race war Long Island Rail Road style.

In general, black aggression toward whites is not so much about hating whitey as it is a reaction and an attempt to overcome the humiliation we continue to heap on them. As with any relationship, people need to be met on their own turf, understood on their own terms, and respected for who they are and what they have to offer. To be black is to feel used, unappreciated, condescended to, to be told you are ugly, stupid, abnormal, inferior, violent. This result is accomplished just as effectively by ignoring, avoiding, or patronizing, someone – or someone's entire area of the city – as it is through active mistreatment. This is as true in the relationships between the races as it is in the relationship between two people

Simply because I went alone to hear Minister Farrakhan, because it was in a black neighborhood, because I took the bus, listened carefully, and clapped when I agreed with him (sometimes even when no one else was clapping – okay, I admit that was kind of rude), it seemed to make the people sitting around me think I was pretty okay. Had I gone to see Farrakhan as part of a group, or waited until he was speaking downtown or on a college campus, or had I gone much further in displaying my disagreement with some of what he said, no doubt I would have been received differently.

Yet these are the very circumstances in which most whites encounter anti-white sentiment: not in a black neighborhood, not by themselves, and not with a basic respect for the speaker. It is this invisible sense of turf, along with the wind at our backs, that so few whites perceive the importance of in race relations. This is why so much anti-white sentiment in America is held, not by slum dwellers, but by successful blacks, educated and living among white people.

But anyone who thinks there is some kind of secret formula to manipulate and get accepted by blacks is sure to be disappointed. Black people will see through you and, more than likely, they'll snicker about you later, or call your bluff outright if they're feeling courageous – oftentimes, even where you are most convinced of your own sincerity. Earning the trust of a wide range of blacks – not just the friendly and servile ones – means turning your world upside down. And that's on top of taking risks, having good intentions, commitment, a sincere interest, and an open mind. It's a weeding out process that few of us understand, much less get very far with. Perhaps it is comparable, in a small way, to the initiation process of blacks into white society.

The most common way whites seek to become initiated – by having black friends or a black-oriented talent – are by themselves flimsy. When asked why he didn't venture into Harlem, an aspiring white rapper from lower Manhattan said he was going to wait until "I get famous and people know who I am, then it'll be cool." Whites who don't need costumes or gimmicks or hip-hop to hang out with blacks, do so because they put black people at ease, not by some superficial trick, but because our basic respect for and familiarity with their culture shines through in all the subtle ways that you can only understand from experience. Learning about black culture at a distance (through music and books) may be even worse than not learning about it at all. Most of the time, we use our knowledge of blacks and their culture as we have always used it, to manipulate them, rather than to repair our own sick habits.

Just because I have gone further than most whites does not mean I belong to some special category, deserving to be judged as anything other than the white boy I am. I was, after all, born biking with my back to the wind. If after eleven years, I decide to swing a U and retrace my path going into the wind for awhile just to see what it's like, it does little to even my personal score. For a long time I denied this, creating an intricate mythology about just how down I was. If you've been reading carefully, you've noticed that I still have that impulse.

But at least now I think I've pretty much come to terms with what my place is. Rather than posturing about the pros and cons of affirmative action as a government policy, I make it my personal policy. Rather than waving signs, "fighting racism" and attacking "sell-outs," I merely spend money in black-owned businesses and work for real-life causes such as the careers of my black friends. I no longer need to dress as a b-boy. Unlike two of my close white friends, I have not become a rapper. Rather than writing as though I myself am black, I work collaboratively with black writers. It took a long time for me to begin to comprehend what Tarek Thorns, my classmate at Oberlin College, refers to as not stepping in people's "cultural space."

American white boys like me have our own space. It's a pretty nice space too. We live somewhere that books like this are available, people have the training to comprehend them, the excess mental energy to think about them, and the luxury to act on them. Keeping in mind that the average earthling survives on less than $2000 per year, I consider myself pretty lucky. Unhampered by bad health, perilous psychological hang-ups, immediate violence, money hardships, etc. I am able, more so than 99 percent of the world's people, to do what I want to in life.

This happy circumstance for me is neither something to feel guilty about, nor to take for granted. It is a rare something that has happened to me, in an important sense, because of the misfortune of others, and relies on my continuing ability to exploit my advantage over them. That is the reason why I am getting paid to write about hip-hop, while the people who taught me about hip-hop are in jail, dead, or strugglin, scramblin 'n' gamblin. This is neither something to fight, nor to gloat, nor to sit back and be thankful over. It is merely a moral debt. There are many moral debts in the world, and one of mine belongs to black America, with some individuals bigger creditors than others. This is not a burden, something to get all martyred out about, and it is not a joke. It is merely an opinion. If I never repay black America in my lifetime, I will have gone unpunished for a permanent theft.

So what is the proper place of whites? I've been toying with this question for more than a decade now, yet I am still so far from being a model white person (as far as I'm concerned, even if such a description is proper, I've yet to meet one who can fill it). I still have a lot more to learn from blacks. I still have irrational fears of them. I still slip into degrading white ways of seeing (one of the worst of these is when I don't expect enough of them). My speech and attitude still slip into caricature and invasions of their cultural space. (They'll be happier to share their culture with us when we begin sharing our spoils, instead of always trying to take, then denying we have taken, what's theirs.) By learning more from them than I give back, I am still accruing a deficit every year on top of the towering debt I already owe.

Like the black trying to make it in white America, we face a Catch-22: We cannot help blacks without undercutting their self-determination; we cannot be cool without encroaching on their cultural space; we cannot take risks without exercising our privilege to take risks; we cannot integrate without invading; we cannot communicate on black terms without patronizing.

Faced with these choices, we need not become paralyzed. Instead we may follow the example of blacks who cross-over in the opposite direction: develop a double consciousness. We must take the risks necessary to do right, yet we must remain sober in recognizing that, unlike blacks trying to make it in white America, our struggle is not the center of importance.

Someone like me takes race so seriously, some have wondered, how can I proceed through life without becoming paralyzed by a million depressing moral dilemmas?

In a land that James Baldwin once described as "dedicated to the death of the paradox," we remain at war with life's indivisible contradictions, unappreciative of their richness. "I'm confused about what your point of view is," an editor of mine once said. "I can't tell from reading this whether you are a hip-hopper or a racist, an insider in black society, or some kind of outside sociologist. Do you like black people or do you hate them?" My answer is that I'm human, meaning that I'm complex enough to be all of these things at once.

If only black people could get away with that.

In this article written with his mother, Allan Bérubé describes growing up as gay "trailer trash": the attitudes of others and the joys and pains of this particular racial, class, and sexual location.

Focus questions:
1 What is Bérubé's notion of the relations between race, class, and sexuality in a 1950s trailer park?
2 What are Bérubé's reservations about making his background seem "hip" and his practice of collecting trailer-related knickknacks? Why does he enjoy that so much?

---

30 Sunset Trailer Park

Allan Bérubé with Florence Bérubé

"I cried," my mother tells me, "when we first drove into that trailer park and I saw where we were going to live." Recently, in long-distance phone calls, my mother – Florence Bérubé – and I have been digging up memories, piecing together our own personal and family histories. Trailer parks come up a lot.

During the year when I was born – 1946 – the booming, postwar "trailer coach" industry actively promoted house traders in magazine ads like this one from the *Saturday Evening Post*:

TRAILER COACHES RELIEVE SMALL-HOME SHORTAGE THROUGHOUT THE HOUSE-HUNGRY NATION

Reports from towns and cities all over the United States show that modern, comfortable trailer coaches – economical and efficient beyond even the dreams of a few years ago – are playing a major part in easing the need for small-family dwellings. Returning veterans (as students or workers), newlyweds, and all others who are not ready for – or can't locate – permanent housing, find in the modern trailer coach a completely furnished (and amazingly comfortable) home that offers the privacy and efficiency of an apartment coupled with the mobility of an automobile.

When I was seven, my parents, with two young children in tow, moved us all into a house trailer, hoping to find the comfort, privacy, and efficiency that the "trailer coach" industry had promised. But real life, as we soon discovered, did not imitate the worlds we learned to desire from magazine ads.

Dad discovered "Sunset Trailer Park" on his own and rented a space for us there before Mom was able to see it. On our moving day in January 1954, we all climbed into our '48 Chevy and followed a rented truck as it slowly pulled our house trailer from the "Sunnyside Trailer Park" in Shelton, Connecticut, where we lived for a few months, into New York State and across Manhattan, over the George Washington Bridge into New Jersey, through the garbage incinerator landscape and stinky air of Secaucus – not a good sign – then finally into the Sunset Trailer Park in Bayonne.

A blue-collar town surrounded by Jersey City, Elizabeth and Staten Island, Bayonne was known for its oil refineries, tanker piers and Navy yard. It was a small, stable, predominantly Catholic city of working-class and military families, mostly white with a small population of African Americans. When we moved there, Bayonne was already the butt of jokes about "armpits" of the industrial Northeast. Even the characters on the TV sitcom *The Honeymooners*, living in their blue-collar world in Brooklyn, could get an easy laugh by referring to Bayonne. "Ralph," Alice Kramden says to her husband in one episode, "you losing a pound is like Bayonne losing a mosquito." My mom was from Brooklyn, too. A Bayonne trailer park was not where she wanted to live or raise her children.

Along with so many other white working-class families living in fifties trailer parks, my parents believed that they were just passing through. They were headed toward a *Better Homes and Gardens* suburban world that would be theirs if they worked hard enough. We moved to Bayonne to be closer to Manhattan, where Dad was employed as a cameraman for NBC. He and his fellow TV crewmen enjoyed the security of unionized, wage-labor jobs in this newly expanding media industry. But they didn't get the income that people imagined went with the status of TV jobs. Dad had to work overtime nights and on weekends to make ends meet. His dream was to own his own house and start his own business, then put us kids through school so we would be better off and not have to struggle so much to get by. My parents were using the cheapness of trailer park life as a stepping-stone toward making that dream real.

As Dad's job and commuting took over his life, the trailer park took over ours. We lived in our trailer from the summer of 1953 through December 1957, most of my grade school years. And so I grew up a trailer park kid.

Sunset Trailer Park seemed to be on the edge of everything. Bayonne itself is a kind of land's end. It's a peninsula that ends at New York Bay, Kill Van Kull and Newark Bay – polluted bodies of water that all drain into the Atlantic Ocean. You reached our trailer park by going west to the very end of 24th Street, then past the last house into a driveway where the trailer lots began. If you followed the driveway to its end, you'd stop right at the waterfront. The last trailer lots were built on top of a seawall secured by pilings. Standing there and looking out over Newark Bay, you'd see tugboats hauling barges over the oil-slicked water, oil tankers and freighters carrying their cargoes, and planes (no jets yet) flying in and out of Newark Airport. On hot summer nights the steady din of planes, boats, trucks and freight trains filled the air. So did the fumes they exhaled, which, when mixed with the incinerator smoke and oil refinery gasses, formed a foul atmospheric concoction that became world-famous for its unforgettable stench.

The ground at the seawall could barely be called solid earth. The owner of the trailer park occasionally bought an old barge, then hired a tugboat to haul it right up to the park's outer edge, sank it with dump-truck loads of landfill, paved it over with asphalt, painted white lines on it and voila! – several new trailer lots were available for rent. Sometimes the ground beneath these new lots would sink, so the trailers would have to be moved away until the sinkholes were filled in. Trailers parked on lots built over rotten barges along the waterfront – this was life on a geographic edge.

It was life on a social edge, too – a borderland where respectable and "trashy" got confused.

"Did you ever experience other people looking down on us because we lived in a trailer park?" I ask my mom.

"Never," she tells me.

"But who were your friends?"

"They all lived in the trailer park."

"What about the neighbors who lived in houses up the street?"

"Oh, they didn't like us at all," she says. "They thought people who lived in trailers were all low-life and trash. They didn't really associate with us."

In the 1950s, trailer parks were crossroads where the paths of poor, working-class and lower-middle-class white migrants intersected as we temporarily occupied the same racially segregated space – a kind of residential parking lot – on our way somewhere else. Class tensions – often hidden – structured our daily lives as we tried to position ourselves as far as we could from the bottom. White working-class families who owned or lived in houses could raise their own class standing within whiteness by showing how they were better off than the white residents of trailer parks. We often responded to them by displaying our own respectability and distancing ourselves from those trailer park residents who were more "lower-class" than we were. If we failed and fell to the bottom, we were in danger of also losing, in the eyes of other white people, our own claims to the racial privileges that came with being accepted as white Americans.

In our attempt to scramble "up" into the middle class, we had at our disposal two conflicting stereotypes of trailer park life that in the 1950s circulated through popular culture. The respectable stereotype portrayed residents of house trailers as white World War II veterans, many of them attending college on GI loans, who lived with their young families near campuses during the postwar housing shortage. In the following decades, this image expanded to include the predominantly white retirement communities located in Florida and the Southwest. In these places, trailers were renamed "mobile" or "manufactured" homes. When parked together, they formed private worlds where white newlyweds, nuclear families and retirees lived in clean, safe, managed communities. You can catch a glimpse of this world in the 1954 Hollywood film *The Long, Long Trailer*, in which Lucille Ball and Desi Arnaz spend their slapstick honeymoon hauling a house trailer cross country and end up in a respectable trailer park. (The fact that Arnaz is Cuban American doesn't seriously disrupt the whiteness of their Technicolor world – he's assimilated as a generically "Spanish" entertainer, an ethnic individual who has no connection with his Cuban American family or community).

A conflicting stereotype portrayed trailer parks as trashy slums for white transients – single men drifting from job to job, mothers on welfare, children with no adult supervision. Their inhabitants supposedly engaged in prostitution and extramarital sex, drank a lot, used drugs, and were the perpetrators or victims of domestic violence. With this image in mind, cities and suburbs passed zoning laws restricting trailer parks to the "other side of the tracks" or banned them altogether. In the fifties, you could see this "white trash" image in B-movies and on the covers of pulp magazines and paperback books. The front cover of one "trash" paperback, "Trailer Park Woman," proclaims that it's "A bold, savage novel of life and love in the trailer camps on the edge of town." The back cover, subtitled "Temptation Wheels," explains why trailers are the theme of this book.

> Today nearly one couple in ten lives in a mobile home – one of those trailers you see bunched up in cozy camps near every sizable town. Some critics argue that in such surroundings love tends to become casual. Feverish affairs take place virtually right out in the open. Social codes take strange and shocking twists . . . "Trailer Tramp" was what they called Ann Mitchell – for she symbolized the twisted morality of the trailer camps . . . this book shocks not by its portrayal of her degradation – rather, by boldly bringing to light the conditions typical of trailer life.

This image has been kept alive as parody in John Waters' independent films, as reality in Hollywood films such as *Lethal Weapon*, *The Client* and *My Own*

Private Idaho, and as retro-fifties camp in contemporary postcards, posters, T-shirts and refrigerator magnets.

I imagine that some fifties trailer parks did fit this trashy stereotype. But Sunset Trailer Park in Bayonne was respectable – at least to those of us who lived there. Within that respectability, however, we had our own social hierarchy. Even today, trying to position ourselves into it is difficult. "You can't say we were rich," as my mom tries to explain, "but you can't say we were at the bottom, either." What confused things even more were the many standards by which our ranking could be measured – trailer size and model, lot size and location, how you kept up your yard, type of car, jobs and occupations, income, number of kids, whether mothers worked as homemakers or outside the home for wages. Establishing where you were on the trailer park's social ladder depended on where you were standing and which direction you were looking at any given time.

To some outsiders, our trailer park did seem low-class. Our neighbors up the street looked down on us because they lived in two- or three-family houses with yards in front and back. Our trailers were small, as were our lots, some right on the stinky bay. The people in houses were stable; we were transients. And they used to complain that we didn't pay property taxes on our trailers, but still sent our kids to their public schools.

On our side, we identified as "homeowners" too (if you ignored the fact that we rented our lots) while some people up the street were renters. We did pay taxes, if only through our rent checks. And we shared with them our assumed privileges of whiteness – theirs mostly Italian, Irish, and Polish Catholic, ours a more varied mix that included Protestants. The trailer park owner didn't rent to black families, so we were granted the additional status of having our whiteness protected on his private property.

The owner did rent to one Chinese American family, the Wongs (not their real name), who ran a Chinese restaurant. Like Desi Arnaz, the presence of only one Chinese family didn't seriously disrupt the dominant whiteness of our trailer park. They became our close friends as we discovered that we were almost parallel families – both had the same number of children and Mrs Wong and my mother shared the same first name. But there were significant differences. Mom tells me that the Wongs had no trouble as Asian Americans in the trailer park, only when they went out to buy a house. "You don't realize how discriminatory they are in this area," Mrs Wong told my mother one day over tea. "The real estate agents find a place for us, but the sellers back out when they see who we are." Our trailer park may have been one of the few places that accepted them in Bayonne. They fit in with us because they, unlike a poorer family might have been, were considered "respectable." With their large trailer and their own small business, they represented to my father the success he himself hoped to achieve someday.

While outsiders looked down on us as trailer park transients, we had our own internal social divisions. As residents we did share the same laundry room, recreation hall, address and sandbox. But the owner segregated us into two sections of his property: Left courtyard for families with children, right courtyard for adults, mostly newlyweds or retired couples. In the middle were a few extra spaces where tourists parked their vacation trailers overnight. Kids were not allowed to play in the adult section. It had bigger lots and was surrounded by a fence, so it had an exclusive air about it.

The family section was wilder, noisier and more crowded because every trailer had kids. It was hard to keep track of us, especially during summer vacation. Without having to draw on those who lived in the houses, we organized large group games – like Red Rover and bicycle circus shows – on the common asphalt driveway. Our activities even lured some kids away from the houses into the trailer park, tempting them to defy their parents' disdain for us.

We defended ourselves from outsiders' stereotypes of us as low-life and weird by increasing our own investment in respectability. Trashy white people lived somewhere else – probably in other trailer parks. We could criticize and look down on them, yet without them we would have been the white people on the bottom. "Respectable" meant identifying not with them, but with people just like us or better than us, especially families who owned real houses in the suburbs.

My mom still portrays our lives in Bayonne as solidly middle-class. I'm intrigued by how she constructed that identity out of a trailer park enclave confined to the polluted waterfront area of an industrial blue-collar town.

"Who were your friends?" I ask her.

"We chose them from the people we felt the most comfortable with," she explains. These were couples in which the woman was usually a homemaker and the man was an accountant, serviceman or salesman – all lower-middle-class, if categorized only by occupation. As friends, these couples hung out together in the recreation hall for birthday, Christmas and Halloween costume parties. The women visited each other every day, shared the pies and cakes they baked, went shopping together and helped each other with housework and baby-sitting.

"There was one woman up the street," my mom adds, "who we were friends with. She associated with us even though she lived in a house."

"Who didn't you feel comfortable with?" I ask her.

"Couples who did a lot of drinking. People who had messy trailers and didn't keep up their yards. People who let their babies run around barefoot in dirty diapers. But there were very few people like that in our trailer park." They were also the boys who swam in the polluted brine of Newark Bay, and the people who trapped crabs in the same waters and actually ate their catch.

When we first entered the social world of Sunset Trailer Park, our family found ways to fit in and even "move up" a little. Physical location was important. Our trailer was first parked in a middle lot. We then moved up by renting the "top space" – as it was called – when it became available. It was closest to the houses and furthest from the bay. Behind it was a vacant housing lot, which belonged to the trailer park owner and separated his park from the houses on the street – a kind of "no-man's-land." The owner gave us permission to take over a piece of this garbage dump and turn it into a garden. My dad fenced it in and my mom planted grass and flowers which we kids weeded. Every year the owner gave out prizes – usually a savings bond – for the best-looking "yards." We won the prize several times.

Yet the privilege of having this extra yard had limits. With other trailer park kids we'd stage plays and performances there for our parents – it was our make-shift, outdoor summer stock theater. But we made so much noise that we drove the woman in the house that overlooked it crazy. At first she just yelled "Shut up!" at us from her second-story window. Then she went directly to the owner, who prohibited the loudest, most unruly kids from playing with us. After a while we learned to keep our own voices down and stopped our shows so we, too, wouldn't be banned from playing in our own yard.

My mom made a little extra money – $25 a month – and gained a bit more social status by working for the owner as the manager of his trailer park. She collected rent checks from each tenant, handled complaints and made change for the milk machine, washers and dryers. "No one ever had trouble paying their rent," Mom tells me; adding more evidence to prove the respectability of our trailer park's residents.

Our family also gained some prestige because my dad "worked in TV" as a pioneer in this exciting new field. Once in a while he got tickets for our neighbors to appear as contestants on the TV game show *Truth or Consequences*, a sadistic spectacle that forced couples to perform humiliating stunts if they couldn't give correct answers to trick questions. Our neighbors joined other trailer park contestants who in the fifties appeared on game shows like *Beat the Clock*, *Name That Tune*, *You Bet Your Life* and especially *Queen for a Day*. The whole trailer park was glued to our TV set on nights when our neighbors were on. We rooted for them to win as they became celebrities right before our eyes. Even the put-down "Bayonne jokes" we heard from Groucho Marx, Ralph Kramden and other TV comics acknowledged that our town and its residents had at least some status on the nation's cultural map.

My dad wasn't the only trailer park resident who gained a little prestige from celebrity. There was a musician who played the clarinet in the NBC orchestra. There was a circus performer who claimed he was the only man in the world who could juggle nine balls at once. He put on a special show for us kids in the recreation hall to prove it. There was a former swimming champion who lived in a trailer parked near the water. Although he was recovering from pneumonia, he jumped into Newark Bay to rescue little Jimmy who'd fallen off the seawall and was drowning. He was our hero. And there was an elderly couple who shared a tiny Airstream with 24 Chihuahua dogs – the kind pictured in comic books as small enough to fit in a teacup. This couple probably broke the world's record for the largest number of dogs ever to live in a house trailer. You could hear their dogs yip hysterically whenever you walked by.

Trailer park Chihuahua dog collectors, game show contestants, circus performers – low-life and weird, perhaps, to outsiders, but to us, these were our heroes and celebrities. What's more, people from all over the United States ended up in our trailer park. "They were well traveled and wise," my mom explains with pride, "and they shared with us the great wealth of their experience." This may be why they had more tolerance for differences (within our whiteness, at least) than was usual in many white communities during the fifties – more tolerant, my mom adds, than the less-traveled people who lived in the houses.

Dangers seemed to lurk everywhere. To protect us, my parents made strict rules we kids had to obey. They prohibited us from playing in the sandbox because stray cats used it as their litter box. We weren't allowed to walk on the seawall or swim in Newark Bay, in which little Jimmy had nearly drowned, and whose water, if we swallowed it, would surely have poisoned us. And they never let us go on our own into anyone else's trailer – or house – or bring any kids into ours.

"Why did you make that rule?" I ask my mom after wondering about it for years.

"Because there were lots of working couples," she explains, "who had to leave their kids home alone with no adult supervision. We didn't want you to get into trouble by yourselves."

But I did break this rule. Once the Chihuahua-dog couple invited me inside their Airstream to read the Sunday comics with them. I went in. But I was so terrified by the non-stop, high-pitched barking, the powerful stench and my own act of disobedience that I couldn't wait to get back outside.

At other times I visited schoolmates in their homes after school. One was a Polish kid who lived two blocks away in a slightly nicer part of town. His house made me think his family was rich. They had an upstairs with bedrooms, a separate kitchen and dining room, a living room with regular furniture, doors between rooms, a basement and a garage. I fantasized about moving into his house and sharing a bedroom with him as my brother. When I visited an Italian boy who lived in a downtown apartment, I learned that not everyone who lived in buildings was better off than we were. Their smelly entry hall had paint peeling from the cracked walls and a broken-down stairway. I was afraid to go upstairs. I visited another schoolmate who lived with his grandfather and a dog inside the Dickensian cabin of a deserted barge on the docks at Newark Bay. They heated their cabin with wood scavenged from the piers and vacant lots nearby. I felt sorry for him because he seemed like the orphans we prayed for in church who had something to do with "alms for the poor." I visited a boy who lived in another trailer park. He was an only child who was home alone when his parents were at work. I envied his privacy and dreamed about us being brothers, too. At times, I'd even go down to the seawall to watch the bad boys swim in Newark Bay.

Alone like that with other white boys in their homes or by the water, I sometimes felt erotic charges for them – affectional desires that moved up, down or across our class positions in the form of envy, pity and brotherliness. Only years later did I learn to identify and group all these feelings together as a generic "homosexual" attraction. Yet that "same-sex" reading of those erotic sparks erased how they each had been differentiated by class and unified by race during my disobedient excursions around Bayonne. Even today, a predominantly white gay identity politics still regards race and class as non-gay issues, refusing to see how they have fundamentally structured male homoerotic attractions and socially organized our homosexual relationships, particularly when they're same-class and white-on-white.

I wasn't the only person around who was a little queer.

"Did I ever tell you about the lesbian couple who lived in the trailer park?" my mom asks me.

"No, Ma, you never did."

I'm stunned that after all these years, she's just now telling her gay historian son about this fabulous piece of fifties trailer-park dyke history coming right out of the pages of her own life!

"They were the nicest people," she goes on. "Grade school teachers. One taught phys ed, the other taught English. Military veterans. They lived in a trailer bigger than ours over in the adult section. I forget their names, but one dressed like a woman and the other dressed like a man. The woman who dressed like a woman had a green thumb. She kept her trailer filled with house plants and took good care of them. She did all the housekeeping – the inside work. The woman who dressed like a man did the outside work – waxed the trailer, repaired their truck. In their yard she built a beautiful patio with a rose arbor and a barbecue – did all the cement work herself. They threw barbecue parties there in the summer – with finger food, hamburgers and wine, They were lots of fun."

I'm as intrigued by Mom's description of a "woman dressed like a woman" as I am by her description of a "woman dressed like a man." The logic of seeing the butch partner acting like the man led to Mom seeing the femme partner acting like the woman, rather than just being a woman. Yet this female couple created a domestic relationship that was familiar enough for my parents and their friends to accept as normal. And like the Wongs, their class respectability – in the form of good jobs, large trailer and well kept yard – seemed to make up for differences that in other neighborhoods might have set them apart.

"Did you know then that they were lesbians?"

"Oh yeah," Mom says. "We never talked about it or used that word, but we all knew. They were a couple. Everybody liked them. Nicest people you'd ever want to meet!" The protection of not having their relationship named as deviant allowed these women to fit into our trailer park world.

It was another woman from the adult section who helped nurture my own incipient queerness. On one of the rare nights when my parents splurged by going to the movies, this woman baby-sat for us. An expert seamstress, she spent her time with us sewing outfits for my sister's Ginny Doll. I was jealous. "Boys can have dolls, too," she reassured me. Sitting on our sofa with me right next to her eagerly watching her every move, she pieced together a stuffed boy-doll for me (this was years before Ken or GI Joe appeared), then sewed him little pants and a shirt. When my parents saw this present, they let me keep him. For a while I cherished this peculiar toy – a hand-made gift that acknowledged my own uniqueness. But before long, "unique" evolved into "weird" and even "queer." My boy-doll embarrassed me so much that I threw him away.

My parents' protective rules were based on an important truth. Whenever I went into other peoples' houses and trailers, or when they came into ours, I *did* find myself getting into trouble – queer trouble, too.

As the distance from the trailer park grew in years, miles and class, I began to manipulate my memory of that world so that it carried less shame. In college I met other scholarship students who adapted to our new middle-class surroundings by working their lower-class origins into cool, competitive, "class escape" stories in which they bragged about how far they'd come. I joined in, "coming out" about my trailer park past. Having grown up in Bayonne made my stories – and my ascent – even more dramatic.

By the nineties, a pop culture, retro-fifties nostalgia resurrected and then commodified the artifacts of trailer park life, reworking their meanings into a campy "trash" style. So I unearthed my own trailer park past once again, this time learning how to take an ironic, parodic, "scare quotes" stance toward it, even using it at times as a kind of white trash cultural – and sexual – currency. I now collect old paperback books, souvenirs and magazine ads having to do with fifties trailer parks. I love the stuff. And I'm glad that the current fascination with white trash icons, like house trailers, has opened up a public discourse big enough to include my own queer, working-class, trailer park voice. Today I can use that voice – and its identity – to challenge the class-based stereotypes that hurt real people. And I can enjoy the pleasures of campy nostalgia along with the pleasures of cross-class sex experienced from many sides. Now that there's a new "rock 'n roll fag bar" in San Francisco called "White Trash," I get to wonder what I'd wear, who I'd want to be and who I'd want to pick up if I went there.

But sometimes it's hard for me to distinguish the camp from the painful realities around which it dances. Ironic distancing has served me as a lens through which I've been able to re-view my trailer park past with less shame. But it has so distorted my vision that I misremember the "reality" of that part of my life. I've caught myself actually believing that we and our neighbors all had fabulous plastic pink flamingoes in our yards. I am sure – and so is my mom – that none of us ever did.

Lately I've searched flea markets for a plastic house trailer just like the one I had as a child. Today it would be a valuable collector's item, and my desire to find it is partly as a collector. But I also want to see it again because it once pointed this working-class boy's way out of being embarrassed about how his family lived, showing him that their trailerpark life was respectable enough to be made into a mass-produced toy.

Recently, at a gay gift shop on Castro Street in San Francisco, I bought a T-shirt that says "Cheap Trailer Trash" over a picture of a fifties trailer that's identical to the one I grew up in – except, of course. it has a pink flamingo. I now can be both cool and authentic when I wear this shirt. When people say, "I like your shirt," I get to say, "Thanks. And it's true, too." When some start telling me their own stories of growing up in trailer parks, I can feel us bond around this weird nineties identity that's built on shared – if distorted – memories rather than on current realities. Sometimes we slip into playing the old class-positioning game. "What kind of trailer did you live in? How wide and how long? How big was your family? Did you own or rent your lot? Did you call it a mobile home? How long did you live there? What kind of trailer park was it? What part of town was it in?" In an inverted form of social climbing, the player with the trashiest past gets to be the winner of this game. We can do this because the distance from our former lives gives us room to play with old degradations as contemporary chic. But back then, actually living inside a trailer park, those who won the game were the ones who got out for good. Nowadays, trailer park folks still try to get out by playing games – not as TV game show contestants, like our neighbors in the fifties who made fools of themselves for prizes, but as "guests" on so called "trash" talk shows, like Geraldo, Richard Bey and Jenny Jones, who "win" celebrity – but no prizes – if they can act out the real dramas of their lives as trashy stereotypes, reassuring viewers that it's someone else who's really on the bottom.

The whole country looks more like a trailer park every day. As our lived economy gets worse, more jobs are becoming temporary, homes less permanent or more crowded, neighborhoods unstable. We're transients just passing through this place, wherever and whatever it is, on our way somewhere else, mostly down.

"I get really scared sometimes," my mom tells me, "that the old days are coming back." She means the Great Depression days she knew in her childhood, and the trailer park days I knew in mine.

I get scared, too. Without any academic degrees, and with the middle dropping out of the book publishing world as it's dropping out of everything else, I find it increasingly difficult to survive as a writer. As I approach 50, I see how closely my economic life history resembles that of my parents as I'm pushed around the edges of lower-middle-class, working-class and "new Bohemian" worlds. Lately, I've been having a perverse fantasy that if times get too tough, I can always retire to a trailer park, maybe in Bayonne.

A few years ago, I actually went back to visit Bayonne, which I hadn't seen since 1957. I wanted to check my distorted fantasies against a tangible reality, to go back "home" to this source of memories that I mine for insights as I try to understand and fight the race and class divisions that are still tearing our nation apart. I asked my friend Bert Hansen to go with me for support because he also grew up white, gay and working-class. I didn't wear my "Trailer Park Trash" T-shirt that day. We took the Path Train from Christopher Street in Greenwich Village over to Jersey City, rented a car and drove out to Bayonne.

To my surprise the trailer park was still there, along with every house, store, bar and restaurant that used to be on our block, all still run by the same families. This was a remarkable testament to the death-defying – and too-often life-threatening – stability of this blue-collar town, despite the enormous social and economic odds working against it.

With my camera in hand, I walked into the trailer park and around both courtyards, taking pictures of the same lots we'd lived in four decades ago. The place was run down now, many lots were empty and littered with car parts and old boards, almost no one was around. A man washing his car in front of his house up the street told me that the trailer park had just been sold to a condo developer. People who worked in Manhattan, he said, would be moving in because it would be cheaper and convenient for commuting. Up the street Roosevelt Grade School and the Police Athletic League buildings were still standing but closed. Slated for demolition, the school was surrounded by chain-link fence and barbed wire until a new one could be built.

When I walked around the trailer park one last time to take my final pictures, two white boys on bicycles suddenly appeared from around a corner. They followed us, keeping their distance, wary and unfriendly, as if protecting their territory from intruders. Watching them watching me, I realized that the distant memory of my boyhood in this trailer park, which was coming alive as I stood there, was now their hard reality. At first glance they seemed really poor. As a kid who never felt poor, did I sometimes look like they do to outsiders? Surely these boys were much worse off than I had been. They seemed hostile, but why should they be friendly towards me – a total stranger taking pictures of their trailers? I could be there to steal their possessions, or to expose their poverty to outsiders, or to design the condos that would replace their house trailers, forcing them to move against their will. Or I might be a graduate student earning an academic degree, wanting to use them as working-class subjects, like the grad student who came here so long ago to give me and my sister intelligence tests, for free, then disrupting our lives by telling us that our high scores might offer us a way out.

I can still see these two boys looking at me as if I am some kind of spy, which indeed I am. I don't belong here any more. Their days belonging here are nearly over, too.

In this passage from his book *Culture of Complaint*, the art critic Robert Hughes attacks the language police of political correctness for debasing meaning. Implicitly, he also attacks the "identity politics" represented by many of the selections in this book, which he believes fragments America.

Focus questions:
1 Why does Hughes use the term "euphemism"? Why does he believe that replacing a word like "crippled" with a phrase like "differently abled" is a useless exercise?
2 Hughes suggests that few serious problems arise from using supposedly sexist bits of language, such as the word "mankind" to mean all persons regardless of gender. Is he right about that?

---

31   Culture of Complaint

Robert Hughes

There are certainly worse things in American society than the ongoing vogue for politically correct language, whether of the left or of the right. But there are few things more absurd and, in the end, self-defeating.

We want to create a sort of linguistic Lourdes, where evil and misfortune are dispelled by a dip in the waters of euphemism. Does the cripple rise from his wheelchair, or feel better about being stuck in it, because someone back in the days of the Carter administration decided that, for official purposes, he was "physically challenged"? Does the homosexual suppose others love him more or hate him less because he is called a "gay" – that term revived from 18th-century English criminal slang, which implied prostitution and living on one's wits? The net gain is that thugs who used to go faggot-bashing now go gay-bashing.

Or take "homophobic," a favorite scatter-word of PC abuse. Today, out of twenty people who use it, scarcely one knows what it means. "Homophobia" is a clinical term for a pathological disorder. It means an obsession with homo-sexuality, caused by the heavily suppressed fear that one may be homosexual oneself. Today it can be, and is, indiscriminately applied to anyone who shows the slightest reserve about this or that same-sexer, or disputes (however mildly) any claims of special entitlement (however extreme) made for them as a group or class. In the 1980s one heard American writers accused of "anti-Semitism" if they were Gentiles, or "self-hatred" if they were Jews, because they didn't toe the extremist political line of the Likud party in Israel and its lobbyists in Wash-ington. In stress, angry people who don't have enough language (or whose language is merely the servant of an agenda) reach for the most emotive word they can find: "racist" being today's quintessential example, a word which, like "fascist," raises so many levels of indistinct denunciation that it has lost what-ever stable meaning it once had. You can be a "racist" for having crackpot theories of superiority based on the lack of melanin in human skin; or for saying the simple truth that the Rev. Al Sharpton hoaxed New York with the entirely concocted abuse of the black teenager Tawana Brawley by imaginary white goons; or for having doubts about the efficacy of welfare; or, in some minds, merely by virtue of being white.

Just as language grotesquely inflates in attack, so it timidly shrinks in appro-bation, seeking words that cannot possibly give any offence, however notional. We do not fail, we underachieve. We are not junkies, but substance abusers; not handicapped, but differently abled. And we are mealy-mouthed unto death: a corpse, the New England Journal of Medicine urged in 1988, should be re-ferred to as a "nonliving person." By extension, a fat corpse is a differently sized nonliving person.

If these affected contortions actually made people treat one another with more civility and understanding, there might be an argument for them. But they do no such thing. Seventy years ago, in polite white usage, blacks were called "colored people." Then they became "negroes." Then, "blacks." Now, "African Americans" or "persons of color" again. But for millions of white Americans, from the time of George Wallace to that of David Duke, they stayed niggers, and the shift of names has not altered the facts of racism, any more than the ritual announcement of Five-Year Plans and Great Leaps Forward turned the social disasters of Stalinism and Maoism into triumphs. The notion that you change a situation by finding a newer and nicer word for it emerges from the old American habit of euphemism, circumlocution, and desperate confusion about etiquette, produced by fear that the concrete will give offence. And it is a peculiarly American habit. The call for politically correct language, though some answer it in England, has virtually no resonance in Europe. In France, nobody has thought of renaming the Frankish king Pepin le Bref, *Pepin le Verticalement Défié*, nor do Velásquez's dwarves show any sign of becoming, for Spanish purposes, *Las gentes pequeñas*. And the chaos that would ensue if academics and bureaucrats decided to overthrow gender-specific terms, in Romance languages where every noun has a gender while, to make things worse, the word for the male genital organ is often feminine and the one for its female counterpart not uncommonly masculine (*la polla, el coño*) hardly bears thinking about.

No shifting of words is going to reduce the amount of bigotry in this or any other society. But it does increase what the military mind so lucidly calls collateral damage in a target rich environment – namely, the wounding of innocent language. Consider the lumpen-feminist assault on all words that have "man" as a prefix or suffix.

"Man-words" are supposed to be gender-specific and thus insulting to women: "mankind," for instance, implies that females aren't human. So in place of *chairman*, we get the cumbersome *chairperson* or simply *chair*, as though the luckless holder of the office had four cabriole legs and a pierced splat. Recently I was sent the Australian Government's State Manual for official publications, which forbids, among other things, such terms as *sportsmanship, workman, statesmanlike* (whose suggested synonyms are "skilful, tactful" – which may say something about the present lack of Antipodean statespersons, given that in October 1992 our Prime Minister, Paul Keating, robustly denounced the Australian Senate as "unrepresentative swill" and "a bunch of pansies"). Even *craftsmanship* is out; its mellifluous alternative is "skill application." Soon my fellow-countrymen, persuaded by American examples to look for euphemisms where no insults exist, will rewrite *Waltzing Matilda* to begin "Once a jolly swagperson camped by a billabong . . ."

But what is this fuss about "man"? Anyone who knows the history of our language knows that, in Old English and Anglo-Saxon, the suffix -*man* was gender-neutral: it had, and retains, the same meaning as "person" today, referring to all people equally. To denote gender, it had to be qualified: a male was called a *waepman*, a female *wifman*. This gender-free use of -*man* gives us forms like *chairman, fisherman, craftsman*, meaning simply a person of either sex who engages in a denoted work or profession. The ancient sexist wrong supposed to be enshrined in the word since the time of Beowulf turns out not to exist.[1] Nevertheless it affords ample opportunities for the display of pettifogging PC virtue, as in the following rebuke from one S. Scott Whitlow, an academic in the College of Communications of the University of Kentucky, to Victoria Martin, a student, who passed it along to the *American Spectator*.

Dear Victoria,
   On your recent scholarship application, members of the review committee noticed the inappropriate use of the word "chairman" . . . of course, it is especially

inappropriate to address a woman as "chairman" unless she has specifically requested such a limiting language. . . . Soon you will be entering the corporate or
media sector as you begin your career. There, too, you will find there are expectations that women not be made invisible through thoughtless use of language . . .
there are a number of books I would be happy to recommend. Please let me know
if you wish a list.

What is so grating about this tidbit is not just the sloppy English ("wish a list"),
or the bureaucratic vagueness ("entering the corporate or media sector" – this,
from someone who is meant to be teaching *communication!*) or even the conde-
scending use of a stranger's Christian name *de haut en bas* ("Dear Victoria"). It is
the anile priggishness of the Puritan marm, lips pursed, seeking nits to pick.

There are, of course, many new terms and usages that seemed picky or un-
necessary to conservatives when they appeared, but are now indispensable. What
letter-writer, grateful for the coinage "Ms," which lets one formally address
women without referring to their marital status, would willingly go back to
choosing between "Mrs" and "Miss"? There is a case to be made for "African
American," though it seems to have no marked advantages over "black" beyond its length, a quality of language many Americans mistake for dignity. Probably the term "Asian American," vague as it is, is better than "Oriental," because
it is at least decently neutral, without the cloud of disparaging imagery that still
clings to the older word: "Oriental" suggests a foreignness so extreme that it
cannot be assimilated, and raises the Fu-Manchu phantoms of 19th-century
racist fiction – treacherous cunning, clouds of opium, glittering slit eyes.
"Native American" for American Indian, or just plain Indian, sounds virtuous –
except that it carries with it the absurd implication that whites whose forebears
may have been here for three, five or even the whole thirteen generations that
have elapsed since 1776 are in some way still interlopers, not "native" to this
country. By the time whites get guilty enough to call themselves "European
Americans" it will be time to junk the whole lingo of nervous divisionism; everyone, black, yellow, red and white, can revert to being plain "Americans" again,
as well they might.

In any case, words are not deeds and mere nomenclature does not change
much. As Barbara Ehrenreich remarked,

I like being called Ms. I don't want people saying "man" when they mean me,
too. I'm willing to make an issue of these things. But I know that even when all
women are Ms., we'll still get sixty-five cents for every dollar earned by a man.
Minorities by any other name – people of color, or whatever – will still bear a huge
burden of poverty, discrimination and racial harassment. Verbal uplift is not the
revolution.[2]

Not only is it not the revolution: it has been a godsend to the right. Where
would George Will, P. J. O'Rourke, the editors of the *American Spectator* and
some of the contributors to the *New Criterion* all be without the inexhaustible
flow of PC claptrap from the academic left? Did any nominally radical move-

ment ever supply its foes with such a delicious array of targets for cheap shots?

Satire loves to fasten on manners and modes, which is what PC talk really is: political etiquette, not politics itself. When the waters of PC recede – as they presently will, leaving the predictable scum of dead words on the social beach – it will be, in part, because young people get turned off by all the carping about verbal proprieties on campus. The radical impulses of youth are generous, romantic and instinctive, and are easily chilled by an atmosphere of prim, obsessive correction. The real problem with PC isn't "post-Marxism," but post-Puritanism. Its repressive weight does not fall upon campus conservatives, who are flourishing, delighted that the PC folk give some drunken creep of a student who bellows "nigger,' and "dyke" into the campus night the opportunity to posture as a martyr to speech-repression. The students it harms are the kids who would like to find a way of setting forth their dissatisfactions with the way America has gone and is going, but now find they can't speak so freely about them in case they use the wrong word and thus set off flares of complaint and little airbursts of contempt from those on their left. In an academic world where an administrator at the University of California in Santa Cruz could campaign against phrases like "a nip in the air" and "a chink in one's armor," on the grounds that such words have expressed racial disparagement *in other contexts*, anything is possible; how about banning "fruit-tree" as disparaging to homosexuals?[3] And their dilemma is made worse on those campuses, like Stanford, which have created speech codes. These are generally not created by students, but imposed by their elders – Baby Boomer academics, members of a moralizing and sanctimonious generation both left and right. As Nat Hentoff pointed out,[4] these codes, "every one of them so overboard and vague that a student can violate a code without knowing he or she has done so," are not always imposed by student demand, for

> At most colleges, it is the administration that sets up the code. Because there have been racist or sexist or homophobic taunts, anonymous notes or graffiti, the administration feels it must do *something*. The cheapest, quickest way to demonstrate that it cares is to appear to suppress racist, sexist, homophobic speech.

Thus a student can be punished under academic law for verbal offences and breaches of etiquette which carry no penalty off-campus, under the real law of the land. This dissociation is rooted in a Utopian fantasy about the nature and role of universities: they are, or should be, Arcadias. But in practice it may impede the student's progress from protected childhood to capable adulthood, which is not an Arcadian state. As one (black, female) community college administrator from Colorado, Gwen Thomas remarked in the course of a panel discussion at Stanford,[5]

> As for providing a non-intimidating educational environment, our young people have to learn to grow up on college campuses. We have to teach them how to deal with adversarial situations. They have to learn how to survive offensive speech they find wounding and hurtful.

Notes

1 See Adam Redfield, letter to *New York Times* dated November 22, 1991.
2 Barbara Ehrenreich, in *Democratic Left*, July/Aug. 1991; repr. in Paul Berman (ed.) *Debating P.C., The Controversy over College Political Correctness on Campuses* (New York: Laureleaf, 1992), p. 336.
3 Reported by William Henry III, "Upside down in the groves of academe," *Time*, April 1, 1991.
4 Nat Hentoff, " 'Speech Codes' on the campus and problems of free speech," *Dissent*, Fall 1991, p. 546.
5 Ibid., p. 549.

[Taken from *Culture of Complaint* (New York: Warner Books, 1994).]

In this dialogue between a Hispanic woman and an Anglo woman, Lugones and Spelman ask this question: to whom is a theory responsible? They argue that a theory is responsible ultimately to the people whom it is about. Their example is feminist theory, which has too often talked about, for example, "woman's experience" without consulting different sorts of women about their experience.

Focus questions:
1 What problems does Lugones identify in traditional feminist theory for women such as herself?
2 What guidelines do Lugones and Spelman think we should follow in talking about kinds of people different from ourselves?
3 What are Lugones's and Spelman's conclusions about how to do respectful and responsible theory?

---

32   Have We got a Theory for You!

María C. Lugones and Elizabeth V. Spelman

Prologue

(In an Hispana voice)

A veces quisiera mezclar en una voz el sonido canyenge, tristón y urbano del porteñismo que llevo adentro con la cadencia apacible, serrana y llena de corage de la hispana nuevo mejicana. Contrastar y unir

> el piolín y la cuerda
> el traé y el pepéname
> el camión y la troca
> la lluvia y el llanto

Pero este querer se me va cuando veo que he confundido la solidaridad con la falta de diferencia. La solidaridad requiere el reconocer, comprender, respetar y amar lo que nos lleva a llorar en distintas cadencias. El imperialismo cultural desea lo contrario, por eso necesitamos muchas voces. Porque una sola voz nos mate a las dos.

No quiero hablar por ti sino contigo. Pero si no aprendo tus modos y tu los mios la conversación es sólo aparente. Y la apariencia se levanta como una barrera sín sentido entre las dos. Sin sentido y sin sentimiento. Por eso no me debes dejar que te dicte tu ser y no me dictes el mio. Porque entonces ya no dialogamos. El diálogo entre nosotras requiere dos voces y no una.

Tal vez un día jugaremos juntas y nos hablaremos no en una lengua universal sino que vos me hablarás mi voz y yo la tuya.

Preface

This paper is the result of our dialogue, of our thinking together about differences among women and how these differences are silenced. (Think, for example, of all the silences there are connected with the fact that this paper is in English – for that is a borrowed tongue for one of us.) In the process of our talking and writing together, we saw that the differences between us did not permit our speaking in one voice. For example, when we agreed we expressed the thought differently; there were some things that both of us thought were true but could not express as true of each of us; sometimes we could not say "we"; and sometimes one of us could not express the thought in the first person singular, and to express it in the third person would be to present an outsider's and not an insider's perspective. Thus the use of two voices is central both to the process of constructing this paper and to the substance of it. We are both the authors of this paper and not just sections of it but we write together without presupposing unity of expression or of experience. So when we speak in unison it means just that – there are two voices and not just one.

Introduction

(In the voice of a white/Anglo woman who has been teaching and writing about feminist theory)
Feminism is, among other things, a response to the fact that women either have been left out of, or included in demeaning and disfiguring ways in what has been an almost exclusively male account of the world. And so while part of what feminists want and demand for women is the right to move and to act in accordance with our own wills and not against them, another part is the desire and insistence that we give our *own* accounts of these movements and actions. For it matters to us what is said about us, who says it, and to whom it is said: having the opportunity to talk about one's life, to give an account of it, to interpret it, is integral to leading that life rather than being led through it; hence our distrust of the male monopoly over accounts of women's lives. To put the same point slightly differently, part of human life, human living, is talking about it, and we can be sure that being silenced in one's own account of one's life is a kind of amputation that signals oppression. Another reason for

not divorcing life from the telling of it or talking about it is that as humans our experiences are deeply influenced by what is said about them, by ourselves or powerful (as opposed to significant) others. Indeed, the phenomenon of internalized oppression is only possible because this is so: one experiences her life in terms of the impoverished and degrading concepts others have found it convenient to use to describe her. We can't separate lives from the accounts given of them; the articulation of our experience is part of our experience.

Sometimes feminists have made even stronger claims about the importance of speaking about our own lives and the destructiveness of others presuming to speak about us or for us. First of all, the claim has been made that on the whole men's accounts of women's lives have been at best false, a function of ignorance; and at worst malicious lies, a function of a knowledgeable desire to exploit and oppress. Since it matters to us that falsehood and lies not be told about us, we demand, of those who have been responsible for those falsehoods and lies, or those who continue to transmit them, not just that we speak but that they learn to be able to hear us. It has also been claimed that talking about one's life, telling one's story, in the company of those doing the same (as in consciousness-raising sessions), is constitutive of feminist method.[1]

And so the demand that the woman's voice be heard and attended to has been made for a variety of reasons: not just so as to greatly increase the chances that true accounts of women's lives will be given, but also because the articulation of experience (in myriad ways) is among the hallmarks of a self-determining individual or community. There are not just epistemological, but moral and political reasons for demanding that the woman's voice be heard, after centuries of androcentric din.

But what more exactly is the feminist demand that the woman's voice be heard? There are several crucial notes to make about it. First of all, the demand grows out of a complaint, and in order to understand the scope and focus of the demand we have to look at the scope and focus of the complaint. The complaint does not specify *which* women have been silenced, and in one way this is appropriate to the conditions it is a complaint about: virtually no women have had a voice, whatever their race, class, ethnicity, religion, sexual alliance, whatever place and period in history they lived. And if it is as women that women have been silenced, then of course the demand must be that women as women have a voice. But in another way the complaint is very misleading, insofar as it suggests that it is women as women who have been silenced, and that whether a woman is rich or poor, black, brown or white, etc. is irrelevant to what it means for her to be a woman. For the demand thus simply made ignores at least two related points: (1) it is only possible for a woman who does not feel highly vulnerable with respect to other parts of her identity, e.g. race, class, ethnicity, religion, sexual alliance, etc., to conceive of her voice simply or essentially as a "woman's voice"; (2) just because not all women are equally vulnerable with respect to race, class, etc., some women's voices are more likely to be heard than others by those who have heretofore been giving – or silencing – the accounts of women's lives. For all these reasons, the women's voices most likely to come forth and the women's voices most likely to be heard are, in the US anyway, those of white, middle-class, heterosexual Christian (or anyway not self identified non-Christian) women. Indeed, many Hispanas, black women, Jewish women – to name a few groups – have felt it an invitation to silence rather than speech to be requested – if they are requested at all – to speak about being "women" (with the plain wrapper – as if there were one) in distinction from speaking about being Hispana, black, Jewish, working-class, etc., women.

The demand that the "woman's voice" be heard, and the search for the "woman's voice" as central to feminist methodology, reflects nascent feminist theory. It reflects nascent empirical theory insofar as it presupposes that the silencing of women is systematic, shows up in regular, patterned ways, and that there are discoverable causes of this widespread observable phenomenon; the demand reflects nascent political theory insofar as it presupposes that the silencing of women reveals a systematic pattern of power and authority; and it reflects nascent moral theory insofar as it presupposes that the silencing is unjust and that there are particular ways of remedying this injustice. Indeed, whatever else we know feminism to include – e.g. concrete direct political action – theorizing is integral to it: theories about the nature of oppression, the causes of it, the relation of the oppression of women to other forms of oppression. And certainly the concept of the woman's voice is itself a theoretical concept, in the sense that it presupposes a theory according to which our identities as human beings are actually compound identities, a kind of fusion or confusion of our otherwise separate identities as women or men, as black or brown or white, etc. That is no less a theoretical stance than Plato's division of the person into soul and body or Aristotle's parcelling of the soul into various functions.

The demand that the "'woman's voice" be heard also invites some further directions in the exploration of women's lives and discourages or excludes others. For reasons mentioned above, systematic, sustained reflection on being a woman – the kind of contemplation that "doing theory" requires – is most likely to he done by women who *vis-à-vis* other women enjoy a certain amount of political, social and economic privilege because of their skin color, class membership, ethnic identity. There is a relationship between the content of our contemplation and the fact that we have the time to engage in it at some length – otherwise we shall have to say that it is a mere accident of history that white middle-class women in the United States have in the main developed "feminist theory" (as opposed to "black feminist theory," "Chicana feminist theory," etc.) and that so much of the theory has failed to be relevant to the lives of women who are not white or middle class. Feminist theory – of all kinds – is to be based on, or anyway touch base with, the variety of real life stories women provide about themselves. But in fact, because, among other things, of the structural political and social and economic inequalities among women, the tail has been wagging the dog: feminist theory has not for the most part arisen out of a medley of women's voices; instead, the theory has arisen out of the voices, the experiences, of a fairly small handful of women, and if other women's voices do not sing in harmony with the theory, they aren't counted as women's voice – rather, they are the voices of the woman as Hispana, black, Jew, etc. There is another sense in which the tail is wagging the dog, too: it is presumed to be the case that those who do the theory know more about those who are theorized than vice versa: hence it ought to be the case that if it is white/Anglo women who write for and about all other women, then white/Anglo women must know more about all other women than other women know about them. But in fact just in order to survive, brown and black women have to know a lot more about white/Anglo women – not through the sustained contemplation theory requires, but through the sharp observation stark exigency demands.

(In an Hispana voice)

I think it necessary to explain why in so many cases when women of color appear in front of white/Anglo women to talk about feminism and women of color, we mainly raise a complaint: the complaint of exclusion, of silencing, of being included in a universe we have not chosen. We usually raise the complaint with a certain amount of disguised or undisguised anger. I can only attempt to explain this phenomenon from a Hispanic viewpoint and a fairly narrow one at that: the viewpoint of an Argentinian woman who has lived in the US for sixteen years, who has attempted to come to terms with the devaluation of things Hispanic and Hispanic people in "America" and who is most familiar with Hispano life in the Southwest of the US. I am quite unfamiliar with daily Hispano life in the urban centers, though not with some of the themes and some of the salient experiences of urban Hispano life.

When I say "we,"[2] I am referring to Hispanas. I am accustomed to use the "we" in this way. I am also pained by the tenuousness of this "we" given that I am not a native of the US. Through the years I have come to be recognized and I have come to recognize myself more and more firmly as part of this "we." I also have a profound yearning for this firmness since I am a displaced person and I am conscious of not being of and I am unwilling to make myself of – even if this were possible – the white/Anglo community.

When I say "you" I mean not the non-Hispanic but the white/Anglo women that I address. "We" and "you" do not capture my relation to other non-white women. The complexity of that relation is not addressed here, but it is vivid to me as I write down my thoughts on the subject at hand.

I see two related reasons for our complaint – full discourse with white/Anglo women. Both of these reasons plague our world, they contaminate it through and through. It takes some hardening of oneself, some self-acceptance of our own anger to face them, for to face them is to decide that maybe we can change our situation in self-constructive ways and we know fully well that the possibilities are minimal. We know that we cannot rest from facing these reasons, that the tenderness towards others in us undermines our possibilities, that we have to fight our own niceness because it clouds our minds and hearts. Yet we know that a thoroughgoing hardening would dehumanize us. So, we have to walk through our days in a peculiarly fragile psychic state, one that we have to struggle to maintain, one that we do not often succeed in maintaining.

We and you do not talk the same language. When we talk to you we use your language: the language of your experience and of your theories. We try to use it to communicate our world of experience. But since your language and your theories are inadequate in expressing our experiences, we only suc-ceed in communicating our experience of exclusion. We cannot talk to you in our language because you do not understand it. So the brute facts that we understand your language and that the place where most theorizing about women is taking place is your place, both combine to require that we either use your language and distort our experience not just in the speaking about it, but in the living of it, or that we remain silent. Complaining about exclusion is a way of remaining silent.

You are ill at ease in our world. You are ill at ease in our world in a very different way than we are ill at ease in yours. You are not of our world and again, you are not of our world in a very different way than we are not of yours. In the intimacy of a personal relationship we appear to you many times to be wholly there, to have broken through or to have dissipated the barriers that separate us because you are Anglo and we are raza. When we let go of the psychic state that I referred to above in the direction of sympathy, we appear to ourselves equally whole in your presence but our intimacy is thoroughly incomplete. When we are in your world many times you remake us in your own image, although sometimes you clearly and explicitly acknowledge that we are not wholly there in our being with you. When we are in your world we ourselves feel the discom-fort of having our own being Hispanas disfigured or not understood. And yet, we have had to be in your world and learn its ways. We have to participate in it, make a living in it, live in it, be mistreated in it, be ignored in it, and rarely, be appreciated in it. In learning to do these things or in learning to suffer them or in learning to enjoy what is to be enjoyed or in learning to understand your conception of us, we have had to learn your culture and thus your language and self-conceptions. But there is nothing that necessitates that you understand our world: understand, that is, not as an observer understands things, but as a par-ticipant, as someone who has a stake in them understands them. So your being ill at ease in our world lacks the features of our being ill at ease in yours precisely because you can leave and you can always tell yourselves that you will be soon out of there and because the wholeness of your selves is never touched by us, we have no tendency to remake you in our image.

But you theorize about women and we are women, so you understand your-selves to be theorizing about us and we understand you to be theorizing about us. Yet none of the feminist theories developed so far seem to me to help Hispanas in the articulation of our experience. We have a sense that in using them we are distorting our experiences. Most Hispanas cannot even understand the lan-guage used in these theories – and only in some cases the reason is that the Hispana cannot understand English. We do not recognize ourselves in these theories. They create in us a schizophrenic split between our concern for our-selves as women and ourselves as Hispanas, one that we do not feel otherwise. Thus they seem to us to force us to assimilate to some version of Anglo culture, however revised that version may be. They seem to ask that we leave our com-munities or that we become alienated so completely in them that we feel hol-low. When we see that you feel alienated in your own communities, this confuses us because we think that maybe every feminist has to suffer this alienation. But we see that recognition of your alienation leads many of you to be empowered into the remaking of your culture, while we are paralyzed into a state of displacement with no place to go,

So I think that we need to think carefully about the relation between the articulation of our own experience, the interpretation of our own experience, and theory making by us and other non-Hispanic women about themselves and other "women."

The only motive that makes sense to me for your joining us in this investigation is the motive of friendship, out of friendship. A non-imperialist feminism requires that you make a real space for our articulating, interpreting, theorizing and reflecting about the connections among them – a real space must be a noncoerced space – and/or that you follow us into our world out of friendship. I see the "out of friendship" as the only sensical motivation for this following because the task at hand for you is one of extraordinary difficulty. It requires that you be willing to devote a great part of your life to it and that you be willing to suffer alienation and self-disruption. Self-interest has been proposed as a possible motive for entering this task. But self-interest does not seem to me to be a realistic motive, since whatever the benefits you may accrue from such a journey, they cannot be concrete enough for you at this time and they may not be worth your while. I do not think that you have any obligation to understand us. You do have an obligation to abandon your imperialism, your universal claims, your reduction of us to your selves simply because they seriously harm us.

I think that the fact that we are so ill at ease with your theorizing in the ways indicated above does indicate that there is something wrong with these theories. But what is it that is wrong? Is it simply that the theories are flawed if meant to be universal but accurate so long as they are confined to your particular group(s)? Is it that the theories are not really flawed but need to be translated? Can they be translated? Is it something about the process of theorizing that is flawed? How do the two reasons for our complaint-full discourse affect the validity of your theories? Where do we begin? To what extent are our experience and its articulation affected by our being a colonized people, and thus by your culture, theories, and conceptions? Should we theorize in community and thus as part of community life and outside the academy and other intellectual circles? What is the point of making theory? Is theory making a good thing for us to do at this time? When are we making theory and when are we just articulating and/or interpreting our experiences?

Some Questionable Assumptions about Feminist Theorizing

(Unproblematically in María's and Vicky's voice)
Feminist theories aren't just about what happens to the female population in any given society or across all societies; they are about the meaning of those experiences in the lives of women. They are about beings who give their own accounts of what is happening to them or of what they are doing, who have

culturally constructed ways of reflecting on their lives. But how can the theo-rizer get at the meaning of those experiences? What should the relation be between a woman's own account of her experiences and the theorizer's account of it?

Let us describe two different ways of arriving at an account of another wom-an's experience. It is one thing for both me and you to observe you and come up with our different accounts of what you are doing; it is quite another for me to observe myself and others much like me culturally and in other ways and to develop an account of myself and then use that account to give an account of you. In the first case you are the "insider" and I am the "outsider." When the outsider makes clear that she is an outsider and that this is an outsider's account of your behavior, there is a touch of honesty about what she is doing. Most of the time the "interpretation by an outsider" is left understood and most of the time the distance of outsidedness is understood to mark objectivity in the inter-pretation. But why is the outsider as an outsider interpreting your behavior? Is she doing it so that you can understand how she sees you? Is she doing it so that other outsiders will understand how you *are*? Is she doing it so that *you* will understand how you are? It would seem that if the outsider wants you to under-stand how she sees you and you have given your account of how you see your-self to her, there is a possibility of genuine dialogue between the two. It also seems that the lack of reciprocity could bar genuine dialogue. For why should you engage in such a one-sided dialogue? As soon as we ask this question, a host of other conditions for the possibility of a genuine dialogue between us arise: conditions having to do with your position relative to me in the various social, political, and economic structures in which we might come across each other or in which you may run face to face with my account of you and my use of your account of yourself. Is this kind of dialogue necessary for me to get at the mean-ing of your experiences? That is, is this kind of dialogue necessary for feminist theorizing that is not seriously flawed?

Obviously the most dangerous of the understanding of what I – an outsider – am doing in giving an account of your experience is the one that describes what I'm doing as giving an account of who and how you are whether it be given to you or to other outsiders. Why should you or anyone else believe me; that is why should you or anyone else believe that you are as I say you are? Could I be right? What conditions would have to obtain for my being right? That many women are put in the position of not knowing whether or not to believe outsiders' accounts of their experiences is clear. The pressures to believe these accounts are enormous even when the woman in question does not see herself in the account. She is thus led to doubt her own judgment and to doubt all interpretation of her experience. This leads her to experience her life differ-ently. Since the consequences of outsiders' accounts can be so significant, it is crucial that we reflect on whether or not this type of account can ever be right and if so, under what conditions.

The last point leads us to the second way of arriving at an account of another woman's experience, viz. the case in which I observe myself and others like me culturally and in other ways and use that account to give an account of you. In doing this, I remake you in my own image. Feminist theorizing approaches this remaking insofar as it depends on the concept of women as women. For it has not arrived at this concept as a consequence of dialogue with many women who are culturally different, or by any other kind of investigation of cultural differences which may include different conceptions of what it is to be a woman; it has simply presupposed this concept.

Our suggestion in this paper, and at this time it is no more than a suggestion, is that only when genuine and reciprocal dialogue takes place between "outsiders" and "insiders" can we trust the outsider's account. At first sight it may appear that the insider/outsider distinction disappears in the dialogue, but it is important to notice that all that happens is that we are now both outsider and insider with respect to each other. The dialogue puts us both in position to give a better account of each other's and our own experience. Here we should again note that white/Anglo women are much less prepared for this dialogue with women of color than women of color are for dialogue with them in that women of color have had to learn white/Anglo ways, self-conceptions, and conceptions of them.

But both the possibility and the desirability of this dialogue are very much in question. We need to think about the possible motivations for engaging in this dialogue, whether doing theory jointly would be a good thing, in what ways and for whom, and whether doing theory is in itself a good thing at this time for women of color or white/Anglo women. In motivating the last question let us remember the hierarchical distinctions between theorizers and those theorized about and between theorizers and doers. These distinctions are endorsed by the same views and institutions which endorse and support hierarchical distinctions between men/women, master race/inferior race, intellectuals/manual workers. Of what use is the activity of theorizing to those of us who are women of color engaged day in and day out in the task of empowering women and men of color face to face with them? Should we be articulating and interpreting their experience for them with the aid of theories? Whose theories?

Ways of Talking or Being Talked About that are Helpful, Illuminating, Empowering, Respectful

(Unproblematically in María's and Vicky's voice)
Feminists have been quite diligent about pointing out the ways in which empirical, philosophical, and moral theories have been androcentric. They have thought it crucial to ask, with respect to such theories: who makes them? for whom do they make them? about what or whom are the theories? why? how are theories tested? what are the criteria for such tests and where did the criteria come from? Without posing such questions and trying to answer them, we'd never have been able to begin to mount evidence for our claims that particular theories are androcentric, sexist, biased, paternalistic, etc. Certain philosophers have become fond of – indeed, have made their careers on – pointing out that characterizing a statement as true or false is only one of many ways possible of characterizing it; it

might also be, oh, rude, funny, disarming, etc.; it may be intended to soothe or to hurt; or it may have the effect, intended or not, of soothing or hurting. Similarly, theories appear to be the kinds of things that are true or false; but they also are the kinds of things that can be, e.g. useless, arrogant, disrespectful, ignorant, ethnocentric, imperialistic. The immediate point is that feminist theory is no less immune to such characterizations than, say, Plato's political theory, or Freud's theory of female psychosexual development. Of course this is not to say that if feminist theory manages to be respectful or helpful it will follow that it must be true. But if, say, an empirical theory is purported to be about "women" and in fact is only about certain women, it is certainly false, probably ethnocentric, and of dubious usefulness except to those whose position in the world it strengthens (and theories, as we know, don't have to be true in order to be used to strengthen people's positions in the world).

Many reasons can be and have been given for the production of accounts of people's lives that plainly have nothing to do with illuminating those lives for the benefit of those living them. It is likely that both the method of investigation and the content of many accounts would be different if illuminating the lives of the people the accounts are about were the aim of the studies. Though we cannot say ahead of time how feminist theory-making would be different if all (or many more) of those people it is meant to be about were more intimately part of the theory-making process, we do suggest some specific ways being talked about can be helpful:

1. The theory or account can be helpful if it enables one to see how parts of one's life fit together, for example, to see connection among parts of one's life one hasn't seen before. No account can do this if it doesn't get the parts right to begin with, and this cannot happen if the concepts used to describe a life are utterly foreign.

2. A useful theory will help one locate oneself concretely in the world, rather than add to the mystification of the world and one's location in it. New concepts may be of significance here, but they will not be useful if there is no way they can be translated into already existing concepts. Suppose a theory locates you in the home, because you are a woman, but you know full well that is not where you spend most of your time? Or suppose you can't locate yourself easily in any particular class as defined by some version of marxist theory?

3. A theory or account not only ought to accurately locate one in the world but also enable one to think about the extent to which one is responsible or not for being in that location. Otherwise, for those whose location is as oppressed peoples, it usually occurs that the oppressed have no way to see themselves as in any way self-determining, as having any sense of being worthwhile or having grounds for pride, and paradoxically at the same time feeling at fault for the position they are in. A useful theory will help people sort out just what is and is not due to themselves and their own activities as opposed to those who have power over them.

It may seem odd to make these criteria of a useful theory, if the usefulness is not to be at odds with the issue of the truth of the theory: for the focus on feeling worthwhile or having pride seems to rule out the possibility that the truth might just be that such-and-such a group of people has been under the control of others for centuries and that the only explanation of that is that they are worthless and weak people, and will never be able to change that. Feminist theorizing seems implicitly if not explicitly committed to the moral view that women *are* worthwhile beings, and the metaphysical theory that we are beings capable of bringing about a change in our situations. Does this mean feminist theory is "biased"? Not any more than any other theory, e.g. psychoanalytic theory. What is odd here is not the feminist presupposition that women are worthwhile but rather that feminist theory (and other theory) often has the effect of empowering one group and demoralizing another.

Aspects of feminist theory are as unabashedly value-laden as other political and moral theories. It is not just an examination of women's positions, for it includes, indeed begins with, moral and political judgements about the injustice (or, where relevant, justice) of them. This means that there are implicit or explicit judgments also about what kind of changes constitute a better or worse situation for women.

4. In this connection a theory that is useful will provide criteria for change and make suggestions for modes of resistance that don't merely reflect the situation and values of the theorizer. A theory that is respectful of those about whom it is a theory will not assume that changes that are perceived as making life better for some women are changes that will make, and will be perceived as making, life better for other women. This is *not* to say that if some women do not find a situation oppressive, other women ought never to suggest to the contrary that there might be very good reasons to think that the situation nevertheless *is* oppressive. But it is to say that, e.g., the prescription that life for women will be better when we're in the workforce rather than at home, when we are completely free of religious beliefs with patriarchal origins, when we live in complete separation from men, etc., are seen as slaps in the face to women whose life would be better if they could spend more time at home, whose identity is inseparable from their religious beliefs and cultural practices (which is not to say those beliefs and practices are to remain completely uncriticized and unchanged), who have ties to men – whether erotic or not – such that to have them severed in the name of some vision of what is "better" is, at that time and for those women, absurd. Our visions of what is better are always informed by our perception of what is bad about our present situation. Surely we've learned enough from the history of clumsy missionaries, and the white suffragists of the nineteenth century (who couldn't imagine why black women "couldn't see" how crucial getting the vote for "women" was) to know that we can clobber people to destruction with our visions, our versions, of what is better. *But*: this does not mean women are not to offer supportive and tentative criticism of one another. But there is a very important difference between (a) developing ideas together, in a "pre-theoretical" stage, engaged as equals

in joint inquiry, and (b) one group developing, on the basis of their own experience, a set of criteria for good change for women—and then reluctantly making revisions in the criteria at the insistence of women to whom such criteria
seem ethnocentric and arrogant. The deck is stacked when one group takes it
upon itself to develop the theory and then have others criticize it. Categories
are quick to congeal, and the experiences of women whose lives do not fit the
categories will appear as anomalous when in fact the theory should have grown
out of them as much as others from the beginning. This, of course, is why any
organization or conference having to do with "women" – with no qualification
– that seriously does not want to be "solipsistic" will from the beginning be
multi-cultural or state the appropriate qualifications. How we think and what
we think about does depend in large part on who is there – not to mention
who is expected or encouraged to speak. (Recall the boys in the *Symposium*
sending the flute girls out.) Conversations and criticism take place in particular
circumstances. Turf matters. So does the fact of who if anyone already has set
up the terms of the conversations.

5. Theory cannot be useful to anyone interested in resistance and change unless
there is reason to believe that knowing what a theory means and believing it to
be true have some connection to resistance and change. As we make theory and
offer it up to others, what do we assume is the connection between theory and
consciousness? Do we expect others to read theory, understand it, believe it,
and have their consciousnesses and lives thereby transformed? If we really want
theory to make a difference to people's lives, how ought we to present it? Do
we think people come to consciousness by reading? only by reading? Speaking
to people through theory (orally or in writing) is a *very* specific context-depend-
ent activity. That is, theory-makers and their methods and concepts constitute a
community of people and of shared meanings. Their language can be just as
opaque and foreign to those not in the community as a foreign tongue or dia-
lect.[3] Why do we engage in *this* activity and what effect do we think it ought to
have? As Helen Longino has asked: "Is 'doing theory' just a bonding ritual for
academic or educationally privileged feminists/women?" Again, whom does
our theory-making serve?

Some Suggestions about how to do Theory that is not
Imperialistic Ethnocentric, Disrespectful

(Problematically in the voice of a woman of color)
What are the things we need to know about others, and about ourselves, in
order to speak intelligently, intelligibly, sensitively, and helpfully about their
lives? We can show respect, or lack of it, in writing theoretically about others no
less than in talking directly with them. This is not to say that here we have a
well-worked out concept of respect, but only to suggest that together all of us
consider what it would mean to theorize in a respectful way.

When we speak, write, and publish our theories, to whom do we think we are accountable? Are the concerns we have in being accountable to "the profession" at odds with the concerns we have in being accountable to those about whom we theorize? Do commitments to "the profession," method, getting something published, getting tenure, lead us to talk and act in ways at odds with what we ourselves (let alone others) would regard as ordinary, decent behavior? To what extent do we presuppose that really understanding another person or culture requires our behaving in ways that are disrespectful, even violent? That is, to what extent do we presuppose that getting and/or publishing the requisite information requires or may require disregarding the wishes of others, lying to them, wresting information from them against their wills? Why and how do we think theorizing about others provides *understanding* of them? Is there any sense in which theorizing about others is a short-cut to understanding them?

Finally, if we think doing theory is an important activity, and we think that some conditions lead to better theorizing than others, what are we going to do about creating those conditions? If we think it not just desirable but necessary for women of different racial and ethnic identities to create feminist theory jointly, how shall that be arranged for? It may be the case that at this particular point we ought not even try to do that – that feminist theory by and for Hispanas needs to be done separately from feminist theory by and for black women, white women, etc. But it must be recognized that white/Anglo women have more power and privilege than Hispanas, black women, etc., and at the very least they can use such advantage to provide space and time for other women to speak (with the above caveats about implicit restrictions on what counts as "the woman's voice"). And once again it is important to remember that the power of white/Anglo women *vis-à-vis* Hispanas and black women is in inverse proportion to their working knowledge of each other.

This asymmetry is a crucial fact about the background of possible relationships between white women and women of color, whether as political coworkers, professional colleagues, or friends.

If white/Anglo women and women of color are to do theory jointly, in helpful, respectful, illuminating and empowering ways, the task ahead of white/Anglo women because of this asymmetry, is a very hard task. The task is a very complex one. In part, to make an analogy, the task can be compared to learning a text without the aid of teachers. We all know the lack of contact felt when we want to discuss a particular issue that requires knowledge of a text with someone who does not know the text at all. Or the discomfort and impatience that arise in us when we are discussing an issue that presupposes a text and someone walks into the conversation who does not know the text. That person is either left out or will impose herself on us and either try to engage in the discussion or try to change the subject. Women of color are put in these situations by white/Anglo women and men constantly. Now imagine yourself simply left out but wanting to do theory with us. The first thing to recognize and accept is that you disturb our own dialogues by putting yourself in the left-out position and not leaving us in some meaningful sense to ourselves.

You must also recognize and accept that you must learn the text. But the text is an extraordinarily complex one: viz. our many different cultures. You are asking us to make ourselves more vulnerable to you than we already are before we have any reason to trust that you will not take advantage of this vulnerability. So you need to learn to become unintrusive, unimportant, patient to the point of tears, while at the same time open to learning any possible lessons. You will also have to come to terms with the sense of alienation, of not belonging, of having your world thoroughly disrupted, having it criticized and scrutinized from the point of view of those who have been harmed by it, having important concepts central to it dismissed, being viewed with mistrust, being seen as of no consequence except as an object of mistrust.

Why would any white/Anglo woman engage in this task? Out of self-interest? What in engaging in this task would be, not just in her interest, but perceived as such by her before the task is completed or well underway? Why should we want you to come into our world out of self-interest? Two points need to be made here. The task as described could be entered into with the intention of finding out as much as possible about us so as to better dominate us. The person engaged in this task would act as a spy. The motivation is not unfamiliar to us. We have heard it said that now that Third World countries are more powerful as a bloc, westerners need to learn more about them, that it is in their self-interest to do so. Obviously there is no reason why people of color should welcome white/Anglo women into their world for the carrying out of this intention. It is also obvious that white/Anglo feminists should not engage in this task under this description since the task under this description would not lead to joint theorizing of the desired sort: respectful, illuminating, helpful, and empowering. It would be helpful and empowering only in a one-sided way.

Self-interest is also mentioned as a possible motive in another way. White/Anglo women sometimes say that the task of understanding women of color would entail self-growth or self-expansion. If the task is conceived as described here, then one should doubt that growth or expansion will be the result. The severe self-disruption that the task entails should place a doubt in anyone who takes the task seriously about her possibilities of coming out of the task whole, with a self that is not as fragile as the selves of those who have been the victims of racism. But also, why should women of color embrace white/Anglo women's self-betterment without reciprocity? At this time women of color cannot afford this generous affirmation of white/Anglo women.

Another possible motive for engaging in this task is the motive of duty, "out of obligation," because white/Anglos have done people of color wrong. Here again two considerations: coming into Hispano, black, Native American worlds out of obligation puts white/Anglos in a morally self-righteous position that is inappropriate. You are active, we are passive. We become the vehicles of your own redemption. Secondly, we couldn't want you to come into our worlds "out of obligation." That is like wanting someone to make love to you out of obligation. So, whether or not you have an obligation to do this (and we would deny that you do), or whether this task could even be done out of obligation, this is an inappropriate motive.

Out of obligation you should stay out of our way, respect us and our distance, and forego the use of whatever power you have over us – for example, the power to use your language in our meetings, the power to overwhelm us with your education, the power to intrude in our communities in order to research us and to record the supposed dying of our cultures, the power to engrain in us a sense that we are members of dying cultures and are doomed to assimilate, the power to keep us in a defensive posture with respect to our own cultures.

So the motive of friendship remains as both the only appropriate and understandable motive for white/Anglo feminists engaging in the task as described above. If you enter the task out of friendship with us, then you will be moved to attain the appropriate reciprocity of care for your and our well-being as whole beings, you will have a stake in us and in our world, you will be moved to satisfy the need for reciprocity of understanding that will enable you to follow us in our experiences as we are able to follow you in yours.

We are not suggesting that if the learning of the text is to be done out of friendship, you must enter into a friendship with a whole community and for the purpose of making theory. In order to understand what it is that we are suggesting, it is important to remember that during the description of her experience of exclusion, the Hispana voice said that Hispanas experience the intimacy of friendship with white/Anglo women friends as thoroughly incomplete. It is not until this fact is acknowledged by our white/Anglo women friends and felt as a profound lack in our experience of each other that white/Anglo women can begin to see us. Seeing us in our communities will make clear and concrete to you how incomplete we really are in our relationships with you. It is this beginning that forms the proper background for the yearning to understand the text of our cultures that can lead to joint theory-making.

Thus, the suggestion made here is that if white/Anglo women are to understand our voices, they must understand our communities and us in them. Again, this is not to suggest that you set out to make friends with our communities, though you may become friends with some of the members, nor is it to suggest that you should try to befriend us for the purpose of making theory with us. The latter would be a perversion of friendship. Rather, from within friendship you may be moved by friendship to undergo the very difficult task of understanding the text of our cultures by understanding our lives in our communities. This learning calls for circumspection, for questioning of yourselves and your roles in your own culture. It necessitates a striving to understand while in the comfortable position of not having an official calling card (as "scientific" observers of our communities have); it demands recognition that you do not have the authority of knowledge; it requires coming to the task without ready-made theories to frame our lives. This learning is then extremely hard because it requires openness (including openness to severe criticism of the white/Anglo world), sensitivity, concentration, self-questioning, circumspection. It should be clear that it does not consist in a passive immersion in our cultures, but in a striving to understand what it is that our voices are saying. Only then can we engage in a mutual dialogue that does not reduce each one of us to instances of the abstraction called "woman."

Notes

1 For a recent example, see Mackinnon 1982.
2 I must note that when I think this "we," I think it in Spanish – and in Spanish this "we" is gendered, *nosotras*. I also use *nosotros* lovingly and with ease and in it I include all members of *La raza cosmica* (Spanish-speaking people of the Americas, *la gente de colores*: people of many colors). In the US, I use "we" contextually with varying degrees of discomfort: "we" in the house, "we" in the department, "we" in the classroom, "we" in the meeting. The discomfort springs from the sense of community in the "we" and the varying degrees of lack of community in the context in which the "we" is used.
3 See Bernstein 1972. Bernstein would probably, and we think wrongly, insist that theoretical terms and statements have meanings *not* "tied to a local relationship and to a local social structure," unlike the vocabulary of, e.g. working-class children.

References

Bernstein, Basil (1972) "Social class, language and socialization," in Giglioli, Pier Paolo (ed.) *Language and Social Context*, Hardmondsworth: Penguin Books, pp. 157–78.
Mackinnon, Catherine (1982) "Feminism, Marxism, method, and the state: an agenda for theory," *Signs* 7/3, pp. 515–44.

In this extract from *Loving in the War Years*, Moraga describes growing up as, and learning to love being, a Chicana lesbian.

Focus questions:
1 How does Moraga describe relations between the genders in her home?
2 What is Moraga's relation to her mother, and how does she say this helps form her identity?
3 What is the connection of the political activism and the eroticism of this piece? What is the connection of both of those to its spirituality?

---

33 A Long Line of Vendidas

Cherríe Moraga

Sueño: 15 de julio 1982
During the long difficult night that sent my lover and I to separate beds, I dreamed of church and cunt. I put it this way because that is how it came to me. The suffering and the thick musty mysticism of the Catholic church fused with the sensation of entering the vagina – like that of a colored woman's – dark, rica, full-bodied. The heavy sensation of complexity. A journey I must unravel, work out for myself. I long to enter you like a temple.

My Brother's Sex was White. Mine, Brown.

If somebody would have asked me when I was a teenager what it means to be Chicana, I would probably have listed the grievances done me. When my sister and I were fifteen and fourteen, respectively, and my brother a few years older, we were still waiting on him. I write "were" as if now, nearly two decades later, it were over. But that would be a lie. To this day in my mother's home, my brother and father are waited on, including by me. I do this now out of respect for my mother and her wishes. In those early years, however, it was mainly in relation to my brother that I resented providing such service. For unlike my father, who sometimes worked as much as seventy hours a week to feed my face every day, the only thing that earned my brother my servitude was his maleness.

It was Saturday afternoon. My brother, then seventeen-years-old, came into the house with a pile of friends. I remember Fernie, the two Steves, and Roberto. They were hot, sweaty, and exhausted from an afternoon's basketball and plopped themselves down in the front room, my brother demanding, "Girls, bring us something to drink."

"Get it yourself, pig," I thought, but held those words from ever forming inside my mouth. My brother had the disgusting habit on these occasions of collapsing my sister, JoAnn's and my name when referring to us as a unit: his sisters. "Cher'ann," he would say. "We're really thirsty." I'm sure it took everything in his power *not* to snap his fingers. But my mother was out in the yard working and to refuse him would have brought her into the house with a scene before these boys' eyes which would have made it impossible for us to show our faces at school that following Monday. We had been through that before.

When my mother had been our age, over forty years earlier, she had waited on her brothers and their friends. And it was no mere lemonade. They'd come in from work or a day's drinking. And las mujeres, often just in from the fields themselves, would already be in the kitchen making tortillas, warming frijoles or pigs feet, albóndigas soup, what-have-you. And the men would get a clean white tablecloth and a spread of food laid out before their eyes and not a word of resentment from the women.

The men watched the women – my aunts and mother moving with the grace and speed of girls who were cooking before they could barely see over the top of the stove. Elvira, my mother, knew she was being watched by the men and loved it. Her slim hips moved patiently beneath the apron. Her deep thick-lidded eyes never caught theirs as she was swept back into the kitchen by my abuelita's call of "Elvirita," her brown hands deepening in color as they dropped back into the pan of flour.

I suppose my mother imagined that Joe's friends watched us like that, too. But we knew different. We were not blonde or particularly long-legged or "available" because we were "Joe's sisters." This meant no boy could "make" us, which meant no boy would bother asking us out. Roberto, the Guatemalan, was the only one among my brother's friends who seemed at all sensitive to how awkward JoAnn and I felt in our role. He would smile at us nervously, taking the lemonade, feeling embarassed being waited on by people he considered peers. He knew the Anglo girls they visited would never have succumbed to such a task. Roberto was the only recompense.

As I stopped to wait on their yearning throats, "jock itch" was all that came to my mind. Their cocks became animated in my head, for that was all that seemed to arbitrarily set us apart from each other and put me in the position of the servant and they, the served.

I wanted to machine-gun them all down, but swallowed that fantasy as I swallowed making the boy's bed every day, cleaning his room each week, shining his shoes and ironing his shirts before dates with girls, some of whom I had crushes on. I would lend him the money I had earned house-cleaning for twelve hours, so he could blow it on one night with a girl because he seldom had enough money because he seldom had a job because there was always some kind of ball practice to go to. As I pressed the bills into his hand, the car honking outside in the driveway, his double-date waiting, I knew I would never see that money again.

Years later, after I began to make political the fact of my being a Chicana, I remember my brother saying to me, "*I've* never felt 'culturally deprived'," which I guess is the term "white" people use to describe Third World people being denied access to *their* culture. At the time, I wasn't exactly sure what he meant, but I remember in retelling the story to my sister, she responded, "Of course, he didn't. He grew up male in our house. He got the best of both worlds." And yes, I can see now that that's true. *Male in a man's world. Light-skinned in a white world. Why change?*

The pull to identify with the oppressor was never as great in me as it was in my brother. For unlike him, I could never have *become* the white man, only the white man's *woman*.

The first time I began to recognize clearly my alliances on the basis of race and sex was when my mother was in the hospital, extremely ill. I was eight years old. During my mother's stay in the hospital, my tía Eva took my sister and me into her care; my brother stayed with my abuela; and my father stayed by himself in our home. During this time, my father came to visit me and my sister only once. (I don't know if he ever visited my brother.) The strange thing was I didn't really miss his visits, although I sometimes fantasized some imaginary father, dark and benevolent, who might come and remind us that we still *were* a family.

I have always had a talent for seeing things I don't particularly want to see and the one day my father did come to visit us with his wife/our mother physically dying in a hospital some ten miles away, I saw that he couldn't love us – not in the way we so desperately needed. I saw that he didn't know how and he came into my tía's house like a large lumbering child – awkward and embarrassed out of his league – trying to play a parent when he needed our mother back as much as we did just to keep him eating and protected. I hated and pitied him that day. I knew how he was letting us all down, visiting my mother daily, like a dead man, unable to say, "The children, honey, I held them. They love you. They think of you." Giving my mother *something*.

Years later, my mother spoke of his visits to the hospital. How from behind the bars of her bed and through the tubes in her nose, she watched this timid man come and go daily – going through the "motions" of being a husband. "I knew I had to live," she told us. "I knew he could never take care of you."

In contrast to the seeming lack of feeling I held for my father, my longings for my mother and fear of her dying were the most passionate feelings that had ever lived inside my young heart.

We are riding the elevator. My sister and I pressed up against one wall, holding hands. After months of separation, we are going to visit mamá in the hospital. Mi tía me dice, "Whatever you do, no llores, Cherríe. It's too hard on your mother when you cry." I nod, taking long deep breaths, trying to control my quivering lip.

As we travel up floor by floor, all I can think about is not crying, breathing, holding my breath. "Me prometes?" she asks. I nod again, afraid to speak fearing my voice will crack into tears. My sister's nervous hand around mine, sweating too. We are going to see my mamá, mamá, after so long. She didn't die after all. She didn't die.

The elevator doors open. We walk down the corridor, my heart pounding. My eyes are darting in and out of each room as we pass them, fearing/anticipating my mamá's face. Then as we turn around the corner into a kind of lobby, I hear my tía say to an older woman – skin and bones. An Indian, I think, straight black and grey hair pulled back. I hear my tía say, "Elvira."

I don't recognize her. This is not the woman I knew, so round and made-up with her hair always a wavy jet black! I stay back until she opens her arms to me – this strange and familiar woman – her voice hoarse, "Ay mi'jita!" Instinctively, I run into her arms, still holding back my insides – "Don't cry. Don't cry." I remember. "Whatever you do, no llores." But my tía had not warned me about the smell, the unmistakable smell of the woman, mi mamá – el olor de aceite y jabón and comfort and home. "Mi mamá." And when I catch the smell I am lost in tears, deep long tears that come when you have held your breath for centuries.

There was something I knew at that eight-year-old moment that I vowed never to forget – the smell of a woman who is life and home to me at once. The woman in whose arms I am uplifted, sustained. Since then, it is as if I have spent the rest of my years driven by this scent toward la mujer.

> when her india makes love
> it is with the greatest reverence
> to color, texture, smell
>
> by now she knew the scent of earth
> could call it up
> even between the cracks
> in sidewalks
> steaming dry
> from midday summer
> rain

With this knowledge so deeply emblazed upon my heart, how then was I supposed to turn away from La Madre, La Chicana? If I were to build my womanhood on this self-evident truth, it is the love of the Chicana, the love of myself as a Chicana I had to embrace, no white man. Maybe this ultimately was the cutting difference between my brother and me. To be a woman fully necessitated my claiming the race of my mother. My brother's sex was white. Mine, brown.

Tired of these Acts of Translation

What the white women's movement tried to convince me of is that lesbian sexuality was *naturally* different than heterosexual sexuality. That the desire to penetrate and be penetrated, to fill and be filled, would vanish. That retaining such desires was "reactionary," not "politically correct," "male-identified." And somehow reaching sexual ecstasy with a woman lover would never involve any kind of power struggle. Women were different. We could simply magically "transcend" these "old notions," just by seeking spiritual transcendence in bed.

The fact of the matter was that all these power struggles of "having" and "being had" were being played out in my own bedroom. And in my psyche, they held a particular Mexican twist. White women's feminism did little to answer my questions. As a Chicana feminist my concerns were different. As I wrote in 1982:

> What I need to explore will not be found in the feminist lesbian bedroom, but more likely in the mostly heterosexual bedrooms of South Texas, LA, or even Sonora, México. Further, I have come to realize that the boundaries white feminists confine themselves to in describing sexuality are based in white-rooted interpretations of dominance, submission, power-exchange, etc. Although they are certainly *part* of the psychosexual lives of women of color, these boundaries would have to be expanded and translated to fit my people, in particular, the women in my family. And I am tired, always, of these acts of translation.[1]

Mirtha Quintanales corroborates this position and exposes the necessity for a Third World feminist dialogue on sexuality when she states:

> The critical issue for me regarding the politics of sexuality is that as a Latina Lesbian living in the US, I do not really have much of an opportunity to examine what constitutes sexual conformity and sexual defiance in my own culture, in my own ethnic community, and how that may affect my own values, attitudes, sexual life *and* politics. There is virtually no dialogue on the subject anywhere and I, like other Latinas and Third World women, especially Lesbians, am quite in the dark about what we're up against besides negative feminist sexual politics.[2]

During the late 1970s, the concept of "women's culture" among white lesbians and "cultural feminists" was in full swing; it is still very popular today. "Womon's history," "wommin's music," "womyn's spirituality," "wymyn's language," abounded – all with the "white" modifier implied and unstated. In truth, there was/is a huge amount of denial going on in the name of female separatism. Women do not usually grow up in women-only environments. Culture is sexually-mixed. As Bernice Reagon puts it:

> we have been organized to have our primary cultural signals come from factors other than that we are women. We are not from our base, acculturated to be women people, capable of crossing our first people boundaries: Black, White, Indian, etc.[3]

Unlike Reagon, I believe that there are certain ways we *have* been acculturated to be "women people," and there is therefore such a thing as "women's culture." This occurs, however, as Reagon points out, within a context formed by race, class, geography, religion, ethnicity, and language.

I don't mean to imply that women need to have men around to feel at home in our culture, but that the way one understands culture is influenced by men. The fact that some aspects of that culture are indeed oppressive does not imply, as a solution, throwing out the entire business of racial/ethnic culture. To do so would mean risking the loss of some very essential aspects of identity, especially for Third World women.

Journal entry: julio 1981
New England. Boston to be exact. Pouring summer rain. We are all immigrants to this town – una hermana de Chicago, una de Tejas, una de Puerto Rico, y yo, de California. And the four of us move out into the rain under the beat of the downpour on the roof of the porch. Cooling off from the evening of enchiladas. I make up a little concoction of a summer drink: jugo de naranja, tequila, limón. Tossing in all kinds of ice cubes, "Try this," I say.

Y mis hermanas drink it up. Dos chicanas y dos puerto-riqueñas getting a little high from the food and the rain and the talk, hablando de nuestras madres.

Sitting out on the porch that night, what made me at home and filled me with ease where I forgot about myself in a fine and fluid way was not just that the Spanish sounds wrapped around the English like tortillas steaming in flour sacks, not just that we all had worked hard to get here from hard-working homes, not just that we understood the meaning of familia, but that we were women – somos mujeres. This is what women's culture means to me.

In failing to approach feminism from any kind of materialist base, failing to take race, ethnicity, class into account in determining where women are at sexually, many feminists have created an analysis of sexual oppression (often confused with sexuality itself) which is a political dead-end. "Radical Feminism," the ideology which sees men's oppression of women as the root of and paradigm for all other oppressions allows women to view ourselves as a class and to claim our sexual identity as the *source* of our oppression and men's sexual identity as the *source* of the world's evil. But this ideology can never then fully integrate the concept of the "simultaneity of oppression" as Third World feminism is attempting to do. For, if race and class suffer the woman of color as much as her sexual identity, then the Radical Feminist must extend her own "identity" politics to include her "identity" as oppressor as well. (To say nothing of having to acknowledge the fact that there are men who may suffer more than she.) This is something that for the most part, Radical Feminism as a movement has refused to do.

Radical Feminist theorists have failed to acknowledge how their position in the dominant culture – white, middle-class, often Christian – has influenced every approach they have taken to implement feminist political change – to "give women back their bodies." It follows then that the anti-pornography movement is the largest organized branch of Radical Feminism. For unlike battered women's, anti-rape, and reproductive rights workers, the anti-porn "activist" never has to deal with any live woman outside of her own race and class. The tactics of the anti-pornography movement are largely symbolic and theoretical in nature. And, on paper, the needs of the woman of color are a lot easier to represent than in the flesh. Therefore, her single-issued approach to feminism remains intact.

It is not that pornography is not a concern to many women of color. But the anti-materialist approach of this movement makes little sense in the lives of poor and Third World women. Plainly put, it is our sisters working in the sex industry.

Many women involved in the anti-porn movement are lesbian separatists. Because the Radical Feminist critique is there to justify it, lesbianism can be viewed as the logical personal response to a misogynist political system. Through this perspective, lesbianism has become an "idea" – a political response to male sexual aggression, rather than a sexual response to a woman's desire for another women. In this way, many ostensibly heterosexual women who are not active sexually can call themselves lesbians. Lesbians "from the neck up." This faction of the movement has grown into a kind of cult. They have taken whiteness, class privilege, and an Anglo-American brand of "return-to-the-mother" which leaps back over a millenium of patriarchal domination, attempted to throw out the man, and call what is left female. While still retaining their own racial and class-biased cultural superiority.

The lesbian separatist retreats from the specific cultural contexts that have shaped her and attempts to build a cultural-political movement based on an imagined oppression-free past. It is understandable that many feminists opt for this kind of asexual separatist/spiritualist solution rather than boldly grappling with the challenge of wresting sexual autonomy from such a sexually exploitative system. Every oppressed group needs to imagine through the help of history and mythology a world where our oppression did not seem the pre-ordained order. Aztlán for Chicanos is another example. The mistake lies in believing in this ideal past or imagined future so thoroughly and single-mindedly that finding solutions to present-day inequities loses priority, or we attempt to create too-easy solutions for the pain we feel today.

As culture – our race, class, ethnicity, etc. – influences our sexuality, so too does heterosexism, marriage, and men as the primary agents of those institutions. We can work to tumble those institutions so that when the rubble is finally cleared away we can see what we have left to build on sexually. But we can't ask a woman to forget everything she understands about sex in a heterosexual and culturally-specific context or tell her what she is allowed to think about it. Should she forget and not use what she knows sexually to untie the knot of her own desire, she may lose any chance of ever discovering her own sexual potential.

Feeding People in all their Hungers

History has taught us that the effectiveness of a movement often depends on its ability to provide what, at least, feels at the time like a spiritual imperative. Spirituality which inspires activism and, similarly, politics which move the spirit – which draw from the deep-seated place of our greatest longings for freedom – give meaning to our lives. Such a vision can hold and heal us in the worst of times, and is in direct opposition to an apolitical spiritualist view of the world or a totally materialistic perspective.

The Civil Rights Movement is probably the best recent example in this country of a movement that was able to reach masses of people through its spiritually-uplifting vision. The power of that vision, however, was based on the fact that in a very profound sense, it was deeply rooted in black culture, and therefore, of necessity, black spirituality. Religious fervor was not manufactured for the purposes of social or revolutionary change, but instead grew directly out of black people's experience, influencing all those who became a part of that movement.

Major missing elements in the Civil Rights Movement, however, were consciousness and activism around specifically female and sexual concerns, as well as an understanding of the entrenchedness of white power and how to move against it. Although the race-related movements that jumped off from the Civil Rights Movement in the late 1960s, such as the American Indian Movement, La Raza, and Black Power were thoroughly coming to terms with the extent and depth of white power, the role of women of color was neither subject for debate nor activism except as women functioned as female members of the race.

But times have changed. The women's movement and lesbian and gay liberation movements in the 1970s brought both the subject of women's rights and sexuality, respectively, to the political light of day. Furthermore, in the 1980s with the increasing conservatism of the country manifested in the reign of Reagan and the rise of the Moral Majority, Third World organizations and organizers can no longer safely espouse the family and, therefore, homophobia, as the righteous *causa* without linking themselves with the most reactionary, and by definition, the most racist political sectors of this county.

The emergence of Third World feminism, then, seemed imminent. Third

World lesbians' disillusionment with the racism and classism of the women's and gay movements and the sexism and homophobia of Third World movements did much to force us to begin to organize ourselves autonomously in the name of Third World feminism.

If any movement, however, could provide a "spiritual" reference point for Third World feminism, it would be the Civil Rights Movement in its culturally-based, anti-separatist, and "humanist" (not to be confused with liberal) approach to political change. As Barbara Smith, black feminist activist and writer, explains:

> I was trying to figure out what the connection was/is for me between the Civil Rights movement and the Black Feminist movement. It is among other things, this. That the Civil Rights movement was based upon the concept of love and deep spirituality. It was a movement with a transcendent vision. *A movement whose very goal was to change the impossible, what people thought could not be changed.*
>
> The women's movement has some of these same qualities, a belief in the human. Actually Black Feminism is a kind of divine coalescing of the two because as Black women we have an identity and therefore a politics that requires faith in the humanness of Blackness and femaleness. We are flying in the face of white male conceptions of what humanness is and proving that it is not them, but us.
>
> That's what the Civil Rights movement was getting to through its divine patience and fortitude – although tactically and strategically it was, at times, flawed – the constant demonstration that we are really the human ones.
>
> Black feminism, lesbian feminism in particular, moves in that direction . . . We will show you what it means to be human, what it means to really care about humanity.[4]

As a Chicana who grew up in a very religious household, I learned early on to respect the terrain of the spirit as the place where some of the most essential aspects of one's life are enacted. The spirit world – my sleeping dreams, my waking fantasies, my prayers and compulsive preoccupations – was and is very rich for me. A place from which I derive strength and perseverance. A place where much internal torture has taken place.

Women of color have always known, although we have not always wanted to look at it, that our sexuality is not merely a physical response or drive, but holds a crucial relationship to our entire spiritual capacity. Patriarchal religions – whether brought to us by the colonizer's cross and gun or emerging from our own people – have always known this. Why else would the female body be so associated with sin and disobedience? Simply put, if the spirit and sex have been linked in our oppression, then they must also be linked in the strategy toward our liberation.

To date, no liberation movement has been willing to take on the task. To walk a freedom road that is both material and metaphysical. Sexual and spiritual. Third World feminism is about feeding people in all their hungers.

Notes

1   Cherríe Moraga, "Played between white hands," in *Off Our Backs*, July 1982, Washington, DC, n.p.
2   Mirtha Quintanales with Barbara Kerr, "The complexity of desire: conversations on sexuality and difference," in *Conditions: Eight* (Box 56 Van Brunt Station, Brooklyn, NY), p. 60.
3   Bernice Reagon, "Turning the century around," in Barbara Smith (ed.) *Home Girls: A Black Feminist Anthology* (Latham, NY: Kitchen Table, Women of Color Press, 1983).
4   Barbara Smith, unpublished paper. (Write: Kitchen Table, Women of Color Press, P.O. Box 908, Latham, NY, 12110.)

Questions about Intersections

1   Describe your own gender, race, sexuality, ethnicity, region, and class, or that of a friend or character from a book or film. How do these things interact in the life of the person you are describing? If that person is a woman, for example, how does her class or race affect the way people view her gender role or the way she herself views it?

2   How do you think language affects social identity? Think here not just of non-English languages but also of vernaculars or slangs associated with class, region, or ethnicity.

3   Is being Native American being a member of a race, of an ethnicity, subscribing to a belief system, belonging to a culture, or some combination of these?

4   What are some of the dangers associated with taking it for granted that white, middle-class people provide the norms for other groups? Think about this question with regard, for example, to family structures, which vary by race, class, sexual orientation, and other factors.

5   What are some of the reasons someone might play (with more or less seriousness) at being a member of a race, gender, or class to which they do not, in fact, belong? What are some of the pleasures and some of the dangers of such play?

6   Has identity politics gone too far? What are some of the drawbacks of "political correctness"? Have you experienced "political correctness" firsthand?

7   What are some of the forms that dialogue or other interactions between members of different groups could take? What are some of the barriers to such dialogue? What are some ways that dialogue between groups could be promoted?

8   What does it mean to be white? What is a white racial identity?

9   The readings in this section have presented a variety of intersections. What are some others, perhaps some that are occupied by yourself or people you know?

10   Have the readings given in this part of the book made you more sympathetic to people unlike yourself? Have you found people similar to yourself in this section? Or have these stories been alienating, or frustrating? Which have and which haven't?

Recommended Reading for Part Five

Allen, Theodore (1994) *The Invention of the White Race*, New York: Verso (a discussion of the economic forces behind the invention of whiteness in the eighteenth century from a variety of ethnicities or regional identities).

Allison, Dorothy (1994) *Skin*, Ithaca, NY: Firebrand (discussions of sex, class, and art by the author of *Bastard Out of Carolina*).

Anzaldúa, Gloria (1987) *Borderlands = La frontera: the New Mestiza*, San Francisco: Spinsters/Aunt Lute (a deep and lovely exploration of various intersections).

Balibar, Etienne and Wallerstein, Immanuel (1991) *Race, Nation, Class: Ambiguous Identities*, New York: Verso (an account of intersectional identities).

Bash, Harry (1979) *Sociology, Race, and Ethnicity*, New York: Gordon and Breach (a comprehensive, if somewhat dated, treatment of its subject).

Cannon, Katie G. (1985) *Black Womanist Ethics*, Atlanta, Ga.: Scholar's Press (a philosophical exploration of black women's values).

Collins, Patricia Hill (1990) *Black Feminist Thought*, New York: Routledge (an excellent survey of and contribution to its topic).

Cox, Oliver (1948) *Caste, Class, and Race*, New York: Modern (an important early discussion of intersectionality).

Davis, Angela (1989) *Women, Race and Class*, New York: Random House (a discussion of intersectionality by the famous philosopher and radical).

Dougherty, Molly C. (1978) *Becoming a Woman in Rural Black Culture*, New York: Holt, Rinehart, and Winston (memoir that explores the relations of gender, race, and region).

Frankenberg, Ruth (1993) *White Women, Race Matters*, Minneapolis, Minn.: University of Minnesota Press (a sociological study of racial attitudes among white women).

Hoch, Paul (1979) *White Hero Black Beast*, London: Pluto (an exploration of race, sexuality, and masculinity).

hooks, bell (1981) *Ain't I a Woman: Black Women and Feminism*, Boston, Mass.: South end Press (a definitive statement of the problems some black women have with some white feminists).

Hull, Gloria T., Scott, Patricia Bell, and Smith, Barbara (eds) (1982) *But Some of Us are Brave*, Old Westbury, NY: Feminist Press (an extremely important collection of papers in black feminism).

Kadi, Joanna (1996) *Thinking Class*, Boston, Mass.: South End Press (essays and poems by a Lebanese American lesbian).

Leacock, Eleanor, and Safa, Helen (eds) (1986) *Women's Work*, South Hadley, Mass.: Bergin and Garvey (a collection of sociological papers on the relation of gender and class).

Lenero-Otero, Luis (ed.) (1977) *Beyond the Nuclear Family Model: Cross-Cultural Perspectives*, Beverly Hills: Sage (throws into question European and European American family norms).

Moraga, Cherríe and Anzaldúa, Gloria (eds) (1983) *This Bridge Called My Back*, Latham, NY: Kitchen Table, Women of Color Press (a collection of feminist essays by women of color).

Roediger, David (1994) *Towards the Abolition of Whiteness*, New York: Verso (essays on the relations of race and economics).

Schlesinger, Arthur (1992) *The Disuniting of America*, New York: Norton (a thoughtful attack on identity politics).

Spelman, Elizabeth V. (1988) *Inessential Woman: Problems of Exclusion in Feminist Thought*, Boston, Mass.: Beacon (an excellent exploration of why feminism has tended to be awfully white and middle class until recently).

Stallybrass, Peter and White, Allon (1986) *The Politics and Poetics of Transgression*, Ithaca, NY: Cornell University Press (gives an account of the "other" in Western culture at the intersections of race, gender, and class).

Swerdlow, Amy and Lessinger, Hanna (eds) (1984) *Class, Race, and Sex*, Boston, Mass.: G. K. Hall (a collection of papers exploring various modes of power).

Zack, Naomi (1993) *Race and Mixed Race*, Philadelphia, Pa.: Temple University Press (a criticism of American racial categories and an exploration of the places between them).

INDEX

sexism, 169, 305
sexual desire, 251, 252
sexual difference, 171, 199, 230
    social organization of, 187
sexual ethics, 269, 296
sexual labor, 253
sexual practices, 251
sexual violence, 308–18
sexuality
    defined, 4
    philosophical accounts, 251
    scientific accounts, 251
Shakespeare, 229
Shapiro, Susan, 167, 212
share-holders, 121
Sharpton, Al, 376
Shay, Daniel (Shay's Rebellion), 19
sickle-cell anemia, 81
signifiers of race, 338
sin, 251
Sinkler, Georgette, 50
Sisterhood is Global, 197–8
skin color, racism and, *see* colorism
slavery, 12, 142
    importance in colonial America, 16–28
    justifications for, 25–6
    one-drop rule and, 76–7
    reparation for, 60–1
slums, trailer parks, 360–1
Smith, Adam, 93–5
Smith, Barbara, 397
Snoop Doggy Dogg, 344
social categories, importance of, 7
social class, 362
social constructionists, 197
social contract, 57
social death, slavery and, 288
social equality, 13
social honor, 116
social identities, 1, 329–30
social locations, 329
social order, 116
social roles, 1
social science, race and, 11
social status, race and, 11
socialist traditions, 228
socialization, gender and, 188–9
sociohistorical idea of race, 39
Solomon, 216–18
Soviet Union, 92
speaking out, 308–9
spectator tradition, 232

Spelman, Elizabeth, 190, 331, 374
Spickard, Paul, 82
Stages on Life's Way, 228
status group, 120–1
stealing
    by employees, 125
stereotypes
    black men, 337
    class, 358–69
    homosexuals, 177
    race, 45–6
    whites, 354
strivings, race and, 31–2
sublime, 229, 232
    concept of nature, 168
Supreme Court of Carolina, 149
Symposium, 270

Tally's Corner, 94
Tan, Amy, 330
Taylor, Kenneth, 50
teenage culture, black male, 338
Theogony, 214
thinness, social desirability of, 136
third world women, 394–6
Thomas, Clarence, 66
Thomas, Laurence Mordekhai, 50
Tolliver, Joseph, 50
torture, 309, 311–13
Tower, John, 151
trade unions, 106
trailer parks, 358–69
Transforming a Rape Culture, 309–10
The Transsexual Empire, 199, 203
transsexuals, 158, 166
Treatise on Marriage, 217
tropes, in Jewish philosophical texts, 221–2
Truth, Sojourner, 328
two-sex body, 206
two-sex system, 195–6
two-stepping, 157
typing, human, 2

unemployment, 123
United Nations Charter, 80
United States House of Representatives Subcommittee on Census, 79
United States Supreme Court, 77, 144
United Way, 145
universal human rights, 12
unskilled labor, 126–7